1999

In a world of increasingly heterogeneous societies, matters of identity politics and the links between collective identities and national, racial, or ethnic intolerance have assumed dramatic significance – and have stimulated an enormous body of research and literature. This research seldom transcends the limitations of a national perspective, however, and thus reproduces the limitations of its own topic; comparative studies are rare, if not altogether absent. *Identity and Intolerance* is an effort to shift the focus toward comparison in order to show how German and American societies have historically confronted and currently confront matters of national, racial, and ethnic inclusion and exclusion. The comparative perspective sheds light on the specific links between the cultural construction of nationhood and otherness, the political modes of integration and exclusion, and the social conditions of tolerance and intolerance. The contributors to this book also attempt to integrate the largely separate approaches offered by the history of ideas and ideologies, social history, and discourse theory.

PUBLICATIONS OF THE GERMAN HISTORICAL INSTITUTE
WASHINGTON, D.C.

Edited by Detlef Junker
with the assistance of Daniel S. Mattern

Identity and Intolerance

THE GERMAN HISTORICAL INSTITUTE, WASHINGTON, D.C.

The German Historical Institute is a center for advanced study and research whose purpose is to provide a permanent basis for scholarly cooperation between historians from the Federal Republic of Germany and the United States. The Institute conducts, promotes, and supports research into both American and German political, social, economic, and cultural history, into transatlantic migration, especially in the nineteenth and twentieth centuries, and into the history of international relations, with special emphasis on the roles played by the United States and Germany.

Identity and Intolerance

NATIONALISM, RACISM, AND XENOPHOBIA
IN GERMANY AND THE UNITED STATES

Edited by
NORBERT FINZSCH
and
DIETMAR SCHIRMER

GERMAN HISTORICAL INSTITUTE

Washington, D.C.

and

CAMBRIDGE
UNIVERSITY PRESS

PUBLISHED BY THE PRESS SYNDICATE OF THE UNIVERSITY OF CAMBRIDGE
The Pitt Building, Trumpington Street, Cambridge CB2 1RP, United Kingdom

CAMBRIDGE UNIVERSITY PRESS
The Edinburgh Building, Cambridge CB2 2RU, United Kingdom
40 West 20th Street, New York, NY 10011–4211, USA
10 Stamford Road, Oakleigh, Melbourne 3166, Australia

First published 1998

Printed in the United States of America

Typeset in Bembo

Library of Congress Cataloging-in-Publication Data
Identity and intolerance: nationalism, racism, and xenophobia in
Germany and the United States / edited by Norbert Finzsch and
Dietmar Schirmer.
    p.   cm. – (Publications of the German Historical Institute)
    Includes bibliographical references and index.
    ISBN 0-521-59158-9
    1. Nationalism – Germany.   2. Nationalism – United States.
3. Racism – Germany.   4. Racism – United States.   5. Xenophobia –
Germany.   6. Xenophobia – United States.   7. Nativistic movements –
United States.   I. Finzsch, Norbert.   II. Schirmer, Dietmar.
                III. Series.
                DD74.I34   1998
    305.8'00943 – dc21   97-21386

*A catalog record for this book is available from
the British Library.*

ISBN 0 521–59158–9 hardback

Contents

Preface

This book evolved from a conference entitled "Racism, Nationalism, Nativism, and Xenophobia in Germany and the United States: A Comparative Perspective on the Conditions of Intolerance," which took place at the German Historical Institute (GHI) in Washington, D.C., June 8–11, 1994.

Every book has many parents; the editors are only those who are, so to say, legally acknowledged and have to take on the respective responsibilities. We wish to thank the Stifterverband für die Deutsche Wissenschaft, whose generous support helped make the original conference possible, and Bärbel Bernhardt, Christa Brown, and Dieter H. Schneider of the GHI, whose organizational talents and administrative efforts were instrumental in carrying through that conference.

We also wish to thank Hartmut Lehmann, director of the Max Planck Institute of History and former director of the GHI, who gave the initial impulse to take on the subject of nationalism, racism, and xenophobia, and Hartmut Keil, professor of history at the University of Leipzig and former deputy director of the GHI, who lent his support to the project in its various stages. Special thanks go to Daniel S. Mattern, the editor of the Cambridge series at the GHI, and to Pamela Abraham and David B. Morris, who assisted in bringing the texts into shape. Sally E. Robertson translated two essays originally submitted in German. Our outside readers gave us invaluable advice, which helped us tremendously to produce a book that is held together by more than only the bookbinder's glue. Thanks also go to Gregg Kvistad of the University of Denver for his constructive criticism and to Andrea Böhm for her critical support in every stage of the project. The editors would also like to extend their gratitude to everyone who, in one way or another, patiently dealt with the idiosyncrasies of the editors and the contributors.

Contributors

Dietz Bering is a professor of German language and literature at the University of Cologne.

Eileen Boris is a professor of political science at Howard University.

W. Fitzhugh Brundage is a professor of history at Queens University, Kingston, Ontario, Canada.

Carl N. Degler is a professor of history at Stanford University.

Norbert Finzsch is a professor of history at the University of Hamburg.

Ute Gerhard is a lecturer in German literature and linguistics at the University of Dortmund.

Lois E. Horton is a professor of sociology and anthropology at George Mason University.

Ralf Koch is a member of the History Department at the University of Hamburg.

Arnd Krüger is a professor of social sciences at the University of Göttingen.

Gregg Kvistad is a professor of political science at the University of Denver.

Dietmar Schirmer is an assistant professor of political science at the Free University of Berlin.

Herbert Shapiro is a professor of history at the University of Cincinnati.

Frank Trommler is a professor of German at the University of Pennsylvania.

Patricia Vertinsky is a professor of human kinetics at the University of British Columbia, Vancouver, Canada.

Peter Weingart is a professor of sociology at the University of Bielefeld.

Introduction

DIETMAR SCHIRMER

SIGNS OF THE TIMES

In the 1990s a mob of extremists firebombs a shelter for asylum seekers in the German town of Rostock. A crowd of bystanders applauds. The police stand idly by. The police in the town of Mölln receive an anonymous call saying, "There's a house burning in Mühlenstrasse. Heil Hitler!" The arson attack leaves nine Turkish immigrants injured and three women dead. A patron at a bar in Wuppertal gets involved in a political argument with neo-Nazi skinheads. They trample him to death, douse him with alcohol, and set him on fire. Several Jewish cemeteries are desecrated. Synagogues and Jewish community centers are under constant police protection. At a bar in Oberhof, Thuringia, Duncan Kennedy of the American bobsled team, which is using the local training facilities, is injured by skinheads when he attempts to defend his African-American teammate, Robert Pipkins, against a crowd of fifteen. The bar is known as a meeting place of the local neo-Nazi scene; a swastika serves as decoration.

An amateur videotapes the beating of Rodney King, an African American, by officers of the Los Angeles Police Department. Despite the video document, the subsequent trial leads to an acquittal – and to the Los Angeles riots of April 1992. In Austin, Texas, a white supremacist attempts to detonate a bomb in a cinema while the movie *Malcolm X* is being shown. Fortunately, the bomb does not go off. On Cable News Network's *Larry King Live* with guest Senator Jesse Helms from North Carolina and with political commentator Robert Novak sitting in for Larry King, a caller suggests that Helms deserves the Nobel Peace Prize for "holding the niggers down all his life." The honored guest thanks the caller for these words of appreciation; the host is helpless to respond. At the "Million Man March" in October 1995, members of the Nation of

Islam sell brochures and videotapes that denounce the Jewish religion as a "gutter religion" and demand "abolition of homosexuality." The publication of *The Bell Curve* triggers heated disputes that demonstrate that the old hypothesis linking race and intelligence has been only in a state of remission.[1]

Approximately one hundred years ago in Germany, prominent conservative historian and writer Heinrich von Treitschke coined the phrase "die Juden sind unser Unglück" (The Jews are our misfortune). Forty years later this phrase became the subtitle of the Nazi newspaper *Der Stürmer*, infamous for its insufferably vulgar anti-Semitism. In the elections of 1893, anti-Semitic parties won sixteen seats in the Reichstag. The decade from 1890 to 1900 witnessed an unsurpassed wave of accusations of "ritual murder" – a virulent anti-Semitic notion of the Middle Ages that claimed that Jews regularly kill Christian children during religious rituals. In 1900, in the province of Posen, Prussian authorities had to prevent a pogrom following an alleged ritual murder.

In the wake of populist success in the late nineteenth century, Jim Crow laws were passed all over the American South. African Americans were systematically disenfranchised. Thus, between 1896 and 1904, the number of "colored people" registered as voters in the state of Louisiana declined from 130,334 to a meager 1,342.[2] "Jim Crow" established a tight system of racial segregation that survived into the 1960s. In 1892 alone, 155 African Americans fell victim to lynching, often witnessed by cheering crowds of onlookers.

Gathering such "signs of the times" is surprisingly easy, no matter what time period is chosen. This is not to say that racism and anti-Semitism are undifferentiated in time and space and unrelated to specific historic, social, and cultural contexts – that is, that they are ontological or anthropological facts. Of course they differ, and they differ tremendously according to phenomenology, the severity and frequency of incidents, the groups that propagate them, and the groups that are affected. In its rationalizations and consequences, the German anti-Semitism of the 1890s, for example, is different from the anti-Semitism of the Nazi era; today's asylum seekers are not the Jews of the 1990s. Jim Crow was not the same as slavery; the multiple racisms African Americans encoun-

---

1 See Richard J. Herrnstein and Charles Murray, *The Bell Curve: Intelligence and Class Structure in American Life* (New York, 1994); Steven Fraser, ed., *The Bell Curve Wars: Race, Intelligence, and the Future of America* (New York, 1995).
2 According to Samuel E. Morison, *The Oxford History of the American People*, vol. 3: *1869 Through the Death of John F. Kennedy, 1963* (New York, 1994), 107.

ter today are different from those they had to suffer in the days of legal segregation.

Although chauvinism, hate, and phobias based on the categories of race, ethnicity, and national origin seem ubiquitous, they often provide only background noise. Sometimes the noise is unpleasant and disagreeable, but essentially ineffective and powerless. Sometimes it is loud and shrill, and it becomes the actual signature of the time. Sometimes it receives support only from a minority within the majority; sometimes it becomes presentable within broader strata of society. And still at other times group hatred and discrimination rise to the status of official state doctrine.

The concept of this book, which attempts longitudinal and horizontal cross sections through the history of intolerance in two largely different national contexts, is based on two major assumptions. We will elaborate on these later; for the moment, however, a brief sketch should suffice. First, we hold nationalist, racist, or ethnocentrist modes of exclusion to be an integral part of modernity, rather than an aberration or a dysfunction. The possibility of emancipation and the grounds for oppression both appear within its horizon. Second, and closely related, we maintain that racism, anti-Semitism, and xenophobia, as aggressive and exclusive practices of the ascription of group characteristics, are only adequately analyzed as a function of collective identity. Collective identity, whether it refers to nation, race, or culture, always depends on the distinction between in-groups and out-groups. The borders may be more or less permeable, but they nevertheless are borders. Collective identification with nation, culture, or race and the aggressive exclusion of people who do not fit the demands of sameness follow the same taxonomic systems.

The reader might notice with some surprise, even with disquiet, that the book does not systematically treat the Holocaust or the nearly total annihilation of the Native American population in the course of the conquest of the North American continent. For a variety of reasons, both events do not fit into the proposed comparative scheme, despite their respective importance in the histories of these two countries. The history of the near extermination of the people and cultures of North America is perhaps best handled in a comparative history of colonialism, one that focuses on the ruthless establishment of European hegemony over many regions of the globe. It might also be told as a parable of the dialectics of the Enlightenment, which, cut off from its roots in universal humanism, transformed the idea of humankind's domination over nature into the ideology of the legitimate domination of some human beings by other human beings. Yet, it does not neatly fit into a German-American comparative design.

In the case of the Holocaust, the problem of comparability poses itself in an even more dramatic manner. The Holocaust is such a singular event, or series of events, that we do not think that comparative research is the adequate methodological tool to address the academic as well as ethical bewilderment and helplessness it produces. To compare the Holocaust to the war against Native Americans is a matter of politics rather than scholarly consideration. The history of postwar Germany is replete with allusions, attempts, and outright strategies to ban the horror of the Holocaust by placing it into a comparative framework with other megacrimes in human history. At least since the so-called *Historikerstreit* (historians' quarrel) of the late 1980s, any attempt to compare the Holocaust is inextricably linked to the politics of "normalization." Thus, drawing comparisons with the Holocaust, no matter how good the academic and ethical intentions, inevitably makes a political statement with which we must disagree. For better or worse, we chose to leave it out of the book as a topic in its own right. Nevertheless, as the ultimate consequence of the racist and nationalist furor, it is present on every single page of this book.

CURRENT CONTEXTS

The political implications of the German discourse on the comparability of the Holocaust vividly illustrate the fact that academic discourse is principally bound up with the public and political discourse taking place outside universities and research institutions. This also applies, as the *Historikerstreit* graphically demonstrated, to the discourse of historians – despite the German tradition of historicism, which for a long time had maintained historians' self-interpretation as members of a disinterested discipline. Historiographic debate structures and is structured by the social, political, and cultural environment in which it takes place. Thus, the book's agenda has been set by observations of current political discourses and practices.

Our starting point is the admittedly banal observation that nationalism, racism, xenophobia, and identity have again become particularly malignant since the end of the 1980s, in Europe as well as in North America. As it turns out, the formation of extreme right-wing parties in Western European countries in the preceding decades was only a prelude to something larger. The Movimento Soziale Italiano (Italy) and

Jean-Marie Le Pen's Front National (France) were the first to establish themselves as nationalist and chauvinist parties in Western democracies during the 1970s and the 1980s; the success of the Republicans (*die Republikaner*) in Germany remained, fortunately, ephemeral, as did that of the British National Front.

What really pushed the subject into the foreground was the collapse of socialism in East-Central and Eastern Europe. As the grip of the pseudointernationalist doctrine weakened, nationalism, nationalist separatism, anti-Semitism, and ethnic chauvinism celebrated a triumphant rebirth. This spurred violent ethnic conflicts, ignited full-blown wars, tore states apart, and even showed long-distance effects, for example, in Canada and Belgium, both of which were, at times, only inches away from dissolution in the name of national purity.

Germany not only was affected but was itself a participant in these postsocialist upheavals. In the wake of reunification, the long-suspended topic of what constituted the German nation became unavoidable. The names of towns such as Mölln and Solingen, Hoyerswerda and Rostock became the violent, eventually murderous, metonymies for the disruptions of the reunification process, inevitably linking the reemergence of a united German nation-state with the specters of nationalism, racism, and xenophobia. Suddenly, the doubts about the reliability of Germany's democratic political culture, which had always existed latently and which became manifest during the discussion of the pros and cons of German unification, seemed validated.

Whereas the violent plebiscites against civility were disturbing enough, they became even more so by coinciding with certain shifts in the fields of politics and intellectual discourse. Political indicators included the abandonment of Germany's liberal asylum law and the German government's egocentric decision to recognize the sovereignty of Croatia and Slovenia, a decision that raised questions about the direction of Bonn's future foreign policy. Intellectually, the revisionist position, which for years had claimed the normalization of Germany's historical self-understanding and the overcoming of Hitler as the prime negative focus of its political ethos, was reinforced by the "course of history" and moved from an outsider position toward the mainstream.[3]

3 For a representative example of the huge number of publications, see Heino Schwilk and Ulrich Schacht, eds., *Die selbstbewusste Nation* [The self-confident nation] (Frankfurt/Main, 1994), which contains essays by the old nobility of German nationalism (e.g., Ernst Nolte, H. J. Syberberg, Alfred Mechtersheimer) and a New Right (Rainer Zitelmann, Roland Bubik, and others), as well as essays by the playwright Botho Strauss, Willy Brandt's widow Brigitte Seebacher-Brandt, and the German-Jewish historian Michael Wolffsohn.

During the *Historikerstreit*, an earlier and largely unsuccessful stage of the national-conservative project aimed at the normalization of Germany and its history, Jürgen Habermas had rightly claimed the "unconditional openness of the Federal Republic toward Western political culture" to be "the preeminent intellectual achievement of the postwar period."[4] The permanence of this achievement seemed to be at stake. The Germans had apparently rediscovered "the Nation" with a capital "N."

In contrast to Germany, the United States was only marginally affected by the European disturbances in the aftermath of the collapse of state socialism in Europe. Nevertheless, in the early 1990s the ongoing discourse about race, ethnicity, and the relation between the majority and minorities was more energized than it had been in over a decade. High-visibility events, such as those referred to previously, were only symbolic representations of a process that could change the social, ethnic, and cultural texture of American society. Immigration from the south, stagnation and backlashes in the relations between blacks and whites, poverty and crime in the predominantly minority inner cities, and, perhaps most important, the persistent stagnation in middle-class incomes – often interpreted as the "end of the American dream" – conspired to spur the debate.

Despite the conservative presidencies of Richard Nixon, Ronald Reagan, and George Bush, measures of social redistribution have been the main tool of race politics. After roughly two decades of declining wages, affirmative action, which had never enjoyed a broad and stable social consensus, and social policies in general are under attack, primarily because two historic laws of American society seem to be losing their validity: The next generation will not be able to surpass or, at least, maintain the living standard of its parents; and, with the increase in white poverty, being white no longer guarantees a better standard of living. At the bottom of the social pyramid, immigration from Latin America drives a "blacks versus browns" competition for low-wage jobs.[5] The volume of benefits and privileges to be distributed is shrinking. The effects are, on the one hand, the revitalization of an antistatist self-help

---

4 Author's translation. The original is "Die vorbehaltlose Öffnung der Bundesrepublik gegenüber der politischen Kultur des Westens ist die grosse intellektuelle Leistung unserer Nachkriegszeit" (originally published under the title "Eine Art Schadensabwicklung" in *Die Zeit*, July 11, 1986; reprinted as "Apologetische Tendenzen," in Jürgen Habermas, *Eine Art Schadensabwicklung* [Frankfurt/Main, 1987], 120–36, 135). See also the anthology *Historikerstreit: Die Dokumentation der Kontroverse um die Einzigartigkeit der nationalsozialistischen Judenvernichtung* (Munich, 1987).
5 For a knowledgeable and thoughtful discussion, see Jack Miles, "Blacks vs. Browns: The Struggle for the Bottom Rung," *Atlantic Monthly*, 270, no. 4 (Oct. 1992): 41–68.

philosophy that generally opposes governmental care for minorities and, on the other, outright pleas for state intervention on behalf of those parts of the majority that live in fear of deprivation. Both these trends have produced general confusion over the traditional political categories of left and right.[6]

Such developments only mark the most recent outbursts of the grand theme of *us versus them* in Germany and in the United States. Matters of homogeneity and heterogeneity, inclusion and exclusion, tolerance and intolerance, although they are topics of modern societies as such, play a preeminent role in the histories of the two countries examined here. It is safe to predict that they will continue do so in the future. Of course, the social structures as well as the institutional conditions in which these topics are debated stand in stark contrast: On the one hand, the American "nation of immigrants" claims the political homogeneity of an ethnically and culturally heterogeneous people, supports it with popular myths such as the "melting pot," the "symphonic nation," or the "color-blind society,"[7] and yet apparently never succeeds in closing the gap between the theory of "freedom and equality" and the practice of repression and inequality. On the other hand, Germany, lacking a unified nation-state for most of its modern history, finds refuge in the romantic concept of the metaphysical homogeneity of the *Volk*, which continues to contradict the empirical evidence of heterogeneity – a contradiction that eventually Nazi Germany attempted to resolve through genocide. The overwhelming historical and current relevance of the topics of identity and intolerance in both countries accounts for the attractiveness of a comparative perspective.

NATIONALISM, RACISM, AND IDENTITY

The semantic fields of nation, race, and identity are polyvalent and over-determined; the literature on these subjects is vast. This introduction is not the place for an extensive discussion of even the most important or recent research. Rather, we would like to restrict ourselves to a brief

---

6 This is what recently made Pat Buchanan's populist drive for state intervention in favor of a deprived segment of America's white and male majority so confusing.

7 *The Melting Pot* is the title of Israel Zangwill's 1909 play and refers, as Michael Lind correctly notes, to "the amalgamation of *European* ethnic groups in the United States" (Michael Lind, *The Next American Nation: The New Nationalism and the Fourth American Revolution* [New York, 1995], 57). "The Symphonic Nation" is a chapter title in Waldo Frank, *The Re-discovery of America* (New York, 1929). The "color-blind society" is the integrationist motto of the civil rights activists and reformers of the 1950s and 1960s.

outline of our understanding of these concepts and of the dynamic ways in which they are linked to one another.

Nationalism

The nation is indisputably the preeminent category of political integration in the modern age, and the nation-state is modernity's preeminent political institution. In the current context, we need not elaborate on how the nation-state is intertwined with other institutional dimensions of modernization. It should be sufficient to note that the rise of nations and nation-states is inseparably bound up with the development and evolution of capitalism, industrialization, and the secularization of processes of political legitimation.[8]

Thus, Ernest Gellner refers to nationalism as an ideological response to the structural demands of industrial society in his study *Nations and Nationalism* when he states: "It is not the case that nationalism imposes homogeneity out of a willful cultural *Machtbedürfnis* (desire for power); it is the objective need for homogeneity which is reflected in nationalism."[9] Only a few pages later, however, Gellner argues: "It is nationalism which engenders nations, and not the other way round."[10] Both statements are, at first glance, mutually exclusive: Nationalism appears to be, on the one hand, a mere reflection of social transformation, or the result of structural change; on the other hand, it can be an autonomous force, itself inducing a new social formation. The question therefore is how to resolve this apparent contradiction.

A nation-state is an abstract system just as its subject, the nation, is an abstract category. Unlike the local communities that generally defined the premodern *Lebenswelt* (life-world), the members of a nation are too numerous and dispersed to allow for face-to-face communication. Thus, social relations on the national level are disembedded, to use Anthony Giddens's fitting term.[11] The citizens of a nation-state are members of an organizational framework that transcends the *hic et nunc* of face-to-face communication and spans remarkable distances in time and space. Consequently, from an individual perspective, the category of the nation is

---

8 See Ernest Gellner, *Nations and Nationalism* (Ithaca, N.Y., 1983), 19–35 and passim.
9 Ibid., 46.
10 Ibid., 55.
11 Anthony Giddens, *The Consequences of Modernity* (Stanford, Calif., 1990), 21–9 and passim; see also Anthony Giddens, *Modernity and Self-identity: Self and Society in the Late Modern Age* (Stanford, Calif., 1991).

empirically empty; the individual will never know, see, or even hear of most of his or her fellow members of the national community. This is what brings Benedict Anderson to describe nations as "imagined communities."[12]

Anderson's characterization is particularly useful because it alludes not only to the contingency of the nation but also to the sense of belonging and the implicit trust it provides for those who participate in it. Again, we are facing an apparent oxymoron, characterizing the nation as contingent and as a source of a sense of belonging at the same time. Hence, the problem is how the transformation of contingency into meaning and anonymity into community works. If we consider a nation a disembedded system in Giddens's sense, this transformation requires reembedding mechanisms.[13] These mechanisms can be found in the symbolic representations of the nation that render the abstract in concrete terms and thus convert anonymity into comradeship and contingency into fate. This symbolic transmutation depends on a system of national myths and legends (most important among them, the myths of origin); a pantheon of national heroes; institutions of remembrance such as museums, monuments, and memorials; the political institutions of the nation-state; the canonization of a national history and a national language; and the representations found in maps, statistics, graphics, and other records that help to consolidate the nation by asserting its existence over and over again.[14]

Thus, we can describe nation and nationalism as resulting contingently but not coincidentally from the dialectics of the demands of a specifically modern social formation and the willful production of a matrix of symbolic representations that, although not consciously designed for

12 Benedict Anderson, *Imagined Communities: Reflections on the Origin and Spread of Nationalism* (London, 1983). The consensus among scholars is that nations should be understood as cultural constructs or inventions, not as quasi-natural facts or historical destiny. Thus, Ernest Gellner expresses the same thought, although a bit more drastically, when he writes, "Nations as a natural, God-given way of classifying men, as an inherent though long-delayed political destiny, are myth. Nationalism, which sometimes takes pre-existing cultures and turns them into nations, sometimes invents them, and often obliterates preexisting cultures: *that* is a reality" (Gellner, *Nations and Nationalism*, 48–9). Similarly, Eisenstadt emphasizes the symbolic and institutional construction of the nation. See, e.g., Shmuel N. Eisenstadt, "Die Konstruktion nationaler Identitäten in vergleichender Perspektive," in Bernhard Giesen, ed., *Nationale und kulturelle Identität: Studien zur Entwicklung des kollektiven Bewusstseins in der Neuzeit* (Frankfurt/Main, 1991), 21–38.

13 Giddens prefers to call these mechanisms disembedding mechanisms, thus emphasizing that they allow disembedding without disrupting social ties altogether. I prefer to call them reembedding mechanisms in order to emphasize their ability to reembed the disembedded.

14 Every census, every political map that represents national territories, every table or graphic representation of whatever kind of data collected on the national level, every bit of information that is presented as a statement on the nation as a whole or a respective average or median (be it the average income, the per capita GNP, or the percentage of households equipped with a personal computer) does, first of all, claim the very existence of the nation.

this purpose, fulfill these demands. This dialectic approach also permits the integration of Gellner's two statements mentioned previously. It frames nationalism as a doctrine, ideology, or belief system that is structured by the social conditions and the cultural resources of modern society and, at the same time, is structuring the nation as the subject of the preeminent form of modern political integration.

The national principle provides a certain taxonomic system for the grouping of people, or, in other words, a dispositive of homogeneity and distinction. The mode of grouping can, in the last instance, be based on culture, history, inheritance, blood, a political faith or mission, or, most likely, a mixture of some or all of them. In principle, the system of nations is universal and egalitarian: Everybody is supposed to be a member of precisely one nation; and every nation has the same claim to independence and to sovereignty.[15] In any case, defining borderlines between in-group and out-groups, or members and nonmembers, is not a side effect but the very essence of the nationalist concept.[16]

Nationalism is not aggressive per se but only potentially. Symbolic re-embedding loads the abstract category of nationhood with often deeply felt affections; and notably a real or supposed violation of the integrity of the nation is, as a consequence of the logic of symbolic representation, equivalent to a violation of the personal integrity of its members. This accounts not only for the willingness to die for one's nation, which gives the ultimate proof of the power of the nationalist mode of integration, but also for foreign wars, which provide the paradigmatic example of nationalism resorting to aggressive means.[17]

Racism and Nationalism

In general terms, we can consider racism to be the hierarchical arranging of group relations on the grounds of a dispositive of bodily properties. Although racism expresses itself in terms of biology, it is not so much a discourse on natural qualities as a discourse on naturalized social relations that deems certain people to be degraded. The question is how the concept of race relates to that of the nation. This question is not easy

---

15 This egalitarian strain is represented in metaphors such as the "concert" or the "community" of nations or in the "one nation, one vote" principle of the United Nations.
16 As a matter of fact, the physical borders of a nation-state are an important element of its reembedding symbolic system.
17 The fact that wars are principally disguised as a defense against aggression – Hitler even masked Nazi Germany's war against Poland as a defensive measure – supports the theory that aggressive nationalism is closely related to a sense of violation of the nationalist code.

to answer because "race" and "nation" constitute two largely separate discourses within academia. When they are brought together, it is mostly in a pejorative manner that tends to eliminate the differences between them and likens one with the other based on their exclusionary character.[18]

Benedict Anderson proposes that we conceive of nationalism as the complete "Other" of racism. Whereas nationalist aggression, such as in a foreign war, manifests itself across national boundaries, he argues, racism is a tool of domestic oppression. Whereas nationalism equalizes individuals into a horizontal community, racism depends on an upper-class strategy to disguise perceived threats. And whereas nationalism, even nationalist hatred, reinforces and respects the nationality of the Other, racism denies the Other its very identity.[19]

We hold this juxtaposition of nationalism and racism to be a misconception that overemphasizes the differences and ignores the intersection of race and nation. Certainly, racism is neither the same as nor the superlative of nationalism. The foremost difference is that, whereas nationalism is only potentially linked to claims of superiority, racism without the notion of a hierarchy of races is unthinkable. Nevertheless, there are logical connections as well as empirical links between them. First, by providing symbolic systems of reembedding, both offer a cure for the coldness of the disembedded existence of modern human beings. Second, both draw on primordial factors, although racism does so more radically than nationalism. Whereas nationalism blends a whole number of unchosen traits — place of birth, ancestors, culture, language — with other, nonprimordial factors, racism depends on a radical reduction of blood or genetic ties. Third, both are modes of transcending time and space. The members of a nation as well as the members of a race know themselves to be united with their most distant predecessors by the thread of their common (natural) history as well as with their most distant co-members by virtue of their mutual affiliation with nation or race. Fourth, there is plenty of empirical evidence for the mutual compatibility of the two ideologies; a study of German citizenship and American immigration laws would prove how legal discourse functions as an interface between nation and race. The most virulently racist organization in world history called itself a "national socialist" political party.

18 See, e.g., J. Weinroth, who argues that thinking in terms of race is racism and thinking in terms of nation is nationalism and racism at the same time (J. Weinroth, "Nation and Race: Two Destructive Concepts," *Philosophy Forum* 16 [1979]: 67–86). Tom Nairn has concluded that racism and anti-Semitism are just "derivatives" of nationalism (Tom Nairn, *The Break-up of Britain: Crisis and Neo-nationalism* [London, 1980], 337).
19 See Anderson, *Imagined Communities*, 141–54.

The Aryan Nation, a decisively racist concept of nationhood, is a stock phrase of American neo-Nazis. Fifth, the exclusive association of nationalism with foreign wars versus that of racism with domestic oppression is empirically invalid. Historically, nationalism has proved all too aware of the "enemy within," and foreign wars – wars between nations – often enough have racist undertones.

Our aim is neither to diminish the conceptual and practical differences between nationalism and racism nor to ignore their correlation on the grounds of the purity of definition. After all, both nation and race signify distinctly modern taxonomic systems for the grouping of people according to a homogeneity-heterogeneity rationale, with the former constituting an essentially cultural discourse and the latter deriving from the discourses of medicine and biology. At times, nationalism may even work as an anti-racist form of political mobilization. Nationalist liberation movements fighting against the racist or, at least, racialized system of colonization provide a graphic example. More often, however, nationalism turns toward racism to strengthen its own homogeneity-heterogeneity rationale and to legitimate claims of superiority. The racialization of nationalism works via the naturalization of culture and, thus, grounds the nationalist dispositive of inclusion and exclusion on the suggestive force of the supposed objectivity of biological knowledge.

To understand the transformability of race into nation and vice versa, and to avoid analytical blindness to the differences between them, it might be useful to remind ourselves of a basic rule of the discursive formation of social reality: Its logic depends on the orientation it provides rather than on its coherence. Concepts of the social world, once they have entered the discursive marketplace, are no longer determined by anything like their original or intended meaning but exclusively by the rules and dynamics of the respective discourse. Thus, Anderson's insistence on the logical incompatibility of race and nation may be meaningful within the academic discourse and its codes of logical conclusion, but it tells us nothing about their mutual compatibility within a social discourse coded according to a rationale of power and domination.

Collective Identity

As described previously, not only nation and race but also culture, ethnicity, and other terms describing or asserting the existence of collective subjects are symbolic representations of otherwise anonymous social entities and provide a symbolic rationale of reembedding. Nationalism and racism are these symbolic representations spelled out in a more or less coherent ideology, doctrine, or faith. Hence, nationalism and racism, as do other "isms," refer to a consciously held cognitive and normative structure – however deficient and twisted it may be. In contrast, national, racial, or other collective identities have a different status. We may understand collective identity as a commonly shared sense of mutual communality that can exist and function without being fully present in the consciousness of those participating in it. Thus, collective identities are a certain aspect of what Pierre Bourdieu describes as the *habitus*, a common disposition to understand oneself as being part of a community, without necessarily being able to spell out its foundations, its reasons, its logic, or its goals. Collective identities are internalizations of common fates, experiences, and histories, both unmediated and acquired through socialization and acculturation, an indisputable and quasi-natural frame of experiencing and perceiving one's social world. Put in terms of disembedding and reembedding, the existence of a collective identity indicates that the crisis of disembedding is banned and a state of reembedding is acquired.

To outline further the relation between collective identity, be it of the nation, race, ethnicity, gender, or class, and the respective "isms" of collectivity, that is, nationalism, racism, ethnocentrism and multiculturalism, feminism, or socialism, it might prove useful to refer to Bourdieu's distinction between doxa, orthodoxy, and heterodoxy. This triadic distinction marks the realms of the natural and indisputable and that of discourse, struggle, and competition, respectively, with the orthodoxy occupying the dominant and the heterodoxy representing the oppositional position. In the absence of crisis, collective identities are part of the doxa. As long as national or ethnic affiliations, gender roles, or class hierarchies maintain their reembedding function and are not challenged by any political or social doctrine or movement, they are not subject to a discourse on their relevance or legitimacy; they exist and function discretely, and it is practically impossible to discuss them in terms of pros and cons. Conversely, the emergence of every political and social doctrine, ideology, and movement concerned with collectivity and identification signals a crisis in the reproduction of existing collectives, marks that collectivity and identification as becoming a problem, and moves that problem into the realm of discourse and the struggle between orthodoxy and heterodoxy.

The existence of a nationalist or racist ideology, or even nationalism or racism institutionalized in a particular political party, normally coincides with and fosters but by no means guarantees the creation or strengthening of national or racial identity. Alternatively, national or racial identities may very well exist without being advocated by a strong racist or nationalist movement. In fact, collective identity does not even necessarily mean that the collective is seen as entirely positive and honorable – although in most cases it will be. The fact that a considerable percentage of postwar Germans, especially those of the so-called 1968 generation, have a distinctly critical and even negative view of the German nation and nationalism – in light of Nazism and the Holocaust – does not necessarily imply a lack of national identity; rather, it points to a negative identification.

Political agitators of race, nation, or class principally seek to frame the category of their obsession as the only kind of collective subject that really matters. So, for example, nationalist propaganda, in a totalizing act of imposing homogeneity, attempts to erase all other possible identifications with class, gender, ethnicity, or religion as a means of fragmentation and as efforts to undermine the common cause of the nation. Similarly, socialism and socialist movements that depended on class as the essentially defining category for social and political power tried to outrule the forces of nationalist identification by imposing the dogma of international worker solidarity.

Nevertheless, collective identities are an indispensable part of the formation of individual identities, insofar as they locate an individual's place in the social space. This location is necessarily defined by a multitude of dimensions. Although one dimension of collective identification, by means of its supposed importance, may outrule others in a specific historical context, principally we have to consider each individual as identifying with more than one collective. This brings into play the question of how different collective identifications, being co-present in one society and flowing together in each individual, compete and interfere with one another politically and socially. These tensions will be a major topic of many of the chapters in this book. Generally, every single device for the sorting of people according to a homogeneity-heterogeneity rationale is not only a struggle of *us versus them* but also a struggle against the legitimacy and validity of other competing categories.

COMPARING INTOLERANCE

Although some of the chapters in this book are explicitly comparative, as a whole the volume does not pursue a systematic approach toward comparative history. The purpose is rather to stimulate further comparative research efforts in the topics discussed by suggesting some dimensions and perspectives that we consider worthy of closer exploration. In light of the current state of research in the field, a modest proposal for starting points for further work is probably all that can be offered. As a consequence, this book investigates the cases of two national histories rather than comparing them. Its methodological status is, so to speak, proto-comparative. Similarly, other recent projects in the comparative study of national and other collective identities – which mostly look at cases from continental Europe – are also methodologically preliminary.[20] Interested scholars are still working toward a prolegomena for systematic and methodologically elaborated comparisons.

Traditional scholarly work on the topics of nationalism and national identity, such as the national character research of the nineteenth and early twentieth centuries or studies on the history of ideas of nationalism, used to be constrained by the limits of the nation as its constitutive category and thus reproduced the limitations of its subject.[21] Modernization theory, another major branch of research relevant to this field, viewed industrialization and the division of labor as the ultimate reason for the emergence of nations and the founding of nation-states and therefore tended to take nations, nationalism, and national movements for granted as the necessary correlates of the development of modern societies. Although it stimulated much comparative research, it was not very interested in the category of the nation. A third tradition of research of immediate importance for this field is the sociopsychological study of nationalism, ethnocentrism, racism, and anti-Semitism – the aberrations of modernity – under the rubric of the study of prejudice. Like modernization theory, it addresses its topics as a problem of modern societies in general, but, unlike modernization theory, it did not trigger any comparative efforts. After all, the specific conditions of national identification seemed to be less important since personality structures were taken to be the result of the alienating effects of modernity as such and, therefore,

---

20 For a survey among European nations see Bernd Estel and Tilman Meyer, eds., *Das Prinzip Nation in modernen Gesellschaften: Länderdiagnosen und theoretische Perspektiven* (Opladen, 1994). For a diachronical and synchronical comparison of the category of the nation in modern history see Bernhard Giesen, ed., *Nationale und kulturelle Identität: Studien zur Entwicklung des kollektiven Bewusstseins in der Neuzeit* (Frankfurt/Main, 1991).

21 This is true despite a tradition of comparing national characteristics that goes back to Herder and Montesquieu because this tradition takes the nation as the subject of history for granted and asks only for the environmental, cultural, or political reasons for the formation of different national characters.

should affect individuals without regard to any national peculiarities.[22] In any case, a comparative effort in the study of nationalism, racism, and anti-Semitism was a logical necessity for none of these traditions.

Only during the last five or ten years has the field witnessed a considerable rise in the number of books that attempt to provide comparative research or, at least, determine dimensions for future comparisons in the study of national and other collective identities. This body of work has been triggered by two entirely independent processes, one taking place in the political field, and the other in the field of social theory. Politically, it was again the collapse of the various state socialisms in Central and Eastern Europe and the reemergence of nationalist and ethnic conflicts in their place that provoked the renewed debate on nationalism. The parallels between these reemerging nationalisms were so striking that they forced social scientists and historians to do something they had rarely done before, namely, take a multinational approach toward nationalism.

Theoretically, it was the development of a "culturalist paradigm"[23] in history and the humanities that stimulated a comparative perspective on collective identities.[24] The culturalization of the categories of nation, race, and sex deprived them of their quasi-natural or ontological status and allowed scholars to conceptualize them as social and cultural constructs. Thus, ethnicity replaced race, and gender was substituted for sex, within intellectual debates. The nation, so far either indisputably accepted as the coherent subject of modern history or dismissed as a transitory and outdated phenomenon on the road to universal humanism, became conceivable as being both a consequence and a condition of political, social, and cultural practice.

ON THE SELECTION OF CASES

In almost every facet of our overall topic, Italy and France share more similarities to Germany than does the United States. Their demographic

---

22 This tradition mainly emerged after and as a result of German Nazism and the success of various fascisms in various European countries. It brought forth classics such as Theodor W. Adorno et al., *The Authoritarian Personality*, Studies in Prejudice, vol. 1 (New York, 1950); Gordon W. Allport, *The Nature of Prejudice* (Reading, Mass., 1954); or Milton Rokeach, *The Open and the Closed Mind: Investigations into the Nature of Belief Systems and Personality Systems* (New York, 1960).

23 Bernhard Giesen, "Einleitung," in Bernhard Giesen, ed., *Nationale und kulturelle Identität: Studien zur Entwicklung des kollektiven Bewusstseins in der Neuzeit* (Frankfurt/Main, 1991), 12.

24 The term "culturalist turn" has been chosen in order to cover a wider area than the popular term "linguistic turn." It refers not only to poststructuralist theories, but also to, e.g., Bourdieu's

structures and their population densities are quite similar; their political and party systems are closer to each other than any of these are to that of the United States; they share the contemporary institutional framework of the European Union; and they are confronted with roughly similar patterns of immigration. Would it not be obvious, therefore, to collect essays on Germany and Italy or France? And, conversely, should the case of the United States not be compared to that of a more similar society, another society of immigrants, for example, neighboring Canada? Although certainly not dismissing a continental European or a Northern American approach as superfluous or fruitless, there are numerous reasons for contrasting the less similar – and yet not completely dissimilar – cases of Germany and the United States.

First, even where it is applied in a less explorative and more systematic manner than at present, the comparative method does not inherently require the maximization of similarities of its cases. As a matter of fact, the dispositives of similarity versus difference, concordance versus divergence, or affinity versus contrast of cases are a general feature of methodologies of comparative social research that allow one to distinguish different comparative strategies.[25] Of course, similarity or contrast of cases is always relative and automatically implicates a metacomparison to still other cases. Thus, a sample containing Germany and the United States can be considered a "difference of systems" approach if metacompared to samples containing Germany and France or the United States and Canada. However, metacompared to a sample consisting of the United States and a non-Western country, such as China, it might appear to follow a "similar systems" approach. In any case, the largely different contexts of Germany and the United States by no means diminish the

---

culturalist revision of class theory, Habermas's theory of communicative action, or Foucault's discourse theory (which is often but falsely subsumed under the label of the linguistic turn).

25 Although the taxonomic systems vary, they all refer to the problem of the selection of cases according to a maximization of similarity or difference with respect to either the independent variables, the dependent variables, or both. See, e.g., Adam Przeworski and Henry Teune, *The Logic of Comparative Social Inquiry* (New York, 1970), 32–9, which favors a contrast of contexts; Arthur L. Stinchcombe, *Theoretical Methods in Social History* (New York, 1978), who features the methodology of "deep analogy" as an extreme case of the "similarity of systems" design. Classic texts advocating a similarity approach are Arend Lijphart, "Comparative Politics and Comparative Method," *American Political Science Review* 65 (1971): 682–93, and Arend Lijphart, "The Comparable Cases Strategy in Comparative Research," *Comparative Politics* 1 (1975): 3–18. For an introduction to the problem of "Small N, many variables," see David Collier, "The Comparative Method," in Ada Finiter, ed., *Political Science: The State of the Discipline* (Washington, D.C., 1993), 111–12. For a brief introduction to comparative method, see also A. G. Heidelberg, "Vergleichende Methode," in Dieter Nohlen and Rainer-Olaf Schulze, eds., *Politikwissenschaft: Theorien – Methoden – Begriffe*, vol. N–Z, Pipers Wörterbuch zur Politik, ed. Dieter Nohlen, 1, no. 2 (Munich, 1985): 1079–85.

chances of acquiring fruitful insights. Comparing apples and oranges is potentially a very productive strategy after all – especially for learning the differences between the subjects undergoing comparison.

Comparative research on Germany and the United States unfolds on the common tableau of the conditions of modern industrial society. Within that context of communality, the comparative strategy has to follow the "contrast of cases" approach. Seen from the perspective of a political history of intolerance, the *us versus them* theme of this book translates into the question of how intolerance toward minorities is hindered or fostered by different types of political integration and identification. The comparison of Germany and the United States provides an almost ideal platform for answering this question because the two cases mark the opposite ends of a scale of different ways of defining nationalism and promoting national integration. Among all Western-type nations, Germany is the purest example of a nation based on common culture and citizenship derived from *jus sanguinis* (blood citizenship), just as the United States provides the prime example of a culturally diverse nation integrated by a common political idea and equipped with an unqualified *jus solis* (territorial citizenship). Practically all concepts of nationhood and citizenship found in the Western world range somewhere between these poles, each promoting its particular and idiosyncratic blend of the pure or almost pure forms represented in our sample. Thus, an exploration of the German and American cases is very well suited for an analysis of the connection between political identity and tolerance toward heterogeneity.

A second reason for the German-American perspective's special appeal is the remarkable attention the discourses on homogeneity and heterogeneity in the two countries pay to each other. This mutual attention makes these discourses codependent rather than autonomous: German discourses on diversity always have the American experience as their backdrop, just as American discourses on nationalism and xenophobia are inherently linked to Germany.

Germany's tendency to define itself by how much it resembles the United States is fed from two different sources. First, as Europeans, Germans throughout the twentieth century perceived the United States as a symbolic representation of modernity's promises and pitfalls. America was the place where one's own future, be it blissful or monstrous, seemed to happen already in the present. It therefore became the yardstick for German and European self-assessment. Second, West Germany's political reorganization after the moral, political, and military disasters of the

Nazi era, the Holocaust, and World War II took place under the supervision and according to the model of the Western democracies under the leadership of the United States. Hence, practically every relevant political discourse in Germany since 1945 is played out with the American example in mind, implicitly or explicitly, often in an affirmative, sometimes in a negative manner. This is especially true for many of the topics discussed in this book, since the United States, for Germans, provides the paradigmatic example of an ethnically and culturally heterogeneous immigrant society. Thus, current German discourses on political integration and alienation, on the relation between immigration and social stability, and on a multicultural versus a culturally and ethnically homogeneous society are essentially structured by different and competing interpretations of America as a society that is civil, liberal, and open-minded, or violent, unstable, and disintegrating.

In any case, German perceptions of America always implicitly determined the course of German political discourse. Likewise, whereas Germany certainly does not – and for obvious historical reasons cannot – play the role of a model for the United States,[26] the American political discourse is particularly sensitive toward Germany with respect to the topics discussed here. Just as the United States has been perceived as the paradigmatic case of modernity, Germany's history over the course of the twentieth century has been taken as a representation of modernity's aberrations and pathologies. On the one hand, two world wars and the Holocaust have established Germany as the prime example of the destructive and murderous consequences of the furies of nationalism, anti-Semitism, and racism. On the other, postwar Germany served and continues to serve as the prime example of successful democratization. Thus, Germany and the United States occupy the extremes on a scale that represents the risks and rewards of Western-style modernity, and both national discourses are linked in a relationship of mutual, if asymmetric, attention.

THE ORGANIZATION OF THIS BOOK

This book is not the result of a unified research project; rather, it evolved out of a scholarly conference. Consequently, the individual contributions emerge from autonomous research interests and display the individual

---

26 Some exceptions do apply. Thus, certain features of German politics and society, especially in education and in social politics, have been, and currently are, discussed as potentially exemplary in parts of the political spectrum of the United States.

intellectual styles of their authors, who represent a variety of academic disciplines – history, political science, cultural studies, linguistics, literature, and sociology – and a large range of theoretical and methodological approaches. Conference volumes are a peculiar type of literature. The very nature of their production does not permit a very high degree of systematology – the intellects they bring together are too obstinate and too idiosyncratic. If things turn out well, such collections make up for this lack of coherence by the originality of their contributions in terms of subject, perspective, theory, and methodology.

The period spanned by the chapters in this book reaches from the Enlightenment to the present day. Some attempt longitudinal cross sections through the whole or large parts of this span, and others focus on specific periods. The connection between nationalism and modernization obviously argues for the study of modes of inclusion and exclusion over a longer time frame. This is necessary for perceiving the covariances in the development of features of social, political, and cultural modernization on the one hand, and of social, political, and cultural tolerance and intolerance on the other. Nevertheless, the pace of modernization is not constant; its history is one of crisis and disruption, of thresholds and transition. Certain historical periods present themselves as times of accelerated change, often accompanied by deep crisis. The correlation of crisis (for example, uncertainty with regard to personal and social prospects, political turmoil, changing moral standards, challenged economic security) with nationalist, racist, or ethnocentrist intolerance is incontrovertible. These moments of rapid transformation in many areas of life – for example, the Napoleonic occupation of many German states, the American Civil War, the emergence of American imperialism in the 1890s, Germany on the eve of World War I, the Great Depression of the 1930s – allow us to study our subjects under the intense pressure of transition.

Methodologically and theoretically, the chapters in this book comprise three clusters that might be labeled "history of ideas and ideologies," "social history," and "discourse theory." We have chosen this approach because we suspect that these areas of thought and research, which all too often appear as competitors on the academic market, actually complement each other. The history of ideas and ideologies, as well as social history, has undeniable merits not only for the study of history in general but also for the understanding of the history of nationalism, racism, and xenophobia in particular. To prove this point, it might be sufficient to point to classics such as Helmuth Plessner's *Die verspätete Nation* or

Oliver C. Cox's *Class, Caste, and Race.*[27] The book also has chapters that employ discourse theory, since we felt that this newer and less established approach, especially the branch linked to Michel Foucault's work, might present the opportunity to integrate both perspectives. In this way, the perspectives are not merely added but are placed into a common theoretical framework that offers an understanding of the formative forces of discursive *and* social practices in the process of creating and redefining social institutions. We have tried to avoid favoring any of the theoretical approaches, because we wanted to incorporate the specific strength of each. After all, in the absence of a common and unified theory of tolerance, intolerance, and of the sorting of people according to a rationale of *us versus them*, eclecticism, understood as the attempt to get the best out of more than one perspective on a topic, seems to be an adequate way to deal with the inadequacies of the available approaches.

The chapters in this book are grouped into three parts that are defined not by chronology, theory, or methodology, but by theme. Part One approaches nations and national identities as cultural and symbolic constructions; Part Two presents chapters that study the social and cultural practices of racism in everyday history; and Part Three discusses the conjunction of race and bodily and biological features, first with respect to the gendering of race and then with a focus on scientific racism.

Entitled "Concepts of National Identity and the Symbolic Construction of Nations," Part One features essays on national identity and the understanding of nationhood as the result of an interplay between cultural dispositions, the needs of modernizing societies, and deliberate efforts in symbolic politics. The prevalent theoretical perspectives in this part of the book are those of a history of ideas and of discourse analysis. *Carl N. Degler's* chapter, "National Identity and the Conditions of Tolerance," takes a macroscopic account of our overall theme in the modern histories of Germany and the United States. In three major steps, he examines the political shaping of national identity in both countries since the turn of the nineteenth century, explores how it affected the definition and treatment of outsiders and their prospects for inclusion, and analyzes how national identity politics determine the social institutions of citizenship, class, and gender. The different paths Germany and the United States took toward national identity are defined by the

---

27 Helmuth Plessner, *Die verspätete Nation: über die politische Verführbarkeit bürgerlichen Geistes* (Frankfurt/Main, 1974); Oliver C. Cox, *Class, Caste, and Race: A Study in Social Dynamics* (New York, 1949).

dichotomy of the politics of ethnic homogeneity versus the creation of a diverse people under the (repeatedly redefined) twin symbols of freedom and equality; this difference can, as Degler's chapter shows, be traced in different social institutions. Thus, Degler proves that national identity transcends the limited doctrine of nationalism and actually works as the political habitus of a nation – a habitus that pervades regions of their political existence and that, at first glance, seems to have nothing to do with matters of nationhood.

Frank Trommler's chapter, "The Historical Invention and Modern Reinvention of Two National Identities," takes a similarly bold approach toward the topics of identity, inclusion, and exclusion. Like Degler, Trommler has an understanding of national identity that includes much more than nationalist doctrine. Unlike Degler, who conceptualizes the political history of national identity formation as the independent variable and examines the determining effects it has on the construction of the socially "Other," Trommler focuses on the identity effects of living and working in an environment of industrial mass production and consumption. He challenges the trend in recent research to analyze matters of identity formation exclusively in terms of symbolic representation and the mediation of experience by insisting on the formative role of unmediated daily experience in the process of shaping national identities. Taking the connection between nationalism and industrial modernization as a starting point, Trommler holds that political symbolism and the politics of representation dominated only the first step – the original invention – of national identities by nineteenth-century elites, while its "modern reinvention" in the age of developed industrialism is essentially a matter of industrial work, status allocation through work, and the development of a national work ethos.

Following Degler's and Trommler's broad and comparative accounts on national identity, *Gregg Kvistad's* chapter, "Segmented Politics," takes a thematically narrower approach and tackles the politics of citizenship and membership in Germany. The chapter makes a historically informed contribution to an issue being debated currently in Germany, namely, the reform of citizenship law as a means to fight xenophobia. Based on the analysis of Prussian and German citizenship concepts in the nineteenth and twentieth centuries, Kvistad makes the case that the pivot of the German understanding of citizenship is not so much the *jus sanguinis* principle but political loyalty toward the state, with *jus sanguinis* being an important but not the only operational mode to distinguish between definitionally loyal and disloyal subjects or citizens. Furthermore, Kvistad argues, a "sorting device" similar to citizenship – which distinguishes horizontally between Germans and non-Germans – is also employed in varying historical forms, in order to differentiate vertically between different kinds of German citizens according to their supposed loyalty to the state and its institutions, with members of the civil service inhabiting a hortatory "state realm" distinguished from the principally suspect "derogatory" realm of society. In a discussion of more recent changes in German political culture since the 1960s, Kvistad finds evidence that the statist demand for loyalty enshrined in citizenship law as well as in civil service politics, which has to be considered one of the most important and historically persistent obstacles to the development of an open and civic society, is increasingly disappearing from the German landscape. It will eventually give way to a democratic, horizontal, and nonhierarchical mode of distinction among different kinds of Germans that will finally allow for the political and social metamorphosis of outsiders into insiders.

The "sorting of people" in order to control the dynamics of modern mass society is also the central topic of *Ute Gerhard*'s chapter, "The Discursive Construction of National Stereotypes." In a case study of nationalist, racist, and identity discourses in Germany before World War I, Gerhard takes the sorting of people into a "We" and an opposing "Them" to be the basic functional analogy of nationalist and racist discourses and of national and racial identities. Applying Foucauldian discourse analysis and the theory of normalization, and drawing upon sources of fiction, demography, national economy, eugenics, and historiography, the chapter reconstructs the formation and deployment of national and racial stereotypes. Gerhard argues that nation and race constitute an interdiscourse that is fed from a wide variety of specialized and nonspecialized discourses and creates a coherent system of symbolic representations of collectives and masses. Within this system of symbols, the dichotomy of *us versus them* is associated with normatively highly loaded dichotomies such as orderly versus chaotic, strong versus weak, normal versus abnormal, healthy versus pathological, or pure versus mingled.

The first part of the book concludes with a chapter by *Dietmar Schirmer* on integration and fragmentation discourses in Germany and the United States. With this chapter, we return to the explicitly comparative format of the contributions by Degler and Trommler but now focus on current rather than historical topics. The analysis employs a two-dimensional concept of collective identity, with history as the vertical and social integration as the horizontal dimension of identity formation.

This concept serves as the analytical framework for a comparison of current German and American discourses on social, cultural, national, and ethnic integration and fragmentation. Based on four case studies, the chapter asserts the two national discourses to be in a state of asynchronicity. Whereas the American discourse on identity can be tracked as a battle of modernism versus postmodernism, the German discourse is a fight over premodernism versus modernism and postmodernism.

Part Two of the book, entitled "The Social and Cultural Practice of Racism," features chapters that employ the methods of social and cultural history in order to analyze racism as a lived and practiced ideology under varying political, social, and economic conditions. This part opens with *W. Fitzhugh Brundage*'s elaboration on the problem of racial violence – lynchings and race riots – in the postbellum South. His chapter uses a new and multifaceted interpretational framework to shed new light on a topic that has already attracted a large amount of scholarly work. Brundage abandons the old categorical dualisms of race/class and race/gender by stressing the dynamic interrelations among all three categories. In this perspective, class identity is inherently not only racialized but gendered as well. By incorporating a multidimensional understanding of class, it becomes possible to interpret racial violence as a systematic rather than an arbitrary means of maintaining status privileges, gender boundaries, and race hierarchies. By applying this interpretational framework to various episodes of racial violence in Spalding and Forsyth Counties, Georgia, spanning the period from the 1890s to the 1910s, Brundage gives impressive proof of its heuristic value. He also suggests its application to racial violence in other societies and different time periods, indicating that the concept might serve as a tool for systematic comparative research.

Herbert Shapiro's chapter examines the links between domestic racist practice and colonial politics. It is a widespread notion that the lack of forceful imperialism sets the United States apart from the development of other Western industrial nations, and that imperialist politics and warfare are merely a temporary aberration in American history. Shapiro's chapter supports this interpretation by demonstrating a double-bind between "Racism and Empire." Not coincidentally, he argues, the period of the American colonial empire was also marked by a ferocious eruption of domestic racial violence. Shapiro presents substantial evidence that the patterns of racism, learned and acquired on domestic turf and practiced in the oppression of African Americans and Native Americans, functioned as a legitimating tool for the Spanish-American War and the establishment of colonial regimes in the Philippines and elsewhere, as, vice versa, the colonial experience of white, Anglo-Saxon dominance reinforced notions of racial superiority and practices of racist violence at home.

In his chapter, "Police, African Americans, and Irish Immigrants in the Nation's Capital," *Norbert Finzsch* draws on sources of the Metropolitan Police Department, established by Congress in 1861, to gain insight into the differential treatment imposed on African-American and Irish minorities by the police force in the nation's capital. The stunning frequency of arrests – their average number per year almost equaling the city's population – leads Finzsch to treat police records as documents of the everyday history of racism. The overall approach of the chapter is to understand crime control not so much as a means of protecting the interests of victims of crime, but as a system of power that reveals at least as much about those who enforce the law as it does about those who break it. Finzsch splits his sample of roughly four thousand cases into white citizens, African Americans, and Irish immigrants, and controls the subgroups according to gender, class – based on profession and literacy – age, offense, disposal, and fine. Surprisingly, the findings suggest the Irish immigrants were most likely to be singled out by the police as suspects, whereas African Americans were not overrepresented in the sample. Finzsch attributes the latter to the existence of the "Black Codes," which still restricted the freedom of movement and ensured the "good behavior" of African Americans without police supervision. However, anti-black racism is revealed by significantly higher fines imposed on African Americans, and by the fact that African Americans were much more likely than white citizens or Irish immigrants to be brought to police attention by private individuals.

The beginning of the Civil Rights movement is closely associated with the Montgomery Bus Boycott, led by Martin L. King Jr. in the mid-1950s. *Ralf Koch*'s chapter, "The Politics of Boycotting," is about the prehistory of Montgomery, focusing on African-American boycotts aimed at discriminatory practices, such as hiring policies, in the decades preceding the Civil Rights movement. The chapter also takes into account other struggles where purchasing power was employed as a political weapon by or against minorities. The list of cases is considerable. It includes the black, Catholic, and Jewish boycotts of KKK-related businesses in Columbus, Ohio, in the 1920s; white, union-led anti-Asian boycotts in the West during the late nineteenth century; African-American streetcar boycotts in the Jim Crow South; the American boycott of

German imports in the Nazi era; and the boycotts of Jewish businesses by German anti-Semitic activists, later sanctioned and endorsed by Nazi authorities and enforced by SA Brownshirts. Clearly, whether boycotts targeted ethnic minorities or the discriminatory practices of majority businesses defines the moral distinction between the politics of boycotting as a means of repression or emancipation. Although this distinction is clear in principle, the debate triggered by the fact that African Americans in the 1930s also targeted, although not systematically, Jewish businesses demonstrates how this distinction can become blurred in the heat of social struggles based on ethnic background.

The rejection of ethnic minorities is often explained in terms of the majority society's inability to accept Otherness. In his chapter on Jews and the German language since the turn of the nineteenth century, *Dietz Bering* shows that eventually the logic of exclusion might be the reverse: The lack of Otherness on the part of a group already recognized as being different may well be at the core of the furor of exclusion. Lacking a unified nation-state, German national identity was, since the late eighteenth century, founded on the notion of the *Kulturnation*, with language being the foremost marker of Germanness. Principally, this concept should have offered German Jews the option of acquiring full integration by acquiring full command of the German language – an option that writers and intellectuals like Jakob Wassermann or Elias Canetti clearly saw and claimed. Bering shows in detail how German anti-Semites nevertheless, and eventually against all empirical evidence, maintained that Jews never were nor would be able to speak German as Germans do, but could only speak it as a foreign language, mimicking true German at best. When the empirical difference between High German and the Jewish languages and dialects of Yiddish and *Jüdeln* vanished and the overwhelming majority of German Jews spoke High German, anti-Semitic propaganda turned from the spoken language to an imagined "spirit" of the language to maintain the obsolete demarcation between Germans and Jews.

Part Three, called "Race, Gender, Body, Biology," features two different perspectives on the conjunction of race and bodily features. The first two chapters deal with aspects of race and gender; the last two chapters analyze scientific racism as it spread from the discourses of medicine and biology; and in between, Patricia Vertinsky's chapter, with its focus on gendered and racialized perceptions of physical ability, builds the bridge leading from the gender perspective to the race perspective. Part Three opens with *Lois E. Horton's* chapter, "Ambiguous Roles," in which discussion of the race-gender nexus moves from eighteenth- and nineteenth-century Germany to the nineteenth- and twentieth-century United States, and from the scientific discourse of white males on women and non-whites to the discourse and social practice of black women. The "feminizing" effect slavery had on black men by preventing them from living up to "manly" role prescriptions has long been a topic for discussion in American social theory and history. This focus on the fate of black men, Horton criticizes, once again obscures the view of the role and fate of black women. Horton argues that throughout American history black women were denied the right to construct their own identity and were pressed into ambiguous and conflicting roles. Whereas slavery "feminized" black women along with black men by disempowering them, at the same time it "masculinized" black women by disregarding traditional gender roles and demanding hard, that is, manly, labor. After abolition, black women remained caught between demands for their strength as laborers and breadwinners and the demands of black men that they support and strengthen their manhood by submitting to traditional roles in child rearing and the household. This ambiguity survived essentially unaltered and can, as the chapter shows, be traced to the debates on gender roles in the 1960s Civil Rights movement, where black women who fought for their rights as women were implicitly and explicitly accused of undermining the common cause of black emancipation.

Eileen Boris's chapter, "Citizenship Embodied," takes up the concepts and politics of citizenship discussed in Kvistad's chapter. Whereas Kvistad approaches the history of citizenship in Germany, Boris's subject is American history. And, whereas Kvistad focuses on loyalty, Boris focuses on the conjunction of race, ethnicity, and gender as a means to determine eligibility for citizenship rights. Thus, the chapter reverts to the race-gender approach already taken up by Horton and Brundage but applies it to policy and institutional analysis rather than to social history. In taking up the extended debate over comparative welfare states, Boris introduces a multilayered understanding of citizenship that differentiates between the political, the civic, and the social dimensions of the concept and examines how the state grants or denies membership rights in all three respects on the grounds of race and gender.

Patricia Vertinsky's chapter, "Body Matters," examines medical and anthropological discourses in Germany from the Enlightenment until the early twentieth century. The chapter demonstrates how perceptions of bodies and physical features constitute a unified order and hierarchy of races and genders that determine social roles and political membership rights on the basis of a rationale of normality versus degeneration. Her starting point is the observation that, by means of analogy, women and members of "inferior" races are located at the same end of a scale of physical ability. The opposing end is occupied by the white "Aryan" male. Dichotomies of physical appearance, such as strength versus weakness or beauty versus ugliness, are then associated with dichotomies describing and prescribing intellectual, moral, political, and military qualities. Vertinsky mainly focuses on the female pelvis and the Jew's foot as bodily features of outstanding significance for the stereotyping of gender and race. Thus, it is the pelvis that becomes the marker for the reproductive function of women and prescribes their image as being complementary to men. In very much the same way, Jews are marked by means of their supposed flat-footedness as a race of inferior physical ability and, therefore, unfit for military service, which of course implies their being unfit for full citizenship.

With the chapters of Arnd Krüger and Peter Weingart, the discussion of the taxonomy of people according to bodily features moves on to the scientific plane. Modern scientific discourses are principally international. Nevertheless, certain scientific discourses tend to take on a distinctively national character. This observation calls for an explanation that, logically, cannot be immanent but has to be drawn from the broader cultural, social, and political context within which scientific discourses are situated. Thus, *Arnd Krüger*'s chapter, "A Horse Breeder's Perspective," reconstructs the peculiarities of the German branch of scientific racism as the result of an interdiscursive constellation that links the scientific and, by nature, international discourses of medicine, anthropology, and demography with the nonscientific discourses of sports and breeding. Krüger's chapter reveals how a specific set of homologies between racism, horse breeding, and sports created a structure of possibilities for the broad appeal of scientific racism in the German public and, under the conditions of a cultural disposition to interpret "fitness" as a collective rather than an individual matter, prepared the ground for its political implementation by the Nazi regime.

Peter Weingart's chapter, "The Thin Line Between Eugenics and Preventive Medicine," continues Krüger's discussion and brings the topic forward to the present day. Weingart analyzes the scientific, social, and political implications of the discourse on eugenics and preventive medicine from the evolution of the anthropological and medical branches of eugenics at the beginning of the twentieth century to today's Human

Genome Project, with the Nazi politics of eugenics defining the moral and ethical watershed. The chapter's main concern is whether society can prevent the rapidly increasing knowledge of the human genetic map from being used for the old selectionist eugenics programs. The answer stresses that there is no built-in barrier, although the ever more complex knowledge of the human gene pool does not easily lend legitimacy to the primitive rationale of racism. On the contrary, Weingart argues that the actual implementation of this knowledge is a matter of ethical and political judgment; reliable barriers against the regression of selectionist politics can be set only by the political system, a cautious and well-informed public, and a democratic political culture.

PART ONE

Concepts of National Identity and the Symbolic Construction of Nations

1

National Identity and the Conditions of Tolerance

CARL N. DEGLER

National identity is a concept frequently raised by a people or by a government, as when we ask, Who are Americans? or What does it mean to be German? Yet, as we also know, the sense of identity that a people or a government arrive at can be a slippery concept and not infrequently a changing one. If national identity is not easy to define precisely, it is, nonetheless, often used, sometimes for necessary and important purposes, like mobilizing a people for war, and sometimes for keeping others out. Since this collection of essays treats the question of the Outsider in the history of Germany and the United States, I should like to offer some suggestions as to how the achievement of national identity in these two countries might throw some light on the issue of xenophobia.

Only by examining the sources and uses of the identity of people over time – that is, through history – can one understand and appreciate the circumstances out of which tolerance emerges or is sustained. Or, to put the matter a little more comparatively: One may learn about the conditions and uses of tolerance by recalling the past presence of intolerance.

Despite the divergent histories of Germany and the United States – about which more will be said later – today they share a concern. Thanks to an upsurge in immigration over the last four or five years, leaders and followers in both countries have been asking an old question, "Who is a German?" or "Who is an American?" On the face of it, the peoples of these two countries do not seem to have a common concern about who they are. After all, one country – the United States – has flourished as a nation of immigrants, whereas the other has proudly defined itself as a nation of emigrants, of people who have departed from their homeland to settle elsewhere. (Indeed, more Germans have settled

3

in the United States than any other single immigrant nationality.) Since the destruction of the Berlin Wall and the consequent influx of refugees and immigrants into Germany, another side of German national identity has emerged. It has been popularly captured by a recent remark by Chancellor Helmut Kohl and by others. Germany, they insist, despite the many new arrivals, is not a country of immigrants.

The United States, for its part, has indeed often described itself as a nation of immigrants, but today that description does not sit well with some Americans. It is not that they deny the immigration history of the country; rather, like Kohl and his supporters, they think immigration today is too threatening, too overpowering, and perhaps too transforming of American identity. In my own state of California, for example, Governor Pete Wilson has pinpointed the threat to national identity from immigration in strikingly strong terms. The governor's concern derives from the stream of legal and illegal immigrants entering California over the last few years, the social costs of which, the governor argues, cannot and should not be borne by the state. Governor Wilson has frankly called for amending the U.S. Constitution to remove the right of citizenship from children born of immigrant parents. This is part of his plan to control the large number of immigrants entering the United States from Asia and Latin America.[1] It seems unlikely, to be sure, that anyone will take Wilson's solution seriously. But that he should even consider such a radical remedy testifies to the present concern about national identity, even in a country – and a state, I might add – in which immigration has been a founding principle.

Wilson's remedy is indeed a radical and insupportable one, but recognizing threats to national identity because of the influx of strangers into the United States is not novel. It is true that even in its colonial days America was a diverse social order with blacks, Jews, Swedes, Scots, Germans, the Dutch, Welsh, French, and Irish all mingling together with the politically dominant English. Yet a widely diversified population by itself did not accept with open arms the great number of Germans and Catholic Irish, who entered the United States in the two decades before the Civil War. One consequence of their arrival was large-scale hostility toward the newcomers. Violence against Irish Catholics in several cities during the 1840s was one form of hostility. Another was the creation of a national political party – the American Party, as it was called – dedicated to separating immigrants from other Americans by lengthening

---

1　*Los Angeles Times*, Aug. 10, 1993, A1; Aug. 11, 1993, A20.

their period of naturalization to twenty-one years and preventing their leaders from holding public office because of foreign birth. That nativist effort failed because of the Civil War, but when large numbers of Chinese entered the country soon after the war, non-Asian Californians sought, often violently, to exclude Chinese from being considered Americans. In 1882 the federal government prohibited the entry of any more Chinese immigrants. That was the first, but not the last, national effort to debate the question of who was to be included as an American.

During the 1890s and the first decade of the twentieth century, when a great wave of immigration broke over the country – this time from eastern and southern Europe – Americans once again began to rethink the nature of their national identity. Many contended that the newcomers were less socially adaptable, more criminal, less intelligent, and less healthy than the resident population. Efforts to restrict immigration began in the 1890s and reached a climax in the 1920s. The aim was to distinguish among national groups since it was believed that some people were less satisfactory as potential Americans than others, that is to say, those newcomers who differed from the Irish and the Germans, who had by then been accepted within American national identity. The first device used to deny entrance to these new arrivals – the Russians, Hungarians, Greeks, Poles, and Italians – was a literacy test, which was defeated by three different presidential vetoes on the ground that such tests discriminated against the disadvantaged, who in time would surely be acceptable Americans.

The most concerted and successful effort to remove the threat posed by immigration to American national identity took place after World War I. The Immigration Act of 1924, for the first time since the exclusion of Chinese and Japanese, severely limited the number of immigrants entering the United States, something that the nativists of the 1850s had never even thought of doing. (The number went from almost a million a year before 1914 to 150,000.) But for our purposes, the most important aspect of this act was the attempt to define American national identity by ascertaining the distribution of nationalities that historically had made up the population. The size of each country's future immigration to the United States would then be set by the historical distribution of past immigration. That distribution would be considered to be the country's proper mix of nationalities.

This approach to American identity prevailed for the next forty years, that is, the years of the Great Depression, World War II, and the postwar dislocation around the world – the years when immigration offered no

threat or challenge to American identity. Then, in 1965, immigration policy was loosened, and the definition of an American culture or society,
which the 1924 legislation had imposed, was abandoned.

The point of all of this, of course, is to recognize that for the United
States, the creation of a diverse population has not been a simple, linear
development, but an uneven and often conflicted one. And at the present
time, as we have already observed, the question of who is a proper
American has once again been publicly and forcefully raised. Yet just
because today many Americans are insistently worried about being overwhelmed by outside arrivals, it is worth reminding ourselves that the
insistence is not new. It is also worth recollecting that among other New
World nations, this history of often hostile and often violent opposition
is peculiarly American. In other countries of immigration, such as Brazil
and Argentina, the kind of nativist restrictions or concern that punctu-
ated the history of the United States simply has not occurred.

In the end, it was the idea of diversity of peoples that eventually
reduced or resolved the antagonisms and conflicts between natives and
newcomers. This is particularly pertinent when one studies the concept
of diversity in America and Germany. How each society deals with
diversity affects the national identity and the conditions of tolerance
in each. Although many Germans believe, as we have seen, that Germany
is not an immigrant country, that cliché may be more a myth than a
fact of German history. Even if one leaves out the French Protestants
who came at the invitation of the Great Elector to Brandenberg in the
seventeenth century, and even if we ignore Frederick the Great's respect
for French friends, one cannot ignore the thousands of Polish peasants
in the mid-nineteenth century who came to the Ruhr River valley to
pull the levers, mine the coal, and pour the steel required of an expanding German industrial economy. Nor ought we to forget the three million Poles in 1890 who lived within the culture of a Polish church and
Polish language inside the confines of Frederick the Great's Prussian
Silesia and Otto von Bismarck's Second Reich.[2] Then, in the course of
World Wars I and II, Germany again brought in millions of *Ausländer* or
foreign laborers to make up for the shortage of native workers. Finally,
in the course of the *Wirtschaftswunder* (economic miracle) of the 1950s
and 1960s, Germany once again encouraged millions more – the so-
called *Gastarbeiter* (guest workers) from Italy, Yugoslavia, and especially

---

2 Harry Kenneth Rosenthal, *German and Pole: National Conflict and Modern Myth* (Gainesville, Fla.,
  1976), 62.

Turkey – to answer a need for industrial workers. In sum, the population of Germany under the Bismarck regime and thereafter has been noticeably diverse. Indeed, as one German historian remarked in 1994, the Federal Republic of Germany today, for all of its concern about the influx of refugees, is "a more homogeneous nation-state than was the Reich of 1871," because, as Heinrich August Winkler put it, at that time Poles, Danes, Alsatians, and Lorrainers were all inside the borders of the old empire.[3]

That history of German diversity, however, lacked an important ingredient: The diversification was not the kind into which the United States had been born. Germans, unlike Americans, did not accept their diversity; rather, they seemed to feel that their sense of identity as Germans, which they relished as well as required, was threatened. "Germany," a German historian has recently written, "once a country of emigration, is today a country of immigration, albeit an unwilling one."[4]

Virtually from the beginning of modern times, Prussia, which would become the dominant force in German nationhood, rejected certain groups within its borders because they were thought to be undesirable in one fashion or another. Frederick the Great was no German nationalist, and acquisition of Silesia in the mid-eighteenth century was his most prized conquest, yet he made no secret of his distress about the Poles, whom his military triumph had brought within Prussia's borders. Persistently and in a variety of ways, he sought to rout out the Poles and replace them with Prussian peasants.

Bismarck and those who followed him continued the pattern that Frederick began. To Bismarck and his supporters, the presence of Poles inside Germany's borders was denounced as a Slavic inundation, a threat to German identity. Bismarck's detestation of the Poles began long before he became chancellor of the new empire. In 1861, for example, he wrote to his sister, "Flay the Poles until they despair of life! I have all sympathy for their position, but if we wish to endure, we can do nothing else but extirpate them."[5] As chancellor, Bismarck certainly did not kill them, but he did insist that the German language be prescribed in the courts and

---

3 Heinrich August Winkler, "Rebuilding a Nation: The Germans Before and After Reunification," *Daedalus* 123 (winter 1994): 108.

4 Klaus J. Bade, "Immigration and Social Peace in United Germany," *Daedalus* 123 (winter 1994): 89.

5 William W. Hagen, *German, Poles, and Jews: The Nationality Conflict in the Prussian East, 1772–1914* (Chicago, 1980), 125.

public administration, something that the Austrians, for example, did not insist on. As historian William Hagen has concluded:

By 1914 Prussian Polish policy depended upon means which glaringly contradicted the principles of the German "state of law." It represented both a massive attack on the very existence of the Prussian Poles as a culturally and ethnically autonomous segment of the Reich's population and a strenuous effort to push the ethnic German border eastwards. This mode of officially promoted Germanization, posited upon the ideas of a Polish menace to the German nation and the necessity of the geographic expansion of the German people eastward, became one of the most fateful of imperial Germany's legacies to Hitler's National Socialist regime.[6]

The Poles were not the only group within the confines of Germany who were perceived as weakening German national identity. Like the Poles, Jews had long lived within the borders of various German states, including Prussia. Medieval anti-Semitism was pervasive in Europe, and even a royal figure of the Enlightenment such as Frederick the Great worked to limit the number of Jews within Prussia. Early German nationalist writers, such as Johann Gottlieb Fichte, made no secret that Jews were a serious danger to the national identity. "There is spread throughout nearly every country of Europe," Fichte wrote in 1733, "a powerful inimical state that wars continually against all others and often succeeds in bitterly oppressing their peoples – this state is Jewry. . . . To protect ourselves against them, again I see no means except to conquer their Promised Land and pack them off to it."[7] By the 1870s and 1880s hostility toward Jews in Germany was sufficiently widespread that a Protestant minister by the name of Adolf Stöcker created in 1878 his frankly anti-Semitic political organization, the Christian Socialist Workers' Party. The whole thrust of Stöcker's appeal and propaganda was to point out again and again the distinction between Jews and Germans, despite the legal and social acceptance that Jews had been gaining in Germany since the eighteenth century.

Even respectable leaders of German society felt free to denounce the "Jewish problem," as Berlin University professor Heinrich von Treitschke pointed out in a famous article in 1879. Soon thereafter Treitschke called for the removal of Jews from Germany because of the "grave danger . . . to the new expression of German life."[8] A broader measure of the so-

6 Ibid., 168.
7 Marvin Lowenthal, *The Jews of Germany: A Story of Sixteen Centuries* (New York, 1936), 229.
8 Quoted in Richard Gutteridge, *Open Thy Mouth for the Dumb! The German Evangelical Church and the Jews, 1879–1950* (Oxford, 1976), 13–15.

called Jewish threat to German identity was a petition signed by a quarter of a million people and sent to Bismarck that called for measures to preserve the German people from the alien domination of the Jews. Although anti-Semitic expressions declined in the 1890s, it was not rare for differences between Jews and Germans to continue to be expressed. As one Protestant clergyman remarked in 1913, "As a human being the Jew remains a Jew, and I am German. There is honestly no way of getting over this."[9] Even after the Empire had collapsed and a more liberal republic had taken its place, public attacks on Jews by respectable German groups or persons persisted. "It cannot be denied," wrote the general superintendent of pastors in 1928, "that in all the manifestations of disintegration in modern civilization Jewry has always played a leading role."[10]

Anti-Semitism was not unknown in the United States. As late as 1842, two states still excluded professing Jews from holding public office, although in more than a dozen states, many public offices were held by Jews.[11] Henry Adams, grandson and great-grandson of presidents, frequently expressed his hostility toward Jews and often in the same manner as some German contemporaries. Henry Adams was especially denunciatory of what he considered the excessive wealth and power of Jews, just as Stöcker frequently referred to Jews as the people of Mammon, who seemed to be threatening German unity and identity. During the 1890s, in the course of agitation over the silver question in the United States, some Populist and other political writers attacked some Jewish bankers for supporting the gold standard. But there was no frankly anti-Semitic political party in the United States comparable to Stöcker's, nor did Adams publicly express his privately held anti-Semitism as his German fellow historian Treitschke certainly did more than once. Indeed, between 1873 and 1890 references to "the Jewish question" appeared in at least five hundred German publications.[12] Anti-Semitic stereotypes appeared in American magazines, but there was no "Jewish problem." American identity had reached a point where Jews did not

9 Quoted in ibid., 26.
10 Quoted in ibid., 1.
11 Frederic Cople Jaher, *A Scapegoat in the New Wilderness: The Origins and Rise of Anti-Semitism in America* (Cambridge, Mass., 1994), 117. See also Leonard Dinnerstein, *Antisemitism in America* (New York, 1994), 250, where his story is harsher than Jaher's but concludes, "Thus, while anti-semitism has always been a problem for Jews in Christian society it has always been weaker in the United States than in European nations."
12 Hans-Ulrich Wehler, *The German Empire, 1871–1918,* trans. Kim Taylor (Leamington Spa, 1985), 106.

threaten the meaning of America, whereas among Germans, Jews, like Poles, were perceived as weakening Germany's newly created identity.

An awareness that Jews differed significantly from Germans may have been widespread in the late nineteenth century, but the sources of the difference were usually said to be based on the grounds of either race or of social achievement such as being wealthy or powerful. Religious doctrine or principle was only peripheral among the central differences many Germans felt about Jews. At the same time, religion played a more significant role in challenging German identity than it did among Americans. Germans, like Americans, may have begun with religious diversity, but the conditions of their tolerance differed greatly. Long before the Bismarckian Empire of 1871 had been thought of, much less created, Germany had been divided by years of war between Catholics and Protestants. By the time Bismarck sought to bring into being a national state in 1871, the religious wars had long since been left behind. Yet differences remained, as the existence of a strong national Catholic political party showed.

Although Bismarck was a committed Protestant, his drive to achieve German identity did not stem from a concern for doctrinal differences. Instead, he feared the alleged power of an international Catholic Church whose center was in Rome, that is, outside Germany. Thus, for almost ten years, beginning with Prussia and then with Germany as a whole, Bismarck sought to limit the authority of the Catholic Church in Germany in what soon became known as the Kulturkampf. It was less a war against cultures than a war in behalf of an alleged threat against German nationhood. Although determined to weld together the various components of his recently established empire, Bismarck exacerbated the very divisions he had hoped to heal. As one recent historian has recalled, "The damage wrought by the Kulturkampf was great. Much that had been won for the cause of national unity during the war against France [in 1871] had been trifled away during the years in which Germans had deliberately been set against Germans on confessional grounds."[13]

If a condition of tolerance has been diversity, as I have been suggesting, then German religious experience has hardly provided much support, but the American religious story does make the point that diversity encourages tolerance. In fact, religious diversity seems to have been the historical underpinning of the conditions of religious tolerance. So diverse were the religions of Americans by the time the Constitution

13 Gordon A. Craig, *Germany, 1866–1945* (New York, 1978), 77.

was drafted that no one could envision a dominant or state church, as was the case in England and most of Europe. Only freedom of religion, not mere toleration, seemed to suit the American scene. Full freedom of religious expression was a novel idea. In fact, the new federal republic was so insistent to realize the idea of separation that it almost brutally cut itself off from all religious groups; no other government of the time was so precipitous or so thorough. No religious test was required of any federal officeholder, and no religion could be supported by the United States. The remarkable result was that it set a new and higher standard of toleration among diverse people.

The closest that America came to Germany's Kulturkampf was the almost fifty-year-long military and legislative persecution of the Church of Jesus Christ of Latter-Day Saints, or Mormons. But the assault on the Mormons, reprehensible as it was, did not stem from a concern about national unity or identity, as Bismarck's effort to Germanize the Catholic Church certainly did. The persecution of the Latter-Day Saints was propelled by the issue of plural marriage, not a question of American identity.

The influence of diversity in both Germany and the United States, as we have seen, still leaves much to be desired in accounting for the conditions of tolerance. We need, therefore, to look further to uncover those historical circumstances that help us find acceptance among strangers. In America that search is best begun by confronting the severest challenge Americans met in the course of their history. It is the divisiveness of race, a problem that settled the question of national identity by paying the price of the most devastating conflict in American history.

The first African Americans, as we are properly reminded, arrived before the *Mayflower*. Yet, they were then, and for centuries thereafter, not considered an integral part of the new society planted on the eastern shores of North America. Even when African Americans were born free, they were seen as strangers, as different. Although hundreds of African Americans bore arms in the Revolutionary War, they were not accepted as true Americans. As Abraham Lincoln himself told a committee of free black men on the eve of emancipation, "On this broad continent, not a single man of your race is made the equal of a single man of ours." That view, Lincoln remarked, needed no discussion because it was a fact of American life. "But for your race among us," Lincoln continued, "there could not be war, although many men engaged on either side do not care for you one way or the other. . . . It is better for us both, therefore, to be separated." And so Lincoln urged them to begin to colonize Central America, even though at that time almost all African Americans, slave or free, had been born in America.[14]

It was not race, of course, that directly brought civil war to America, but certainly race was used to make slavery acceptable. It was slavery that made the South different enough from the rest of the country to raise deep questions about the nation's identity. Indeed, the differences were sufficiently compelling to shatter that identity in civil war.

So what was the identity of the nation, what defined Americans? Although diversity has characterized the United States, as I have been suggesting, it could hardly define a single people, that is, a nation. Indeed, precisely because Americans were diverse from the beginning, we need to ask what held those varieties of people together to enable them to call themselves Americans. Unlike the historical circumstances that brought German identity to a head — a place, a locale — that unifying force was lacking in America. By the very novelty of its locale — an open continent — and the diversity of people who came there, America could not identify itself as every European nation did by defining boundaries around people who had always been there. Boundaries, as we will see a little later, would prove to be an important ingredient in the creation of a German identity, but there was never any doubt that Germans and the land on which they lived had always been there, from "time out of mind," as ancient English legal usage phrased it.

Americans, however, came from elsewhere, and what they came for was not really a place or a location, but an idea; their physical destination began as a wilderness stretching along the edge of a continent and ended as a country of farms and cities. Their identity had to be self-created, drawn not from where they had been, but for what they hoped. (Only later were Amerindians and African Americans let into the pattern.) Working out American identity took a long time, perhaps over a century and a half, after which Americans discovered that they were no longer subordinates of Britain, but a new people. What they had learned in the process was not only the freedom and independence that they had gained from Britain, but also the religious freedom that diversity had bestowed on them. As we remember from the Declaration of Independence, with that freedom Americans arrived at the principle that "all men are created equal." In short, rather than being a people of a place or locale, Americans became and remain an attitude of mind, a set of ideas

14 Speech given on Aug. 14, 1862, in Abraham Lincoln, *Speeches and Writings, 1859–1865: Speeches, Letters, and Miscellaneous Writings: Presidential Messages and Proclamations* (New York, 1989), 353–4.

that determine what it means to be an American. It is a set of ideas that knits together the diversity of peoples to which America has come, and from which American identity has been forged.

Freedom and equality have long been the central elements in American identity, but the meaning of those two values has altered as Americans have struggled to say who is to be included in America. We know, for example, that when Thomas Jefferson wrote that "all men are created equal" he did not include black men in that phrase any more than he meant to include white or black women or Indians. "Men" in Jefferson's mind meant those white men who had been accepted as members of a polity that a century and a half of colonial experience had hammered out. Those who were outside that polity were set aside because of race or sex. And so the Founding Fathers excluded them from the new constitution. Yet that exclusion challenged the very meaning of the established American identity and thus threatened the destruction of the country because of African-American slavery. Bondage based on race threatened American nationality on several counts.

The first and most obvious count, of course, was that the social and economic differences between a North without slavery and a South with slavery created such tension and conflict that the South felt compelled to disrupt the polity the American Revolution had founded. A southern success would have closed the era of American national identity because it would have brought two new identities into being. (It was similar to Bismarck's effort, after the Battle of Königgrätz, to create a new German identity, one deliberately and clearly separate from German-speaking Austria.) The attempt to disrupt the political basis of American identity was not the primary challenge. Rather, the twin values of equality and freedom underlay the political challenge. Slavery was recognized as a threat to freedom in America long before the Civil War edged above the horizon. It was, after all, Jefferson the slaveholder who wrote the impassioned words carved in his monument in Washington, D.C.: "Indeed, I tremble for my country when I reflect that God is just." Lincoln recognized that slavery was a hostage to American identity when he argued before the war began that slavery must either take over the whole country or be removed entirely. A house divided against itself, he insisted, cannot stand. With slavery ended, Lincoln's hope for freedom throughout America was realized. Lincoln also reshaped the meaning of American identity by including African Americans within the concept of equality. In the Gettysburg Address, Lincoln included African Americans for the first time in Jefferson's "proposition that all men are created equal."

Equality, however, was more difficult to realize than freedom. After all, as we have seen, even Lincoln had to wrestle with the obstacle of race, finding it difficult, as he once admitted, to envision an American nation in which blacks and whites could live in peace and profit. It would take another century for Americans to recognize the acceptance of equality, and even now racial conflict and tension have not been eliminated, even though the principle is no longer an issue. Fundamental values of American identity have not in and of themselves created the conditions of tolerance; full implementation of these values still waits.

The historical roots of German identity are considerably deeper. The term "German nation," for example, goes back centuries, as in the title of the Holy Roman Empire of the German Nation. A wit once said that it was neither holy nor Roman, and today we must add that Germans then were also not a nation. The emergence of either a country named Germany or a people with a national identity is hardly recognizable before the nineteenth century. Even then, what contemporaries referred to as Germany was at best a collection of several dozen states, some very large, such as Prussia and Bavaria, and some tiny, such as the cities of Lübeck and Hamburg. Although other Europeans referred to Germany, they did not consider the place a country or state, such as France, England, or even the United States, nor as a people who had once been a recognized country and still aspired to be one, like the Poles. At the same time, those Europeans whose native tongue was German numerically dominated central Europe. German speech was heard from the eastern shores of the Baltic Sea to the western edge of the Rhine, from the shores of the North Atlantic to the Tyrolean Alps in the south. Dozens of governments divided German speakers into Prussians, Austrians, Swiss, Saxons, Bavarians, Bohemians, and many more.

Who was a German, then? many asked. The question became especially pointed as the new nationalist forces of the French Revolution violently spread across central Europe. In the face of French military power and the defeat of much of German-speaking Europe, a new sense of national identity began to emerge. To be a German, for many, was to oppose the French, who under Napoleon had largely occupied central Europe for two decades; to be a German also meant to resist the revolution that Napoleon had seeded across Europe. And for some, to be a German was to hope that the revolution France had begun would bring about an identified Germany, one that was united, freer, and more open than the loosely organized and traditional Germany of the past. The failure of the revolutions of 1848 in German-speaking Europe dimmed the hopes of a freer and more open Germany (or what today we would call a liberal and democratic Germany), but it did not end the hope that a single German identity, comparable to that of Europe's major nations, could somehow be brought into existence. That hope achieved its realization and much of its subsequent character through the actions of Bismarck, whose interest in national identity was considerably less than his interest in Prussian influence and security.

Bismarck's easiest as well as his earliest decision in defining German identity was to include the German-speaking areas of Denmark within his new Germany while excluding the German-speaking part of the Austrian Empire. That required two brief wars. Finalizing the boundaries of Bismarck's Germany required an additional war, this time against the old enemy, France. That was done to bring together the still separate German kingdoms and duchies into an empire under the leadership of Prussia. There can be little doubt that the authority and actions of Bismarck constitute the heart and marrow of German identity. Probably no German outshines Bismarck as the quintessential personification of his country's national identity. Indeed, if one concentrates only on Lincoln's central role in saving the American union, then perhaps Bismarck might be seen as the Lincoln of German national unity. Both men, after all, used war as the cement of their respective unions.

Did the different paths to national identity that Germany and the United States followed help shape their social institutions? Let me suggest differences in three of their institutions: citizenship, class awareness, and the social condition of women. Citizenship should be first since it at once reflects and embodies identity. In the United States, defining citizenship was directly related to the ideas that underlay the American sense of national identity.[15] When slavery was ended, the question of what would be the position of the freed people was answered in the Fourteenth Amendment to the Constitution: Any person, regardless of ancestry, who is born in the United States is a citizen. This meant, of course, that the children of immigrants would achieve citizenship automatically. Thus, American citizenship became an explicit expression of the two great national values of freedom and equality.

The road to German identity was quite different, as we have seen, since from the beginning the definition of a German had often meant the exclusion of certain groups − Poles and Jews. Citizenship thus became

15 See James H. Kettner, *The Development of American Citizenship, 1608–1870* (Chapel Hill, N.C., 1978).

a matter of German parentage. Just as the American version of citizenship reflects the freedom, equality, and individualism of American identity, so the German version reflects the exclusive identity that has run through the story of Germany diversity. As Wolfgang Schäuble, Chancellor Kohl's party chairman, remarked, "We gain our identity, not from commitment to an idea, but from belonging to a particular *Volk*," or people.[16] Significantly, that definition of citizenship has been the law in Germany to this day, despite two intervening world wars and their subsequent revolutions. It is, in short, the legal underpinning of the oft-repeated slogan that Germany is not a land of immigration, since naturalization in Germany is also difficult to achieve.

That Bismarck and Prussia were the architects of the new Germany further shaped its identity. In Bismarck's mind, Germany would be a stronger and safer Prussia, not only in the face of foreign military threats around its borders, but also in the face of modern liberal and radical challenges. Bismarck, it is true, was willing to let universal manhood suffrage prevail in his empire, but he never believed, in Lincoln's words, in governments "of the people, by the people, for the people." Just as Bismarck himself was never elected by voters, so his king, who became emperor, dominated the new Reichstag, which thereby fell short of being a parliament like others in most of Europe. Put another way, the popular sovereignty that provided the conditions for tolerance in America was absent in the emerging identity of Bismarck's empire.

The meaning of German identity was infused with Prussian political and social values. In the consciousness of traditional Prussians, ethnic or racial differences were not the only kind of threatening divisions to be feared in bringing about a national identity for Germans. There was also the danger of class divisions, especially as the rise of industry and urban growth began to transform a once unchallenged traditional and largely agricultural society. One source of that challenge was the emergence of socialist ideas and the formation and growth of a socialist political party, the Social Democratic Party (Sozialdemokratische Partei Deutschlands, or SPD). Bismarck and his political allies saw socialism not only as a threatening sign of political and social change but also as a danger to German unity. Thus, for thirteen years, at Bismarck's insistence to a compliant Reichstag, socialist party activities were illegal in Germany. It is true that after Bismarck's dismissal and by the time of World War I

---

16 Quoted in Mary Fulbrook, "Aspects of Society and Identity in the New Germany," *Daedalus* 123 (winter 1994): 227.

the socialists were the largest party in Germany. Yet in the eyes of many German voters a strong socialist party continued to be a threat to German unity and identity – as the agonizing end of the Weimar Republic reminds us.

Socialism wore a different face in the United States from that in Germany. The difference lay in diverse roads to national identity that the two countries had taken. The very strength of the German socialist party, which frightened Bismarck and his successors, also reflected a German group identity based on the idea of the *Volk*, which subordinated or reduced the individual freedom that Americans took for granted. This comparison can best be seen in social terms by noting the well-known weakness of socialism in the United States in contrast to Germany's powerful socialist party. It can also be observed in the fact that America's labor unions have historically been far weaker than Germany's.

After all, to be a socialist or to join a labor union requires a worker to reduce to some degree his or her individuality, to subordinate oneself to the group in the name of a larger and lasting purpose. This is something that Americans did not find easy to accept, for history had encouraged them to be competitive individuals. Part of that history came from their having been immigrants, from being people who were prepared to start afresh and escape old ways. And those who freely left the Old World for the New mostly sought the opportunities that freedom and equality of American identity promised. Thus, it was the emphasis on individual opportunity that in the end largely closed off the possibility of large-scale trade union or socialist movements in the United States comparable to those that emerged in Germany.

One final example of the individualism implicit in the meaning of American identity can be suggested by contrasting the rise of the early women's movements in the United States and in Germany. As we have seen, the phrase "all men are created equal" left out of American political inclusiveness not only African Americans, but women as well. It is true that the recognition of women as equal Americans has been long in coming, but for our purposes here, it is worth recalling that the beginnings go far back in the American past. Just as the appeal for black equality depended for its success on the recognition of the right of an individual to achieve equality and freedom, so the opening guns in the century-long struggle for women's equality were first heard in the middle of the nineteenth century at almost the same time and for the same reason that African-American freedom and equality were vigorously asserted. It was in 1848 that Elizabeth Cady Stanton wrote her parody of the Declaration of Independence in which she put "man" in place of George III as the oppressor against whom women were declaring their independence.

A women's movement came much later and more slowly in Germany, but by World War I, several large women's organizations had been formed, including a women's section of the socialist party. But when World War I came to the two countries, the effect on women revealed in another way the striking differences in the national identity of the two societies. Like the SPD's affirmative vote in the Reichstag to finance the war, the bourgeois women's organization rallied behind the kaiser's famous declaration in 1914: "I recognize no parties, only Germans."[17] Even a radical feminist like Minna Cauer admitted in 1915 that the war effort "made it clear to women for the first time that they belong to a greater whole, that a higher and stronger power has the right to exercise compulsion over them." This means, Cauer continued, "a step forward from a fully individual egotism, which only allows validity to the individual's own needs, to a higher development as a member of the state."[18] This was, of course, the same kind of outlook that had long characterized the German search for a *Volk*, which thought in terms of community rather than of individuals and which found little place for diversity. Socialist feminists, despite their long assertion of the cause of women, also subordinated the interests of individual women to the good of the group, in this case the socialist movement and party.[19]

The women's movement in wartime America also acted within its national identity. The emphasis, however, was on individual rights and the acceptance of differences, in this case, differences in sex. The radical Women's Party seized the opportunity created by the war to press the Wilson administration for women's suffrage, even in the face of imprisonment of some of the more vocal dissenters. Nor could the government, given the historical identity of Americans, long resist the women's claims for equality for all in a society of diversity. Women's suffrage through a constitutional amendment was achieved in 1919. Suffrage came for German women that same year, but it required the political and social overthrow of Bismarck's Germany. Yet even that alteration in

---

17 Quoted in James J. Sheehan, *German Liberalism in the Nineteenth Century* (London, 1982), 278.
18 Quoted in Richard J. Evans, *The Feminist Movement in Germany, 1894–1933* (London, 1976), 267.
19 Jean H. Quataert, *Reluctant Feminists in German Social Democracy, 1885–1917* (Princeton, N.J., 1979), chaps. 9–10.

German national identity did not reach fulfillment until the coming of the Federal Republic of Germany.

In both Germany and the United States, cities and factories flourished during the late nineteenth and early twentieth centuries, for the two nations became the great industrial juggernauts of the time. Despite that common experience, some of the social and political institutions of the two countries, such as those connected with women's rights, trade unions, and socialism, were strikingly different. They differed principally because they were shaped by divergent paths to national identity. Those national identities, in turn, provided different conditions of tolerance.

2

The Historical Invention and Modern Reinvention of Two National Identities

FRANK TROMMLER

PATTERNS OF INVENTION

An old saying describes a nation as a group of people united by a common mistake about their ancestry and a common dislike of their neighbors. Pointing to a tenuous link with the past and a heartfelt detachment from other peoples, this witticism is as helpful an introduction to the dynamics of inventing a nation as any scholarly definition. Unless an "us" is created that is separate from "them," organizing human beings into a political unit can hardly succeed. The maintenance and historical adjustment of this collective identity, as fictitious as its symbols might be, serves an important political function by providing a framework for the difficult integration of diverging social groups, religions, and lifestyles – even antagonistic ideologies.

In terms of scholarly definitions, the understanding of the nation as an imagined political community, though not new, has received much attention in recent years. Political scientists and historians have even become fearful that the discussion is shifting precariously from the realm of constitutional law and political ideologies to that of cultural mentalities and generalities. Yet, although social scientists such as Ernest Gellner and Miroslav Hroch have made the connection between nationalism and modernization watertight,[1] Gellner himself, in his criticism of Durkheim, recognized the problems of specifying the different twists and turns of

---

1 Ernest Gellner, *Nations and Nationalism* (Ithaca, N.Y., 1983); Miroslav Hroch, *Social Preconditions of National Revival in Europe: A Comparative Analysis of the Social Composition of Patriotic Groups Among the Smaller European Nations* (Cambridge, 1985); Edward A. Tiryakian and Neil Nevitte, "Nationalism and Modernity," in Edward A. Tiryakian and Ronald Rogowski, eds., *New Nationalism of the Developed West* (London, 1985); Bernhard Giesen, ed., *Nationale und kulturelle Identität: Studien zur Entwicklung des kollektiven Bewusstseins in der Neuzeit* (Frankfurt/Main, 1991); Bernd Estel, "Grundaspekte der Nation: Eine begrifflich-systematische Untersuchung," *Soziale Welt* 42 (1991):

national allegiance on the part of individuals and groups.[2] It seems that the macrosociological approach, which exposes the economic and social dimensions of nationalism, omits too many factors in the realm of everyday individual experience. For a comparative look at national identities that does not result from quantitative research, the current refocusing on the interaction of individual and collective dynamics provides helpful arguments vis-à-vis this omission.

The widely applied concept of the symbolic construction of reality has made the interplay of historical consciousness and technological progress – the creation of a public sphere by the mass production of books and newspapers – accessible, illuminating both the abstract nature of the imagined nation and the individual contribution to its upkeep. In *Imagined Communities*, Benedict Anderson articulated a timely insight when he insisted that national identities grow out of "large cultural systems" rather than specific political ideologies. Anderson avers that national identity is a particular style of imagining the community. His thesis encourages cross-cultural comparisons of the forms in which the social processes of modernity develop in different cultures. These processes include mass literacy and mass communication, secular rationalism, political participation, and technological progress.

For the comparison of American and German traditions of generating a national identity, I take as my point of departure Anderson's practice of linking national consciousness to the processes of modernization, although I reject the exclusivity of his definition of "lived reality" as a reality lived in and through representations, not in direct communal solidarity.[3] To be sure, the concept of the nation, whether in political declarations of state building or in the individual imagination, is to a large extent an abstraction. But the current tendency to ascribe to the sphere of the media and its techniques of mediation an all-encompassing power in shaping experience through representation does not justify the reduction of national identities to mere systems of cultural signification. If nation is equated with narration, whereby strategies of textual inquiry – "textuality, discourse, enunciation, *écriture*, 'the unconscious as a language'"[4] – determine the key insights into the political reality of a

---

208–31; Mikulas Teich and Roy Porter, eds., *The National Question in Europe in Historical Context* (Cambridge, 1993).

2 Ernest Gellner, *Culture, Identity, and Politics* (Cambridge, 1987), 27.

3 Benedict Anderson, *Imagined Communities: Reflections on the Origin and Spread of Nationalism* (London, 1983), 15.

4 Homi K. Bhaba, "Introduction: Narrating the Nation," in Homi K. Bhaba, ed., *Nation and Narration* (London, 1990), 4.

nation, the notion of modernity easily dwindles into a system of manip-
ulated signifiers.

In its reliance on symbolic communication, such an approach echoes
the traditionally romantic projections of nationalism. This might account
for the fact that the interest in the composition of national identities is
still growing, especially among intellectuals. Given the illustrious tradition
of intellectual expressions of national greatness, one cannot but restate
the old dictum according to which intellectuals, even more eagerly than
politicians, regularly update the importance of this area of discourse.[5]
This time it is mostly done by highlighting the techniques of public representation as a far-reaching social operation.[6] Although it provides new
insights into the workings of the politics of representation, this endeavor
is distressingly isolated from much of the concrete legislative, administrative, and economic actions that determine national consciousness in the
sphere of production and social welfare. Vis-à-vis such semiotic reduc-
tionism, George Mosse's earlier exploration of the political symbolism in
modern Europe offered a more comprehensive picture of the techniques
of creating nationalist movements in the twentieth century, although he
was criticized for being overly beholden to ideological notions.[7] Illuminating the nonrational substructures within the internally rationalized
institutions of education and administration, Mosse already went far beyond the established views of manipulation of "the masses."

In short, defining "lived reality" primarily in terms of a reality lived in
representations has its heuristic flaws. It is itself a product of the technological transformations that have shaped the concept of the individual in
the world of capitalist productions of things and realities. It points to the
mediating factors in the individual's encounter with reality, but it is not
"lived reality" in its innumerable shapes and instances, in the individual's
plight between love, angst, work, and death. By establishing the concept
of "the invention of tradition," which has been exploited as proof of
the symbolic politics in the nineteenth century, even Eric Hobsbawm was

---

5 A recent example for this updating is Liah Greenfeld, *Nationalism: Five Roads to Modernity* (Cambridge, Mass., 1992).
6 See the review essay by Philip Schlesinger, "On National Identity: Some Conceptions and Mis-
conceptions Criticized," *Social Science Information* 26 (1987): 219–64.
7 See esp. George L. Mosse, *The Nationalization of the Masses: Political Symbolism and Mass Movements
in Germany from the Napoleonic Wars Through the Third Reich* (New York, 1977), and the comparative article, "National Self-Representation During the 1930s in Europe and the United States," in
George L. Mosse, *Confronting the Nation: Jewish and Western Nationalism* (Hanover, N.H., 1993),
27–40. See also Seymour Drescher et al., eds., *Political Symbolism in Modern Europe: Essays in Honor
of George L. Mosse* (New Brunswick, N.J., 1982).

cautious in his generalizations, leaving room for the effects of the industrial experience on the formation of collective identities.[8]

In this chapter, I argue that the experience of living and working in the twentieth-century world of mass production and consumption created an agenda for national identities different from the politics of symbolism developed by nineteenth-century elites, but that is still framing the discussion concerning the matrix of nationalism and representation. As the title of this chapter indicates, I assume a multistage or at least two-stage process in which invention and reinvention of national identity occurred on different levels of experience, rationalization, and symbolization. As an individual's self-image takes shape according to a variety of social, political, ethnic, and biological dependencies and relationships, which cannot be summed up as *one* identity but rather has to be understood as a set of multiple identities, the perception of national identity must account for a diversity of identities. It can include antinationalist sentiments, and it can be devoid of any concept of nation. In the course of a lifetime, the individual can shift conscious and unconscious references of national identity from war events to technological achievements and the experiences of work or ethnicity, mostly not to the exclusion of the other. Given the dialectic of identity-through-lived-experience and identity-through-representation, I concentrate on the impact of work and everyday routines in the hope of shedding some light on the connection between the identity formation in the work world and certain factors of national identity in the United States and Germany.

THE POLITICS OF SYMBOLISM

The endless succession of pageants, fairs, celebrations, expositions, commemorations, and monuments, which fostered national pride in the later nineteenth century, is an international phenomenon. In the cases of the United States and Germany, the celebrations were marked by a comparable sense of a unified nation whose material progress merited citizen loyalty and respect. The increasingly opulent public display of the imperial status of Germany after unification in 1871 coincided with the colorful celebrations in which American cities after the centennial year 1876 honored the Founding Fathers and the revolutionary upheaval on national holidays.[9] Dates such as 1871 and 1876 mark a decisive step

---

8 Eric Hobsbawm and Terence Ranger, *The Invention of Tradition* (Cambridge, 1983).
9 Wallace Evan Davies, *Patriotism on Parade: The Story of Veterans' and Hereditary Organizations in America, 1783–1900* (Cambridge, Mass., 1955).

toward a more aggressive and professional use of historical representation. Legitimizing the *Kaiserreich* as a sequence to the medieval Reich drew no less on invented history as the "search for a usable past," as Henry Steel Commager defined the new historicism in the United States, which superseded the long-held conviction that "the Americans had no need of a past because they were so sure of a future."[10] Historians such as C. Vann Woodward and Daniel Boorstin later generalized the fact that Americans use "their history not only as a source of myth and an object of filial pity, but as a substitute for political theory."[11]

From what has been called the "unregulated memory" of the nineteenth century, commemoration progressed to local and regional forums and eventually came under the domination of an increasingly powerful nation-state.[12] Based on the "invention of traditions," to use Hobsbawm's term, the state established strategies by means of which social integration could be maintained. Hobsbawm and his collaborators see a break in the 1870s when it became obvious "that the masses were becoming involved in politics and could not be relied upon to follow their masters."[13] After the 1870s, rulers and middle-class observers rediscovered "the importance of 'irrational' elements in the maintenance of the social fabric and the social order."[14] They learned to address the emergence of mass politics by providing a sense of invariance through national rituals and symbols. These cultural constructions of a stable past enforced the claim of political legitimacy in a secularized age. It was at this time that the French Revolution became "institutionalized" as the prime focus of national thinking in France; the celebration of Bastille Day on July 14, begun in 1880, was to transform the heritage of the Revolution into a combined expression of state pomp and power and the citizens' pleasure.[15]

Examples of the various techniques of bringing the national heritage to life abound. American political parties used the iconography, themes, and symbols of revolutionary events to present themselves as natural mediators between citizens and state, teaching individuals how to be true Americans. Election ceremonies brought Americans together in a highly stylized political drama "that helped to make their national life more

---

10 Henry Steele Commager, *The Search for a Usable Past and Other Essays on Historiography* (New York, 1967), 7.
11 C. Vann Woodward, *American Attitudes Toward History: An Inaugural Lecture* (Oxford, 1955), 7.
12 John Bednar, *Remaking America: Public Memory, Commemoration, and Patriotism in the Twentieth Century* (Princeton, N.J., 1992), 28–35.
13 Hobsbawm and Ranger, *The Invention of Tradition*, 268.
14 Ibid.
15 Ibid., 271.

coherent."[16] In Germany, where Bismarck had emasculated the political parties, rendering them mere vehicles of economic interests, political ceremonies drew heavily on the power of the German state and its civilizing mission, personified, after 1888, by Kaiser Wilhelm II and his insatiable appetite for public representation.[17]

In both countries, as elsewhere, the prevailing forces pursued an antipluralist, one-nation principle, homogenizing history as one great ascent to the present heights of national glory. In the United States, this meant a dismissal of minority claims for inclusion in the national self-understanding. German Americans, for instance, were hardly successful in the 1880s and 1890s when they attempted to legitimize themselves as historical contributors in the national narrative of the American fight for independence. They felt compelled to express their identity as Americans in their own celebrations, founding their own historical society modeled after Scotch-Irish, Irish-American, and Jewish initiatives.[18] Yet, whereas the northern European ethnic groups enjoyed a somewhat respectful treatment within the Anglo-Saxon racialism and the melting-pot idea,[19] the millions of new immigrants from eastern Europe and the Mediterranean found a rather hostile reception in the decades before World War I. These groups were given a chance to gain legitimacy within society through their contributions to the enormous expansion of productive industries, but Native and African Americans remained mostly outside the social parameter.

In Germany, the discrepancy between the official one-nation, one-culture doctrine and the divergent views of substantial segments of society was no less obvious. For large sections of the Catholic population the power and civilizing mission of the German nation and state was not a topic and certainly no source of new identity. They were as little inclined to support the symbols of the Wilhelmine state as were many workers who were under suspicion of being traitors to the fatherland, especially as members of the Social Democratic Party. Neither the German government's Kulturkampf against the Catholic Church nor the antisocialist law helped to generate a new quality of national identity in

16 Jean H. Baker, "The Ceremonies of Politics: Nineteenth-Century Rituals of National Affirmation," in William J. Cooper Jr. et al., eds., *A Master's Due: Essays in Honor of David Herbert Donald* (Baton Rouge, La., 1985), 166.
17 Wolfgang Hardtwig, "Bürgertum, Staatssymbolik und Staatsbewusstsein im Deutschen Kaiserreich, 1871–1914," *Geschichte und Gesellschaft* 16 (1990): 269–95.
18 Frank Trommler, "The Use of History in German-American Politics," in Charlotte L. Brancaforte, ed., *The German Forty-eighters in the United States* (New York, 1989), 279–95.
19 Philip Gleason, "American Identity and Americanization," in Stephan Thernstrom, ed., *Harvard Encyclopedia of American Ethnic Groups* (Cambridge, Mass., 1980), 31–58.

Catholics and workers. Instead these political measures enhanced the affiliation of the individual to a world that, in the cases of Catholicism and socialism, was at once larger and smaller than the Wilhelmine nation-state, carried by a different symbolism.

Obviously, the hegemonic use of national symbols vis-à-vis the adherence to separate symbolic agendas was not dissimilar in both countries. Whereas the middle classes generally participated in the public celebration of the nation and its broadly displayed traditions, the enforcement of such loyalty in the society at large remained public and formal, visibly serving the interests of the political elites. It allowed, even invited, ritualistic participation, superseding but not extinguishing specific ethnic, religious, or political identities.

NATIONAL IDENTITY IN THE MODERN WORK WORLD

These practices have been studied fairly thoroughly, although rarely compared. Underlying these studies is the assumption that national identity and nationalism can be generalized across geographical boundaries as components of modernization. Whereas the differences are thought to be conditioned by the particular cultures, the strongest proponents are believed to belong to an international class of intellectuals and politicians. Reflecting this social bias, the focus on the manipulation and strategic action seems logical. Once the hegemonic projection of the nation in public rituals is generalized as a communicative practice, the highlighting of agents who achieve a particular sophistication – or ruthlessness – in the manipulation of national symbols follows with certainty. Overlooking the techniques of theatrical brain washing in twentieth-century dictatorships and democracies, from Mussolini and Hitler to de Gaulle and Reagan, one cannot but conclude that there is more than just a continuity with nineteenth-century practices, namely, a new and technologically improved version of making the national community imaginable, indeed accessible. Thus, Anderson's linking of national consciousness to the processes of modernization seems to be confirmed by the enormous advancement of media technologies that enable mass participation far beyond the wildest dreams of the nineteenth century. Perfected in the acoustic spatialization of the German Reich as a gigantic radio hall with which the National Socialists created their version of the nation, the preferred focus is on an unalienated community that becomes (virtual) reality, thanks to the most modern projection techniques in film, radio, and visual and print media.

The modernization of communicative practices since the nineteenth century is beyond question. Yet, to what extent does this entail those shifts in constituting national identities that occurred under the impact of both the new production technologies and the transformation of the working and living space, and that cannot easily be retrieved from the study of textual and visual strategies? It is telling that most scholars of nationalism have anchored their theories in the concept of modernization yet put the emphasis on preindustrialist sources, thereby avoiding the study of the everyday work world of industrial societies, which Gellner outlined in *Culture, Identity, and Politics*.[20] Anthony Giddens, who recognized the peculiarities of "day-to-day social life" in his analysis of the "Janus-faced character" of nationalism, has rightly been criticized for erasing it again in the conflation of nationalism and national identity. In his critique of Giddens's pioneering work *The Nation-State and Violence*, Philip Schlesinger has formulated an important distinction between nationalism and national identity:

Nationalism, one may agree, is a particular kind of doctrine, but the term tends to carry the sense of community mobilized (in part at least) in the pursuit of a collective interest. National identity may be invoked as a point of reference without thereby necessarily being nationalistic. There are undoubtedly historical periods when the construction of a national identity may be part of a nationalist programme, and therefore involve a good deal of intellectual labour. However, once the political boundaries of the nation-state have been achieved, a national identity, with all the accompanying mythico-cultural apparatus, may be in place and is not necessarily identical with nationalism as such.[21]

Following Schlesinger's definition, we have good reason to distinguish between the intellectual and political conceptualization of nationalism, on the one hand, and the functional realization of national affiliations, on the other, which combine with notions of family and religion as well as particular moral visions of work and social relations. The latter composite is not necessarily less explosive in terms of emotions, politics, and exclusions. At its core stands the traditionally held opinion that work defined as paid labor is the major source of social identity in industrialized societies. Although increasingly contested, this belief requires reconsideration of the sociopolitical repercussions of work in its highly varied actuality, from skilled to unskilled labor, from absolute alienation to compensatory or genuine satisfaction within the social context.[22] And, as

---

20 Gellner, *Culture, Identity, and Politics*, 91–110.
21 Schlesinger, "On National Identity," 253.
22 "The links between skill (also work more generally) and national identity are important and little studied"; Patrick Joyce, "The Historical Meaning of Work: An Introduction," in Patrick

indicated earlier on, the notion of *the* identity that Schlesinger resurrects in his otherwise useful distinction needs to be replaced by that of multiple identities.

For this, a look at turn-of-the-century America provides much evidence. As the appearance of millions of new immigrants triggered a rather vicious national debate about the racial inferiority of the newcomers, their primary access route to becoming American led through work, industrial work. The problem was not totally unknown in Germany, where a comparable transformation from an agrarian state to a powerful industrial state with a strong agrarian sector took place and where labor, mainly from the East, was imported. The plight of the "Ruhr Poles" confronted the authorities with difficult decisions between social integration and national segregation. In both countries administrative and economic criteria, together with the new structures of industrial production, engendered expressions of national identity that could be absorbed into neither the parameters of middle-class education nor those of the traditional public sphere.

Nowhere was the transformation of industrial production techniques more apparent than in the United States. The assembling of large-scale systems of manufacturing by engineers and managers full of obsessive concern for control became a symbol of the new America.[23] Profoundly questioning the efficiency of traditional manufacturing practices, the new managerialism asserted the primacy of a new collectivism of productivity, claiming the need for a conscious, scientifically informed control of complex social processes that culminated in what David Riesman later described in *The Lonely Crowd* as a change from the older forms of personality toward a more marketable personality structure. I refer to Riesman because he avoided undue reveling in American technological exceptionalism, keeping a clear focus on what most participants in the revamping of industrial organization claimed to have created: a novel personality type who, by shedding the old work habits, became the new American.

Joyce, ed., *The Historical Meaning of Work* (Cambridge, 1987), 22. About the impact of work on political attitudes, see Michael X. Delli Carpini, "Work and Politics: A Decomposition of the Concept of Work and an Investigation of Its Impact on Political Attitudes and Actions," *Political Psychology* 7 (1986): 117–40.

23 Thomas P. Hughes, in *American Genesis: A Century of Invention and Technological Enthusiasm, 1870–1970* (New York, 1989), 295ff., speaks of "The Second Discovery of America." The general phenomenon is well outlined by Charles S. Maier, "Between Taylorism and Technocracy: European Ideologies and the Vision of Industrial Productivity in the 1920s," *Journal of Contemporary History* 5 (1970): 27–61.

The urgency behind this transformation has many sources. A favorite clue among historians is the Progressive movement, but the fact that between 1880 and 1924 more than 25 million immigrants entered the United States deserves equal if not stronger emphasis, not to mention the dynamics of capitalist expansion. For many Americans there was a clear and threatening relationship between the breathtaking shifts in industrial organization and the realization that most of the workforce that carried the country's modern mission into the twentieth century was foreign-born. Was it still the America that those pageants on national holidays projected? Was it still sustained by the work ethic that President Theodore Roosevelt celebrated with a nod toward the frugal days of the nineteenth century?[24]

In "American Identity and Americanization," Philip Gleason states, "Especially during the first quarter of the twentieth century, the ethnic factors of 'race,' nationality, language, and so on were the issues that sprang immediately to mind when Americans asked themselves, 'What does is mean to be an American? What kind of Americanism do we want?'"[25] Gleason distinguishes four perspectives on American identity in this period: the unifying idea of the melting pot, the Americanization movement, the far-reaching Anglo-Saxon racialism, and the liberal cultural pluralism (for which Horace Kallen provided the concept). Yet, the classification of these perspectives seems incomplete without defining their relationship to the dynamics of radical industrial transformation. Even the concern with ethnicity can be a deficient clue if it does not grasp the momentum of fear or at least ambiguity with which the majority of Americans experienced the very matrix of mass immigration and the unsettling effects of modernization.

The reaction to this encounter obviously fed the hope that Taylorist production managers, who tried to hammer the indigenous and the immigrant workers into one collective work personality, would forge a new type of American identity. What came to be called "Americanization" was the development of techniques of habituating the immigrants to the discipline of industrial employment, culminating in the production of a new "American" personality.[26] It often meant the use of categories of national propriety against the social opposition, ethnic unrest, and

24 John M. Blum, "Exegesis of the Gospel of Work: Success and Satisfaction in Recent American Culture," in Clarence Morris, ed., *Modern American Society* (Philadelphia, 1962), 21.

25 Gleason, "American Identity and Americanization," 46.

26 Gerd Korman, *Industrialization, Immigrants, and Americanizers: The View from Milwaukee, 1866–1921* (Madison, Wis., 1967), David F. Noble, *America by Design: Science, Technology, and the Rise of Corporate Capitalism* (New York, 1877), 304ff.; John F. McClymer, "The Americanization Movement

working-class politics. However, it also meant that the acculturation of millions of foreigners was a concrete project of behavioral adjustment, as long as each individual, usually a male, was immersed in the work world. The landmarks of symbolic nationalism allowed a ritualistic integration in which women and families were included on national holidays, but the behavioral acculturation in the work world entailed factors of cultural emancipation and social descent as well as gains and losses in male self-respect.

Still, Riesman and other sociologists, in their studies of the American character in the twentieth century, documented the far-reaching shifts in the manifestation of national identity itself, shifts that transcended the premises of the industrial education of the immigrant masses. Whereas the acculturation of these masses occurred inside and outside the work world, exposing the traces of the factory discipline as well as the rituals of the informal neighborly contacts with the "established" population, it was also strongly mediated by the nickelodeon and later the movie house.[27] Simultaneously condemned and praised, the motion picture became a great homogenizer of conduct and fantasy among Americans and foreigners. It is hardly coincidental that the culmination of the Americanization movement and the severe restriction of immigration in 1924 occurred at a time when national identity was increasingly defined by a common tendency to certain attitudes and emotional signals. In the everyday routine recognition of the "American character," the emphasis was on thrift, success, and work efficiency rather than on Wilson's democratic virtues. Spreading the term "Americanism" was motivated by the desire to pronounce national identity as a credo of a particular – the "right" – conduct in the modern world.

By comparison, the most visible challenges to the politics of national symbolism in Germany came from the working class as well as segments of the middle classes that were strongly involved in the manufacturing and trading sectors. They focused mainly on the anachronistic representation of the modern Reich by the theatrical feudalism of the kaiser and his caste.[28] Unable to respond to the need for a thorough democratization, middle-class professionals aimed at a modernized notion of *Volk* as

---

and the Education of the Foreign-Born Adult, 1914–25," in Bernard J. Weiss, ed., *American Education and the European Immigrant, 1840–1940* (Urbana, Ill., 1982), 96–116.

27 Anton Kaes, "Mass Culture and Modernity: Notes Toward a Social History of Early American and German Cinema," in Frank Trommler and Joseph McVeigh, eds., *America and the Germans: An Assessment of a Three-Hundred-Year History* (Philadelphia, 1985), 2:317–31.

28 See esp. Helmuth Plessner, "Die Legende von den Zwanziger Jahren," in Helmuth Plessner, *Diesseits der Utopie: Ausgewählte Beiträge zur Kultursoziologie* (Frankfurt/Main, 1974), 93ff.

the quintessence of national identity. Although racist tendencies entered the redefinition of "high" and "low," "them" and "us," and national terminology was used in the suppression of working-class organizations, the shift toward a concept of *Volk* that encompassed the industrial expansion gained much momentum before World War I. Due to the lack of democratic practices, one learned to refer to work and its ethos, which had been romanticized in the nineteenth century, as an authentic expression of a new social identity that united different classes toward a collective purpose.

This redefinition of work constituted an important part of the reinvention of national identity in Germany. It was by no means the only component; the energizing effects of radical nationalism on parties and institutions on the political right after 1880, for instance, spilled over into public life in general,[29] transforming the military accoutrements of the Franco-Prussian War into aggressive symbols of power and self-aggrandizement. In addition, there was a similar symbolic ascent to self-aggrandizement in the realm of culture, which culminated in the professorial conjoining of *Kultur* and *Militär* in 1914.

World War I became the high point of this flag-waving nationalism, not only for Germans. However, when the initial speeches, proclamations, and parades were over, the everyday war began. It was experienced as a gigantic machinery of working and dying.

WORLD WAR I AS CATALYST

No event did more to unravel the politics of national symbolism than World War I. The fact that the war also created new symbols for the national discourse needs no comment unless one elaborates on the different qualities of these symbols.[30] The crucial shifts concerned both the impact of the everyday experience of survival on the loyalty to the country and the unprecedented encounter with "the other." As Americans observed how thousands of immigrants were called back to serve in the armies of their homelands, they were shocked not only by the eruption of ethnic nationalism but also by their own blind spot, not having realized "just how 'foreign' the sentiments and attachments of

---

29 Roger Chickering, *We Men Who Feel Most German: A Cultural Study of the Pan-German League, 1886–1914* (Boston, 1984).
30 Klaus Vondung, ed., *Kriegserlebnis: Der Erste Weltkrieg in der literarischen Gestaltung und symbolischen Deutung der Nationen* (Göttingen, 1980).

the foreign-born population actually were."[31] Consequently, the war unleashed thousands of militant nationalists who had been engaged in using the factories for teaching immigrants the gospel of Americanism;[32] they now proclaimed, especially against the German Americans, the goal of "100 percent Americanism." The concept of the melting pot, which Americans had inherited from their simpler, agricultural days, was replaced by a system of controls and restrictions that resulted in the prohibitive Immigration Act of 1924. In the words of Korman, "Their faith in an unregulated system of immigration shaken, Americanizers proposed to replace the melting pot with a pressure cooker."[33]

A similar trend, although on a lesser scale of immigration politics, can be discerned in the case of Germany. Taking the treatment of the comparably small percentage of foreigners in the workforce as an indicator of the changes in the period of World War I, one can detect a similar tightening of laws and work permits. Before the war a majority in the Reichstag pleaded, in the debates on the *Reichs- und Staatsangehörigkeitsgesetz* (Reich citizenship law), for approval of a regulation that foreigners were given legal access to citizenship after only two years of residence.[34] German governments since World War I never took such a relatively liberal approach. On the contrary, they intensified the fortress mentality with *völkisch* arguments. The ethnic exclusiveness was instituted before the ascent of National Socialism and survived it with some corrections that eliminated the blatantly racist formulations. At the same time that the authors of the Basic Law of the Federal Republic guaranteed, in the Western tradition, basic rights, in particular the rights of freedom and equality, as well as the principle of political cooperation, division of power and the rule of law, they also reconfirmed – for instance, in Article 116 – the ethnic definitions of German citizenship that were invented to shield the nation from contamination.

In retrospect, the comparison of American and German developments points to a general tendency toward self-proclaimed ethnic identities in the interwar years. The differences between the countries were, of course, more pronounced in those areas where victory and defeat in the war influenced the attitudes toward industrial production and their social

---

31 Gleason, "American Identity and Americanization," 40.
32 Korman, *Industrialization*; James R. Barrett, "Americanization from the Bottom Up: Immigration and the Remaking of the Working Class in the United States, 1880–1930," *Journal of American History* 79 (1992): 996–1020.
33 Korman, *Industrialization*, 138.
34 See the critical account in Dieter Oberndörfer, *Die offene Republik* (Freiburg/Breisgau, 1991).

consequences. Whereas in Germany the sense of empowerment through work often was conjured up in order to sustain the faith in national survival after Versailles, in the United States it was but one aspect in the search for a common purpose that, for the first time, generated a state-run managerial apparatus. In 1919, engineers, economists, and management scientists stood "at the center of an administered economic system devoted to a clearly defined public purpose,"[35] but the chances for a transformation into the democratic system soon evaporated together with the sense of a common purpose. For a large and diverse population that had learned, through war, of its boundless resources, the mystique of production was soon enhanced by the mystique of consumption, as Henry Ford had predicted and initiated. While work was becoming an attribute of productive conduct, the individual found new sources for self-realization by learning the standards and styles of consuming.[36]

The heyday of the celebration of work came, of course, when work became scarce in the Great Depression. During the 1930s, even left unions overcame the stigmatization of un-Americanness and capitalized on the claim that the creation of the great American civilization was due to the workers, not to the closed world of the rich.[37] Indeed, under the pressure from a state machine that became powerful under wartime conditions after 1941, such working-class Americanism with its focus on more equality in capital-labor relations was transformed into a pluralism that promised the elimination of racial, ethnic, and religious prejudices. It was not until the 1960s and 1970s that this premise was again addressed by the state. In between lay a period when anticommunism dominated the debate of what it meant to be an American.

THE GERMAN COMMUNITY OF ETHNICITY AND WORK

Taking the Basic Law of the Federal Republic as the parameter for an enlightened response to the failure of German governments in the twentieth century, one cannot overlook its strong attachment to the politics of ethnicity in the interwar years. The disjunction between the Enlightenment traditions of fundamental freedoms, rights, and access to citizen-

35 Richard P. Adelstein, "'The Nation as an Economic Unit': Keynes, Roosevelt, and the Managerial Ideal," *Journal of American History* 78 (1991): 167.
36 For an insightful comparison of the American and German attitudes toward work organization and industrial rationalization, see Mary Nolan, *Visions of Modernity: American Business and the Modernization of Germany* (New York, 1994).
37 Gary Gerstle, *Working-Class Americanism: The Politics of Labor in a Textile City, 1914–1960* (Cambridge, 1989), 166–87.

ship, on the one hand, and the politics of ethnicity, on the other, has remained a source of friction and inconsistency. In their diagnoses, historians have seldom addressed the underlying causes. They instead maintained the narration of the well-documented morality tale of German nationalism.

When Max Scheler, in the first years of World War I, diagnosed the causes for the hatred against the Germans, he stressed the fact that the Germans had taken the lead in making the identification with the modern industrial work process the core of their national identity.[38] Other nations, shaken up by this obsession, blamed Germans for the expulsion from the paradise of a more serene and carefree lifestyle. Indeed, contrary to the French practice of conceptualizing "national work" as one of the constitutive principles of the nation,[39] Germans tended to distill identity directly from the experience of labor, which led to a stylization and aestheticization of work far in excess of similar trends in other countries. Since the mid–nineteenth century, Germans had developed a fairly consequential policy of status allocation to work, which was soon adopted at the state level.

Whether a strategy of countering the threats inherent in political alienation – "a sense of not having a recognized position in the civic community in an emerging industrial society"[40] – or a ploy to undermine the Marxist theories of alienation and exploitation, the allocation of status to work, and in particular to skilled work, found a resounding echo in the different strata of German society. The distinction between skilled and unskilled labor was crucial. It continued the highly cherished – and reinvented – tradition of craftsmanship once associated with the guilds and now furthered by the middle classes, yet it also played an important role in the organizational thrust of social democracy. The ensuing distinctions provided the primary basis for a feeling of superiority over foreign workers, a phenomenon that Max Weber had mentioned in his inauguration speech at the University of Freiburg in 1895. Weber referred to the increasing unwillingness of German farmworkers to assume the seasonal work of modernized agriculture; rather than being made into proletarians, they left this work to the migrant workers from the

---

38 Max Scheler, "Die Ursachen des Deutschenhasses," in Max Scheler, *Gesammelte Werke*, ed. Manfred S. Frings (Bern, 1982), 4:316ff.

39 Werner Conze, "Arbeit," in Otto Brunner et al., eds., *Geschichtliche Grundbegriffe: Historisches Lexikon zur politisch-sozialen Sprache in Deutschland* (Stuttgart, 1972), 208–15.

40 Reinhard Bendix, *Nation-Building and Citizenship: Studies of Our Changing Social Order* (Berkeley, Calif., 1977), 426.

East, usually from Czarist Russia.[41] Weber called it a phenomenon of
mass psychology.

The allocation of status is, of course, incomplete without the projection of representative forms of conduct. In the early decades of the
twentieth century, creating typical modes of modern behavior met with
broad interest within the middle classes, especially among the younger
and upwardly mobile groups. Designers, architects, and engineers developed a strong sense of leadership by shaping the forms of everyday
dwelling, working, relaxing, and communicating. Much ingenuity went
into the stylization of the new German as the quintessential Aryan or
vegetarian, but more sober-minded contemporaries favored the *sachlich*
(objective) type who, by exemplifying a goal-oriented *Haltung* (attitude)
toward things and problems, would help the nation to make the biggest
jump into the modern world. Compared with the broadly based search
for the "American character" on the other side of the Atlantic, the German effort relied more on an aesthetic sense of middle-class elitism
modeled on the English. More important, however, was the infatuation
with the concept of work itself. If Americans are said to have attracted
more character studies than any other people,[42] Germans can be described as having done more than others to dignify work despite the
alienating effects of industrialization,[43] thereby drawing political legitimacy from it.

In the early stages of the Weimar Republic, references to work – "German work" – were often placed in the center of official proclamations of
a democratic *Volksgemeinschaft* (national community).[44] In 1919, shortly
after the fall of the kaiser, this notion provided some identification for
the broad masses of the population, which were not accustomed to
embracing democratic institutions. After the destruction of the republic,
when National Socialists set out to establish a clearly antidemocratic
Volksgemeinschaft, the notion of work, German work, received a new
boost that was, especially with the brutal actions on May 1, 1933, directly
related to the destruction of the workers' organizations. "If popular par-

---

41 Max Weber, *Gesammelte politische Schriften* (Munich, 1921), 13.

42 Rupert Wilkinson, "Journeys to American Character: Margaret Mead, David Potter and David
    Riesman," in Brian Holden Raid and John White, eds., *American Studies: Essays in Honor of
    Marcus Cunliffe* (New York, 1991), 297.

43 Joan Campbell, *Joy in Work, German Work: The National Debate, 1800–1945* (Princeton, N.J.,
    1989).

44 Frank Trommler, "Die Nationalisierung der Arbeit," in Reinhold Grimm and Jost Hermand, eds.,
    Arbeit als Thema in der deutschen Literatur vom Mittelalter bis zur Gegenwart (Königstein/Taunus,
    1979), 118–19.

ticipation of the German people in the realm of the state is at all possible," Hitler exclaimed at a mass meeting in the Berlin Sportpalast in October 1933, "it happens only through work. In this sense the Third Reich is the Reich of German socialism, a state of work and the workers."[45] There is little dispute that, at least in the early years and with the end of the Depression, the National Socialist regime gained much of its legitimacy among broad segments of the German population by "providing work," as it was called, thereby reinstilling a feeling of worth and dignity – the most commonly invoked ingredient of national identity.

There are good reasons to ask the obvious question whether this redefinition was just another politics of symbolism, removed from the alienating experience of industrial work. The lack of studies, however, as a result of long-standing avoidance of national and nationalist issues by social historians, makes the answer difficult.[46] With his assessment that any popular participation of the Germans in the affairs of the state was based on *Arbeit* (work), Hitler reformulated an important truth about the political functioning of the concept of work in a society that only recently had learned some democracy. To be sure, the *völkisch* romanticizing of work had retrograde traits; yet in this period of the highly touted Soviet experiment of modernization through industrialization, when in the United States too "the idea of work survived the era of its basic relevance,"[47] this reference held a key to bringing the collective sense of purpose together with the individual quest for "ontological security," as Giddens has called it.[48]

The fact that the symbolism of work only rarely dominated the public articulation of national issues does not speak against its importance for identity formation. Illuminating the aforementioned distinction

---

45 Quoted in Friedrich Heiss, *Deutschland zwischen Nacht und Tag* (Berlin, 1934), 202. See also Martin H. Geyer, "Soziale Sicherheit und wirtschaftlicher Fortschritt: überlegungen zum Verhältnis von Arbeitsideologie und Sozialpolitik im 'Dritten Reich,'" *Geschichte und Gesellschaft* 15 (1989): 382–406.

46 So far the best study of the political strategies underlying the concern with the symbolism of work under National Socialism is Alf Lüdtke, "'Ehre der Arbeit': Industriearbeiter und Macht der Symbole: Zur Reichweite symbolischer Orientierungen im Nationalsozialismus," in Klaus Tenfelde, ed., *Arbeiter im 20. Jahrhundert* (Stuttgart, 1991), 343–92. Yet Lüdtke hardly extends his findings on the integrating power of this symbolism to the much contested issue of national identity. Others have avoided it altogether. A recent example is the instructive study of the history of everyday life of German workers in Dietmar Brock, *Der schwierige Weg in die Moderne: Umwälzungen in der Lebensführung der deutschen Arbeiter zwischen 1850 und 1980* (Frankfurt/Main, 1991). See also Tilman Mayer, "Die nationale Frage in Deutschland," *Neue Politische Literatur* 28 (1983): 310ff.

47 John M. Blum, "Exegesis of the Gospel of Work," 21.

48 Anthony Giddens, *The Nation-State and Violence: A Contemporary Critique of Historical Materialism* (Berkeley, Calif., 1985), 2:218.

between nationalism (with its public rhetoric) and everyday manifestations of national identity, the individual experienced his or her allegiance usually in a less conspicuous way than in public speeches: often in the practices of exclusion and discrimination through regulations against foreign workers, which was accompanied by the internalization of the hierarchies of industrial production. Although generally comparable to the tension-ridden policies toward the immigrant workers in the United States and other countries, the National Socialists' discriminatory agenda soon became especially aggressive in separating the "others" in the realm of work. Based on the tradition of enhancing the skilled craftsman as the embodiment of respectability at the expense of the unskilled worker,[49] this separation increasingly included cultural, biological, and even race-related characteristics. As the juxtaposition of working and nonworking (or pseudoworking) had become a discriminatory feature in anti-Semitic rhetoric, it was used to reinforce "modern" elements in the everyday use of *völkisch* arguments.

Similarly, the customary distinction between the German culture of respectability through work and the foreign practice of mere laboring or mass producing found new and seemingly more concrete applications. Thus, the National Socialists were able to create a climate of tolerance for some of the worst excesses of their politics against people of other nationalities who appeared as workers in lower functions, as exploited masses, as *Fremdarbeiter* (foreign workers). This encounter had become significant on the eve of World War I, when more than a million foreign workers were employed in Imperial Germany;[50] it assumed unprecedented proportions during World War II, when about eight million foreigners worked for the German war machine. Expanding the legal codification of the difference between German and foreign nationals into a systematic application of racist ideology, the Nazis arrived at the distinction of *Herrenmensch* (member of the master race) and *Arbeitsvölker* (working peoples), to which the population rarely objected publicly.[51] Although the reference to the hierarchies of the work world did not seem the most efficient tool for spreading the gospel of the race, the Nazis got what they wanted from the population: compliance.[52]

---

49 Lüdtke, "Ehre der Arbeit," 363–4, 370.
50 Klaus J. Bade, "Transatlantic Emigration and Continental Immigration: The German Experience Past and Present," in Klaus J. Bade, ed., *Population, Labour and Migration in 19th- and 20th-Century Germany* (Leamington Spa, 1987), 141.
51 Ulrich Herbert, *Geschichte der Ausländerbeschäftigung in Deutschland, 1880 bis 1980: Saisonarbeiter, Zwangsarbeiter, Gastarbeiter* (Berlin, 1986), 176–7.
52 Ulrich Herbert, *Fremdarbeiter: Politik und Praxis des "Ausländer-Einsatzes" in der Kriegswirtschaft des Dritten Reiches* (Berlin, 1985), 131, 358.

As the war went on and the Germans grew ever more preoccupied with their own survival, the attitude toward the *Fremdarbeiter* coalesced into matter-of-fact disinterest – they simply took them for granted. This might account for the scant recollection of this experience after 1945. Nonetheless, many of the distinctions survived not only the end of the war but also the promotion of the more accommodating term *Gastarbeiter* in the Federal Republic since the late 1950s. Typically, cultural distinctions were – and still are – deeply intertwined with status allocation, as Hermann Korte avers when he speaks of

the thinking of a large part of the German population that tends to believe there is such a decisive and insuperable difference of culture between them and the foreign migrants, that the latter will never be capable of reaching the higher German standards. This line of thought can be found on other subjects among politicians. It is deeply rooted in the emergence of the nation-states in the nineteenth century and is still part of the ideological background of Western European states in general and the Federal Republic of Germany in particular.[53]

Although West Germans assumed a new identity as *Bundesbürger* (federal citizens) – an identity based in part on the German work ethic and the efficiency and quality of production – the debate about foreigners in Germany was charged with many older value judgments.[54] Omitting the specific reference to the inhuman side of these older distinctions, people focused on the fact that only work, even an obsession with work, had saved both individuals and the nation from perishing in the self-made catastrophe. Indeed, this time it had been history itself, a sullen and disparate history, that had accorded work a higher status. Rather than the saving grace of German music and art or the humanism of Goethe and Schiller, it was this focus that provided a source of identity and continuity for the millions of survivors in the war-torn and fragmented country.[55]

Remnants of this thinking remained eminently visible in the self-understanding of the two successor states to the Reich, the Federal Republic and the German Democratic Republic, during the decades

---

53 Hermann Korte, "Guestworker Question or Immigration Issue? Social Sciences and Public Debate in the Federal Republic of Germany," in Bade, ed., *Population, Labour and Migration*, 181.
54 Herbert, *Geschichte der Ausländerbeschäftigung*, 211.
55 A more extensive discussion in Frank Trommler, "Arbeitsnation statt Kulturnation? Ein vernachlässigter Faktor deutscher Identität," in Albrecht Schöne, ed., *Akten des VII. Internationalen Germanisten-Kongresses Göttingen 1985*, vol. 9: *Deutsche Literatur in der Weltliteratur* (Tübingen, 1986), 220–9; Frank Trommler, "'Deutschlands Sieg oder Untergang': Perspektiven aus dem Dritten Reich auf die Nachkriegsentwicklung," in Thomas Koebner et al., eds., *Deutschland nach Hitler: Zukunftspläne im Exil und aus der Besatzungszeit, 1939–1949* (Opladen, 1987), 220ff.

before their eventual unification in 1989. No other allusion to a collective purpose invoked stronger consensus among each of the two populations than praising the achievements that resulted from common work. Each society found legitimacy as a *Leistungsgesellschaft* (society of achievement); although in East Germany the consensus – or what could be understood as such – only lasted from about 1965 to 1975. The rush of East Germans to unite with the West after the fall of the Berlin Wall proved those right who had maintained that enhancing the status of work by itself, without sufficient material rewards in the realm of consumption, had become an ineffectual tool for identity formation, even among Germans.

The West Germans, following the example of the Americans, had transformed their gospel of successful reconstruction into a consumerist Magna Carta. The East Germans, in their state, had to accommodate themselves to a worn-out socialist edition of the German community of work, purified of the *Volk* – a dubious venture. It meant rubbing additional salt into the wounds of the East Germans when the West Germans articulated the ultimate put-down as a failure in the work world: that the East Germans had lost the ability to work hard.

BETWEEN THE WELFARE STATE AND THE AMERICAN DREAM

Comparing constitutional and institutional conditions in the United States and Germany for the formation of national identity has not been of central concern to scholars.[56] The matrix of ethnicity and work has been of even less concern. Yet, the topic has sparked new interest since the decline of the work ethos and the democratization of the concept of ethnicity have made necessary a rethinking of social and national allegiances. I suggest that we need to sharpen the focus on the intermingling of ethnicity and the work ethos that shaped so much of twentieth-century national identity, not just in the United States and Europe.

In Germany, where the Basic Law mirrored the strictly ethnic policy of inclusion and exclusion, pertinent discussions and decisions concerning the national status of guest workers, and their families (anywhere from two to three million people) rarely took place. The public debate about national identity did not reflect the problem. This debate had become a captive of the political division into West and East Germany,

---

56 Characteristically, this aspect is missing in Paul Kirchhof and Donald P. Kommers, eds., *Germany and Its Basic Law: Past, Present and Future* (Baden-Baden, 1993).

ritualistically affirming the common history and culture as the established frame of reference.[57] Instead, the problem was transferred to the social welfare bureaucracy, the labor ministry, and regional and local institutions, thus confirming a long-established tradition. Begun under Bismarck, the tradition of the German welfare state had come into its own after World War I, in correspondence with the politics of ethnic exclusion in favor of the *Volksgemeinschaft*.

It appears logical that the debate on the ethnic foundations of German nationality was thrown open after the unification of the two successor states to the Reich became a political fact. The debate was overdue since the legal remnants of the *Volksgemeinschaft* do not fit well into the new framework of European unity. Despite the interest in the patterns of national and nationalistic revival – which is the other consequence of the unification and the breakdown of the dual world order – the parameters of this debate are set by the overriding reality of the welfare state. It is not enough to assert that the worldwide rise of ethnic identities is closely related to the decline in the status of the work ethic. One needs to include in the diagnosis the fact that the expansion of the welfare state in Europe and especially in Germany has generated an allegiance that can rightly be seen as an heir to the identity that was shaped within the collectivity of the "working nation." What once developed as a response of personal and collective ethics to the challenges of industrialization, gathered around the internalization of production, has been replaced by an allegiance whose compensatory benefits are truly privileging, providing the internalization of the nation as a security net. The state-sponsored allocation of status is transferred to the realm of social security and health and old-age benefits. One might call it another turn in the growth of national identity from the everyday experience of rationalized collectivity; at any rate, it has shifted the encounter with "the other" to the "question of access to legal positions and the right to benefits within the welfare state."[58] This issue constitutes the focus around which the debates about nationality become truly heated: Whether people of different ethnicity, even if they were born in the country, will be allowed into the entitlement system. Only those who look through the continuities in the German rhetoric of exclusion and inclusion realize that since *social* citizenship rights have been granted to many of "the others," the battle about the *political* citizenship rights often plays a compensatory role.

---

57 Cf. Werner Weidenfeld, ed., *Die Identität der Deutschen* (Munich, 1983).
58 Hubert Heinelt, "Immigration and the Welfare State in Germany," *German Politics* 2 (1993): 79.

It was not until the late 1950s that Americans began to address fully the restrictions in the worlds of work and education that had been reinforced with ethnic and racial stereotypes in the preceding decades. After the Civil Rights movement took the lead in reversing and abolishing segregation, the search for solutions shifted to the matrix of work and ethnicity, resulting in the policy of affirmative action, an agenda of continuous struggle for equality and diversity at the workplace that has included women within the same framework.

Since the 1980s, the debate on multiculturalism has affected more of the world of education than that of the industrial and postindustrial economy. Indeed, it has gained its momentum as a debate about national identity or identities among educated elites. There is little attention to the everyday experience of national identity among the population at large. Within the dialectic of forming identity through experience, representation, or both, many manifestations still reflect, if only dimly, the old entitlements of being an American: having the freedom of pursuing economic, competitive, and, above all, conspicuous success — a freedom from government, though not from taxes, and the self-imposed guilt when it does not work out. Although tarnished, identity is still realized as a form of conduct, monitored through the ever-present standards of behavior, including that of ethnicity. The concept of the nation as an entitlement system, as it developed in Europe, is left to the lower classes, although the middle classes have long become dependent on the same system. The continuities in the American rhetoric of exclusion and inclusion are evident in the assertion that social cohesion should be maintained by reliance on "the American character" and "the American conduct" alone, without the policy of a specific security net. Obviously, the polemic directed against such a policy because of its inclusiveness toward "the others" also plays a compensatory role in the maintenance of national identity.

3

Segmented Politics

Xenophobia, Citizenship, and Political Loyalty in Germany

GREGG KVISTAD

This chapter explores the complex relationship between xenophobia and the politics of membership in the Federal Republic of Germany. The horror of xenophobic violence in the Federal Republic since unification in 1990 – with Hoyerswerda, Rostock, Mölln, and Solingen becoming shorthand for thousands of acts of right-wing violence perpetrated against foreigners – left politicians and commentators desperately searching for public policy solutions.[1] Two main calls for change surfaced after this violence: As conservatives defined "too many foreigners" to be the problem, the solution advocated and adopted by the federal government in the early spring of 1993 was to tighten considerably Germany's constitutionally guaranteed right to asylum;[2] as liberals and leftists alternatively defined Germany's citizenship law to be the problem – based on the principle of *jus sanguinis* – calls for a liberalization of Germany's restrictiveness were advanced.

Efforts to reduce complexity in order to yield pragmatic public policy solutions are common among modern Western societies grappling with difficult social problems; witness the current obsession in the United States with building prisons. Pragmatically, the drive to keep foreigners out of the Federal Republic and criminals behind bars in the United States might, respectively, reduce xenophobia and crime rates; but by identifying too many foreigners and too few prisons as the problems, the

---

1 See Karsten Schröder and Hermann Horstkotte, "Foreigners in Germany," *Sozial-Report* 2 (1993): 1–6.
2 Dieter Roth, "*Volksparteien* in Crisis? The Electoral Successes of the Extreme Right in Context," *German Politics* 2 (1993): 12–15; Alan Watson, *Focus on Germany: Dangers from the Right?* (Washington, D.C., 1993), 8.

questions of why xenophobia and crime are such widespread phenomena in these societies remain unaddressed.[3] The problem of xenophobia in Germany *is* more fundamentally addressed by reformers who demand change in the country's restrictive citizenship and naturalization laws. Reformers argue that easing the acquisition and attribution of German citizenship would improve the lives of foreigners in Germany, reduce violence against official "outsiders," and contribute to making Germany a more tolerant and multicultural society.[4]

Two main objections, however, are typically raised against this position, both informed by ethnocultural and ethnonational concerns. First, there is the response that "Germany is not a country of immigration," frequently joined by "Germany is not a country of naturalization." This position rejects the "mere transformation of foreigners into citizens" and questions the ability and willingness of foreigners to assimilate themselves to German social, cultural, and political life. The focus is on the will and capacity of the foreigner to adjust.[5] Second, there is the response that recognizes the ethnocultural and ethnonational impediments to the adjustment demanded of foreigners in the first place. Focusing on Germany and not on the foreigner, it is argued that liberalizing the law to allow for easier citizenship acquisition and attribution is perhaps a necessary, but no means sufficient, answer to xenophobic discrimination in the Federal Republic.

This chapter endorses the latter objections to the legalism of "merely transforming foreigners into citizens" in Germany, especially given Germany's *jus sanguinis* tradition. It attempts to wedge itself between the abstract response to German xenophobia in the form of liberalized citizenship, the most extreme example of which would be to "deny the necessity of any borders,"[6] on the one hand, and the protodeterminism of an ethnocultural attribution of certain relatively constant and objectionable "German" proclivities, on the other.[7] It is argued that membership in Germany since the early nineteenth century has been a distinctly *political* and not a merely legal or ethnocultural and ethnonational phenomenon.

---

3 For an excellent recounting and critique of the alleged relationship between immigration pressures and nationalist aggressiveness in the Federal Republic, see Jürgen Fijalkowski, *Aggressive Nationalism, Immigration Pressure, and Asylum Policy Disputes in Contemporary Germany* (Washington, D.C., 1993), 11–14.
4 Kay Hailbronner, "Citizenship and Nationhood in Germany," in William Rogers Brubaker, ed., *Immigration and the Politics of Citizenship in Europe and North America* (Lanham, Md., 1989), 72.
5 Ibid., 77–9.
6 Fijalkowski, *Aggressive Nationalism*, 22.
7 See Liah Greenfeld, *Nationalism: Five Roads to Modernity* (Cambridge, Mass., 1992), 277–395.

As a result, there are significant *political* limitations to the legal reform of citizenship as a response to German xenophobia and antiforeigner discrimination, but those limitations, it also concludes, have increasingly eroded in the Federal Republic.

Political limitations to the legal reform of membership in Germany rest on a lingering nineteenth-century tradition of segmenting public life into hortatory and derogatory beliefs and practice within the status of legal German citizenship. Since the early nineteenth century, the status of legal German citizen (or official "subject") has not prohibited significant instances of political marginalization, discrimination, persecution, and worse against "legal" Germans. These include Catholics during the Kulturkampf, Social Democrats during and after the period of anti-Socialist legislation, Jews most virulently (but by no means exclusively) during the late Weimar and the Nazi periods, Communists throughout the postwar era, radicalized university students in the 1960s and 1970s, Greens since the 1980s, and even some *Aussiedler* (ethnic Germans) and former East Germans since the collapse of the Berlin Wall. Whereas political discrimination, persecution, and marginalization do not compare to murderous xenophobic right-wing violence, this chapter argues that these phenomena all share at least one common political root: a lingering statist political ideology segmenting legal German public life into legitimate-hortatory and illegitimate-derogatory agents, beliefs, and actions.

The other side of political impedance, however, is political opportunity. This chapter also argues that the nineteenth-century segmentation of German public life into hortatory and derogatory realms has come under concerted attack in the Federal Republic, especially since the 1960s. Indicators of that are too numerous even to mention, but they include the consolidation of the very successful *Parteienstaat* (party-state);[8] the growth of subjective citizen competence attitudes among ordinary German citizens;[9] the political-cultural and partial institutional "revolution" of "more democracy" of the early 1970s;[10] the appearance of the Greens in the early 1980s and their subsequent survival;[11] and, as this chapter tries to develop, the protracted and divisive political battle over the so-called *Radikalenerlass* (radicals decree) in the 1970s and

---

8 Kenneth H. F. Dyson, *Party, State, and Bureaucracy in Western Germany* (Beverly Hills, Calif., 1977).
9 David Conradt, "Changing German Political Culture," in Gabriel A. Almond and Sidney Verba, eds., *The Civic Culture Revisited: An Analytic Study* (Boston, 1980), 221–72.
10 See Arnulf Baring, *Machtwechsel: Die Ära Brandt-Scheel* (Stuttgart, 1982).
11 Gregg Kvistad, "Between State and Society: Green Political Ideology in the Mid-1980s," *West European Politics* 10 (1987): 211–28.

1980s. Specifically, the battle over the *Radikalenerlass* revealed two important features about public life in this period: First, the political tradition of vertically differentiating a "state" realm populated by politically hortatory civil servants with "reliable" political beliefs and actions from a "society" realm of ordinary German citizens with potentially "unreliable" political beliefs and actions remained powerful in the Federal Republic in the 1970s. Second, this political tradition was no longer ideologically hegemonic in the Federal Republic in the 1970s and 1980s, as was revealed by a powerful antistatist popular mobilization against the decree.

This chapter includes, first, a discussion of the nature of citizenship in the modern nation-state; second, a treatment of German citizenship law, which is based on the Wilhelmine concept of *jus sanguinis*, including the reforms of 1991 and 1993; third, a discussion of the traditional political ideology in Germany that vertically segments legal universal membership into hortatory and "lower" political beliefs and actions; fourth, a brief recounting of both the embodiment and the rejection of that segmentation in the battle over German civil service policy and German naturalization policy; and finally, a speculation on the vertical segmentation of public life, political discrimination, xenophobia, and the political determinants of a multicultural society.

CITIZENSHIP IN THE MODERN NATION-STATE

The history of the concept of political citizenship is obviously rich and variegated. Whereas Aristotle and Rousseau emphasized the creative, voluntary, and open-ended self-ruling capacities of citizens in small communities, Max Weber focused instead on the nonvoluntary "legitimate domination" of "compulsory members" of an institutionalized political community.[12] The first suggests political creativity, whereas the second suggests management. If the Weberian state management perspective on the nature of modern citizenship has any relevance anywhere in the 1990s, it is in Western Europe. As nation-states in Europe sort out the consequences of the end of the Cold War and the collapse of the Iron Curtain, the problem of managing who is, who is not, and who might become citizens of wealthy industrialized democracies has acquired immense significance.[13] Consistent with this perspective, Rogers Brubaker's

---

12 Max Weber, *Economy and Society*, ed. Guenter Roth and Claus Wittich, 2 vols. (Berkeley, Calif., 1978), 2:901ff.
13 See William J. Serow et al., eds., *Handbook on International Migration* (New York, 1990), 1–5.

OUTSIDERS   INSIDERS

(citizens of *other* nation-states)   (citizens of nation-states)

Figure 3.1. Citizenship as Differentiation

recent comparison of German and French immigration treats modern citizenship as an instrument to effect "exclusion," "inclusion," "separation," "differentiation," "closure," and "restriction."[14] Tomas Hammar similarly refers to states acting as "controller, regulator or gatekeeper" with their citizenship laws.[15]

The institution of citizenship can thus be viewed, although by no means exclusively, as a sorting mechanism for modern nation-states to determine who is "in" and who is "out," especially in periods of large-scale migration and attempted migration. Legally, "insiders" constitute a single status, typically entailing residence rights, the right to enter the nation-state, and some level of political participation, but also obligations such as compulsory military service. "Outsiders," in contrast, are a more variegated group: All "foreigners," some are temporary visitors, some are resident aliens (both long- and short-term), and some are more ambivalently "denizens," or foreigners with nearly fully guaranteed residence status and, for some at least, particular political rights.[16] "Outsiders" are vertically differentiated by legal rights and obligations (denizens, if they exist, typically have the most, and temporary visitors have the least), whereas "insiders" inhabit a "region of legal equality." As Brubaker writes, "[to] be defined as a citizen is not to qualify as an insider for a particular instance or type of interaction; it is to be defined in a general, abstract, enduring, and context-independent way as a member of the state."[17] Furthermore, "outsiders" are legally differentiated from "insiders" horizontally, in the sense that citizen and noncitizen are exclusive classes of rights- and duties-bearing persons. Noncitizens of one nation-state are virtually always citizens of another, and the metaphorical wall that separates these two classes is, from a global nation-state perspective, legally separating level territory – regardless of the views of particular migrating individuals (see Figure 3.1).

14 Rogers Brubaker, *Citizenship and Nationhood in France and Germany* (Cambridge, Mass., 1992), ix–xi.
15 Tomas Hammar, *Democracy and the Nation-State: Aliens, Denizens, and Citizens in a World of International Migration* (Aldershot, 1990), 29.
16 Ibid., 30–3.
17 Brubaker, *Citizenship*, 21, 29.

For the recent debate in the Federal Republic of Germany, it is this last differentiation – the horizontal distinction between German citizens and non-Germans – that is most relevant. In the late 1980s, the potential differentiation among types of "foreigner" in the Federal Republic acquired relevance as local voting rights were advocated by Social Democrats for long-term foreign residents. But the Federal Constitutional Court's unanimous decision in October 1990 to prohibit the extension of local voting rights to non-Germans effectively rendered "non-German" the most relevant political status of all foreigners living in the Federal Republic.[18] "Who is German?" as opposed to "What kind of foreigner?" was then the operative question in the Federal Republic's recent political debate: Conservatives suggested limiting the number of "non-Germans" in the Federal Republic, thereby removing non-German *persons* targeted by xenophobia; liberal and leftist reformers, in contrast, advocated making the acquisition of the status "German" easier, thereby limiting the non-German *status* targeted by xenophobia. In each case, the status of German citizen was treated as a legal phenomenon, disaggregated by neither ethnocultural nor political considerations.

THE MODERN HISTORY OF CITIZENSHIP IN GERMANY

The formal "region of equality" that constitutes the current status of German citizenship has been delineated since 1913 by the principle of *jus sanguinis*.[19] This principle holds that citizenship status is transmitted genealogically, by the "blood" of a person's biological father or (since 1974) mother. Location of birth, the fact that is relevant for the principle of *jus soli*, is in itself meaningless for German citizenship. Yet the contradictory blood and territory bases of *jus sanguinis* and *jus soli*, respectively, were combined in German citizenship law prior to 1913. In nineteenth-century Germany, a joining of these two principles was possible within what Brubaker calls a "state-national" citizenship law: "Prolonged residence in the territory no longer [as it had in Prussia prior to 1842] sufficed to acquire citizenship. Prolonged absence from the territory, however, still occasioned the loss of citizenship."[20] Foreigners living within Germany's

---

18 Hammar, *Democracy*, 19; Barbara Marshall, "German Migration Policies," in Gordon Smith et al., eds., *Developments in German Politics* (Durham, N.C., 1992), 250–1.
19 "Bericht der Beauftragten der Bundesregierung für die Belange der Ausländer über die Lage der Ausländer in der Bundesrepublik Deutschland, 1993," *Mitteilungen der Beauftragten der Bundesregierung für die Belange der Ausländer* (1994): 84.
20 It should be mentioned that before 1913 German citizenship was mediated: One was a citizen

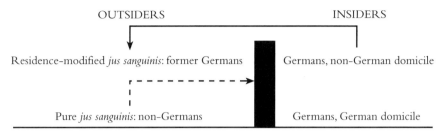

Figure 3.2. Pre-1913 German "State-National" Citizenship

borders acquired no right to citizenship, whereas Germans living abroad could be transformed (after ten years) into "outsiders" to the German community by their chosen place of residence. "Blood" excluded foreigners from German citizenship, whereas chosen domicile could lead to the same for German citizens.

This "state-national" understanding of German citizenship prior to 1913 was fundamentally a political understanding. Its pivot was loyalty, or the purported intensity of the tie between an individual citizen and the modern nation-state. Brubaker writes:

From a state-national point of view . . . descent creates a more substantial community than the "accidental fact" of birthplace. Descent binds the individual more closely to the destiny of the state; and the strength of the ties between state and citizen is a central concern in the age of the nation-state, particularly at the historical moment of the nation at arms.[21]

On the one hand, this understanding assumed that a genealogical transmission of citizenship provided a deeper and more reliable tie to the German nation-state than the accidental physical location of birth. On the other hand, German law – consistent with a "state-national" understanding – posited that this genealogical tie was not determinative but could be ruptured by extended periods of residence abroad that would justify rescinding citizenship status. This assumption modified pure *jus sanguinis* by holding the tie between German citizens and the German nation-state to be potentially but not universally variable, dependent for Germans (but not non-Germans) on the choice of territorial residence (see Figure 3.2).

of Bavaria, Prussia, and so forth, and only by being a citizen of a federal state did one acquire membership in the Reich. Passports, for example, were issued by member states (Brubaker, *Citizenship*, 115).

21 Ibid., 123.

A residence-modified *jus sanguinis* understood extended residence outside of the nation-state as producing, by legal implication, political unreliability. Extended German residence in the nation-state by non-Germans, however, was not at the same time seen to produce the binding ties of loyalty required for political membership. For "ethnic non-Germans," genealogy alone, and not birthplace, residence, or political will, necessarily implied insufficient loyalty to the German nation-state. Similarly, for "ethnic Germans," genealogy and residence, but not birthplace or political will, were taken to indicate loyal ties to the nation-state. Loyalty was not in any sense "tested" for either group, yet that was the object at stake in the residence mediation of "blood" membership in the nation-state. State-national political considerations modified the "blood" understanding of loyal bonds to the "destiny of the nation-state" by introducing prolonged residence outside of the territory as indicating an inadequate linkage to that destiny. Germans by descent who were resident in the nation-state were loyal; "ethnic Germans" living outside the nation-state for a lengthy period – as well as "ethnic non-Germans" – were not.

After 1913, an ethnonational adjustment to the state-national understanding of German citizenship meant that loyalty lost its legal relevance for the retention – although not acquisition – of German citizenship. That occurred by removing the residence modification of *jus sanguinis* that had previously allowed the loss of German citizenship for extended periods of residence abroad; indeed, the new law even allowed the reacquisition of German citizenship by those who had lost it under the old.[22] With the removal of all traces of residence considerations from the law, "ethnic Germans" joined "ethnic non-Germans" in having citizenship attribution and retention be controlled solely by descent. This formal "de-statification" of German citizenship, by which political membership ties were reconceptualized as unalterable bonds to an ethnonational German community, meant that political loyalty was no longer regarded as variable for "ethnic Germans" regardless of residence. For "ethnic non-Germans," the assumption of nonloyalty – regardless of residence, place of birth, or political belief and actions – remained unchanged. This shift to an ethnonational understanding of German citizenship occurred in a highly politicized context, one not unlike that found in the Federal Republic after the collapse of the Iron Curtain in 1989.

22 Ibid., 115.

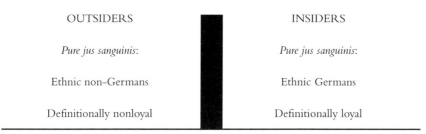

OUTSIDERS		INSIDERS
Pure jus sanguinis:		*Pure jus sanguinis:*
Ethnic non-Germans		Ethnic Germans
Definitionally nonloyal		Definitionally loyal

Figure 3.3. Post-1913 German Ethnocultural Citizenship

By the early twentieth century, Germany had become an economic magnet for immigrants, especially Poles, working in heavy industry, mining, and commercial agriculture.[23] As migration increased, the Pan-German League's concern for the "preservation of German *Volkstum*" (nationhood) enveloped virtually all of Wilhelmine Germany's political parties as they supported the retention (and reacquisition) of German citizenship for foreign-domiciled Germans (*Auslandsdeutsche*).[24] Over a million foreigners working in the Reich encouraged German lawmakers to view the potential political falling away of long-term German residents abroad with much less disfavor. The ethnocultural threat of the alleged *Drang nach Westen* (drive to the West) of Slavs and Jews to Germany's "flourishing economy" and "free institutions" was to be met, according to the Reich Interior Ministry, by the promotion of *Deutschtum* (Germanness) both in Germany and abroad, wherever "ethnic Germans" and their blood descendants resided.[25] Gone was the "state-national" concern for the lapsed political loyalty of Germans who had left the fatherland. The only valid legal differentiation now was the ethnonational horizontal one between definitionally loyal "ethnic Germans," on the one hand, and definitionally nonloyal "ethnic non-Germans," on the other, regardless of domicile (see Figure 3.3). *Jus soli*, or the principle of attributing citizenship on the basis of some consideration of the place of birth (automatically *at* birth, or by acquisition after some period of residence), was left completely out of the government policy debate in 1913. The principle of *jus soli* implied assimilation to "Germanness" as a means to acquire membership status. Conservatives in 1913 saw that as both undesirable and impossible: undesirable, given Germany's "front-line" status facing

23 Peter O'Brien, "German-Polish Migration: The Elusive Search for a German Nation-State," *International Migration Review* 36 (1991): 379.
24 Brubaker, *Citizenship*, 16.
25 Ibid., 134, 136.

the East; and impossible, because the "accident" of the location of birth could never, it was held, equal the blood tie to the German ethnonational community.[26]

The ethnonational rendition of pure *jus sanguinis* thus turned on the definition of "ethnic German." After World War II, "ethnic Germans" included not only Germans inhabiting the Federal Republic but also Germans carrying a GDR passport – who were officially treated as citizens of the Federal Republic – and "ethnic Germans" outside the combined territory of the FRG and the GDR. Officially, this last group included only those who qualified as postwar *Vertriebene*, or "expellees," from Eastern Europe and the former Soviet Union because of their German "ethnicity." A combination of Cold War policy and the acknowledgment of the powerful political clout of the organization of expellees in the Federal Republic, however, led Germany to "consider virtually all ethnic German immigrants from Eastern Europe and the Soviet Union as *Vertriebene*, without inquiring into the actual circumstances of their emigration."[27] The *Sonderprogramm Aussiedler* (Special Program for Ethnic Germans) of August 1988 provided these "ethnic Germans" with German citizenship and complete legal equality with Germans in the Federal Republic.

Pure *jus sanguinis* suggested the ethnocultural assumption of definitional political loyalty to be attached to many immigrants who had never set foot in the Federal Republic, knew nothing of its political and social system, and spoke no German. The absurdity of this assumption, combined with the collapse of communism and attendant flood of "ethnic German" migrants to the Federal Republic (nearly 1,200,000 between 1988 and 1991), led to a slight tightening of the treatment of "ethnic German" *Aussiedler* in 1991. This included more stringent application procedures, some demonstration of connection to German "culture," and limitations on freedom of settlement once in the Federal Republic.[28] The operative principle for citizenship in the Federal Republic remained, however, *jus sanguinis* and its accompanying definitional assumption of powerful and loyal ties to the German nation among "ethnic Germans," regardless of domicile. For "ethnic non-Germans" seeking naturalization, the obverse definitional assumption of

---

26 Ibid., 136–7.
27 Peter J. Katzenstein, *Policy and Politics in West Germany: The Growth of a Semisovereign State* (Philadelphia, 1987), 212–13; Brubaker, *Citizenship*, 206–7 n. 19.
28 Marshall, "German Migration Policies," 256–7; James F. Hollifield, *Immigrants, Markets, and States: The Political Economy of Postwar Europe* (Cambridge, Mass., 1992), 35.

nonloyalty provided a significant hurdle to acquiring German citizenship. The hurdle could be cleared but, until 1993 when the formal requirements for naturalization were lowered, only by relatively few.

During the 1980s, foreigners became "Germans" at an average annual rate of less than one-tenth of the corresponding figures in France, with its combination of *jus soli* and *jus sanguinis*. Controlling for France's attribution of citizenship in response to birth location and subsequent residence – which Germany did not and still does not allow – German naturalization alone was still roughly one-sixth of that of France's in the same period.[29] These figures suggest that naturalization applicants must scale a rather high wall in the Federal Republic. Part of that height was constructed, until 1993, by the rigorous formal demands made by the German state on the political beliefs and actions of naturalization applicants. Because the principle of pure *jus sanguinis* makes a person's country of birth or residence, irrelevant, long-term residents in the Federal Republic, including even second- and third-generation "ethnic non-Germans" who had never visited the country of their citizenship, were forced to demonstrate clearly a number of extraordinary characteristics to qualify for German citizenship – characteristics not legally required of lifetime Germans of the Federal Republic, former East German *Übersiedler*, or "ethnic German" *Aussiedler* from Eastern Europe and the former Soviet Union.[30] Most generally, these were captured in what was referred to as a "positive attitude toward German culture." Specifically, these included a long period of permanent residence and adequate accommodation in the Federal Republic; a good reputation; the ability to make a living for self and dependents without reliance on welfare; fluency in spoken and written German language; a "voluntary attachment" to Germany; a basic knowledge of Germany's political and social structures; no criminal record; and a positive commitment to the Federal Republic's "free democratic basic order."[31] The strong ties to the ethnonational community that were assumed to be in place among "ethnic Germans" had to be positively demonstrated by "ethnic non-Germans" seeking naturalization. Naturalization remained discretionary, controlled by state authorities whose job it was to determine the public interest in naturalizing any particular applicant. No private legal right to citizenship existed among "ethnic non-Germans," regardless of place of birth or residence.

29 Brubaker, *Citizenship*, 82.
30 Fijalkowski, *Aggressive Nationalism*, 19.
31 Hailbronner, "Citizenship," 68–9.

Whereas citizenship status was of course legally nonpoliticized for Germans in the Federal Republic during this period – for them there existed the *legal* assumption of a "realm of equality" without a positive demonstration of political loyalty – for non-Germans seeking naturalization, citizenship law was highly politicized (although not "party-politicized"). A law professor and Administrative Appeals Court judge in Baden-Württemberg argued, "To my mind, it is perfectly reasonable to require loyalty to the basic principles of the constitution as long as a clear distinction is made between fundamental constitutional principles and the existing political regime." He continued, "Political activities in emigrant organizations are usually taken as evidence against a permanent attachment to Germany. Activities in extremist or radical organizations justify, in general, the conclusion that the applicant is not committed to the democratic order of the Federal Republic."[32] This requirement of heightened demonstrable political loyalty – and not mere political legality – reveals in clear detail the implicit assumption of deep and significant attachment to the German ethnonation that accompanies pure *jus sanguinis*. "Blood" is argued to be a more significant tie to the German nation than accidental location of birth or residence. If an "ethnic non-German" wishes to become a German, he or she must demonstrate an extraordinary tie to the German ethnonation and its political institutionalization in order to remove the definitionally nonloyal status he or she harbored as an "outsider."

RECENT LEGAL REFORM OF GERMAN CITIZENSHIP

One obvious response to German xenophobia and ethnocultural discrimination suggested by the previous analysis would be to lower the wall between "insiders" and "outsiders" in the German community. If German citizenship were made less difficult to attain – via acquisition, attribution, and naturalization – fewer "foreigners" would exist in Germany, and what might appear to be an officially sanctioned definition of "otherness" would end. That would entail either getting rid of *jus sanguinis* entirely, or substantially modifying it with the addition of elements of *jus soli* and residency considerations. With the demise or amendment of an ethnonational *jus sanguinis* would go a corollary concern for a strong and loyal attachment to a German political community. For citizenship, the elevated demands on the political loyalty of "ethnic non-

32 Ibid.

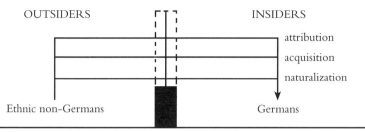

Figure 3.4. Proposed Legal Reform of Citizenship in the FRG: Lowering the Wall

Germans" would disappear and more closely resemble the presumptively loyal political status of ordinary German citizens who formally occupied a "region of legal equality."

Jürgen Fijalkowski's call for a quota system of immigration in the Federal Republic incorporates this recommendation:

A modernized understanding of citizenship and nation . . . could be based only on the rejection of an ethnonational understanding of citizenship. It would represent a turn toward an understanding of nation as a self-governing society formed by heterogeneous citizens. The nation of common ethnic descent would be transformed into a post-national society characterized by the will of citizens to live together under the common law of constitutional democracy irrespective of race, gender, ethnicity, descent, origin, social group, religion, and political thinking, looking to the future rather than to the past.[33]

The pragmatic policy choice to lower the barriers to legal German citizenship could thus be informed by an eloquent modernist appeal to increased tolerance, constitutional liberalism, and a multicultural Federal Republic. The "region of legal equality" enjoyed by German citizens would be extended to "ethnic non-Germans" by means of citizenship acquisition, attribution, and naturalization (see Figure 3.4).

In fact, a new Aliens Law, which took effect in January 1991 after considerable political wrangling, significantly altered some but not all of the characteristics a naturalization applicant must embody.[34] Most important for the discussion here, a *Regelanspruch auf Einbürgerung* (legal eligibility for naturalization) was granted to foreigners who had renounced their previous citizenship and met a number of conditions. For foreigners between the ages of sixteen and twenty-three, these included legal residence and school attendance in the Federal Republic for six years; for

---

33 Fijalkowski, *Nationalism*, 26–7.
34 Marshall, "German Migration Policies," 251–2.

foreigners over the age of twenty-three they included legal residence for fifteen years, a permanent address, a means of maintenance that did not include welfare and unemployment benefits, and no convictions for a criminal offense.[35] Gone was the explicit ethnonational demand to demonstrate an attachment and "positive attitude toward German culture." Remaining in the 1991 law was, however, a continued reliance on bureaucratic discretion – *Ermessen der zuständigen Behörden* – for determining the public interest in granting German citizenship to any particular naturalization applicant. Although that was to be granted *in der Regel* (as a rule), these "eligible" foreigners possessed no right to German citizenship.

The Aliens Law of 1991 in no way altered German citizenship law, which continued to be based on the principle of pure *jus sanguinis*. It also did not affect the definition of the Federal Republic as "not an immigrant country." It finally did not reverse federal government policy, in force since October 1982, to strive for "integration" but not the "assimilation" of foreigners. The government minister in charge of the affairs of foreigners defined the government policy of "integration" as a "peaceful coexistence between people of different origins."[36] The continued validity of pure *jus sanguinis* suggested that "origins" – or genealogical descent – continued to matter for defining membership in the German community. "Peaceful coexistence" among "insiders" and "outsiders" within Germany's national-state borders, and not the assimilation of foreigners, was all that the German government formally declared to be desirable. Cutting across these remnants of an ethnonational understanding of German membership, however, was the legal granting of a *Regelanspruch* for German naturalization as detailed in the 1991 law. This removed the demand for a positive demonstration of an attachment to "Germanness." For adult foreigners, "peaceful coexistence" among "ethnic Germans" for fifteen years, among other formal universalistic criteria, produced an "eligibility" for naturalization *in der Regel*. The odd juxtaposition of "peaceful coexistence" and eligibility for naturalization was, on the one hand, an artifact of the government's reluctance to encourage "ethnic non-German" immigration and assimilation, whereas on the other hand, it recognized the perils to social peace of doing nothing to ease the naturalization prospects of almost 10 percent of the population of the Federal Republic.

The retention of bureaucratic discretion in the 1991 Aliens Law for

---

35 Schröder and Horstkotte, "Foreigners," 4; "Bericht der Beauftragten der Bundesregierung," 84.
36 Schröder and Horstkotte, "Foreigners," 2–3.

individual naturalization cases remained meaningful enough for government and opposition at the end of 1992 to agree to amend the law to replace the *Regelanspruch* (legal eligibility) for naturalization to a *Rechtsanspruch* (legal *right*) to naturalization for the persons defined in the 1991 prescriptions.[37] Coming into force in 1993, this amendment was not trivial. It appeared in a nation-state with ethnonational traditions of defining citizenship according to *jus sanguinis* and naturalization as an extraordinary process available only to those who are able positively to demonstrate deep attachment to "German culture" and its political institutions. In this context, as long as naturalization remained a matter defined by the public interest and not by private right, and as long as government policy continued to identify Germany as "not a country of immigration" striving for "integration" but not "assimilation" of foreigners, bureaucratic discretion could very easily continue to make naturalization an arduous exception, even for those legally eligible.

With the 1993 amendment granting a legal right to naturalization, Germany's formal naturalization policy lost its ethnonational character and acquired – or reacquired – a more secure state-national identity. Reinstituting Germany's pre-1913 concern for choice of domicile, the 1993 law gave long-term foreign residents of Germany the right to acquire German citizenship. That status would not flow automatically, by attribution, but it could legally be claimed by persons meeting other formal and universalistic requirements. Hence, we have a return to a state-national understanding of German membership, but with the actors and proscriptions reversed from the pre-1913 legal context. Before 1913, national-state boundaries mattered for "ethnic Germans" who chose to live outside the borders of the Reich for a lengthy period; since 1993, national-state boundaries matter for "ethnic non-German" foreigners who choose to live legally inside the borders of the Federal Republic for a lengthy period and who have formally applied for naturalization. This reform of pure *jus sanguinis*, with its ethnonational understanding of membership, to a residence-modified *jus sanguinis*, with a state-national understanding of German membership, marked a clear but limited liberalization of German citizenship law (see Figure 3.5).

Legal reformism, however, runs up against ethnoculturalists and ethnonationalists – by conviction and in their critique – who argue that sixty years and four German regimes of pure *jus sanguinis* pose major impediments to transforming ethnic "Turks," for instance, into "Germans" by

37 "Bericht der Beauftragten der Bundesregierung," 85.

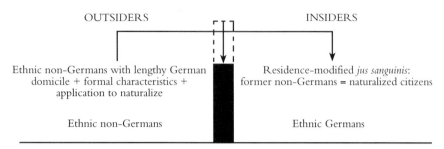

Figure 3.5. Post-1993 German "State-National" Citizenship

"merely" changing citizenship or naturalization law in the Federal Republic. Although the substantial modification of German naturalization law in 1991 and 1993 may indeed go some way in moving in the direction toward Fijalkowski's "postnational" society of "heterogeneous citizens," there exist, in addition to ethnocultural and ethnonational impediments, distinctly German *political* impediments – reaching back to the end of the eighteenth century – to understanding citizenship as a status of persons inhabiting a "region of equality." Understanding citizenship as a status enjoyed within a metaphorically walled "region of legal equality" obscures not only ethnocultural and ethnonational inequalities, but, in the historical case of Germany, also the vertical *political* segmentation of legal "insider" status. For an account of that segmentation, we must return to reform-era Prussia.

THE HISTORICAL SEGMENTATION OF
LEGAL POLITICAL MEMBERSHIP IN GERMANY

The Prussian General Code of 1794 establishing a *Gesetzesstaat*, or codified law state, placed the state "above" all persons in Prussia, including the monarch who was mentioned only as a legal personality, or *Oberhaupt*, in relation to the Prussian state.[38] At this time the Prussian "state" itself was a diffuse entity. Reinhart Koselleck argues that an acknowledged *Geist*, or spirit, provided Prussia with an identity in the early nineteenth century in lieu of territorial, ethnic, linguistic, and religious unity. Politically, Prussia's *Geist* took the form of the "idea" of the Prussian state.

---

38 Ernst Rudolf Huber, *Deutsche Verfassungsgeschichte seit 1789*, vol. 2: *Der Kampf um Einheit und Freiheit, 1830–1850* (Stuttgart, 1968), 16–19; Kurt G. A. Jeserich, "Die Entstehung des öffentlichen Dienstes, 1800–1871," in Kurt G. A. Jeserich, Hans Pohl, and Georg-Christoph von Unruh, eds., *Deutsche Verwaltungsgeschichte*, vol. 2: *Vom Reichsdeputationshauptschluss bis zur Auflösung des Deutschen Bundes* (Stuttgart, 1983), 304–5.

The *Geist*-informed idea of the Prussian state was regarded as a universal value that transcended all concrete particularity in Prussian society – even the particularity of the personality of the Prussian monarch, as articulated by Frederick the Great's claim that he was the state's "first servant."[39] Prussia's bureaucrats were legally no longer the "king's servants" or "royal servants" but, rather, *Beamte des Staates* (state officials) or *Diener des Staates* (servants of the state).[40]

For the subsequent understanding of both German civil-service politics and the politics of German citizenship, the logical inability for any person fully to embody the abstract *Geist* of the Prussian state was of singular importance. It meant that some citizens, as *Träger* of the state's idea, were "closer" to the Prussian state than others, but they were never unequivocal embodiers of the state's *Geist*. Since the early nineteenth century, the *Dienst an sich* demanded of civil servants was, as a category, vague, insufficient, and formed the foundation for testing the adequacy of that "service" in German politics.[41] According to Liah Greenfeld, the concept of the German state in this period "implied . . . dissociation and fostered the development of loyalty to an impersonal, secular political entity, the well-being or power of which, presumably, meant the common well-being."[42] But from the perspective of the ordinary citizen (or subject), even meaningfully "loyal" service to the Prussian state and subsequent nearness to its *Geist* was impossible. The "state estate" of the civil service in the Prussian *Vormärz* was understood, according to Robert Berdahl, "as the guardian of the public interest, elevated above the conflicting interests of the other *Stände*."[43] Bernd Wunder describes the "ideology of the state service" consolidating in this period: "In the belief of service for the 'common good,' the civil service saw itself way above a society following only individual or group interests. . . . All criticisms from society were rejected as egoistic special interests."[44]

The factualness of the Prussian civil service estate's singular ability to serve the "common good" in this period is not a central question here.[45] In any case, the political instrumentalization of civil servants ideally

39 Reinhart Koselleck, *Preussen zwischen Reform und Revolution: Allgemeines Landrecht, Verwaltung, und soziale Frage von 1791 bis 1848* (Stuttgart, 1967), 399; Jeserich, "Entstehung," 306.
40 Rosenberg, *Bureaucracy, Aristocracy, and Autocracy: The Prussian Experience, 1660–1815* (Boston, 1966), 191.
41 Huber, *Deutsche Verfassungsgeschichte*, 22.
42 Greenfeld, *Nationalism*, 286.
43 Robert Berdahl, *The Politics of the Prussian Nobility* (Princeton, N.J., 1988), 312.
44 Bernd Wunder, *Geschichte der Bürokratie in Deutschland* (Frankfurt/Main, 1986), 67.
45 John R. Gillis, *The Prussian Bureaucracy in Crisis, 1840–1860: Origins of an Administrative Ethos* (Stanford, Calif., 1971), 16.

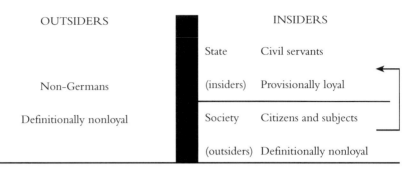

Figure 3.6. The Political Ideology of Bureaucratic Paternalism

devoted to *Dienst an sich* occurred as political "outsiders" in Prussia – including mercantile wealth, the urban poor, landless peasants, and the educated bourgeoisie – increasingly challenged political "insiders" and their alleged special relationship to the *Geist* of the Prussian state.[46] The societal challenge "from below" in the *Vormärz* led to the consolidation of a political ideology that segmented a hortatory "state" estate devoted to a more or less classical Greek concept of the "common good" and inhabited by civil servants, and a politically derogatory realm of "society" that included an assortment of estates, classes, groups, and, as 1848 approached, nascent political parties.[47] The consolidating political ideology of bureaucratic paternalism viewed German citizens inhabiting "society" not just as irrelevant for determining and acting on the common good, but – because of their definitional nonloyalty produced by their inability to serve the *Geist* of the Prussian state – as positively dangerous to the success of that effort (see Figure 3.6).

Not only was there the consolidation of a vertically segmented political space placing a hortatory "state" inhabited by civil servants above a derogatory "society" of ordinary citizens and subjects; there also appeared a vertical political segmentation *within* "society." For this we need to turn briefly to German liberalism and its antecedents. The persons relegated to the realm of "society" in the institutional ideology of bureaucratic paternalism in *Vormärz* Prussia were obviously not all of one group. Among them included the *Bildungsbürgertum*, the university-educated class, which had been growing since the end of the eighteenth century and which simply could not be absorbed by either the universities or the state civil service. Also locked out of provincial *Landtagen* (diets) for

46 Berdahl, *Politics of the Prussian Nobility*, 312.
47 Koselleck, *Preussen zwischen Reform und Revolution*, 342–3, 381–4, 387, 447.

lack of property ownership, the *Bildungsbürgertum* became, according to Greenfeld, "victims of status inconsistency": they "identified with the aristocracy [who occupied the civil service], which would not merge with them, and despised the bourgeoisie, to which they were inseparably tied. Elevated above the common lot, they remained a lower class nevertheless, and were vexed and made unhappy by their position in society."[48] Greenfeld holds this "status inconsistency" ultimately responsible for the growth of a virulent middle-class romantic nationalism among a displaced German intellectual elite, in other words, for reinforcing with nationalist argument the wall horizontally separating German insiders from non-German outsiders.[49] This status inconsistency was also responsible for a further segmentation of "insider" political life – not only between a state realm and a societal realm but also between a hortatory societal realm and a derogatory societal realm.

This further segmentation is captured in the tenets of nineteenth-century German liberalism.[50] In contrast to Anglo-American variants of this political ideology, German liberalism on the whole did not define individual liberty in terms of pushing back state power. According to James Sheehan, most nineteenth-century German liberals saw the problem not to be state power as such, but how to reconcile their hatred for official, monarchical, and bureaucratic despotism – the antithesis of *Dienst an sich* in the name of the common good – with their recognition of state power as the only possible means for securing political freedom.[51] German liberalism idealized state power with its critique of a political *Willkür*, or arbitrariness, regarded as the antithesis of the "norms of rational law" embodied in the *Rechtsstaat*.[52] Only the *Rechtsstaat*, according to the liberals Rotteck and Welcker, as they argued in the *Staatslexikon* in 1843, could defend against "anarchy," which was dually defined as despotic state rule, on the one hand, and the "naturally" antipolitical condition of society, on the other.[53] Both *Fürstensouveränität* (princely

---

48 Greenfeld, *Nationalism*, 297–8.
49 Ibid., 310–14.
50 The dangers of reducing at least nine different strands of German liberalism in the nineteenth century to a single concept are enormous, but not relevant for the level of argument here. See James J. Sheehan, "Liberalism and Society in Germany, 1815–1848," *Journal of Modern History* 45 (1973): 588–91.
51 James J. Sheehan, *German Liberalism in the Nineteenth Century* (Chicago, 1978), 39–43.
52 Karl-Georg Faber, "Strukturprobleme des deutschen Liberalismus im 19. Jahrhundert," *Der Staat* 14 (1975): 214; Dirk Blasius, "Bürgerliches Recht und bürgerliche Identität: Zu einem Problemzusammenhang in der deutschen Geschichte des 19. Jahrhunderts," in Helmut Berding et al., eds., *Vom Staat des Ancien Régimes zum modernen Parteienstaat* (Munich, 1974), 214–16.
53 Peter Christian Ludz, "Anarchie," in Otto Brunner, Werner Conze, and Reinhart Koselleck, eds.,

sovereignty) and *Volkssouveränität* (people's sovereignty) were rejected by German liberalism in the *Vormärz* as particularistic and illegitimate; only *Staatssouveränität* (state sovereignty) could defend against despotism from above and the will of the "mob" from below.[54]

German liberalism thereby introduced a further segmentation of society into the primary dichotomy of a state of civil servants, on the one hand, and a society of ordinary citizens, on the other. Citizens (or subjects) inhabiting society could be divided between those who acknowledged *Staatssouveränität* as good politics and radical *Ungebildeten* (uneducated) who demanded popular democratic rule. On the latter, the "wounding sword" of the state, to adopt the language of the early liberal Friedrich Dahlmann, would need to be deployed.[55] By the 1830s, a significant shift in the meaning of the concept of society had thus occurred: As the reality of a class-divided industrializing society set in, the old liberal concept of a harmonious, moderate, "classless" *Gesellschaft* (society) dominated by the *Mittelstand* (middle class) was replaced by the notion of *bürgerliche Gesellschaft* (bourgeois society), a realm of self-interested dependence, spiritual degradation, atomization, unenlightenment, and particularistic politics.[56] The members of *bürgerliche Gesellschaft* were "incapable ever of being transformed into *Staatsbürger* (citizens of the state) by the German state as healing *Erziehungsanstalt*, or educative institution."[57] *Bürgerliche Gesellschaft* had become a "negation" of the "political," a "negation" of the "state," and at best, a completely "governed body of the people."[58]

Nineteenth-century German political ideology thus vertically segmented "insiders" into three levels of political reliability. At the top were inhabitants of the state realm, professional civil servants whose political loyalty to the German idea of the state was extraordinary but always provisional: *Dienst an sich* to an ultimately unembodiable *Geist* of the state

---

Geschichtliche Grundbegriffe: Historisches Lexikon zur politisch-sozialen Sprache in Deutschland, vol. 1: *A–D* (Stuttgart, 1972), 69–70; Blasius, "Bürgerliches Recht," 216; Huber, *Deutsche Verfassungsgeschichte*, 322.

54 Huber, *Deutsche Verfassungsgeschichte*, 377.

55 Quoted in Sheehan, *German Liberalism*, 39.

56 Lothar Gall, "Liberalismus und 'bürgerliche Gesellschaft': Zu Charakter und Entwicklung der liberalen Bewegung in Deutschland," in Lothar Gall, ed., *Liberalismus* (Cologne, 1976), 166–7; David Blackbourn, "The Discreet Charm of the Bourgeoisie: Reappraising German History in the Nineteenth Century," in David Blackbourn and Geoff Eley, eds., *The Peculiarities of German History: Bourgeois Society and the Politics of Nineteenth-Century Germany* (Oxford, 1984), 257.

57 Sheehan, *German Liberalism*, 43; Koselleck, *Preussen zwischen Reform und Revolution*, 403; Manfred Riedel, "Gesellschaft, bürgerliche," in Brunner, Conze, and Koselleck, eds., *Geschichtliche Grundbegriffe*, 2:777.

58 Riedel, "Gesellschaft," 777–9.

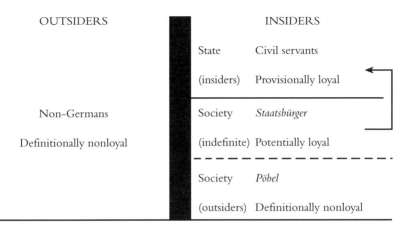

Figure 3.7. Nineteenth-Century Political Segmentation of German "Insiders"

promoted the common good of the political community. The next level of "insiders" constituted the *Staatsbürger* who recognized the positive role of a rationally organized and well-functioning state for controlling both despotical *Willkür* (arbitrariness) and the "mob rule" of the *Pöbel* (rabble). From these "insiders" civil servants could sometimes – but not usually and certainly not by right – be fashioned. Their political reliability was relatively high, their status as members remained somewhat undefined, and their loyalty to the political community could be characterized as potential. Finally, "insiders" also included ordinary *Bürger* in civil society whose political reliability vis-à-vis the idea of the state was nonexistent. These definitionally nonloyal members of the German political community were usually tolerated, sometimes "contained," and always politically suspect (see Figure 3.7).

Although all German citizens (or subjects) have been members of a German "region of legal equality" horizontally differentiated from non-German "regions of legal equality," Germans occupying this region since the nineteenth century have been vertically differentiated by the ascribed reliability of their political loyalty. To demonstrate that this vertical political differentiation is not merely a historical artifact, we now turn to a brief discussion of the so-called *Radikalenerlass*, or loyalty-oath decree, and the controversy this caused over citizenship policy in the Federal Republic in the 1970s and 1980s.

THE SEGMENTATION OF LEGAL POLITICAL MEMBERSHIP
IN THE FEDERAL REPUBLIC

The *Radikalenerlass* appeared in January 1972 as a federal-level agreement among *Länder* minister presidents and the federal chancellor, who, adopting a recommendation of a standing conference of federal state interior ministers, called on each state employee to "guarantee that he would intervene on behalf of the free democratic basic order at all times." Such a "guarantee" was positive in nature: If doubts about the candidate's loyalty surfaced, the burden of proof rested on the candidate to expunge them. Furthermore, this "guarantee" was to be demonstrated during work and nonwork hours, and it was to be determined not only by the actions but also by the beliefs of state employees and applicants. Although "each individual case" was to be decided on its own merits, "membership" in organizations "hostile to the constitution" (*verfassungsfeindlich*) would *in der Regel* justify either dismissal or denial of employment.[59]

The political context of the appearance of the decree in 1972 was very complicated. It followed on the heels of a similar measure adopted in Hamburg and was regarded by its signatories, including Federal Chancellor Willy Brandt, as not "a new law" but only an effort to "unify implementation" of standing civil-service law at the *Länder* and federal levels.[60] However, it appeared in a highly politicized environment caused by two important phenomena: first, the massive political mobilization of German university students and intellectuals that began in 1967 with the APO, continued in 1968 with the anti-Emergency Laws demonstrations, and was encouraged by the *Machtwechsel* (change of government) of the SPD-FDP coalition's coming to power in 1969; and second, the new government's active efforts to jump start *Deutschlandpolitik* and *Ostpolitik* immediately after forming the federal coalition.[61]

These contextual determinants heightened considerably the political stakes of German state-employment policy in 1972. The first threatened a "march through the institutions," in Rudi Dutschke's memorable phrase, by politically radicalized university students, many of whom had

---

59 For the text of the decree, see "Dokument Nr. 43: Beschluss der Regierungschefs des Bundes und der Länder vom 28. Januar 1972," in Erhard Denninger, ed., *Freiheitliche demokratische Grundordnung* (Frankfurt/Main, 1977), 2:518–19.
60 "Demokratie und Sicherheit: Interview des Bundeskanzlers," *Bulletin* 55 (April 15, 1972): 773.
61 See Baring, *Machtwechsel*; Klaus Hildebrand, *Geschichte der Bundesrepublik Deutschland*, vol. 4: *Von Erhard zur Grossen Koalition, 1963–1969* (Stuttgart, 1984); and Wolfgang Jäger, "Die Innenpolitik der sozial-liberalen Koalition, 1969–1974," in Karl-Dietrich Bracher, Wolfgang Jäger, and Werner Link, eds., *Geschichte der Bundesrepublik Deutschland*, vol. 5, pt. 1: *Republik im Wandel, 1969–1974* (Stuttgart, 1986).

recently discovered Marxism. It has been claimed that if Dutschke had never uttered that phrase at a rally in 1967, the *Radikalenerlass* would never have appeared.[62] The second drove the SPD, according to its leaders, to attempt to detach the historical opprobrium of unreliable *vaterlandslose Gesellen*, or men without a fatherland, from the party's identity without at the same time derailing its new foreign policy. To that end, a series of *Abgrenzungen*, or lines of demarcation, needed to be drawn to demonstrate especially to the opposition CDU/CSU that the SPD would also govern as a post–Bad Godesberg party. The first of these lines was drawn in November 1970, in a party document that detailed the strict separation between dealing with communists in foreign-policy matters and cooperating with communists at home.[63] The second was the *Radikalenerlass* of January 1972, which SPD leaders subsequently (but not at the time) explained as "ransom" paid to the CDU/CSU not to petition to ban the newly reconstituted German Communist Party (Deutsche Kommunistische Partein, or DKP), which, in the eyes of the Social Democrats, would have derailed the government's quickly moving *Ostpolitik* and *Deutschlandpolitik*.[64]

Both contextual determinants – the radicalization of the political culture by university students and intellectuals and the extraordinary "normalization" of relations with communist Eastern Europe – turned on the purported political reliability and loyalty of *legal* citizens of the Federal Republic. So "natural" was this concern that what Peter Graf Kielmansegg has called the most divisive domestic political conflict in the history of the Federal Republic – over the *Radikalenerlass* – was evidently produced after very little discussion within the federal government.[65] The depth and rancor of the subsequent battle over the *Radikalenerlass* further revealed the "naturalness" for many political actors and commentators in the Federal Republic of the idea of a protective state of hortatory political actors, with extraordinary and positive demands on their political loyalties, acting for ordinary German citizens in a protoanarchic and non–self-regulating civil society.[66]

---

62 Kurt Sontheimer, *Die verunsicherte Republik* (Munich, 1979), 27.

63 Baring, *Machtwechsel*, 358.

64 For a perceived linkage between the decree and foreign policy, see Willy Brandt, *". . . wir sind nicht zu Helden geboren"* (Zurich, 1986), 133; for an earlier denial of that linkage by the same actor, see Willy Brandt and Helmut Schmidt, *Deutschland 1976: Zwei Sozialdemokraten im Gespräch* (Hamburg, 1976), 48.

65 Peter Graf Kielmansegg, "The Basic Law – Response to the Past or Design for the Future?" *Forty Years of the Grundgesetz* (Washington, D.C., 1989); "Extremisten," collected papers of Willy Brandt, file 13, Friedrich Ebert Stiftung, Archiv der Sozialdemokratie, Bonn.

66 See Gerard Braunthal, *Political Loyalty and Public Service in West Germany* (Amherst, Mass., 1990);

This reiteration of the institutional ideology of bureaucratic-paternalistic statism in the 1970s occurred in a politicized context that saw the challenge of *das Establishment* and the *formierte Gesellschaft* (established society) by citizens demanding rights of participation, "more democracy," a "politics of the first person," and substantial reform of what some characterized as feudalism-encrusted institutions occupied by former Nazis.[67] Part of this "silent revolution" involved a massive public mobilization in the Federal Republic directed against the *Radikalenerlass* and the practice of using political loyalty as a sorting device to divide German public life vertically into agents embodying "reliable" and "unreliable" political beliefs and actions. A segmentation of legal German citizenship was embodied in the decree; a massive mobilization *against* that political segmentation was embodied in the various forms of protest against it. After the decree underwent multiple revisions and amendments at both the federal and *Land* levels – typically characterized as "corrections" of the "mistaken implementation" of the decree – the controversy gradually abated. That abatement, however, was never combined with a fundamental amendment to, or removal of, article 33 of the Basic Law, which still posits the "traditional principles of the professional civil service" as informing civil-service policy in the Federal Republic – including the special loyalty of the civil servant that reaches back, according to recent commentary, to tenth-century feudal law.[68]

Similarly, the politics of German citizenship and naturalization law historically have been overwhelmingly preoccupied with internal security and the potential threat that foreigners pose. In the early 1980s, concerns for the "undivided loyalty" of German citizens still drove the CDU/CSU to reject a liberalization of German naturalization policy in the name of the "German nation's right to protect its own culture and identity."[69] Regular official reports in the Federal Republic on the criminality of foreigners, which strike outside observers as an odd question to address, are entirely consistent with the traditional dichotomization of hortatory

and Gregg O. Kvistad, "Radicals and the State: The Political Demands on West German Civil Servants," *Comparative Political Studies* 21 (1987): 95–125.

67 See Hans-Joachim Winkler, *Das Establishment antwortet der APO* (Opladen, 1968), 7–12; Jürgen Habermas, *Toward a Rational Society*, trans. Jeremy Shapiro (Boston, 1970), 15–27; Hildebrand, *Geschichte der Bundesrepublik Deutschland*, 164, 375, 381; Baring, *Machtwechsel*, 63; Wilfried Röhrich, *Die Demokratie der Westdeutschen: Geschichte und politisches Klima einer Republik* (Munich, 1988), 94.

68 Anke Warbeck, "Die hergebrachten Grundsätze des Berufsbeamtentums im Wandel der Zeiten und ihre Bedeutung," *Recht im Amt* 37 (1990): 295.

69 Laura M. Murray, "*Einwanderungsland Bundesrepublik Deutschland?* Explaining the Evolving Positions of German Political Parties on Citizenship Policy," *German Politics and Society* 33 (1994): 28.

state political actors "above" a society of unreliable citizens – or, even more problematic in this case, foreign residents in Germany.[70] Peter O'Brien argues that it is the Federal Republic's substantial success with its liberal democracy that rationalizes not only humane welfare-state assistance for migrants but also a determined effort to protect German democracy from the political threat of foreigners. For its part, the SPD has stressed the need for foreigners in the Federal Republic to be provided opportunities to assimilate, such as education, that would allow them to "earn" the "trust to respect democratic politics and eschew extremism"; the CDU/CSU, meanwhile, has stressed integration and assumes the desire of many foreigners to return to their countries of origin. O'Brien concludes that "both parties claim to protect pluralist democracy by excluding a large contingent of potentially antidemocratic voters [foreigners] from the political process."[71]

But not only is liberal pluralist democracy at stake in this debate. In citizenship/naturalization policy, as with civil-service policy, German political discourse has historically registered a much deeper concern for the reliable political "protection," from "above," of an already-formed entity – now the "free democratic basic order" – in contrast to the Anglo-American discourse of continuously creating a new political community via steady immigration and assimilation. The concern to "protect" German democracy from the *political* threat of foreigners on German soil replicates bureaucratic paternalism's concern to "protect" the political community from unreliable citizens.

CHALLENGES TO THE SEGMENTATION OF POLITICAL MEMBERSHIP IN THE FEDERAL REPUBLIC

The furor over the *Radikalenerlass* embodied a fundamental and powerful *political* challenge that hastened the decree's slow and uneven demise. Vast numbers of mobilized West Germans from all parties, religious denominations, and countless interest groups rejected the traditional segmentation of German public life into politically "reliable" state civil servants with hortatory beliefs and actions, on the one hand, and politically "unreliable" ordinary citizens with derogatory beliefs and actions, on the other. After the battle over the *Radikalenerlass* finally died down in the

---

70 James Sperling, "(Im)migration and German Security in Post-Yalta Europe," *German Studies Review* 17 (1994): 542.
71 Peter O'Brien, "The Civil Rights of West Germany's Migrants," *German Politics and Society* 19 (1990): 34–8.

late 1980s, the question of the political loyalty of civil servants once more pressed itself onto the political agenda as the GDR acceded to the Federal Republic in 1990. The civil-service policy that was adopted in the unification treaty of 1990 for state employees from the former GDR was substantially more liberal than what appeared in the Federal Republic in the 1970s. Only the employment of former Stasi members in unified Germany's civil service was categorically regarded as "unreasonable." Adopting the "single-case test," neither membership in the Communist party nor previous employment in the state service of the GDR, as such, disqualified one for state employment in the unified Federal Republic.[72] This move away from paternalistic institutionalism marked a considerable step toward functional pragmatism in the politics of German membership. It is also relatively more consistent with a universalistic state-national rather than a particularistic ethnonational citizenship/naturalization law.

The reforms of German naturalization law in 1991 and 1993 similarly revealed a slow and uneven demise of an ethnonationalistic pure *jus sanguinis* in the face of millions of legal foreigners with permanent residence in the Federal Republic. All political parties, including the most reluctant members of the CDU/CSU, recognized the undesirability of having vast numbers of foreign nationals living in the Federal Republic.[73] After the murderous violence against foreigners, especially in 1991 and 1992, hundreds of thousands of Germans from all parties, interest groups, and religious denominations protested in candlelight marches against intolerance and the mistreatment of foreigners on German soil. Although the 1993 law still requires fifteen years of "integration" before the status of citizenship becomes a legal right, it – like Germany's more pragmatic civil-service personnel policy – marked a considerable shift away from the historical politicization and segmentation of political membership in Germany.

CONCLUSION

German political culture since the 1960s has revealed that a number of citizens and institutions reject as anachronistic a vertical segmentation of public life based on positive demands of political loyalty. On the one

---

72 Bundesministerium für innerdeutsche Beziehungen, ed., *Texte zur Deutschlandpolitik*, series 3, vol. 8a–1990 (Bonn, 1991), 7–17; Gregg O. Kvistad, "Accommodation of 'Cleansing': Germany's State Employees from the Old Regime," *West European Politics* 17 (1994): 52–73.

73 Murray, "*Einwanderungsland*," 23–56.

hand, the traditional segmentation and ethnonationalization of the politics of political membership continue to be powerful; pure *jus sanguinis* remains the principle informing Germany's citizenship law, and the "traditional principles of the professional civil service" remain constitutive parts of the Federal Republic's state bureaucracy. On the other hand, the "new politics" of the Federal Republic since the 1960s demonstrates that this "loyalty politics" is not a permanent "German" barrier to the gradual development of a more heterogeneous, multicultural, and horizontally differentiated public sphere. Both the liberalization of civil-service policy and the residence modification of naturalization law point in this direction. We must therefore wedge ourselves between the abstract optimism of a simple legal solution to xenophobia, and the dark pessimism of a cultural determinism that argues against the ability of Germans ever to accept "foreigners" as full-fledged members in "legal equality."

As ordinary German citizens increasingly demonstrate the will and competence to engage in meaningful, successful, and creative "politics of the first person," positive and extraordinary political demands will be made of professional German civil servants, and demands placed on foreigners wishing to become German citizens will become increasingly anachronistic. Eminently political, and not merely legal and ethnocultural, this process is slow and uneven. But with the demise of the vertical segmentation of German public life and the creation of a vibrant and active democratic horizontal differentiation among different kinds of "Germans" that this process promises, xenophobia and intolerance of the "other," however defined, will increasingly disappear from the German landscape.

4

The Discoursive Construction of National Stereotypes

Collective Imagination and Racist Concepts in Germany Before World War I

UTE GERHARD

The mechanism and power of nationalist and racist ideas and movements raise a series of questions regarding both theory and methods. Traditional boundaries of scientific and academic disciplines are confounded not merely by the profusion of research subjects but even more significantly by the immediate explosive political context. These issues frame the following reflections in which I examine, from a perspective of discourse, literary, and cultural theory, the production of nationalist and racist concepts and their social function in Germany before World War I. In this chapter, I emphasize discoursive schemes of collective identity and the part they play in the self-description and basic knowledge of modern societies.

Any analysis of processes involving culture, politics, and the history of mentalities in the broadest sense must necessarily take an interdisciplinary approach. It is precisely in this regard that the discourse theory of Michel Foucault opens up new and productive lines of inquiry. To explore the concept of national identity it is important, first of all, not to view phenomena such as national character as more or less naturally occurring but instead to investigate them for their specific discoursive and historic composition. The emphasis on discourse is by no means intended to cast doubt on the relative validity of nondiscoursive practices,

This chapter is based in part on a larger project entitled "'Flucht,' 'Wanderung' und 'Lager' nach dem 1. Weltkrieg im Diskurs der Medien und der Literatur." Research for the project has been supported by the Volkswagen Foundation. Sally E. Robertson of Arlington, Virginia, translated this essay from the German.

such as material reproduction cycles, but rather to take into account the functional and constitutive linkage of the two moments in historical processes. Thus, bodies of texts, statements, and knowledge are viewed not as reflections or articulations of existing subjective perceptions, but as functional aspects of the formation of individual and collective subjectivity.

I am particularly interested in symbolism, a set of discoursive elements whose meaning in the context of nationalist and racist developments has already been addressed by many scholars, particularly by George Mosse.[1] For Mosse, symbols are fundamental elements of the "nationalization of the masses" and, in general, of a new political style that developed along with the opening of the political arena to mass participation. Sacred fire, flags, songs, and monuments are some of the most notable national symbols fostering identity that Mosse associates with a politics of aesthetics and ritual. Contrasted with truth, intellectualism, knowledge, and theory, he claims that the pictorial quality of symbols tends to acquire a somewhat archaic, or at least deficit, status. As accurate as these observations may be for certain forms of political movements, this restrictive and disparaging determination cannot encompass the important overall role played by symbolic processes in politics. Even a brief look at public discourse in the nineteenth and twentieth centuries shows a multitude of symbols that can be described as image complexes to which additional layers of meaning are assigned. The structural and functional variety of such symbols is indicated by examples such as the "floods," the "volcanoes," and the "fires" of revolution, the "train" of progress, the "healthy growth" of the economy, "rampant" inflation, or the "collapse" of the stock market.[2] Detailed research into collective symbols shows that the entire body of basic and everyday knowledge of modern societies is constituted symbolically. Symbols play a central role in the development of subjectivity, both individual and collective. Because they can set into motion or stabilize cultural processes of integration and identification, they become constitutive factors in the formation of national identity.

From this perspective, the contrast between image and truth, or symbolism and knowledge, must be abandoned, although not without addressing the question of the subjective effects of political symbolism. Rather, it is possible to reconstruct the connection between such symbols and

---

1 George L. Mosse, *The Nationalization of the Masses* (New York, 1975).
2 For a more precise definition of collective symbolism, see Axel Drews, Ute Gerhard, and Jürgen Link, "Moderne Kollektivsymbolik: Eine diskurstheoretisch orientierte Einführung mit Auswahl-bibliographie," *Internationales Archiv für Sozialgeschichte der deutschen Literatur*, Special Supplement, no. 1, Research Reports (Tübingen, 1985), 256–375.

the constitution of thoroughly modern knowledge, a connection that was probably necessary for the success of nationalistic movements, and particularly for National Socialism.

In the context of the question of nationalist and racist concepts, there is another reason for more detailed analysis of symbolism. It is often overlooked that the phenomena regarded from various research angles as stereotypes, clichés, prejudicial schemes, or enemy images have a significant pictorial element.

Against the background of these observations, the symbolic processes of a nationalist and racist formation of society are subsequently examined. First, however, in order to elucidate the underlying theory, I use several examples to outline the most important mechanisms of the nationalist identifications that appeared to be such natural developments at the beginning of the twentieth century. I begin with two literary texts set in the late 1920s that depict the nationalist escalation at the outset of World War I in an alienating style through the eyes of an outsider.

NATIONAL "SORTING" AND THE BIG "WE"

In Ernst Glaeser's novel *Jahrgang 1902* (1928), written in the first person from the perspective of a child living with his mother in Switzerland, the narrator speaks of the "days of the first sorting," in which the "mood" in the hotel "changed":

Where previously citizens of different nations had sat together in a colorful mix, gone on outings, danced on the terrace in the evenings, the guests began around this time to be sorted according to the colors of their countries' flags. . . . People were sorted, placed together by force of some unknown law, each one an item belonging to a certain line of business.[3]

Through the symbolism of the lively, colorful mix, contrasted with the quasi-economic classifications and color arrangements, the child's view depicted here provides a counterimage to the familiar, enthusiastic national identifications described later in the novel. The latter appear as something forced, and the passive voice draws attention to the question of the unknown laws and rules of this process.

These rules are the subject of Siegfried Kracauer's novel *Ginster*, which Joseph Roth in his positive review welcomed as the first realistic portrayal of the *Drückeberger* (shirker).[4] The catchword *Drückeberger*, which

---

3 Ernst Glaeser, *Jahrgang 1902* (Berlin, 1931), 178–9.
4 Interestingly enough, Joseph Roth's review emphasized, above all, the ironic perspective on

has a generally negative and primarily anti–Semitic connotation, accurately describes the outsider status of the novel's main character. Ginster coincidentally finds himself in the town square when the declaration of war is announced: "Our armies, they said. We have been attacked; we'll just show those others. Suddenly, they were a *Volk*. Ginster thought of Wilhelm Tell; he could not make himself pronounce that 'we.'"[5] This passage in Kracauer's text illuminates a fundamental yet banal rule of national identifications. In order to become a "we," one must first say "we" and "our." There is a simultaneous, dualistic counterpart linked to the "we," namely the "other." The reference to Wilhelm Tell adds an important dimension to this word game. It adds the discursive process of applying pithy phrases, pictures, or, in general, collective identity schemes that have already acquired an automatic cultural response. One such pithy phrase is the line from Schiller's drama to which Kracauer alludes: "We want to be a single nation of brothers." This line was already part of the "quotation treasury of the German people" – according to the subtitle of the popular Büchmann collection – in the second half of the nineteenth century because it was so often quoted in the context of collective association.[6] Kracauer's character acquires his outsider position by being unable to identify with this application at this point in time. Interestingly, the subsequent text depicts this outsider perspective through a description of the "Ginsterian" view and memories, which can be characterized overall as a narration of dispersion. Discrepancies, gaps, and details destroy the sense of identity. Instead of a uniform picture, an identical "we," a fragmentary mosaic develops.

A foil for these literary portrayals of alienation is formed by texts that sought to design and redesign the national identity at the outset of the war. Typical of this vigorous activity on the part of German professors and philosophers is Max Scheler's book *Der Genius des Krieges und der Deutsche Krieg* (The genius of war and the German war), published in 1915. One of the many philosophical, pedagogical, and theological significances that he attributes to war is that it facilitates "recognition . . . of

normality through which the figure of the abnormal *Drückeberger*, an important anti-Semitic stereotype, obtained its positive connotation. The review appeared under the title "Wer ist Ginster?" *Frankfurter Zeitung*, Nov. 25, 1928. Joseph Roth, *Werke 2: Das journalistische Werk, 1924– 1928*, ed. Klaus Westermann (Cologne, 1990), 996–9.

5 Siegfried Kracauer, *Ginster* (Frankfurt/Main, 1972), 9.

6 Georg Büchmann, *Geflügelte Worte: der Zitatenschatz des deutschen Volkes* (Berlin, 1864). Known simply as "the Büchmann," this work has been an institution since the nineteenth century and has been published repeatedly in expanded, updated form. On the functionality of the Schiller reception, see Ute Gerhard, *Schiller als "Religion": Literarische Signaturen des 19. Jahrhunderts* (Munich, 1994).

the reality of the nation as having a collective spiritual personality."[7] In war, he argued, "those large, powerful, collective intellectual personalities that we call 'nations' become fully aware of their existence and their nature." Symbolically, this "collective personality" acquires additional contours of subjectivity. It awakens in war and seems to sleep during peacetime. And this "great spiritual being" finally acquires a "beating heart" to which it "wildly pulls us as mere 'appendages.'"[8] Whereas this example still refers to the general symbolism of the state as an organism, national stereotypes are constituted only by the interaction of a wide variety of symbols and character attributions, thus shaping very complex and historically specific subjectivity schemes surrounding the "we" of the nineteenth and twentieth centuries. The "collective personality" symbolically becomes an "individual personality" with a corresponding character, so that individual people can identify with it and, in this manner, form a large "we."

The process of distinction is of primary importance in the discursive production of such identifying "collective personalities." For example, Scheler speaks elsewhere in his text of "English rigidity, southern Italian gesturing, German heaviness," and "French agility and charm."[9] Based on the symbolic paradigm of movement, character traits are assigned to the different nations corresponding to the distinctions necessary for identification. In terms of physical symbolism, the English nation – from the German perspective – has no "heart" but is said to be dominated by the "bowel" or "stomach" (when the subject is "congestive symptoms" of the "English soul"), or by the "head" (when it is a matter of the cold calculations of the "petty-minded" English).[10]

With these attributions, Scheler's text is clearly based on the configuration of symbolic national characters, which had been undergoing a process of stabilization since the second half of the nineteenth century and through which the political and economic constellation of major European and non-European nations obtained its particular embodiment and subjective contours.[11] Subsequently, I illustrate this discursive production

---

7 Max Scheler, *Der Genius des Krieges und der Deutsche Krieg, Gesammelte Werke*, vol. 4: *Politisch-Pädagogische Schriften* (Bern, 1982), 81.
8 All preceding quotes, ibid.
9 Scheler, *Genius*, 160.
10 Ibid., 225.
11 See Ute Gerhard and Jürgen Link, "Zum Anteil der Kollektivsymbolik an den Nationalstereo-typen," in Jürgen Link and Wulf Wülfing, eds., *Nationale Mythen und Symbole in der zweiten Hälfte des 19. Jahrhunderts: Strukturen und Funktionen von Konzepten nationaler Identität* (Stuttgart, 1991), 16–52.

of national stereotypes using the primary example of concepts of German identity toward the end of the nineteenth century.

As the configuration of national stereotypes develops, we can observe the general process of symbolically placing the different nations within a wide variety of image fields. For example, on the vertical scale, England lies directly on the "bottom." France and Germany are both "bottomless," whereas France is positioned "high," in the "air," and Germany "deep." These positions and the corresponding character traits allow the symbolic representation of a wide variety of historical conditions, including inventions and scientific findings, economic systems, styles of thought, lifestyles, or other dominant practices of the nation in question. The realistic pragmatism and "flat" empiricism of the English is associated with their industrial orientation and the invention of the railway, the "capricious ingenuity" and spirit of the French with the hot-air balloon as a French invention, and finally the "deep," "fundamental" reflectiveness of the Germans with their philosophy and philology. An example of this "deep" symbolic coding of the German language is the following text of the Germanist Wilhelm Scherer: "The clustering of consonants gives our language a secure, measured tone, a full sound, a distinct, firm step that never rushes headlong but strides with dignity as do Germans. . . . The elements of our language are masculine and strong."[12] The connection between styles of movement and physical and gender-specific characteristics emphasizes the significance of the entire system of collective symbolism in developing such national stereotypes. It should also be noted that, in the image field of the gendered body, France is depicted primarily as female, in particular as a "whore" and "hysterical woman," and England more likely as a "cold" and often "aging man."

The symbolism of movement in Scherer's text, which is expanded to a "distinct, firm," and therefore military "step," as well as the symbols of masculinity and strength, refer to contours in the stereotype of German identity that represent an important prerequisite for the military escalation of German nationalism. With its positive military connotations, the quotation is typical of a wide variety of German texts from the last third of the nineteenth century. The basis of the generally positive self-identification with the military involves not only the pragmatic event of

12 Wilhelm Scherer, *Jacob Grimm*, 2d ed. (Berlin, 1885), 41.

the victory in the Franco-Prussian War of 1870–1, but also the special symbolic function of the military within the configuration of the national character. It is part of a context of discursive developments that led to a change in stereotypical characteristics of the German self-image.

With the end of the revolution of 1848 and the phase of political stabilization and increased industrialization, "realism" developed into a central interdiscursive concept. Based on its most general symbolic coding as "standing on the foundation of the facts," it became an integrating concept for science, politics, literature, and everyday knowledge. The symbolic shifts associated with this are demonstrated clearly by the positive economic depiction of Bismarck and his realpolitik using the figure of the "honest broker."[13] The symbolic integration of the economy produced shifts that confused the set of symbolic character traits making up the national stereotype of Germany. For example, the concepts of national character and national identity basically demand continuity and permanence. In other words, the "idealism" and "transcendence of Germany," the "land of poets and thinkers," slogans that were often invoked, even from the perspective of other nations, with greater or lesser irony, for this reason alone simply could not be abandoned. At the same time, the "realistic turn" within the configuration of European national stereotypes called into question important distinctions between Germany and England. To this extent, the discursive play between distinction and identity seemed to demand an integration of idealism and realism. Anticipating the mythical figure of the "realist-idealist" Bismarck, Max Duncker suggested in a letter to historian Gustav Droysen at the end of 1853 that the "fanciful idealism of philosophy that had filled and contorted the heads of the youth before 1848 be replaced with the realistic idealism of history."[14]

The mechanism of semantic differentiation and shifting of the various definitions of realism and idealism emerging here also managed to reintegrate the previously idealistic national character. The symbols for "depth," "inwardness," "profundity," and "weight" were retained as fundamental traits and, through connections with other discursive areas, could identify idealism as realism, and vice versa. The conservative

---

13 Bismarck used this symbol in his speech before the sixth session of the German *Reichstag* on Feb. 19, 1878.

14 Letter of Dec. 11, 1853, in Johann Gustav Droysen, *Briefwechsel*, ed. Rudolf Hübner (1929; reprint, Osnabrück, 1967), 2:54. On the mythologization of Bismarck, see Rolf Parr, *"Zwei Seelen wohnen, ach! in meiner Brust!" Strukturen und Funktionen der Mythisierung Bismarcks, 1860–1918* (Munich, 1991).

historian Heinrich von Treitschke used this connection in a modified Hölderlin quotation to state the future central characteristics of Germany as follows: "Prussia is building up a state that, strong in weapons and heavy with ideas, will march proudly from century to century."[15] Within the configuration of national stereotypes, the Prussian military formed a central element distinguishing Germany from the other nations. It was, however, an extremely ambivalent element, indeed often a negative one, even from the internal German perspective, when viewed as Prussian militarism. The emphatically positive identification is no surprise coming from Treitschke's well-known "Prussian" perspective. The fact that this position was able to establish itself in the following decades is attributable, as mentioned previously, to the war against France and its symbolic processing, but also to the discursive rules for creation of national characters and national stereotypes. This demonstrates the intensive interrelatedness of pragmatic factors and discursive processes that cannot be reduced to a simple cause-and-effect relationship. Militarism, through its symbolic attributions, guarantees the integration of idealism and realism, thus marking a distinct aspect of the German national character and, simultaneously, signaling an important difference. According to Treitschke, it is "Germany's glorious task [to guard] both the idealism of science and the idealism of war,"[16] which seems to point the way for the conspicuous war fervor among German professors in 1914.

This identity scheme was again stabilized by symbolic linkage of the military to other practical areas. In 1907, Walther Rathenau's *Die Vier Nationen* (The four nations), which the author described as an "attempt at a comparative psychological evaluation," linked some aspects of the national stereotypes for England, France, the United States, and Germany to the economy.[17] With reference to Germany, he writes: "The transcendent and individualistic mind of the German, which previously wore itself out with internal battles, religious squabbles and fruitless speculation, has now found in the scientific, organizational, and confrontational tasks of economic life a sphere that raises it to a level of high reality."[18] The strange-sounding wording of an idealism "raised" to "high" reality is explained by the symbolic shift of stereotypical traits that converted

15 "Was fordern wir von Frankreich?" (Aug. 30, 1870), in Heinrich von Treitschke, *Aufsätze, Reden und Briefe*, ed. Karl Martin Schiller, vol. 3: *Schriften und Reden zur Zeitgeschichte I* (Meersburg, 1929), 489.
16 "Die Feuerprobe des Norddeutschen Bundes" (Aug. 30, 1870), in ibid., 441.
17 Walther Rathenau, *Vier Nationen*, in Walther Rathenau, *Gesammelte Schriften*, 5 vols. (Berlin, 1918), 4:123.
18 Rathenau, *Vier Nationen*, 4:140.

idealism to realism and simultaneously had to prevent a landing on "flat ground." Whereas "economic life" appears to be the element that integrates the contradictory traits, the emphasis on "organization" and "confrontation" indicates a symbolic dominance of the military. This is particularly clear since the same text states: "The German works for the sake of the task. . . . Conscientious and modest, he gladly submits to organization and discipline. He wants to imperiously obey."[19]

The conspicuous recurrence of symbolic references is further evidence that the military realm functioned as a guarantee of the identity of the German national character at the beginning of the twentieth century. Indeed, military practice in Germany at this point in time had become one of the most important identity-fostering factors, as reproduced in many texts and statements, of which Rathenau's description of the "four nations" is exemplary.

Scheler claimed in 1916 that "German militarism" is more like "an artwork than a tool."[20] Werner Sombart, in his "patriotic reflections" published in 1915 under the title *Händler und Helden* (Tradesmen and heroes), delivered an incisive and even more pointed expression of the stereotypical contrast between England and Germany.[21] Many references to the title in the press, political speeches, and other publications testify to the popularity of this book. By contrasting "shopkeepers and warriors," he accentuated idealism as an important distinction, but it was an idealism that symbolically always produced new realism.[22] The two were chiastically connected using the tree symbolism that is so notoriously important for the German national stereotype: "German patriotism thrusts its deep roots into the fruitful mother earth of a heroic weltanschauung, and around its crown gleam the rays of the highest critical culture."[23] The vertical symbolism of height and depth made it possible to situate even the trenches at the "highest heights." According to Sombart, "Militarism is the heroic spirit elevated to the spirit of the warrior. It is 'Faust' and 'Zarathustra' and 'Beethoven' in the trenches."[24] The discursive mechanism for symbolically "elevating" the trench to the place of "highest culture" and thus to the place of the idealist-realist German national character helps us reconstruct at least partially two phenomena

19 Ibid., 4:138.
20 Max Scheler, *Krieg und Aufbau* (Leipzig, 1916), 172.
21 Werner Sombart, *Händler und Helden: Patriotische Besinnungen* (Berlin, 1915).
22 Sombart, *Händler*, 81.
23 Ibid., 71.
24 Ibid., 74–5.

of 1914 relevant to mentality history that are put forth as typical. The first is the particular enthusiasm of high school and university students, as well as literary figures, for volunteering to serve in these trenches. The second is the extraordinary significance of classical texts – be it Schiller, Goethe, or Hölderlin – as "provisions" in the soldier's "kit bag."

This raises the question of how the discursive interplay of identification and distinction of symbolic character traits is actually involved in forming national identity. The positive self-identification with militarism has already been mentioned, and the example of the classical texts in the "kit bag" shows that such processes of collective identity formation can take place, among other means, through direct application of the symbolic structures in various practical situations. It becomes possible for the individual not only to speak the "we" but also do it and live it.

Max Scheler's text outlines an introduction to such an application and simultaneously articulates by example the tendency to stabilize this identity by transferring symbolic character traits to the various practical realms. I quote him rather extensively here since he emphasizes particularly clearly some of the aspects I have described:

The incomparable German fortitude in warfare and tirelessness in pursuing the enemy until he is completely annihilated . . . is the same power that gave form to the monumental works of Mommsen and Leopold von Ranke with their incomparable tenacity in pursuing their chosen purpose and the thoroughness of their execution. German science and warfare are characterized by a certain ponderousness and too great a love of method, in contrast to that French property manifested in science as "ingenuity" and in war as a bold fighting spirit and preference for open battle but without the persistent power to thoroughly exploit an advantage once attained.[25]

In this way, even the desks and studies of German professors could become symbolic trenches. If the stereotypical character traits are connected by symbolism with the different practical fields, then any individual can recognize himself as typically German by operating in that field.

Military escalation is generally accompanied by an escalation of the discursive mechanisms of national stereotypes and their application for purposes of identification. Imagined future "explosions" are depicted as early as Rathenau's aforementioned text, *Vier Nationen*. Germany is symbolically described in this text as a steam engine, linking the national character to modern discursive positions as well: "And when he [the

---

25 Scheler, *Genius*, 145.

French 'pensioner,' as he is called in the preceding sentence] looks out the window of his borders and sees the German national boiler quivering under the pressure of sixty million people, he wonders anxiously if the western vacuum is adequately protected."[26] In this case, the two nations acquire their subjective contours through the symbolism of the "pensioner" in his house, on the one hand, and the "steam boiler" under pressure, on the other. Whereas the image of the "steam boiler" automatically places the modern arena of industry dominantly on the side of Germany in relation to France, mentioning the number of people brings in the dimension of population statistics. The element of expanding "steam" corresponds to the high birthrate, and the "western vacuum" to the "shortage of people" that was given as a characteristic of France in a slightly earlier part of Rathenau's text. The birthrate, which was still climbing in Germany, unlike in France, at the end of the nineteenth century, had already become a trait of the German and French national stereotypes via the symbolism of body and genealogy as "strong" versus "weak," "young" versus "old." The catachresis between "pensioner," "house" and "national boiler," and "vacuum" in the Rathenau text shows that statistical knowledge can involve a tendency that confounds the conception of nations as "collective personalities." The "quivering steam boiler" in this case seems not only to lend a certain embodiment to statistical phenomena and forecasts by means of imaginary visibility, but also to clearly outline the possibility of a bursting of borders through mass enthusiasm, a hearty explosion that is yet another reference to military escalation. The aforementioned Glaeser novel also captures nicely the possible connection between military enthusiasm and the discursive presence of the birthrates when the father of the narrator says in 1914, certain of victory, "Just look at France's birthrates. That speaks volumes!"[27]

All in all, detailed analysis of the discursive processes shows that the symbolic mechanisms behind the concept of national "identity" described here play a significant part in the strangely "excessive" readiness for war that characterizes German history in the first half of the twentieth century. At the same time, however, there was also a racist escalation, particularly in Germany. With respect to both German history and current events, this raises the second important question regarding the possible relationship between national identification and racist concepts.

---

26 Rathenau, *Vier Nationen*, 4:131.
27 Ibid., 156.

"STATISTICAL MICROSCOPE" AND "BODY POLITIC"

If we look at Glaeser's metaphor of "sorting" cited previously, which he uses to describe the nationalist identification process among hotel guests in the summer of 1914, we immediately recognize an important functional analogy between nationalism and racism. Racism also "sorts" people according to certain "laws" and draws boundaries between population groups – boundaries that do not necessarily coincide with, indeed often cross, the boundaries of nations or nation-states. For example, the "we" to which Alfred Ploetz appeals in his address on "Neomalthusianism and Eugenics" at the International Congress of Eugenics in London in 1912 is not merely the traditional, national "we." Another collective identity scheme is indicated when Ploetz speaks to European and American eugenicists of the "love of our nation and our race, which still face serious battles," which may appear paradoxical, at least in light of the events of 1914.[28]

Scheler's aforementioned text on the "genius of war" solves this paradox by outlining a future in which "Europeanness" and "the 'other,' the different, the non-European" are the central opposing forces. In preparation for this future, the soldiers are called upon to look "carefully" at these "others" in the field – a variety of "others" are named, from "Cossacks" to "rock-throwing negroes."[29]

The knowing glance that the text describes here and wishes to initiate in the soldiers is well known to have been central even for many race theorists in determining distinct boundaries between people, again emphasizing the importance of visibility, imagery, and embodiment. I do not want to address here the well-known difficulty of formulating strict racial boundaries from a biological or medical perspective. At any rate, this "unsolved problem" does not seem to have been of particular significance in the activation of racism, which is not to say that the scientific disciplines and specialist discourses did not have an important part to play in this development. This sort of converse conclusion drawn by recent works on racism shifts the question of the functionality of modern knowledge onto a contrast between rationality and irrationality that is much too simple for the issue of racism.[30] This categorical scheme

---

28 *Archiv für Rassen- und Gesellschaftsbiologie: Einschliesslich Rassen- und Gesellschaftshygiene* (hereafter cited as *Archiv*) 1–2 (1913–14): 172, published by Ploetz Verlag.
29 Scheler, *Genius*, 175.
30 For this sort of simplistic contrast of science and racism, see Detlev Claussen, *Was ist Rassismus?* (Darmstadt, 1994).

misses the interplay between scientific or technocratic fields on the one hand and phenomena more related to mentality history on the other.

It remains to be stated that, particularly with regard to the question of collective imagination and identification, racism outlines and creates new boundaries between population groups. To do so, it relates to a different *socius*, a different collective identity than national concepts. It deals namely with the "body politic," as a medicalized, statistically recorded, and regulatable ensemble. In 1908, the *Archiv für Rassen- und Gesellschafts-biologie* printed the translation of a lecture by Karl F. Pearson in which he states: "The study of eugenics concentrates on a statistical treatment of human society in all its stages, healthy as well as pathological." All "things that affect the strength or weakness of the character," Pearson went on, must "be put under the statistical microscope." Only in this way, he said, can we recognize "why nations rise and fall" and "recommend an appropriate cure."[31] But to put things under the "statistical microscope" means primarily to constitute these "things" and conditions as mass phenomena. Another claim in the text shows how these concepts of recording are actually connected to notions of historical processes based on mass dynamics: "Statistics concerning the prevalence of diseases in the army of a conquered nation can tell us more than any scholarly treatise on the brilliant commanders and astute statesmen of their victorious enemy."[32]

These "treatises" on commanders and statesmen represent the notion of historic events as an interaction of subjects. The statistical method converts these subject categories and even the characters of nations to dependent variables determined by anonymous mass phenomena. When we consider that the central strategies of racism – selection and "eradication" – are based on mass dynamics, we can see the horrible manner in which racist theoreticians and practitioners, as controllers of these processes, can ensure themselves an even more elevated subject status.

It is certainly wrong to suspect statistical population records of being racist as a rule. Modern racism, however, is conspicuously linked with procedures of statistical recording, evaluation, and forecasting that increased enormously around the turn of the century. Foucault has called these activities the central strategies of normalization.[33] The concept of

---

31 Karl F. R. S. Pearson, "Über den Zweck und die Bedeutung einer nationalen Rassenhygiene (National-Eugenik) für den Staat" (lecture before the Oxford University Junior Scientific Club on May 17, 1907; authorized translation by Hans Fehlinger), *Archiv* 1 (1908): 74.
32 Pearson, *National-Eugenik*, 72.
33 Michel Foucault, "Faire vivre et laisser mourir: la naissance du racisme," *Les Temps Modernes* 535 (Feb. 1991). For a more precise description of the strategy of normalization, see Jürgen Link,

normalization underscores the fact that "statistical treatment" – as Pearson's text clearly called it – is oriented toward determining normal and abnormal ranges, and toward corresponding regulation, that is, the symbolic "cures."

Toward the end of the nineteenth century, statistical recording and forecasting developed into a "true discourse" on society and appear to have played an important part in the new spread of anti-Semitism.[34] One important example of this further development is the census of Jews in the German army carried out in 1916 at the instruction of the army command. It turned out to be extremely functional and effective for constituting and stabilizing the abnormal (from a German perspective) *Drückeberger* as an important anti-Semitic stereotype. The fact that the results of this "census" were not published has always provoked a variety of suppositions. The debate over the possible political reasons for the suppression overlooks the fact that simply performing such a statistical survey accomplishes the segregation. Such statistics show at least the first signs of identification, isolation, and concentration that Raul Hilberg has described as the phases of the subsequent extermination process.[35]

RACIST CONCEPTS AND THE "MASSES"

The observations regarding the normalizing effect of statistical recording and its significance for modern societies allow a new look at the correlation stressed in numerous studies between "mass societies" and racist developments.[36] Hannah Arendt's writings on totalitarianism lay a foundation for formulating such a correlation. In these writings, the complex of the masses and the fascination of the dynamic are essentially constitutive. For Arendt, an important function of ethnic and racist ideas is to form population groups that, unlike nation-states, are independent of territorial references. Her example of the Great Trek of the Boers effects the symbolic connection between "rootlessness" and movement.[37] In this way, it is natural to conclude that the concept of a "racial society" is a

---

"Normalismus-Konturen eines Konzeptes," *Kulturrrevolution: Zeitschrift für angewandte Diskurstheorie* 27 (1993): 50–70; Jürgen Link, *Versuch über den Normalismus – wie Normalität produziert wird* (Opladen, 1996).

34 Francois Ewald, *Der Vorsorgestaat* (Franfurt/Main, 1993).

35 Raul Hilberg, *The Destruction of the European Jews*, 2d ed., 3 vols. (New York, 1985), 1:53–80.

36 See, e.g., Claussen, *Rassismus*, 108.

37 Hannah Arendt, *Elemente und Ursprünge totaler Herrschaft* (Munich, 1991), 321; Hannah Arendt, *The Origins of Totalitarianism*, new ed. with added prefaces by Hannah Arendt (San Diego, 1975), 195–6.

fitting "response" to "the needs of the shifting masses of modern cities," to "the rightful apprehensions of . . . isolated individuals in an atomized society," and in general to "their situation of spiritual and social home-lessness."[38] In a striking way, this echoes symbolic structures of self-description of the early twentieth century and, particularly, the period between the wars. The same symbolic schemes, however, are also embod-ied in the ideas of mass society, disintegration, and disorientation as nega-tive characteristics of modernity that determine the current debate over racist tendencies in the present.

The strategy of "statistical treatment" already described, however, sug-gests that we should perhaps first disconnect the causal relation given by Hannah Arendt and inquire as to the discursive formation of the as-sumed subjective mass experience. In doing so, the interrelatedness of two factors should be looked at in more detail: first, the normalizing per-spective, which records populations as an ensemble of mass phenomena; and, second, the symbolic identity scheme thereby developed, which can apply this perspective to the culture as a whole. Possible connections be-tween discoursive production of mass ideas and racist structures can be shown in the migration movements that, since the late nineteenth cen-tury, have repeatedly been viewed as problems involving phenomena of mass dynamics.

THE "MINGLING" OF NATIONAL BORDERS

Statistical recording and the subject of population movements have been important factors in the spread and stabilization of modern racism and anti-Semitism. This was true even of the debates of the 1870s and 1880s. Treitschke's notorious, scandalous verdict of 1879, "the Jews are our mis-fortune," was already associated with the warning "Year by year, our eastern boundary is penetrated by a stream of ambitious, trouser-selling youngsters from the inexhaustible Polish cradle."[39] Statements like this from a respected professor, publisher of the Prussian Yearbooks, serve to make presentable the anti-Semitic positions being articulated to an increasing degree at this point in time. Accordingly, Treitschke's essay caused a sensation, and numerous public statements were made in response.[40] Statistics, or rather

38 Arendt, *Origins of Totalitarianism*, 235–6, 352.
39 Heinrich von Treitschke, "Unsere Aussichten," *Preussische Jahrbücher*, Nov. 15, 1879; cited here from Treitschke, *Deutsche Kämpfe*, new series: *Schriften zur Tagespolitik* (Leipzig, 1896), 23.
40 See the documentation in Walter Boehlich, ed., *Der Berliner Antisemitismusstreit* (Frankfurt/Main, 1965).

attempts at statistical forecasts, permeated the entire debate. All parties were demanding numbers. Treitschke himself expressed regret that the authorities no longer recorded religious faith as a differentiating feature upon immigration; he referred instead to older or general "Jew statistics." Others objected that his figures were taken from a statistician "not at all considered an authority by professional statisticians" since "his data are not based on reliable calculations." A "significant statistician" was said to be in the process of "proving with figures that Jewish immigration from Poland and Galicia in the last decade has been infinitesimally small."[41] Only Hermann Cohen, in his reply to Treitschke, criticized what he called the "predictive nature of his statistics on Jews" and, in general, "this whole manner of statistical concern regarding the state system of providing welfare to eligible members of the state."[42] The segregating effect of such statistical analyses of a population group, to which Cohen alluded, was confirmed by the records made from a variety of perspectives in the subsequent period. Since they promised to tell the truth, statistics could be used either by those wishing to call anti-Semitic claims into question, or by those wishing to confirm them. The dominant effects, however, as mentioned previously with the example of the army's Jewish census, were those of segregation and constitution of a population group with a supposedly clearly distinguishable identity.

In the debate triggered by Treitschke's essay, certain symbols are also connected to the statistics. One critic remarked: "When one reads his description, one thinks of an invading flood, like the Chinese in California. Wouldn't he like to give us a few statistics on the subject from recent years?"[43] Collective symbolism and imagination are placed here in relation to the statistics. Statistics can substantiate the symbols as true, whereas the symbols, in turn, can give the statistics an embodiment, and – through explicit images such as that of a flood – subjective meaning. This relationship is conspicuous in the racist, anti-Semitic articles that welcomed Treitschke's position. They echoed the symbolism of "overgrowth" and "flooding" threatening from the East. The wandering Jews, who were contrasted with the "peoples who were and remained sedentary in a compact mass," were said to have come to Germany, not in a "mass isolated onto itself" but "dispersed among the Germans."[44] There was re-

---

41 Heinrich Graetz, "Mein letztes Wort an Professor von Treitschke," in Boehlich, *Antisemitismusstreit*, 46.
42 Hermann Cohen, "Ein Bekenntnis zur Judenfrage," in Boehlich, *Antisemitismusstreit*, 144.
43 Ludwig Bamberger, "Deutschthum und Judenthum," in Boehlich, *Antisemitismusstreit*, 162.
44 Wilhelm Endner, "Zur Judenfrage," in Boehlich, *Antisemitismusstreit*, 101, 106, 111–12.

peated mention of "parasites" breaking through "national barriers" to "infest other peoples." "Just as one bad apple spoils the whole bunch," it was charged, "German morality [has] already acquired more moldy Jewish spots than are evident from the crime statistics." Referring to rudimentary statistics from Berlin, it was claimed that "the burden on the country is distributed too unevenly," which was further exacerbated by the "endless influx from day to day." Finally, the method of statistical forecasting was used. It was necessary, one article read, to "calculate the development based on the experience of the last ten years." Since a "progressive acceleration" was occurring, after only "another twenty years," it would be a matter of the "life of the nation." This forecast was followed by the proposal "The existing Jews shall be evenly distributed," but the "tolerated head count . . . in the individual communities may not increase."[45]

When these clearly anti-Semitic articles talk of "progressive acceleration" side by side with "overgrowth," "flooding," and "parasites," then one might well conclude that this is a case of the well-known procedure of naturalization of social processes or the effectiveness of archetypical schemes and, to that extent, a repetition of the same old thing. This hasty conclusion, however, overlooks the mechanisms and effects of the power of symbolism and statistics, for collective symbolism acquires its historically specific materiality precisely as a result of the bodies of knowledge that it incorporates.[46]

The examples cited demonstrate several important aspects of the interrelatedness of symbolism and modern normalizing knowledge.[47] The contrasting of "compact mass" and dispersion, as well as the envisioned uniform distribution, refers to negative concepts of mass and dynamics as well as to normalizing models for regulating them. The movement of the dispersed multitude leads to unevenness, which can be derived from statistical records, as can the model of regulation. The "parasitic infestation"

---

45 H. Naudh, "Professoren über Israel: von Treitschke und Bresslau," in Boehlich, *Antisemitismusstreit*, 189, 192, 196, 199.

46 On the modern constitution of parasitic symbolism, see Peter Friedrich and Wolfgang Tietze, "Einbruch der Epidemie, Vernetzung des Untergrundes: Cholera und Typhus als Psychosemodell des modernen Massenstaates," *Kulturrevolution: Zeitschrift für angewandte Diskurstheorie* 29 (Mar. 1994): 20–30.

47 E.g., clear parallels are evident between the call for even distribution or establishment of a "tolerated head count" and the regulatory model of American immigration policy in the twentieth century. The Quota Law of 1921 limited future immigration to a certain percentage (3 percent per year) of the population groups living in the United States in 1910. The proportional composition of 1910 was thus defined and established as the normal condition of the American population.

and the "contagion" or "spreading of mold" are the symbols of negative mass dynamics that clearly focus on the problems of optimal distribution of bodies in space, which Foucault described as an important strategy of modern power technologies.[48] At the end of the nineteenth century, it was primarily the growing discourse on hygiene that centered on the problem of the relationship between health, body, and space. The field of hygiene calculated "exactly" the optimal, that is, healthy, relationships among work space, living space, bed, air, fresh water, sewerage, and number of bodies. The establishment of limits – "tolerated head counts" in the previous quotations – is particularly important in this regard.

In the early 1880s, the openly anti-Semitic contributions to the Treitschke debate illustrated the trend toward the interlinking of statistical recording with the hygienic perspective and a complex of symbols regarding mass dynamics that contained a negative bias. For one thing, this allowed known Jewish stereotypes to be integrated into the normalizing approach to migration movements and thus acquire a new embodiment. For another, this provided the possibility of constituting the Jewish population group together with the migration movements as an object of hygiene. A good example of the linking of anti-Jewish stereotypes and modern dynamics is the popular racist text by Eugen Dühring *Die Judenfrage als Frage der Rassenschädlichkeit für Existenz, Sitte und Cultur der Völker*, which was published in 1880 and was in its fifth printing in 1901. In the chapter entitled "Proliferation of Jews in Recent Times," "free movement" as a "good thing" is contrasted with "civilized nomadism" as a "bad thing," for the latter is based on "aberration and exploitation," whereas the former promotes "settlement in the proper place": "Economic freedom of movement is not a peddler's principle. It should serve to shift sedentary life to the proper places but not to sanction the fluctuations of the Jews as a model for other peoples."[49] The symbolic linkage of possible new dynamics with anti-Jewish stereotypes was associated here, too, with symbols of parasites or pests, and foreshadows the later extension of the racist approach to the "vagrants."[50] At the same time, con-

---

48 Michel Foucault, *Sexualität und Wahrheit*, vol. 1: *Der Wille zum Wissen* (Frankfurt/Main, 1977), 167, 170.
49 Eugen Dühring, "Die Judenfrage als Frage der Racenschädlichkeit für Existenz, Sitte und Cultur der Völker," cited from an excerpt in Claussen, *Rassismus*, 58.
50 In the 1930s, the infamous "gypsy researcher" Ritter carried out a "genetic study" of "drifters" at the behest of the Imperial Office of Health. He treated drifting as "innate imbecility." The eugenic debate over the migrants had already been going on for some time, however. As early as 1911, American scientist Charles H. Davenport ("Heredity in Relation to Eugenics") claimed to be able to detect not only criminality but also the "migratory instinct" as a genetic trait, with

tours of a positive mass dynamic were being developed that, as a corrective "shifting of sedentary life," is clearly a territorialized, regulated movement and satisfies the perspective of normalization.

In the following decades, immigration from the East became a subject of political discourse in which racist and anti-Semitic positions were repeatedly involved. Motions by the anti-Semitic fraction in the Reichstag to close the border or block further Jewish immigration continuously gave rise to debates in which the symbolism of pests and pathogens was again used in a stereotypical manner. The debate of 1895 showed early trends toward broader dissemination of anti-Semitic positions. A group of conservative politicians also called for measures against Jewish immigration from the East. As justification, Delegate Jacobskötter referred on February 27 to the supposed "devastation" of the "sedentary trades" by the Jewish "roving warehouses." Delegate Bindewald, who subsequently spoke in favor of the motion of the anti-Semitic fraction, seized upon the symbolic aspects of this contrast and honed them further with a series of negative symbols – from "nomadism" to "trash and bargain bazaars," "proliferation," "nesting," "undermining," and several reiterations of the "parasitic" theme.[51] Later in the debate, on March 6, the speaker of the anti-Semitic faction, Ahlwardt, even described the Jews as "cholera germs" and claimed they were contagious. This was followed by a call for a "calm and reasonable separation of the Jews from the Germans" and the hope that "we will someday close the door to prevent even more from getting in."[52] The "amusement" over this anti-Semitic staccato noted in the stenographic record of the debate did not stop delegates from the conservative fraction from also pointing out the supposed health risks of continued immigration of eastern Jews. The embodiment of the need for segregation and exclusion is provided symbolically using the model of hygienic defense against epidemics.

Also within the fields of demography and population policy, the movement of populations across boundaries became a crystallization point for racist ideas, showing again their unique interlinkage with the concept of national identity. At first glance, the main problem appears to have been the crossing of the territorial border of the nation-state. Upon closer examination, however, it is evident that the idea of a territorial

---

the corresponding consequences, namely institutionalization or sterilization. These ideas were already being discussed in Germany as well.

51 Session of Feb. 27, 1895, *Stenographische Berichte über die Verhandlungen des Reichstags* (Berlin, 1895), 2:1144–9.

52 Session of Mar. 6, 1895, *Stenographische Berichte*, 2:1298.

boundary is overshadowed by the idea of boundary of cultural mingling, interpreted as a limit for purposes of normalization. This is particularly true of immigration policy in the United States in the early twentieth century. This policy was observed with great interest by German eugenicists, who generally focused positively on the supposedly much greater social and political acceptance of eugenics.[53] This led to certain ambivalences, however, regarding the increasingly restrictive treatment of immigration in the United States. In 1913 the *Archiv für Rassen- und Gesellschaftsbiologie* contained a review of a publication on eugenics in the United States. It is stressed in positive terms that "in twenty years, America denied residence to 190,000 inferior persons and threw this mass of parasites back into their native lands." For the European nations, however, this meant an overall "increasing wretchedness of the body politic."[54] The symbolism underscores the fact that the boundary drawn by measures to regulate immigration defined not nations but conditions of disease versus health.

One of the many publications on demography and population policy appearing in Germany around 1910 shows how racist boundary-setting converged on this point even with relatively moderate positions. An introductory book published in 1913 mentions as an object of "increased attention" the problematic "inundation with culturally or economically inferior elements" and calls for "constant oversight of the hundreds of thousands of immigrants pouring into the German Empire from culturally low-level peoples and classes," because they "can easily have an unfavorable effect on native people who mingle with them."[55] But this oversight and potential regulation also extended to migrational phenomena within national boundaries, namely, migration as a permanent condition, "drifting with no fixed address (for example, vagabonds, Gypsies)," and domestic migration such as rural-urban migration, which demonstrated the continued increase in the "uprooting of man from his native ground."[56]

---

53 However, this supposedly much greater acceptance is not so certain. The primary pieces of evidence cited from the German perspective were the well-known laws in various states permitting eugenically motivated sterilization. Yet, the problems that arose in performing such acts indicate a lower level of acceptance, at least on the part of civilian society.

54 *Archiv* 1–2 (1913–14): 215.

55 Otto Most, *Bevölkerungswissenschaft: Eine Einführung in die Bevölkerungsprobleme der Gegenwart* (Berlin, 1913), 80.

56 Most, *Bevölkerungswissenschaft*, 77, 129.

DANGEROUS MINGLING OF BODIES

The assumed effects of unfavorable mingling and a risk of instability owing to the distribution of bodies in space made the migration movements a negative mass dynamic and a phenomenon of denormalization. Through the corresponding symbolism, this perspective led to development of important and effective cultural identification schemes in Germany at the beginning of the twentieth century. An example of the extent to which these schemes, in turn, offered anti-Semitic and racist concepts a place to settle and spread can be seen in texts by Werner Sombart, the dangerous tendencies of which have received far too little acknowledgment. The ambivalence of Sombart's familiar description of the Jews as "sourdough" or "expediters" of capitalism is given a clearly negative accent by his general descriptions of cultural typology. When Sombart wrote of "masses" and "change" as the central "characteristics" of the time in his *Einführung in die Nationalökonomie* in 1903, he was speaking primarily of population movements and distinctly negative mass dynamics.[57] Statistics on population movements, said to make those of the *Völkerwanderung* era "shrink to trivial events," are repeatedly accompanied by conspicuously repetitive symbols. For example, the German Empire was said to resemble "an anthill into which the wanderer has thrust his walking stick."[58] "Hill" or "pile," along with "swarm," "flood," and "inundation" make up the central symbols of negative mass dynamics in Sombart's texts. The symbolism is assigned to the various economic and cultural phenomena and, in this way, establishes the imaginary identity of an entire epoch, the central feature of which is instability and thus uncertainty. With regard to the population, Sombart's conclusion is that "[t]he old communities, whether generated by blood relations or place of residence, have been dissolved; the population has been thrown together like a pile of sand grains in the new commonalty where there are no longer any bonds binding one to another."[59]

Sombart's clearly negative mass symbolism of the "pile of sand" is associated, in turn, with other symbolic attributions of the time: the "reduced level" diagnosed in a wide variety of fields, the lack of "depth," and the general "broadening" and "flattening" of cultural and intellectual life. They also seem to provide an embodiment for racist concepts. The

---

57 Werner Sombart, *Die deutsche Volkswirtschaft im 19. Jahrhundert und im Anfang des 20. Jahrhunderts: Eine Einführung in die Nationalökonomie* (Berlin, 1903; reprint, Darmstadt, 1954).
58 Sombart, *Volkswirtschaft*, 407–8.
59 Ibid., 474.

lack of bonds in the "pile of sand" corresponds, namely, to unstructured and disorganized states, and especially the state of being "thrown together" – the negative mingling. According to Sombart, mass and change had "jumbled the components together in such a way" as to create a "colorful mixture . . . whose contribution to the fitness of the race we are not yet able to foresee." However, the "hodgepodge" does not appear "very promising," he continued, if one "inspects the bow-legged, pasty-faced, raceless offspring in the sandboxes of our cities' playgrounds."[60] The "sandbox" as an urban institution and the fact that it can be experienced physically actualize and stabilize the symbolism of the negative mass. The "inspection" underscores the normalizing and classifying approach. Military inspection is an important paradigm of eugenic study. Sombart immediately emphasized that no "scientifically verifiable conclusions" could yet be drawn regarding the effects "of intermarriage in Germany" or "of the city as such on racial quality," since social circumstances would have to be measured as a "determining factor." This disclaimer seems, however, to have already been canceled out by the recurrent symbolic constitution of negative mass dynamics.

Another text by Sombart, which appeared in 1912 under the title *Die Zukunft der Juden* (The future of the Jews), shows how racist concepts of segregation were able to attach themselves to these symbolic images as regulations of negative mass dynamics. The book, "which is intended simply as a confession of faith," was intended to promote public debate "of the greatest problem of humanity," a debate that, in the opinion of the author, had so far been prevented by the liberal press.[61] Whereas by themselves these claims are reminiscent of Treitschke's interventions described earlier, there are also other, quite surprising similarities to that debate. According to Sombart, the starting point for any study must be the "oversight of the number and spatial distribution of Jews."[62] Statistical figures are then given. Against this background, Sombart wrote, the "problem" of the eastern Jews was a "settlement or resettlement problem." To solve this problem, and also to assist and rescue the suffering eastern Jewish population, "ways and means" must be found, he argued, "to accommodate the eastern Jews in compact masses in some other place on earth (thereby avoiding the invasion of another body of people)."[63] The parenthetical comment underscores the "resettlement" of

---

60 Ibid., 418.
61 Werner Sombart, *Die Zukunft der Juden* (Leipzig, 1912), 8–9.
62 Ibid., 9.
63 Ibid., 27.

"compact masses" as a countermodel to negative movement associated with the idea of dangerous mingling. Sombart does regard the "colorful variety" engendered by the migrants as a necessary counterbalance to the uniformity of the modern "conformist" or the "American Man," and he sees the "mobility" of the Jewish spirit as an enriching "piece of the Orient" in the "gray world of the northland." This balance, however, is based for Sombart on segregation and "uniform" distribution, as he calls it.[64] Mingling and excessive proximity had to be prevented, he believed, for they would disturb the "equilibrium" and cause "tensions." Finally, according to Sombart, statistically speaking, mixed marriages led to increased infertility or to children deprived of "spiritual equilibrium" and "much too frequently" to "people lacking in intellectual or moral equilibrium."[65]

A review of the book in the *Archiv für Rassen- und Gesellschaftsbiologie* welcomes the observations on resettlement of eastern Jews in "compact masses" and criticizes only the fact that Sombart apparently does not wish to exclude the Jews altogether.[66] A positive assessment of this publication by Zionist groups does not change the fact that the call for segregation and imposed distribution are important aspects of racist positions. It is also irrelevant whether Sombart was a racist or not. The important matter is the functionality of his writing in the discursive process of spreading and stabilizing racist and anti-Semitic positions, and these texts clearly show the linkage between the normalistic symbolism of modern mass dynamics and racist concepts. For, as a concrete version of Hannah Arendt's descriptions, if the various fields of study view population migrations as a problem and a dangerous confounding of the normal distribution of bodies, then racism is an adequate response to the extent that it delivers imposed regulatory concepts. Territorial placement of people is replaced by statistical recording and classificatory inspection of their bodies, whereas territorial, national boundaries are replaced with mingling boundaries related directly to the bodies. The symbolic outlines of dangerous mass dynamics that have been described – the "swarms," the "parasites" and "bacilli," the "piles" thrown together, the "floods" and "inundations," the "infestation," the "nomadism," the "dispersion" – give people a subjective means of identifying with the necessity of such territorialism, not least of all by producing "anxieties" on the part of the "uprooted."

64 Ibid., 56, 70–1.
65 Ibid., 44.
66 *Archiv* 5 (1913): 687.

This sort of linkage between regulatory concepts and subjective attitudes can also be seen in the symbolic outlines setting in motion, in turn, the positive identification with regulated movement. For example, the physician Grassl, who is represented with numerous articles in the *Archiv für Rassen- und Gesellschaftsbiologie*, speaks emphatically in 1913 of "taking up the systematic migration" in order to "evade the *völkisch* risk of the dwarf family."[67] Werner Sombart's 1915 publication on the war gives an example of what the "systematic" indicates, namely the production of possible positive images by connection to known national stereotypes: "How we, who have so often wrinkled our noses at the swarms in our land and likened many of our provinces to rabbit hutches, do now bless these diverse peoples as they roll in vast, tight columns to defend the fatherland against impertinent enemies."[68]

The symbolic realm of the military that was so central to national identity apparently offers positive images of a specific mass dynamic identity: the "columns" in contrast to the "swarms" (of "vermin"). Elias Canetti's definition of the army as a central German "mass symbol" therefore very nicely captures both aspects – that of the traditional national identity and that of the newly formed mass identity. The "marching columns" also suggest the mass events staged by the National Socialists. They were characterized by the steady movement of compact masses performed by uniformed bodies at precise distances from one another.

It remains to be noted that the discursive processes of normalizing the population movements were interlinked with corresponding political and police measures. As early as the turn of the century, there were mass expulsions of eastern immigrants, and during the imperial period it was customary practice to transport immigrants from the East through Germany to the port cities in special closed trains that, in some cases, were sealed and guarded. Under the extraordinary conditions of war and postwar periods, such measures are intensified with deportations, expulsions and the establishment of concentration camps. The establishment of such camps specifically for eastern Jews in the early 1920s was accompanied by a discursive escalation of the symbolism previously described. The symbolism of inundation, vermin, and disease permeated statements on the subject of eastern Jews from the widest variety of newspapers, journals, and political parties, from the German National People's Party (Deutschnationale Volkspartei, or DNVP) to the Social Democrats. Stabi-

---

67 Josef Grassl, *Der Geburtenrückgang in Deutschland, seine Ursachen und seine Bedeutung* (Kempten, 1914), 159.
68 Sombart, *Händler*, 120.

lization of this constellation of symbols made this debate a fateful event for the subsequent spread of anti-Semitism in Germany.

MIGRATION: DENORMALIZATION OR NORMAL TURBULENCE?

In summary, the still somewhat sketchy description of the discoursive processes in the late nineteenth and early twentieth centuries allows at least one important conclusion. It is not, as often presumed, the deficiency of identity, values, and orientation that makes the "mass character" of modern societies so susceptible to racist concepts, but rather specific discoursive formation and the corresponding symbolic staging of mass identities. Both are closely coupled with strategies of normalization. This perspective lends a precarious status to the increase in mobility since the nineteenth century, especially, to the major migration movements; for the precise recording and regulation of these movements is directly connected to the prognostic determination of possible denormalization tendencies. A demand for limits arises. The racist concepts developed by physicians, hygienists, and eugenicists imposed organizational schemes in this regard: clear boundaries against mingling and reterritorialization of bodies according to "ancestry." The regulatory and disciplinary measures that were developed as a result became matters of survival; their rigidity therefore made them even more evident. In addition, this form of reterritorialization promised not a standstill but an orderly dynamic of progress.

The constitution of migration movements through collective symbolism in the early twentieth century played an important part in the spread of such normalization concepts and, through subjective application, simultaneously supported development of a societal mentality in Germany that ultimately permitted a certain amount of approval of a murderous political movement. As a defense against the "swarming parasites," securing national borders against immigrants could simultaneously be experienced symbolically as a hygienically necessary reinforcement of the body's own boundaries. The development of a disciplined, delineated mass and movements thereof safeguarded against the "dispersion," "contagion," and "swarm" of a negatively portrayed mass identity. In this way, the mobility of the masses, their "homelessness," first became (and probably remains) a threatening experience to which racist identity concepts can be an adequate response. The "normal" national identity now frequently criticized as a defect in the Federal Republic of Germany of the 1990s cannot prevent the development of such panics and dangerous divisive phantoms. This is because the symbolic mechanism of national stereotypes and national characters stabilizes the subjective identification with boundary-setting and "sorting" that are based on a long continuum of history and are therefore fixed.

On the other hand, other cultural perspectives of the migration movements of the twentieth century appear truly helpful. Critical discussion of the different ideas of normality and their symbolic structures is indispensable in this regard. Both aspects characterize the text that Hans Magnus Enzensberger places at the beginning of his "thirty-three markings" of the "great migration." The accent on the aesthetics of a climatic map of the world on which "swarms" of colored arrows "combine into whirls" and then "disperse" again is associated here with the following note: "The normal state of the atmosphere is turbulence. The same is true of the settlement of the earth by human beings."[69] Enzensberger's text raises many questions regarding the "great migration," this "chaotic process that destroys every planned intention, every long-term forecast." One of the few certainties reads: "The more vigorously a civilization defends itself against an external threat, and the more it walls itself in, the less it has to defend in the end."[70]

69 Hans M. Enzensberger, *Die Grosse Wanderung: Dreiunddreissig Markierungen: Mit einer Fussnote "Über einige Besonderheiten bei der Menschenjagd,"* 7th ed. (Frankfurt/Main, 1993), 9.
70 Ibid., 11, 65-6.

5

Integration and Fragmentation Discourses

Demanding and Supplying "Identity" in Diverse Societies

DIETMAR SCHIRMER

INTRODUCTION

In the spring of 1995, Andrew Sullivan in the *New Republic* wondered about Phil Gramm's chances of winning the Republican nomination for president. Concluding his argument, he asked, "Is he too mean to win? Possibly. But on race, the issue where meanness most hurts, Gramm is inoculated. Thanks to his Asian-American wife and Amerasian sons, he's an archetype of this country's transracial, conservative future."[1] Some issues later, the *New Republic* published a letter to the editors saying:

Phil Gramm's Asian American wife hardly "inoculates" him on matters of race. . . . The dominant American culture's acceptance of Asian feminine sexuality has preceded acceptance of ethnic Asians as genuine Americans. Sullivan refers to Gramm's Eurasian American sons as "Amerasian." This description is erroneous, since Wendy Gramm is just as American as Phil Gramm – but perhaps understandable, since Sullivan isn't.[2]

Although neither Sullivan nor Andrew Chin, the writer of the letter, speaks of identity, they obviously refer to it – but in quite different manners. The writer of the letter rejects not only Sullivan's judgment of Gramm but also his semantics of ascribing group identities to individuals. Chin refers to Wendy Gramm as Asian American, as does Sullivan. But he rejects the notion that the offspring of a WASP American and an Asian American can be referred to as Amerasians, while himself referring to them as Eurasians. Obviously, he carries out a semantic program:

---

1 All translations, unless otherwise noted, are the author's own. Andrew Sullivan, "The Washington Diarist," *New Republic*, Mar. 20, 1995, 42.
2 *New Republic*, Apr. 17, 1995.

97

"Asian American," analogous to "African American" or, for that matter, "European American," gives a closer description of somebody of American nationality by adding information on his or her ethnicity. The compound term "Eurasian," however, refers to somebody of mixed ethnicity – "Eur" plus "Asian." On the same principle of analogy, Sullivan's use of the compound "Amerasian" for the Gramm sons would refer to their mixed American and Asian ethnicity. This cannot be, since being American is a category of citizenship, not of ethnicity – a political category, not one of culture or descent. Hence, the letter's point is that Sullivan, in applying the compound form "Amerasian," which signifies ethnicity, reveals that in his view Americans are principally white (European) whereas nonwhite Americans exist only in and through their qualification as "ethnic" Americans. Andrew Chin is, of course, perfectly right, although Sullivan probably did not consciously carry out a semantic rule, but did as members of the majority often do: take themselves for the whole.

This is only about half of the interpretation of this tiny ten-line letter, since it deals with only the interference of political, legal, or ethnic categories. The letter also refers to the equally relevant interference of cultural and gender categories. I have described this in some detail because it tells much about the complex implications of social identities: first, the multidimensional character of the concept, which comes as ethnic, cultural, national, and gender identity aspects; second, the categorical complications that result from multiple group memberships and their interference; and third, the political significance of identity discourses, which are ultimately power struggles for inclusion and recognition.

Identity discourses are currently occurring almost everywhere – in Germany as well as in the United States. They are triggered by the irritating effects of immigration, by internal fragmentation according to ethnic, cultural, and lifestyle milieus, and by debates on the interpretation of history. In the case of Germany, this all takes place under the unique conditions of unification, which is nothing short of a redefinition of the German nation-state itself.

The omnipresence of identity discourses, both in Germany and the United States, indicates a crisis of the mechanisms of social, cultural, and political integration and expresses fears of a fragmentation or compartmentalization of society. For a political scientist, the most interesting aspects of this crisis are those that affect the integrational capacity of the political system on the national level itself. After all, that specific form of political organization we call a nation-state largely depends on the shared belief of its members that there is a good reason for its existence. Theoretically, the sheer efficiency of its institutions might do. Empirically it will not. There actually is no nation-state that would not try to assure itself of the loyalty of its members by referring to a system of symbols that elevates its existence beyond the more or less arbitrary considerations of expediency, such as the supposedly primordial factors of common blood, culture, language, and history, a national mission, or some sort of state or civil religion. These systems of symbols constitute what we commonly refer to as national identity.

Identity and identity politics are a particularly fuzzy topic. The term itself has to be considered a political symbol rather than an analytical concept. Therefore, the attempt to define clearly social identities in general and political identity in particular, even with the best pragmatic intentions, is not particularly helpful. On the contrary; in order to learn about the social, cultural, and political significance of identity discourses, one has to live with the term's ambiguities and overdeterminations. What is required is not the definition of the term but the reconstruction of the multitude of its semantics and pragmatics.

To do so, I wish to suggest an interpretational framework that understands collective identity as a two-dimensional concept of symbolic integration, with the two dimensions being integral wholeness in space and continuity in time. The former refers to those symbolizations that determine the reach of the identical collective. In the case of the nation, these might be institutions such as the constitution, citizenship laws, possession of a common language and certain cultural knowledge, and ethnic and racial ascriptions. Cultural knowledge refers to the totality of historical narratives, myths, and representations that constitute what Michael Kammen metaphorically described as the "collective memory."[3] Examples are history books and curricula, a pantheon of national heroes, historic sites and museums, and battlefields and memorials.

Collective identity, thus, is a specific symbolic means of time-space distanciation[4] that links the past to the present (or, to put it more precisely, that invents and reinvents the past in and for the present) and that integrates individuals who have never and probably never will. Although it aims to stabilize the collectivity that is its subject of reference, identity is itself the subject of permanent redefinition in both of its

---

3 Michael Kammen, *The Mystic Chords of Memory: The Transformation of Tradition in American Culture* (New York, 1991), 4.
4 On time-space distanciation, see Anthony Giddens, *The Consequences of Modernity* (Stanford, Calif., 1990), 17–24.

	Integration in time	*Integration in space*
United States		
Germany		

Figure 5.1. Representing German and American Discourses

dimensions. History undergoes reinterpretations in the light of present needs and reshapes the contents of the "collective memory," as does the understanding of who belongs to the identical social unit and who does not. The task of exploring and comparing contemporary German and American discourses on identity and fragmentation along the two dimensions of the interpretational framework discussed can be schematically depicted in a matrix of four fields as shown in Figure 5.1.

This chapter fleshes out the fields of this matrix. It features four case studies. For the axis of integration over time, the cases are the American debate on affirmative action and the German argument on history and normality. For the dimension of horizontal integration, the cases are the American argument on diversity and the German debate on nationhood and civil society.

Our interest in these cases is, nevertheless, limited by the extent that they can reveal something about identity discourses. Our prime concern is not the political character of these debates but the concepts of national and group identities that implicitly or explicitly underlie them. Our interpretation, therefore, aims to reveal and compare the structure and logic of identity discourses as represented in this sample. The lead questions are: How are identity, integration, and fragmentation conceptualized in these texts? What constitutes the homogeneity of an identical social unit, and what determines the heterogeneity of others? And how do these texts relate social identities of all kinds to the integrational capacity of the political system?

I formulate answers to these questions in three steps. First, I develop characteristics of the American discourse on identity, integration, and fragmentation that I interpret as a conflict between modernism and postmodernism. Second, I paint a picture of the German debates on the country's historical self-interpretation and its concepts for its present and future identity. These can be described, *cum grano salis*, as a conflict between premodernism and modernism. Third, I explore, in a comparative perspective, structural similarities and dissimilarities of both national discourses.

THE CASE OF THE UNITED STATES

The type of political identity that evolved during the process of nation building in the United States[5] has been described as a "civil religion."[6] The term refers to "a public perception of our national experience, in light of universal and transcendent claims upon human beings, but especially Americans: a set of values, symbols, and rituals institutionalized as the cohesive force and center of meaning uniting our many peoples."[7]

Thus, the United States claims a type of national identity that is founded on political values – foremost the symbolic duality of freedom and democracy – rather than on supposed primordial factors such as ethnic and cultural homogeneity, tradition, language, and so forth.[8] The values and beliefs that constitute the core of American political culture find their objectifications in a well-known set of national heroes and semi-divinities (foremost Washington and Lincoln), holy scriptures (such as the Constitution and the Declaration of Independence, Abraham Lincoln's Gettysburg Address and Martin Luther King Jr.'s "I Have a Dream" speech), national monuments, and mythic narratives and representations (such as the myth of the frontier or the different variations of the melting-pot myth). For our purposes, the most important among these constitutive myths and symbolizations are those that relate to that system of individual freedom, equal opportunity (the pursuit of happiness),

---

5 The term "nation building," normally assigned to decolonized countries after World War II, has been applied to the United States by Seymour M. Lipset. For example, see *The First New Nation: The United States in Historical and Comparative Perspective* (New York, 1979).

6 On the concept of civil religion, see Robert N. Bellah, "Civil Religion in America," *Daedalus* 96 (1967): 1–21; Robert N. Bellah, "American Civil Religion in the 1970s," in Russell E. Richey and Donald G. Jones, eds., *American Civil Religion* (New York, 1974); Jürgen Gebhardt, "Politische Kultur und Zivilreligion," in Dirk Berg-Schlosser and Jakob Schissler, eds., *Politische Kultur in Deutschland: Bilanz und Perspektiven der Forschung* (Opladen, 1987), 49–60; Wilbur Zelinsky, *Nation into State: The Shifting Symbolic Foundations of American Nationalism* (Chapel Hill, N.C., 1988), 232–45.

7 Michael Novak, *Choosing Our King: Powerful Symbols in Presidential Politics* (New York, 1974), 127. This quotation is a fine example of the discursive dynamics that an appealing theoretical concept may develop. Civil religion had been introduced as a concept to establish the link between societies and political institutions – at least in nation-states as the typical form of political organization in modernity: "all politically organized societies have some sort of civil religion" (Bellah, "American Civil Religion," 257). Nevertheless, taken as a matter of figurative speech rather than as a theoretical framework, it seemed to match especially the American type of political culture. For Novak, it is already the symbolization of "our national experience." Civil religion shares this type of career with concepts like Gramsci's "cultural hegemony" or the "civil society."

8 We must keep in mind, however, that there has always been a hegemonial segment of society that considered itself to be the core population. Those political values that have constituted the American civil religion for most of the history of the United States applied to the entitled members of this group of insiders (which originally consisted of white, Protestant, property-owning males of Anglo-Saxon descent).

and the universal people which constitutes what is popularly considered the American Dream.[9]

Since the very beginning of the construction of American national identity, these myths and symbolizations have stood in a relationship of triple tensions. These tensions are, first, between the individual lifestyle they suggest and the social obligations they require or, to put it in other terms, a tension between individualism and communitarianism; second, between mythical ideality and social practice; and third, between the various interpretations that occur at different times or in different perspectives. Thus, whereas the symbolic and mythical system itself, although it has changed in time, proved to be amazingly stable, enormous dynamics characterize the permanent struggles for establishing its interpretations – with the most dramatic confrontations to appear in the dimension of inclusiveness and exclusiveness.[10] In this chapter, I argue that the current debate over political integration and identity is the result of a major struggle in society to preserve an old interpretation of that symbolic and mythical system, or to modify it or establish a largely new general one. That is why it can be described as a semantic struggle or a struggle about systems of classification.

A survey of the current discourse on political identity and political segmentation in the United States shows that the discussion is structured by the cleavages of race and ethnicity, immigration, class, gender, generation, religion, and sexual orientation.[11] For our purposes, we will focus on the first three cleavages. The causes of extensive discussions along the cleavages of whites versus nonwhites, middle and upper class versus poor, and natives versus immigrants are to be found in every field of social action – politics, social relations, economy, and culture – and have

9 Ironically, according to the GOP's 1994 "Contract with America," the American Dream now takes the shape of a $500-per-child tax credit - perhaps one of the most radical and unintentional demythologizations ever. See Newt Gingrich et al., "The American Dream Restoration Act" in *The Contract with America: The Bold Plan by Rep. Newt Gingrich, Rep. Dick Armey, and the House Republicans to Change the Nation* (New York, 1994), 10, 85–90.

10 Indeed, the history of American national identity would have to be written as a history of the dialectics of demands for participation in the American Dream on the side of deprived minorities and their rejection or (partial) admission on the side of the hegemonic majority.

11 I am borrowing the term cleavage from Seymour M. Lipset and Stein Rokkan. Although the cleavage concept was developed in the first place to describe voting patterns in different party systems, the application of the term in this context seems justified, since the cleavages that determine voter alignments and those mentioned here are structurally quite similar. See Seymour M. Lipset and Stein Rokkan, "Cleavage Structure, Party Systems, and Voter Alignments: An Introduction," in Seymour M. Lipset and Stein Rokkan, eds., *Party Systems and Voter Alignments: Cross-National Perspectives* (New York, 1967), 1–64.

recently been stimulated by a whole variety of trends and events. This variety reaches from the Los Angeles riots to the Crown Heights attack, from the decline of the inner cities to the decline of the middle class, from illegal aliens crossing the Rio Grande to the illegal aliens illegally employed by members of the political establishment, from historically black colleges to black-majority voting districts, from the breakup of the civil-rights coalition of Blacks and Jews to the anti-Semitic rhetoric of prominent leaders of the Nation of Islam, and from Proposition 187 to *Adarand Constructors v. Penna.*

Obviously, the cleavages defined by race, class, and immigration are far from independent of each other; the notorious race–class nexus is present here as in any discussion concerned with social structure in the United States. Generally, all these classifications are representations of social perceptions of differentiations. And their actual analytical weakness, the fact that they are conceptually close to empty, does not at all affect their power to determine social relations.

What all these various trends and events have in common is that although they are mainly political, economic, social, or cultural in nature, they are widely interpreted as symbolizations of *cultural* conflicts. Thus, they appear to be the result of either the dissolution of the traditional American consensus (this is the interpretation I would like to call conservative) or the failure of integrating aspiring groups into this consensus (the liberal interpretation) or its dismantling as an ideology of the ruling majority, maintained in order to deceive the oppressed about the permanence of their deprivation (the left-wing liberal and radical interpretation). Thus, the discourses stimulated by these trends and events are about their relationship, first, between different subcultures and, second, between these subcultures and that set of symbols and myths that traditionally guaranteed and maintained a sense of identity and integration.

Affirmative Action: "Reverse Racism" or "Equality Through Inequality"?

A briefing paper prepared by the Office of the U.S. Commission on Civil Rights provides the following definition:

Affirmative action is a contemporary term that encompasses any measure, beyond simple termination of a discriminatory practice, that permits the consideration of race, national origin, sex, or disability, along with other criteria, and which is adopted to provide opportunities to a class of qualified individuals who have either historically or actually been denied those opportunities and/or to prevent the recurrence of discrimination in the future.[12]

Two aspects referred to in this definition are of particular importance for our purpose: those of historicity and collectivity. Affirmative action is designed not only to fight discrimination when and where it appears, but also to compensate for past discrimination; and it does not apply to individuals, but to classes of individuals. These aspects make affirmative action a topic highly relevant for matters of identity, both national and social.

First, affirmation for classes of people discriminated against can be considered a rather strong expression of the intention to include groups that have been and are excluded; it is thus an attempt to extend the reach of the integrational framework of the nation at large. History is one of the main legitimations for this affirmation, especially after the termination of legal discrimination – a past social wrong that not only must be terminated but demands compensation. Thus, the debate on affirmative action is, implicitly, a debate on the relationship society establishes toward its own past. In this respect, the debate on affirmative action, structurally, comes as close as it can get to the German debate on what historical normality can mean if this history includes National Socialism and the Holocaust.[13]

Second, the determination of entitlements obviously requires a method of defining classes of people who experienced and experience discrimination. This method is a combination of semantic determinations and

12 U.S. Commission on Civil Rights, Office of General Counsel, *Legislative, Executive, and Judicial Development of Affirmative Action,* Washington, D.C., Mar. 1995.
13 Stanley Fish, in a much disputed article rejecting the conservative notion of affirmative action as "reverse racism," actually defended the application of preferences for excluded minorities in the United States by drawing an analogy with the exclusiveness of Zionism and the foundation of Israel after World War II. He quotes an address former President George Bush gave to the United Nations, in which he rejected the UN resolution equating Zionism with racism on the ground of its ahistoricity. "Zionism," Fish quotes Bush, "is the idea that led to the creation of a home for the Jewish people. . . . And to equate Zionism with the intolerable sin of racism is to twist history and forget the terrible plight of Jews in World War II." Fish adopts the structure of the argument and applies it to affirmative action: "What I want to say, following Bush's reasoning, is that a similar forgetting of history has in recent years allowed some people to argue, and argue persuasively, that affirmative action is reverse racism. . . . Not to make the distinction [between the original racism against blacks and the race based preferences of affirmative action programs] is, adapting George Bush's words, to twist history and forget the terrible plight of African Americans in the more than 200 years of this country's existence" (Stanley Fish, "Reverse Racism or How the Pot Got to Call the Kettle Black," *Atlantic Monthly* 272, no. 5 [Nov. 1930]: 128–36). Interestingly, although all six letters to the editor that the *Atlantic Monthly* published in one of its following issues objected to Fish's argument, none of them took offense at this analogy (see the letters in *Atlantic Monthly* 273, no. 2 [Feb. 1994]: 8–12).

statistical measures. The semantic part of the procedure lies in attaching significance, first, to distinctive features that define groups and, second, to fields of social achievement that allow for the measurement of discrimination. The group-forming features are race, gender, and ethnicity; the variables on which discrimination is to be measured are income, education, employment, and contracting. The statistical part of the procedure is, of course, those techniques that compare the scores of semantically defined classes with those of the population at large in order to confirm or reject the assumption of significant disadvantage.

Functionally, if not historically, affirmative action can be described as the second phase of civil rights politics. The first phase was about finally granting that legal equality that the Constitution had promised from the beginning. Under the rubric of "color blindness," the classic civil rights movement had struggled for tearing down legal and bureaucratic walls that separated the white American majority from the black and other minorities, which remained largely excluded from the social, cultural, and economical surplus of society. Affirmative action, as a measure of social advancement, draws the consequences of lasting and grinding inequality and provides the legal tools against a wide and, in the course of the years, widening array of social practices of discrimination not only against blacks but also against other ethnic minorities and women.

On a pragmatic level, the affirmative action controversy is about the distribution of benefits. Politically, the turn in focus from legal to social equality left the civil rights movement in an awkward position much weaker than the one it had occupied during its first phase. When the subject of its struggle still was legal equality, it could build a broad consensus for a fight for the higher good of the universal principles of the Constitution. In the new constellation, its supporters – organizations that had evolved with and through the classic civil rights movement, such as the NAACP or the National Urban League – had to take on a role that often resembled that of any special-interest group.[14] Moreover, other than in the case of the struggle for legal equality, a considerable part of the majority population perceives affirmative action as a vital threat toward their personal chances for social achievement. These are the reasons why affirmative action failed to build a consensus that substantially transcended the coalition between the liberal establishment and the aspiring groups. The decline of the American middle class since the 1980s,

---

14 See Steven A. Holmes, "Affirmative Action: For the Civil Rights Movement, a New Reason for Living," *New York Times*, July 9, 1995, sec. 4, 1.

which pushed more and more whites toward the edge of poverty, even hardened the opposition toward social policies especially designed for the advancement of minorities.

On a semantic level, this controversy is played out as a controversy over the interpretation of the meaning of "equality" as one of the elements of the very symbolic core of the American civil religion. This exegetic controversy has two main aspects. First, it is about whether equality is to be understood in a legal or in a social sense, with the former being linked to a conservative antistatist or libertarian notion of a passive government and the latter correlating either with the liberal idea of an interventionist state actively involved in the shaping of social relations or with a conservative-paternalistic understanding of a caring state. The second main interpretational aspect is whether equality is to be interpreted as a property that applies exclusively to individuals or as a quality that essentially transcends personal assignability. Accepting the legitimacy of affirmative action obviously requires an equality-inequality rationale that takes into account collective and historical rather than individual fates, whereas opposition toward affirmative action applies a concept of equality that is restricted to the absence of legal discrimination of individuals *hic et nunc.*

For supporters of affirmative action, the history of discrimination against African Americans, of slavery and lynching, of disenfranchisement and segregation, and of resentment and prejudice constitutes a moral argument. According to this argument, past wrongs spill into the present, both as the moral debt of the majority and the lasting effect they have had on the oppressed and excluded minority. Former generations, cut off from the opportunities society presented to the majority of its members, were unable to acquire even a fraction of the social, economic, and cultural capital others had. This, combined with the lasting resentments of the majority, determines the chances of their present-day descendants. Lower wealth and income, less access to grants, inferior education, crime-ridden neighborhoods, and the prejudice of the majority conspire to prevent them from fulfilling their potential.

History served as one of the very first major legitimating tools for affirmative action. President Lyndon B. Johnson metaphorically referred to slavery in his famous phrase "You do not take a person who, for years, has been hobbled by chains and liberate him, bring him up to the starting line of a race and then say, 'You are free to compete with the others.'" Another often quoted phrase on affirmative action, by Supreme

Court Justice Blackmun, adopts the same logic: "In order to get beyond racism, we must first take account of race. . . . And in order to treat some persons equally, we must treat them differently."[15] A recent speech by President Bill Clinton not only refers to history as a legitimation of affirmative action but explicitly links the rationale of righting a historical wrong to that of national unity and future strength. This text, a fine example of the general logic of legitimating affirmative action, deserves closer examination.

In order to "prepare our nation" for the challenges of a rapidly transforming world, Clinton said, "we must reach beyond our fears and our divisions to a new time of great and common purpose." Still stressing the rationale of national unity, he proceeded: "Our challenge is twofold: first, to restore the American dream of opportunity and the American value of responsibility; and second, to bring our country together amid all our diversity into a stronger community so that we can find common ground [and] move forward as one." Then, Clinton argued that the norms and practice of affirmative action are integral to the project of national unity, serve as a precondition for future success, and lie at the root of American values and American history more generally:

"We hold these truths to be self-evident: that all men are created equal; that they are endowed by their Creator with certain inalienable rights; that among these are life, liberty, and the pursuit of happiness." Our whole history can be seen, first, as an effort to preserve these rights, and then as an effort to make them real in the lives of all our citizens. We know that from the beginning there was a great gap between the plain meaning of our creed and the meaner reality of our daily lives. Back then only white, male property owners could vote. Black slaves were not even counted as whole people, and Native Americans were regarded as little more than an obstacle to our great national progress. . . . Emancipation, women's suffrage, civil rights, voting rights, the struggle for the rights of the disabled, all these and other struggles are milestones on America's often rocky but fundamentally righteous journey to close the gap between the ideals enshrined in these treasures here in the National Archives and the reality of our daily lives. . . . Our search to find ways to move more quickly to equal opportunity led to the development of what we now call affirmative action. The

---

15 This comment, referring to the Supreme Court's decision in the 1978 *Regents of the University of California vs. Bakke* case, is probably the most quoted comment on affirmative action in both the pro and contra camps. See Lino L. Graglia, "Affirmative Discrimination," *National Review* 45, no. 13 (July 5, 1993): 26; Jared Taylor, *Paved with Good Intentions: The Failure of Race Relations in Contemporary America* (New York, 1992), 138; Clint Bolick, *Changing Courses: Civil Rights at the Crossroads* (New Brunswick, N.J., 1988), 68; Nicolaus Mills, "Introduction: To Look like America," in Nicolaus Mills, ed., *Debating Affirmative Action: Race, Gender, Ethnicity, and the Politics of Inclusion* (New York, 1994), 29.

purpose of affirmative action is to give our nation a way to finally address the systemic exclusion of individuals of talent, on the basis of their gender or race, from opportunities to develop, perform, achieve, and contribute.[16]

Clinton's speech reveals a coherent system of symbolic meanings and locates the divisive issue of affirmative action within the larger symbolic framework of American identity. It links the American dream to the unity of a diverse people; it draws upon the moral authority of the Constitution; and it even offers a teleological interpretation of American history as a continuous effort to bring social practice into harmony with the promises of the Constitution, with affirmative action as one link in a chain of struggles leading toward justice and inclusion for all. The narrative of a national history of progress thereby supports and compliments the ethic of transpersonal responsibility, which forms the foundation of a remedial rationale for affirmative action: Social responsibility transcends individual accountability because the nation does not just group together individuals at random, but interlinks its members horizontally through shared values and practices, and vertically through a common historical narrative.

Opponents of affirmative action base their case, just as the supporters do, on the notion of equality. They adopt the moral authority of the civil rights movement's concept of a "color-blind society" and dismiss race- or gender-based privileges as "reverse racism" or "reverse sexism," respectively. Thus, rather than understanding affirmative action as poetic justice for past exclusion, they hold that it perpetuates the old wrong with reversed signs. As Supreme Court Justice Antonin Scalia put it, "To pursue the concept of racial entitlement even for the most admirable and benign of purposes is to reinforce and preserve for future mischief the way of thinking that produced race slavery, race privilege and race hatred."[17] Instead of racialist remedies for past racism, all that government can legitimately do is provide a "level playing field" of legal equality. The symbolic dispositive for that point of view is the American tradition of individualism and the principle of merit.

Nevertheless, the decisive features of race and gender regularly reenter the rationale of the anti–affirmative action camp, despite its insistence on colorblindness. They do so in the form of statistical dispositives that include race as a grouping variable – just as supporters of affirmative action do in order to prove the persistence of discrimination. But where-

16 Quoted according to "Give All Americans a Chance," *Washington Post*, July 20, 1995, A12.
17 Supreme Court Justice Antonin Scalia in his concurring opinion in *Adarand v. Penna*, quoted in the *New York Times*, June 13, 1995, D24.

as the pro-affirmative action calculation uses education, employment, and income as dependent variables, the opponents turn to SAT scores, trying to prove discrimination against whites. The topic here, of course, is the practice of college and university admission; the point to prove is that minorities, especially African Americans and Hispanics, are admitted with lower average scores than whites. Lina A. Graglia displayed that line of argument in an essay published in the *National Review.*

After a brief recollection of the history of the legal and judicial abandonment of race discrimination since *Brown v. The Board of Education*, and a sketch of the representational logic of the affirmative action rationale, Graglia points out: "The fact is that there is a very large, longstanding and apparently unyielding difference between blacks as a group and whites as a group – despite, of course, large areas of overlap – in academic ability as measured by standard aptitude tests," such as the SAT, LSAT, MCAT, and GREQ. Here, racial distinctions are, so to say, back in business, despite statements to the contrary. Graglia then dismisses the argument that these tests are culturally biased against minorities. She goes on to suggest that even supporters of affirmative action have long abandoned the hope that blacks and Hispanics could ever match the scores of whites and Asians, and then she again turns against the concept of proportional representation: "The problem is undoubtedly a severe one: if a stable multiracial society requires that all racial groups be more or less proportionately represented in all important institutions and activities, it requires what no multiracial society has ever achieved."[18]

At this point, "colorblindness" has been abandoned. If discrimination has long been a thing of the past, and cultural biases cannot be held responsible for the lower test scores of some racial groups, what then is the explanation for the obvious differences in achievement? Graglia avoids being explicit, but the deduction is an easy one: It must have something to do with race. The argument against racialized politics turns into a latently racist one.

Thus, neither position can avoid the fact that social practice relies on race, ethnicity, and gender as modes of distinction. The pro-affirmative action camp, as defensive as it might appear at times, takes an offensive stance toward that observation and includes the categories of race, ethnicity, and gender in a concept that attempts to counteract discriminatory practice. The anti-affirmative action camp chooses a passive approach, practically affirming the status quo, because it thinks the government is

18 Graglia, "Affirmative Discrimination," 26–31.

not a legitimate provider of social redistribution, or because it considers the goal of equal opportunity has already been achieved, or because it simply wants to protect a given mode of social reproduction, or even for all these reasons. Both points of view are rooted in two different concepts of equality and are legitimated by involving the values and symbols of the Constitution and the American civil religion, as well as national history. The fact that the same symbolic dispositives can serve to legitimate opposing views indicates the overdetermination of symbols and symbolic texts, whether it is the Constitution or the narrative of American history.

Diversity: "Balkanization" or "Cultural Pluralism"

In a letter to the editors of the *Washington Post*, referring to an article on multiculturalism, the writer mentioned that her point of view was that "we are a multiethnic, but monocultural society," thus putting the most powerful myths of America – the "melting pot" and the "universal people" – against the idea that America could be a multitude of cultures rather than a cultural synthesis.

In some way, the concept of "diversity" can be seen as homologous to affirmative action. It does in the field of culture what affirmative action does in the field of social politics. Both indicate a shift from the perspective of individuals to that of groups. Both are based on the use of variables such as race, ethnicity, and gender to aggregate individuals into groups of people of a common fate and interest. But whereas affirmative action does this mainly in the sense of statistical aggregation in order to prove and fight practices of discrimination, the concepts of "diversity" or "multiculturalism" aim at constituting cultural identities. That signifies an important inversion in the application of the underlying variables. Affirmative action uses them in a defensive way; race, ethnicity, and gender define groups of disadvantaged minorities that deserve special protection against discrimination by the (white, male, heterosexual) ruling majority. Diversity uses attributes such as race, ethnicity, and gender to define groups that draw strength, self-esteem, and identity from the notion of a common culture, lifestyle, or heritage. The fact that "diversity" attracts so much attention, although it is mainly a campus issue, indicates the potential threat it poses. As a concept of cultural distinctiveness, it attacks the orthodoxy's myth of a common American culture more directly than the concept of social redistribution contained in affirmative action.

The opposing camps in the "diversity" discourse resemble those in the affirmative action debate. A conservative orthodoxy battles it as the politics of racial and ethnic separation and an assault on the predominance of a Western tradition that made America; left-wing liberals, black nationalists, Afrocentrists, and the spokespersons of other ethnic minorities support it as a movement that defends minorities against the humiliation of being different in a society dominated by whites and against the pressure to adapt to white values and ways of life, validates non-European cultures and histories, and thus highlights progress from a Eurocentrist to a truly pluralistic perspective. Between the conservative opponents and the supporters of diversity and multiculturalism are liberals, both white and nonwhite, who resist the sensitivity codes of political correctness in the name of the First Amendment, and who feel uneasy about or oppose the segregationist tendencies within the diversity movement out of concern for the universalistic-integrationist tradition of the older civil rights movement. The observation that the camp of nonconservative opponents here is considerably larger than in the case of affirmative action indicates how radical the concept is. Whereas the goals of the "classic" civil rights movement and affirmative action remain within the framework of the American mythology, the idea of diversity is widely seen as a threat.

The attraction — as well as the threat — of "diversity" and "multiculturalism" is fostered by two different sources: (1) a social and cultural demand and (2) the philosophy of postmodernity that transforms the Western philosophical tradition predominant since the Enlightenment.

1. Diversity is probably a result of the failure of civil rights policy as well as of its success. The persistence of racial and ethnic resentments and social exclusion, despite the accomplishment of legal equality, betrayed the hopes for an equal society. This set the stage for a movement that focused on ethnic consciousness and the cultural bonds of heritage rather than on the integrational appeal of the American mythology. But it is important to see that this rejection of Western universalism is less a voluntary decision than a symbolization of a history of unfulfilled promises and betrayed hopes. It is necessary to recall the history of struggles for inclusiveness in order to understand the demand for exclusive identities, and not to mistake them as the simple reverse of white separatism. These identities are based on some of those supposedly primordial factors that the concept — if not the reality — of American political identity had apparently abolished. In addition to a change in expectations, another development important for the emergence of the idea of diversity is

demographic change. In this respect Hispanic and Asian immigration it-self is not changing the landscape as much as the fact that these groups – like others not defined by ethnicity – are becoming increasingly visible through their own emerging political representation. "Now, there are more players on the field, with Hispanics and Asians, and women and other groups also making claims."[19] Thus, what used to be perceived as a black versus white opposition changed toward a continuum of differen-tiations among a multitude of groups.

2. The unifying principle of that collection of ideas commonly labeled "postmodernism" is the skepticism about objectivity and truth as uni-versal principles. The postmodernist shifts from objectivity toward objec-tification, from reality toward the "fantasies of realism,"[20] and from truth toward perception indeed indicate an epistemological break – whether we interpret it as a break of epoch and the eclipse of modernism or, probably more appropriately, as just another step in the history of the critique of reason within the framework of modernity. In any case, the de-construction of two centuries of Western philosophy based on the idea of self-centered subjectivity and the notion of universal truth is the phi-losophical background of the diversity approach. The demystification of the holistic myths of modernism made way for something that critics called an eclectic and superficial attitude of "anything goes," and that followers emphasize is the surmounting of the modernist self-deceptions about truth, reality, history, and objectivity. If there is not one objectivity, not one reality, but manifold perceptions of manifold representations, none with an exclusive pretension to truth, then the predominance of Western civilization in all its expressions – philosophy, culture, sciences, historical achievements, lifestyles, modes of production and reproduction, social and political organization – can only be based on power, not on superiority.[21] Thus, the postmodern critique of Western modernism pro-vides the philosophical foundation for scholars and students – not only of minorities – to refuse to conceptualize their perception of the world according to the works of "dead white males."

Thus, the socially induced demands for ethnic, cultural, gendered, and

---

19 Andrew Hacker, *Two Nations: Black and White, Separate, Hostile, Unequal* (New York, 1992), 134.
20 Jean-François Lyotard, *The Postmodern Condition: A Report on Knowledge* (Minneapolis, 1993), 74.
21 Asante, e.g., explicitly refers to this relation between postmodernism and diversity: "[W]hat we see going are the vestiges of a system of racial domination – it was a wrong-headed system in the first place – what we see coming is a postmodern society that is sympathetic to diversity and committed to plural views. Thus, no longer can European studies of Africa parade as African studies; the overthrow of the dominating canon has already begun" (Molefi Kete Asante, *Kemet, Afrocentricity, and Knowledge* [Trenton, N.J., 1990], 7).

other identities on a subnational level that emerged in the aftermath of the failing success – or successful failure – of classic civil rights policies coincide with the postmodern dismantling of Western modernism. But that would constitute only an academic battlefield of minor public interest, if it were not for the fact that the system of political myths that constitutes the idea of America itself is perhaps one of the most powerful political expressions of classic modernism. Individual liberty, representative democracy, legal equality, the "universal race" that emerges from the "melting pot," the voluntary association of a people of immigrants – each of these constitutive myths is an objectification of the paradigms of modernism. "Diversity" and the American civil religion in the political field, and postmodernism and modernism in the field of ideas, inhabit homologous positions. Therefore, the concept of diversity is perceived as no less of a threat to the American way of life than postmodernism is to the established canon of Enlightenment philosophy.

It might be useful to stick to the analogy between the systems *cultural assimilation versus diversity* and *modernism versus postmodernism* for a moment. A central metaphor of the latter is linearity versus net. It applies to the conceptualization of such basic categories as progress (here they mean intentional action versus systemic autopoeisis as formative forces), history (continuity and synchronicity versus discontinuity and asynchronicity), the narrative organization of events (linear plot versus intertextuality), social interaction (communication versus discourse), the structure of society (classes organized on a power-deprivation continuum versus classes defined by a multitude of relations according to economic, social, cultural, political positions), and knowledge (accumulation versus transformation).

The central metaphor of the system *assimilation versus diversity* is the opposition of the melting pot versus the patchwork of multiculturalism; and it is obvious how it fits into the pattern of the symbolic dispositive of the modernism-postmodernism system. The basic idea of the melting pot is the homogenization of heterogeneous substances in time – no matter whether this means a metaphor of assimilation or fusion.[22] The

---

22 In Zangwill's 1908 play *The Melting Pot*, the metaphor describes America as a utopian crucible that breeds the universal race: "Germans and Frenchmen, Irishmen and Englishmen, Jews and Russians – into the Crucible with you all! God is making the American." Nevertheless, most applications of the melting-pot metaphor have a clear bias toward assimilation of heterogeneous elements into a well-established American culture. Julian L. Simon, for example, recently based his whole argument for a liberal immigration policy on the notion that "immigration does not substantially alter American institutions and culture. Rather, the immigrants absorb American ways, and are absorbed into them" (Julian L. Simon et al., "Why Control the Borders? An Immi-

underlying concept of the diversity patchwork is the equal coexistence of a multitude of subcultures that cross-refer to each other through people who belong to more than only one of them and constitute wholeness only through their mutual particularity. Diversity is multidimensional, offering the possibility of multiple identifications; whereas one belongs to one subculture according to his or her ethnicity, he or she might include him- or herself in other subcultures according to gender, sexual orientation, or lifestyle. Thus, diversity is an inclusive concept – but only if its diverse subcultures are seen to be based on permeable differentiations rather than impermeable oppositions. On the other hand, if the subcultural identities that exist within that patchwork are perceived according to the model of the traditional national identities, that is, as exclusive and (scarcely) impermeable, it indeed is threatening – in more than only one sense.

First, the homogeneous majority perceives it as a threat to its own traditional and still predominant form of American identity. Thus, the patchwork of diversity appears to endanger the perpetuation of an Anglo-Saxon and European-biased culture by means of assimilation and, consequently, the status advantages of those who represent it by virtue of birth. The most visible counterstrategy for securing the perpetuation of the traditional hierarchies is the application of a narrow and inflexible concept of normality that distinguishes between mainstream Americans and all sorts of political, ethnical, and other "countercultures."

Second, and farther reaching, diversity threatens the legitimation of a unified political organization of society at large. This expresses itself usually in the semantics of "balkanization," "lebanonization," or "tribalism." It was Schlesinger who eloquently set the standards for the old-time liberal critique of diversity. He devises a plot that contrasts the melting-pot type of American unity with its multicultural "decomposition":

The ethnicity rage in general and Afrocentricity in particular not only divert attention from the real needs but exacerbate the problems. The recent apotheosis of ethnicity, black, brown, red, yellow, white, has revived the dismal prospect that in happy melting-pot days Americans thought the republic was moving safely beyond – that is, a society fragmented into separate ethnic communities. The cult of ethnicity exaggerates differences, intensifies resentments and antago-

gration Debate," *National Review*, 45, no. 2 [Jan. 2, 1993]: 27), thus proving the current validity of Schlesinger's notion about nineteenth-century America that "the melting pot . . . had, unmistakably and inescapably, an Anglocentric flavor" (Arthur M. Schlesinger Jr., *The Disuniting of America: Reflections on a Multicultural Society* [New York, 1993], 28).

nisms, drives ever deeper the awful wedges between races and nationalities. The endgame is self-pity and self-ghettoization.[23]

The consequence of this compartmentalization seems to be a vital threat to the very base of political unity itself:

The cult of ethnicity has reversed the movement of American history, producing a nation of minorities – or at least of minority spokesmen – less interested in joining with the majority in common endeavor than in declaring their alienation from an oppressive, white, patriarchal, racist, sexist, classist society. . . . [W]hen a vocal and visible minority pledges primary allegiance to their group, whether ethnic, sexual, religious, or, in rare cases (communist, fascist) political, it presents a threat to the brittle bonds of national identity that hold this diverse and fractious society together.[24]

Thus, the liberal orthodoxy applies a (modernist) concept of oppositions to a (postmodernist) concept of differentiations. Multiculturalism, from this perspective, looks rather like an explosive and aggressive scheme of hostile tribes and sects – therefore the metaphorical recourses to Lebanon and the Balkans – than the cultivation of a cultural patchwork.

Third, this perception is nurtured by a considerable number of minority spokespersons who, under the label of diversity, indeed behave like leaders of sects and tribes and therefore have to be held accountable for the majority's animosity toward a diverse redefinition of the American concept of identity. Basically, they transform diversity into a threatening concept by applying the same means of interpretation as the majority. They take as dichotomies or oppositions what should be taken as differentiations and conceptualize their peculiar and particular cultural identities as exclusive and superior.

One of the major representations of this claim for superiority is the battle over Egypt and ancient Greece that is fought by Afrocentrists in order to establish the African origins of Western civilization.[25] Literature that claims the blackness of ancient Egypt and disputes the European perception of a white Mediterranean antiquity has been around for decades; but the current struggle for diversified curricula in public schools

---

23 Schlesinger, *Disuniting*, 102. Alas, Schlesinger – like other liberal critics of the "new tribalism" – in general overestimates the voluntariness of "self-ghettoization." E.g., Douglas S. Massey and Nancy A. Denton, *American Apartheid: Segregation and the Making of the Underclass* (Cambridge, 1993) show in their careful study the implications of persisting and nonvoluntary residential segregation for the perpetuation of racial inequality.

24 Schlesinger, *Disuniting*, 112–13.

25 See, e.g., Cheik Anta Diop, *The African Origin of Civilization: Myth or Reality* (Chicago, 1974); Mary Lefkowitz, "Not Out of Africa (Review Essay on Afrocentrist Literature)," *New Republic* 206, no. 6 (Oct. 2, 1992): 29–36; Schlesinger, *Disuniting*, 60–71.

and the establishment of African and African-American studies in colleges and universities make it a highly symbolic political issue. Whereas the tone in this "Whose Greeks are they?" debate is quite tame, the goal clearly is to unmask Western civilization since Greek antiquity as either a free rider or a thief of African civilization. Afrocentrism sounds considerably shriller when it comes to Leonard Jeffries's melanin theory.[26] This theory is by no means less narrow-minded and chauvinist than white supremacist theories, and less racist only if one applies a definition that inherently links racism to possession of dominating power. Jeffries also has been said to be anti-Semitic[27] as have other Afrocentrists and Black Nationalists who have recently made headlines by focusing specifically on the supposed overrepresentation of Jews in the slave trade in particular and the oppression of blacks in general.[28] But we should not forget that black anti-Semitism is also readily instrumentalized to prove the threat and unpredictability of nonassimilationist black movements and of multiculturalism in general. This becomes obvious in the expectations of many whites that blacks should dissociate themselves consistently and explicitly from black anti-Semites, and thus holding them responsible for the stupidity of others only on basis of their ethnicity – as if whites were always expected to dissociate themselves from white supremacists.

Thus, the concept of diversity in practice turns out to be not as peaceful as it has been in theory. As a matter of fact, ethnic separation on campus seems to be flourishing. My thesis, however, is that segregationist tendencies and a rise in ethnic tensions within the context of diversity are due, first, to the fact that diversity seriously challenges the established hierarchy of ethnicities and erodes the pressure for assimilation customarily exerted on everybody who wants recognition, and, second, to

26 The theory contrasts white, low-melanin "ice-people" and black, high-melanin "sun-people," whose character is either "cold" or "warm," according to their environment.

27 *Emerge*, in a positive article on Leonard Jeffries, quotes from a speech of his that gives much evidence for this accusation. See Michael H. Cottman, "Professor Leonard Jeffries: Afrocentric Profs Under Constant Pressure," *Emerge* 5, no. 6 (Mar. 1994): 26–31.

28 Recent examples include the anti-Semitic polemics of Khalid Abdul Muhammed, minister of Louis Farrakhan's Nation of Islam, in New Jersey and at Howard University. See, e.g., "Time-Forum: The Rift Between Blacks and Jews," *Time*, Feb. 28, 1994, which collects essays by Leon Wieseltier, Thulani Davis, Midge Decter, Cornel West, Michael Lerner, and Randall Kennedy. See also Paul Berman, "The Other and the Almost the Same," *New Yorker* 70, no. 2 (Feb. 28, 1994): 61–71. Muhammed also established one of the currently most notorious subjects in this respect, the role of Jews as slave traders and slave holders, by estimating that 75 percent of enslaved Africans were owned by Jews. (The real rate is approximately 3 percent, according to Michael Lerner, "Victims and Victimizers: Farrakhan's Jewish Problem," *Tikkun* 9, no. 2 [1994]: 9; see also Ralph A. Austen, "The Uncomfortable Relationship: African Enslavement in the Common History of Blacks and Jews," *Tikkun* 9, no. 2 [1994]: 65–8, 86.)

the interpretation of a concept of normative neutral differentiations as normative oppositions by both spokesmen and opponents of the diversity approach. But, of course, the peaceful patchwork approach is somewhat idealistic and idyllic since it does not adequately consider the fact that cultural conflicts are not only about attitudes and prejudice but also about power and the distribution of opportunity.

THE CASE OF GERMANY

Whereas American political identity is founded on the common possession of a set of genuinely political ideas, the traditional German identity rests primarily on the nonpolitical and supposedly primordial factors of homogeneous ethnicity and common language and culture. It has often been pointed out that until the present day the German concept of citizenship has depended on the atavistic principle of blood ties.[29] Even in the forty years during which two ideologically antagonistic German states existed, both regimes agreed on the continued existence of a common *Kulturnation.* The history of Germany as a nation-state is in fact the history of its permanent redefinition in terms of territory and in terms of its political system. The establishment of a German cultural nationalism preceded the foundation of a political nationalism – or, to put it more precisely, the construction of political nationalism used the notion of cultural nationalism as a strategically legitimating tool. Culture remained the dominant source of national identity in a society that could not develop a reliable system of political norms and assumptions. This is most obvious when we consider the pantheon of German national heroes. They are either cultural heroes – foremost Goethe and Schiller – or legendary heroes that emerge from the deep and dark world of ancient Teutonic myths.[30]

Discredited by the Nazis and dysfunctional in a Western-oriented and

---

29 Nevertheless, the traditional link between citizenship status and ancestry has recently been challenged. In response to the demographic realities of Germany's immigrant population, the third generation of "guest workers" is now legally entitled to apply for German citizenship. This reform is the first major step in the erosion of the traditional *jus sanguinis* definition of German national identity and may, in the long term, ultimately change its frame of reference.

30 During the nineteenth and the first half of the twentieth century, German nationalism used Hermann, Barbarossa, or – less successfully – the Nibelungs as a mythical frame of reference for the conceptualization of Germanness. See Wulf Wülfing, Karin Bruns, and Rolf Parr, *Historische Mythologie der Deutschen, 1798–1914* (Munich, 1991); Andreas Dörner, "Die Inszenierung politischer Mythen: Ein Beitrag zur Funktion der symbolischen Formen in der Politik am Beispiel des Hermannsmythos in Deutschland," *Politische Vierteljahresschrift* 34, no. 2 (1993): 199–218; Herfried Münkler and Wolfgang Storch, *Siegfrieden: Politik mit einem Deutschen Mythos* (Berlin, 1988).

rapidly modernizing Germany, the tradition of the mythologization of Germanness broke off after World War II. What remained is the legal concept of German citizenship as a matter of blood and the cultural concept of cultural heritage and homogeneity. Nationalism as a tool of political integration generally was rejected and replaced by a mode of political integration based on the political, social, and economic success of the Federal Republic. But the fact that the overwhelming support for democratic institutions in West Germany was accompanied by a unique economic success story also induced the assumption of a causal relationship and therefore the fear that German democracy could be seriously challenged by an economic crisis. It remained unclear whether or not Germany was developing a democratic identity that would protect the system against the withdrawal of loyalty in times of crisis – whether the support for democracy was merely instrumental or owing to genuine democratization of political assumptions.

During the first two decades of the history of the Federal Republic, the most crucial determinations of German national identity – Nazism and the Holocaust – were a well-protected taboo, based on what Lübbe affirmatively called the "asymmetric discretion" between those involved and those not involved in Nazism.[31] That changed radically with the student movement of the 1960s. The establishment of a nexus between Auschwitz and every later reference to the semantic field of the nation as an integrative tool is among the most important achievements of the student movement. Since the memory of National Socialism effectively blocked the positive use of nationalism as a source of identity, the legitimation of the democratic West German state depended largely on its efficiency. Thus, the parameters of success – economic growth and prosperity, individual wealth, social peace, and international recognition – became the very symbols of a rational and sober state. Eventual attempts at a renationalization of German self-interpretation and politics in the early and mid 1980s – the so-called *Historikerstreit*, for example – were widely unsuccessful.

The whole pattern changed in the aftermath of the dissolution of the GDR and German unification. First, the unification of the two German states inevitably set the agenda for revisiting the question of national self-interpretation. Second, the enormous financial transfers from western to eastern Germany and the claim for western solidarity with the eastern

---

31 Hermann Lübbe, "50 Jahre danach – Der Nationalsozialismus im politischen Bewusstsein der Gegenwart," *1933 – Deutschlands Weg in die Diktatur: Internationale Konferenz zur nationalsozialistischen Machtübernahme* (Berlin, 1983).

parts of the country could be legitimated only with reference to that German national identity that had not played very much of a role during the preceding four decades. Third, the resulting economic dislocations challenged the parameters of success that used to stabilize the old Federal Republic. Finally, the influx of immigrants from former Warsaw Pact countries – both asylum seekers and people who claimed German citizenship because of German ancestors – confronted a people already in a state of uncertainty and disorientation with the question of how to deal with other people who were visually and culturally different. The results are well known: Germany at present is a country unsure of its basic political options both within the international framework and at home, one that is deeply divided between east and west, between integrationists and national exclusivists, and over the question of its self-interpretation and identity.

A survey of some of the most relevant newspapers and magazines shows that the resulting discourses on political identity, and political and social integration and disintegration, are organized along the dimensions of eastern versus western Germans, Germans versus non-Germans, and the political and the historical self-understanding of the newly unified Germany. These discourses deal with various current events and the shaping of possible future policies for the cultural, social, political, and economic process of unification. Examples are the wave of xenophobic, anti-Semitic, and racist attacks that has swept Germany since 1989 and the related debates on the asylum guarantee for the victims of political repression;[32] the redefinition of German citizenship and revision of immigration laws; the struggle over Germany's future role in international politics, and the debates over internal political alienation and the general question of the relation between state and civil society. Finally, complicating the discussion, the discourses also cover the nation's historical self-interpretation in Hitler's fading shadow.

Nation, History, Normality

"Deutschland in der Zeitmaschine,"[33] *Zeitenwende*, change, turning point, threshold, end, and beginning – many of the keywords of the post-unification discourse on political and historical self-interpretation indicate

32 This debate, meanwhile, has come to an end with the de facto abandonment of the asylum guarantee.
33 This sentence recurs as a kind of leitmotif in the title and at the beginning of each major paragraph – there are three of them – in the fourteen-page essay of Michael Müller and Wolfgang

a vital consciousness of historical acceleration and break – after 1918, 1933, and 1945, the fourth fundamental break in this century – and thus contribute to what we might call the fragmentation of identity *in time*. Generally, the disappearance of Germany's political division as a constant reminder of the consequences of Germany's hypertrophic nationalism is considered to mark the end of the postwar era. It is much less clear what this might mean for the political and historical self-consciousness of Germans.

The commonly used categorical system for the political self-description of Germany in relation to its history is the opposition of normality versus anormality or normality versus pathology. This is the underlying rationale of such theoretical topoi as the "German *Sonderweg*" or the "belated nation,"[34] the widespread practice of the Weimar analogy ("Bonn ist nicht Weimar"[35] or "Das Weimar-Syndrom"),[36] the conflicting assessments of the legitimacy of national pride and patriotism, and various policies in the field of international relations. It was also the basic argument of the notorious *Historikerstreit*, which focused on the "historicization" versus the "incomparability" of National Socialism, or the "normalization" of German history.[37] The normality versus anormality dispositive usually defines the prevailing position of Germany and the Germans in relation to their National Socialist past, with the Third Reich as the ideal pathology. The ideal normality, in contrast, is an assumed state in which German politics would finally be free of the limitations and concerns brought about by the experience of Nazism and would "step out of Hitler's shadow," to use a popular phrase. One of the major issues of the current "historical identity" discourse is whether the fact of unification and the end of the postwar era is to be considered as a step toward "normalization" of German conditions, or whether the accompanying upheavals – mass unemployment, the federal deficit, the falling off of broad-based support for the political system, the crisis of the party system, and, above all and most disturbing, the wave of neo-Nazi violence and the increase in xenophobic attitudes – indicate a step toward denormalization.

Thierse, "Deutschland in der Zeitmaschine," in Christoph Hein et al., eds., *Deutsche Ansichten: Die Republik im Übergang* (Bonn, 1992), 11, 17, 22.

34 Thus the title of the book by Helmuth Plessner, *Die verspätete Nation: über die politische Verführbarkeit bürgerlichen Geistes* (Frankfurt/Main, 1974).

35 See Fritz Rene Allemann, *Bonn ist nicht Weimar* (Cologne, 1956).

36 See Volker Ulrich, "Das Weimar-Syndrom," *Die Zeit* 48, no. 28 (July 9, 1993): 28.

37 See the documentation of the major contributions: *"Historikerstreit": Die Dokumentation der Kontroverse um die Einzigartigkeit der nationalsozialistischen Judenvernichtung* (Munich, 1987).

The normalization versus denormalization dispositive bases the political discourse on a whole variety of issues: constitutional reform, Germany's role in international politics and foreign military missions, immigration politics, European integration, and so on. Unfortunately, the normality versus anormality binary produces quite a complex structure that is hardly consistent with other systems of classification such as conservative versus progressive or right versus left. Nevertheless, there seems to be some underlying pattern in the application of the normality versus anormality dispositive. My thesis is that (1) conservatives tend to hold the normalization view in a macroscopic perspective as far as Germany as a whole and its role in international politics are concerned and see denormalization at work in several perspectives on the microscopic level of domestic issues, whereas (2) the Left insists on the anormality position in general and claims normality for certain issues. In between are (3) dissidents, mostly on the Left, who feel the urge to redefine their political assumptions in the light of the revolutionary change Germany and the world underwent in the recent past.

1. The conservative and national-liberal camp interprets the fact of German unification and unified Germany's future role in the international framework as a matter of normalization. From this perspective, not only the existence of two antagonistic German states but also the totality of the political results of World War II – Germany's limited sovereignty, its restraint in international politics, a special moral obligation to provide asylum to oppressed people, and, in rare cases, even the politics of strict orientation to the West – constituted an anormality that at the end of the postwar era must be overcome. Normalization in this sense means – mostly implicitly, sometimes explicitly – the restitution of past conditions. The focus therefore shifts from supranational consensus toward national interest, growing skepticism about European integration and decreasing willingness to transfer national sovereignty to institutions of the European Union (EU), stronger impetus for EU expansion as opposed to EU extension, a revival of the topic of the "land in the middle" in a geopolitical sense (which is the traditional symbolization of a special German role between East and West and expresses reservations against "Western" rationalism as well as ideas of German domination in Eastern Europe), and occasionally doubts about whether the old Federal Republic's Western orientation is still appropriate for the newly unified Germany.[38] Whereas normalization here means renationalization of

---

38 Thus, the neoconservative authors Zitelmann, Weissmann, and Grossheim pledge that Germany's

politics, anormality is claimed for those political restrictions in German politics that reflect moral obligations Germany had taken over after, and as a consequence of, National Socialism and are now considered a legacy of its postwar conditions, that is, the generous and far-reaching asylum law and the strict limitations on military action.[39]

From a conservative-nationalist perspective, unification marks the national catharsis of Germany and demands the redefinition of its self-understanding as well as its material politics according to its newly developed "national interest." The restorative character of that claim for national normality is visible in the resurrection of the rhetoric of German political romanticism, which was thought to be permanently discredited. Arnulf Baring interpreted the unification as the revival of Bismarck's Germany; Botho Strauss claimed that we, "in our liberal-libertarian self-referentiality," cannot understand anymore that "a people wants to maintain its moral law against another and is ready to bring blood sacrifices for that purpose."[40] And, in a review essay about a book on the reason for Germany's Western orientation, Heinrich August Winkler was reminded of the rhetoric of the so-called "Conservative Revolution" during the Weimar Republic:

Nowhere is it more obvious than here, where the supposed demythologization of the West can lead to: back to the German myths of the interwar period. Even in the style of language there appears to be an echo of that "conservative revolution" that, during the Weimar Republic, called for a struggle for German self-assertion.[41]

2. Like the conservatives, the Left and left-wing liberals also discuss the relation between history and identity in unified Germany by applying the normality-anormality dispositive. But the conservatives' anormality is the Left's normality, and vice versa. From a liberal perspective, the

---

Western orientation has "almost the character of a political utopia aimed at the totalitarian penetration of the whole society" (Rainer Zitelmann, Karlheinz Weissmann, and Michael Grossheim, "Einleitung," in Rainer Zitelmann, Karlheinz Weissmann, and Michael Grossheim, eds., *Westbindung: Chancen und Risiken für Deutschland* [Frankfurt/Main, 1993]).

39 In the context of anormality and asylum law, it is interesting and revealing that the federal government introduced the term *Asylnotstand* (emergency refuge) into the debate over altering the asylum article 16 of the *Grundgesetz* (Basic Law), thus emphasizing the allegedly "anormal" situation caused by the existing law; see also Friedrich Karl Fromme, "Noch kein Notstand," *Frankfurter Allgemeine Zeitung*, Nov. 3, 1992.

40 Author's translation. The original quotation is "Dass ein Volk sein Sittengesetz gegen andere behaupten will und dafür bereit ist, Blutopfer zu bringen, das verstehen wir nicht mehr und halten es in unserer liberal-libertären Selbstbezogenheit für falsch und verwerflich" (Botho Strauss, "Anschwellender Bocksgesang," *Der Spiegel* 47, no. 6 [1993]: 202).

41 Heinrich August Winkler, "Westbindung oder was sonst? Bemerkungen zu einem Revisionsversuch," *Politische Vierteljahresschrift* 35, no. 1 (1994): 117.

break with the German tradition of political romanticism and *völkisch* nationalism, the strict Western orientation, and a political identity based on the political values outlined in the constitution and institutionalized in the political order – "Verfassungspatriotismus," as Habermas calls it with reference to Dolf Sternberger[42] – constitute a still fragile state of relatively normal liberal democracy that developed in the old Federal Republic, especially after 1968, and must be maintained and strengthened in the future. Hence, it is not Germany's division after the war that constitutes its pathology, but the history of aggressive nationalism that culminated in Nazism and, as a by-product, led to the country's division into two states. The historic singularity of National Socialist crimes is considered a permanent delegitimation of the German nationalist tradition; and the relative normality established in the postwar era depends exactly on the absence of a conventionally constructed national identity. Therefore, by insisting on the persistent national anormality of a people responsible for Auschwitz, the Left and liberals reject conservative attempts to renationalize German politics and political culture. This notion of anormality also supports the Left's resistance against the redefinition of Germany's military role: Past aggression carried an obligation to practice current and future restraint.

Thus, whereas the big picture is one of the anormality of German nationalism and national identity, the Left de-emphasizes and de-dramatizes the Right's fear of ethnic heterogeneity as it is expressed in the debates on asylum and citizenship law by pointing out Germany's dependence on immigration and the empirical normality of heterogeneous societies.[43] Moreover, the pro-immigration and promulticulturalism position of the German Left plays a strategic role in the taming of the nationalist

42 See Dolf Sternberger, "Verfassungspatriotismus: Rede bei der 25-Jahr-Feier der 'Akademie für Politische Bildung,'" in Dolf Sternberger, *Verfassungspatriotismus*, Schriften 10 (Frankfurt/Main, 1990), 17–31. In this 1982 speech, Sternberger explicitly attempts to separate patriotism from nationalism and designate the Basic Law as the new point of reference. Habermas adopted the term in 1986 in his reply to Ernst Nolte, "Vergangenheit, die nicht vergehen will," *Frankfurter Allgemeine Zeitung*, June 6, 1986, the text that basically initiated the *Historikerstreit*. Here Habermas calls "Germany's unconditional opening toward the West the great intellectual achievement of the postwar era" and links it to *Verfassungspatriotismus* (loyalty to the constitution) as "the only kind of patriotism that will not alienate us from the West." See Jürgen Habermas, "Apologetische Tendenzen," in Jürgen Habermas, *Eine Art Schadensabwicklung* (Frankfurt/Main, 1987), 120–36, 135. The text was first published in *Die Zeit*, July 11, 1986, under the title "Eine Art Schadensabwicklung."

43 In light of the normality-anormality dispositive, the German government's often-criticized insistence on Germany as a "nonimmigration country," against all empirical evidence, makes sense: It excludes immigration from the ruling concept of what should be considered "normal" and delegitimates all demands for a liberal practice in immigration policy. As such, the notion is less descriptive than imperative, less an interpretation of reality than an attempt to shape reality.

beast: It serves the attempt to redefine political identity by replacing the *völkisch* concept of a nation of common heritage, both culturally and biologically, with a mode of integration that is based on the liberal-democratic pattern of universalist values, and that finds its symbolic expression in the emphasis on a normatively elevated "civil society."

3. The breakdown of socialism and the unification of Germany threw the Left into a deep crisis of self-confidence and self-interpretation. The ongoing discourse on "What's Left?"[44] is far from reaching a consensus. Meanwhile, the former leftist dogma of an "open-door policy" on asylum and immigration has given way to a more differentiated position that tries to preserve the core of asylum law while admitting certain limitations and, as a countermove, that demands redefinition of the citizenship law and introduction of an immigration law. At the same time, there are some indications that even liberal and leftist suggestions for a more modern concept of citizenship do not completely abandon the German tradition, which frames citizenship as a quality that is normatively loaded and founded on primordial categories of inclusiveness. Thus, discussions on supposed conflicts between a German civil society and the allegedly premodern, unsecularized, Islam-based and even fundamentalistic political culture of Turks living in Germany refer to citizenship as a matter of who one is and what one thinks, a matter of membership in a community rather than in a polity. Also, the fact that dual citizenship became the major battleground for attempts to change German citizenship law shows that even the reformers stick to a concept of citizenship that is not free of notions of a quasi-natural affiliation to one's national descent.

Even more delicate is the question of foreign military missions. Whereas the Left unanimously rejects sovereign German decisions on military actions other than defense, there is a deep cleavage between supporters and opponents of German participation in UN peace-keeping missions. This conflict emerged first in the context of the Gulf War when, for example, Enzensberger called Saddam "Hitler's reincarnation."[45] In the proceedings of this inner-left discussion, the opponents of any military intervention introduced the new classification of "pacifists versus belligerents," the latter a neologism for all those who principally

44 Thus the title of the book by Norberto Bobbio, Antje Vollmer, and Tony Judt, eds., *What's Left? Prognosen zur Linken* (Berlin, 1993), which collects essays on the Left, most of which originally were published by the *Frankfurter Allgemeine Zeitung*. See also Bernd Guggenberger and Klaus Jansen, eds., *Die Mitte: Neuvermessungen in Politik und Kultur* (Opladen, 1993).

45 The original notion was "Hitlers Wiedergänger." See Hans-Magnus Enzensberger, "Hitlers Wiedergänger," *Der Spiegel* 45, no. 6 (1991): 26–8.

considered military action a legitimate means of political action. The issue was on the agenda after the war in Bosnia started, and the Left's support for military action has since been growing. The ironic dialectic of the relation between ethic responsibility and military action was on display when a delegation from the German Green Party recently tried to convince Washington of the necessity of military intervention in Bosnia, while arguing against German military participation in just such a mission. In any case, the fact that many on the Left have abandoned the principally pacifist position that emerged during the era of bloc confrontation as a response to the threat of nuclear war indicates a considerable political convergence between left and right.

National Identity, Liberal Democracy, Civil Society

With respect to political identity as the cultural foundation of political integration, we can distinguish two largely different conceptions within the current discourse. The political Right thinks of political identity in terms of national identity (which, given the traditional German concept of nationhood, means identity based on blood ties and common culture); the Left argues in favor of a "postconventional identity" based on a system of commonly shared political assumptions, namely, norms and values and proper processes and institutions to maintain and enforce them as a result of the permanent self-constitution of the civil society.

The prerequisite for political identity as national identity is a positive national consciousness combined with the institutional framework of the nation-state. The restitution of national consciousness under Germany's current circumstances requires, first, the breakup of the Nazism-nationalism nexus and, second, the restoration of the traditional source of German nationalism, namely, cultural and ethnic homogeneity. The conservatives' tools to dissociate Nazism and nationalism are the qualification and normalization of fascism in a horizontal and a vertical dimension: horizontally by comparison with other "evils," above all Stalinism, and vertically by emphasizing the positive achievements of Germany's national history.[46] The conservative support for the concept of cultural and ethnic homogeneity of the Germans – which is actually a myth largely independent

---

46 The project of reacquiring history as a source of national identity started around 1982, when Kohl took office and promised a "geistig-moralische Wende." Its major episodes have so far been Bitburg, the *Historikerstreit*, the founding of national museums in Bonn and Berlin, the reburial of Frederick the Great in Potsdam, and the rededication of Schinkel's "Neue Wache" in Berlin as a national memorial.

of reality – translates politically into a defensive position on immigration and citizenship law. Thus, according to conservatives' own interpretation, their fears of ethnic and cultural heterogeneity are not the result of animosity against foreigners but reflect a demand for national distinctiveness and uniqueness. (Nevertheless, this position serves the manifest xenophobia of the far right, since it produces a predisposition to hold foreigners generally responsible for ethnic tensions, even when the roles of aggressors and victims are as clearly defined as they in fact are in the current wave of antiforeigner attacks.) Institutionally, the rationale of *political identity as national identity* enforces skepticism against further European integration in order to preserve the sovereignty of the nation-state. Interestingly, the reasons that are given for this skepticism mostly do not refer to issues of technical, bureaucratic, and economic practicability and efficiency, but stress identity and homogeneity as preconditions for democratic government. Peter Graf Kielmansegg, for example, refers to the democratic principle of majority rule and claims that the minority can accept the legitimacy of majority decisions only if there is consciousness of a collective identity:

Why does an overruled minority accept the decision? When does an overruled minority accept this decision? In other words, under which conditions will the legitimacy of majority rule be accepted reliably enough to keep the democratic decision-making process functioning? . . . Obviously, the majority's decision will only be accepted as legitimate as a matter of course if there is a sense of a common collective identity that transcends majority/minority and that prevents the majority's decision from being perceived as an act of heteronomy.[47]

The fact that this skepticism, especially in the Christian Social Union and in considerable parts of the Christian Democratic Union, emerged shortly after German reunification is not surprising, since recovery of Germany's full national sovereignty in 1990 provided for the first time a realistic institutional foundation for traditional national politics. In this context, relinquishing sovereignty to EU institutions only recently regained from the Allies of World War II is a painful process.

The German Left has so far shown little interest in the question of political integration on the national level[48] and now focuses on the re-

47 Peter Graf Kielmansegg, "Ein Mass für die Grösse des Staates," *Frankfurter Allgemeine Zeitung*, Dec. 2, 1992, 35. Similar, if less elaborated, is Nonnenmacher's argumentation: "Die Bürger wollen kein technokratisches Europa, sondern ein demokratisches; der Raum, in dem demokratische Verantwortung glaubhaft vermittelt werden kann, ist bis auf weiteres der Nationalstaat" (Günther Nonnenmacher, "Frankreichs Lehren für Europa," *Frankfurter Allgemeine Zeitung*, Sept. 22, 1992).
48 This notion is valid mainly for a younger generation on the Left that has been socialized and acculturated in the Federal Republic. It is certainly not true for members of an older genera-

placement of the reemerging nationalist mode of identification with a still vague concept represented by the buzzwords of civil society and multiculturalism. "Civil society" owes its brilliant career to the utopian vacuum of the Left after the demise of socialism, on the one hand, and to the impulses of successful civil self-organization during the break-up of state socialist regimes in Eastern Europe, on the other. Within less than a decade, the concept became a powerful symbol that merges a holos of associations. These include naive hopes for a less violent and more civilized society (as it is represented in the political practice of civil self-organization on the grassroots level), as well as elaborate concepts that emerge from the discourses of experts on social philosophy and the democratic theory – where the common denominator is the radical sec-ularization of the legitimating foundations of politics: the replacement of transcendent *pouvoir constituant* with the self-constitution of the society of active citizens.[49]

The public discourse, however, perceived "civil society" as a reimport from Eastern Europe, where its significant role as a frame of reference for the civil movements at the dawn of the socialist regimes had associated it with a highly normative and almost utopian program. Thus, it was well prepared to become the slogan of a deeply irritated Left and to prepare it for its reconciliation with a liberal tradition purified of its infection with capitalism. As a matter of fact, categories of interest and economy have been largely absent from the civil society discourse.[50] The "round-tables" – informal ad hoc institutions that spread all over Eastern Europe during the period of transition from communism – and Václav Havel, the "writer-president," were taken as representations of the potential for a civil society; yet the mixed experience of the roundtables, as well as the civic movements, which soon had to make room for conventional political parties as the main intermediate institutions of representative

---

tion, such as Willy Brandt, who in 1989 was perhaps the West German political figure most gen-uinely moved by the sudden chance of unification.

49 On the current scholarly debate on civil society, see, e.g., Ulrich Rödel, Günter Frankenberg, and Helmut Dubiel, *Die demokratische Frage: Ein Essay* (Frankfurt/Main, 1989); Ulrich Rödel, ed., *Autonome Gesellschaft und libertäre Demokratie* (Frankfurt/Main, 1990); Volker Heins, "Ambivalen-zen der Zivilgesellschaft," *Politische Vierteljahresschrift* 33, no. 2 (1992): 235–42; Rainer Schmalz-Bruns, "Civil Society – ein postmodernes Kunstprodukt? Eine Antwort auf Volker Heins," *Politische Vierteljahresschrift* 33, no. 2 (1992): 243–55.

50 The concept, as perceived in Germany, refers largely to the neo-Aristotelian republicanism of Hannah Arendt and therefore bears an idealistic bias that so far makes it largely incompatible with the categories of material interest. In fact, in the context of the civil society debate, refer-ences to the polis democracy of the Greek classic are just around the corner. For example, see Bernd Guggenberger, "Die politische Aktualität des Ästhetischen," *Leviathan* 21, no. 1 (1993): 146–61.

democracies, did not diminish the fascination of the civil society idea. Nevertheless, however vague the concept, it might very well become highly relevant in the future for the constitution of a genuinely political and postconventional identity in Germany.

Multiculturalism, which as a buzzword has been around in the German discourse considerably longer than *civil society*, initially meant not much more than a response to popular antiforeigner resentments. It mainly signified a foreigner-friendly attitude on the part of alternative subcultures – by then almost exclusively represented by the Green Party – and general support for an open-door policy on immigration. In this sense, the earlier notion of multiculturalism had a touch of romanticism and idealism. It did not really reject the classification of people according to their ethnic and cultural background, but only reversed it by replacing negative with positive resentments.[51] Thus, it failed to address the major issue of the cultural institutionalization of tolerance in the absence of empathy. This theoretical and empirical deficit diminished when the multiculturalism debate merged with the discourse on civil society, since the focus now shifted from habitual friendliness toward the principles of political integration and participation in a democratic society. The idea of the civil society thus provides the background to discuss ethnic and cultural diversity with respect to the demands of a postnationalist political culture. Similarly, it also offers a normative reference point for the overdue discussion of a redefinition of the German concept of citizenship as well as for the outlining of future immigration policy.

FRAGMENTATION AND INTEGRATION IN COMPARATIVE PERSPECTIVE

The material examined here, as well as the selectivity of the topics discussed so far, is certainly insufficient for a systematic comparison of the integration-fragmentation discourses in Germany and the United States. Nevertheless, it should be possible to lay out an exploratory outline in comparative perspective.

Some similarities of both discourses reflect social and political constellations that are not specifically American or German but rather characterize the conditions of late modernity in general. The shift from class to culture as the predominant category of analysis does not mainly reflect, as

---

51 Thus, the *Ausländerbeauftragte* (official in charge of resident foreigners) in Berlin started a campaign entitled "Mein Freund ist ein Ausländer" (My friend is a foreigner).

is often maintained, the delegitimization of communist ideology through the breakdown of state socialism. As a matter of fact, this shift had begun long before state socialism's imminent demise. One of the landmarks of this shift was the emergence of a postmaterialist set of values, which Ronald Inglehart characterized as a "Silent Revolution." In Inglehart's theory, postmaterialism corresponds to a postindustrial cleavage structure, as materialism corresponds to an industrial society.[52] Inglehart also pointed out that this new postindustrial cleavage, although it cancels out the industrial cleavage, does not in the same way affect enduring preindustrial cleavages such as "religion, race, and other ethnic ties"[53] and thus anticipated precisely those variables that determine the cultural unities of today's multiculturalism and diversity movements.

The shift from class to culture is based primarily on the assumption of a postindustrial existence that includes the dialectics of globalization and fragmentation; and in both discourses we find an interpretation of this dialectic that emphasizes the growing demand for cultural and ethnic distinctiveness in order to create protected refuges of cultural and ethnic identity in an increasingly homogenized world.[54] The underlying rationale is that of globalization versus fundamentalism, and it is thought to correspond to the clashes between particularistic ethnic and cultural groups on a worldwide scale, as well as the fragmentation within each individual society and even within local communities and neighborhoods. It is quite common, for example, to label gang fights over territory in American inner cities as expressions of a "new tribalism," and eventually someone else discovers a potential "Bosnia *en miniature* in every subway car."[55]

Postmodernity is another and closely related general trend that influences the respective discourses in both countries. I use the term here in a very broad sense to cover that cultural totality that relates time diagnoses like the postindustrial society, information society, simulation

52 See Ronald Inglehart, *The Silent Revolution: Changing Values and Political Styles Among Western Publics* (Princeton, N.J., 1976). For other major contributions to the 1970s and 1980s debate on changing values, voting behavior, and party affiliation, see Norman H. Nie, Sidney Verba, and John R. Petrocik, *The Changing American Voter* (Cambridge, Mass., 1976); and Helmut Klages and Peter Kmieciak, eds., *Wertwandel und gesellschaftlicher Wandel* (Frankfurt/Main, 1984).

53 Inglehart, *Silent Revolution*, 216.

54 See Samuel P. Huntington, "The Clash of Civilizations?" *Foreign Affairs* 72, no. 3 (1993): 22–49; Benjamin R. Barber, "Jihad vs. McWorld," *Atlantic Monthly* 269, no. 3 (Mar. 1992); Hans Magnus Enzensberger, "Ausblicke auf den Bürgerkrieg," *Der Spiegel* 47, no. 25 (1993): 170–5; Norberto Bobbio, "Die Linke und ihre Zweifel: Eine Bestandsaufnahme," in Bobbio, Vollmer, and Judt, *What's Left?*, 18–19.

55 The original is "Auf diese Weise kann jeder U-Bahn-Wagen zu einem Bosnien en miniature werden" (Enzensberger, "Ausblicke," 172).

society, communication society, postmaterialism, postconventionalism, and various other "postisms" with theoretical approaches like poststructuralism and deconstruction and with political concepts like the civil society, diversity, and multiculturalism. Since postmodernism is often used in a normatively loaded sense, I want to point out that I use it in a largely descriptive manner and want to subsume theories and standpoints into that category – whether their respective advocates would accept this label or not.[56] The relation between postmodernism and modernity is dialectical. Whereas the term expresses a sense of discontinuity, at the same time it includes modernity within itself as its significant other.

As far as the integration-fragmentation discourses explored here are concerned, the influence of postmodernism is visible mainly in the diversity framework in the United States and in the civil society-multiculturalism dispositive in Germany. In both cases, these discourses are located left of center. Owing to the more positive reputation postmodernism enjoys among the American Left, the category is more likely to be applied as a self-interpretation. More important than the question of labeling is the fact that the American discourse on diversity and the German discourse on civil society aim at a redefinition of the respective modes of political socialization and integration. Whereas diversity rejects the traditional assimilationist melting-pot myth as well as the "color blindness" dictum of the modernist civil rights movement of the 1950s and 1960s, instead fostering the coexistence of diverse cultures, the German discourse on civil society focuses on the secularization of the normative foundations of democracy and challenges the culturalist-racist German conception of *Volk* nationality as its metaphysical derivative. Multiculturalism supplements the civil society discourse insofar as it shifts the focus from the legitimating foundations of democracy in general to the civil rights of those who so far do not meet the categorical imperatives of Germanness in particular.

56 The reputation of postmodernism in Germany is generally worse than in the United States. It is therefore not so easy – at least outside the linguistics departments – to find intellectuals willing to accept the label. Postmodernity in Germany is considered to be anti-Enlightenment, affirmative, and neo-conservative on the one hand, eclectic and frivolous on the other. As far as I can see, it is mainly Jürgen Habermas who deserves credit for the postmodernity-neoconservative nexus (see Jürgen Habermas, *Die Neue Unübersichtlichkeit* [Frankfurt/Main, 1985], esp. the two essays under the common title of "Neokonservativismus," 11–56). I want to point out that Habermas himself would actually fit into my usage of the term postmodernism. His theory of communicative action, which rests on the decentering of the subject of philosophy, as well as his adoption of the concept of postconventional identity and his focus on *Lebenswelt* as the endangered part of the dichotomy "system-*Lebenswelt*," make him at least a partial postmodernist in this very broad and non-normative sense. Klaus von Beyme, e.g., locates Habermas "between modernity and postmodernity." See Klaus von Beyme, *Theorie der Politik im 20. Jahrhundert: Von der Moderne zur Postmoderne* (Frankfurt/Main, 1991), 252, 260–76.

Whereas the relation of the American diversity movement to postmodernity is indisputable, things are considerably more complicated in the case of Germany's discourse on civil society. Although this discourse shows indisputable postmodern elements – such as the idea of the autonomous self-constitution of society, or the problem of balancing the demands of particular groups and needs of the society with the communicative competence of the citizens and their associations – it remains a decisively modernist discourse insofar as the secularization of political legitimation through universal values is modern. This observation indicates an asynchronicity – *Ungleichzeitigkeit* (asynchronicity) in Bloch's sense – of the respective discourses. Since its founding, the United States has been based on a radical political secularization that in Germany is still a work in progress.[57] German notions of national identity and citizenship must be thought of as premodern, whereas their American counterparts are objectifications of classic modernity. And whereas the German discourse on civil society, as far as questions of citizenship are concerned, tries to elevate Germany from a premodern to a modern level, the American diversity discourse, as far as questions of cultural coexistence are concerned, struggles to transform a modern concept into a postmodern one.

Thus, the major opponents in the American discourse on integration and fragmentation can be described as cultural modernists and postmodernists, whereas in the German case cultural premodernists square off against modernists and postmodernists. This cultural asynchronicity also explains why the notions of civil society and multiculturalism can be located on the same (progressive) side of the German discourse and on opposing sides of the American discourse. American multiculturalism acts within a society that considers itself "civil" and unified by a common civil religion; its critics attack the difference between the proclaimed universalism and the real particularist distribution of access to power, social status, and so on. Programmatically, multiculturalism tries to overcome

---

57 I am oversimplifying here. First, the secularization of the state in the United States was dialectically intertwined with a theologization of politics. Brumidi's "Apotheosis of Washington," which decorates the Great Rotunda of the U.S. Capitol, illustrates most colorfully the success and the empirical validity of the civil-religion concept quoted above. Second, the secularization of the foundations of political legitimation certainly does not mean that modernism captured the whole population. Many kinds of nativist and racist movements demonstrate the persistence of premodernism. But it is still true that the United States, for better or worse, has always had to rely on the self-constitution of society that the civil-society discourse proclaims for contemporary Germany, and that fact explains why German civil-society advocates refer so often to the act of democratic self-foundation in the American Revolution. Similarly, to categorize the German concept of national identity as premodern is oversimplifying. Although certain changes of citizenship law in the last few years have weakened the determination of nationality through blood ties, they have not abandoned it altogether.

the particularist reproduction of the given power structure by strengthening the particularist identity of minorities and demanding their equal
share – and occasionally more – of the economic, social, and cultural
surplus. Within the German framework, multiculturalism and the notion
of cultural and ethnic diversity serve as tools for dismantling the traditional concept of cultural and ethnic homogeneity by proving its lack
of empirical validity, and for fostering a concept of political integration
that is based on a universal political ethic instead of the bonds of blood
and culture.

The different status of multiculturalism in the two discourses is also
reflected in different systems of classification for cultural and ethnic
groups. In the American case, with the introduction of diversity as a
major competitor in the discursive field, the traditional binary distinction between white and black – which basically signifies white versus
nonwhite – was overcome and replaced by a more complex system
that is attuned to the various cultural and ethnic groups on the scene.
Although the effects of the older binary code are still observable in many
ways,[58] legitimate participation in the discourse requires the use of the
newer and more sophisticated system not only for the supporters of the
diversity movement, but also for its liberal and conservative opponents.
In the German case, the binary code of Germans versus non-Germans is
still in place – even on the side of the advocates of multiculturalism.[59]
This lack of differentiation does not reflect a lack of diversity, but simply
the largely instrumental character of non-German cultures within a discourse that is mainly about Germanness.

If, as suggested above, we think of the construction of political identity
as essentially a two-dimensional process, with historical self-interpretation
as the vertical axis and political integration as the horizontal axis, then it
is possible to compare the structure of the respective discourses on identity in relation to these two axes. The dominant axis of the German discourse is history, whereas the dominant axis of the American discourse
is integration. The German discourse is mainly about the interpretation
of history and the production of a meaningful tradition, whereas the
respective positions on diversity and integration – multiculturalism on

---

58 See Jack Miles, "Blacks vs. Browns: The Struggle for the Bottom Rung," *Atlantic Monthly* 270,
   no. 4 (Oct. 1992): 41–68; Hacker, *Two Nations*, 10–11. A good example of the potentially bizarre
   outcomes from the coexistence of both, the classification of race and ethnicity, is the U.S. Census, which in an effort to adjust to new needs without abandoning old classifications, was forced
   to introduce a "Hispanic" race.
59 See Zafer Senocak, "Die ethnische Brille der Linken," *Die Tageszeitung*, Apr. 11, 1994, 10.

the one hand and fear of cultural alienation on the other – are treated as dependent variables. Thus, for progressives the history of Germany's aggressive nationalism demands the abandonment of the nation as the frame of reference of its political identity and a multicultural redefinition of its self-understanding.[60] The conservative counterargument is that this kind of identity has no tradition in Germany and therefore cannot qualify as a source of integration; on the contrary, it is the history of the German nation that demands the preservation of a discernible cultural and ethnic homogeneity. The structure of the American discourse is the converse. Here the matter under discussion is the horizontal axis of integration, whereas the vertical axis of history mainly delivers arguments for one or the other side in the debate over the main issue.[61]

These structures reflect a hierarchy of problems: The German discourse is predominantly about history because the main threat to its identity is its fragmentation in time, or as Plesser's still valid notion on the late nineteenth century puts it, "not a lack, but an oversupply, a competition of too many incompatible traditions" is what produces the need for historical legitimation.[62] The American discourse is able to use history as a source of legitimation for arguments referring to the horizontal axis of political identity because it so far has been much more successful in integrating a consistent interpretation of American history and tradition than in integrating the multitude of ethnic and cultural groups that make up the American nation.

Each discourse reflects and reacts to a disruption of the established reproduction of political and cultural relations on the macrolevel of its respective society. Whereas these disruptions immediately affect the integrative capacity of the political system, the search for their causes leads both discourses, again, into the sphere of culture. What is considered to be at stake is the acceptance of those norms and values that are supposed to form the core of political and social culture and guarantee the rather frictionless coexistence of individuals and groups, on the one hand, and loyalty and support for the political system, on the other. In both the German and the American cases, the loss of this ethic of common sense by both conservatives and progressives leads to the revival of a "discourse of virtues" that includes discussions on the conditions of those institutions that are supposed to instill them: the family and the school. And

---

60 This is the background of the popular bumper sticker saying, "Dear foreigners, Don't Leave Us Alone with These Germans!"
61 See, e.g., the status of "History as a Weapon" in Schlesinger, *Disuniting*, 45–72.
62 Plessner, *Verspätete Nation*, 95–6.

this might be the single most important similarity between these otherwise different discourses on identity. The field of virtues and teaching virtues is exactly the field where the conservative and progressive camps seem to converge. Whereas family values and the failure of education are traditional topics of the political Right, more and more liberal and leftist voices are joining the chorus.[63] The reason for this unanimity is, first, the general discursive shift from class to culture on both the Right and the Left and, second, the fact that the postmodernization of the Left's discourse testifies to the loss of the Left's traditional trust in redistributive policy, which is now being replaced by small-scale self-organization and social self-constitution, including the establishment of codes of good behavior in the name of sensitivity and political correctness.

Whereas there is a convergence between Left and Right regarding the general attentiveness toward virtues, the conceptions differ with respect to the bearer of virtuousness: The Left's discourse on virtue is centered on community, whereas the Right's discourse on virtues is traditionally family-centered, with abortion and illegitimacy as the symbols of decay. Liberals oppose both concepts, emphasizing categories of individual liberty over an unitary definition of the common good.

---

63 Two examples are the following: Jesse Jackson gets strongly involved in the issue of the breakup of the black family and joins the campaign against Gangsta Rap, and Claus Leggewie recently published a "Plädoyer eines Antiautoritären für Autorität" in *Die Zeit*, Mar. 5, 1993, 93, where he holds antiauthoritarian education responsible for youth violence.

PART TWO

The Social and Cultural Practice of Racism

6

Race, Class, and Southern Racial Violence

W. FITZHUGH BRUNDAGE

No observer of life in the American South during the late nineteenth and early twentieth centuries, and certainly no African American, could overlook the thread of violence woven into race relations. Lynchings, race riots, and all manner of violence defined the boundaries of black life. Between 1865 and 1950, mobs hanged, shot, burned alive, and tortured to death thousands upon thousands of African Americans.[1] Indeed, so widespread and frequent was mob violence that lynching became at once a measure of both American and southern exceptionalism. As early as 1903 James Cutler, an American sociologist, labeled lynching a distinctly American crime. He might well have added that it was an increasingly southern one. More recently, scholars of comparative race relations have reached similar conclusions; in South Africa, for example, where white racism was at least as virulent as in the American South, no comparable tradition of extralegal violence developed. With good reason, then, scholars and observers may be inclined to conclude that racist violence in the modern American South had its own unique rhythms, intensity, and form.

Antiblack violence, without question, was rooted in historically contingent economic conditions and cultural formations in the American South. Yet, by concentrating on the impulses behind antiblack violence rather than the specific form that the impulses assumed, it may be possible to see similarities with racist violence and exclusionary behavior elsewhere. Much about racist violence in the postbellum South was rooted in a struggle over work and status, as well as racial and gender identities that had parallels in other modern societies. Wherever privileges were

---

1 The best survey of antiblack violence is Herbert Shapiro, *White Violence and Black Response: From Reconstruction to Montgomery* (Amherst, Mass., 1988). See also W. Fitzhugh Brundage, *Lynching in the New South: Georgia and Virginia, 1880–1930* (Urbana, Ill., 1993); George C. Wright, *Racial Violence in Kentucky, 1865–1940: Lynchings, Mob Rule, and "Legal Lynchings"* (Baton Rouge, La., 1990).

tied to ethnicity or race, including essential privileges tied to work, the reassertion of boundaries was an ongoing trauma that necessarily accompanied modernization. The recurring contest in the South over class, racial, and gender privileges had counterparts in many other modern societies plagued by eruptions of bigotry, racism, and xenophobia.

The pathology of racial violence, despite appearances, was neither random nor entirely irrational. A brutal logic, it may be argued, underlay the violence of lynch mobs, vigilantes, and rioting whites. Because southern racial violence was a glaring symbol of black oppression as long as it endured, scholars have attempted to uncover that logic and to explain fully its role in American race relations. Recent scholarship on southern racial violence has revealed new dimensions of the phenomenon, such as the role of honor and political culture in sustaining and legitimating it. Even so, approaches to racial violence have yet to resolve several conceptual problems, in particular the question of the class dimensions of racial violence.

Early scholars of lynching, writing during the 1920s and 1930s, were sensitive to the class status of lynch mob participants and the role of capitalist development in southern racial violence. Yet, their sensitivity did not lead them to incorporate class into their explanatory framework. Intent on spreading the blame for antiblack violence broadly, these early scholars emphasized the shared commitment of virtually all southern whites to maintaining white domination. At a time when accounts of mob violence still filled newspapers, they took for granted the existence and perpetuation of racism itself; the question that attracted their interest was why racism found an outlet in violence against blacks. The answer, they concluded, could be found in the failure of southern institutions to provide adequate controls to stifle mob violence. For these observers, lynchings marked a phase in the economic and social maturation of the South; as the South underwent economic modernization and became increasingly urbanized and industrialized, lynching would no longer be condoned and the practice finally would be suppressed. In a sense, the economic dimensions of racial violence were a recognized feature rather than a historical problem that needed to be investigated or explained.[2]

Other scholars have adopted methods and concepts derived from psychology to explain racial violence. Racial violence, they suggest, vented

2 Arthur F. Raper, *The Tragedy of Lynching* (Chapel Hill, N.C., 1933), 41–3, 51–4. See also Earl Fiske Young, "The Relations of Lynching to the Size of Population Areas," *Sociology and Social Research* 12 (1928): 348–53.

whites' accumulated and deeply rooted psychological tensions about sexuality and status. Whites, one early student of mob violence has argued, projected forbidden fantasies onto blacks and then deflected their anger on the creature of their own creation, the black rapist.[3] Some scholars, influenced by the frustration-aggression school of psychology, have suggested that the root of racial violence could be found in the socially accepted channels for aggression in the South. Because day-to-day life generates continual frustrations, psychologist John Dollard contended, each individual must either turn his or her aggression inward and release it at some future time or else direct it toward some acceptable target. In the South, social conventions welcomed the release of white frustrations on blacks, a defenseless group who were associated with whites' repressed fears and desires.[4] Scholars who attempted to pinpoint the sources of this aggression traced the rise and fall in the frequency of lynchings to the economic conditions of whites. The rate of lynching, then, was a barometer of the economic frustration of white southerners. Although class dynamics can, and have been, incorporated into psychohistorical interpretations of southern racial violence, matters of class typically assume importance only as a catalyst for aggression rooted in deeper, more fundamental psychological tensions.[5]

Recently, cultural explanations for racial violence, and lynching in particular, have emerged. Mob violence, several historians have suggested, was one of the most hideous manifestations of ingrained cultural attitudes of the patriarchal, honor-bound South. The central peculiarity of southern culture, the persistence of honor long after it had withered elsewhere

---

3 Historian Joel Williamson has suggested that "black men were lynched for having achieved, seemingly, a sexual liberation that white men wanted but could not achieve without great feelings of guilt." Tortured by their frustration, white men projected their thoughts on black men "and symbolically killed those thoughts by lynching a hapless black man. . . . In effect, the black man lynched was the worst part of themselves" (Joel Williamson, *The Crucible of Race: Black-White Relations in the American South Since Emancipation* [New York, 1984], 308). For similar conclusions, see Trudier Harris, *Exorcising Blackness: Historical and Literary Lynching and Burning Rituals* (Bloomington, Ind., 1984), 19–24; Paul Hoch, *White Hero, Black Beast: Racism, Sexism, and the Mask of Masculinity* (London, 1979), 54–5; Philip Resnikoff, "A Psychoanalytic Study of Lynching," *Psychoanalytic Review* 20 (1933): 421–7.
4 John Dollard, *Caste and Class in a Small Southern Town* (New Haven, Conn., 1937); and John Dollard et al., *Frustration and Aggression* (New Haven, Conn., 1939).
5 The correlation between cotton prices and lynchings is described in Carl Iver Hovland and Robert R. Sears, "Minor Studies of Aggression: VI. Correlation of Lynchings with Economic Indices," *Journal of Psychology* 9 (1940): 301–10; and Raper, *Tragedy of Lynching*, 30–1. See also E. M. Beck and S. E. Tolnay, "The Killing Fields of the Deep South: The Market for Cotton and the Lynching of Blacks, 1882–1930," *American Sociological Review* 55 (1990): 526–39; Alexander Mintz, "A Re-examination of Correlations Between Lynchings and Economic Indices," *Journal of Abnormal and Social Psychology* 41 (1946): 154–65.

in the nation, created a climate particularly prone to ritualized affirmations of traditional values. Lynchings, in one fell swoop, confirmed inherited, inflexible attitudes toward blacks, women, and patriarchal rule.[6]

Many of these explanations of racial violence in the Jim Crow South
have a commonsense plausibility, which in part explains why they are,
either implicitly or explicitly, incorporated into most recent explanations
of racial violence. Yet, despite the renewed interest in racial violence,
much about it remains incompletely understood. As has already been
noted, accounts of southern racial violence often overlook or inadequately address the role of class in the phenomenon. Not since the work
of leftist activists and scholars at midcentury has scholarship prominently
stressed the class dimensions of antiblack violence. In contrast, scholars of
northern racial violence, including Dominic Capeci, Roberta Senechal,
and William Tuttle, have been especially sensitive to the role of class in
the riots they have studied. For these scholars, northern racial violence
cannot be understood without reference to class. Roberta Senechal, for
example, is explicit in her account of the 1908 Springfield, Illinois, riot:
"For Springfield's white working class, collective violence represented
the extreme end of a wide spectrum of strategies to keep blacks in their
place."[7]

The absence of careful discussions of the role of class in southern
racial violence is easily explained. Race, understandably, has long been
seen as the primary division within southern society and a "central theme"
in the region's history. Abundant evidence confirms the grip that white
supremacy and all of its attendant slogans have had on white southerners until the present day. And given that the overwhelming majority of
victims of lynch mobs and racial violence were black, only the most
closed-minded observer would deny the centrality of race and racism to
that violence. For all these reasons, scholars often conflate class and race
in the Jim Crow South, so that the color line divides property holders
from the dispossessed and the master class from the proletariat.

One scholar who never underestimated the significance of class or

---

6 Edward L. Ayers, *Vengeance and Justice: Crime and Punishment in the Nineteenth-Century South* (New
York, 1984), chap. 7; Jacquelyn Dowd Hall, *Revolt Against Chivalry: Jesse Daniel Ames and the
Women's Campaign Against Lynching* (New York, 1979), chap. 5; and Bertram Wyatt-Brown, *Southern Honor: Ethics and Behavior in the Old South* (New York, 1982), chap. 16.
7 Roberta Senechal, *The Sociogenesis of a Race Riot: Springfield, Illinois, in 1908* (Urbana, Ill., 1990),
196. See also Dominic J. Capeci Jr., and Martha Wilkerson, *Layered Violence: The Detroit Rioters of
1943* (Jackson, Miss., 1991); Dennis B. Downey and Raymond M. Hyser, *No Crooked Death:
Coatesville, Pennsylvania and the Lynching of Zachariah Walker* (Urbana, Ill., 1991), chap. 5; William
M. Tuttle Jr., *Race Riot: Chicago in the Red Summer of 1919* (New York, 1970).

the dynamics of class and race in the American South was the pioneering black sociologist Oliver C. Cox. His work offered an explicit and nuanced discussion of the role of class in the origins and manifestations of racist behavior. Writing from a perspective as both a sociologist and socialist, Cox argued that we are gravely mistaken if we assume that racism alone explains either racial oppression in general or racial violence in particular. Racism, he stressed, is the epiphenomenon of capitalism and cannot be understood independently of it. "Economic relations," he explained, "form the basis of modern race relations." Seen in this light, racism is "the socio-attitudinal concomitant of the racial exploitative practice of a ruling class in a capitalistic society." Accordingly, racial violence must be understood in the context of southern class relations. Lynching, "the whip hand of the ruling class," served the "indispensable social function of providing the ruling class with the means of periodically reaffirming its collective sentiment of white dominance."[8] Cox almost certainly nodded in agreement when Jessie Daniel Ames, director of the Association of Southern Women for the Prevention of Lynching, remarked that the purpose and consequence of mob violence was "intimidated, inarticulate, and cheap labor."[9]

Much of Cox's line of argument has been bolstered by the work of recent scholars who have reasserted the importance of class dynamics in the rural economy and the role of coercion in the perpetuation of the economic and political power of white rural elites. The systemic violence directed against African Americans was not random or indiscriminate, but rather had the intended goal "of encouraging deferential and discouraging egalitarian behavior by blacks."[10] Violence supplemented vagrancy laws, debtor legislation, and the crop lien, creating a system of "bound labor" in sharp contrast to the free-labor practices outside of the South.[11]

The broad strokes of Cox's interpretation of racial violence, supplemented by recent scholarship, help to clarify the violence of the plantation

---

8 Oliver C. Cox, *Race Relations: Elements and Social Dynamics* (Detroit, Mich., 1976), 6; Oliver C. Cox, *Class, Caste, and Race: A Study in Social Dynamics* (New York, 1949), 440, 555.

9 Quoted in Hall, *Revolt Against Chivalry*, 140.

10 Jay Mandle, *The Roots of Black Poverty: The Southern Plantation Economy After the Civil War* (Durham, N.C., 1978), 31.

11 Jack M. Bloom, *Class, Race, and the Civil Rights Movement: The Changing Political Economy of Southern Racism* (Bloomington, Ind., 1987), 18–58; Mandle, *The Roots of Black Poverty*; Joseph P. Reidy, *From Slavery to Agrarian Capitalism in the Cotton Plantation South: Central Georgia, 1800–1880* (Chapel Hill, N.C., 1992); Jonathan M. Wiener, "Class Structure and Economic Development in the American South, 1865–1955," *American Historical Review* 84 (1979): 970–92.

belt of the South. In central Georgia and Alabama, and in the Mississippi Delta, for example, racial violence was one tool among many used by white landed elites to secure and preserve their control over both economic and political resources. The pressing issue they faced following the Civil War was what system of labor would replace slavery. As the rural labor system evolved during the late nineteenth century, the landlords' controls over agricultural laborers expanded, and the rural workers' options diminished.

Even in the best of times, the relationship between white landlords and black tenants was charged with tensions. Tenants and sharecroppers chafed under the close scrutiny of landlords. The hierarchy of plantation agriculture sanctioned the discipline of black farmhands not only for economic reasons but also for perceived transgressions only remotely connected to the economic functioning of the plantation. A planter kept close scrutiny over the conduct of a laborer because "[w]hen he steals, fights, assembles 'unlawfully,' plots, marries secretly, indulges in fornication, has illegitimate children, spends his time in gambling, cockfighting, or courting, the planter suffers some loss or threat of loss."[12] Planters assumed the right to regulate, prohibit, or punish these practices as they saw fit.

Violence became an enduring feature of labor relations throughout the plantation belt. For the white population in the region that was dependent on black labor, mob violence, as Cox observed, was "the culminating act of continuing white aggression against the Negro."[13] Landlords, like their slave master predecessors, vouched for the healthy effects of intimidation and an occasional flogging of dilatory laborers. So rooted was violence in the time-honored privileges of planters that neither the courts nor public opinion impeded its routine application. Whipping and other forms of intimidation of black laborers attracted the attention of local authorities only when they reached epidemic proportions and threatened to lead to an exodus of black laborers. The behavior of county officials reflected the widely shared belief that "any crime which occurs among the propertyless Negroes is considered a labor matter to be handled by the white landlord or his overseer."[14]

The atmosphere of violence that was so pronounced in plantation-belt

---

12 Edgar T. Thompson, *Plantation Societies, Race Relations, and the South: The Regimentation of Populations* (Durham, N.C., 1975), 93; see also Mandle, *The Roots of Black Poverty*, 46–8.
13 Cox, *Caste, Class and Race* (New York, 1949), 561.
14 Raper, *The Tragedy of Lynching*, 56. See also Neil R. McMillen, *Dark Journey: Black Mississippians in the Age of Jim Crow* (Urbana, Ill., 1989), 125–7.

race relations was evident in both the frequency of and the alleged pretext for lynchings. In Georgia, for example, not only were there more lynchings in the plantation belt than anywhere else in the state, but mob violence also became more frequent over time, increasing sharply during the early twentieth century. Also, murder or violent assault, not rape, was the allegation most often leveled against mob victims in the region. Prior to 1900, alleged sexual offenses prompted the largest number of lynchings, but in the subsequent three decades murder topped the list of causes of mob violence. Between 1910 and 1919, for example, lynchers executed fifty-five victims for violent attacks and murders, nine for a variety of lesser affronts, and eight for alleged sexual transgressions.[15]

Although the immediate causes of lynchings in the South's plantation belt were often violent confrontations between whites and blacks, the deeper cause lay in the planters' reliance on the threat of violence to silence black protests and to secure their hold over subdued and inarticulate black laborers. When blacks refused to be cowed by the threat and remained defiant, or defended themselves, whites responded with swift and brutal retribution. In countless instances, ranging from the unrecorded murders of individual farmhands to the slaughter of perhaps two hundred blacks in the "Race War" of 1919 in Elaine, Arkansas, white planters, with the open complicity of local officials, imposed or restored their authority through a reign of terror.[16] Across the South, the presence of staple crops, white landlords, and black laborers may serve as an index of mob violence. In these parts of the South, mob violence became part of the very rhythm of life: Deeply rooted traditions of violent labor control, unhindered by any meaningful opposition from either institutions or individuals, sustained a tradition of mob violence that claimed thousands of lives and persisted for decades.

However compelling the evidence that racial violence in the rural South served as a primitive weapon of class domination, the region was too complex and the phenomenon of racial violence too multifarious to be explained so simply. Research on Tennessee has revealed the complex and uneven evolution of postbellum systems of rural labor and underscores the essential point that the comparatively uncomplicated racial and class hierarchy of the plantation belt was not duplicated in other areas of

---

15 See Brundage, *Lynching in the New South*, 110–11.
16 Ibid., 110–3, 118–20; Richard C. Cortner, *A Mob Intent on Death: The NAACP and the Arkansas Riot Cases* (Middletown, Conn., 1988), 5–23; James Weldon Johnson, *Along This Way: The Autobiography of James Weldon Johnson* (New York, 1933), 341–3; Wright, *Racial Violence in Kentucky*, 127–54.

the South.[17] Historians also have pointed out the precarious economic status of many rural whites and the widening class divisions that separated whites no less than blacks in the upcountry.[18] Recent scholarship has reminded us of the extent and significance of class dynamics within the black community.[19] Taken together, these works call into question any understanding of race and class in the South that assumes that the stark class-race stratification of the plantation belt was normative.

A full understanding of the class dimensions of racial violence in the South should also integrate recent insights into the dialectic of race and class. Scholars now are less likely to oppose class and race to each other or to elevate one as more essential, more important, or more real. Older interpretative dualisms – race/class and gender/class – that emphasize the immutable "fact" of class have undergone revision as scholars have concluded that class formation entails much more than job classifications and relations to the means of production. Class identity, like racial and gender identity, may be seen as an ideological creation that must be understood in relation to evolving social formations. Each individual's identity emerges from the interactions of class, race, ethnicity, and gender, with no single identity inherently taking precedence in defining behavior. By stressing the interrelationship of class, gender, and race, scholars seek to replace ahistorical and universal categories – essentialist notions of class, for example – with historically and culturally specific ones.

The insights offered by this recent scholarship emphasize the need for approaches to southern racial violence that are more sensitive to the agency of all whites in the construction of the southern racial ideology. Barbara Fields, David Roediger, and Alexander Saxton have already alerted us that racism, like all ideologies, was uniform neither across class lines nor over time.[20] Saxton cogently observes that ruling classes

17 Robert Tracy McKenzie, "Freedmen and the Soil in the Upper South: The Reorganization of Tennessee Agriculture, 1865–1880," *Journal of Southern History* 59 (1993): 63–84.
18 Charles L. Flynn Jr., *White Land, Black Labor: Caste and Class in Late Nineteenth-Century Georgia* (Baton Rouge, La., 1983); Steven Hahn, *The Roots of Southern Populism: Yeoman Farmers and the Transformation of the Georgia Upcountry, 1850–1890* (New York, 1983).
19 Willard B. Gatewood, *Aristocrats of Color: The Black Elite, 1880–1920* (Bloomington, Ind., 1990); Thomas Holt, *Black over White: Negro Political Leadership in South Carolina During Reconstruction* (Urbana, Ill., 1977); Earl Lewis, *In Their Own Interests: Race, Class, and Power in Twentieth-Century Norfolk, Virginia* (Berkeley, Calif., 1991); George C. Wright, *Life Behind the Veil: Blacks in Louisville, Kentucky, 1865–1930* (Baton Rouge, La., 1985).
20 Barbara Fields, "Ideology and Race in American History," in J. Morgan Kousser and James M. McPherson, eds., *Race, Region and Reconstruction* (New York, 1982); David R. Roediger, *The Wages of Whiteness: Race and the Making of the American Working Class* (New York, 1991); Alexander Saxton, *The Rise and Fall of the White Republic: Class, Politics, and Mass Culture in Nineteenth Century America* (New York, 1990).

in the nineteenth century did not monopolize "ideological construction" and that working-class whites participated in forging racist ideologies. Similarly, Roediger argues convincingly that working-class whites constructed their own racial ideology, which gave voice to their fears and ideals and at times fueled and legitimated deadly violence against African Americans and other minorities.

Similarly, the call for gender to be conceived as a fundamental category of historical analysis prods us to revise our understanding of southern racial ideologies. There is common recognition that historical analysis must move beyond the assumption that women have been defined by their sexuality and men by their gender-neutral class identity. Recent scholarship has insisted that gender and class always operate together and that class identity always takes a gendered form. Joan Wallach Scott and others have revealed how normative definitions of gender became embedded in class relations and even became the language of class. Indeed, Ava Baron has proposed that in order to discern the roles of men and women in reproducing class hierarchies, "we must understand men's and women's efforts to construct and defend a collective gender identity."[21]

Let us begin with the premise that class and race in the South were, in fundamental ways, gendered. Southern men and women, like all others, lived in a discrete social system within which gender, class, and race identities were continually forged, contested, reworked, and reaffirmed. The concatenation of gender, race, and class situated men and women within the social order and worked to entrench gender and racial categorization at every level of the southern legal, political, economic, and social formation.

Racial violence, more than most forms of behavior, became a forum for the expression and reaffirmation of these identities. The linkages of gender, race, and class in the lynchings of black men accused of rape are perhaps self-evident. Jacquelyn Dowd Hall, Martha Hodes, and Nancy MacLean have skillfully delineated the sexual politics that mobilized the lynch mobs that strung up alleged rapists and black men who defied conventions of sexual propriety.[22] But the same linkages were also

---

21 Ava Baron, "Gender and Labor History: Learning from the Past, Looking to the Future," in Ava Baron, ed., *Work Engendered: Toward a New History of American Labor* (Ithaca, N.Y., 1992), 30. See also Joan Acker, "Class, Gender, and the Relations of Distribution," *Signs* 13 (1988): 473–97; Leonore Davidoff and Catherine Hall, *Family Fortunes: Men and Women of the English Middle Class, 1780–1850* (Chicago, 1987), 13–35; Joan Wallach Scott, *Gender and the Politics of History* (New York, 1988), 28–50, 53–67.

22 Hall, *Revolt Against Chivalry*, 129–58; Martha Hodes, "The Sexualization of Reconstruction Politics: White Women and Black Men in the South After the Civil War," *Journal of the History of*

fundamental to other manifestations of racial violence, ranging from riots against black industrial workers to attacks on black sharecroppers. By incorporating a multifaceted understanding of class into interpretations of southern racial violence, it becomes possible to gain insights into the class hostilities, the maintenance of gender boundaries, the concerns about masculine authority, and the economic currents that all contributed to the motives and rationale for antiblack violence. Two episodes of violence in Spalding County, Georgia, in 1899 and Forsyth County, Georgia, in 1912 may serve to illustrate the intersection of gender and class in events in which, on first glance, neither may appear central.

In May 1899, the management of the Kincaid Cotton Mills in Griffin, Georgia, hired three blacks to work in the mills. White male workers responded by organizing a "Laborers' Union League" to overturn the new policy. Late on the evening of May 22, a mob of perhaps thirty men dragged the blacks to the outskirts of the town and flogged them nearly to death. The next morning a party of white men warned African-American laborers who were building an addition to the mill and others employed near the mill to leave the community. For the next several weeks, "a band" of white men, which newspapers numbered at five hundred, carried out "nightly depredations" against blacks. The "midnight marauders" also issued proclamations, signed "Jack the Ripper," that ordered the replacement of all black mill workers, tradesmen, and draymen with white men. "We trust that managers and merchants will discharge the negro promptly," one proclamation announced, "and save us the embarrassment of going through the negro, for we certainly will."[23]

As the violence escalated, local officials arrested the alleged ringleaders and called out the state militia. Always vigilant against labor activism or any form of working-class protest, the local elite were, predictably, anxious to suppress the "Laborers' Union League." During the tense weeks in which the cases of the alleged leaders progressed through the courts, an informal patrol of town leaders, bolstered periodically by the militia, patrolled Griffin at night and maintained order. Eventually, after a

---

Sexuality 3 (1993): 402–17; Nancy MacLean, "The Leo Frank Case Reconsidered: Gender and Sexual Politics in the Making of Reactionary Populism," *Journal of American History* 78 (1991): 917–48. For a gender analysis of lynching flawed by poststructuralist interpretative excess, see Robyn Wiegman, "The Anatomy of Lynching," *Journal of the History of Sexuality* 3 (1993): 445–67.

23 *Griffin News*, May 26, 1899, 1–1; *Atlanta Constitution*, May 24–7, 1899. See also Melton A. McLaurin, *Paternalism and Protest: Southern Cotton Mill Workers and Organized Labor, 1875–1905* (Westport, Conn., 1971), 65; Mercer G. Evans, "The History of the Organized Labor Movement in Georgia," Ph.D. diss., University of Chicago, 1929, 89.

week of trials, juries failed to convict any of the "marauders." The participants in the campaign of terror presumably judged it a success; they drove many blacks from the community and intimidated some white employers into replacing black workers with whites.

At one level, the outbreak of violence in Griffin may be explained as a predictable consequence of economic competition between white and black workers. Undeniably, the white working-class men resorted to violence as a crude tactic to defend and expand their economic opportunities. Yet the response of the white men seems entirely out of proportion to the threat that the three black employees represented. As the local newspaper protested, "the only crime [the black laborers] were charged with [by their attackers] was that they were earning salaries upon the mill."[24] The newspaper, however, could not grasp the full dimensions of the violence because it failed to recognize that the hiring of three black men violated in fundamental ways some white men's sense of racial entitlement.

Conceptions of respectability, gender, and racial entitlement were bound up in the gendered and racial division of labor in the South. Throughout the region the routines of work were explicitly organized to coincide with both gender and racial hierarchies. Notions of respectable labor, which had roots in slavery and traditions that exalted economic independence as a masculine ideal, attached dignity to some forms of work and disrepute to others. Simultaneously, the gendered division of labor and authority was essential to the construction and reproduction of masculine identity. As Stephanie McCurry explains, "the control and discipline of women's labor and the assumptions of natural authority that accompanied it" emerged as one measure of male independence in the early nineteenth century.[25]

This gendered division of labor and authority faced profound challenges following the Civil War. The impoverishment of many white male heads of households, who were reduced to tenancy and wage labor, and the dramatic expansion in the number of young white women wage earners shifted the power that different groups of men were able to wield over their subordinates, black and white. Industrialists shrewdly

---

24 *Griffin News*, May 23, 1899, 1–1.
25 Stephanie McCurry, "The Politics of Yeoman Households in South Carolina," in Catherine Clinton and Nina Silber, eds., *Divided Houses: Gender and the Civil War* (New York, 1992), 28. See also Laura F. Edwards, "Sexual Violence, Gender, Reconstruction, and the Extension of Patriarchy in Granville County, North Carolina," *North Carolina Historical Review* 68 (1991): 237–60; Elizabeth Fox-Genovese, *Within the Plantation Household: Black and White Women of the Old South* (Chapel Hill, N.C., 1988), 192–241.

adapted the tenets of both white and male supremacy to their needs in the New South. By adopting the family labor system in textile mills, for example, they seemingly recognized patriarchal authority within mill families, thereby mitigating the charge that mill work subverted traditional male authority by promoting women's economic independence. Simultaneously, mill owners pledged that white women would not risk the loss of their respectability by working in mills. With this in mind, women workers were strictly separated from black laborers, especially black males.[26]

Labor practices, however, could erode these social distinctions between white workers and blacks. The hiring of the black men in Griffin, for instance, threatened to expose the myth that southern gender conventions applied to all white women. Older definitions of feminine propriety conflicted with the new circumstances of female employment; the proximity of white workers, especially white women, to black workers communicated inferior status and powerlessness. In the minds of some white workers, the three black workers must have represented a dire threat to reorder the southern hierarchy of subordinates and superordinates.

The controversy over the three black workers almost certainly took on added significance because of the contemporary context. Only weeks before the incident in Griffin, the entire state, and especially central Georgia, had been electrified by the notorious alleged crimes of Sam Hose, an itinerant black farmhand accused of murder and rape. After a week-long manhunt, a mob lynched Hose in a spectacle of torture and mutilation that attracted nationwide attention and amplified a furious debate about the menace that black criminality posed to white women.[27] Coming so fast on the heels of the Hose lynching, the hiring of the blacks inflamed anxieties over the prerogatives of class power, status, and gender.

Had white male workers at the Griffin mills conceded the hiring of the black men, they would have revealed their inability to "protect" their wives and daughters and made manifest their own loss of power, authority, and status. White industrialists may have established the system of a

---

26 Jacquelyn Dowd Hall et al., *Like A Family: The Making of a Southern Cotton Mill World* (Chapel Hill, N.C., 1987); Dolores E. Janiewski, *Sisterhood Denied: Race, Gender, and Class in a New South Community* (Philadelphia, 1985), Dolores E. Janiewski, "Southern Honor, Southern Dishonor: Managerial Ideology and the Construction of Gender, Race, and Class Relations in Southern Industry," in Baron, ed., *Work Engendered*, 70–91; MacLean, "The Leo Frank Case Reconsidered," 922, 927–33.

27 *Atlanta Constitution*, Apr. 13–16, 1899; *Atlanta Journal*, Apr. 13–25, 1899; *Macon Telegraph*, Apr. 13–26, 1899; Brundage, *Lynching in the New South*, 34, 82–4.

labor force segregated by race and gender, but white workers elevated the exclusion of black workers to a moral principle. The moral principle, of course, also protected "white" jobs. When confronted by the menace of downward mobility that the black workers represented, white men predictably responded with violence and protest. Three years earlier, 1,400 white workers of the Fulton Bag and Cotton Factory in Atlanta had walked off the job and formed a rock-throwing mob when twenty "nasty, black, stinkin' nigger wimmin" were employed at the plant. The enraged workers were protecting more than their pay; they attempted to reaffirm publicly the status of their jobs. Undoubtedly, they found satisfaction in the subsequent dismissal of the black women and the adoption of a policy of strict racial segregation in the factory. Across the late nineteenth and early twentieth centuries, then, white laborers replenished and reinvigorated the justifications for occupational segregation.[28]

The conflicts at the Griffin and Fulton mills, unquestionably, were sparked by economic grievances. But those grievances cannot be separated from the simultaneous dispute over gender and racial boundaries.[29] Competing groups of men contested the privileges of class and masculinity. The white mill owners took for granted their power to draw and redraw the precise boundaries of economic and racial entitlement. Their decisions over mill staffing ignored the implications for their white workers' sense of status and economic security. Simultaneously, the black

28 John W. Cell, *The Highest Stage of White Supremacy: The Origins of Segregation in South Africa and the American South* (New York, 1982), 128–30; Janiewski, "Southern Honor, Southern Dishonor," 84; McLaurin, *Paternalism and Protest*, 61–5; John M. Matthews, "Studies in Race Relations in Georgia, 1890–1930," Ph. D. diss., Duke University, 1970, 218–9; Allen H. Stokes Jr., "Black and White Labor in the Development of the Southern Textile Industry," Ph.D. diss., University of South Carolina, 1977, 204–8; Gavin Wright, *Old South, New South: Revolutions in the Southern Economy Since the Civil War* (New York, 1986), 189–90.

29 That the nightriders in Griffin, who were especially intent on defending the respectability and status of white women workers, chose to sign their proclamations "Jack the Ripper" is an intriguing curiosity. The misogynist violence of Jack the Ripper in 1888 had long since achieved the status of a Victorian myth. Perhaps the men simply adopted the sobriquet because it was both sensational and ominous. Or perhaps the title contained a coded reference to male dominance and deep-seated gender antagonisms. Several scholars have suggested that female employment in mills tested parental and male authority and the methods of its enforcement. The conscious adoption of the title of "the Ripper" may have been intended to exploit female terror and buttress male authority. Finally, the appropriation of the notorious nickname may have revealed the investment of blacks, who were the victims of the whipping spree, with the attributes of helplessness, immorality, and inappropriate behavior that were attached to the Ripper's victims. The violence against the blacks perhaps was a reenactment of violence against women, a form of violence with its own powerful mystique that permeated society. Whatever the case, the reference to Jack the Ripper is suggestive, but extant sources unfortunately render any interpretation of its significance inherently speculative. For a provocative discussion of Jack the Ripper, see Judith R. Walkowitz, "Jack the Ripper and the Myth of Male Violence," *Feminist Studies* 8 (1982): 543–74.

men presumably accepted jobs at the Griffin mills in hopes of securing the economic standing that undergirded masculine status in the black community no less than in the white. Finally, the white men who formed the "Laborers' Protective Union" intended to set boundaries on the prerogatives of white mill owners, to defend the "honor" of white women against the threats represented by both white industrialists and blacks, and to remind blacks of enduring hierarchies. To do this, they adopted a traditional form of justice that had long been used to impose moral as well as rough justice.[30]

Similar gender, class, and racial dynamics sparked violence in rural communities as well as in mill towns. In the upcountry, for example, the expansion of cotton cultivation and the crop lien caught large numbers of whites in the web of tenancy. Landless whites, who chafed when they found themselves caught in a system of labor they believed fit only for blacks, insisted that they deserved loftier positions on the agricultural ladder than blacks. But the swelling white population, in combination with the tribulations of cotton cultivation, placed increasing pressures on hard-pressed yeoman farmers; they watched with frustration as they sank into debt, as their farms shrank with each division among their children, and as cotton prices fell.[31]

The downward economic spiral of many white yeoman farmers undercut their inherited notions of respectability and eroded their social standing in a profoundly hierarchical society. The economic dependency inherent to sharecropping and tenancy allowed for only a skeletal version of the masculine ideal of responsible breadwinners able to satisfy the needs of their dependents. Instead, white men were left with the token advantages they received from white landlords – modestly better land to till and a degree of latitude denied blacks.[32]

But even these privileges had to be defended. Throughout the upcountry of Georgia, and especially along the borders of the region where mountain whites pressed down into the Upper Piedmont and in turn Upper Piedmont whites pushed into the plantation belt, white tenant farmers confronted landlords who preferred black tenants or croppers. The pent-up discontent of white sharecroppers and struggling farmers periodically surfaced in terrorist racial violence against blacks.[33]

30 Flynn, *White Land, Black Labor*, 29–56; Wyatt-Brown, *Southern Honor*, 435–61.
31 Flynn, *White Land, Black Labor*, 136–49; Hahn, *The Roots of Southern Populism*.
32 On the privileges of white tenants and sharecroppers, see Allison Davis et al., *Deep South: A Social Anthropological Study of Class and Caste* (Chicago, 1969), 266–9; Jack Temple Kirby *Rural Worlds Lost: The American South, 1920–1960* (Baton Rouge, La., 1987), 147; Theodore Rosengarten, *All God's Dangers: The Life of Nate Shaw* (New York, 1974), 511–2.
33 Brundage, *Lynching in the New South*, 120–7.

In 1912, for example, white tenant farmers in Forsyth County, a county on the northern border of the region, determined to force all black landowners to sell their farms and to drive all black tenants out of the county. They whipped and murdered an undetermined number of blacks, burned their homes and barns, and warned them to leave. The white planters who depended on black laborers tried to prevent the exodus of blacks by refusing to hire white tenants or to extend credit to the leaders of the terrorist campaign. Even so, almost all blacks were driven out of the county, and it remained "lily-white" until almost the present day.[34]

In important ways, the events in Forsyth County shared similarities with the violence in Spalding County. The event that precipitated the campaign of terror against blacks in the county was the rape and murder of a local white woman.[35] Despite that pretext, in the eyes of white planters and urban editors, the violence against blacks was an indefensible outrage. Like the mill owners and town fathers of Griffin, planters in the upcountry assumed the prerogative to divvy out jobs as part of their dominion. They took for granted that the interests of black and poor white men were dependent on and subsumed by their own interests. But whereas these planters saw their paternalism as benevolent and protective, white tenant farmers and sharecroppers saw it as exploitative and deeply resented it. Indignant about encroachments that threatened to render cosmetic their authority and prestige, some white men in Forsyth resorted to violence to reassert their power in the face of planter encroachments. With a moral and cultural authority that was rooted within a gendered concept of class, they imposed their moral authority not only within their community but also on the planter class. Yeoman whites, who were painfully aware of their own economic and political weakness relative to white elites, prudently used intimidation and violence in a manner that the ideology of white supremacy arguably sanctioned. Their tactics did not so much turn blacks into scapegoats as challenge the white elites at their most vulnerable point. In attacking black tenants and farmers, they drew a direct line between the threat of impoverishment, black encroachments, planter abuses of class power, and

---

34 *Atlanta Constitution*, Oct. 13, 1912; for other examples, see *Atlanta Constitution*, Jan. 8, 1900; Nov. 20, 1900; Jan. 13, 1916; June 1, 1916; Matthews, "Studies in Race Relations in Georgia, 1890–1930," 163; Royal Freeman Nash, "The Cherokee Fires," *Crisis* 11 (1916): 265–70; Robert Preston Brooks, "A Local Study of the Race Problem," *Political Science Quarterly* 26 (1911): 193–221. For a discussion of similar patterns of whitecapping in Texas and Missouri, see *Nation* (1897): 253; David Thelen, *Paths of Resistance: Tradition and Dignity in Industrializing Missouri* (New York, 1986), 88–99.

35 *Atlanta Constitution*, Sept. 11–13; Oct. 2–13, 1912; *Marietta Journal*, Sept. 13, 1912.

their claims to the prerogatives and the power of wealthier white men.

To view the violence in Spalding and Forsyth counties as a contest over race, class, and gender boundaries is to take one step toward reintegrating class into interpretations of southern racial violence. As the events across the South reveal, class dynamics were present in antiblack violence from the plantation belt to the upcountry. Rather than applying class analysis to some lynchings (that is, lynchings of black sharecroppers) and gender analysis to others (that is, lynchings of alleged sexual offenders), the goal instead should be to reveal the salience of class and gender in all lynchings.

This reading of southern racial violence encourages a recognition of the diversity and complexity of motives behind racial violence in the New South. We make a serious mistake if we assume that racial violence inherently affirmed race or gender interests that united southern white men across class lines. To the contrary, the unrest in Griffin, Georgia, is only one example of the ongoing contest between industrialists and mill workers over class prerogatives and gender status. Similarly, the terrorist violence in Forsyth County vividly exposed the differing meanings that yeoman and elite whites attached to the ideology of white supremacy. Precisely because racial violence was extralegal it was an exceptionally flexible method of controlling blacks that could be and was adopted by a broad array of whites with complex and contradictory motives. The simple truth that lynching was susceptible to the personal whims of each lyncher insured that the jurisdiction of the lynch mob was both expansive and capricious. White elites periodically urged southern whites to restrict the boundaries of "legitimate" forms of racial violence, but the imprecise and contested meaning of white supremacy made it almost impossible to do so.[36]

This approach to southern racial violence also helps clarify the underlying causes of that violence that were distinctive to the South and those that had counterparts in other societies. However singular the form of violence, the continuing contest over boundaries in the American South

---

36 That racial violence was a weapon in the arsenal of lower class whites does not mean that southern elites were not its beneficiaries. White workers may have fortified the racial barriers that kept blacks out of southern mills, but mill owners also profited from the hostility and suspicion that separated black and white workers. Periodic attacks on black sharecroppers may have inconvenienced some white planters, but just as often such campaigns forced blacks to accept the personal authority and guardianship of elite whites as the best possible guarantee of their rights. As Oliver C. Cox explains, the black man "prostrates himself, as it were, before white men in recognition that Negroes may enjoy a degree of well-being only by the sufferance of their white neighbors" (Cox, *Caste, Class and Race*, 564).

had parallels elsewhere. As Frank Trommler has pointed out, the links between "status accumulation," work, and notions of ethnic and national identity became tightly bound together in both Germany and the United States during the late nineteenth and early twentieth centuries. Similarly, a fusion of masculinity, status, racial identity, and work privileges emerged in South Africa in the early twentieth century. In each of these societies, the ongoing process of defining identity boundaries generated anxieties and hostilities that could, and often did, find expression in racist violence. Certainly, the attacks on Jews in modern Germany (and more recently, attacks on immigrants throughout western Europe) and anti-black violence by American white supremacists reveal a similar violent reassertion of class, gender, and racial boundaries by displaced, alienated young men.

Yet, at the same time, the tools available for southern whites to preserve and establish the boundaries that circumscribed race, gender, and class reflected distinctive American traditions of political culture, government institutions, and race relations. Working-class white South Africans during the early twentieth century, for example, prodded the state to fix their status to a degree unmatched in the Jim Crow South. As pervasive as segregation was in the South, it left large areas of economic activity unregulated with regard to race. The weak state apparatus in the South could not easily have extended its authority into such matters. But if white southerners could only partially cement the privileges of "whiteness" through the extension of state authority, they still had the tool of extralegal violence at their disposal. Precisely because the state did not have and could not easily secure a monopoly on violence in the South, whites retained an exceedingly powerful means of demarcating their perceived racial entitlements. Consequently, antiblack violence remained a forum for contested expressions of class hostilities, gender anxieties, and racial boundaries well into the twentieth century and indeed even to the present day.

7

Racism and Empire

A Perspective on a New Era of American History

HERBERT SHAPIRO

The notion that the emergence of American imperialism in the 1890s was an aberrant, temporary phenomenon has had some influence in the historical literature. It is expressed, for example, in Julius W. Pratt's study of the expansionists of 1898 and implied in Richard Hofstadter's emphasis on the psychic, even benevolent, factors leading to acquisition of colonies.[1] (Hofstadter suggested that the Spanish-American War originated "not in imperialist ambition but in popular humanitarianism.") Samuel Flagg Bemis writes that imperialism "was never deep-rooted in the character of the people" and indeed found that the American experience was one of "an imperialism against imperialism."[2] The historian Rubin Francis Weston observes that American imperialism lacked "vigor and persistence."[3]

Imperialism's abiding significance in American history is confirmed by the evidence that our colonial adventures spurred the fuller flowering of racism that has endured ever since the 1890s and still threatens us with disaster. Well known, of course, are the racist writings of the publicists Lothrop Stoddard and Madison Grant, filled with dehumanization of blacks and strident pleas for exclusion of immigrants in the interest of preserving the supposed Anglo-Saxon character of the American population.

Theodore Roosevelt, key architect of the Spanish-American War, wrote in 1901 that "what has taken us thirty generations to achieve, we cannot expect to see another race accomplish out of hand," especially

---

1 See Richard Hofstadter, "Cuba, the Philippines and Manifest Destiny," in *The Paranoid Style in American Politics and Other Essays* (New York, 1966), 145.
2 Samuel Flagg Bemis, quoted in Rubin Francis Weston, *Racism in U.S. Imperialism* (Columbia, S.C., 1972), 257.
3 Weston, *Racism in U.S. Imperialism*, 1.

when non-Caucasians allegedly were behind where whites were at the start of those thirty generations.[4] Perhaps central to Roosevelt's view was his rejection of the thesis that the color question was essentially one of class, one of the few against the many. Race conflict, he insisted, was deep and fundamental.[5]

The National Education Association declared that teachers supported the Spanish-American War because "the solidarity of the American people and the Anglo-Saxon races is vastly increased by such an armed contest."[6] America's wars have repeatedly evoked racism from those in the armed forces, from the officer who characterized the Filipinos as "an illiterate, semi-savage people who are waging war, not against tyranny, but against Anglo-Saxon order and decency" to the troops who referred to Koreans and Vietnamese as "gooks."[7] As the Spanish-American War unfolded, Senator Albert Beveridge (an Indiana Republican) proclaimed, "We are of the ruling race of the world; . . . ours is the blood of government; ours the heart of dominion; ours the brain and genius of administration."[8]

It was in the aftermath of that war, in 1900, that Charles Carroll's diatribe *The Negro a Beast* was published, describing the Negro as "simply an ape" and concluding that "the pure-blooded White is the creature whom God deigned should perform the mental labor necessary to subdue the earth; and that the Negro is the creature whom God designed to perform the manual labor." The book exuded classism as well as racism in connecting labor to the activity of nonhuman creatures. Carroll also carefully noted that white men were not corrupted by sexual relations with black women. He hoped to have his writings accepted as the product of scientific thought, at the same time as he contended that viewing black people as human was a misconception fostered by evolutionists.[9]

That same year Mississippian James K. Vardaman referred to the black as a "lazy, lying lustful animal which no conceivable amount of training can transform into a tolerable citizen."[10] Southern Democrat John T.

---

4 Roosevelt, quoted in Weston, *Racism in U.S. Imperialism*, 42.
5 See George Sinkler, *The Racial Attitudes of American Presidents* (Garden City, N.Y., 1971), 419.
6 See Thomas G. Gossett, *Race: The History of an Idea in America* (Dallas, 1963), 318.
7 U.S. Army officer Frederick Funston, quoted in H. W. Brands, *Bound to Empire: The United States and the Philippines* (New York, 1992), 58.
8 Beveridge, quoted in Weston, *Racism in U.S. Imperialism*, 46.
9 Charles Carroll, "*The Negro a Beast*" (St. Louis, 1900; reprint, Salem, Mass., 1991), 102, 126, 159 (page citations are to the reprint edition).
10 Gossett, *Race: The History of an Idea*, 271.

Morgan, who voted for annexing the Philippines, said in the same year that "in physical, mental, social, inventive, religious, and ruling power the African race holds the lowest place."[11] American opposition to Hawaiian statehood was long rooted in racism, as was Washington's Puerto Rican policy. American officials, particularly in the Wilson administration's Kapp report, spoke of Haitians as savages, liars, and cannibals to justify occupation of the country.[12] American Haitian policy, according to a statement made by prominent public figures in March 1994, is still marked by considerations of race.[13]

America's reformers were often contaminated or at least thrown on the defensive by racism. New York's anti-Tammany crusader the Reverend Charles Parkhurst declared in 1898 that the nation had conquered "a people ten times our inferior in brute force, military genius, and personal fibre."[14] Albion Tourgee was a Radical Republican during Reconstruction and, although appalled in the 1890s by renewed racial violence in North Carolina, supported the Philippine conquest. "The natives," he stated, "are about as hard material as civilization ever had to deal with. I do not know what we can do with them, but even if we have to kill them off, it is better than to abandon the relics at Cavite." In 1899, Tourgee rather unhappily observed that "civilization and Christianity are irredeemably committed to the theory of white supremacy and the assertion in fact, if not in theory, of a world-wide difference between the inherent rights of a white man and a colored 'individual.'"[15] At the 1911 Universal Races Congress, Felix Adler, the liberal leader of the Ethical Culture Society, referred to "backward races" and "uncivilized races," and in keeping with the educational philosophy of Booker T. Washington, urged agricultural and industrial training for these people. Adler sought "humane treatment" of the "backward" races, but there is clearly the note of paternalism.[16] The writings of muckraker Upton Sinclair were sprinkled with an assortment of racist references to black people.[17]

American racism flourished in the context of the racism that permeated much of public life in Western nations. Oliver C. Cox writes, "Racial

---

11 Weston, *Racism in U.S. Imperialism*, 11.
12 Ibid., 232.
13 *New York Times*, Mar. 23, 1994.
14 Sinkler, *Racial Attitudes*, 356.
15 See Otto H. Olsen, *Carpetbagger's Crusade: Life of Albion Wingear Tourgee* (Baltimore, 1965), 344, 347.
16 See G. Spiller, ed., *Inter-racial Problems: The Complete Papers of the First Universal Races Congress, London 1911* (Secaucus, N.J., 1970), 267.
17 See Herbert Shapiro, "Muckrakers and Negroes," *Phylon* (Jan. 1970): 76–88.

antagonism attained full maturity during the latter half of the nineteenth century, when the sun no longer set on British soil and the great nationalistic powers of Europe began to justify their economic designs on weaker European peoples with subtle theories of racial superiority and masterhood."[18] Perhaps symbolic of an entire tradition was Arnold Toynbee's observation that the "only one of races not to make a contribution to civilization is the black race."[19] The racism expressed by Rudyard Kipling was quite influential in the United States at the end of the 1890s. In "The White Man's Burden," the poet wrote that the colonizers served their captives' needs but that these captives were "sullen peoples, half devil and half child." The task of the white man was to "fill full the mouth of Famine, and bid the sickness cease," but Kipling added that when the goal of helpfulness was nearest the European would watch "sloth and heathen folly" bring hopes for progress to naught. Those ruled over by white society were clearly inferior, and paternalism was most significant in what it did to enhance the character of the colonizers.[20]

Tourgee had another view of the "white man's burden" when he defined it as "a view of the relation of white Christian duty which makes injustice done to colored people not only righteousness but the noblest of Christian duties."[21]

Imperialism encouraged the development of scientific racism – sets of ideas supposedly based on empirical research that justified white superiority and the inherent right of whites to rule over darker people. A characteristic expression was formulated in 1906 by anatomist Robert Bennett Bean. Contending that the availability of the bodies of black people for anatomical study indicated "less respect for the dead among Negroes," Bean argued that the evidence derived from measurements of brains explained the qualities he claimed to observe among blacks. "instability of character incident to lack of self-control, especially in connection with the sexual relation . . . lack of *orientation* of recognition of position and condition of self and environment, evidenced by a peculiar bumptiousness, so called, that is particularly noticeable." His general conclusion was that "the Negro has the lower mental faculties (smell, sight, handicraftmanship, body-sense, melody) well-developed, the Caucasian the higher (self-control, will-power, ethical and aesthetic senses and reason)."[22]

18 Oliver C. Cox, *Caste, Class, and Race: A Study in Social Dynamics* (New York, 1970), 330.
19 Toynbee, quoted in Stephen Jay Gould, *The Mismeasure of Man* (New York, 1981), 41.
20 Rudyard Kipling, "The White Man's Burden," *McClure's Magazine* (Feb. 1899): 290–1.
21 Albion Tourgee, "Black and White," manuscript, Chautauqua County Historical Society, 1899.
22 Robert Bennett Bean, "Some Racial Peculiarities of the Negro Brain," *American Journal of Anat-*

In an era marked by technological transformation and the growth of industry, priority was given to natural law, to justification of the status quo in terms of what must be. The rule of whites was justified because it was the end product of evolution. Gunnar Myrdal wrote of the biological rationalizations for racism, "They have been associated in America, as in the rest of the world, with conservative and even reactionary ideologies." He explained that this is related to the fact that the biological sciences and medicine came into existence within American universities much earlier than the social sciences "and have not yet the same close ideological ties to the American Creed."[23] A variant of this racism was eugenics, originally conceptualized by Francis Galton. Stefan Kuhl has recently observed that racism was at the core of the eugenics movement.[24] In a society marked by substantial inequality of opportunity between races, the concept that a dominant position of economic and political superiority is a reflection of superior biology is bound to foster racism.

Such was the case with the eugenicists, and their case has not been substantially strengthened by recent efforts to find redeeming worth in sociobiology.[25] It is disquieting to read uncritical references to the views of a psychologist, Leonard Carmichael, who urged investigation of supposed racial differences in behavior. One of the more crass eugenicists was horse breeder W. E. D. Stokes, a member of a patrician New York family. Stokes appeared to be unclear about the difference between race horses and human beings, urging selective breeding of the laboring classes through use of a "labor registry." Citing the existence of the Eugenics Bureau at Cold Spring Harbor and the support given eugenics research by Carnegie, Rockefeller, and Harriman funds, Stokes urged sterilization of "defectives." He argued that superior New Englanders could "no longer cross with or assimilate the rotten, foreign, diseased blood of ages" allowed by immigration. Stokes further wrote that when

---

omy 4 (1906): 379, 412. A reply to Bean's view is found in the study edited by W. E. B. Du Bois, *The Health and Physique of the Negro American* (Atlanta, 1906), 27. Du Bois wrote that the facts "seem to indicate that what has been described as being peculiar in the size, shape, and anatomy of the Negro brain is not true of all Negro brains. These same peculiarities can no doubt be found in many white brains and probably have no special connection with the mental capacity of either race."

23 Gunnar Myrdal, *An American Dilemma: The Negro Problem and Modern Democracy*, 2 vols. (New York, 1964), 1:91.

24 Stefan Kuhl, *The Nazi Connection: Eugenics, American Racism, and German National Socialism* (New York, 1994), 70.

25 Carl Degler, *In Search of Human Nature: The Decline and Revival of Darwinism in American Social Thought* (New York, 1991), 218.

the black child reached a certain age "we find an impenetrable wall, beyond which there can be no future accomplishment." The future of blacks was hopeless, as "the pure-blooded Negro in America has in him no elements that will ever lift him above his present condition." Stokes found Jews to be an "admirable race of people," but they were also people who breed "with money-getting and money-keeping in view."[26] The notions held by advocates of sociobiology still run up against the view Gunnar Myrdal set forth in *An American Dilemma*. Myrdal argued that differences in human behavior are to be explained in terms of social and cultural factors and that if we approach such differences primarily "in terms of heredity, we do not have any scientific basis for our assumption."[27]

In the 1930s, scientists in Nazi Germany drew on American eugenics as a model for policies of racial purification, and a number of American eugenicists hailed the flowering of so-called population science in Germany. From the mid-1920s on, German eugenicists often referred favorably to the American sterilization practices instituted by various states, most extensively by California. In 1935 the American eugenicist Clarence G. Campbell commented that German racial policies promised "to be epochal in racial history." The Pioneer Fund, which has consistently supported racist-oriented research – offering to fund Arthur Jensen's work, for example – praised Nazi racial policies. Adolph Hitler, who declared that Madison Grant's *The Passing of the Great Race* was his Bible, was quoted as having praised the laws of several American states that prevented reproduction. In 1935 Alabama's state health officer, J. N. Baker, told the state legislature, "With bated breath, the entire civilized world is watching the bold experiment in mass sterilization recently launched by Germany." In 1939–40, the eugenicist T. U. II. Ellinger visited Germany and reported that the Nazi treatment of Jews was a "large-scale breeding project, with the purpose of eliminating from the nation the hereditary attributes of the Semitic race." American eugenicists, according to Stefan Kuhl, allowed themselves to take a sympathetic view of Nazi race policy by separating science from politics, unwilling or unable to recognize that the Nazi rulers insisted that science function as the instrument of ideology. Kuhl observes that the racist ideology at the root of genocide was not limited to German scientists.[28] There was a long road between sci-

26 W[illiam] E. D. Stokes, *The Right to Be Well-Born, or, Horse-Breeding in Its Relation to Eugenics* (New York, 1917), 48, 81, 101, 168, 175.
27 Myrdal, *American Dilemma*, 149.
28 Kuhl, *Nazi Connection*, 5, 34, 37, 60, 85, 106; Edward J. Larson and Leonard J. Nelson III, "Invol-

entific racism at the turn of the century and the Holocaust experience of World War II, but these phenomena are connected.

A particularly destructive manifestation of American racism was the distortion of educational psychology to contend that there was an inherent intelligence differential between whites and African Americans. This distortion relied on the intelligence tests administered to servicemen during World War I. Henry Fairfield Osborn, head of New York's Museum of Natural History, once commented in regard to these tests, which modern scholarship has subjected to withering criticism, that they showed "we have learned once and for all that the Negro is not like us." The psychologist Lewis Terman predicted in 1916 the discovery of "enormously significant racial differences in general intelligence, differences which cannot be wiped out by any scheme or mental culture." The psychologist Robert M. Yerkes, director of the World War I testing program, generalized from the tests and concluded that the "Negro lacks initiative, displays little or no leadership and cannot accept responsibility." Walter Lippmann and others demonstrated the twisted logic at the base of the program; nevertheless, the army tests served the purposes of ideological racism.[29] As Thomas Gossett writes, "the conclusion readily reached was that a great number of people – in fact, the majority – were incapable of benefiting from improved education."[30] The IQ tests fitted in with a broadly reactionary social agenda.

Some have argued that turn-of-the-century African-American leaders, such as W. E. B. Du Bois, at times responded to white racism with their own racism. In the case of Du Bois, this argument rests on the points he lays out in his 1897 essay "The Conservation of Races." In reality however, Du Bois's essay is a forceful expression of anti-racism and furnishes a contrast to white supremacist ideology. Du Bois wrote that the American black had "been led to deprecate and minimize race distinctions, to believe intensely that out of one blood God created all nations," and against that he insisted that the race idea was "the central thought of all history." Blacks, he also said, must not offer a servile imitation of Anglo-Saxons. But Du Bois argued further that, despite physical differences, such distinctions between people "do not explain all the differences of their history." Each race has its own ideal, and the point was that the

untary Sexual Sterilization of Incompetents in Alabama: Past, Present and Future," *Alabama Law Review* 43, no. 2 (1992): 417, quoting J. N. Baker; in 1996 the Pioneer Fund again drew public attention owing to the role of fund director Thomas Ellis in the campaign of Republican presidential aspirant Steve Forbes. See *New York Times*, Feb. 12, 1996, A13.

29 Gould, *Mismeasure of Man*, 174, 179, 180, 191, 197, 231.
30 Gossett, *Race: The History of an Idea*, 368.

messages to the world of the African, the Asian, and the Slavic had not
been fully revealed. Each race idea, he observed, advances the world
toward perfection. Blacks had a responsibility to "speak to the nations of
earth a divine truth that shall make them free." Du Bois insisted that
blacks must strive for the "broader humanity which freely recognizes differences in men, but sternly deprecates inequality in their opportunities
for development." He hoped that blacks and whites would develop side
by side "in peace and mutual happiness" and contribute what each had
to offer American culture.[31]

Racism and imperialism were inextricably linked at the turn of the
century. Rubin Weston was on target when he wrote that it was "highly
significant that the age of American imperialism overlapped what one
historian [Rayford Logan] called the nadir of black history."[32] White
supremacy served national decision makers both at home and abroad,
and domestic and foreign policy tended to reinforce each other. Racism
justified the American annexation of the Philippines and was utilized to
defend the brutal measures taken against Filipino nationalists. Racism
also supplied the ideological force propelling disfranchisement, de jure
segregation, and lynching at home. Under cover of white supremacy, as
John W. Cell has shown, southern racists reached new levels of violence
in their drive to extinguish the rights of African Americans.[33] And contrary to the views of those contending that southern racists, after the
Spanish-American War, opposed America's embrace of empire, it must be
noted that Philippine annexation would not have been adopted without
southern congressional votes and that the first concern of numerous
southern politicians was not one of principled opposition to colonialism
but of using the issue to strengthen white supremacy at home. Their
anti-imperialism was – to a considerable degree – demagogic.

Following a suggestion made by Frederick Merk, George Frederickson
contends that prior to 1898 racism was a deterrent to imperialism and
that later extreme racism and imperialism did not harmonize. The "white
man's burden" was linked to paternalism rather than to racist frenzy.[34]
Frederickson's hypotheses, I believe, merit some investigation. He cites
racism as instrumental in obstructing earlier Mexican annexation and the

31 See W. E. B. Du Bois, "The Conservation of Races," in *The Seventh Son: The Thought and Writings of W. E. B. Du Bois*, ed. Julius Lester, 2 vols. (New York, 1971), 1:176–87.
32 Weston, *Racism in U.S. Imperialism*, x.
33 See John W. Cell, *The Highest State of White Supremacy: The Origins of Segregation in South Africa
   and the American South* (Cambridge, 1982).
34 George M. Frederickson, *The Black Image in the White Mind: The Debate on Afro-American Character and Destiny, 1817–1914* (New York, 1971), 305–9.

failure to win congressional approval for annexation of the Dominican Republic. But were the operative factors here racism, or did they concern what the incorporation of nonslaveholding Mexico might mean for the stability of the slave system and the reluctance of the United States at the time, which had not yet completed settlement of the continent, to embark on foreign adventures? Was racism altogether irrelevant to American willingness to wage war against a non-Anglo-Saxon Spanish empire? Racism definitely played a role in cultivating a chauvinism and jingoism in the American consciousness that sustained the intervention in the Cuban struggle against Spanish rule. As Richard Hofstadter tells us, an American society shaped by constant warfare with the Indians and proslavery arguments was "thoroughly grounded in notions of racial superiority."[35] Without doubt, the brutal treatment of American Indians prepared the way in the 1890s for the harsh treatment of overseas populations that the United States conquered. In 1894, John Fiske divided the Indians into three groups, "savage, barbarous and half-civilized."[36] If racism did nothing else, it produced national habits of arrogance and self-centeredness.

Even before the Spanish-American War there were voices arguing the case for empire in racist terms. Theodore Roosevelt told the students at the Naval War College in 1897 that "all great masterful races have been fighting races."[37] The previous year he described the temporary failure of Hawaiian annexation as a crime against "white civilization." George Sinkler has observed that Roosevelt's racial frame of reference "recognized the white as the superior race and the yellow and black as alien and inferior."[38] This mind-set clearly predated the Spanish-American War. Integral to Roosevelt, as Daniel Boone Schirmer notes, "was his sense of white, Anglo-Saxon superiority."[39]

Imperialism was linked to the American missionary spirit, the racism that according to Forrest G. Wood was inherently unable to leave another people alone.[40] There is a connection between McKinley's rhetoric about the duty to Christianize the Filipinos and the long-established evangelical missionary dogma that held everyone else in contempt and obligated

---

35 Hofstadter, quoted in Weston, *Racism in U.S. Imperialism*, 35.
36 John Fiske, quoted in Forrest G. Wood, *The Arrogance of Faith: Christianity and Race in America from the Colonial Era to the Twentieth Century* (New York, 1990), 34.
37 See Daniel Boone Schirmer, *Republic or Empire: American Resistance to the Philippine War* (Cambridge, Mass., 1972), 50.
38 Sinkler, *Racial Attitudes*, 391, 409.
39 Schirmer, *Republic or Empire*, 85.
40 Wood, *Arrogance of Faith*, 22.

Americans to rescue the heathen. Undoubtedly, the Congregationalist minister Josiah Strong was the quintessential American imperialist. Strong asserted that "Christian individuals and nations had a primary obligation to fulfill the missionary charge of world evangelization and that . . . Americans as Christians had a special obligation and opportunity to fulfill this charge." In 1893, Strong wondered if it were unreasonable "that this race is destined to dispossess many weaker ones, assimilate others, and mould the remainder, until in a very true and important sense, it has Anglo-Saxonized mankind?"[41] By the outbreak of World War I, 175,000 copies of his book *Our Country* were sold; chapters in pamphlet form had been reprinted in numerous magazines and newspapers. A reading of this book suggests that imperialism was closely interconnected with nativism and nationalism long before 1898.

Some of the themes are outlined in the book's introduction, written by Austin Phelps, a clergyman from Andover Theological Seminary. "Our national salvation," Phelps wrote, "demands in supreme exercise certain military virtues," qualities of daring, vigilance, and force. The colonizing races and nations, he asserted, have been the favorites of Christianity.[42]

Strong envisioned the American West as a future giant, "in each of whose limbs shall unite the strength of many nations." He sharply indicted immigration and socialism as imperiling American development. It was his view that immigrants provided the greater portion of American criminals and harmed the morals of the native population. The typical immigrant was a peasant "whose ideas of life are low." Although cognizant of legitimate workers' grievances, Strong connected socialism to anarchism and bomb throwing. Like W. E. B. Du Bois, Strong believed that each race was the representative of some great idea, but for him these ideas did not have equal validity. The Anglo-Saxon represented civil liberty and a pure spiritual Christianity. These, it turned out, were mankind's two great needs. The Anglo-Saxon, whose great home was North America, excelled in pushing his way into new countries, and it was clear that the future of the continent belonged to the United States. Of the Anglo-Saxon future, he wrote:

---

41 Strong quoted in Wood, *Arrogance of Faith*, 22, 213.
42 See Austin Phelps's introduction to Josiah Strong, *Our Country: Its Possible Future and Its Present Crisis* (New York, 1885). Phelps was a racist, as shown in his comment about black Reconstruction legislators that they were men "who not only could neither read nor write, but whose guffaws in derision of parliamentary order, as they sat with feet higher than their heads, betrayed scarcely more of intelligence than the bray of an ass" (Austin Phelps, *My Portfolio: A Collection of Essays* [New York, 1882], 94–5).

Then this race of unequaled energy, with all the majesty of numbers and the might of wealth behind it – the representative, let us hope, of the largest liberty, the purest Christianity, the highest civilization – having developed peculiarly aggressive traits calculated to impress its institutions on mankind, will spread itself over the earth.

The Anglo-Saxon would move on Mexico, Central and South America, the island countries, and eventually Africa and beyond.[43]

Forrest Wood poses the intriguing question of how much more imperialistic the United States might have become had Strong been secretary of state at the time of the Spanish-American War. One wonders about the humanitarianism of this pastor of Cincinnati's Central Congregational Church, who wrote that "the extinction of inferior races before the advancing Anglo-Saxon certainly appears probable." Yet, it must be remembered that social gospel spokesman Walter Rauschenbusch considered Strong one of the "pioneers of Christian social thought in America."[44]

Rubin Francis Weston relates Henry Cabot Lodge's racism to his advocacy of war and empire. Lodge's support for Hawaiian annexation was permeated with a racism that claimed that Americans and Englishmen represented all there was of character and intelligence in Hawaiian society. He downplayed the significant role played by blacks in the Cuban revolution.[45] To suit his purposes he pandered to the racial climate existing in the United States.

The evidence indicates that extreme measures against African Americans were paired with extremism directed against Filipinos. The suppression of the Filipino nationalists was accomplished only by wholesale recourse to savage methods of warfare. This is a much neglected and truly shameful chapter in American history, and the record is obscured if this counterrevolutionary war becomes transformed into an American venture in paternalism. The war involved use of concentration camps and an assortment of other terrorist methods to destroy Filipino resistance. Copying methods used by the Spanish in Cuba, the Americans confined inhabitants of an area in fenced, guarded compounds, and anyone found outside was declared a guerrilla and subject to execution. There was evidence that the American commander on the island of Samar had ordered his soldiers to make the place a "howling wilderness" and, writing on American policy in the Philippines, the reporter of the pro-administration *Philadelphia Ledger* stated:

43 Strong, *Our Country*, 29, 40, 42, 85–112, 159, 161, 167, 175.
44 Wood, *Arrogance of Faith*, 353, 378–9.
45 Weston, *Racism in U.S. Imperialism*, 43–4.

The present war is no bloodless, fake, opera bouffe engagement; our men have been relentless, have killed to exterminate men, women, children, prisoners and captives, active insurgents and suspected people from lads of 10 up, an idea prevailing that the Filipino as such was little better than a dog.

William Howard Taft was asked what would happen in the event of war between Americans and Filipino revolutionaries, and he agreed such conflict would lead to inhuman warfare. The war was justified by such officers as Frederick Funston, who declared that the Filipinos were "an illiterate, semi-savage people, who are waging war, not against tyranny, but against Anglo-Saxon order and decency." Funston affirmed that the American objective in the Philippines was to "raw-hide these bulled-headed Asians until they yell for mercy." He had praise for his troops, who "go for the enemy as if they were chasing jackrabbits." To elicit information American troops sometimes resorted to the "water cure," in which a large volume of water was forced down the throat of the victim, following which interrogators jumped up and down on the prisoner's abdomen. Historian H. W. Brands concludes about American tactics, that "evidence indicating American participation in torture is irrefutable." During the course of operations the *Boston Herald* reported that the policy of the McKinley administration was influenced by Lord Kitchener's brutal plan of operations in South Africa.[46]

The other side of extreme cruelty in the Philippine War was the vicious brutality directed at African Americans in the South, most clearly in the November 1898 massacre in Wilmington, North Carolina. John W. Cell has added greatly to our understanding of turn-of-the-century racism by setting it in context, pointing out that segregation was one of the harshest form of racism, accompanied as it was by draconian "solutions" of the race question.[47] Whereas some within American society were determined to crush the assertiveness of Filipinos, others vowed that black people were to be kept down in perpetuity, allowed at best to live as menial servants of white people. Terror was to be systematically used to maintain the status quo. In Wilmington a mob shot up the black community, drove a black newspaper editor, Alex Manly, from the city, and forcibly displaced a lawfully elected municipal government. Hundreds of black Wilmingtonians sought refuge from violence in other parts of the country. One leading white supremacist said "only" twenty or thirty blacks had been killed, but a black minister declared that the

---

46 Brands, *Bound to Empire*, 56–8; Schirmer, *Republic or Empire*, 143, 225, 227, 234, 237.
47 Cell, *Highest State of White Supremacy*, 172.

mob had dumped hundreds of black bodies into the Cape Fear River.[48] The federal government did nothing to protect the black people of Wilmington.

The writings of several observers reflect the relationship between racism at home and abroad. Albion Tourgee asked if the political questions confronting the supposed Anglo-Saxon nations, "the United States in the Antilles and the Orient and Great Britain in South Africa, are not steps toward the solution of this greatest of all world problems – the relation between white peoples and brown-skinned men and women?"[49] The white supremacist Thomas Dixon, glorifier of the Ku Klux Klan, ardently embraced the new thrust of imperialism. Hailing the Spanish-American War, Dixon wrote that

America, united at last and invincible, waked to the consciousness of her resistless power. And, most marvelous of all, this hundred days of war had reunited the Anglo-Saxon race. This sudden union of the English-speaking people . . . confirmed the Anglo-Saxon in his title to the primacy of racial sway.

According to Dixon, the war revealed that blacks had no place in the "new-born unity" of American life. "When the Anglo-Saxon race was united into one homogeneous mass in the fire of this crisis," he wrote, "the Negro ceased that moment to be a ward of the nation." Dixon has one of his characters say that Americans now dreamed of the conquest of the globe and that in this crisis, "our flag has been raised over the millions of semi-barbaric black men in the foulest slave pen of the orient." This character asks if at such a solemn hour a "grand old commonwealth" of the South was to sink "into the filth and degradation of a Negroid corruption" – all of this set out in a novel portraying the triumph of white supremacy in North Carolina. [50]

Imperialism furthered the solidification of racism in the United States. The expansion of governmental powers inherent in the nation's acquisition of a colonial empire legitimized the various practices of de jure segregation now being imposed within the United States. What was, above all, new in the Jim Crow system was its sponsorship by official institutions of power, its being underwritten by the Supreme Court's *Plessy v. Ferguson* decision and innumerable state ordinances. In the sense of their

48 See Jerome Anthony McDuffie, "Politics in Wilmington and New Hanover County, North Carolina, 1865–1900: The Genesis of a Race Riot," Ph.D. diss., Kent State University, 1979, 738.
49 Tourgee, "Black and White," 16.
50 Thomas Dixon Jr., *The Leopard's Spots: A Romance of the White Man's Burden, 1865–1900* (New York, 1902), 412–13, 439–40.

dependence on state action, both segregation and imperialism were pro-gressivism writ large. If, as George Frederickson writes, the implanting of segregation resulted in an "elaborately formalized pattern of caste domi-nation," imperialism also produced a system of colonial administration.[51]

The McKinley administration's commitment to empire facilitated the triumph of racism. The federal government was hardly likely to inter-vene on behalf of black people's civil and political rights when it denied independence and political rights to the populations of the Philippines, Hawaii, and Puerto Rico and imposed a thinly veiled protectorate on Cuba. The Spanish-American War became an occasion for sectional rec-onciliation, for white harmony within the United States, for celebrat-ing, for example, the valor on the battlefront of ex-Confederate officer Fightin' Joe Wheeler. William Jennings Bryan laid out the situation when in the summer of 1898 he declared: "When the president of the United States gave a general's commission to General Fitzhugh Lee and General Wheeler the sectional question was forever settled and hereafter there will be no Dixie line."[52] The Spanish-American War became an instrument for closing the books on the Civil War and putting aside the issues of human rights at the core of that struggle. The architects of imperialism were not about to alienate southerners in Congress by seri-ously challenging white supremacy. Denial of rights to Filipinos and to black Mississippians reinforced each other.

The white racism generated by American society was carried in the baggage of the colonizers who took control of the Philippines. American personnel repeatedly referred to Filipinos as "niggers." One American soldier was quoted as stating "it kept leaking down from sources above that the Filipinos were 'niggers,' no better than Indians and were to be treated as such." Commodore George Dewey referred to Filipinos as "Indians."[53] If a feature of racist rhetoric at home was the characteriza-tion of African Americans as children, this language also become a cus-tomary reference to the Filipinos. Josiah Strong compared the Filipinos to "an undeveloped child who is incapable of self-government."[54] Rep-resentative is missionary Stealy B. Rossiter's observation that the Filipinos were "a simple minded people and have all the impulsiveness and preju-dices of children."[55] Taking account of the blatant expression of racism

---

51 George M. Frederickson, *The Arrogance of Race: Historical Perspectives on Slavery, Racism, and Social Inequality* (Middletown, Conn., 1988), 240.
52 *Wilmington Messenger*, July 21, 1898.
53 Schirmer, *Republic or Empire*, 89, 143.
54 Strong quoted in Gould, *Mismeasure of Man*, 119.
55 See Kenton J. Clymer, *Protestant Missionaries in the Philippines, 1898–1915: An Inquiry into the*

toward the Filipinos, it is little wonder that, as Willard Gatewood tells us, "many black American soldiers in the Philippines were painfully conscious of their position as the opponents of a movement by a 'colored people' to achieve independence and freedom."[56] It was really not surprising that a large number of African-American soldiers deserted during the Philippine War.

The Wilmington Massacre brings into sharp focus the linkages between domestic racism and imperialism. As Hayumi Higuchi writes, "the national government joined European imperialism by ruling non-white natives. . . . In North Carolina, Democrats understood either consciously or unconsciously that national policy implicitly encouraged their own commitment to white supremacy."[57] What appears clearly in this case is the class nature of the racist movement to destroy the Republican-Populist alliance, and the evidence here counters the notion that poor whites were the fundamental source of opposition to black aspirations. Wilmington's reality should lead us to scrutinize more carefully the sources of decision making in American society, both with regard to domestic issues and questions of foreign policy. Wilmington also places in bold relief the role imperialism played in furthering the establishment of white-supremacist government.

The Wilmington experience contradicts James Bryce's view that most of "the leading business men and professional men and many of the large landowners" held blacks in better regard than did poor whites.[58] During the Wilmington struggle reporter Henry L. West of the *Washington Post* came to the city and wrote a series of articles in which he stressed the claims of property holders to control the machinery of government. He quoted a Wilmington businessman as saying,

Every cent I have in the world is invested in and around Wilmington, but I would rather sacrifice all and leave the locality rather than endure another two years of what we have patiently suffered here since 1896. . . . We have organized now for the protection of the property-holding, tax-paying class.[59]

American Colonial Mentality (Urbana, Ill., 1986), 73. That this version of antiblack racism was exported can be seen in James Bryce's comment that blacks are "children of nature whose highest form of pleasure had hitherto been to caper to the strains of a banjo" (James Bryce, *The American Commonwealth* [New York, 1914], 516).

56 Willard B. Gatewood Jr., *"Smoked Yankees" and the Struggle for Empire: Letters from Negro Soldiers, 1898–1902* (Urbana, Ill., 1971), 14.

57 Hayumi Higuchi, "White Supremacy on the Cape Fear: The Wilmington Affair of 1898," M.A. thesis, University of North Carolina, 1980, 142.

58 James Bryce, *The American Commonwealth* (New York, 1923), 563.

59 *Wilmington Messenger*, Nov. 1, 1898, quoting the *Washington Post*.

West reflected the ideology of disfranchisement advocates who believed, as Guion Griffis Johnson notes, that the suffrage was a privilege to be enjoyed by "the educated, tax-paying, property-owning and virtuous citizenry."[60] Wilmington's Democratic Party was dominated in the 1890s, according to Jerome A. McDuffie, by "the merchant, banker, industrialist, entrepreneur, railroad promoter, and lawyer." The city's business interest opposed Republican-Fusion proposals for city ownership of electrical, sewer, water, and street-rail systems. Statewide, the party was dominated by railroad interests backed by J. P. Morgan.[61] *Baltimore Sun* correspondent and Johns Hopkins University historian Guy Carleton Lee reported from Wilmington on how the white supremacy campaign was organized: "The business men, with but three exceptions, commenced the work of organization. It is of special note that the committee in charge was composed of the most substantial business and professional men, the combined wealth of whom would approximate $20,000,000."[62]

The *Wilmington Messenger*, the city's leading conservative newspaper, articulated the views of the business community. The paper attacked Governor Daniel Russell for having "made war upon the corporations. . . . So far from bringing in northern capital and encouraging home investment his reign of terror has alarmed capital that is ever sensitive, and stifled in the incipiency plans and promises."[63] The paper declared that columns could be filled with interviews from merchants, bank presidents, clergymen, lawyers, "and reputable citizens generally" agreeing with the businessman quoted by the *Washington Post* in urging organization by property-holders. The *Messenger* flatly stated that "the anti-negro movement began with and was stimulated by the business men as a matter of self-preservation."[64] The paper ran the full text of the speech by white supremacist Alfred M. Waddell indicting blacks for voting against white interests although whites had paid the taxes to support black education and employed them as artisans and laborers.[65] On November 5, 1898, the *Messenger* quoted a Richmond newspaper report that described a gathering of Wilmington Democrats: "These are businessmen – those who own the property here and who cannot be called politicians."[66] The key strat-

---

60 Guion Griffis Johnson, "The Ideology of White Supremacy," in Fletcher Melvin Green, ed., *Essays in Southern History* (Chapel Hill, N.C., 1949), 133.
61 McDuffie, "Politics in Wilmington and New Hanover County," 187, 509, 545–6.
62 *Wilmington Messenger*, Nov. 17, 1898.
63 Ibid., Aug. 12, 1898.
64 Ibid., Nov. 1, 1898.
65 Ibid., Oct. 25, 1898.
66 Ibid., Nov. 5, 1898.

egy group planning the Wilmington violence was the Secret Nine, composed of representatives of various cotton mill, dry goods, lumber, and banking interests.[67]

Business also supported imperialism in its operations abroad. Daniel Boone Schirmer explains that, at the inception of the American empire, both supporters and opponents believed that the demand by industry for new markets played a large role. Schirmer criticizes Julius Pratt for neglecting the business newspapers that supported intervention.[68] The depression of 1893 provoked deep anxieties about America's economic future and was influential in the shaping of policy. William Appleman Williams pioneered in revealing business interest in overseas empire.[69] A textile-industry newspaper wrote in July 1898, "Supremacy in the world appears to be the destiny of race to which we belong." A good example of business opinion was New Englander Nathan Matthews Jr., who told a Boston audience that greater opportunities were needed for the investment of surplus capital "in order to prevent the duplication of industries for which there can be no adequate domestic market." According to Matthews, the possibilities of China as a field for capital investment were the centerpiece of American foreign economic policy.[70]

There is substantial evidence that demonstrates the use made of imperialism in reinforcing racist policies at home. Schirmer writes that "the imperialist posture, in attitude and ideology, as well as in practice, stimulated white racism." The *Springfield Republican* asked, "Is the contempt we have shown for the rights and protests of the natives of the Philippines . . . calculated to increase the southern white's regard for the Negro as a fellow-being of like feelings and claims to life and liberty as himself?"[71] The *Wilmington Messenger* pointed to North Carolina as the exception to the global rule of white supremacy, claiming that "there is no country or domain or state of white men or Aryan stock being ridden over roughshod by the descendants of the black men of African wilds."

One of the factors in the racist seizure of power in Wilmington was the Wilmington Light Infantry, an organization of Spanish-American War veterans that patrolled the city following the coup. One of the unit's officers was told, "You have just been through the war and so you know

67 McDuffie, "Politics in Wilmington," 618.
68 Schirmer, *Republic or Empire*, 19, 62.
69 William Appleman Williams, *The Contours of American History* (Cleveland, 1961), 363–70.
70 Schirmer, *Republic or Empire*, 87, 167–8.
71 Ibid., 83, 147.

about what should be done, so let's get started and be through with it." Jerome McDuffie writes that the Light Infantry and the naval reserve unit searched black churches with military precision. Among others patrolling the city was a group named the "Rough Riders," echoing the name of Theodore Roosevelt's troops in Cuba.

In the weeks before the November violence, a Winston-Salem leader proposed that since the previous slogan had been "Remember the *Maine*," what was now called for was "Remember North Carolina."[72] Alfred Waddell expressed the view in 1900 that since the annexation of Hawaii, Puerto Rico, and the Philippines, conditions would become more favorable for repeal of the Fifteenth Amendment.[73] The *Atlantic Monthly* asked, if the right to vote could be curtailed abroad, why not in Mississippi and South Carolina?[74]

It is also appropriate to note that "Pitchfork" Ben Tillman, the South Carolina white supremacist, involved himself in the 1898 North Carolina struggle. Tillman drew on the experience of British imperialism in India to support American white supremacy. The Englishman, he contended, "governs by law where law will do, and by force where force is necessary." Tillman told an interviewer, "England has more to do with colored races than any other nationality – than all the other nations combined – and the Englishman goes about the conquest and governing of Chinese, Hindoos, Malays and Africans in the sole principles of inherent superiority and right to rule."[75] During the campaign of 1898, Tillman carried his message of white supremacy to Democratic rallies in North Carolina. To a crowd of thousands gathered at Fayetteville on October 20, he lauded the example of South Carolina, which had amended its state constitution in order to deny the ballot to blacks.[76]

The *Wilmington Messenger* reported with approval the comments of the *Chicago Interior*, a Presbyterian publication. This journal declared that

nowhere in the world today, in Carolina or Massachusetts, in India or China or Africa or the Philippines will the Anglo-Saxon submit to the rule of another race, be that race white or yellow or brown or red or black. Whatever the future may reveal, just at this hour in the world's history, the Anglo-Saxon is supreme.

72 *Wilmington Messenger*, Aug. 24, Sept. 27, 1998; Higuchi, "White Supremacy," 57, 72–4; McDuffie, "Politics in Wilmington," 686, 713, 716, 718.
73 Weston, *Racism in U.S. Imperialism*, 13.
74 See C. Vann Woodward, *The Strange Career of Jim Crow* (New York, 1974), 72.
75 *New York Herald*, Nov. 14, 1898, quoting Tillman.
76 *Wilmington Messenger*, Oct. 22, 1898.

The *Messenger* unified domestic white supremacy and colonialism in its boast that it "has had much to say of the great conquering, civilizing, dominating, colonizing, educating, humanizing White Race."[77]

The interconnection of empire and racism in American history suggests the inaccuracy of the view that the United States has been exceptional in the development of the great industrial nations. The systems of corporate capitalism in the United States, Germany, France, and Britain have all spawned the growth of racism, and in each of these nations the conquest of other nationalities, most often nonwhite nationalities, has been of decisive importance. The United States moved on to more indirect postcolonial versions of empire in which economic penetration and export of ideology were key, but in fostering the racism that bedevils us still, the nation linked itself to the destiny of all nations that substitute conquest for democratic self-development.

77 Ibid., Oct. 25, 1898.

8

Police, African Americans, and Irish Immigrants in the Nation's Capital

A History of Everyday Racism in Civil War Washington

NORBERT FINZSCH

This is the situation the LAPD does not want to happen.
They do not dig this gang truce. They want to keep them
separate. Once you sit down with twenty thousand guys
who used to be fighting each other in groups of five or
five hundred, and you set them all together, you've got
some kind of new phenomena.[1]

THEORY

Everyday History, Everyday Racism

Racism, nationalism, and xenophobia are likely to increase during critical periods in the history of a society. Racism appears not only in written or spoken texts but also in acts. David Theo Goldberg has argued that there is no generic racism and that therefore one has to historicize the different racisms:[2]

There is no single [set of] transcendental determinant[s] that inevitably causes the occurrence of racism – be it in nature, or drive, or mode of production, or class formation. There are only the minutiae that make up the fabric of daily life and specific interests and values, the cultures out of which racialized discourse and racist expressions arise. Racist expressions become normalized in and

1 Ice T, *The Ice Opinion as Told to Heidi Siegmund* (New York, 1994), 39.
2 David Theo Goldberg, *Racist Cultures: Philosophy and the Politics of Meaning* (Oxford, 1993), 90. His earlier writings on the topic of racism include Davis Theo Goldberg, ed., *The Anatomy of Racism* (Minneapolis, 1990).

through the prevailing categories of modernity's epistemes and institutionalized in modernity's various modes of social articulation and power.[3]

Racism is more than just a reaction to problems and difficult passages in the life of individuals and groups. It is a fact of life, even in stages of relative economic stability and social equilibrium. Two examples that stem from different historical backgrounds explain this. According to a poll taken by *Der Spiegel*, in 1992 one-third of Germany's population believed that Jews are at least partly responsible for the hate crimes committed against them.[4] Studs Terkel's book *Race* has demonstrated how deeply the "American obsession" with racial matters is ingrained into everyday culture.[5] Racist assumptions about people believed to be the "Other" are tenacious and often lie below the surface of conscientious behavior. But they can easily be reactivated and acted on if one's own social, economic, or cultural position seems to be threatened or questioned.[6] The recent discourse about the allegedly greater amount of criminal activity of "foreigners" in Germany in connection with the debate on a "reform" of German laws that grant asylum to refugees – who come to Germany for political reasons – is a case in point. In this sense, racist assumptions are part of *mentalité* and of that highly heterogeneous historiography that Germans call *Alltagsgeschichte*, or the history of everyday life.[7] One largely ignored aspect of the history of everyday life is that its proponents seek to recapture subjective historical experience of people "from below." Those who attack this method of historiography fear, for example, that it ignores Nazi atrocities and the silent complicity of ordinary people. It should nevertheless be emphasized that the concept of everyday history

3 Goldberg, *Racist Cultures*, 90.
4 Original poll in the issues of Jan. 13, 1992 and Jan. 20, 1992, under the heading "*Spiegel* Umfrage: Deutsche und Juden." See also Rafael Seligmann, "Republik der Betroffenen," *Der Spiegel*, April 4, 1994, 92.
5 Studs Terkel, *Race: How Blacks and Whites Think and Feel About the American Obsession* (New York, 1992).
6 The long-term history of racism, ethnocentrism, and anti-Semitism has led some sociobiologists to conclude that they may not be social phenomena, but "natural" ones; see George J. Stein, "The Biological Bases of Ethnocentrism, Racism and Nationalism in National Socialism," in Vernon Reynolds, Vincent Falger, and Ian Vine, eds., *The Sociobiology of Ethnocentrism: Evolutionary Dimensions of Xenophobia, Discrimination, Racism, and Nationalism* (Athens, Ga., 1986), 251.
7 There has been a paradigmatic discussion on the importance and the meaning of *Alltagsgeschichte* in Germany since the mid-1980s. Compare Klaus Gerteis, "Zur Thematik der Alltagsgeschichte im Zeitalter der Aufklärung," *Aufklärung* 5, no. 2 (1990): 3–8; Carola Lipp, "Writing History as Political Culture: Social History versus *Alltagsgeschichte*: A German Debate," *Storia della Storiografia* 17 (1990): 66–100; Geoff Eley, "Labor History, Social History, Alltagsgeschichte: Experience, Culture, and the Politics of the Everyday – A New Direction for German Social History?" *Journal of Modern History* 61, no. 2 (1989): 297–343. For further information, see Alf Lüdtke, ed., *Alltagsgeschichte: Zur Rekonstruktion historischer Erfahrungen und Lebensweisen* (Frankfurt/Main, 1989). Klaus Tenfelde, "Schwierigkeiten mit dem Alltag," *Geschichte und Gesellschaft*, no. 10 (1984): 376–94.

is not as theoretically blind as its antagonists suggest and that it has critical potential. To study subjective experience does not necessarily mean
to oppose structural historical explanations. Everyday history can also
serve as a complement to achieve a richer picture of a historical epoch.[8]
  In contrast to some historians, I do not think that the study of the
everyday past has provided German historians with a means of using the
methods of deconstruction without accepting its theoretical implications.[9] For one thing, as a theoretical concept, deconstruction is almost
unknown among German (social) historians; and for another, critics of
this methodology alienate *Alltagsgeschichte* from its context, which can
only be understood by looking at the so-called *Geschichtswerkstätten*, or
"history workshops," groups of freelance, nonacademic historians who
started to do research in their immediate environment, for example, their
neighborhood, church community, or social clubs, mostly to rediscover
the history of fascism and the resistance against it in the 1930s and
1940s.[10] To see that kind of historiographic practice in connection with
deconstruction fails to understand the atheoretical or antitheoretical position of many early historians of everyday life in Germany. A theoretically more enriched position was only gained after professional historians
like the late Detlev J. K. Peukert used *Alltagsgeschichte* to gain a different
access to the history of the fascist period in German history.[11] Others,
such as Lutz Niethammer, very early on helped to introduce the concept
of everyday history into academic historiography.[12] If *Alltagsgeschichte* has

---

8 This point is made by Martin Jay, "Force Fields: Songs of Experience: Reflection on the Debate
  over *Alltagsgeschichte*," *Salmagundi* 81 (1989): 29–41. The methodological advantages of *Alltagsgeschichte* over conventional social history are emphasized by James H. Jackson Jr., "*Alltagsgeschichte*, Social Science History, and the Study of Migration in Nineteenth-Century Germany,"
  Central European History 23, nos. 2–3 (1990): 242–63; Jackson, "*Alltagsgeschichte*, Social Science
  History, and the Study of Mundane Movements in Nineteenth-Century Germany," *Historical
  Social Research* 16, no. 1 (1991): 23–47.
9 David F. Crew, "*Alltagsgeschichte*: A New Social History 'From Below?'" *Central European History*
  22, nos. 3–4 (1989): 394–407. The theoretical limitations of early *Alltagsgeschichte* have aptly been
  demonstrated by Mary Nolan, "The *Historikerstreit* and Social History," *New German Critique*, no.
  44 (1988): 51–80.
10 Dagmar Freist, "Alltagsgeschichte der Juden: In Search for New Approaches to Jewish History,"
  German History 7, no. 2 (1989): 248–51. The article constitutes a report on issue no. 15 of
  Geschichtswerkstatt, a journal of the history workshop movement, attempting to reconstruct Jewish daily life in nineteenth- and twentieth-century Germany and Europe.
11 Detlev J. K. Peukert, "Ist die neuere Alltagsgeschichte theoriefeindlich?" in Herta Nagl-Docekal
  and Franz Wimmer, eds., *Neuere Ansätze in der Geschichtswissenschaft* (Vienna, 1984), 7–17;
  Richard Bessel, "Detlev J. K. Peukert (1950–1990)" [in memoriam], *German History* 8, no. 3
  (1990): 321–4; Detlev J. K. Peukert, "Neuere Alltagsgeschichte und Historische Anthropologie,"
  in Hans Süssmuth, ed., *Historische Anthropologie: Der Mensch in der Geschichte* (Göttingen, 1984),
  57–72.
12 Lutz Niethammer, "Das kritische Potential der *Alltagsgeschichte*," *Geschichtsdidaktik* 10, no. 3

gained increasing acceptance among social historians, this is owing to a stronger linkage with positions of the French Annales school and reception of anthropological techniques of description and analysis.[13]

In this chapter, I describe and analyze racism as a fact of everyday life, part of a necessary system of "social differentiation." This is not to say, however, that racism itself is necessary. This racism becomes visible in everyday actions taken by individuals or institutions – for example, the legal apparatus or the police. The administration and execution of the law are indeed phenomena of the *Alltag* (the everyday). Most of the time we deal with them in our daily routine without even being aware of it. In addition, I do not construct criminal law and its procedures, of which the police is only a part, as a means of protecting the "interests of people who suffered as victims of crime,"[14] but as a system of power, in which "prosecutions reflect changes in the behaviour of those who control the law at least as much as the acts of those who break it."[15] If crime control is a system of power, it follows that power relations defined by ethnicity or racism must be reflected in the daily routines of that system. Leon Higginbotham Jr., one of the most eminent lawyers in the United States, has gone so far as to speak of the "interrelationship of race and the American legal process."[16]

This concept of the law contrasts sharply with the image of justice as "color-blind": The allegory of "Justitia" is depicted as blindfolded, sword and balance in both hands, thus able to decide what is the law of the land without regard to class, gender, or ethnicity of the defendant. Justice and its administration should be impartial and blind to social position, sex, and color. In fact, since colonial times, the law and the courts vacillated over the question of whether or not African Americans were people and, if so, "whether they were a species apart from white humans."[17] Thus, this chapter examines the daily racism of white policemen directed against African Americans in Washington, D.C., during a critical period of American history. To make my findings comparable to other

---

(1985): 245–7. By the same author, see "Anmerkungen zur Alltagsgeschichte," *Geschichtsdidaktik* 5, no. 3 (1980): 231–42.

13 For a discussion of the importance of the *Annales* for a history of criminality, see Dirk Blasius, "Kriminologie und Geschichtswissenschaft: Bilanz und Perspektiven interdisziplinärer Forschung," *Geschichte und Gesellschaft*, no. 14 (1988): 143–9.

14 J. H. Langbein, "Albion's Fatal Flaws," *Past and Present* 98 (1983): 97.

15 Douglas Hay, "War, Dearth, and Theft in the Eighteenth Century: The Record of the English Courts," *Past and Present*, no. 95 (1982): 118.

16 A. Leon Higginbotham Jr., *In the Matter of Color: Race and the American Legal Process: The Colonial Period* (New York, 1978), 5.

17 Higginbotham, *In the Matter of Color*, 7.

ethnic groups, I use Irish immigrants as a control group. Before dealing with the archival material, I develop some ideas about the relationship between discourse analysis and social history, ideas that are somewhat disconnected from the main body of this chapter. A discussion of these ideas is nevertheless essential for a full development of the historiographical methodology.

Discourse Versus Social History

Social history, as it has been understood, is out. Discourse analysis, as currently practiced, is definitely in. As a consequence of the "linguistic turn," literary criticism and literary history have developed into fields, in which, based on the writings of Friedrich Nietzsche and Martin Heidegger and ideas brought to the United States by authors such as Michel Foucault and Jacques Derrida, Western rationality has become a focus of critique.[18] At the same time, a shift had occurred in what was perceived as "evidence," not only within literary studies but also in historiography. Critiques of what is called a "vogue" by some, a "fashion" by others, focus on the fact that exactly the same intellectual traditions central to the rise of irrationality, fascism, and Nazism are supposed to have become components of modern theory. This may be deplorable in the context of literary criticism, but according to some critics, it becomes outright unbearable if used for the explanation of fascism, racism, or studies of the Holocaust. It is hard, in fact, to face millions of victims of German fascism or of American chattel slavery on the basis of discourses if one "envisions" at the same moment the corpses of victims piled up in German concentration camps in 1945.

The same principle applies to the historiography of American slavery and of the thousands of African Americans who were victims of lynchings. It is difficult to imagine hundreds of thousands of slaves, who barely escaped from death from starvation, illness, or violence on the slave ships and who were sold into captivity after the infamous "middle passage," exclusively as part of a discourse. This is not intended to deny that different discourses on slavery, racist exclusions, racisms, and fascisms have in fact taken place in different times and under different circumstances. The problem we have to tackle, though, is whether discourse can embrace "matter," "reality," and "bodies" – whether there is "reality" outside of discourse or whether we cannot escape the iron cage of language

18 Adrian M. S. Piper, "Xenophobia and Kantian Rationalism," *Philosophical Forum* 24 (1992): 188ff.

even when talking about practices. Let me give just one example: When the African American James Irwin was killed by a white mob, his death, as cruel and bestial as it was, nevertheless followed a certain preordained pattern that bore significance in itself. I quote from one of the earlier books on lynching, a 1933 study by Arthur Raper:

Mobs are capable of unbelievable atrocity. James Irwin at Ocilla, Georgia, was jabbed in his mouth with a sharp pole. His toes were cut off joint by joint. His fingers were similarly removed, and his teeth extracted with wire pliers. After further unmentionable mutilations [that is, castration], the Negro's still living body was saturated with gasoline and a lighted match was applied. As the flames leaped up, hundreds of shots were fired into the dying victim. During the day, thousands of people from miles around rode out to see the sight. Not till nightfall did the officers remove the body and bury it.[19]

It is important to note that (1) the atrocity of the murder of James Irwin, as undeniably as it had happened, itself had strong resemblance to a text, because it "meant" something to onlookers and the absent African Americans who were supposed to "understand" it as a warning not to transgress the limits assigned to them by a racist white majority, and (2) it is equally important that we – as nonwitnesses – know about this event only from texts like that by Raper. We have no access to that death except through texts. One of the most eminent historians of Germany, Jane Caplan, has expressed serious doubts about the applicability of postmodern theory (that is, deconstruction) to history:

What can one usefully say about National Socialism as an ideology or a political movement and regime via theories that appear to discount rationality as a mode of explanation, that resist the claims of truth, relativize and disseminate power, cannot assign responsibility clearly, and do not privilege (one) truth or morality over (multiple) interpretations?[20]

To be fair, however, it is important that there are as many postmodern theories as there is coal in Newcastle. Deconstruction may be the least useful theory in coping with problems of racism and National Socialism. But it should also be noted that rationality is by no means a safeguard against racist discourses and racist practices, as David Theo Goldberg and Zygmunt Baumann have shown.[21] It is too easy to dismiss postmodern

19 Arthur F. Raper, *The Tragedy of Lynching*, Patterson Smith Reprint Series in Criminology, Law Enforcement, and Social Problems, publication no. 25 (Chapel Hill, N.C., 1933; reprint, Montclair, N.J., 1969), 6–7.

20 Jane Caplan, "Postmodernism, Poststructuralism, and Deconstruction: Notes for Historians," *Central European History* 22, nos. 3–4 (1989): 274.

21 See Goldberg, *Racist Cultures*. Bauman's writing very much constitutes the theoretical backbone

theory in history generally as a case of historical amnesia or historical ignorance. Among the most influential postmodern theoretical contributions to the broad field of discourse analysis are the writings of Foucault, but other authors would have to be quoted as well for the picture to be complete. I do not want to add my observations on the apparent rediscovery of Foucault in recent years or point out the fact that his impact may finally be felt even in German historiography, which is traditionally less open to theoretical innovation and over which the Bielefeld school still exerts a major influence.[22] Foucault, who is often quoted in the debate between postmodern "scholars of discourse" and "modern" scholars of structural social history, does not in fact lend himself easily to abuse as propaganda for discourse analysis, as the only viable way of dealing with complex historical problems. To choose Foucault as a starting point in this debate is also appropriate because more recent schools, such as new historicism, cultural poetics, new cultural history, or cultural materialism, draw heavily on Foucault's ideas.[23] Some of those links can be defined as the exchange, some as the containment of ideas.

for Goldberg's analysis of racism. Zygmunt Bauman, *Modernity and Ambivalence* (Ithaca, N.Y., 1991). On problems of modernity and how they influence racist thinking, see Zygmunt Bauman, *Legislators and Interpreters: On Modernity, Post-Modernity and Intellectuals* (Cambridge, 1987).

22 Martin Dinges, "Foucaultrezeption in Deutschland," in Norbert Finzsch and Robert Jütte, eds., *Institutions of Confinement: Hospitals, Asylums, and Prisons in Western Europe and North America, 1500–1950* (New York, 1996).

23 H. Aram Veeser, ed., *The New Historicism* (New York, 1989). Especially interesting also is the introductory article by Veeser, "The New Historicism," in H. Aram Veeser, ed., *The New Historicism Reader* (New York, 1994), 1–34, in which the author underlines the theoretical influence of cultural anthropology *à la* Clifford Geertz. So far a literary critic has written the best German introduction to the New Historicism; see Ansgar Nünning, "Narrative Form und fiktionale Wirklichkeitskonstruktion aus der Sicht des *New Historicism* und der Narrativik: Grundzüge und Perspektiven einer kulturwissenschaftlichen Erforschung des englischen Romans im 18. Jahrhundert," *Zeitschrift für Anglistik und Amerikanistik* 40 (1992): 197–213; also very helpful is the article by Annette Simonis, "*New Historicism* und *Poetics of Culture: Renaissance Studies* und Shakespeare im neueren Licht," in Ansgar Nünning, ed., *Literaturwissenschaftliche Theorien, Modelle und Methoden* (Trier, 1995): 153–72; see also Heide Ziegler, "Directions in German–American Studies: The Challenge of the 'New Historicism,'" in Peter Freese, ed., *Germany and German Thought in American Literature and Cultural Criticism: Proceedings of the German-American Conference in Paderborn, May 16–19, 1990* (Essen, 1990), 363; Udo J. Hebel, "Der amerikanische *New Historicism* der achtziger Jahre: Bestandsaufnahme einer neuen Orthodoxie kulturwissenschaftlicher Literaturinterpretation," *Amerikastudien/American Studies* 37, no. 2 (1992): 325–47. One of the major critiques of the new paradigm is Brook Thomas, *The New Historicism and Other Old-Fashioned Topics* (Princeton, N.J., 1991), 179–218. The lack of concepts stemming from social history (old style) within New Historicism is criticized by Peter Nicholls, "Old Problems and the New Historicism," *Journal of American Studies* 23, no. 3 (1989): 423–34. The importance of New Historicism for American historiography is discussed in Shirley Samuels, "The Family, the State, and the Novel in the Early Republic," *American Quarterly* 38, no. 3 (1986): 381–95; Robert M. Calhoon, "The Constitution and the New Historicism," *Pennsylvania Magazine of History and Biography* 114, no. 2 (1990): 271–9; Gillian Brown, *Domestic Individualism: Imagining Self in Nineteenth-Century America*

It is obvious that Foucault does not deny the existence of a (socially and conventionally constructed) reality outside of discourses. In his treatise on the structure of discourses, *L'archéologie du savoir* (The archaeology of knowledge), written in 1969 and translated into German in 1988, Foucault made clear that, with its relatively recent tendency to avoid any resemblance with a "collective memory" of past events that actually happened, history had taken a position that turned historiography into a discipline closer to archeology because it tended to interpret documents immanently as "monuments."[24] Another text of relevance here is Foucault's *Les mots et les choses* (translated into English as *The Order of Things*), an archeology of humanities, as the subtitle indicates. Thus far, the worst expectations of those historians who understand Foucault as a theorist of the dissolution or "death" of the individual subject and as an advocate of a discourse removed from contemporary political and social consequences have been confirmed.[25] If everything is discourse, according to antipostmodern theorists, how then can bodies have a reality?[26]

This view, however, has a blind spot. First of all, discourses are not just "talks" or "texts"; they are not simply what one finds in the newspapers if one randomly opens the society or style section, nor are they what one can overhear in casual conversations. It is important to understand that discourses are "serious" and not just contingent performative "speech acts" *à la* Austin and Searle.[27] Second, Foucault analyzes discourses according to their positivity. He is, as he himself claims, a "happy positivist" and content with this ascription.[28] There needs to be a certain "thickness" of "texts" or "speech acts" on a serious matter to qualify these discoursative events as discourses. Most important, contradicting Derrida's famous dictum, there indeed is a "hors-texte."[29] This "hors-texte," this praxis, is

---

(Berkeley, Calif., 1990); Gesa Mackenthun, "Vom Nutzen und Nachteil Historischer Anfänge in den Early American Studies," *Amerikastudien/American Studies* 38, no. 2 (1993): 223–36. Under the rubric of New Cultural History, New Historicism is discussed by Lynn Hunt, ed., *The New Cultural History* (Berkeley, Calif., 1989).

24 Michel Foucault, *Archäologie des Wissens* (Frankfurt/Main, 1988), 15.

25 Judith Butler, "Kontingente Grundlagen: Der Feminismus und die Frage der 'Postmoderne,'" in Seyla Benhabib, Judith Butler, Drucilla Cornell, and Nancy Frazer, *Der Streit um die Differenz: Feminismus und Postmoderne in der Gegenwart* (Frankfurt/Main, 1993), 46, later published in English as Seyla Benhabib et al., *Feminist Contentions: A Philosophical Exchange* (New York, 1995).

26 Butler, *Kontingente Grundlagen*, 51.

27 Hubert L. Dreyfus and Paul Rabinow, *Michel Foucault: Jenseits von Strukturalismus und Hermeneutik* (Frankfurt/Main, 1987), 70–2. See also Susanne Krasmann, "Silmultaneität von Körper und Sprache bei Michel Foucault," *Leviathan: Zeitschrift für Sozialwissenschaft* 23, no. 2 (1995): 241.

28 Michel Foucault, *Archäologie des Wissens*, 182.

29 Jacques Derrida, *De la Grammatologie* (Paris, 1967), 227.

called nondiscursive practice.[30] Its domain is that of materiality, work, and the body. Foucault establishes this area of nondiscursive practice in his attempt to explain what discourse analysis is not: It is not a history of the referent, although "such a history of the referent is no doubt possible."[31] He continues, "In one word, one wants to be abstinent from 'the things' completely; [one wants to] "de-present" them; [one wants to] ban their rich, heavy and immediate fullness."[32] That means, of course, that there is a rich and immediate fullness of "things" like economic or technical events. This does not mean, however, that those areas are sealed off from discourse completely. They are no actual part of discourse, but they are bound within discourses. "One has to understand discourse as a power that we exert on things; a practice, in any case, that we force on them."[33]

Here again, we find this conspicuous dichotomy of (visible and material) "things" and discourse that have a dialectical relationship, although Foucault always claimed to want to do away with dialectics.[34] What is visible ("things") cannot simply be transformed into things that are said. Bodies are not simply represented in language, and language is no mirror of bodies' physical existence, since bodies belong to the realm of things visible and constitute unformed matter, a surface on which language may place signs. The body thus is the result of the inscription of language onto that matter. It comes into existence simultaneously through the combination of visible matter and inscription of signs by language.[35]

Simultaneity thus dissolves the dichotomy of "reality" and "construction," on the one hand, and "materiality" and *écriture*, on the other. Bodies become "things" that cannot be dissolved from "discourses" that shape our thoughts and imagination.[36] Whether there is a reality outside of discourses and how we have to deal with the "reality" of burned bodies and tortured flesh as evidence of the material side of racism, it is helpful to remind ourselves constantly of the simultaneity of body and language.

---

30 Bernhard Waldenfels, "Ordnung in Diskursen," in Ewald François and Bernhard Waldenfels, *Spiele der Wahrheit: Michel Foucaults Denken* (Frankfurt/Main, 1991), 280.
31 Foucault, *Archäologie des Wissens*, 72.
32 Ibid. All translations from the German edition provided by the author.
33 Michel Foucault, *Die Ordnung des Diskurses: Mit einem Essay von Ralf Konersmann* (Frankfurt/Main, 1991), 34–5.
34 Wolfgang Welsch, "Präzision und Suggestion: Bemerkungen zu Stil und Wirkung eines Autors," in Ewald and Waldenfels, eds., *Spiele der Wahrheit*, 141. The dichotomy of visibility and discourse is the topic of Susanne Krasmann's enlightening article "Simultaneität von Körper und Sprache," 249–53.
35 Butler, *Kontingente Grundlagen*, 52–3. Quoted in ibid., 253.
36 Krasmann, "Simultaneität von Körper und Sprache," 253.

Burns and scars are real, but they are the ultimate inscription of discourses onto the body at the same time. The binary opposition of social history versus discourse analysis is "false," that is, ideologically motivated. We can close this artificial gap by writing social history that nevertheless includes discourses and their analysis while also taking into account the "real world." Social history is discourse analysis with nondiscoursive practices left in.

FREE BLACKS

Washington had always had a large proportion of free blacks, owing to its geographic position south of the Mason-Dixon Line and its relatively benign treatment of African Americans. Despite repressive "black codes" and the slave trade that was conducted out of Washington City, laws affecting blacks were milder, and they were not as vigorously enforced as elsewhere in the South. The situation of educational institutions reserved for blacks in the city can even be described as "exceptional."[37] Nevertheless, the lives of black Americans in the District of Columbia remained marked by sharp contradictions. Although slavery within the city had virtually disappeared by 1860 and most of the city's blacks were free, they witnessed the growth of the slave trade in the capital and its vicinity.[38] The presence of slave traders in the city constituted a direct menace to the freedom of blacks because "[they] were sometimes kidnapped into bondage and sold South."[39] While the slave population of Washington kept declining gradually after 1800, first relatively and then absolutely, the free-black citizens of the District increased twelvefold in the antebellum decades. Most of them came from the adjoining states, namely, Maryland and Virginia. Statistical evidence drawn from the 1860 census suggests, however, that at the beginning of the Civil War, most black Washingtonians, like the white majority, had been born inside the city limits.[40]

Although some of the free blacks were economically prosperous and the population of color enjoyed greater freedom of movement than in most other prewar American cities, "black codes" restricting the move-

---

37 David L. Lewis, *District of Columbia: A Bicentennial History* (New York, 1976), 44.
38 James O. Horton, "The Making of Black Washington," in Francine C. Cary, ed., *Urban Odyssey* (Washington, D.C., 1994), 10.
39 James O. Horton, *The Making*, 12.
40 48.6 percent as compared to 14.8 percent from Maryland and 16.7 percent from Virginia. Calculations based on a randomly collected sample of 418 blacks and mulattos.

ments of free blacks limited this freedom. "Free blacks were forbidden to operate or frequent gambling or drinking establishments, to swear in public or to be found drunk. They could not keep dogs, race horses through the streets [or] carry fire arms."[41] Besides these infringements on the civil liberties of blacks, they were forced to post bail for their good behavior and their solvency, something that put them on the same level as convicted criminals. After 1812 they were required to register with the city authorities and to produce their "freedom papers" whenever required to prove their free status.[42] Antiblack racism increased with the anticipated flood of African-American migrants from the neighboring slave states and the emergence of abolitionist activities in the city during the 1830s, since Washington was the one place in the United States where federal authority could and did – however reluctantly – interfere with slavery.

Two incidents in the prewar history of Washington, D.C., demonstrate that with all the comparative lenience that was practiced against free blacks in the capital, the amount of racism should not be underestimated. The alleged attempt of a slave to murder the widow of a notable citizen led to a riot that left the fashionable property of African-American restaurateur Beverly Snow in ruins and led to the destruction of other black-owned property in the city. Fortunately, the "Snow Riot" of 1835 did not result in the loss of life.[43] As a direct consequence of the violence directed against African Americans, however, the city council passed an ordinance blocking blacks from ownership of commercial businesses.[44] Another incident of an openly racist attack on African Americans occurred in 1848. An attempt to free seventy-seven slaves onboard the ship *Pearl* failed after one slave had informed the furious owners that their "property" had left the city on a vessel anchored downstream in the

---

41 Horton, *The Making*, 14.
42 Ibid.
43 Carl E. Price argued that the 1834–5 riots, numbering more than twenty-four nationwide, were largely nativist responses to competition for employment, whose targets were free blacks and Irish immigrants. He sees the riots, taken as a whole, as a result of the dynamic transformation and pressures brought on by rapid urbanization, heavy Irish immigration and rapid industrialization. But agrarian disruption and the emerging abolitionist movement also influenced this unrest, which cracked the facade of Jacksonian egalitarianism. See Carl E. Price, "The Great 'Riot Year': Jacksonian Democracy and Patterns of Violence in 1834," *Journal of the Early Republic* 5, no. 1 (1985): 1–19. The Philadelphia riot of August 1834, however, was a direct outcome of racist Irish attacks on African Americans. John Runcie, "'Hunting the Nigs' in Philadelphia: The Race Riot of August 1834," *Pennsylvania History* 39, no. 2 (1972): 187–218. The Snow Riots are discussed in the context of Jacksonian politics by David Grimsted, "Rioting in Its Jacksonian Setting," *American Historical Review* 77, no. 2 (1972): 361–97.
44 Lewis, *District of Columbia*, 48.

Chesapeake Bay. On April 18, 1848, a steamboat caught up with the *Pearl* and forcibly brought the ship's passengers and crew back to Washington where they were imprisoned. The recaptured slaves were sold off to new owners in Georgia and Louisiana. The captain of the *Pearl*, Daniel Drayton, was sentenced to life in prison but was released two years later after having received a presidential pardon.

The city was affected by the *Pearl* Affair in many ways: Both the Senate and the House of Representatives discussed the matter, not without the exchange of insults and violent threats from defenders of the system of slavery against those who questioned the justification of chattel slavery. City authorities, police, judges, and juries reacted both to the Snow Riot and the *Pearl* Affair by indicting more free blacks and securing more verdicts against African Americans in the months immediately after both incidents.[45] This will be important for the further discussion of the interrelationship of racism with the legal apparatus during the Civil War. One of the direct consequences of the *Pearl* Affair was abolition of the slave trade in the District of Columbia as part of the "Compromise of 1850."

The Civil War dramatically transformed Washington. The hitherto sleepy town became a bustling city with a steep population growth during the war years and after. In 1860, the city's population numbered 75,000 people, one-fifth of whom were African Americans. Only four years later, reliable estimates rated the population at 150,000 inhabitants. This was not caused by a temporary swelling of the urban population; most newcomers had come to stay. The 1870 census listed 132,000 residents. But the changes were not only numerical. The city, which had become one of the major centers of both the Southern and the Northern military activities in the initial stages of the war, was transformed from a former southern town with its political and economical ties to Maryland and Virginia to a city that was facing north, literally, because the lines of communication with the South no longer existed. Southern politicians and officers had left the city in 1861 and were replaced by Northern troops, businessmen, and financiers, who were eager to equip the Army of the Potomac.

New jobs were thus created, and the capital was filled with runaway slaves who had left the plantations in the vicinity.[46] It took until April

45 Norbert Finzsch, "'To Punish as Well as to Reform': Das Gefängnis in Washington, D.C., 1831–1862," in Norbert Finzsch and Hermann Wellenreuther, eds., *Liberalitas: Festschrift für Erich Angermann*, Transatlantische Historische Studien, vol. 1 (Stuttgart, 1992).

46 Lois E. Horton, "The Days of Jubilee: Black Migration During the Civil War and Reconstruction," in Cary, ed., *Urban Odyssey*, 1–3.

Table 8.1. *Change and growth in Washington's African-American population according to the 1860 and 1870 censuses*

	1860	1870
Total population[a]	75,000	132,000
African Americans[a]	14,000	43,000
Percentage black[a]	18.7%	32.6%
Profile of African Americans in sample		
Number in sample	418	873
Real property per capita	$42.46	$48.19
Percentage without real property	94.7%	95.9%
Personal property per capita	$61.29	$6.19
Percentage without personal property	88%	96%
Semiskilled and unskilled labor	40.7%	45.1%
No profession or occupation	54.8%	53.3%
Other	4.5%	1.6%
	100%	100%
Literacy rate	30.40%	17.20%

Note:
[a] Rounded figures

16, 1862, for Congress to pass a law that provided for the compensated emancipation of more than 3,000 slaves in the District of Columbia. "Contraband" slaves, placed under jurisdiction and custody of the U.S. Army as early as 1861, and accommodated in makeshift camps and in army barracks under questionable sanitary conditions, were set free in July 1862. More former slaves kept pouring into the city.[47] In contrast to the 1860 census, which had shown that most black residents had been born in Washington, the 1870 census suggests that less than one-third of Washington's African Americans had lived here before 1860. More than 40 percent had been born in Virginia, and more than 25 percent had moved to the District of Columbia from the state of Maryland.[48]

Table 8.1 depicts the dramatic changes that the black community

47 Horton, "Days of Jubilee," 3–7.
48 The calculations are based on a random sampling of 2,621 cases taken out of the census manuscripts for 1870, of which 873 contain information on blacks and mulattos. I thank James O. Horton and Lois E. Horton for collecting the data and making them accessible to the public. The raw

underwent during the Civil War decade.[49] It not only shows the demographic growth but also proves that the economic and living conditions of the newly arrived migrant African Americans had deteriorated. The number of semi- and unskilled workers among Washington blacks increased, and the indices for property owned by blacks dropped, with the exception of a slight nominal increase in real estate. Five years after the end of the Civil War, the black community was poorer and less educated than in the decade prior to it. This did not help to reduce the racist beliefs held by a majority of white inhabitants of Washington. On the contrary, "[white] and black citizens alike were increasingly apprehensive of the migration of thousands of plantation blacks, destitute, ignorant of urban ways, and swamping the meager relief provisions provided by the federal government and private charity organizations."[50] Enormous problems and, consequently, terrible social tensions arose. One-third of the city's population was black, and most of them had to live in improvised shanties or camps that were unhealthy and unfit for families.[51] Diseases, destitution, and crime were consequences of these living conditions.

IRISH IMMIGRANTS

Between 1830 and 1860 more than 1.8 million Irish left Europe and emigrated to the United States. It would be a euphemism to describe relations between African Americans and Irish immigrants as difficult. Summing up the recent research on Irish and blacks in mid-nineteenth-century America, historians James O. Horton and Hartmut Keil have concluded that "Irish immigrants shared with . . . blacks a position at the

data were available in Dbase format, which I transformed into an SPSS system file. Some of the variables therefore had to be renamed. My findings for 1860 are confirmed by the results of Melvin R. Williams, "Blacks in Washington, D.C., 1860–1870," Ph.D. diss., Johns Hopkins University, 1975. See also Melvin R. Williams, "A Blueprint for Change: The Black Community in Washington, D.C., 1860–1870," *Records of the Columbia Historical Society* 48 (1971–2): 359–93.

49 Source: U.S. Department of Commerce, Bureau of the Census, *Historical Statistics of the United States: Colonial Times to 1970*, 2 vols. (New York, 1975), vol. 1, Series A 195–209, 26. Samples collected by James O. Horton and Lois E. Horton, taken from census manuscripts, 1860 and 1870. The sampling process is explained in James O. Horton and Lois E. Horton, "Race, Occupation, and Literacy in Reconstruction Washington, D.C.," in James O. Horton, *Free People of Color: Inside the African American Community* (Washington, D.C., 1993), 191–2. Table 8.1 gives number of readers only; 11.8 percent of those in the sample could write. Missing values were counted as illiterates in both instances.

50 Lewis, *District of Columbia*, 58.

51 Constance McLaughlin Green, *The Secret City: A History of Race Relations in the Nation's Capital* (Princeton, N.J., 1967), 81–2.

economic bottom of American society, and they were blacks' most notorious adversaries."[52] Although Irish immigration was strongest in the urban centers of the Northeast and Middle West, a considerable minority had also migrated into the Southern states, and their political weight was felt south of the Mason-Dixon Line before and after 1860.[53] The political influence of the Irish was not always organized around a formal political machine. But in contrast to blacks, who did not have the theoretical right to vote before 1866, Irish immigrants, despite open discrimination and victimization in nativist anti-Catholic riots, could be and were actively involved in politics well before the end of the Civil War.[54]

When Irish and German immigrants poured into East Coast cities after 1815, free blacks who worked in skilled and semiskilled jobs in northern cities, such as Boston,[55] and in southern cities, such as Baltimore, were pushed out of their economic niches and had to accept lower-paid semiskilled and unskilled jobs.[56] In some cities around the Chesapeake Bay, such as Wilmington, Delaware, free-black workers were able to resist the tide of the competing Irish for a while, but with the advent of the new immigration, the outcome was usually the same: The Irish came to dominate the male labor market, and African Americans lost their previous status in the skilled trades.[57] The results of such economic displacement were bitter for both sides because of the ethnic tension building up between them. The 1830s had seen nativist-nationalist propaganda, leading to anti-Irish riots. During and after the Civil War, Irish mobs participated in anti-black excesses as in the case of the Draft Riots in

52 James O. Horton and Hartmut Keil, "African Americans and Germans in Mid-Nineteenth-Century Buffalo," in James O. Horton, ed., *Free People of Color: Inside the African American Community* (Washington, D.C., 1993), 170.

53 Kathleen C. Berkeley, "Ethnicity and Its Implications for Southern Urban History: The Saga of Memphis, Tennessee, 1850–1880," *Tennessee Historical Quarterly* 50, no. 4 (1991): 193–202; Randall M. Miller, "The Enemy Within: Some Effects of Foreign Immigrants on Antebellum Southern Cities," *Southern Studies* 24, no. 1 (1985): 30–53, in which the author emphasizes the economic competition between blacks on the one side and Irish and Germans on the other.

54 Stephen Erie, *Rainbow's End: Irish-Americans and the Dilemmas of Urban Machine Politics, 1840–1985* (Berkeley, Calif., 1988). Studying six Irish-controlled cities, Erie debunks myths about machine politics. Eugene C. Cornacchia and Dale C. Nelson, "Historical Differences in the Political Experiences of American Blacks and White Ethnics: Revisiting an Unresolved Controversy," *Ethnic and Racial Studies* 15, no. 1 (1992): 102–24.

55 James O. Horton and Lois E. Horton, *Black Bostonians: Family Life and Community Struggle in the Antebellum South* (New York, 1979), 76–8.

56 D. Randall Beirne, "The Impact of Black Labor on European Immigration into Baltimore's Old-town, 1790–1910," *Maryland Historical Magazine* 83, no. 4 (1988): 331–45; Frank Murray, "The Irish and Afro-Americans in U.S. History," *Freedomways* 22, no. 1 (1982): 21–31.

57 Yda Schreuder, "Wilmington's Immigrant Settlement: 1880–1920," *Delaware History* 23, no. 2 (1988): 140–66.

New York in 1863 and in Memphis, Tennessee, in 1866.[58] Some blacks actively retaliated or developed strong anti-Irish stereotypes.[59]

THE POLICE

In 1861 Congress established the Washington Metropolitan Police Department.[60] Before the organization of a professional police force, the nation's capital was not well policed. Prior to the 1850s the police force was too often used for political purposes and was closely tied to the national government.[61] Before 1861, as in other American cities, a night watch and a day constabulary, assisted by guards from the U.S. Marine Corps, caught criminals, served warrants, and acted as agents of the court system.[62] After the creation of the more professional Metropolitan Police, things in Washington did not change much for the better. Before the outbreak of the Civil War and with slavery as a "peculiar institution" still firmly in the saddle even in the nation's capital, constables, judges, and juries did not treat African-American arrestees and defendants impartially. In their racism, they only reflected the latent and open racism of a city that was as much southern in its culture as it was national in its function. Since most of the policemen were of Anglo-American stock, some of the ubiquitous ethnic tensions must have been part of the daily police work of the District of Columbia.[63] Accordingly, that police officers working in Washington, D.C., during the Civil War were biased against African Americans and Irish immigrants comes as no surprise. The already existing tensions were aggravated by the influx of "contraband" blacks from the vicinity and thousands of soldiers, who had volunteered or were drafted to fight in the Union Army.

58 Altina I. Waller, "Community, Class and Race in the Memphis Riot of 1866," *Journal of Social History* 18, no. 2 (1984): 233–46.
59 Jay Rubin, "Black Nativism: The European Immigrant in Negro Thought, 1830–1860," *Phylon* 39, no. 3 (1978): 193–202; David J. Hellwig, "Black Attitudes Toward Irish Immigrants," *Mid-America* 59, no. 1 (1977): 39–49.
60 *U.S. Congressional Globe*, 37th Cong., 1st Sess., 1861, 288 (Aug. 3, 1861).
61 Keneth G. Alfers, *Law and Order in the Capital City: A History of the Washington Police, 1800–1886*, Washington Studies, no. 5 (Washington, D.C., 1976), 12–23.
62 Catrien C. J. H. Bijleveld and Eric H. Monkkonen, *Cross-Sectional and Dynamic Analyses of the Concomitants of Police Behavior*, UCLA Statistics Series, no. 41 (Los Angeles, 1989), 1.
63 The daily returns of the ten precincts for 1861 to 1878 suggest that D.C. patrolmen were selected from among the lower strata of society. Fluctuation among the force was tremendously high. German Americans and apparently also Irish were a tiny minority within the police force, which attracted rather marginal personnel before 1865. After the war the typical policeman in the city was recruited from among the veterans of the Union Army (list of 452 police officers compiled from a sample of 7,000 of the 140,000 cases of arrests made by the Metropolitan Police Department between 1861 and 1878. NARA, RG 351, Records of the Government of the District of Columbia).

The legal basis for action against alleged criminals was the "Act for the Punishment of Crimes in the District of Columbia" of March 2, 1831, which was a direct result of Jacksonian reforms of the law and abolition of most of the harsh corporal-punishment statutes on the books.[64]

The criminal offenses or misdemeanors for which police arrested individuals were very different, and it is fair to speak of "catchall" services that the police had to render, for their activities included catching loose dogs as well as returning lost children or inspecting the canals of the capital. This is another point that justifies speaking of everyday history, since police activities had almost nothing to do with criminals in the proper sense of the word but were almost exclusively confined to the less precisely defined areas of social control and crime prevention. The following examples of police actions were exceptional and, therefore, not mentioned in the usual forms to be filled out by every policeman on patrol. They were recorded freely in the space provided on the back of each form.

[1.] In 1864 police officer George B. Harrison owned a house, situated on L Street between Fourth and Fifth Street East, that he had rented out to a black family. On March 15, an unknown party set the dwelling on fire, probably in order to drive its inmates out, before entering and stealing their property. Fortunately the fire was noticed and extinguished before the building was damaged and its inhabitants suffered major injuries.[65]

[2.] Rachel Smith, age 30, working as a servant, was found guilty of intentionally killing a black boy child in the home of Mary Parker in Chestnut Alley (7th precinct) on November 5, 1865. Rachel Smith was jailed until the court had reached a final decision.[66]

[3.] A fire occurred in a frame house owned by Emanuel Brickert situated on B Street South, between 3rd and 4th Street West. The alarm was given by Patrolman Weeden from Box Nr. 19, the engines were soon on the spot and extinguished the fire before the flames broke out. The interior was considerably damaged, loss about $300. Eliza Johnson (coloured) was arrested by roundsman Vernon charged with having robbed and set fire to the house. The prisoner confessed to the crime this morning before Justice Handy, who sent her to jail for court.[67]

---

64 Twenty-first Congress, Sess. II, chap. 37, Statutes II, Mar. 2, 1831. It defined certain crimes as felonies that were to be punished with imprisonment of at least six months or the death penalty.

65 Metropolitan Police Department (hereafter cited as MPD), Daily Return of Precincts (hereafter cited as DRP), Mar. 15, 1864. National Archives, Washington, D.C. (hereafter cited as NARA), Record Group (hereafter cited as RG) 48.

66 MPD, DRP, Nov. 5, 1865, in NARA, RG 351, Records of the Government of the District of Columbia.

67 MPD, DRP, July 2, 1865, 10th precinct, in NARA, RG 351, Records of the Government of the District of Columbia.

The three episodes cited here are atypical both for the routine work of policemen in Washington, D.C., and the relationship between African Americans and the newly established Metropolitan Police Department. I would like to discuss these relations by using a hitherto neglected source, namely, the "daily returns of the precincts" collected between 1861 and 1878 and deposited in the National Archives. Each of these thirty-eight unwieldy red volumes contains five hundred pages of notes taken in the ten precincts on the activities of the various policemen and on the force generally. They list the full names and professions of the persons arrested, their race, their age, their gender, their marital status, their literacy, the reasons for the arrest, who had filed a complaint against them, the police officer who had dealt with the case, how these cases were disposed of, how the persons were punished, and if they were convicted or deferred to a judge. Since about fifty people were arrested on an average day, that meant that more than 18,000 people were arrested in the course of a year. For the Civil War years, the number of arrests was probably higher. On this basis, it is reasonable to assume that between 1861 and 1866 more than 90,000 individuals were, at least temporarily, taken into police custody in Washington, and this in a city of approximately 100,000 inhabitants (75,000 in 1860; 132,000 in 1870). This should suffice to explain why I deal with these arrests as a phenomenon of "everyday" life.

For a certain section of Washingtonians, contact with policemen in the form of being harassed or even taken to the precinct headquarters were routine. Out of these 90,000 arrests made I have pulled a randomly chosen sample of 4,530 cases.[68] This represents a sample of about 5 percent.[69] There is no objectively measurable correlation between officially recorded crime (or misdemeanors) and actual levels of criminal or deviant behavior, and my data should not be interpreted in that way. Crime statistics and the like are not totally divorced from reality, just as they are not totally reflective of reality. "For example, the same economic changes that increased the potential disruption of theft and white-collar crime also made them easier to commit."[70] In other words, crime statistics and

---

68 A computer program that created random numbers decided what days to choose between August 1, 1861, and December 31, 1865. A chosen day was then fully recorded for all of the ten precincts. This method avoided the impractical selection of every *n*th case, since it was not possible to ascertain beforehand whether the data for a specific case would be complete. It also made sure that the distances between days would oscillate, so that the bias typical for equidistant sampling methods would be avoided.

69 My gratitude goes out to my diligent research assistant Susanne Saygin, who did most of the actual data recording in the National Archives.

70 Michael Stephen Hindus, *Prison and Plantation: Crime, Justice, and Authority in Massachusetts and South Carolina, 1767–1878* (Chapel Hill, N.C., 1980), 60.

police records tell us more about the perception of those who collected them than about the deeds of those who were the targets of police activities. Yet complaints of third parties were very often the reason for arrests made on the basis of a violation of city ordinances or other non-criminal actions. The pattern of offenses for which people were arrested is not the mere creation of the police or justice system. To make things more complicated, the spread of news through media like the "crime section" in the local newspapers increased the awareness of crime and led to a changed perception of crime in the context of urban politics.[71] For the documents under discussion here, it may suffice to say that only a minimal number of arrests led to actual indictments or convictions by courts. This shows that policing had to some degree much more to do with "preemptive" social control and also that most of the arrests made were not based on evidence that would lead to a criminal conviction with a prison term. They often led only to dismissals or fines.[72]

Before concentrating on African Americans and the Irish, I describe the results with a few general remarks on the quality of the data and the overall findings for the whole sample. In order to say something about the attributes of those who were arrested by the police, I compare them to the samples drawn from the 1860 and 1870 census discussed earlier. (See Tables 8.2 and 8.3.)

For each of the three subcategories the gender ratio is strikingly out of balance. The median age is lowest for white Americans, whereas Irish immigrants, with a highly disproportionate gender distribution, showed the greatest departure from the statistical average. In 1860, only every third Irish immigrant was male. This fits with the median age of Irish, who were much older, statistically speaking, than the average native-born inhabitant of Washington, D.C.

For research in criminal or deviant behavior, it is paramount to know the age structure and the gender ratio of the population under study because it is a long-held truism of criminologists that most criminal acts are committed by males under twenty-five years of age. This is a "general law" believed by most criminologists to be valid for all kinds of societies in different historical epochs. Explanations for an apparent lesser inclination of women to commit violent crimes vary from "judicial paternalism" to a theory of the "masked female criminal."[73] One very

---

71 Ibid., 61.
72 Compare Table 8.4.
73 For a discussion of the impact of age and gender on criminality, see Michael R. Gottfredson and Travis Hirschi, *A General Theory of Crime* (Stanford, Calif., 1990), 123–53. There is heated debate

Table 8.2. *Censuses for 1860 and 1870, from the
original manuscript records*

	1860	1870
Total number of cases	2,348	2,621
Blacks and mulattos	419	873
Percentage of sample	17.8%	33.3%
Irish immigrants	204	173
Percentage of sample	8.7%	6.6%
U.S.-born whites	1,564	1,434
Percentage of sample	66.6%	54.7%
Ratio of males:females	47:53	47:53
Median age	20	22

Table 8.3. *Censuses for 1860 and 1870 – U.S.-born whites,
African Americans, and Irish*

	1860	1870
U.S.-born whites		
Total number of cases	1,564	1,434
Ratio of males:females	49:51	49:51
Median age	16	18
African Americans		
Total number of cases	419	873
Ratio of males:females	41:59	43:57
Median age	20	20
Irish		
Total number of cases	204	173
Ratio of males:females	38:62	46:54
Median age	30	33

on the causes of the apparently lower criminality among women that goes back to antebellum American tracts and memoranda. In present times, with a slight increase of violent female criminal behavior, some historians of crime have constructed a "masked criminal offender," and some attribute the "lack" of female offenders to socially constructed roles that tend to confine women in their homes. For a recent debate see Dorie Klein, "The Etiology of Female Crime: A Review of the Literature," *Issues in Criminology* 8, no. 2 (1973): 3–4; Jocelynne A. Scutt, "Debunking the Theory of the Female "Masked Criminal," *Australian and New Zealand Journal of Criminology* 11,

telling explanation was given by New York Secretary of State Samuel Young, who in 1842 wrote, "This . . . remarkable disproportion . . . may be accounted for partly by the reluctance to prosecute females, partly by their domestic life and habits, leaving them less exposed to temptation, and partly by the unavoidable inference that they are superior to men in moral honesty."[74] Restricted to their homes and separated from the outside world by a theory of "two spheres" and a "cult of true womanhood," attributing to them a higher standard of morality, Victorian women had, at least in the expectations of their male contemporaries, few reasons to commit crimes.[75] Once they fell off that pedestal, they could be sure to receive harsher punishment than males convicted of the same crimes.[76]

These high moral standards could not be expected from African-American women, who stereotypically were perceived either as female correlates of the "Sambo," that is, "Mammies," or as uncontrollably passionate "Jezebels," neither of which deserved to be treated according to the same moral standards as white women.[77] As for African-American men, as early as 1830 it was clear that they represented the "born criminal,"

no. 1 (1978): 23–42; Meda Chesney-Lind, "Judicial Paternalism and the Female Status Offender: Training Women to Know Their Place," *Crime and Delinquency* 23 (1977): 121–30. The problem is dealt with in historical perspective in the very instructive book by Lucia Zedner, *Women, Crime, and Custody in Victorian England* (Oxford, 1991), 11–90.

74 Quoted in Estelle B. Freedman, *Their Sister's Keepers, Women's Prison Reform in America, 1830–1930* (Ann Arbor, Mich., 1981), 12.

75 Peter W. Bardoglio, "Separate Spheres and Sisterhood in Victorian America," *Reviews in American History* 18, no. 2 (1990): 202–7. The factual existence of these separate spheres in the early nineteenth century was recently questioned by Karen V. Hansen, "'Helped Put in a Quilt': Men's Work and Male Intimacy in Nineteenth-Century New England," *Gender and Society* 3, no. 3 (1989): 334–54; Karen V. Hansen, "Challenging Separate Spheres in Antebellum New Hampshire: The Case of Brigham Nims," *Historical New Hampshire* 43, no. 2 (1988): 120–35. For a more conventional interpretation, see Linda K. Kerber, "Separate Spheres, Female Worlds, Woman's Place: The Rhetoric of Women's History," *Journal of American History* 75, no. 1 (1988): 9–39; Barbara Todd, "Separate Spheres: Woman's Place in Nineteenth-Century America," *Canadian Review of American Studies* 16, no. 3 (1985): 329–37; Gary R. Kremer, "Strangers to Domestic Virtues: Nineteenth-Century Women in the Missouri Prison," *Missouri Historical Review* 84, no. 2 (1990): 293–4.

76 The pedestal metaphor was most widely used for southern women. See Anne Firor Scott, *The Southern Lady: From Pedestal to Politics, 1830–1930* (Chicago, 1970).

77 Finzsch, "To Punish as Well as to Reform." For the (male) Sambo stereotype, see Joel Williamson, *The Crucible of Race: Black-White Relations in the American South Since Emancipation* (New York, 1984), 22–3. The mammy stereotype is analyzed in Margaret Rose Gladney, "Lillian Smith's Hope for Southern Women," *Southern Studies* 22, no. 3 (1983): 274–84. For a discussion of the Jezebel stereotype see Ida Jeter, "Jezebel and the Emergence of the Hollywood Tradition of a Decadent South," *Southern Quarterly* 19, nos. 3–4 (1981): 31–46. Only recently have feminist historians begun to research the history of sexuality of African-American women. See Catherine Clinton, "Bloody Terrain: Freedwomen, Sexuality and Violence During Reconstruction," *Georgia Historical Quarterly* 76, no. 2 (1992): 313–32, which emphasizes the sexual violence committed against black women in Reconstruction Georgia by white racists.

since they were statistically overrepresented in most jails and penitentiaries of Victorian America. Postbellum state penal systems in the South became themselves instruments of social stratification, since blacks comprised over 95 percent of most prison populations.[78]

THE STATISTICS OF DISCRIMINATION

The "returns of the precincts" list more than 130 different felonies, misdemeanors, and transgressions for which inhabitants of Washington, D.C., were arrested and (sometimes) punished. The offenses varied from first-degree murder to such unobtrusive violations of the public order as "absenting from the asylum," "suspicion," or "vagrancy." It would have been impossible to draw conclusions from such a variety of deviant behaviors. Therefore, I clustered them into eight main categories, such as property crimes, violent crimes, criminal cases, violations of the moral code, violation of the public order, and other offenses. Among the latter were included suspicion and lodgers, which did not even constitute an apparent or alleged transgression of specific rules or laws. "Suspicious people" were individuals who, for reasons nowhere specified, were sufficiently conspicuous for the police to arrest them. Most of them were citizens from the Confederacy and were believed to be Southern spies. Lodgers (vagrants) were people who were taken into custody by policemen because they did not have a place to stay and were either permanently or temporarily homeless. Property crimes included felonies and misdemeanors, such as the "attempt to swindle," "breaking in [a] door," "burglary," "having a stolen horse in his possession," "larceny," "receiving stolen money or goods," and so forth.[79] Violent crimes included reproaches like "accessory to robbery," "assault," "attempt to commit rape," "highway robbery," or "throwing vitriol on ladies' clothes."

The common denominator of criminal felonies, as specified here, is that they were neither violent nor property-related crimes, but that they all were punishable with prison terms exceeding six months. They include patently criminal offenses, such as "arson," "desertion," "rioting," or "forgery," but also less common charges, such as "blockade runner," "imposter," or "bogus military patrol." Moral transgressions, persecuted by the police, were cases of bastardy, bigamy, profanity, cross-dressing ("dressed in female attire" or "wearing men's apparel"), "indecent expo-

---

78 Christopher R. Adamson, "Punishment After Slavery: Southern State Penal Systems, 1865–1890," *Social Problems* 30, no. 5 (1983): 555–69.
79 All quotes taken from NARA, RG 351.

sure," "keeping disorderly house," which meant enticement of prosti-
tution, "seduction," and "sodomy" (homosexuality), among others. The
least clearly defined group was the catchall transgressions of "disorderly
conduct" and the like. Offenses such as "abusive language," "asleep in
lumberyard," "[blacks] cursing, in company with white men," "cutting
corporation trees," and other violations of city ordinances fall into this
category. In addition, this group contains misdemeanors like "drunkenness," "dog without license," traffic violations, and the like.[80] This was
definitely the group of complaints that gave the police most leeway in
deciding whom to take in and whom to let go. In Table 8.4, I present the findings for the whole sample and then break them down
into white Americans, African Americans, and Irish in Tables 8.5 to
8.7. These findings are then compared to (1) the census data and (2)
among themselves.

The first and most general conclusion that can be drawn from the
comparison of the census data and the police records is that the population in the police files is not representative of the population at large.
The police files contain an expected, but disproportionately high amount
of single-male suspects, which represent a minority in the census records.
Thus, these results confirm what is a commonplace among historians of
crime and deviance: Men commit most (violent) crimes. The difference
lies in the age structure: The arrestees were relatively old. In fact, the
average age of twenty-nine years for all arrestees is congruent to the
census data, if one excludes from the latter those cases where suspects
were younger than eleven years.[81] The arrestees are best described as unskilled and semiskilled workers or as small-time shopkeepers at the lower
strata of society. More than 20 percent were laborers. The four most
often recorded professions (laborer, soldier, prostitute, servant) make up
more than half of the whole sample.

Illiteracy rates were relatively high by contemporary American standards, which is partly explained by the high proportion of African Americans and Irish immigrants in the city's population. Contrary to what
could be expected given the racist mood in antebellum Washington,
African Americans were not overrepresented in the sample. They constituted 17.8 and 33.3 percent of the population in the censuses of 1860
and 1870, respectively. That corresponds very well with their share of

---

80 All quotes taken from NARA, RG 351.
81 Census 1860. Median age 29, mean age 31.76, standard deviation 15.92, curtosis 0.759, with
16,448 valid observations. Census 1870: Median age 29 years, mean age 31.51 years, standard
deviation 14.99, curtosis 0.545, with 1,934 valid observations.

Table 8.4. *Demographic structure of arrestees as compiled from police records,*
1861–5 (4,530 valid cases)

Gender ratio	
Men	81.00
Women	18.70
Sum	99.70
Missing values	.30
Total	100.00
Age	
Mean	29.25
Standard deviation	10.18
Curtosis	.75
Skewness	.82
Marital status	
Married	38.30
Single	61.70
Sum	100.00
Literacy	
Can read and write	66.50
Cannot read and write	29.10
Sum	95.60
Missing values	4.40
Sum	100.00
Delicts	
Property	11.30
Violence	8.30
Criminal	3.10
Moral	4.70
Order	66.10
Suspicion	1.30
Others	.40
Lodgers	3.90
Sum	99.10
Missing values	.90
Total	100.00
Race	
Whites	77.80

Table 8.4. *(cont.)*

Blacks	20.70
Sum	98.50
Missing values	1.50
Total	100.00
Nationality	
U.S.-Americans	59.00
Irish	29.40
Germans	6.80
Sum	95.20
Others	4.80
Total	100.00
Professions	
Laborer	20.40
Prostitutes	7.70
Soldier	17.30
Servant	5.40
Sum	50.80
Disposal	
Workhouse	4.90
Dismissed	28.40
Fine	34.50
Trial	3.80
Imprisoned as punishment	2.30
Bail	3.70
Military	12.80
Imprisoned for trial	3.30
Sum	93.70
Others	6.30
Total	100.00
Fine	
Average fine in dollars	4.98
Standard deviation	17.91
Curtosis	692.30
Skewness	25.20
Ratio of police vs. private complaints	58:42

Table 8.5. *Demographic structure of arrestees as compiled from police records, 1861–5: White U.S. citizens (1,705 valid cases)*

Gender ratio	
Men	86.20
Women	13.70
Sum	99.90
Missing values	.10
Total	100.00
Age	
Mean	28.12
Standard deviation	9.76
Curtosis	.64
Skewness	.86
Marital status	
Married	30.00
Single	68.00
Sum	98.00
Literacy	
Can read and write	88.60
Cannot read and write	9.00
Sum	97.60
Missing values	2.40
Sum	100.00
Delicts	
Property	10.40
Violence	8.00
Criminal	3.20
Moral	5.40
Order	67.30
Suspicion	1.70
Others	.80
Lodgers	2.30
Sum	99.10
Missing values	.90
Total	100.00

Table 8.5. *(cont.)*

Professions	
Laborer	12.30
Prostitutes	8.60
Soldier	21.90
Servant	.90
Sum	43.70
Disposal	
Workhouse	3.70
Dismissed	28.60
Fine	33.10
Trial	3.50
Imprisoned as punishment	2.10
Bail	3.80
Military	16.50
Imprisoned for trial	3.40
Sum	94.70
Others	5.30
Total	100.00
Fine	
Average fine in dollars	4.38
Standard deviation	5.44
Curtosis	29.64
Skewness	4.68
Ratio of police vs.	
private complaints	61:39

Table 8.6. *Demographic structure of arrestees as compiled from police records,*
1861–5: African Americans (934 valid cases)

Gender ratio	
Men	68.10
Women	31.50
Sum	99.60
Missing values	.40
Total	100.00
Age	
Mean	25.71
Standard deviation	9.94
Curtosis	2.47
Skewness	1.33
Marital status	
Married	28.10
Single	70.80
Sum	98.90
Literacy	
Can read and write	13.10
Cannot read and write	85.80
Sum	98.90
Missing values	1.10
Sum	100.00
Delicts	
Property	20.20
Violence	7.60
Criminal	2.10
Moral	6.40
Order	60.80
Suspicion	1.20
Others	.20
Lodgers	1.00
Sum	99.50
Missing values	.50
Total	100.00

Table 8.6. *(cont.)*

Professions

Laborer	32.20
Prostitutes	11.30
Soldier	.90
Servant	21.50
Sum	65.90

Disposal

Workhouse	5.40
Dismissed	26.70
Fine	46.70
Trial	7.10
Imprisoned as punishment	3.00
Bail	3.00
Military	1.00
Imprisoned for trial	3.90
Sum	96.80
Others	3.20
Total	100.00

Fine

Average fine in dollars	6.13
Standard deviation	33.07
Curtosis	217.10
Skewness	14.62
Ratio of police vs. private complaints	50:50

Table 8.7. *Demographic structure of arrestees as compiled from police records, 1861–5: Irish (1,323 valid cases)*

Gender ratio	
Men	80.70
Women	19.30
Sum	100.00
Missing values	0.00
Total	100.00
Age	
Mean	31.62
Standard deviation	9.73
Curtosis	.63
Skewness	.71
Marital status	
Married	40.40
Single	56.20
Sum	96.60
Literacy	
Can read and write	72.50
Cannot read and write	23.80
Sum	96.30
Missing values	3.70
Sum	100.00
Delicts	
Property	7.30
Violence	7.70
Criminal	3.70
Moral	3.30
Order	73.30
Suspicion	.70
Others	.20
Lodgers	3.60
Sum	99.80
Missing values	.20
Total	100.00

Table 8.7. *(cont.)*

Professions

Laborer	28.20
Prostitutes	6.20
Soldier	22.40
Servant	1.50
Sum	58.30

Disposal

Workhouse	7.30
Dismissed	29.20
Fine	30.40
Trial	2.60
Imprisoned as punishment	2.60
Bail	2.90
Military	16.00
Imprisoned for trial	3.60
Sum	94.60
Others	5.40
Total	100.00

Fine

Average fine in dollars	4.41
Standard deviation	5.08
Curtosis	15.01
Skewness	3.45
Ratio of police vs. private complaints	65:35

20.7 percent among the arrestees. Irish immigrants, in contrast, seem to have been the major offenders, at least in the eyes of Washington policemen. Their share of the city's population, which dropped from 8.7 percent in 1860 to 6.6 percent in 1870, has to be seen in comparison with their share of arrestees, which make up almost a third of all cases. Irish Americans were proportionately three to four times more numerous among alleged offenders than within the whole population. Explanations of this indicator of discrimination against the Irish may be found in the nature of offenses and the way the police and justice system disposed of alleged transgressors. White Americans in general, like any other group, were most frequently arrested for "disorderly conduct" or public drunkenness, that is, for disorderly conduct, and here Irish immigrants figured most prominently in alleged offenses against the public order.[82] The "typical" offense for which African Americans were arrested was a crime against property, such as larceny or petty larceny. They were three times more likely to be arrested for this offense than the Irish and two times more likely than white American citizens. Yet, blacks tended to be underrepresented in the area of violent and criminal acts. They accounted for the highest rate of complaints against (sexual) immorality.

The punishments varied according to these data. In all three categories about one-fourth of the cases were dismissed without any further action by the authorities. But, strikingly, African Americans were punished the hardest of all. Not only did they have to pay a fine in 46.7 percent of the cases, more than 7 percent had to appear in court. The fines that African Americans had to pay were exorbitant in comparison to what Irish or whites had to pay. The average fine was 40 percent higher than that of white American citizens or Irish immigrants. Conspicuously absent among blacks was deference to military authorities, despite or because of the fact that the contraband camps were subordinate to military authority. By contrast, a high percentage of American citizens and Irish immigrants were soldiers or otherwise subject to military law and were transferred accordingly to the provost marshal.[83]

One final observation is the number of complaints filed by private individuals in comparison to those filed by policemen on patrol. Two-thirds of all the cases under scrutiny here were brought in by policemen on their rounds or on duty in the precinct headquarters. Private individuals were responsible for complaints in only one-third of all cases.[84] This reflects less a high "professionalization" of the police force, but rather the effort of the newly founded Metropolitan Police to prove its efficiency, as well as the fact that informers among the citizenry of Washington, D.C., were rather rare. This is totally different for the African Americans, whose names were usually given to the police by neighbors and employers. One explanation may be a high percentage of property crimes, allegedly committed by blacks. It also reflects the high percentage of African-American (female) house servants or housekeepers, who were

---

82 67.3 percent for whites, 60.8 percent for blacks, and 73.3 percent for Irish. Other violations than that of the public order make up only one-third to 40 percent of all complaints filed.
83 American citizens 16.50 percent, Irish 16.00 percent, blacks 1.00 percent.
84 61:39 for white citizens, 65:35 for the Irish.

more prone to be indicted for theft or petty larceny than any other professional group.[85]

An analysis of police behavior toward different ethnic categories, no matter how superficial it may have to be, would be incomplete without a look at the gender difference. It can be shown that the police's major concern with men was largest in the area of social and crime control. Women, in contrast, were perceived as primarily a moral threat. Whereas property crimes seem not to have been the prerogative of either sex,[86] and violent crimes were almost as common among women of all races as among men,[87] men were more likely to be indicted for criminal charges,[88] and women were ten times more likely to be cited for moral offenses.[89] This is, of course, partly the result of the fact that men were not accused of being prostitutes, and women, as a rule, were confined to their homes or workplaces.[90] If they left their part of the "two spheres," they automatically revolted against the "cult of true womanhood" and could thus become the target of public scorn and police action.[91] These findings are in concordance with the fact that African-American and Irish women were judged on a different standard: Since they were black or Irish, that is, immoral by definition, it was not necessary to dedicate special attention to their moral behavior. Only 12.6 percent of all black women were charged for moral offenses, whereas 19 percent of them were indicted as thieves or in other property charges.[92] The same tendency can be shown for Irish women.[93]

85 Gender ratio among blacks 68:32; 21.50 percent of all arrested African Americans were servants.
86 11.30 percent for males, 11.60 percent for females.
87 7.30 percent as compared to 8.50 percent.
88 3.60 percent versus 0.90 percent.
89 Of the crimes committed by men, 1.80 percent were moral crimes, in comparison to 17.50 percent of the alleged female crimes.
90 41.1 percent of the women arrested were reported to be prostitutes, but most of them were indicted for other offenses; 19.3 percent worked as housekeepers, 16.8 percent as servants.
91 I do not quote the extensive literature on the cult of domesticity here. See Christine Stansell, "Women, Children, and the Uses of the Streets: Class and Gender Conflict in New York City, 1850–1860," in Ellen Carol DuBois and Vicki L. Ruiz, eds., *Unequal Sisters: A Multi-Cultural Reader in U.S. Women's History* (New York, 1990), 92–108. See also Barbara Leslie Epstein, *The Politics of Domesticity: Women, Evangelism, and Temperance in Nineteenth-Century America* (Middletown, Conn., 1981).
92 The figures for black women are as follows: property charges 19 percent; violent crimes 5.8 percent; criminal charges 0.70 percent; moral transgressions 12.60 percent; violations of the public order 60.50 percent. The sample contained 294 valid cases.
93 They were charged for the following offenses: crimes against property, 7.80 percent; violent crimes, 7.8 percent; criminal charges, 2.3 percent; moral transgressions, 12.9 percent; offenses against public order, 66.4 percent. The sample contained 256 valid cases. Irish-American women were grossly overrepresented, as were their male counterparts, for they were held responsible for 30.3 percent of all offenses committed by women. The same is true for African-American women, though to a lesser degree: They constituted 34.8 percent of all persons charged.

CONCLUSION

The initial hypothesis, that to a high degree African Americans were targets of racist police actions, could not be totally verified. Blacks were not overrepresented statistically in the samples. It is important, however, to differentiate between gender roles if one wants to get a more complete picture. Irish immigrants, in contrast, were very likely to be singled out by policemen, although their low conviction rate shows that actual crimes could seldom be proved in court. With regard to free blacks, it is important to see gender boundaries as important for an understanding of racial or ethnic divisions. I could speculate that the low representation of African Americans among the offenders may have to do with their only recent emancipation and the fact that the "black codes" were still being enforced. These codes restricted the freedom of movement of African Americans and assured "good behavior" without police supervision.

On the basis of these preliminary results, it may be important to keep the following points in mind for future research: (1) Individuals accused of deviant or criminal offenses have statistically belonged to the lower strata of society, which has made them more "visible" to police and legal authorities for purposes of social control. (2) Ordinances and legal measures, like the "black codes," have to be taken into account for the actual behavior of those controlled by them and for law officers' expectations about how the groups affected by these laws behave. Racist assumptions about minorities on the part of police officers need not necessarily lead to tighter police control, if those minorities can be checked by means other than policing. (3) Ethnicity and race as useful categories for understanding how racism affected everyday life in nineteenth-century America have to be controlled by the categories of gender and age.

9

The Politics of Boycotting

Experiences in Germany and the United States Since 1880

RALF KOCH

I

On December 29, 1930, the Associated Negro Press (ANP) offered its membership, which included nearly all of the major black newspapers in the United States, a feature listing the "most significant happenings" of the year. In the opinion of the leading African-American news agency, one of the thirteen events "which have meant most to the Negro race" was the "employment campaign of the Chicago Whip which won 5,000 new jobs for Negroes and had as its highlight, picketing, boycott (new forms of economic protest by Negroes), and the agreement of the Woolworth chain stores to employ colored clerks."[1] What had been "new" at the beginning of 1930 had become a widely used tactic by the end of the year. After the success of the boycott campaign in the South Side of Chicago, black communities in other cities quickly adopted the "new" weapon against discriminatory hiring policies of white-owned businesses.[2] During the summer and fall, journalists reported campaigns on Detroit and Los Angeles. At the end of 1930, at least two consumer boycotts were going on in Ohio, one in Toledo and another in Columbus.

---

1 The ANP documents are included in the Claude A. Barnett papers at the Chicago Historical Society. Barnett founded the news agency in 1919 and was one of the most influential black journalists until his death on August 2, 1967. Claude A. Barnett papers (hereafter cited as CAB), box 6, folder 1, ANP, Dec. 29, 1930, Archives and Manuscripts Collection, Chicago Historical Society. For background on the ANP, see Linda Evans, "Claude A. Barnett and the Associated Negro Press," *Chicago History* 7, no. 1 (spring 1983): 44–56.
2 In this essay the terms consumer boycott or boycott are used interchangeably and defined as an "attempt by one or more parties to achieve certain objectives by urging individual consumers to refrain from making selected purchases in the marketplace." This definition deliberately excludes some boycott types, for example, school boycotts and embargoes. It is borrowed from Monroe

The editors of the *Chicago Whip* had been the first to promote successfully the idea that the black community should use its buying power as a political weapon to get jobs in companies that discriminated against African-American applicants.[3] In 1929, this black newspaper had launched the first boycott campaign against some stores of the Consumers Corporation in the "colored district" of Chicago. But it was not until the spring of 1930 that the efforts of the *Whip* received nationwide coverage in the black press, which was essential for the spread of the "new" tactic to other cities, since the white media tried to ignore the boycotts. On March 1, 1930, the ANP distributed its first feature about the campaign of the *Chicago Whip*. Under the headline "NEWSPAPER WINS FIGHT AGAINST CHAIN STORES," the news agency enthusiastically reported that after enduring nearly a year of picketing and boycotting, the Consumers Corporation had agreed to employ black sales personnel for the first time in the history of the company:

The victory was notable because the issue between the newspaper and the management of the concern was so clear. Although other chain store units in the district, such as the Atlantic and Pacific stores [A & P], the Loblaw grocerterias, and others, had admitted the justice and benefit of employing colored help, the Consumers management had openly stated that it would not employ any Negroes. Thus the issue was stated and the battle was joined.

The fight against the stores was pressed through the churches and various other public agencies. Volunteer groups of women picketed the Consumers stores on Saturdays and counselled housewives not to do their trading in them. The effect was to create a growing boycott of the stores so that they would either be forced to yield through the loss of business or suspend business.[4]

According to the ANP, three women were already placed at work, and Henry Porter, one of the boycott leaders, estimated that the capitulation of the Consumers' management would mean "a total of forty or more jobs for Negroes in these stores alone."[5]

Friedman, "Consumer Boycotts in the United States, 1970–1980: Contemporary Events in Historical Perspective," *Journal of Consumer Affairs* 19, no. 1 (summer 1985): 97–8.

3 Historically, the *Whip* was not the first newspaper that promoted selective buying campaigns as a means to get jobs for African Americans. In the mid-1920s, the *New York Amsterdam News*, e.g., had attempted to launch a similar campaign but never attracted nationwide attention. See Jefferson B. Kellogg, "A Study of Negro Direct Action Activity During the Depression: The Selective Buying Campaigns in Chicago, Baltimore, Cleveland, Washington, New York and Richmond," M.A. thesis, Kent State University, 1974, 5–6.

4 CAB, box 260, folder 7, ANP, Mar. 1, 1930; Joseph D. Bibb papers (hereafter cited as JDB), box 1, folder 16, printed, letter-size leaflet (8.5 × 11 inches) "Jobs f[or 2]00 Girls!" (winter 1929–30), Archives and Manuscripts Collections, Chicago Historical Society.

5 CAB, box 260, folder 7, ANP, Mar. 1, 1930.

These new jobs were especially valuable because thousands of black workers had been dismissed since the stock market collapse in October 1929. During the early years of the Great Depression, African Americans were the first to be discharged, very often to be replaced with white workers who were now forced to compete for jobs that were "once regarded beneath the dignity of a Caucasian."[6] Most African Americans worked as unskilled laborers or in domestic and personal services. Prior to the boycott movements of the 1930s, white-collar positions as clerks and sales personnel in supermarkets and department stores were considered to be exclusively "white jobs." Even in the black urban ghettos, where most of the customers of these businesses were black, African Americans usually had no chance of being hired for a vacancy in a white-owned shop. Since 1929, the situation and embitterment in the black community had become even worse. African-American elevator operators, waiters, porters, cooks, and maids had "seen their jobs downtown shrink away and their places taken by white workers."[7] The unemployment rates of blacks were relatively much higher than those of whites. In Chicago, for example, at the end of 1930, 40.3 percent of the male African Americans and 55.4 percent of the black women were without jobs, whereas only 23.4 percent of white males and 16.9 percent of white women were reported unemployed.[8] In the spring of 1930, the seriousness of the economic crisis "was reflected in discussions wherever Negroes assembled – whether on the corners, in literary societies, in lodges or in churches. The dominant note of public meetings was always some economic subject."[9]

African Americans who were interested in knowing more about the "new" boycott tactics that had been successfully introduced in Chicago could find a first comment on the campaign in the monthly magazine of the National Association for the Advancement of Colored People (NAACP), one of the two leading civil-rights organizations in the United States. In the March issue of *Crisis*, W. E. B. Du Bois wrote an editorial in which he promoted consumer boycotts as a "tremendous and most effective weapon." According to Du Bois, "the colored people have a right . . . to agree among themselves not to trade with certain stores until

---

6 Eugene Kinckle Jones, "Twenty Years After," *Opportunity* 8, no. 3 (Mar. 1930): 78; for a general overview of the situation of African Americans during the Depression years, see Raymond Wolters, *Negroes and the Great Depression: The Problem of Economic Recovery* (Westport, Conn., 1970).
7 Claude McKay, "Labor Steps Out in Harlem," *Nation* 145, no. 16 (Oct. 16, 1937): 399–402.
8 Fifteenth Census of the United States: 1930, Unemployment, vol. 2, 370–3.
9 Jones, "Twenty Years After," 78.

they either get better treatment or until the stores hire colored clerks or until other changes in policy are made."[10] For members of the NAACP this "semi-official" approval of the politics of boycotting by one of the most influential black intellectuals was a first hint about the position of their organization.[11] Even more important was that Du Bois also gave the first account of the concrete way in which the campaign in Chicago was prepared and conducted, information that was extremely useful for the quick adoption of the boycott tactic by black communities in other cities. The recognition of the ANP and Du Bois that the movement in Chicago was more than just local news drew nationwide attention to the "new" form of protest pioneered by the *Whip*.[12] Without the coverage by the black news agency and *Crisis*, the campaign probably never would have become what it is known as today: the initial model for "Don't Buy Where You Can't Work" boycotts in cities all over the United States.[13] Although the black press played a key role in the spread of the "Don't Buy Where You Can't Work" idea, it would be misleading to believe that newspapers were the only source of information; the influence of the written word should not be overestimated. Almost equally important were informal patterns of communication: word-of-mouth propaganda, as well as letters or telephone calls from friends and relatives in other cities.

In April 1930, four weeks after the first reports of the ANP and *Crisis*

10 W. E. B. Du Bois, "The Boycott," *Crisis* 37, no. 3 (Mar. 1930): 102.
11 Although Du Bois often had his own opinion on political issues, traditionally "what appeared in the [*Crisis*] was referred to as the NAACP's official stand" (Joseph V. Baker, "NAACP and the Negro Press," *Crisis* 41, no. 5. [May 1934]: 131).
12 There is no evidence that the simultaneously published reports were a coordinated effort to stir a nationwide debate about the politics of boycotting, but it is well known that Barnett had close ties to the national offices of the NAACP and the Urban League. See Lawrence D. Hogan, *A Black News Service: The Associated Negro Press and Claude A. Barnett, 1919–1945* (Rutherford, N.J., 1984), 103, 146.
13 For an overview, see Gary Jerome Hunter, "'Don't Buy from Where You Can't Work': Black Urban Boycott Movements During the Depression, 1929–1941," Ph.D. diss., University of Michigan, 1977; in particular the campaigns in New York City are well researched. Recent studies include Ralph L. Crowder, "'Don't Buy Where You Can't Work': An Investigation of the Political Forces and Social Conflict Within the Harlem Boycott of 1934," *Afro-Americans in New York Life and History* 15, no. 2 (July 1991): 7–44; Cheryl Lynn Greenberg, "Don't Buy Where You Can't Work," in *"Or Does It Explode?": Black Harlem in the Great Depression* (New York, 1991), 114–39; for Washington, see Michele F. Pacifico, "'Don't Buy Where You Can't Work': The New Negro Alliance of Washington," *Washington History* 6, no. 1 (spring–summer 1994): 66–88; for Baltimore, Andor Skotnes, "'Buy Where You Can Work': Boycotting for Jobs in African-American Baltimore, 1933–1934," *Journal of Social History* 27, no. 4 (summer 1994): 735–61; for Cleveland, see Kenneth M. Zinz, "The Future Outlook League of Cleveland: A Negro Protest Organization," M.A. thesis, Kent State University, 1973, and Christopher G. Wye, "Merchants of Tomorrow: The Other Side of the 'Don't Spend Your Money Where You Can't Work' Movement," *Ohio History* 93 (winter–spring 1984): 40–67.

about the boycott in Chicago had been published, the national head-quarters of the Urban League in New York City reacted. The staff of this civil-rights organization, which was as important as the NAACP, invited Joseph D. Bibb, editor of the *Chicago Whip* and one of the masterminds of the Chicago campaign, to lecture in New York. Explaining the positive experiences with the tactic of boycotting in Chicago, Bibb suggested that a similar effort should be launched in New York.[14] But nothing happened. It is unclear why it took two more years until the first boycott campaign actually started in Harlem, the "Negro-Capital of the world."[15] Other black communities considered to be much less radical and progressive than Harlem adopted the "new" tactic much faster.

During the spring and summer of 1930, the nationwide interest and coverage of the boycott campaign in Chicago intensified. On May 7, 1930, eight weeks after the ANP and *Crisis* had published their first accounts of the boycott, the agency offered its member newspapers a detailed background feature that was almost twice as long as the first report. The ANP journalists used a short press release from A. C. McNeal, general manager of the *Chicago Whip*, to retell the success story of the boycott, which was based on "the theory that 'enough talk had been done and it was now time for action.'" According to McNeal, "more than 2,600 Negro men and women had secured jobs directly or indirectly through the campaign . . . against [white] merchants on the South Side who profited from Negro patronage, but who refused to give employment to the members of the group."[16] This ANP feature seems to be the first account in which the catchy slogan of the Chicago campaign, "Do Not Spend Your Money Where You Can Not Work," was brought to the attention of a national audience. Slightly changed and shortened to "Don't Buy Where You Can't Work," it became the battle cry of most of the black boycotts in the 1930s and was still in use during the 1950s, 1960s, and 1970s.[17] The journalists of the ANP had a professional feeling for the persuasiveness of the slogan and tried to stress its adoption by using capital letters in their news release. Because of their

---

14 Greenberg, *Black Harlem*, 116; Crowder, "'Don't Buy Where You Can't Work,'" 19.
15 Neither Greenberg's nor Crowder's case studies give any explanation for this astonishing time lag.
16 CAB, box 4, folder 4, ANP, May 7, 1930.
17 A bad record concerning the hiring and promotion of minorities can still trigger a boycott. In August 1990, the sportswear manufacturer Nike, for example, became the target of a national boycott launched by PUSH, a black civil rights organization founded by Jesse Jackson. The controversy was extensively covered by all the major American media; see, e.g., Isabel Wilkerson, "Challenging Nike, Rights Group Takes a Risky Stand," *New York Times*, Aug. 25, 1990, 10A.

excellent connections, Claude A. Barnett, the agency's founder, and his staff already knew that the boycotts in Chicago had attracted national interest and that "several publications in other cities . . . [were] planning to launch similar campaigns."[18]

In the first week of June 1930, delegates from all over the United States traveled to Buffalo to attend the four-day national conference of the Urban League.[19] The congress's theme was "Vocational Opportunities for Negro Workers," and one of the speakers was Joseph D. Bibb.[20] His speech at the convention must have been impressive. Shortly after the end of the meeting, T. Arnold Hill, Director of Industrial Relations of the National Urban League, wrote an editorial for his organization's monthly magazine, which was obviously inspired by Bibb's lecture. Hill's commentary, published in the July edition of *Opportunity*, gave the local chapters of the Urban League their first idea about the official position of the headquarters in New York. Referring to the successful campaign of the *Whip* in Chicago, Hill stated:

This movement has penetrated far into the consciousness of Negroes. . . . The buying-power argument is a good one. It should be pushed vigorously all over the country. . . . But this movement should not stop with chain stores. It should be extended into the realm of public utilities. . . . Our telephone systems, our water companies, gas, electric light and transit systems should be included among those to which the Negro appeals for jobs.[21]

When Bibb returned to Chicago, a new boycott drive on the South Side was started. The target of the summer campaign was well known: F. W. Woolworth & Company, "the only national chain store group which [did] a large business in the colored district that [did] not employ colored clerks."[22] There is no evidence that the attacks against the Consumers and Woolworth chain stores were linked to the general anti–chain store sen-

18 CAB, box 4, folder 4, ANP, May 7, 1930.
19 T. Arnold Hill, "Vocational Opportunities for Negro Workers," *Opportunity* 8, no. 6 (June 1930): 184.
20 JDB, box 1, folder 1. Bibb was not only a journalist but also a practicing attorney, who had graduated from the Yale University law school in 1918. In 1952, Bibb, a Republican, and at this time managing editor of the Chicago edition of the *Pittsburgh Courier*, became State Director of Public Safety in Illinois. According to newspaper reports it was "the first time in the history of Illinois or any other northern state that a governor has appointed a Negro to a cabinet post." See JDB, box 3, undated newspaper clippings (1950s); Joseph J. Bros, ed., *Who's Who in Colored America: A Biographical Dictionary of Notable Living Persons of Negro Descent in America*, 2d ed. (New York, 1929), 31.
21 T. Arnold Hill, "Picketing for Jobs," *Opportunity* 8, no. 7 (July 1930): 216; cf. also Dean S. Yarbrough, "Facing the Future After Twenty Years: Impressions of the National Urban League Conference," *Opportunity* 8, no. 7 (July 1930): 208.
22 CAB, box 4, folder 6, ANP, June 18, 1930.

timent so prevalent in America's white mainstream society during the 1930s.[23] The "Don't Buy Where You Can't Work" movements targeted chain stores as well as independent white-owned groceries and department stores that refused to hire black sales personnel. Since the 1920s, black business organizations like the Colored Merchants' Association and the National Negro Business League had promoted black cooperatives and even tried to copy the marketing strategies of the successful white chains.[24] But despite the efforts of these organizations to support African-American retailers, in the 1930s the vast majority of the stores in black neighborhoods were owned and operated by whites.

On June 7, 1930, pickets with sandwich signs began to walk in front of two Woolworth stores on the South Side of Chicago.[25] This was probably the first time that African Americans used continuous pickets to enforce a boycott and not just sporadic leafleting and agitation. The black community watched this attack against Woolworth with very mixed feelings. On the one hand, many African Americans were fascinated and impressed that "Negroes" dared to challenge an economic giant like Woolworth. On the other hand, there was also much insecurity and fear, because it was hard to imagine how a powerful company like Woolworth and the local law enforcement agencies would react. The report from the ANP about the new campaign, distributed on June 18, mirrored the anxiety and the fear of a backlash very clearly. Once again, the news agency stressed the slogans of the movement written on the banners by capitalizing them: "THIS STORE IS UNFAIR TO NEGRO LABOR – DO NOT SPEND YOUR MONEY WHERE YOU CAN NOT WORK." According to the feature, the pickets were extremely successful:

The effect of the picketing for the past several days has been to almost completely cut off the trade of the stores affected by the boycott. Few colored shoppers will enter in the face of this organized protest, and there are only a few

23 For a short overview of the anti–chain store movement, see Mansel G. Blackford, *A History of Small Business in America* (New York, 1991), 88–93; for a more detailed account, see Richard S. Tedlow, *New and Improved: The Story of Mass Marketing in America* (New York, 1990), 182–226; for reasons for African Americans to buy in chain stores, see also Lizabeth Cohen, *Making a New Deal: Industrial Workers in Chicago, 1919–1939* (Cambridge, 1990), 152.
24 See, e.g., Albon L. Holsey, "The C.M.A. Stores Face the Chains," *Opportunity* 7, no. 7 (July 1929): 210–13 and "Business Points the Way," *Crisis* 38, no. 7 (July 1931): 225–6; W. E. B. Du Bois, "Buying and Selling," *Crisis* 38, no. 11 (Nov. 1931): 393; Ira de A. Reid, "Social Problems of Negro Business," *Crisis* 43, no. 6 (June 1936): 166–7, 186; Gunnar Myrdal, *An American Dilemma: The Negro Problem and Modern Democracy*, 2 vols. (New York, 1944) 1:307–11, 2:815–17; Hunter, "Black Urban Boycott Movements," 52–5, 137–8.
25 St. Clair Drake, "Churches and Voluntary Associations in the Chicago Negro Community," Report of Official Project 465–54–3–386 (3), Work Projects Administration, Chicago, Illinois, 1940 (mimeographed), 249.

white shoppers in the community. From every indication, the stores will either be forced to employ colored clerks or go out of business. There is, however, observers point out, some real danger in carrying the plans of coercion this far, for although definite gains have been made by newspaper publicity and other methods of appeal, there are instances where retaliation may be made positive and harmful.[26]

African Americans had good reasons to fear a white backlash. In the 1930s, most of the people who lived on Chicago's South Side and in other predominantly black urban ghettos were not born in the North but had migrated to the metropolis from the more oppressive southern states. Chicago's black population, for example, which stood at 44,100 (2 percent) in 1910 mushroomed to 233,900 (6.9 percent) by 1930.[27] Certainly, the situation of African Americans in Chicago was less repressive than in Mississippi, Alabama, or Louisiana. Nevertheless, the black experience with police brutality, hostile courts, threats by the Ku Klux Klan, bombings, and lynchings was not limited to the Deep South.[28] In the opinion of many African Americans in Chicago, it was a risky step to dare boycotting and picketing Woolworth's stores.

The company's top management in its New York City headquarters quickly became involved: After suffering serious losses, the local manager of the chain store group in Chicago wrote and wired the Woolworth's office repeatedly to secure a change in the company's discriminatory employment policy.[29] While the "battle" against Woolworth in Chicago was still going on, the ANP reported the first adoption of the boycott tactic in another city:

One more satisfactory demonstration of just what can be accomplished through united effort, in almost any direction, was clearly brought home to John Rosink, white owner of the Detroit Stars baseball team, by the successful boycott of

---

26 CAB, box 4, folder 6, ANP, June 18, 1930.

27 During the same period, the black population of New York increased from 91,700 (1.9 percent) to 327,700 (4.7 percent); the black community in Columbus, Ohio, went from 12,700 (7 percent) to 32,800 (11.3 percent); and in Detroit, the city that became the center of the American automobile industry, the black population rose from 5,700 (1.2 percent) to 120,000 (7.7 percent) (Robert B. Grant, *The Black Man Comes to the City: A Documentary Account from the Great Migration to the Great Depression, 1915–1930* [Chicago, 1972], 28).

28 Joseph Boskin, *Urban Racial Violence in the Twentieth Century* (Beverly Hills, Calif., 1969), 21–37.

29 CAB, box 4, folder 6, ANP, June 18, 1930. Although business historians have focused on company founders and top managers in company headquarters, little is known about the experiences and attitudes of average store managers. For a first attempt to fill this gap see Alan A. Raucher's study, which examines the recruitment and promotion practices for these positions. Raucher also points out the limited career opportunities for women and certain ethnic groups in the five leading dime store chains. Alan R. Raucher "Dime Store Chains: The Making of Organization Men, 1880–1940," *Business History Review* 65, no. 1 (spring 1991): 145, 152–60.

Rosink's Stadium by baseball fans here who stayed away from the park three weeks and just at the time when the Stars are playing the best ball of their career.[30]

According to the ANP correspondent, the boycott was led by Russell J. Cowan, a sports journalist, and grew out of Rosink's failure to advertise in "shine" newspapers, his arrogant, insulting attitude toward black patrons, and the alleged unfair treatment of his African-American players. The ANP reporter beamed with satisfaction about the outcome of the campaign: "Playing to empty benches brought Rosink down from his 'high horse.'" The economic losses and the racial tensions must have been great. After three weeks of boycotting, Rosink not only turned the park management over to Mose L. Walker, his "colored lieutenant," but also signed an agreement that he would stay away from the park himself. After the end of the campaign, paid "advertisements in the Negro newspapers" were asking the fans to again support the team.[31] The character of the boycott of the Detroit Stars' baseball stadium clearly differed from those of the job campaigns in Chicago. Although the motivations of the leaders were partly shaped by their own economic interests, the primary goal of the boycott in Detroit was not to gain jobs but to protest against racist attitudes and to make a collective political statement. This experience – that boycotts could also be successfully used in such a broader way – opened new possibilities for the fight of African Americans against segregation. Of course, the objective of getting jobs dominated the campaigns during the Depression years of the 1930s; nevertheless, for the first time boycotts were also used to combat racism and discrimination in sports. The boycott against the owner of the Detroit Stars in August 1930 pioneered a strategy that has remained in the tactical repertoire of civil rights activists to this day.[32]

Black boycotters succeeded not only in Detroit but also in Chicago. In the first week of October 1930, after more than four months of picketing

30 CAB, box 5, folder 2, ANP, Aug. 27, 1930.
31 Ibid.; in the 1930s, major league baseball in the United States was also segregated. For background on the Detroit Stars and other black baseball teams, see Robert Peterson, *Only the Ball Was White* (Englewood Cliffs, N.J., 1970), 268–9.
32 For a detailed discussion of black boycotts in sports, see the thorough case study by Donald Larue Hoover. He focused not only on the debate about the proposed boycott of the Olympics 1968 but also on the preceding boycott of the New York Athletic Club, which discriminated against African Americans and Jews. Donald Larue Hoover, "Should We Stay or Should We Go ? – America's Black Athletes, the Civil Rights Movement, and the Proposed Boycott of the 1968 Olympic Games," M.S. thesis, Kansas State University, 1990; for a more recent example of a successful boycott threat in the sports arena, see "NAACP Called Off Boycott of LPGA Event," *Chicago Tribune*, Aug. 15, 1990, sec. 4, p. 7.

on Chicago's South Side, the Woolworth management finally yielded and abandoned the "company's fifty-year-old policy against the employment of colored girls as clerks." The local manager hired twenty-one African-American women for the opening of the newest and largest of Woolworth's five-and-ten cent stores in the "colored district." The black community celebrated its victory and, according to the ANP, "several thousands of curious persons elbowed their way" through the store. According to the report, the boycott activists indicated that the pickets "will now be used against other businesses in the district which ignore the claim of the Negro Worker."[33]

The news that the black community in Chicago had "defeated" the powerful Woolworth Company impressed African Americans all over the country. It stimulated debates and calls for action, but only a few communities dared to adopt the "radical" boycott tactic in the fall of 1930. Although there was an outpouring of sympathy and verbal support, the direct action approach pioneered in Chicago was still considered to be a very "drastic" and "dangerous" step.[34] In the streets and bars, at church meetings and in the national headquarters of the NAACP and the Urban League in New York City, people discussed the victory over Woolworth. But neither the NAACP nor the Urban League were all-black organizations. Although the majority of their members in the 1930s were African Americans, both organizations stood for an interracial approach and also had white Protestant and Jewish members and executives.[35] Possibly afraid of alienating its white followers and contributors, the National Urban League, in particular, hesitated to take a clear position on boycotts of white-owned businesses.[36] Whereas the two leading civil-rights organizations, despite their early favorable comments, were undecided, the predominantly black National Negro Business League (NNBL) had excellent connections to the leaders of the Chicago boycott. Founded by Booker T. Washington in 1900, the NNBL promoted self-help by African-American merchants and businessmen and hoped that vocational training, scientific management, and professional marketing would help

33 CAB, box 260, folder 7, ANP, Oct. 6, 1930.
34 CAB, box 5, folder 4, ANP, Oct. 20, 1930.
35 The role of whites in these organizations is discussed in August Meier and Elliot Rudwick, "The Rise of the Black Secretariat in the NAACP, 1909–35," and "Attorneys Black and White: A Case Study of Race Relations Within the NAACP," both in August Meier and Elliott Rudwick, *Along the Color Line: Explorations in the Black Experience* (Urbana, Ill., 1976), 94–173; Nancy J. Weiss, *The National Urban League, 1910–1940* (New York, 1974), on the financial situation, see especially, 242–5; also Hunter, "Black Urban Boycott Movements," 183.
36 See T. Arnold Hill, "What Price Jobs," *Opportunity* 8, no. 10 (Oct. 1930): 310.

black entrepreneurs to compete successfully in the American market-place.[37] In a warm letter to Joseph D. Bibb, editor of the *Whip*, the secretary of the NNBL, Albon L. Holsey, wrote on October 27, 1930: "My dear Friend Bibb: The entire Negro race owes you a debt of gratitude for the courageous fight with its happy conclusion that you led against the Woolworth Company."[38] Some days later, in the new edition of *Crisis*, W. E. B. Du Bois again urged his readers to use the boycott systematically as a means to fight for jobs:

> The American Negro who suffers most in crises like this, has concentrated his activities on a feverish search for work. He has begun systematically to bargain, offering to buy only of those business institutions which give him work in turn. He has used, particularly in Chicago, against notorious chain stores, the systematic boycott. We are delighted to learn that the boycott carried on there against the Woolworth stores has at last been successful. What Chicago, led by The Whip, has done can be done elsewhere. We hope it will. It is one of the paths leading out of our economic wilderness.[39]

Although in New York sympathy for the movement in Chicago was great and the economic situation very similar, strangely enough the black community in Harlem did not adopt the boycott tactic in 1930. It was not in New York but in Toledo and Columbus, Ohio, where the first follow-up campaigns after the success in Chicago were initiated in October 1930. On the same day that the ANP reported the "happy" end of the boycott against Woolworth's, African Americans in Columbus started to prepare the first systematic "Don't Buy Where You Can't Work" campaign in the capital of Ohio.[40] The target of the boycott was the Kroger Grocery and Baking Company, at this time the second largest grocery chain in the United States, with more than 5,500 stores, most of them in the Midwest.[41] The company operated twelve outlets in Columbus's predominantly

---

37 For background, see Albon L. Holsey, "The National Negro Business League: Forty Years in Review," *Crisis* 48, no. 4 (Apr. 1941): 104–5; for the early years of the NNBL, see Louis R. Harlan, "Booker T. Washington and the National Negro Business League," in William G. Shade and Roy C. Herrenkohl, eds., *Seven on Black: Reflections on the Negro Experience in America* (Philadelphia, 1969), 73–91.

38 JDB, box 1, folder 1, TLS, Oct. 27, 1930. Holsey was also a close friend of Barnett, see Hogan, *Associated Negro Press*, 103.

39 W. E. B. Du Bois, "Jobs," *Crisis* 37, no. 11 (Nov. 1930): 389.

40 Unfortunately, the surviving documents do not reveal exactly which organizations composed the boycott committee, but the sources suggest that the Urban League, the NAACP, the Independent Voters League, and several churches supported the campaign (Urban League Columbus, records [hereafter cited as ULC], box 13, folder "Kroger Matter," minutes, Oct. 6, 1930, TMs, manuscript collection no. 146, Ohio Historical Society, Columbus, Ohio).

41 C. H. Shoenberger, "How Kroger Makes Friends for 5,500 Stores," *Chain Store Age*, administration ed. 5, no. 5 (May 1929): 46; George Laycock, *The Kroger Story: A Century of Innovation* (Cincinnati, Ohio, 1983), 37.

black East End. But despite the fact that up to 90 percent of its customers were African Americans, the local Kroger management stated that
it would not hire any "Negroes." During negotiations with representatives of Columbus's black community, the white managers had said
frankly, "This is a matter of cents and dollars. We believe our prices will
appeal to your group and we do not believe you can keep your people
out of our stores in sufficient numbers to affect us."[42] To the majority of
the committee members it seemed clear that a boycott was the only way
to react. After careful preparations that took several weeks, leaflets were
printed, and the boycott against all Kroger stores launched. Unfortunately,
neither the ANP nor the local white newspapers covered the campaign
in Columbus.

During the early 1930s, the Chicago-based black news agency was
still struggling to build up a reliable network of correspondents, and it
was not before the mid-1930s that the ANP was able to find a regular
contributor in Columbus. Until 1935, news about happenings in Ohio's
capital was very rare in the releases of the ANP. On the other hand, the
journalists of the financially weak agency tried their best to get news not
only from the big cities like Chicago, New York, Atlanta, or Detroit but
also from smaller towns. In a special service called "Business and Industry,"
the ANP reported on January 7, 1931, from Toledo: "In the first actual,
systematic boycott ever conducted here, hundreds of citizens and hired
picket men with sandwich signs picketed two Kroger and an independent meat store in the midst of the colored section last week until they employed colored help."[43] The picketing was supported and organized by the
local branch of the NAACP.[44] It is unclear if the boycotters in Toledo
knew about the ongoing campaign against Kroger in Columbus, just
some 150 miles to the southeast, and if they coordinated their tactics.
However, for the management of Kroger's in Cincinnati the "Christmas
news" that African Americans had started boycotting and picketing
Kroger stores not only in Columbus but also in Toledo must have been a
warning signal. The campaigns at the end of 1930 were only the beginning: In the years to come Kroger as well as many other companies that
discriminated against African Americans would become frequent targets
of black consumer boycotts.

---

42 ULC, box 13, folder "Kroger Matter," minute, Oct. 6, 1930.
43 CAB, box 6, folder 2, ANP, Jan. 7, 1931.
44 *Pittsburgh Courier*, Dec. 27, 1930, 3.

II

The successful campaign of the *Whip* in 1930 stirred up a nationwide debate among black intellectuals about the advantages and risks of consumer boycotts. Advocates of the "new" tactic clashed with leaders who condemned it and predicted a "deadly boomerang" effect for the African-American community if purchasing power were to be used as a weapon in the struggle for civil rights.[45] For the first time, the politics of boycotting were a topic of controversy in all black newspapers and political magazines. Between 1930 and 1941, boycott movements all over the country copied the "Don't Buy Where You Can't Work" idea.[46] The tactic itself was not really new. Since the 1880s the labor movement in the United States and other countries had frequently used consumer boycotts to support its demands. But because American unions, with the exception of the Knights of Labor, systematically barred African Americans, blacks were usually not involved in these early boycotts.[47]

American unions not only banned "inferior races" from their membership, they were also in the forefront of the anti-Asian campaigns in the West during the late nineteenth century. Since Chinese workers were excluded from all but the most menial occupations in white companies, many Asian immigrants in California, Nevada, and Montana had successfully tried to establish their own small businesses. During the 1870s, Chinese laundries, grocery stores, restaurants, and hotels became an increasingly common sight in the cities and towns of the western United States. Simultaneously, anti-Chinese sentiments rose, and agitators, many of them members of all-white unions, realized that the economic prosperity of Chinese businesses was strongly determined by the demand for their services and products by European Americans. Consequently, from 1880 to

---

45 The term "deadly boomerang" is borrowed from George S. Schuyler, "To Boycott or Not to Boycott? – A Deadly Boomerang," *Crisis* 41, no. 9 (Sept. 1934): 259–60, 274.

46 For a thorough analysis that includes an incomplete but still useful listing of cities where "Don't Buy Where You Can't Work" boycotts occurred, see August Meier and Elliot Rudwick, "The Origins of Nonviolent Direct Action in Afro-American Protest: A Note on Historical Discontinuities," in Meier and Rudwick, *Along the Color Line*, 316.

47 For more background, see the early analyses of Harry W. Laidler, *Boycotts and the Labor Struggle: Economic and Legal Aspects* (New York, 1913) and Leo Wolman, "The Boycott in American Trade Unions," *Johns Hopkins University Studies in Historical and Political Science* 34, no. 1 (1916): 1–148; for a more recent case study, see Michael A. Gordon, "The Labor Boycott in New York City, 1880–1886," *Labor History* 16 (spring 1975): 184–229; Dana Frank, *Purchasing Power: Consumer Organizing, Gender, and the Seattle Labor Movement, 1919–1929* (Cambridge, 1994), 108–38; for the first account of the new "American" tactic of boycotting in a German scholarly magazine, see A[ugust] Sartorius von Waltershausen, "Boycotten, ein neues Kampfmittel der Amerikanischen Werkvereine," *Jahrbücher für Nationalökonomie und Statistik* 45 (1885): 1–18.

1910, nativists in many western American cities launched boycotts to oust Chinese and Japanese competitors and drive them first out of business and then out of town. "The Chinese must go" was the war cry of these movements, a racist demand that commonly was supplemented with economic rationales.[48]

One of the popular claims, which could be heard in almost every anti-Asian boycott campaign, was that the Chinese employers and workers created unemployment by underbidding the wages of European-American laborers. This widespread belief was based on the myth that Chinese Americans and white workers would compete for the same jobs. But like African Americans, Asian Americans were usually forced to earn a living in fields that European Americans normally avoided because of the hard work and long hours. Although economic motivations surely played an important role in the mobilization process of anti-Chinese boycotts, it is evident that the campaigns generally were deeply rooted in a spirit of white supremacy that sought to expel all Asians from the country whether they were competitors in business or in the job market or not.[49] The rumors that launched during boycotts mirrored the underlying nativist mentality that shaped anti-Asian actions: Chinese laundrymen, for example, were stigmatized with the charge of infecting customers with syphilis through the laundrymen's practice of spraying clothes prior to ironing by spurting water from their mouths.[50] Decoded, the subliminal message of these claims branded Chinese as carriers of sexually transmitted diseases and therefore as a dangerous threat not only to the mental but also to the physical health of America and especially to American womanhood.

Given these racist undertones, it comes as no surprise that unionists in Butte, Montana, for example, conducted their boycott campaigns in the year 1897 against the Chinese businesses in town under the battle

48 For a comprehensive analysis of the distinctive characteristics of American nativism, see John Higham, *Strangers in the Land: Patterns of American Nativism, 1860–1925,* 2d ed. (New Brunswick, N.J., and London, 1988); hereafter, the term nativism is used following Higham's definition on pages 3–11; for a reexamination of Higham's classic and the topic it treats, see also the essays in *American Jewish History* 76 (1986): 107–226.

49 For conclusions of a contemporary scholar, see Laidler, *Boycotts,* 73–5; for a case study, Stacy A. Flaherty, "Boycott in Butte: Organized Labor and the Chinese Community, 1896–1897," *Montana* 37, no. 1 (winter 1987): 34–47; on boycotts in Los Angeles, see Raymond Lou, "Chinese American Agricultural Workers and the Anti-Chinese Movement in Los Angeles, 1870–1890," in Robert Asher and Charles Stephenson, eds., *Labor Divided: Race and Ethnicity in United States Labor Struggles, 1835–1960* (Albany, N.Y., 1990), 49–62; for San Francisco, see H. Brett Melendy, *Chinese and Japanese Americans* (New York, 1984), 102–9; on Chinese counterboycotts, see Delber L. McKee, "The Chinese Boycott of 1905–1906 Reconsidered: The Role of Chinese Americans," *Pacific Historical Review* 55, no. 2 (May 1986): 165–91.

50 Lou, "The Anti-Chinese Movement in Los Angeles," 60.

cry "America versus Asia." In newspaper ads and leaflets the Silver Bow Trades and Labor Assembly, an umbrella organization of the city's more than thirty labor unions, appealed to their fellow European Americans to assist them "in this fight against the lowering Asiatic standards of living and of morals." Whites who criticized the boycott of the Chinese and continued to patronize their businesses or to give employment to them quickly became themselves targets of the boycotters, who labeled them un-American. For nativists it was beyond question that "anyone who opposes anything that is so American in its nature as the general boycott against the Asiatic races simply put themselves in a ridiculous light."[51] During the boycotts, activists used graphic images painted on muslin to convince the public that the "sneaky, treacherous" Asians should never be trusted. According to an eyewitness, one of the propaganda pictures paraded by the boycotters showed a "Chinaman baking bread, and holding a rat" over it as if he intended to drop it into the bread.[52] Using one of the most common and effective patterns to legitimize racist attacks, the boycotter's caricature transformed the victims of their campaign into offenders. From the imagery that these vilifications connoted, it was only a small step to completely dehumanize Asians and depict them as "cute . . . rats."[53] The nativist message was clear: Asians could only be regarded as subhuman beings, a plague that had come over America and that could only be fought off by a joint effort and with drastic measures.

In Butte as well as in many other cities in California, Nevada, and Montana, the calls for boycotting Chinese businesses and for the expulsion of all Asians created an atmosphere full of racial hatred. In several cases pogrom-like riots were the outcome; the bloodiest of them became known as the Rock Springs Massacre, in which twenty-eight Chinese were killed by whites. Although anti-Asian violence was not unusual, nativist activists mainly resorted to more subtle strategies against the Asian minority in the American West. In Congress, for example, representatives of the western states successfully lobbied for the Chinese Exclusion Act (1882), which prevented further immigration of Chinese to the United States, although the borders were kept open for European immigrants.[54]

---

51 Flaherty, "Boycott in Butte," 34, 41.
52 Ibid., 38.
53 Ibid., 37.
54 Chinese and Japanese immigrants who had come to the United States prior to the Exclusion Act were also excluded from becoming American citizens, and in most states Asians were forbidden by law to marry European-American women (McKee, "Chinese Boycott," 172; Lou, "The Anti-Chinese Boycott Movement in Los Angeles," 56).

On the local level, nativists realized that economic pressure through special taxes and boycotts could be an effective means to get rid of the "leprous" Asians and the "pest houses," as Chinese laundries were labeled.[55] Despite the general anti-Asian sentiment, it should be noted that several boycotts of Chinese businesses ended in obvious failure. In Los Angeles, for example, the campaigns collapsed because most white customers of the Chinese did not support the campaigns.[56] Nonetheless, in most cases the boycotts caused serious losses, and attempts of Chinese to obtain court injunctions against these actions, which threatened their economic survival, were usually not successful. Hence, in the long run, boycotts forced many Asian-American businessmen to give up their enterprises and leave the hostile communities. In Butte alone, more than three hundred Chinese left the Rocky Mountain city as a consequence of the boycott.[57]

At roughly the same time, African Americans in the Deep South gained their first experience using the tactic of boycotting as a means of defense against discrimination. In the years between 1890 and 1906, black communities in more than thirty cities, all of them located in states of the former Confederacy, boycotted Jim Crow streetcars to protest against the enactment of segregation laws that assigned special sections to white and black passengers in the trolleys. The African-American streetcar boycotts at the turn of the century lasted from a few weeks to as long as two or three years. In several cases the companies that operated the streetcars reported losses of up to $50,000. Some of the black communities even bought motor buses and tried to start an independent black transportation system. At a time when white shotgun sovereignty was still the rule in many towns of the South, such a massive protest was a courageous step for black Americans. Nonetheless, it should not be overlooked that the general character of these early boycott movements "can be best described as a 'conservative protest.'" The boycotters were seeking to "preserve the status quo" – to prevent the introduction of stricter segregation laws. Therefore, the goal of the streetcar boycotts was defensive in nature without the intention to fight for equal rights in the future.[58] Given the repressiveness in the former slave states at this time, it was no

---

55 Flaherty, "Boycott in Butte," 37.
56 Lou, "The Anti-Chinese Movement in Los Angeles," 57–60.
57 Flaherty, "Boycott in Butte," 42.
58 Inspired by the "recent boycotts against southern bus segregation" (in Montgomery, Alabama [1955–56] and Tallahassee, Florida [1956–57]), August Meier presented his first tentative findings on the forgotten history of streetcar boycotts in 1957. In the late 1960s, after a decade of intensive research and exhausting the available source materials, Meier and his partner Elliot Rudwick

wonder that the boycotts of African Americans could not stop the white backlash and the enactment of racial segregation.

Since these early boycotts of transportation monopolies at the beginning of the twentieth century had failed, contemporaries and historians credited the campaign directed by the *Chicago Whip* in 1930 with being the first *successful* black consumer boycott in the United States.[59] Nonetheless, source materials discovered during the research for this study prove that the historiography has been partially misleading. There is good reason to assume that at least some cities had a local tradition of boycotting years before the efforts of the *Whip* attracted nationwide attention. The African-American community in Columbus, Ohio, for example, had successfully used consumer boycotts as a political weapon long before the *Whip* started its first campaign at the beginning of the 1930s.

III

In August 1923 the managers of the Columbus-based Budd Dairy Company made a fatal mistake that would finally cost them their jobs: An advertisement in the Ku Klux Klan's weekly newspaper, intended to increase product sales, particularly of a newly introduced soft drink, unintentionally triggered a consumer boycott against the dairy, which caused tremendous financial losses. Some months later, in April 1924, a local competitor bought the struggling company.[60] Although the new management "at once acknowledged that there had been a great falling off in the Budd Dairy Company's sales as a result of the advertisement," it generally refused to give any more details. Since the former owners and the top management stonewalled, a contemporary scholar, J. Wesley

published a series of studies that remain standard works. See August Meier, "Boycotts of Segregated Street Cars, 1894–1909 – A Research Note," *Phylon* 18, no. 3 (1957): 296–7; August Meier and Elliot Rudwick, "The Boycott Movements Against Jim Crow Streetcars in the South, 1900–1906," *Journal of American History* 55, no. 4 (Mar. 1969): 770; August Meier and Elliot Rudwick, "Negro Boycotts of Jim Crow Streetcars in Tennessee," *American Quarterly* 21, no. 4 (winter 1969): 755–63. August Meier and Elliot Rudwick, "Negro Boycotts of Segregated Street Cars in Virginia, 1904–1907," *Virginia Magazine of History and Biography* 81, no. 4 (Oct. 1973): 479–87. For a more recent case study, which is mostly based on materials already used by Meier and Rudwick, see Lena R. Marbury, "Nashville's 1905 Streetcar Boycott," M.A. thesis, Tennessee State University, 1985; for earlier conflicts over racial segregation on streetcars, see also Roger A. Fischer, "A Pioneer Protest: The New Orleans Street-Car Controversy of 1867," *Journal of Negro History* 53, no. 3 (July 1968): 219–33.

59 Interestingly, none of the contemporary journalists who covered the boycotts in the 1930s mentioned the earlier streetcar boycotts in the South, although at least W. E. B. Du Bois knew about them (see Meier and Rudwick, "Negro Boycotts of Jim Crow Streetcars," 763).

60 *Columbus Citizen*, Apr. 16, 1924, 9; *Ohio State Journal* [Columbus], Apr. 17, 1924, 16.

Hatcher, who tried to collect information about the boycott, contacted the drivers of delivery wagons and foremen. Under the assurance that he would not print their names, Hatcher finally managed to get the interviews he wanted. A former foreman of the Budd Dairy Company told him the following story:

> The thing was astonishing. . . . It did not seem possible that it could be done as it was. The paper was put on sale on Friday [August 31, 1923]. On Saturday morning, early, customers began calling into the office by phone [,] ordering their milk stopped. This continued through several days and was almost continuous. Generally they stated frankly that their action was due to the "ad in the paper. . . ." It made the Catholics and the "niggers" mad. And this falling off in the sales of milk continued until there was a loss of over 600 gallons per day. In some cases the customers of an entire street would discontinue. The thing was done in a hurry. A representative was sent out by the company . . . to convince them that Mr. Budd was not a Klansman, but it had no effect. The thing was on. It went like wild fire.[61]

It was not the text of the advertisement that triggered the boycott against the Budd Dairy but its appearance in the *Ohio Fiery Cross*, the Ku Klux Klan weekly, which since its revival in the turbulent years after the end of World War I had strongly intensified its agitation against African Americans, Jews, Catholics, and immigrants.[62] Within days, delivery drivers of the dairy lost first their customers and then their jobs. One man who delivered milk in a district with a large number of African-American and several Roman Catholic families said that he "lost all the Negro families and all of those connected with the Roman Catholic church except one." The driver was desperate and tried everything possible to persuade his customers to continue purchasing from him, but his efforts were in vain. Eventually, several drivers had to give up their routes completely. The heaviest losses were sustained in the neighborhoods with a "concentration of Negro population."[63] An African-American woman told Hatcher

> No one knows what I suffer and what we all suffer. . . . And the Kluxers more than anything else have brought about this change and are creating all this trouble for us. So you see the colored people just can't afford to buy goods from them or do anything else which will in any way contribute to a body of peo-

61 J. Wesley Hatcher, "The Effect of Coercion upon the Attitudes and Organizations of the Suppressed Group," M.A. thesis, Ohio State University, 1925, 41–2.
62 According to Hatcher, the advertisement (5.5 × 17.5 inches) was published in the *Ohio Fiery Cross*, Aug. 31, 1923, 2. Unfortunately, a copy of this edition did not survive; the Ohio Historical Society owns only some issues of the year 1924.
63 Hatcher, "The Effect of Coercion," 40–2.

ple or to an individual who takes the attitude toward our people the Kluxers have. We couldn't keep our self-respect and be true to our future or loyal to our race and do it. We are compelled to quit buying milk from Budd or anything else from anybody else who is identified with the Kluxers or is in sympathy with them.[64]

According to Hatcher's informants, the boycott against the Budd Dairy was not the first occasion when residents of Columbus withdrew their purchasing power for political reasons: "Whenever it was found that a certain individual was a Kluxer, or was suspected of being, word was passed along and every colored person quit buying from him immediately."[65] Apparently, the use of the boycott tactic against the Ku Klux Klan was inspired by the Klan's own agitation in Ohio's capital for systematically boycotting Catholic, Jewish, foreign-born, and black businesses.[66] The anti-Klan boycotts in the early 1920s worked informally, without any committee or formal organization: "That is not necessary. We all feel the situation so deeply that it is only necessary to tell a colored person that anyone is a Kluxer and that settles it all." It is crucial that the anti-Klan boycott was interracial – supported not only by African Americans but also by Catholics and Jews.[67] One black businessman on the East Side who stopped selling Budd's products explained his motivation as follows:

Well, I never believed in paying people to injure me. When I know they are doing it and I can find any way to protect myself I am going to do it. Likely there are plenty of others from whom I am buying who are Kluxers but if I don't know it I am not so much to blame. But when I do know it I am not going to help him along in his dirty work. Every colored man knows, as well as does every Catholic and Jew, that the Kluxers are our enemies and are always against us. The Kluxers, after we began cutting off business from them at the East End Market, Budd's dairy and such places, got scared.[68]

Businessmen, who were boycotted because they supported the Klan, started goodwill actions and tried to persuade the African-American community that the "Klan was not the enemy of the Negro" in general, but

---

64 Ibid., 44.
65 Ibid., 45.
66 For the use of boycotts by the Ku Klux Klan, see Frank Bohn, "The Ku Klux Klan Interpreted," *American Journal of Sociology* 30, no. 4 (Jan. 1925): 390; and Kathleen M. Blee, *Women of the Klan: Racism and Gender in the 1920s* (Berkeley, Calif., 1991), 147–53; for an interpretation of the Klan as a reactionary, fraternal "business organization," see Charles C. Alexander, "Kleagles and Cash: The Ku Klux Klan as a Business Organization, 1915–1930," *Business History Review* 39, no. 3 (autumn 1965): 348–67.
67 In the early 1920s, Columbus's East Side, although predominantly black, was still a multiethnic neighborhood; Nimrod B. Allen, "East Long Street," *Crisis* 25, no. 1 (Nov. 1922): 12–16.
68 Hatcher, "The Effect of Coercion," 46–7.

that it was "only after the bad fellows." But the Klan's propaganda was
fruitless and could not stop the boycotts. Seven months after the boycott
against Budd had started, a local competitor bought the financially weakened dairy.[69] The black community of Columbus interpreted this as a
clear victory and consequence of the withdrawal of its purchasing power.
The outcome of the boycott was crucial for the self-esteem of African
Americans in Ohio's capital. One might argue that the boycotts in
Columbus in the early 1920s had marginal significance because they
were only informally organized. But more essential for the changing attitude of African Americans than a formal organization of the boycott with
institutionalized committees was the collective experience of successful
resistance. In his conclusion, written in 1925, Hatcher prophesied what
would happen in the years to come:

> The boycott is most significant. It reveals beyond question the presence of un-
> yielding attitudes of antipathy [toward white supremacists] as being almost uni-
> versally among the Negro group. It also shows their awareness of their power in
> the economic situation. Let the opposition which has occasioned the boycott of
> the present continue and organization for the more effective wielding of the
> newly found power is the inevitable. Necessity will forge the tool.[70]

IV

Whereas the boycotts in Columbus in the early 1920s apparently were
inspired by the Ku Klux Klan's own boycotting policy, it remains uncertain where the leaders of the campaigns in Chicago in 1930 got the idea
to promote the boycott as a political weapon. Ralph Crowder's claim
that the use of consumer boycotts was an "indigenous and unique creation by the Black community" that was not inspired by forces outside is
not substantiated.[71] Obviously, black leaders did not exist in an intellectual vacuum but were influenced by the contemporary discussions on
the political pages of both the black and the white press.[72] Thus the question some historians ask, whether the idea of using consumer boycotts
was an adoption of an established method of social pressure from the

69 Ibid., 47–8.
70 Ibid., 49–50; for black boycotts in the 1920s, see also "Italians Shoot and Beat Man," *Detroit Inde-
    pendent*, Oct. 7, 1927, 1.
71 Crowder, "'Don't Buy Where You Can't Work,'" 9.
72 The struggle for independence of the Indian people, e.g., and the tactics of economic noncoop-
    eration and boycotting employed by Mahatma Gandhi were widely covered. Advertisements for
    his books appeared in the *Crisis*, and in 1929 the editors of the same journal labeled Gandhi
    "the greatest colored man in the world, and perhaps the greatest man in the world" (*Crisis* 36,
    no. 7 [July 1929]: 225); see also *Pittsburgh Courier*, Feb. 28, 1931, 10, and Mar. 7, 1931, 10.

repertoire of other groups or an independent reinvention of the black community, seems not to be very helpful.[73] The debate in the 1930s shows that African-American intellectuals were well aware that they were not the first group to employ their buying power as a political weapon but that "other races have used the boycott" before.[74] On the other hand, it is also true that it was the first time that blacks all over the country discussed the pros and cons of the politics of boycotting with regard to their fight for equal opportunities in the United States.

During the controversy from 1930 to 1941, despite the early favorable commentaries in their monthly magazines, the national headquarters of the two major civil-rights organizations, the NAACP and the Urban League, never took a clear stand on the use of consumer boycotts. Because of this lack of central leadership, the local branches decided independently whether they considered a boycott an adequate means to improve the situation of African Americans in their own community. In some cities NAACP chapters organized and led boycotts, whereas in others the local branches supported boycott campaigns only behind the scenes or opposed the efforts of black activists to launch a "Don't Buy Where You Can't Work" movement. The same ambiguous pattern toward boycott campaigns emerges if one analyzes the attitudes of the various chapters of the Urban League in the 1930s. This ambivalence makes it difficult to prove the claim of Meier and Rudwick that branches of the Urban League were "far more supportive" than those of the NAACP.[75]

Books about boycotting were not as rare in the 1930s as one might assume. Although how-to manuals with detailed tips for boycott activists did not become popular before the 1960s,[76] the trained black attorneys who were involved in the campaigns of the 1930s, like Joseph D. Bibb (Chicago), John Farrison (Columbus), Charles V. Carr (Cleveland), or Belford W. Lawson (Washington), surely had no problem finding Harry W. Laidler's and Leo Wolman's standard works on boycotting. Less well

---

73 Crowder, "'Don't Buy Where You Can't Work,'" 9; cf. also Meier and Rudwick, "The Origins of Nonviolent Direct Action," 382, 387, 389.

74 NAACP, Ohio Branch Records (hereafter cited as NAACP-OBR), box 5, folder 7, "Proceedings Second Special Conference, Apr. 3, 1932," TMs, Manuscripts Collection no. 13, Ohio Historical Society, Columbus, Ohio; Ralph Bunche, "A Critical Analysis of the Tactics and Programs of Minority Groups," *Journal of Negro Education* 4, no. 3, (July 1935): 313; Kelly Miller, "The Negro Uses the Boycott," *Pittsburgh Courier*, Dec. 23, 1933, sec. 2, p. 2; Schuyler, "To Boycott or Not to Boycott?" 260; John A. Davis, "We Win the Right to Fight for Jobs," *Opportunity* 16, no. 8 (Aug. 1938): 234; Charles Harold Loeb, *The Future Is Yours: The History of the Future Outlook League, 1935–1946* (Cleveland, Ohio, 1947), 25.

75 Meier and Rudwick, "The Origins of Nonviolent Direct Action," 331.

76 See Martin Oppenheimer and George Lakey, *A Manual for Direct Action* (Chicago, 1965), 17, 35, 40, 73–114.

known, but also available in the 1930s, was Clarence Marsh Case's book, one of the first studies in methods of social pressure, which included chapters about boycotting and influenced Mahatma Gandhi.[77]

From 1930 to 1941, the main arguments used in the debate about the chances and risks of consumer boycotts for the black community were often reiterated. One of the strongest objections to the use of the boycott strategy by African Americans was the possibility of retaliation. The concern was widespread that boycotts against white companies with discriminatory hiring policies would increase the tension between blacks and whites and finally result in a backlash by white employers inside and outside the black neighborhoods. The agitation against white shops in the ghetto apparently "bred fear in the minds of some non-ghetto, colored workers – especially those holding preferred jobs."[78] During the *Whip's* campaigns in Chicago, for example, rumors circulated that downtown stores had dismissed black employees as a retaliatory measure.[79] But white businessmen in Chicago were very pragmatic and less emotional than some African Americans believed. The *Whip's* prophecy proved to be true: "There will be no wholesale discharge of colored people for they are not holding their jobs because white employers love them or are interested in the race and its civic welfare," but because blacks were not unionized and worked for lower wages.[80] Indeed, the fear of retaliation by white employers outside the ghetto proved to be groundless in Chicago.[81]

Nonetheless, the argument remained popular.[82] Throughout the 1930s, adversaries of the boycott tactic like George Schuyler, who denounced the "Don't Buy Where You Can't Work" campaigns as "crackpot agita-

77 Clarence Marsh Case, *Non-Violent Coercion: A Study in Methods of Social Pressure* (New York, 1923; reprint, New York, 1972), 305–46.

78 Oliver Cromwell Cox, "The Origins Of Direct-Action Protest Among Negroes," unpubl. M.S., 133; Oliver Cromwell Cox was a contemporary who studied the boycott campaigns on Chicago's South Side while a student at the University of Chicago in the 1930s. His manuscript "The Negroes' Use of Their Buying Power as a Means of Securing Employment," written for the Department of Economics, was finished in 1933; Cox rewrote and edited the study in the early 1970s, but it was never published.

79 CAB, box 4, folder 6, ANP, June 18, 1930.

80 *Chicago Whip*, June 21, 1930 (quoted after Cox, "The Origins of Direct Action," 134), see also A. E. Patterson, "Woolworth Store Picketing Keeps Our Girls Out of Work," *Chicago Defender*, Sept. 13, 1930, 2.

81 Apparently only in a few cases did whites threaten that blacks would be laid off if the boycotts did not stop. Arnold T. Hill, "What Price Jobs," *Opportunity* 8, no. 10 (Oct. 1930): 310; William Jones, "A History and Appraisal of the Economic Consequences of Negro Trade Boycotts," M.A. thesis, Atlanta University, 1940, 36–7; Hunter, "Black Urban Boycott Movements," 146; Claude McKay, *Harlem: Negro Metropolis* (New York, 1940), 202.

82 See, e.g., Bunche, "A Critical Analysis," 314.

tion," "stupidity," and "race chauvinism," spread the misinformation that as a consequence of the boycott in Chicago "more Negroes lost jobs *outside* the colored section than won jobs *inside* it [Schuyler's italics]. . . . With sixteen Negroes working outside the black belts to every one inside, the boycott ballyhooers are clearly asking us to cut off our heads to cure a cold."[83] Schuyler's polemic attacks did not remain unanswered. In a letter to the editors of *Crisis*, one writer from Chicago categorized Schuyler's claim "as a mystical rationalization based upon a personal fear of reprisal."[84]

Another point of criticism was that the demand to employ black clerks would cause dismissals of white employees and therefore increase the tension between the races. Usually boycott advocates replied that they did not ask for the immediate replacements of white clerks by blacks, but that the next vacancies caused by turnover, retirements, or the opening of new stores should be filled by African Americans. In reality, the activists, of course, were eager to see quick results and frequently did not accept a company's excuse of not needing additional employees.[85] A major point critics of the "Don't Buy Where You Can't Work" movements often raised was that the boycotts would work only in the urban ghettos and that the few jobs that could be won in groceries would not solve the problem of mass unemployment among African Americans. Indeed, only in very rare cases did blacks try to organize boycotts and pickets outside the black districts. The politics of boycotting depended strongly on the sympathetic environment and mass support that could only be found in predominantly black neighborhoods. It was much more difficult to employ boycotts against discriminatory policies of companies or factories not located in the ghetto.[86]

Although the tactic of boycotting to get jobs was new and radical for African Americans, the underlying ideology was not. The boycotters never attempted to challenge the economic system in the United States. The short-term goal of the campaigns in the 1930s was to open clerical positions for African Americans, the long-term objective to build black

83 Schuyler, "To Boycott or Not to Boycott?" 259; see also Schuyler's editorial in *Pittsburgh Courier*, Oct. 6, 1934, sec. 1, p. 10, and the anonymous letter to the editor "Sure Way to Suicide," *Pittsburgh Courier*, Oct. 27, 1934, sec. 2, p. 2.
84 See letters of Jack Ovington and Nathaniel Henderson, "The Boycott Discussion," *Crisis* 41, no. 11 (Nov. 1934): 344–5.
85 Davis, "We Win the Right to Fight for Jobs," 234–5; Zinz, "Future Outlook League," 44–5.
86 For some rare cases of boycotts outside the black neighborhoods, see Greenberg, *Black Harlem*, 136; Kellogg, "Negro Direct Action," 98–9; Loeb, *Future Is Yours*, 75.

businesses functioning in a free market economy. The idea was that after some years of experience, learning the trade, and moving up the management ranks in ghetto-based white stores, young black entrepreneurs would ultimately establish ventures of their own.[87] Black communists, like Harry Haywood, therefore attacked the "Don't Buy Where You Can't Work" campaigns as a "reformist, petit bourgeois" movement that operated against the interests of the black working class.[88] From a Marxist point of view, racism had to be seen as an "integral part of white capitalist ideology" that could not be challenged with scattered boycotts. Communists criticized the boycott as an inadequate tactic for solving the problems of mass unemployment and impoverishment of hundreds of thousands of black workers:

There is no substance to the "use our buying power" proposal: it can only be raised by those whose social vision is bounded by petty industry and petty trade, who see everything not from the viewpoint of the Negro workers (the great mass of the Negro people) but rather from that of the Negro small business man.[89]

Although Marxist intellectuals were among the sharpest theoretical critics of the black boycott movements of the 1930s, in several cities African-American and white communists, for whom class solidarity was a matter of political principle and personal commitment, encouraged the "spirit of rebellion" and supported the mass action in the streets.[90] Whereas black and white Marxists argued for a revolutionary and interracial labor movement, the perspective of a united working class seemed to be rather unrealistic for the majority of African Americans, who were excluded from most of the "white" unions in the United States. During the early 1930s, the leading organization, the American Federation of Labor

---

87 Cf. Davis, "We Win the Right to Fight for Jobs," 236; William Muraskin, "The Harlem Boycott of 1934: Black Nationalism and the Rise of Labor-Union Consciousness," *Labor History* 13 (summer 1972): 368; Wye, "Merchants of Tomorrow," 42; Hunter, "Black Urban Boycott Movements," 137.

88 Haywood also attacked the sympathy of "Negro reformism" for Gandhian tactics. Harry Haywood, "The Crisis of the Jim-Crow Nationalism of the Negro Bourgeoisie," *The Communist* 10 (Apr. 1931): 330–8, reprinted in Philip S. Foner and Herbert Shapiro, eds., *American Communism and Black Americans: A Documentary History, 1930–1934* (Philadelphia, 1991), 70–8.

89 Will Herberg, "Shall the Negro Worker Turn to Labor or to Capital?" *Crisis* 38, no. 7 (July 1931): 227.

90 For the involvement of communists in boycott movements, especially during the campaigns in New York, see Greenberg, *Black Harlem*, 119, 126, 130–1; Crowder, "'Don't Buy Where You Can't Work,'" 15–16; Hunter, "Black Urban Boycott Movements," 141, 183, 187; cf. also Meier and Rudwick, "The Origins of Nonviolent Direct Action," 332–44; for more background on the role of communists in the struggle for equal opportunities, see Harvard Sitkoff, *A New Deal For Blacks: The Emergence of Civil Rights as a National Issue*, vol. 1: *The Depression Decade* (New York, 1978), 139–68.

(AFL), openly discriminated against black workers: Most of its affiliates did not admit them as members. The situation gradually changed in the mid-1930s with the emergence of the Congress of Industrial Organizations (CIO), which actively recruited black laborers. Nonetheless, the relationship between African-American workers and the predominantly white labor movement remained tense.[91] Black activists who used boycotts to desegregate the workforces of dairies, bakeries, breweries, and meat markets frequently faced the opposition of all-white unions. AFL locals of milk- and bakery-wagon drivers, meat cutters, and butchers often went on strike when, after boycotts, employers agreed to open traditionally "white" jobs to African Americans.[92]

The bitterness and disillusionment of black intellectuals about the AFL became particularly evident during the year 1934, when the union joined the American anti-Nazi boycott. Since 1933 Jewish groups in the United States and around the world had urged consumers not to buy German goods. They argued that the anti-Nazi boycott should force the dictatorship in Berlin to stop its racist policy against German Jewry. It is important to note, especially since the Nazis' propaganda machinery claimed the opposite, that the campaign against German products in the United States was a counter-boycott that started only after the new regime had openly advocated and organized the persecution of the Jewish minority in the Reich. Equally crucial for an understanding of the politics of boycotting, although hardly known, is the fact that anti-Semitic and ethnically motivated boycotts were nothing new in Germany. For decades, German Jewry had had to live with a "silent" boycott by anti-Semites against businesses that were known to be Jewish or were presumed to be because of their "Jewish-sounding" names.[93] At the turn of the century, at a time when an independent Polish state did not exist and western Poland still was part of Prussia, German and Polish nationalists had used their purchasing power in the so-called *Volkstumskampf*. During this fight, which was ideologically rooted in the ideal of an ethnically homogeneous national state, both groups employed consumer boycotts as a weapon in their attempts to *Germanize* or *Polonize* the border regions with their mixed, multi-ethnic population.[94]

91 For more background, see Philip S. Foner, *Organized Labor and the Black Worker, 1619–1981*, 2d ed. (New York, 1982), 188–237; William H. Harris, *The Harder We Run: Black Workers Since the Civil War* (New York, 1982), 77–122; Hunter, "Black Urban Boycott Movements," 224–34.

92 Loeb, *Future Is Yours*, 54–5, 65–73, 89, 110; Cox, "The Origins of Direct Action," 64–7.

93 For background on the stigmatization of "Jewish" names, see Dietz Bering, *Der Name als Stigma: Antisemitismus im Deutschen Alltag, 1812–1933* (Stuttgart, 1987; new edition, Stuttgart, 1992), 159, 325–34.

94 Waldemar Mitscherlich, "Die polnische Boykottbewegung in der Ostmark und ihre Aussichten,"

At approximately the same time, in 1906, Germany's Imperial Court had more or less sanctioned anti-Jewish boycotts and "Buy Christian" campaigns in the Reich.[95] Despite the mainly covert anti-Semitic boycott attempts between 1871 and 1918, however, many Jewish shopkeepers were successful in their trade. After World War I and the founding of the democratic Weimar Republic, the situation changed slowly as the radical *völkisch* movements gained momentum. Beginning in the mid-1920s, boycotts increasingly became a problem for Jewish storekeepers in Germany because the Nazis and other *völkisch* groups were gradually intensifying their propaganda for the systematic boycott of Jewish businesses. On February 21, 1924, the *C.V.-Zeitung*, the weekly newspaper of the Central Association of German Citizens of the Jewish Faith, reported that for the first time since the establishment of the new republic the *Völkischen* had openly employed the "rusty weapon of economic boycott against Jewish Germans."[96] During the Weimar Republic, however, German Jews were able to defend themselves in the courtrooms. Despite the unfavorable 1906 verdict of the Imperial Court and widespread anti-Semitic attitudes in Germany's judiciary, in the 1920s Jewish shopkeepers in many cases successfully fought for court injunctions against *Hetz-Boykotte* (hate boycotts), which targeted businessmen only because of their Jewishness.[97]

After the National Socialist takeover in January 1933, the situation changed drastically. Under the Nazi regime, the carefully planned destruction of the economic base of German Jewry became an essential component of the government's policy. On April 1, 1933, the Nazi party organized a nationwide boycott of all Jewish stores, lawyers, and physicians in Germany.[98] SA Brownshirts stood guard in front of Jewish-

---

Jahrbuch für Gesetzgebung, Verwaltung und Volkswirtschaft im Deutschen Reich 35, no. 3 (1911): 31–65; Maxim Anin, "Der Judenboykott in Polen," *Sozialistische Monatshefte*, Berlin, no. 6 (Mar. 26, 1914): 350–5; for a general overview, see William W. Hagen, *Germans, Poles, and Jews: The Nationality Conflict in the Prussian East, 1772–1914* (Chicago, 1980) 116, 158, 261–3, 296–319.

95 Reichsgericht, Germany, *Entscheidungen des Reichsgerichts in Zivilsachen*, 64, n.s. 14 (Leipzig, 1907), 62.

96 "Boykott!" *Central Verein-Zeitung: Blätter für Deutschtum und Judentum, Organ des Central-Vereins deutscher Staatsbürger jüdischen Glaubens* [Berlin] (hereafter cited as *C.V.-Zeitung*) 3, no. 8 (Feb. 21, 1924): 71; see also Georg Baum, "Der völkische Boykott und seine Rechtsfolgen," *C.V.-Zeitung* 4, no. 13 (Mar. 27, 1925): 221–2; cf. also Paul Oertmann, *Der politische Boykott* (Berlin, 1925), 31, 58–60.

97 Rudolf Wertheimer, *Der Hetz-Boykott: Einige Gedanken zum Boykott-Problem* (Wiesbaden, 1931); Rudolf Callmann, *Zur Boykottfrage: Ein Gutachten* (Berlin, 1932); see also Sibylle Morgenthaler, "Countering the Pre-1933 Nazi Boycott Against the Jews," *Leo Baeck Institute Year Book* [London] 36 (1991): 127–49.

98 Avraham Barkai, *Vom Boykott zur "Entjudung": Der wirtschaftliche Existenzkampf der Juden im Dritten Reich, 1933–1943* (Frankfurt/Main, 1988), 23–35; this study is also available in English,

owned department and retail stores hindering "Aryans" from shopping in "non-Aryan" businesses. These actions in the spring of 1933 were just the prelude to the total expulsion and annihilation of German Jewry in the years to come. In 1933, the destruction of Germany's democratic institutions and the beginning of the persecution of Jews by the Nazi dictatorship caused worldwide protests that were especially strong in the United States.

In October 1933 the American Federation of Labor decided to join the Jewish anti-Nazi boycott and also declared "a boycott against German-made goods . . . until Germany ceases its repressive policy of the persecution of Jewish people."[99] In the black American press, the policy of the AFL to openly discriminate against African Americans at home and at the same time to support a boycott against racial discrimination in a foreign country was seen as additional proof of white America's mendacity. After the decision, editorials in African-American newspapers asked, "Why cannot the AFL boycott the goods of southern manufacturers who are the backbone of the persecution of Negroes in Dixie? . . . The fact is that this boycott move is another piece of A. F. of L. hypocrisy. The Federation has never been sincerely interested in helping the Negro worker."[100] Throughout 1934, when black boycott campaigns against racial discrimination in the United States were going on in New York, Baltimore, Washington, Columbus, and various other American cities, black journalists continued their attacks on the AFL. For African Americans, the union's policy was simply hypocritical, since the labor leaders "suggested 'boycott' as the weapon to break the power of Hitlerism, but not for a moment [did they propose] the boycott as the weapon to break the power of Ku Kluxism, Nordicism, Lily-Whiteism" in the United States.[101]

Although the AFL was hostile to the efforts of African Americans to employ boycotts as a means to fight discrimination, there were some cases in which religious groups used interracial boycotts to protest against Jim Crowism in hotels and restaurants. In May 1934, more than two

---

Avraham Barkai, *From Boycott to Annihilation: The Economic Struggle of German Jews, 1933–1945*, Tauber Institute for the Study of European Jewry, series 11 (Hanover, N.H., 1989); Moshe Gottlieb, "The First of April Boycott and the Reaction of the American Jewish Community," *American Jewish Historical Quarterly* 57, no. 4 (1968): 516–56.

99 Moshe Gottlieb, "The Anti-Nazi Boycott Movement in the American Jewish Community, 1933–1941," Ph.D. diss., Brandeis University, 1967, 165, 343; see also Moshe Gottlieb, "The Anti-Nazi Boycott Movement in the United States: An Ideological and Sociological Appreciation," *Jewish Social Studies* 35, nos. 3–4 (July–Oct. 1973): 198–227.

100 *Pittsburgh Courier*, Jan. 6, 1934, 10.

101 Ibid., Mar. 17, 1934, 1.

thousand black and white delegates to the Young Women's Christian Association convention in Philadelphia canceled reservations and boycotted hotels that barred African Americans. Some months later, in September 1934, more than one thousand black and white members of the National Council of Methodist Youth, which held its national convention in Evanston, Illinois, decided to boycott all restaurants there that discriminated against African Americans. In a resolution the delegates declared: "We, as Christian youth working together with God for a new world, believe that the present racial discrimination in restaurants, drug stores and eating places . . . constitutes one of the greatest barriers to the realization of our goal."[102] Despite these isolated boycott actions of black and white conference delegates and some efforts of white communists and socialists to organize interracial pickets, the "Don't Buy Where You Can't Work" movements of the 1930s were all-black. During its first years, the Future Outlook League (FOL) in Cleveland, for example, explicitly prohibited whites from joining the organization and did not accept any contributions from Caucasians. Later it changed its policy, but nonetheless whites never played an active role in the FOL or in the other "Don't Buy Where You Can't Work" movements of the 1930s.[103]

V

In January 1934 supporters of the anti-Nazi boycott started to picket Macy's in New York City, at this time one of the largest department stores in the United States. The highly publicized picketing ended in March when Macy's management finally decided to stop importing German goods and to close its office in Berlin. In a press release the company declared that "consumer resistance to goods of German origin" was responsible for this decision and that orders placed in Germany had "declined 98 percent in the past six months, from $127,000 to $2,800."[104] Three days after the Macy's announcement, the Woolworth Company also announced, "We have discontinued importation [of German goods] owing to extreme sales resistance."[105] Editorials in the black press interpreted the decisions of these large American retail companies as further

102 *Cleveland Call and Post*, May 19, 1934, 1; *Pittsburgh Courier*, Sept. 15, 1934, 5.
103 Zinz, "Future Outlook League," 28–9.
104 Gottlieb, "Anti-Nazi Boycott Movement in the American Jewish Community," 170; for a personal account by one the leaders of the anti-Nazi boycott, see Joseph Tenenbaum, "The Anti-Nazi Boycott Movement in the United States," *Yad Washem Studies* 3 (1959): 141–59.
105 Gottlieb, "Anti-Nazi Boycott Movement in the American Jewish Community," 173.

proof that "there is no nerve more sensitive than that of the pocket."
With unhidden admiration, one African-American commentator wrote:

This boycott engineered by Jews in America, has seriously injured German
trade. . . . The Jews, who possess considerable organized economic power, know
how to apply pressure when they are hurt. . . .
    Negroes have also used the boycott successfully on several occasions. It is . . .
an effective and prompt means of bringing pressure to bear to reward friends
and punish enemies. . . . The Jews have great organized economic power with
which to defend themselves from counter-attack; unfortunately we have not.
    And yet there is much we can do. We can refrain from buying the goods of
those firms discriminating against Negro labor and buy from those who do not.
We can patronize those firms that think enough of colored patronage to advertise in Negro newspapers. We can purchase the goods of those firms who do
not insult us over the air and in display advertising [as Pepsodent toothpaste
does]. Such effective boycotting, minus the ballyhoo usually accompanying
efforts of this kind, will prove most helpful.[106]

Ironically, although African Americans were impressed by the effectiveness of the Jewish anti-Nazi boycott, they in turn boycotted Jewish businesses and stores. In New York as well as in Boston, Detroit, Philadelphia,
and other northern cities, the black urban ghettos had emerged during
the 1910s and 1920s in districts that previously had been predominantly
Jewish. Since the beginning of the Great Migration and the influx of
African Americans from the Deep South to these neighborhoods, more
and more white families had moved to "better" sections of the cities, but
had kept their businesses in the now black districts. Consequently, during
the 1930s, many of the groceries and department stores operating in the
black ghettos were still owned and operated by Jews. This experience
could easily lead to the popular misconception among African Americans
in Harlem, Roxbury, and other now black neighborhoods that "*all* white
landlords and shopkeepers were Jews."

    For an understanding of the racial tensions in the American ghettos it
is crucial to realize that the daily encounters between African Americans
and Jews "were scarcely the kind that promoted goodwill and intergroup
understanding." Typically, they involved Jewish storekeepers and landlords
on one hand and black consumers and tenants on the other. These were
"unequal-status, friction-generating contacts," and in almost every instance
the African American was in a subordinate position. In many cases white
retailers, no matter what their ethnic background or faith, treated black

106 *Pittsburgh Courier*, Mar. 24, 1934, 10.

customers disrespectfully, overcharged and shortweighted, sold food of low quality, and generally refused to employ African Americans in white-collar jobs despite the fact that the great majority of their customers were black.[107] In such a climate of distrust and embitterment, it was not difficult to stir up anti-white and anti-Jewish sentiments.[108]

In 1934, Jewish businessmen in New York, for example, "protested to Mayor LaGuardia against the anti-Semitic character of the boycott campaign [of Sufi Abdul Hamid] in Harlem."[109] The controversy about anti-Semitic tendencies in Hamid's job crusade in New York was one of the rare exceptions in which a black boycott movement received coverage by the local white press. Hamid was soon labeled a "Black Hitler," an expression used not only by white newspapers but also by some black journalists. From the few surviving documents it is almost impossible to know whether Hamid was motivated by a specific anti-Semitic ideology. His boycott campaign, at least, did not exclusively single out Jewish businesses but was also directed against Woolworth and other stores that were not Jewish-owned.[110]

The issue of anti-Semitism polarized the boycott activists in America's black community. Whereas some African Americans admitted that prejudices against Jewish store owners and merchants played an important role, others denied the charge and argued that there was no difference between specific anti-Jewish feelings and anti-white feelings in general. However, the discussion about anti-Semitic tendencies in the black community on the one hand and "parallels between Hitlerism and the persecution of Negroes in America" on the other remained one of the hot topics in the mid-1930s.[111] African-American newspapers, for example,

---

107 Robert G. Weisbord and Arthur Stein, *Bittersweet Encounter: The Afro-American and the American Jew* (Westport, Conn., 1970), 40–3. Many African-American consumers were suspicious and assumed that avaricious white retailers tried to sell products of a lower quality in black neighborhoods. During the 1930s, the African-American press frequently published stories that groceries sold rotten food or meat in the "colored districts"; see, e.g., *Cleveland Call and Post*, Mar. 24, 1934, 1.

108 On the other hand, it should also be noted that it was a Jewish-owned department store in Chicago that first voluntarily desegregated its work force without any boycott pressure; see Stephen Breszka, "And Lo! It Worked," *Opportunity* 11, no. 11 (Nov. 1933): 342, 344, 350.

109 *Pittsburgh Courier*, Oct. 6, 1934, 10.

110 *New York Times*, Aug. 1, 1938, 1, 3; *Pittsburgh Courier*, Oct. 20, 1934, sec. 2, p. 1; Crowder, "'Don't Buy Where You Can't Work,'" 19; Greenberg, *Black Harlem*, 126–7; Hunter, "Black Urban Boycott Movements," 187–9; Kellogg, "Negro Direct Action," 91–2; see also the forthcoming essay by Winston C. McDowell, "Conflict and Cooperation: African Americans, Jews and the Harlem Jobs Boycotts, 1932–35," paper presented at the conference "Blacks and Jews: An American Historical Perspective," Washington University, St. Louis, Dec. 1993.

111 The NAACP tried to moderate between both minority groups, see [Rabbi] Stephen S. Wise, "Parallel Between Hitlerism and the Persecution of Negroes in America," *Crisis* 41, no. 5 (May 1934): 127–9; [Rabbi] Jacob J. Weinstein, "The Jew and the Negro – The Negro and the Jew:

not only covered the Nazis' attacks on the Jewish minority in Germany but also reported in detail on the racial discrimination of children of white German mothers and black fathers, most of them French-African soldiers, who had been stationed in Germany after its defeat in World War I.[112]

In 1936, Abram L. Harris, a well-known African-American professor of economics at Howard University in Washington, D.C., harshly attacked the tactic of certain black American boycott leaders to preach "extreme racial chauvinism against other minorities, especially the Jew." As Harris observed, anti-Semitism was not a new phenomenon in the black community of the United States, but "the feeling of the Negro against the Jew [had] been increased and widened" since the beginning of the Great Depression. Harris argued that "it is silly to see anything especially Jewish in the exploitation" of the black masses. He accused parts of the black middle class of instrumentalizing anti-Semitic feelings for its own business interests and making "the Jew the scapegoat of the depression." In doing so, Harris concluded, parts of the "Don't Buy Where You Can't Work" movement became "a spiritual ally of German Fascism."[113]

Brochures of the Jewish Anti-Defamation League B'nai B'rith indicate that the Nazis' anti-Semitic propaganda tale claiming that Jews had gained control of the retail trade with unfair tricks was also prevalent in the United States.[114] William Jones, for example, "explained" that "because

A Comparative Study in Race Prejudice," *Crisis* 41, no. 6 (June 1934): 178–9, and no. 7 (July 1934): 197–8; "Fascism and Minority Groups" was also the topic of several speeches and discussions at the NAACP's annual conferences in 1935 and 1936; on contemporary African-American opinions on German Anti-Semitism, see also Lunabelle Wedlock, *The Reaction of Negro Publications and Organizations to German Anti-Semitism* (Washington, D.C., 1942), and Weisbord, *Bittersweet Encounter*, 50–62.

112 *Pittsburgh Courier*, Feb. 17, 1934, 10; ibid., Oct. 20, 1934, sec. 2, p. 2; for personal impressions of a well-known African-American writer who had visited Germany during the 1920s, see Claude McKay, "Once More the Germans Face Black Troops," *Opportunity* 17, no. 11 (Nov. 1939): 324–8; also Sally Marks, "Black Watch on the Rhine: A Study in Propaganda, Prejudice and Prurience," *European Studies Review* 13, no. 2 (1983): 297–333; Keith L. Nelson, "The 'Black Horror on the Rhine': Race as a Factor in Post-World War I Diplomacy," *Journal of Modern History* 42, no. 4 (1970): 606–27; Rosemarie K. Lester, "Blacks in Germany and German Blacks: A Little-Known Aspect of Black History," and Reinhold Grimm, "Germans, Blacks, and Jews; Or Is There a German Blackness of Its Own?," both essays in Reinhold Grimm and Jost Hermand, eds., *Blacks and German Culture* (Madison, Wis., 1986), 113–14, 150–84; Georg Lilienthal, "'Rheinlandbastarde', Rassenhygiene und das Problem der rassenideologischen Kontinuität," *Medizinhistorisches Journal* 15 (1980): 426–37; on the fate of black Germans during the Nazi dictatorship, see esp. Reiner Pommerin, *"Sterilisierung der Rheinlandbastarde": Das Schicksal einer farbigen deutschen Minderheit, 1918–1937* (Düsseldorf, 1979).

113 Abram L. Harris, *The Negro as Capitalist: A Study of Banking and Business Among American Negroes* (Philadelphia, 1936), 183–4.

114 For background on anti-Semitism in the United States, see the essays in David A. Gerber, ed., *Anti-Semitism in American History* (Urbana, Ill., 1986).

of centuries of dexterous merchandising the Jewish merchant has been able to out-smart the Negro merchant in getting the Negro dollar."[115] In the 1930s, B'nai B'rith in defense published a booklet against the "Myth of Jewish Economic Dominance" stating that the big American department store chains, like Woolworth, Kress, and A & P, for example, were all "non-Jewish."[116]

New York was not the only place where Jewish stores became targets of black boycotts during the 1930s.[117] For America's Jewish community the experience of systematically organized boycotts against Jewish businesses in Germany and the emergence of black boycott movements in the United States at the same time must have been a shocking development.[118] However, seen in retrospect, the Nazis' boycotts and the "Don't Buy Where You Can't Work" campaigns are not comparable. What happened in Germany was a staged, nationwide campaign organized by a dictatorship that used its bureaucratic infrastructure to ensure an effective boycott against a minority. The long-term goal of the Nazis' anti-Jewish boycott, which became an integral component of the dictatorship's racist policy, was the so-called *Arisierung* of the German economy and society, which meant nothing but the total destruction and annihilation of German Jewry. In contrast, the black campaigns in the United States were local grassroots movements that employed the boycott tactic to combat racial discrimination.

From a Jewish perspective, however, the Nazi boycott guards in front of Jewish stores in Germany and the pickets of African Americans in the United States must have been a similarly frightening experience, especially since many of America's Jews had heard the graphic personal accounts of the Nazi terror from relatives and friends, many of whom had recently emigrated.[119] Although Jewish stores were often among the

---

115 Jones, "Economic Consequences Of Negro Trade Boycotts," 42.
116 Anti-Defamation League B'nai B'rith, Fireside Discussion Group, *The Myth of Jewish Economic Dominance*, brochure no. 11 (Chicago, 1930), 9–10.
117 For Cleveland, see Loeb, *Future Is Yours*, 31–2; for Baltimore, see ANP report in the *Pittsburgh Courier*, Dec. 23, 1933, 2.
118 It should not be forgotten that during the 1930s fascist movements were also active in the United States and that it was considered to be an open question whether under certain conditions America could turn fascist too. Compare Sander A. Diamond, *The Nazi Movement in the United States, 1924–1941* (Ithaca, N.Y., 1974) 204–8, 244; on anti-Jewish boycotts organized by Nazis in the United States, see esp. 137–9, 230. For a short overview, see also Ronald H. Bayor, "Klan, Coughlinites and Aryan Nations: Patterns of American Anti-Semitism in the Twentieth Century," *American Jewish History* 76 (1986): 181–96.
119 Some tactics of stigmatization used to intimidate customers into not breaking the boycotts were identical: Nazis as well as black activists in the United States took pictures of people who continued to shop in boycotted stores and published the photographs or the addresses of "race

targets of black job crusades in the United States, it would be misleading to interpret this fact as a clear expression of anti-Semitic sentiments.
The African-American boycott movements during the 1930s were not
specifically aimed at Jewish groceries or department stores but attacked
white businesses with discriminatory hiring policies in general. As one
member of the Future Outlook League, a black civil-rights organization
in Cleveland, put it; "The fact that the Hoicowitz family [whose department store became a boycott target] was Jewish is incidental; what is
important is . . . their attitude toward the employment of Negro clerks."[120]

VI

The leaders of the various black boycott movements in the 1930s do not
fit into one single socioeconomic category. Their personal backgrounds,
educational and professional experiences, as well as their political goals
differed from city to city. Mystical, charismatic street prophets like Sufi
Abdul Hamid, the controversial leader of the campaigns in Harlem, or
"Bishop" Kiowa Costonie, who started a boycott movement in Baltimore, had little in common with characters like Joseph D. Bibb or the
members of the boycott committee in Columbus. An analysis of the education and careers of the journalists, ministers, and professionals who were
active organizers of boycott campaigns reveals that the majority of them
had a middle-class rather than a working-class background. Usually they
were middle-aged men and women in their thirties or forties who already
had some professional experience.[121] Nonetheless, the following that the
boycott movements attracted was a much more diverse and mixed crowd
in which unemployed, semiskilled workers could be found, as well as
high school and university students, maids, housewives, and clerks.

traitors." Muraskin, "The Harlem Boycott of 1934," 364; Hunter, "Black Urban Boycott Movements," 253; Barkai, *Vom Boykott zur "Entjudung,"* 28, 44; Philip S. Bernstein, "The Fate of German Jews," *Nation* 145, no. 17 (Oct. 23, 1937): 424; Hazel Rosenstrauch, *Aus Nachbarn wurden
Juden: Ausgrenzung und Selbstbehauptung, 1933–1942* (Berlin, 1988), 149.

120 Loeb, *Future Is Yours*, 31–2; cf. Davis, "We Win the Right to Fight for Jobs," 235.

121 For background information on Sufi Abdul Hamid, see *New York Times*, Aug. 1, 1938, 1, 3; and
the chapter entitled "Sufi Abdul Hamid and Organized Labor," in Claude McKay, *Harlem: Negro
Metropolis*, 181–262; for background on Kiowa Costonie, see Skotnes, "Buy Where You Can
Work," 737–51, and Hunter, "Black Urban Boycott Movements," 113–14; on the leaders in
Chicago, see Cox, "The Origins of Direct Action," 12–13; for Cleveland, see Zinz, "Future Outlook League," 3–9, 142–3; for Washington, see Davis, "We Win the Right to Fight for Jobs,"
230–7; Kellogg, "Negro Direct Action," 20; Hunter, "Black Urban Boycott Movements," 131;
for Toledo (1932), see *Crisis* 40, no. 1 (Jan. 1933): 17; for Columbus, see ULC, box 13, folder
"Kroger Matter."

The division of activities along gender lines during the boycott campaigns of the 1930s seems to have been less strict than one might assume. African-American women were in the front line of the movements. They picketed, agitated, and leafleted in front of stores, got beaten and arrested by police.[122] However, gender remained an important force shaping the activities and perception of women during the campaigns. Public speaking, for example, at least to bigger audiences, was commonly left to male activists, and the intellectual debate in the black press was also dominated by men. Female boycotters played a key role in the everyday work, but they usually did not take part in the "more prestigious" negotiations with managers of the boycotted companies.[123] Female boycott activists found – probably not only in Toledo – that they were the ones who started to "do things, and when they were accomplished, it was the male members . . . who did them – according to themselves."[124]

The use of pickets was the most visible and the most effective tactic to make "Don't Buy Where You Can't Work" campaigns successful. For African Americans it was also a very risky step, since in 1930 picketing was often not tolerated by the local law enforcement agencies, and conflicts with the police were therefore likely. Arrests and injunctions were indeed common characteristics of almost every black boycott movement. During the 1930s, the legal situation changed gradually through the more labor-friendly New Deal legislation and a Supreme Court decision in 1938 that legalized the picketing of stores that discriminated against African Americans.[125] Nonetheless, public opinion still considered

---

122 For confrontations of female pickets with the police, see Loeb, *Future Is Yours*, 56, 121–2; *Atlanta Daily World*, July 6, 1934, 2.

123 CAB, box 260, folder 7, ANP, Mar. 1, 1930; Cox, "The Origins of Direct Action," 31–2, 35. Women were in a stronger position when they joined campaigns as leaders of all-female organizations like women's clubs or chapters of the National Negro Housewives' League, which played an important role during job campaigns in Columbus, Detroit, Baltimore, and Richmond; see Detroit Housewives League papers, box 2, "Declaration of Purpose of the National Negro Housewives League," printed, letter-size leaflet (8.5 × 11 inches), undated (1930s), Burton Historical Collection, Detroit Public Library; George Streator, "Detroit, Columbus and Cleveland," *Crisis* 41, no. 6 (June 1934): 172–3; *Atlanta Daily World*, July 6, 1934, 2; Skotnes, "Buy Where You Can Work," 751; Kellogg, "Negro Direct Action," 105; Hunter, "Black Urban Boycott Movements," 115.

124 Mrs. S. B. Bagnall, an activist during the "Don't Buy Where You Can't Work" campaigns in Toledo, made this caustic comment at a conference of Ohio's NAACP branches (NAACP-OBR, box 5, folder 7, "Minutes 3rd Annual Ohio NAACP Branches Convention," manuscript [Sept. 1932]); for a rare acknowledgment of women's contributions to the success of a boycott movement, see Loeb, *Future Is Yours*, 48. For background on boycotts in Toledo, see also the account on "Chain Store Jobs" of Lillian Upthegrove at the NAACP's national annual conference in 1933, NAACP papers, group 1, series B, box 10, folder "Annual Conference Chicago, Speeches 1933," Manuscript Division, Library of Congress, Washington, D.C.

125 U.S. Supreme Court, *New Negro Alliance v. Sanitary Grocery Company*, United States Reports

picketing radical. In 1930, the black press perceived the use of pickets in Chicago as something fundamentally new and interpreted it as an impressive step ahead in the struggle against racial discrimination.[126] Whereas the ANP reports emphasized the courage of the boycott activists, it would be misleading to believe that the first pickets during black boycotts in the 1930s were similar to the mass action of labor unions during strikes. In Chicago as well as in Columbus, the picketing was conducted by only a single man who stood or walked in front of the store with his sandwich sign or banner. The initial goals of the pickets were to be visible and to signal that the boycott was still going on, but usually not to block the entry of the shop.[127] Only later, in the mid-1930s, did picketing in larger groups become common during campaigns.

Boycotters knew that any violence at picketed sites would be used against them.[128] Even peaceful picketing could easily be interpreted by the local courts as a "disturbance of the peace."[129] The pickets were therefore usually carefully chosen and instructed "that they should rather take a blow than start a physical combat that might result in shedding of blood and probably discredit" the campaign.[130] Generally speaking, African-American boycotters tried to avoid violence and clashes with the police not because they believed in non-violence as a tactic of social pressure, as many civil rights activists did twenty years later, but because an open challenge of the police would not have had any chance to succeed. The

303, 552–64; *Pittsburgh Courier*, Jan. 27, 1934, sec. 5, p. 1; Davis, "We Win the Right to Fight for Jobs," 230–7. For background, see Charles O. Gregory and Harold A. Katz, *Labor and the Law*, 3d ed. (New York and London, 1979), 97–104, 158–99; Herbert Hill, *Black Labor and the American Legal System: Race, Work, and the Law* (Washington, D.C., 1977), 93–106.

126 CAB, box 4, folder 4, ANP, May 7, 1930. Actually, in some rare cases African Americans had used pickets before, see Meier and Rudwick, "The Origins of Nonviolent Direct Action," 311.

127 This aspect was also essential for the favorable decision of the Supreme Court in 1938; see U.S. Supreme Court, New Negro Alliance, 557–8; Cox, "The Origins of Direct Action," 25, 29; ULC, box 13, folder "Kroger Matter," undated report by J. D. McKarn (Oct. 28, 1930?), typescript.

128 Drake, "Churches and Voluntary Associations," 251; Cox, "The Origins of Direct Action," 33, 40, 157.

129 In the 1930s, experienced African-American lawyers who could handle civil rights cases or labor law efficiently were still scarce. For a detailed overview of the situation in the different states, see Charles H. Houston, "The Need for Negro Lawyers," *Journal of Negro Education* 4, no. 1 (Jan. 1935): 49–52. For background on tension and cooperation between black and white civil rights attorneys, see August Meier and Elliot Rudwick, "Attorneys Black and White: A Case Study of Race Relations Within the NAACP," in Meier and Rudwick, *Along the Color Line*, 128–73. For a study of black lawyers' experiences in the 1920s, 1930s, and 1940s, and the transformation of black law schools from "third rate law centers" into nationally renowned legal institutes specializing in civil rights law, see Vibert Leslie White, "Developing a 'School' of Civil Rights Lawyers: From the New Deal to the New Frontier," Ph.D. diss., Ohio State University, 1988, 54–77.

130 Drake, "Churches and Voluntary Associations," 251; Cox, "The Origins of Direct Action," 33, 40, 157.

boycotters in the 1930s were non-violent simply of necessity and did not have a specific pacifist ideology. Despite frequent arrests and injunctions against picketing, which were a common experience of almost every boycott movement, the more successful campaigns apparently took place in cities with a less oppressive and relatively "tolerant" attitude on the part of white politicians and law enforcement agencies toward black protest. A contemporary sympathizer of the boycott movement in Chicago, for example, admitted that it "cannot be said that the police [was] particularly unrestrained or hostile" during the job drives on the South Side.[131]

Despite the fact that some leaders gave lectures about their campaigns in other cities, the boycotts and their goals in the 1930s were local in scope.[132] Although many movements attacked stores that belonged to big retail chains, such as Woolworth, A & P, and Kroger, a nationwide coordinated boycott campaign did not yet emerge. Nonetheless, at the beginning of the 1940s, African-American leaders already discussed the chances for national consumer boycotts against large companies, among them Procter & Gamble.[133] In general, blacks were well aware that a boycott, even if it did not achieve its economic goals, could be an effective means to politicize their community. In 1930, an African American from Columbus, Ohio, who considered boycotting a movie theater and knew that the chance of winning the fight was small, since the revenue lost through a "Negro boycott" would be negligible, concluded:

While the boycott is meaningless as a lever with which to lift the white man's prejudice, it will be found to be a powerful force in educating Negroes to appreciate themselves as human beings deserving human consideration; in educating them in the worth of personality to the point where they will refuse the humiliation of the segregated theatre seat. Wholesale rejection of the whole idea [of racial segregation] would immediately follow.[134]

---

131 CAB, box 4, folder 4, ANP, May 7, 1930; Cox, "The Origins of Direct Action," 33; for Columbus, see *Atlanta Daily World*, July 6, 1934, 2; for New York, cf. Crowder, "'Don't Buy Where You Can't Work,'" 12–13; Meier and Rudwick, "The Origins of Nonviolent Direct Action," 317.

132 Hunter, "Black Urban Boycott Movements," 114, 125, 145; Only after years of groundwork, the FOL in Cleveland felt strong enough to threaten the National Biscuit Company with a statewide boycott in Ohio (Loeb, *Future Is Yours*, 96–7). The only attempt by African Americans to launch a nationwide boycott against a private-owned enterprise in the 1930s was the crusade for the removal of the "Amos 'n' Andy" radio program, which exploited racial stereotypes. Target of the campaign was the program's sponsor, the Pepsodent Toothpaste Company; see Arnold Shankman, "Black Pride and Protest: The Amos 'n' Andy Crusade," *Journal of Popular Culture* 12, no. 2 (fall 1979): 236–52.

133 Jones, "Economic Consequences of Negro Trade Boycotts," 39.

134 Jonathan Queer, "Your Best People Come Here," *Crisis* 37, no. 10 (Oct. 1930): 357–8.

It is difficult to assess how the boycott movements influenced mentalities and attitudes of the black communities in which they occurred. For active leaders and supporters of boycotting, the campaigns were surely an important political and social experience, especially if a boycott achieved its objective. Certainly, not all of the campaigns were successful and not everyone in the community was sympathetic toward the politics of boycotting. Nonetheless, the "new" tactic made many African Americans aware of their collective power as consumers. The long-promoted use of black purchasing power was no longer an abstract construction of intellectuals but became very concrete when ministers in New York, for example, asked their congregations to collect the receipts they got from a certain department store against which a campaign was to be started. After several days, the boycott leaders had some $7,000 in sales slips – good ammunition for negotiations with the store's management.[135] The experience of solidarity was important not only for the activists but also for the black community as a whole, a community that consisted largely of people who had migrated to the city just some years before. The politics of boycotting allowed participation: People invited pickets who were standing in the cold to warm up in their cars, and neighbors sent them free coffee or ice cream in the summer. These were gestures of solidarity people still remembered years later.[136]

Movements that lasted longer slowly developed their own "boycott culture": The boycotts became an inspiration for poems, songs, and cartoons. Mass meetings, fund-raising parties, annual banquets, "benefit dances," or "victory parades" were important cultural and social events in the community.[137] Some boycott groups even had their own mascots: One famous member of the FOL in Cleveland was "Bobby," a white rabbit, who "paid" dues for several years until he died.[138] Songs and support from black musicians such as Duke Ellington, Mamie Smith, or Bill Robinson were also important to strengthening solidarity.[139] To focus on such previously neglected aspects of the campaigns does not mean to romanticize them, but to understand that the developing "boycott culture" was an essential factor in stabilizing a social movement.

---

135 Vere E. Johns, "To Boycott or Not to Boycott? – We Must Have Jobs," *Crisis* 41, no. 9 (Sept. 1934) 258.
136 Hunter, "Black Urban Boycott Movements," 118; Loeb, *Future Is Yours*, 121–2.
137 Loeb, *Future Is Yours*, 22, 50, 73; Hunter, "Black Urban Boycott Movements," 116, 136, 143; Kellogg, "Negro Direct Action," 106; Crowder, "'Don't Buy Where You Can't Work,'" 7–8.
138 Loeb, *Future Is Yours*, 121.
139 Dominic J. Capeci Jr., "From Harlem to Montgomery: The Bus Boycotts and Leadership of Adam Clayton Powell, Jr. and Martin Luther King, Jr.," *Historian* 41, no. 8 (1979): 725; Hunter, "Black Urban Boycott Movements," 117, 278.

Although most of the targets of black campaigns were retail stores, boycotts were not only employed against groceries, department stores, bakeries,
or meat markets. The variety of companies against which boycotts were
used was much bigger. From 1930 to 1941, black activists launched campaigns against dairies, insurance companies, restaurants, telephone companies, breweries, bus and streetcar companies, baseball stadiums, skating
rinks, movie theaters, and radio stations. Even though some skeptics had
said that "merchants . . . will not accede to the demands of an impover-
ished people," losses during boycotts often were high enough to convince
managers that it would be more profitable to yield and to employ "colored clerks."[140] How many jobs really were won through boycott activities
in the different cities is impossible to assess, especially because successful
campaigns often triggered a domino effect: managers of other companies
in the community decided to desegregate their work force "voluntarily,"
rather than risk a campaign against their stores in the near future. It is
also evident that black newspapers and news agencies sometimes exaggerated the gains of boycott campaigns.[141]

The "Don't Buy Where You Can't Work" movements could not, of
course, solve the problem of mass unemployment during the Great Depression, nor did they change discriminatory hiring and promotion policies
in companies outside the ghettos. Nevertheless, it is clear that the campaigns in the 1930s gradually prompted a significant change in the
employment pattern in urban black neighborhoods. At the end of the
decade, most of the shops in the ghettos employed African-American
clerks and sales personnel.[142] In 1939, the *Whip* reminded its readers of
the change during the last years: "Look at Walgreens, A & P stores, the
butcher shops, Woolworths, and all over the business in our districts, and
note the Colored people working. They were not there ten years ago."[143]

---

140 CAB, box 149, folder 4, Richard I. Durham, "Don't Spend Your Money Where You Can't
   Work," unpubl. manuscript (ca. 1939), 6.
141 Whereas the *Whip* claimed in May 1930 to have already won over 2,600 jobs for African
   Americans in Chicago, Cox's survey of 213 businesses on the South Side in 1932 suggests that
   the total number of job opportunities created by the campaigns in Chicago was approximately
   1,500. The FOL in Cleveland claimed to have opened more than 1,200 positions between 1935
   and 1938, a figure that also seems to be inflated. The same is true for Hunter's optimistic esti-
   mate that "75,000 new jobs were secured for black workers through urban activism" in the
   years 1930 to 1941. Kellogg's figures, on the other hand, are too low because he did not consider the domino effect that many campaigns prompted. Cf. CAB, box 4, folder 4, ANP, May 7,
   1930; Cox, "The Origins of Direct Action," 108; Wye, "Merchants of Tomorrow," 44; Hunter,
   "Black Urban Boycott Movements," 284, 299; Kellogg, "Negro Direct Action," 147–8.
142 Loeb, *Future Is Yours*, 58.
143 Chicago *Whip*, Jan. 28, 1939, quoted after Durham, "Don't Spend," 4.

With the entry of the United States into World War II in 1941, the desperate need for jobs ceased, and black boycott campaigns dwindled, as the mobilization of the American economy ended more than ten years of depression and created thousands of new jobs. While black soldiers were fighting for human rights all over the world, however, African Americans still faced discrimination in their own country – a fact that would prompt new boycotts in the years to come.

VII

Seen in retrospect, the successful consumer boycotts in Columbus in the 1920s against businesses that sympathized with the Ku Klux Klan suggest that the thesis of August Meier and Elliot Rudwick, who emphasized the "discontinuities" of black protest and claimed that "there was nothing in the Afro-American experience that could be called a tradition of direct action," has to be modified.[144] Newly discovered source materials prove that African Americans in Ohio's capital, and probably other cities as well, had a continuous tradition of boycotting that, although it did not attract the media's attention, shaped local attitudes. However, the 1930s were unquestionably a much more important period for black protest, for it was the first time that African-American leaders discussed the risks and chances of the politics of boycotting in a nationwide debate and not only in their local communities. The extensive media coverage of the successful campaigns of the *Whip* in 1930 by African-American journalists encouraged other communities to copy the strategies that had been used in Chicago. At the end of the decade consumer boycotts had established themselves as an effective weapon in the tactical repertoire of black civil-rights activists in the United States. Although the boycotts of the 1930s became famous under the slogan "Don't Buy Where You Can't Work" it is important to note that the campaigns were not one homogeneous movement but consisted of various different local movements that knew about each other through the black press but rarely coordinated their campaigns. Depending on the local situation and the reaction of the targets, boycotters modified and improved their strategies, independently adapting their actions to the specific political and social environment.

It should not be overlooked that African-American boycotts in the 1930s did not always aim to end the racist hiring practices of white employers or to win jobs. Although this was clearly the dominant objective

144 August Meier and Elliot Rudwick, "The Origins of Nonviolent Direct Action," 382–4.

in most of the campaigns in the United States during the Great Depression, the boycott of the Detroit Stars' baseball stadium shows that African Americans realized the potential of the "new" tactic: Boycotts could not only be used to fight for jobs, but also as a means to make a political statement against racism.[145] Whereas the character of the early black streetcar boycotts at the turn of the century was clearly defensive, the boycotts of the 1930s had a different spirit. In the 1930s, African Americans in various cities experienced their collective power as consumers, an experience that in the decades to come would make the boycott one of the most frequently used weapons in the struggle for equal rights.

Consumer boycotts have always been much more common in the United States, the "classic home of the boycott," than in any other country. Boycotting is a peculiar part of national political culture.[146] In the historical memory of Americans, for example, the yearlong bus boycott in Montgomery, Alabama, led by Martin Luther King Jr. in 1955–6, marks the beginning of the Civil Rights movement.[147] This long-lasting but finally successful boycott against racial discrimination became a landmark in American history and reinforced the prevailing positive attitude toward the politics of boycotting in the United States: Most Americans think there is nothing wrong with using their purchasing power as consumers in a fight for a just cause.

It was not until the 1990s, with the rising fear of "ethnic fragmentation" and "tribalism," that warning voices could be heard arguing that Americans should be more careful in employing boycotts – particularly if the campaigns target minorities, as was recently the case in New York and Los Angeles, where boycotts were launched by African Americans against several Korean businesses. It comes as no surprise that an especially thoughtful editorial in the *New York Times* on the risks of racial

---

145 For boycotts launched without the intention of winning jobs, see also CAB, box 5, folder 5, ANP, Nov. 12, 1930; *Pittsburgh Courier*, Dec. 8, 1934, sec. 3, p. 2; *Detroit Independent*, Oct. 7, 1927, 1.

146 G[regorii] Schwittau, *Die Formen des wirtschaftlichen Kampfes (Streik, Boykott, Aussperrung usw.): Eine volkswirtschaftliche Untersuchung auf dem Gebiete der gegenwärtigen Arbeitspolitik* (Berlin, 1912), 240; Arthur S. Hayes and Joseph Pereira, "Marketing: Facing A Boycott, Many Companies Bend," *Wall Street Journal*, Mar. 8, 1990, 1B; David Kiley, "The Whole World Is Watching," *Adweek's Marketing Week*, July 23, 1990, 19; Adam Snyder, "Do Boycotts Work? No Brand Is Immune from the 'Non-Buy' Movement," *Adweek's Marketing Week*, Apr. 8, 1991, 16–18.

147 The bus boycott in Montgomery is probably the most thoroughly documented and researched boycott in American history. For background and bibliography, see, e.g., the studies in David J. Garrow, ed., *The Walking City: The Montgomery Bus Boycott, 1955–1956* (New York, 1989).

boycotts was written by an American journalist who in his youth had personally experienced the anti-Jewish hate boycotts in Germany during the 1930s.[148]

148 Fred M. Hechinger, "Racial Boycotts, Then and Now," *New York Times*, Oct. 13, 1990, 24A. The boycotts of several Korean-owned grocery stores in predominantly black neighborhoods of New York and Los Angeles occurred for different reasons. In New York the shopkeepers were accused of mistreatment of black patrons; in Los Angeles the boycott started in June 1991 after a Korean store owner killed a black customer who allegedly was threatening him. The boycotts, which lasted several months, received extensive coverage by the local, national, and international media.

10

Jews and the German Language

The Concept of Kulturnation and Anti-Semitic Propaganda

DIETZ BERING

THEORETICAL PERSPECTIVES

One does not need to have a Zionist outlook to conclude that the history of the Jewish people is unique, absolutely unlike the fate of any other people. Although this is certainly true of the near extermination of the Jewish community in Germany, the conclusion would be flawed if it could not be verified on several levels. One might well have a perception that there is something unique about the linguistic fate of the German Jews from the eighteenth to the twentieth century – and that that perception can also be documented. Take, for example, Jakob Wassermann, who reported in detail on his "path as a German and a Jew":

> Up to now, I was innocently convinced that I was not merely a part of German life and the German people, but that it was an innate part of me. I breathe in the language. It is much more than my means of communicating. . . . Its words and rhythm make up my innermost being. . . . It is familiar to me, as if I had been bonded with this element for all eternity. It has shaped my features, illuminated my eye, guided my hand, taught my heart to feel and my brain to think.[1]

Is the German language, then, the core piece of proof that one is a German? Or is this the eccentric argument of an oversensitive spirit?

Apparently the first is true, for Elias Canetti, a man with a sensitive but fundamentally strong, independent nature, says the same thing, although with even more extravagant intensity: "The language of my

---

Sally E. Robertson of Arlington, Virginia, translated this essay from the German.
1 Jakob Wassermann, *Mein Weg als Deutscher und Jude* (Munich, 1994), 48.

spirit will always be German, because I am a Jew."[2] So the German language is inextricably linked to being Jewish! Is it only literary figures who assume such a curious amalgamation of the two identities? No, even sober scientists come out with startling statements. According to the American Judaist Theodor Kwasmann, Judaistics is very similar in this regard to Semitics, of which it is claimed that "the most important Semitic language is German." Kwasmann made this claim in his inaugural lecture at the University of Cologne as he was demonstrating that the most important, basic works for every Judaist were written in German, for it is in that language that the "science of Judaism" was articulated for the first time.[3]

I have begun with this topic because I believe I can prove the implied thesis. This thesis states that the linguistic circumstances of the Jews and the Germans reveal especially clearly the peculiarities of this singular relationship. My style of argumentation may be new, or at least unorthodox. Therefore, I start with three principles of analysis. I attempt to defend two of these here. The third principle, the urgency of which became increasingly clear, is intended as a perspective for future research and can be addressed here only in passing.

The Perspective of Although

The development of cultural and ethnic tension within a society has frequently been explained using an approach that emphasizes difference. The clearer and more irreversible the difference between groups – in language, social circumstance, physical constitution (especially skin color), and ingrained social behavior patterns, and so forth – the more successful is this analytical method. Bolstered by such success, it then appears to have such strong explanatory power that it is applied even when the evidence really does not support it, for example, in the case of the German Jews between 1800 and 1945. To save the analysis, one latches onto the following conclusion: "Although the Jews were so attached to Germany, and were already so extensively assimilated, blatant rejections occurred." I base my remarks on the opposite reasoning: "Precisely because the Jews" – then continuing in exactly the same way – "were so attached to Germany and were already so extensively assimilated, particularly obvious rejections occurred." An obscure relationship may have existed on an his-

2 Cited in Leonore Schwartz, "Nachruf auf Elias Canetti," *Kölner Stadtanzeiger*, Aug. 19, 1994.
3 Inaugural lecture of Feb. 2, 1994, unpublished.

torical and sociocultural, essentially ethnopsychological level,[4] so that the decisiveness and brutality of the rejection could be explained by the energy that hate gains when it is directed not at those far away and foreign but at those closely related – who appear so threatening precisely because they are living in one's own house.

The Theory of Proximity

The rejection must be particularly harsh when the ostracized minority has achieved similar or even higher value than the rejecting majority in precisely those parameters by which the majority defines itself. As a concrete goal of research, therefore, the following questions must be posed and answered: Can it be shown that language functioned as a constituent of German identity in the nineteenth and twentieth centuries? Can it be shown that the Jews had moved particularly close to the Germans in the area of language? Can it be shown that it was precisely those classes of society promoting the concept of the German *Kulturnation* (cultural nation) to whom the Jews were especially close? Was it precisely those classes who were most consistent, unerring, and unyielding in their rejection of the Jews? My answer to all of these questions is yes.

The Theory of Universal Structures

Future research should take into account the following perspective, which is to be defined as its own comprehensive project. Are the techniques of rejection of minorities in Germany and in America the same, similar, or completely different? We cannot expect reliable answers to this question until the target terrain has been searched for predetermined, universal structures, that is, necessary patterns with an imperative psychological or even cognitive anchor. It has been repeatedly emphasized, for example, that the same accusations used to fight the Christian missionaries in China were also used against the Jews in Germany. Similarly, Norman Cohn has demonstrated that the early modern "witch" stereotype was used not only in the Middle Ages against the heretics but also

---

4 I have sketched an initial outline of this theory in a very rudimentary manner in several places: Dietz Bering, "Eine Tragödie der Nähe? Luther und die Juden," in Ulrich Ernst and Bernhard Sowinski, eds., *Architectura poetica: Festschrift für Johannes Rathofer zum 65. Geburtstag* (Cologne, 1990), 327–44; Dietz Bering, "Rezension zu B. Martin und E. Schulin, *Die Juden als Minderheit in der Geschichte* (3d ed., 1985)," *Geschichte in Wissenschaft und Unterricht* 37 (1986): 45–8.

in a similar manner in ancient Rome against the Christians.[5] In the context of our research, this means that we cannot speak of a surprising and
significant parallel until we have ruled out the possibility that the similarities between German and American conditions are simply the result
of such universal structures that are (and must be) found in all cultures.
For example, the pejorative description of the psychological (cowardly)
and physical (flat-footed) constitution of blacks in the United States
and of Jews in Germany could be an imperative structure, as could the
"black codes" mentioned by Norbert Finzsch, with their bans on carrying weapons and traveling on the streets with racehorses.[6] These measures
are comparable to the longtime Prussian/German proscription of Jews
in the military cadres[7] and to the ingrained scorn of the Jews because of
their particular incompetence as horsemen.[8] All of these could be predictable manifestations of an underlying universal principle: rendering
the representatives of a minority defenseless and militarily weak.[9]

This universal perspective could also include denigration of the language of the Jews and the blacks. It is a long tradition; even the classical
Greeks used the terms "barbarians" and "stammering ones" to banish
everything that did not belong to them behind the demarcation line of
self-identification. The uniqueness of the German-Jewish relationship in
the area of language could therefore not have developed simply from
the linguistic ostracism of the minority. There must be specific, additional peculiarities most likely derived from the individual historical
structures of the particular case. Just such singular peculiarities should be

5 Quoted in Peter Burke, "Stärken und Schwächen der Mentalitätsgeschichte," in Ulrich Raulff, ed.,
   Mentalitäten-Geschichte: Zur historischen Rekonstruktion geistiger Prozesse (Berlin, 1989), 139.
6 See the chapters by Patricia Vertinsky and Norbert Finzsch in this book.
7 Dietz Bering, *Der Name als Stigma: Antisemitismus im deutschen Alltag, 1812–1933*, 2d ed. (Stuttgart,
   1988), 343–5, 352–4; published in English as *The Stigma of Names: Antisemitism in German Daily
   Life, 1812–1933* (Cambridge, 1992), 243–5, 250–2.
8 See Dietz Bering, *Kampf um Namen: Bernhard Weiss gegen Joseph Goebbels*, 2d ed. (Stuttgart,
   1992), 258–60, 295–6.
9 Borrowing from cognitive sciences such as linguistics, this field of research would therefore have
   to be investigated on three separate levels: (1) the universal, abstract, "underlying" cognitive structures of distance-creating markings of foreignness (= the parameters); (2) the many concrete
   manifestations thereof in the various fields of tension between minorities and the majority
   (= concrete assignment of value to the universal parameters); (3) searching of these manifestations
   for relationships of implications between types: if marking x is manifested, then marking y is certainly present; in other words, no marking x without the presence of marking y, but y possible
   without x (= one-sided foundation). For ideas regarding cognitive structures in the area of language, see the recent works of Noam Chomsky, well summarized in Gisbert Fanselow and Sascha
   W. Felix, *Sprachtheorie: Eine Einführung in die Generative Grammatik, Band I: Grundlagen und Zielset-
   zungen* (Tübingen, 1987); for the relationships of implication in particular, see Elmar Holenstein,
   Sprachliche Universalien: Eine Untersuchung zur Natur des menschlichen Geistes (Munich, 1985), 11–12,
   35–41, 128–30, 155–7.

evident in investigating the relationship "German language – Germans – German Jews."

The discussion so far may seem interesting but also somewhat speculative. It must be placed on a realistic basis. If this chapter is to make a contribution to a book on racism and minority problems, however, then the following must be proved now that the research principles have been established: The German language played a central, or at least a special role for both Germans and German Jews in the period being addressed. This role was such that, rather than driving the minority and the majority further apart, it brought them closer together. The hate was nevertheless maintained, provoking an ever stronger defensive reaction because the minority, which was still being accused of being threatening and foreign, had in reality approached the majority so nearly as to be indistinguishable, or had perhaps even surpassed it. The supposed (linguistic) difference, which was stressed ever more desperately by the rejecters, therefore found less and less basis in reality. An emphasis on contrast – indeed, on the imagining of contrast – was needed. Accordingly, a disproportionate demonization had to be put into action, a continuous caricature of the actual normal, day-to-day state of affairs, so that the merely supposed difference, which was no longer supported by reality, could be delivered up by (ultimately murderous) fantasy.

THE CENTRAL FUNCTION OF LANGUAGE AMONG THE GERMANS

The particularly ardent efforts of the Jews to learn and perfect the High German language (*Hochdeutsch*) cannot be explained or properly assessed without knowing the function that the German language served for Germans in general at the beginning of the nineteenth century.

We must draw a somewhat wider circle so that the core theses of this book are addressed. The subject of this chapter, then, is the German language among Jews and Germans in the last decades of the eighteenth century and throughout the nineteenth. The perspectives established by this collection are (1) development of minority status, (2) strategies of exclusion on the cultural and sociopsychological levels, and (3) state responses to intolerance. Many of the facts are certainly familiar. The only new element in this first part of the chapter, which serves to augment existing knowledge on the subject, is the manner in which the facts are juxtaposed to create contrasts.

I begin with the German perspective. One of the few undisputed

views is that by the time its official end was declared in 1806, the Holy
Roman Empire of the German Nation (*Heiliges Römisches Reich deutscher
Nation*), if indeed it ever existed in any kind of effective way, had in any
case already been dissolved through a long process of erosion. This is the
genetic background to that motley map that comprised Germany and
German-speaking lands for centuries and, to a certain extent, still does.
The most significant and successful countermovements to this fragmentation in the eighteenth century were not political but cultural. They
can be referred to collectively as the "German movement"[10] – the effort
to give birth to a German spirit to counter the dominant French spirit.
Although the period from 1770 to 1830 delimits the "classical" movement, it must be said that the politico-cultural forces that claimed this
motivation, even when their objectives were purely those of power politics, remained in power for the entire nineteenth century, and indeed
until 1945. It is of fundamental importance that the German language
was a central anchor for the German character and consciousness both in
the initiation phase from 1770 to 1830 and in the phase of political
implementation from, let us say, 1870 to 1914. This was true in two fundamental dimensions.

The Dimensions of Culture and Nation

In the search for unifying dimensions to override petty particularism,
attention was repeatedly directed to the language. There is agreement
that Johann Gottfried Herder was one of the first to do this, and that he
was the most effective at it. There have been considerable, unsuccessful attempts to find evidence that representatives of the national movement themselves made reference to him.[11] To quote one of the primary
Herder scholars: "The actual force through which a nation constitutes
itself is neither a biological one such as 'race,' which Herder, unlike
Kant . . . tends to discount . . . nor a metaphysical principle (Hegel's
Volksgeist), but rather the *language* with its individual national peculiarities."[12] In Herder's own words, "Thus, every nation speaks as it thinks

---

10 For the general relationship between the German language and the German nation, see Claus
   Ahlzweig, *Muttersprache – Vaterland: Die deutsche Nation und ihre Sprache* (Opladen, 1994); for a
   comprehensive presentation focusing on the aspects discussed here, with extensive bibliography,
   see Otto Dann, "Herder und die Deutsche Bewegung," in Gerhard Sauder, ed., *Johann Gottfried
   Herder, 1744–1803*, special issue of *Studien zum 18. Jahrhundert* 9 (1987): 312–16.
11 See Dann, "Herder und die Deutsche Bewegung," 309.
12 Hans Dietrich Irmscher, "Nationalität und Humanität im Denken Herders," *Orbis Litterarum* 49
   (1994): 198.

and thinks as it speaks."[13] The conclusion is clear and had decisive consequences for the Jews of the emancipation period. Different speech leads to different thought, and both lead to exclusion from a nation.

This kind of thinking, with precisely these conclusions, was immediately emphasized in two ways and thus became an increasingly exacting standard for determining national consciousness. Ernst Moritz Arndt, Theodor Körner, *Turnvater* Jahn,[14] and the other agitators for an uprising against Napoleon found ever more vivid pictures and ever harsher words for these connections.[15] Johann Gottlieb Fichte, with many emulators after him, was the first to interpret consistently the nation using the metaphor of the "organism,"[16] which by the laws of nature must inevitably cast off the "inorganic." In 1854, in the famous preface to the first volume of his *German Dictionary* (*Deutsches Wörterbuch*), intended as a monument to the nation, Jakob Grimm, still longing for German unity after the failure of 1848, invoked that rare moment of joy in which the ascendant German philology and the people's receptiveness to their mother tongue were joined: "How they both were moved by intensified love for their fatherland and an unquietable yearning for its more solid unity. What do we have in common but our language and our literature?" He then showed the far-reaching power of language in his concluding appeal:

Beloved German countrymen, regardless what state, regardless what faith you may be, enter the great hall of your native, ancient language, which is open to all of you, learn it and sanctify it and hold fast to it, your strength and endurance as a people rests in it. Still it reaches across the Rhine into Alsace to Lorraine, across the Eider deep into Schleswig-Holstein, along the Baltic shore to Riga and Reval, beyond the Carpathians in Transylvania's old Dacian lands.[17]

13 Quoted in ibid. For other documentation of early equating of mother tongue and nation, see Claus Ahlzweig, "Die deutsche Nation und ihre Muttersprache," in Konrad Ehlich, ed., *Sprache im Faschismus* (Frankfurt/Main, 1989), 40–2, with quotes from Adelung, Herder, and Jean Paul.

14 A nickname for Friedrich Ludwig Jahn; *Turnvater* is German for "father of gymnastics."

15 E.g., Arndt wrote, "Why is it that the inhabitants of border regions, where three or four nations abut, mixing languages, customs and mores, are usually a roguish, deceitful, fainthearted lot?" (Ernst M. Arndt, *Geist der Zeit* [Berlin and London, 1807–18], 135), and "But language draws the proper boundary between peoples. . . . What lives together and speaks one and the same language belongs together according to God and Nature" (Ernst M. Arndt, *Der Rhein, Teutschlands Strom, aber nicht Teutschlands Grenze* [Leipzig, 1813], 12–13). For additional relevant quotations, see Ahlzweig, "Die deutsche Nation und ihre Muttersprache," 55.

16 See Irmscher, "Nationalität und Humanität," 201.

17 Quoted in Johannes Janota, ed., *Eine Wissenschaft etabliert sich, 1810–1870* (Tübingen, 1980), 126, 134. Alan Kirkness says the language purifiers of the period from 1840 to 1860 acted not as linguists but consciously as patriots, for "they considered a pure and uniform German language to be the sign of national (German) unity and autonomy" (Alan Kirkness, *Zur Sprachreinigung im Deutschen, 1789–1871: Eine historische Dokumentation*, 2 vols. [Tübingen, 1975], 2:418). Kirkness

These are decidedly "German" tones, so characteristic that one would tend to look with skepticism on the thesis that there is a concealed harmony with the Jewish view. But let us imagine for a moment the effect from a Jewish perspective of this urgent invitation – "beloved countrymen, regardless what state, regardless what faith you may be, enter" – and let us listen at the same time to Ludwig Börne, who described it in 1833 as a particularly great mercy of God

> that I can become simultaneously a German and a Jew. . . . Indeed, because I was born to no fatherland, I desire a fatherland more fervently than you, and because my place of birth was no greater than the ghetto, behind the closed door of which a foreign land began, because of all this, the city is not fatherland enough for me, nor a territory, nor a province; I am satisfied only with the whole immense fatherland, as far as its language reaches. And if I had the power, I would not tolerate even a gutter the width of my hand separating territory from territory, German family from German family. And if I had the power, I would not tolerate a single German word coming from a German mouth on the other side of the border.[18]

The parallels, indeed several parallels, are evident: (1) a point of departure involving an isolated, particularist existence that begs for unification; (2) pent-up desire (providing unparalleled energy) for the day of fulfillment; (3) language as the actual defining value for both groups because the Jewish people were widely dispersed within the broad circle the Germans envisioned as their political home; (4) the Jews as predestined participants in the intended unification process; and, above all, (5) Börne's claim, which must not be overlooked, of the structural parallelism with his clear declaration that he desired "more fervently than you" the (linguistic) unity of the fatherland, a declaration that must have shocked the "German" Germans by outdoing them.

We can try to reduce this affirmation to the following formula: the Jews as the most German of Germans, or, more cautiously, as the heralds

---

also includes an abundance of quotations to this effect. I offer here the stated positions of one person and one institution. The laughably strict language purifier J. D. C. Brugger wrote, "The pure German language is and should be the *great tie* which binds together the approximately forty thousand *Germans of all provinces and tribes into one inseparable unified whole, into a people,* who all understand it and who speak and write it as their mother tongue. . . . It is the emblem of German greatness and unity" (ibid., 2:325). A manifesto of the "Potsdam Society for the German Language," founded in 1848, states that purification and education in the mother tongue is "an obligation of self-preservation, since in the *mother tongue* we are protecting the sacred, mysterious tie which unites us as a people and the only thing which holds us together . . . for *language is the common, intellectual homeland of a people*" (ibid., 344).

18 Quoted in Nicoline Hortzitz, *"Früh-Antisemitismus" in Deutschland (1789–1871/72): strukturelle Untersuchungen zu Wortschatz: Text und Argumentation,* Germanistische Linguistik, no. 83 (Tübingen, 1988), 62.

of especially German developments. This thesis plays a significant role in our analysis because it can be verified using several parameters.

Wilhelm von Humboldt gave this central category of language a particularly strong foundation, and it is still discussed. As one of the most powerful minds of his time, on the political stage as elsewhere, he joined in the same refrain: "The language is, basically and above all, the nation."[19] He gave it a much firmer status, however, than had the impotent Herder with his somewhat muddled wording. Von Humboldt presented a complete linguistic theory in which the identical nature of (national) spirit and language (spirit) was presented in an impressive manner. It was not the case, he argued, that a preexisting national spirit manifested itself in the language and that a worldview (also identical with the national spirit) was then formed from the structure of the language. Neither was the opposite the case, that is, there was no pre-existing world structure that was simply reflected in the language. Rather, language was not a finished product, an *ergon* just lying there for a nation to make use of, but a continually applied creative force, an *energeia* creating new language with every act of articulation (in constant confrontation with existing language and with the world, which has already been interpreted, and thus made accessible, by language). In other words, steadily changing or confirming itself in a constant process of new creation, language perpetually *reformulates* its forms of expression *and* its semantic content (phonetics/phonology/syntax, on the one hand, and meaning, on the other). In this way, it keeps (national) spirit and interpretation of the world in a state of equilibrium. One does not exist prior to the other; rather, the two must be created simultaneously on a mutual foundation.[20]

There is no doubt that, after all of these developments and position statements, many had built into their intellectual foundation the idea that German language, German nation, and German spirit were manifestations of one and the same thing. As long as unity was not achieved, it had to at least be imagined through the idea of a *Kulturnation* led by language.[21] This kind of basic outlook must have offered the newly emancipated Jews a desired yet fragile foundation. A truly firm footing could

19 Quoted in Hans Feist, *Sprechen und Sprachpflege*, Sammlung Göschen, no. 1122 (Berlin, 1938), 5.
20 On Wilhelm von Humboldt, see summary in Volker Heeschen, "Die Sprachphilosophie Wilhelm von Humboldts," Ph.D. diss., University of Bochum, 1972.
21 Historians agree on this point of departure, e.g., Thomas Nipperdey, *Deutsche Geschichte, 1800–1866: Bürgerwelt und starker Staat* (Munich, 1983), 300–5, with multiple references to language as constituent; Dann, "Herder und die Deutsche Bewegung," 315. Consensus likewise prevails among linguistic historians, e.g., Oskar Reichmann, *Deutsche Nationalsprache: Eine kritische Darstellung* (Tübingen, 1978), 390–1, or, in a detailed form with extensive citations from the literature,

only be achieved under favorable conditions – above all, real acceptance by the majority culture. Yet a second dimension made the problem even more difficult.

The Dimensions of Class and Prestige

The language question actually could have moved to the margins around 1870, because at least a provisional harmonization between language, nation, and state had emerged. However, language had the function of establishing not only state and nation but also classes and social strata.

One of the sweeping structural dilemmas of the (German) middle class is that it had to come into conflict with its own ideals. From a linguistic perspective, this means that with the legacy of the French Revolution, German middle-class principles and self-descriptions (*Bürger/ citoyen*/citizen) had an emancipatory, universalist element to them. Liberty, equality, and fraternity should prevail for all the people, for the entire nation, for all *citoyens*. Parallel to that, the language of the German nation, meaning the High German of the German classical period, should also be a (unifying) means of communication for the entire people. In fact, however, the language as a whole, as well as its central political concepts in particular,[22] was caught in a field of tension between different purposes of communication (situational variants) and between classes, social strata (social, ideological variants), or both. The "liberty" of middle-class economic activity brought not "equality and fraternity" but tension-generating relations of superiority and inferiority.

The same was true of the language of the *Kulturnation*. It did not become a common possession but rather the prestige language of the middle class, which saw itself as the leading class, progressively distinguished from the nobility, on the one hand, and defending its privileges in a reactionary manner against the growing working class, on the other. Many general[23] as well as linguistic historians have pointed this out

---

Ahlzweig, *Muttersprache – Vaterland*. The linguists make the same judgment, e.g., Wolfgang Frühwald, "Die Idee kultureller Nationbildung und die Entstehung der Literatursprache in Deutschland," in Otto Dann, ed., *Nationalismus in vorindustrieller Zeit* (Munich, 1986), 129–41.

22 Regarding the utopian content of the terms *Bürger/citoyen*, see Willibald Steinmetz, "Die schwierige Selbstbehauptung des deutschen Bürgertums: begriffsgeschichtliche Bemerkungen in sozialhistorischer Absicht," in Rainer Wimmer, ed., *Das 19. Jahrhundert: Sprachgeschichtliche Wurzeln des heutigen Deutsch* (Berlin and New York, 1991), 29; regarding the fight of the conservatives against the progressive content of these terms, see Jürgen Kocka, "Bürgertum und Bürgerlichkeit als Probleme der deutschen Geschichte vom späten 18. zum frühen 20. Jahrhundert," in Jürgen Kocka, ed., *Bürger und Bürgerlichkeit im 19. Jahrhundert* (Göttingen, 1987), 33.

23 For middle-class linguistic prestige in the writings of general historians, see Thomas Nipperdey,

repeatedly.[24] One of the most prominent of these, Peter von Polenz, succeeded in tracing the often-invoked "language crisis" of the late nineteenth century to nothing more than the lost battle of the middle class – which was committed to classical High German – against the modern age with its banal culture, mass media, and mass organizations of workers, and the linguistic reflection thereof. This could not simply have consisted of the ratification of that which was established and promoted as the cultural linguistic standard by the elite, highly educated strata of the bourgeoisie.[25] The middle class was thus (1) the supporter of the German language as a harbinger of, and a substitute for, unity and (2) the defender of the classical language because of the power it gave them to distance themselves from competing groups.

Since we have already described the German-Jewish parallel on the first battlefield of unity, we must ask the same question regarding the position of the Jews on the second battlefield. What position did the Jews have within the (economic) middle class as they wrestled for power and differentiation from other classes? The answer is clear, yet it yields amazing conclusions. The Jews were thoroughly middle class. The center of their life and activity was independent trade and commerce. Their success in this area was amazing. When one further considers that the German middle class wanted to compensate with "culture" for the lack of political power, and that the Jews were the middle-class group with the least political power, and therefore in a certain sense forced to compensate, then the circumstance noted above is seen by this measure as well: The Jews were the "most German" German citizens, for they

---

Deutsche Geschichte, 1866–1918, vol. 1: *Arbeitswelt und Bürgergeist* (Munich, 1990), 382–9, with several references to the system of academic qualification. Hans-Ulrich Wehler stated pointedly in 1987 that the educated middle class, under the spell of neo-humanist educated religion, held up "High German and cultured German" as a "social barrier" to the "uneducated": "This 'power to define' the High German language constituted a power potential on the part of the 'educated' that should not be underestimated" (Hans-Ulrich Wehler, *Deutsche Gesellschaftsgeschichte*, vol. 2: *Von der Reformära bis zur industriellen und politischen "Deutschen Doppelrevolution" 1815–1845/49* [Munich, 1987], 564–5). Regarding the general delineation of the middle class against the lower classes, see Jürgen Kocka, "Bürgertum und bürgerliche Gesellschaft im 19. Jahrhundert: Europäische Entwicklungen und deutsche Eigenart," in Jürgen Kocka and Ute Frevert, eds., *Bürgertum im 19. Jahrhundert: Deutschland im europäischen Vergleich*, 3 vols. (Munich, 1988), 1:21.

24 For middle-class language as a standard of prestige in the writings of linguists, see overview article with ample bibliography by Klaus J. Mattheier, "Standardsprache als Sozialsymbol: Über kommunikative Folgen gesellschaftlichen Wandels," in Wimmer, *Das 19. Jahrhundert*, 41–72, with the key phrases "socially symbolic tasks" (41), "educated German" (42), and "standard language is no longer a social symbol of one social group but is becoming a national symbol, the symbol of a nation state" (vs. *Kulturnation*) (49).

25 Peter von Polenz, "Die Sprachkrise der Jahrhundertwende und das bürgerliche Bildungsdeutsch," *Sprache und Literatur* 14, no. 2 (1983): 3–13.

embodied the characteristics of the German middle class in particularly
distinct form. They probably also placed the strongest emphasis on the
"culture language," which functioned as an instrument of compensation
and prestige. Thus, given the further rejection of Jews in the society, it is
hard to imagine any more delicate, complicated dilemma (because it is
also filled with paradoxes) than the relationship between Germans, Jews,
and the German language.

Summarizing what has been presented thus far: The Jews did not
come into a well-established, self-confident nation but rather into a
community that itself was still seeking an identity,[26] especially in terms
of prestige and in its language. In other words, the Jews were graciously
admitted, under the condition, of course, that they do not enter with
their old, native, Jewish identity (which was already faltering as a result
of the Enlightenment) but that, instead, they divest themselves of things
Jewish and fit themselves into a new German identity – which itself was
also faltering. It makes good sense to interpret Jews and "Germans" as on
a parallel path in this entire process.

This demonstration of the central position of language leads inevitably
to the following question: What were the linguistic customs and self-
assessments of the Jews when they were entering German society and
attempting to establish themselves within it?

YIDDISH

At the end of the eighteenth century, the Enlightenment, with its pre-
cepts of equality and the perfectibility of man, seized the imagination of
at least a small, powerful elite – in Prussia, primarily a group of high-
level government officials – if not a broad cross section of society. At
that time it was not really possible to say that the Jews were an example
of the equality of man. Indeed, they could be seen as a very definite
example of inequality. As a completely discrete group, they stood out
distinctly from the Germans – placard-like for all to see – in their clothing, their lifestyle, their entire demeanor, and their language as well.
They could, however, be used as a positive example of the second fundamental principle of the Enlightenment – perfectibility, or the belief in
the general capability of man to educate and improve himself. Putting
these facts into the first analytical dimension (development of minority

---

26 See Jacob Toury, "Die Sprache als Problem der jüdischen Einordnung im Deutschen Kultur-
  raum," *Jahrbuch des Instituts für deutsche Geschichte*, supp. 4 (1982): 93.

status), the difference between majority and minority did not develop in the nineteenth century. Rather, it was a traditional status that had been handed down; it was actually a preserved artifact of the Middle Ages. The roots of the rigid religious and socioeconomic differences – and the linguistic difference as well, once Yiddish evolved during the fourteenth century – were that deep. A new type of explosiveness was created when two different elements, which had previously been kept apart, were now practically forced together.

At the time of their emancipation in Germany around 1800, the Jews consistently spoke Western Yiddish (often written in the Hebrew alphabet) in addition to Hebrew, or they used a mixed dialect that was an approximation of pure German and came to be known as *jüdeln* and later *jargon*.[27] Almost no one spoke pure German. What kind of boundary did Yiddish draw? What sort of tension did it create? More precisely, how did it differ in its style from German and, even more important, how did its style fit into the direction in which linguists, linguistic and other philosophers, makers of cultural policy, and statesmen wanted German to develop?

Yiddish is a mixture or amalgamation of three ingredients, the dominant one being (medieval) German, with lesser contributions from Slavic languages (primarily Polish) and a smattering of Hebrew.[28] In contrast, Klopstock had attributed to the envisioned homogeneous German national language a certain "primordial form," whereas Schottelius and Harsdörffer credited it with a "basic, certain correctness" that freed it of everything "nonnative" (von Zesen) and "unnatural" (Klopstock).[29] Just such properties of original "purity," which later had to be defended against adulteration, made it superior, for example, to the despised French, a mixed language derived from Latin. How infinitely superior it must then have been to Yiddish! Furthermore, the linguistic structure of this Yiddish conglomerate differed from German by having much less inflection and a greater degree of analyticity. In other words, as in English, the relationship of words in a Yiddish sentence is indicated more often than

---

27 Evidence of this is everywhere; e.g., for the general facts of the matter, see Shulamit Volkov, *Die Juden in Deutschland, 1780–1918* (Munich, 1994), 5, under the rubric "The Jews as a discrete, isolated group"; and, for details, see Jacob Toury, "Die Sprache als Problem," 95–6; and Peter Freimark, "Sprachverhalten und Assimilation: Die Situation der Juden in Nordwestdeutschland in der 1. Hälfte des 19. Jahrhunderts," *Saeculum* 31 (1980): 240–61, both containing evidence that this was the case as late as the mid-nineteenth century.

28 See Dietz Bering, "Sprache und Antisemitismus im 19. Jahrhundert," in Wimmer, *Das 19. Jahrhundert*, 329 (with extensive references to linguistic literature).

29 Quotations from Reichmann, *Deutsche Nationalsprache*, 406.

in German by separate, added words rather than by inflected forms.[30] Nothing could have been more contrary to the dominant views of the value of language and the correctness of linguistic development than these Yiddish structures. It must also have been a stumbling block in the dominant path of nineteenth-century linguistic development in general.

Consider the linguistic landscape of the day. At the beginning of the nineteenth century, the German language had only just acquired a "pure" standard form above the level of the dialects, and an image as the "language of the classics." As already indicated, this language allowed a nation that was, in reality, politically divided to appear as a whole, as a (cultural) nation that was, ideally, linguistically unified. Then came the homogenizing pressures of the Napoléonic Wars, in the context of which national partisans such as Arndt, Körner, and *Turnvater* Jahn also raised a "linguistic" flag against the pernicious French language. The virtually futile fight of the middle class for political influence followed, and a significant part of their argumentation was grounded on their role as upholders of civilization and culture. Finally, beginning in 1870, as the goal of "unity" loomed larger, and the goal of "liberty" smaller, the systematic restructuring of the German Empire, including linguistic restructuring, began in earnest. All dialects were repressed in favor of a uniform written language and a more and more clearly developing uniform colloquial language.[31]

Moreover, this development took place in an era of imperialism with a renewed drive for homogenization. Determined resistance was offered to all foreign influences. One need think only of the chauvinistic battle against foreign words waged by tens of thousands of members of the German Language Society (*Allgemeiner Deutscher Sprachverein*), who no less enthusiastically launched and extolled volumes of poetry on the beauty of the German language.[32] In this category was also the establishment of periodical literature on the teaching of the German language, of which the *Zeitschrift für den deutschen Unterricht* (1887) was particularly consequential. It articulated its strictly patriotic viewpoint as follows:

For German instruction is nothing but instruction in the art of using . . . the German language in such a way that the German spirit and essence, German style and morals achieve perfect expression among all circles and all social

---

30 E.g., the genitive is not formed synthetically with the ending -s, as in German, but rather as a periphrastic form with the preposition "fun/fin."
31 Mattheier, "Standardsprache als Sozialsymbol," 52–5.
32 Paul Pietsch and Günter A. Saalfeld, *Deutscher Sprache Ehrenkranz: Was die Dichter unserer Muttersprache zu Liebe und zu Leide singen und sagen* (Berlin, 1898).

strata, among people of all vocations and all ages. *Language is the people.* (emphasis added)[33]

Against this broad linguistic panorama, it is likely that nothing would have been more repugnant, nothing would have stood out to such a degree as a crass counterpart to all the developing trends, as Yiddish and its Germanified offshoot, the Jewish *jargon*.

Unlike this ostracism of mixed languages, which lasted throughout the century and gained fairly broad acceptance, the linguistic philosophy of Humboldt and his adherents was probably restricted to academic circles. All adherents of this philosophy believed that the more inflective and synthetic languages were of higher value than the analytical ones.[34] Nevertheless, the diagnosis must be that every ideology in the years between 1770 and 1914 ran contrary to the native language of the Jews. As a result, anti-Semites found a well-stocked arsenal of arguments.

How these basic facts look when inserted into the line of inquiry I established at the outset indicates the fate of the Jewish minority in Germany. Did the conflict acquire fierceness because of a particular closeness or because of an alien strangeness? It is no less interesting to approach these problems with the second issue of this book in mind and ask: What of the strategies of exclusion, and what is the sociocultural dimension of these developments? The answers to both questions are surprising.

Regarding the first, unlike the Polish, Serbian, and French linguistic minorities in the German Empire, the irritation of Yiddish was not that it was completely foreign and absolutely incomprehensible; it was precisely its relatedness that aroused aggression. A Jew speaking *jargon*, or even Yiddish, was not completely incomprehensible. The language was so close that one could say that it was German that had *missed the mark*. This miss is a worse failing and carries with it a greater potential for

---

33 Supplement to the *Zeitschrift für den deutschen Unterricht* 3 (1889): 356–7, quoted in Franz Gress, *Germanistik und Politik: Kritische Beiträge zur Geschichte einer nationalen Wissenschaft* (Stuttgart, 1971), 115.

34 Wilhelm Wackernagel, Friedrich Schlegel, and, above all, Wilhelm von Humboldt interpreted less inflection and more analyticity (in terms of the ideology of "organic" vs. "mechanical") as a sign of lesser status; on this point, see Ruth Römer, *Sprachwissenschaft und Rassenideologie in Deutschland* (Munich, 1985), 105–10. Lest I give the impression that such opinions were expressed solely in these "gentlemen" studies and elite conversational circles, I shall also cite the Hamburg educator quoted in more detail below, Anton Rée, *Die Sprachverhältnisse der heutigen Juden, im Interesse der Gegenwart und mit besonderer Rücksicht auf Volkserziehung* (Hamburg, 1844), 73. Rée was intent on talking his fellow Jews out of using Yiddish, with its dearth of conjugations and declinations. As the loyal follower of those great predecessors, he believed, "The more original a language is for its people, the more inflective it is, and vice-versa. . . . The closer a race of people is to the actual core of the nation, the more inflective is its dialect, and vice-versa."

both irritation and attack. As it was often put, this "contaminated, corrupted"[35] dialect simply "insults" the German ear because it can be interpreted as a *distortion* rather than being seen as something completely different. One finds just this sort of harsh judgment of the specifically Jewish manner of articulation in examples to be presented subsequently.

The answer to the second question is perhaps even more surprising. One cannot speak of strategies of linguistic exclusion at all, at least on the governmental level. Governments subscribed to the idea of perfectibility in this regard by ordering conformity wherever they could. Linguistic emancipation, like emancipation in general, was therefore not an offer to become a citizen and adapt as one saw fit but rather an obligation to adapt. The linguistic dimension demonstrates this particularly clearly.

THE REACTION OF THE STATE

Although the liberal Prussian reformers were able to avert compulsory assimilation in matters of clothing and beards in 1812, there clearly was compulsory linguistic assimilation, as had existed in Hesse-Kassel since 1739. Paragraph 2 of the emancipation edict obligated all Jews "to use the German language not only in keeping their business records, but also in drafting their contracts . . . and in signing their names to use no other characters than German or Latin ones." Moreover, they were required to adapt to the German system of names, that is, adopt permanent surnames. Certainly, in the general conservative rollback in the period to 1848, the Jews lost more and more rights that the edict had generously granted them (although it had not, of course, granted them the right to enter the civil service). A clean sweep was made in questions of language. The compulsory adoption of names was carried out within six months, and the obligation to use German was not only decreed but also enforced through decisive administrative measures. I shall now present

---

35 "Contaminated," said Karl Friedrich von Klöden in the 1790s in the memoirs of his youth, quoted in Julius Carlebach, "Der Säkulierungsprozess in der Erziehung," in Hans Liebeschütz and Arnold Paucker, eds., *Das Judentum in der Deutschen Umwelt, 1800–1850* (Tübingen, 1977), 57; that article contains additional contemporary judgments, 71: "contaminated gibberish," "vernacular hermaphroditism," "contaminated dialect"; Johann Wolfgang von Goethe said "contaminated and distorted," quoted in Hans Peter Althaus, "Die jiddische Sprache: Eine Einführung, Erster Teil," *Germania Judaica*, n.s. 14, no. 4 (1965): 3 ("Die jiddische Sprache: Eine Einführung, Zweiter Teil," *Germania Judaica*, n.s. 23, no. 1 [1968]); "nearly incurable disease" was the opinion of Hartwig Wessely, a member of the Enlightenment circle around Mendelssohn, transmitted by none other than Leopold Zuns, who was absurdly optimistic in matters of language. See the Zuns's *Die gottesdienstlichen Vorträge der Juden* (Berlin, 1832), 452.

previously unknown sources regarding both processes that demonstrate serious efforts and astonishing benevolence on the part of Prussian authorities in the matter of language and that, on the names issue, yield evidence of what has, to date, been merely a plausible suggestion, namely, the influence of Herder.

The First Indicator: Forcible Introduction of the German Language and Script

On November 1, 1814, the Prussian Ministry of the Interior opened a dossier with the following heading: "Regarding the ban contained in § 2 of the edict of March 11, 1812, on use by the Jews of the Hebrew alphabet in their signatures, and the handling of offenders."[36] It is telling that, although the dossier was not closed until November 26, 1855, more than forty years later, ministry officials had filed only twenty-one records. One typical case was presented to the minister of the interior in Berlin on October 21, 1814, by President von Stettin. A Jew had signed his name in Hebrew script, although the police authorities of the royal Prussian government of Pomerania, through "all district officials, police constables and magistrates," had announced to the synagogues and Jewish schools that – in accordance with said paragraph – the citizenship of offenders would be revoked. What decision did the minister of the interior make? And what decision did he make in a Königsberg case in which the magistrate had already imposed a sentence of deportation? His decisions were lenient. A single offense, he argued, could not justify such a harsh penalty as loss of citizenship. The offender should receive a hearing at his own expense. If he claims it was simply a mistake, then the police should issue a warning. If he will not submit, then one should not hesitate to deport him.

In 1849, the senior district president of the province of Posen led a rearguard action. He referred to § 6 of the law of July 23, 1847, which called on the Jews to draft contracts in German or another living language, or face a penalty of fifty talers or six weeks in jail. He argued that this was in violation of § 11 of the constitutional charter, which stated that no disadvantage shall accrue as a result of religious affiliation. On April 15, 1849, the minister in fact rescinded the regulation, stating that it was "without a doubt a restraint on the general rights of a citizen based on the religious affiliation of the Jews." This opinion was soon

36 Kingdom of Prussia, Ministry of the Interior, Rep. 77, Tit. 30: *Generalia*, doc. no. 31.

confirmed by a judgment of the upper tribunal in 1855, which gave the signal finally to close both the dossier, with its meager records, and the chapter as a whole.

Jewish Attitudes Toward Yiddish

The apparent rapidity and ease with which the switch to the German script and German language were accomplished is somewhat astounding. The speed seems almost logical, however, when one investigates the Jews' own attitude toward Yiddish. One is faced with yet another amazing characteristic of the German-Jewish relationship.

We do not need to provide any new sources at this point, for there is a well-documented, commonly held opinion among historians and linguists that the reform-minded Jews felt no less contempt for their idiom than did the champions of the German majority culture, with whom they shared exactly the same ground in terms of ideology and linguistic philosophy. They prized linguistic homogeneity and "purity" above all else.[37] In the case of Mendelssohn, this was also true of Hebrew: "simply no mixing of languages"[38] was his general maxim; for him, violations of this dealt a blow to the moral foundation: "I fear that this *jargon* has contributed not a little to the immorality of the common man, and I foresee a very good effect from the use of the pure German dialect, which has been on the rise among my people for some time now."[39]

This feeling was shared by the many Jews who, unlike the exceptional Mendelssohn, were not able to achieve flawless integration of the Jewish-Hebraic and German cultures and in most cases did not even want to. The judgment of many Jewish opinion leaders regarding Yiddish was only barely surpassed by the verdict of the famous Jewish historian, Heinrich Graetz, who found it a "semi-animalistic language."[40]

---

37 There has yet to be a systematic search of the Jewish periodicals, but they offer much material, e.g., *Sulamith* 7 (1848): col. 87: "coarse *jargon*."

38 Quoted in Toury, "Die Sprache als Problem," 77. He also implored on the basis of the *Mishnah* that Hebrew be kept pure and free of mixings; see *Sulamith* 7 (1845): 208.

39 Quoted in Sander L. Gilman, "Moses Mendelssohn und die Entwicklung einer deutsch-jüdischen Identität," *Zeitschrift für deutsche Philologie* 99 (1980): 516. To show that this was not an incidental comment but part of the basic arsenal of argumentation of Jewish language educators, see the extensive appeal for German language instruction by Emmanuel Wohlwill, teacher at the Free School of Hamburg, in *Sulamith* 7 (1845): 85, where it is stated that a "clear, robust, powerful, genuine language of truth is the characteristic feature of a masculine, educated spirit, of an honorable, forthright mind; it also testifies to clear and orderly emotions, indeed it is the most effective means of producing this clarity and harmony of emotion."

40 Quoted in Siegbert S. Prawer, "'Das verfluchte Gemauschel': Jiddische Dichtung im Kampf der Sprachen," in Albrecht Schöne, ed., *Kontroversen: Alte und neue: Akten des VII. Internationalen*

But let us not quote only famous persons. Hermann Makower, in a biography of his father, a relatively unsuccessful grocer but fervent admirer of Mendelssohn, Lessing, and, above all, Schiller, reports, "He insisted absolutely that I speak German as purely as possible. He hated nothing more than the *jargon* that you heard all around. My grandfather also spoke beautiful German."[41]

The efforts of Jewish champions of emancipation to establish Jewish free schools that systematically taught High German are well documented.[42] Just as well known is the large program book written in 1844 by Anton Rée, a Hamburg Jew, entitled *Die Sprachverhältnisse der heutigen Juden, im Interesse der Gegenwart und mit besonderer Rücksicht auf Volkserziehung.* This text only demonstrates how resolutely the assimilation-minded Jewish opinion leaders assumed the typical viewpoint of the German citizen in matters of language. They asked what "nationality" meant and whether anything could be found that, unlike the religious differences, unlike the factual differences in opinion and circumstances, "produces a total impression and at the same time yields a *definite* characteristic? Something of the sort most definitely exists, and we have already mentioned it once, it is language."[43]

This text can also be used, however, to show just as clearly how the anti-Semites reacted to *jargon* − very differently from the state, which appeared to be compassionately and cautiously supportive in the realm of languages. First, though, let us look at the counterattack of the conservative forces on a second linguistic level, because, here again, it becomes evident how Jews, former Jews and German representatives of the majority culture stood on precisely the same ground. It is becoming increasingly clear that the Jews, driven by the pent-up hope of finally having

Germanisten-Kongresses, 11 vols. (Tübingen, 1986), 1:97. "Revolting gibberish," said Ludwig Börne in 1818 regarding the language of the − admittedly anti-Semitic − burlesque, "Unser Verkehr," in Ludwig Börne, *Sämtliche Schriften*, ed. Inge Rippmann and Peter Rippmann (Düsseldorf, 1964ff.), 1:417.

41 Monika Richarz, ed., *Jüdisches Leben in Deutschland*, vol. 1: *Selbstzeugnisse zur Sozialgeschichte, 1780−1871* (Stuttgart, 1976), 445.

42 See the comprehensive essay by Freimark, "Sprachverhalten und Assimilation," 240−61. The Jewish press monitored these efforts with continuous commentary and supportive essays, e.g., the 38-column essay by the Hamburg educator Emmanuel Wohlwill in *Sulamith* 7 (1848): cols. 25ff., with such core statements as "We all agree that, in our institutions, there is the need for double the attention to the language education of our youth, because neglect of this area is at the same time the cause and effect of the isolation, backwardness and one-sidedness which have yet to be completely eliminated" (ibid., col. 86). A report entitled "Jüdische Zustände in Hamburg," *Der Israelit des 19. Jahrhunderts* 6 (1845): 318, stated that "a good method of instruction in German language and style is being used." (I am grateful to Harald Egerland for assistance in the reading of these Jewish journals.)

43 Rée, *Die Sprachverhältnisse der heutigen Juden*, 118−19.

somewhere they could call home, identified very strongly with the receiving German culture and language, perhaps not least of all with the German because they sensed a structural identity there. It was precisely this identification that blinded them to such a degree that they ultimately saw eye to eye with the aggressors, trying with the fervor of converts even to outdo them.

It must be added that the old Jewish identity, centered on Yiddish (providing internal cohesion) and Hebrew, had its defenders among the orthodox Jews. The dominant direction of development, however, is so little disputed that one of the older studies draws a conclusion that is no different from the most recent position: Under the pressure and direction of the state, the transition from Jewish religious education to secular education "was completely successful."[44]

The Second Indicator: The Problem of Jewish Names

The second target aspect of language was names. This had significant anti-Semitic potential, since it was here that it would be decided whether the Jews were to be recognizable as Jews by their names, which – if so – would turn them into important identifying symbols for the anti-Semites.

When they were emancipated, the Jews had been given free choice of names in all states except for West Galicia.[45] Accordingly, their choices had been a mixture of typically new-style names such as *Rosenthal, Silberstein, Rosenberg*, and so forth, and typically old-style names such as *Levin, Kohn, Katz*, and so forth. Given names could be assigned anew each time a child was born. When the Jews, in their general scramble to do anything in their power to fulfill the assimilation pact, began to give their children more and more "German" names (*Friedrich, Wilhelm, Siegfried, Bernhard*, and so forth), the real Friedrich Wilhelm intervened in 1836 and – in keeping with the general, notorious anti-Semitic rollback of the restoration period – attempted by means of a language decree to broaden the dividing line between the Jews and the majority culture. The Jews were forbidden from choosing "Christian baptismal names."

---

44 Carlebach, "Der Säkulierungsprozess," 93 and, as the most recent position, Helmut Berding and Dorothee Schimpf, "Assimilation und Identität: Probleme des jüdischen Schul- und Erziehungswesens in Hessen-Kassel im Zeitalter der Emanzipation," in Bernhard Giesen, ed., *Nationale und kulturelle Identität: Studien zur Entwicklung des kollektiven Bewusstseins in der Neuzeit* (Frankfurt/Main, 1991), 382: "In short, right down the line, the state pushed through its right to regimentation and control."

45 Bering, *Der Name als Stigma*, 52–3, 409–10.

The difficulties this decree presented the otherwise willing royal ministries, difficulties that were ultimately acknowledged to be insurmountable, are described in detail in my study *Der Name als Stigma* (The stigma of names).[46] The book describes how and why the administration finally had to admit that there was no fundamental difference between Christian and Jewish forenames. There could be none, for the Christian names – *Joseph, Maria, Joachim* – were Hebrew/Jewish names, names of the very religion from which Christianity arose. Both Jews and Christians were at home – including onomastically – in the ancient world with its Greek and Roman names. And Jews had lived in the lands of the Teutons and Celts since the fourth century! Thus, nearly all forenames were more or less common European property, unsuitable for drawing the desired sort of boundary. Similarly, the surnames chosen in 1812 really offered no basis for a new strategy of exclusion through stigmatized marking of names. The Jews had been allowed to choose freely in 1812. Thus, they chose "German" names (cf. *Rosenberg*, already cited), just as the Germans, in turn, had carried surnames of Old Testament origin since time immemorial, and particularly since the Reformation, including such "core Jewish" names as *Levi* and *Israel*.

Although I need only repeat the conclusions of this study here, I also wish particularly to emphasize a significant, although previously unknown, source to which I paid only minimal attention in the book – the names report written by Dr. J. H. R. Biesenthal (1800-86), a converted Jew and employee of the Berlin Jewish Mission.[47] Its drafting was commissioned by the Prussian minister of the interior, who was actually quite amenable to renewing the exclusion of the Jews. The report was to recommend the best restrictions to be placed on the minority in their selection of names. Biesenthal produced a counterpart – completely unknown until recently – to Leopold Zunz's famous work on the *Namen der Juden* (Jewish names). Quite unlike that founder of the science of Judaism, Biesenthal argued at the conclusion of his text of 248 pages not for the maintenance of existing freedoms but for the institution of restrictive measures.[48] It is interesting to discover the theoretical basis he

---

46 Bering, *The Stigma of Names*, 44–75.
47 The title read: "Kritischer Versuch über den Sprach-, Volks- und Religionsgeschichtlichen Ursprung der jüdischen Vornamen, nebst einer Beantwortung der Frage: Ist es den Juden gestattet, sich christlicher Vornamen zu bedienen." The original was incorporated into the files of the Royal Civil Cabinet, Central State Archives, Merseburg, Civil Cab. 23687, 175–91.
48 He argued against Christian names and for a list of "names in the Hebrew language," to be sanctioned by the synagogue.

used. Even on the title page, he inserted a quotation from Herder. He then states in the introduction:

The reason I have dealt with language and the national character as a general introduction in the second chapter is to express my views regarding the historical and moral value of these things, in order to indicate the vantage point from which I observe Jewish history, which is at times judged too highly and at other times not highly enough.[49]

His argument was therefore based on linguistic philosophy. Referring again to Herder, he then took forty pages to demonstrate that there was nothing that defined the Hebraic people more clearly than its language.[50] Hebrew, according to Biesenthal, was on an undeniably lower level because, not unlike the language of the Hottentots, it could express only concrete concepts and could arrange the parts of a sentence only in a natural sequence and not according to their intellectual force; the subject was always at the beginning because it was the symbol of the old patriarchal structure of the people; science was not possible in Hebrew, because the language could never address objects without their attributes, that is, always "birds *of the sky*," which was yet another hindrance to real thinking, to *putare*, which means "to cut off, separate." Envy, suppressed hate, imitation, hypocrisy, Biesenthal continued, this repertoire of the Slavs, who had no more sensitivity than Negroes or house pets, also dominated among the Jews, who – expelled from all civil circumstances – were left with only the Talmud, out of the murk of which Mendelssohn alone had attempted to lead the way. Obviously, a misunderstood, trivialized Herder – that gateway figure of the German movement – was godfather to the deductions of this raving convert, and to those of others as well.[51]

In keeping with his Herder-based viewpoint, Biesenthal proceeded directly from the necessary parallel between the spirit of the language and the intellectual constitution of an entire people to the recommendation of his report. Because the Jews were still a separate (peculiar) ethnic group, he counseled, certain names had to be allotted to them, so that the internal and the external would be in agreement. Yet, Prussian ministerial officials were not so blind in 1841 that they could not see the intermixing that had been practiced in the world of names since time

---

49 Biesenthal, "Kritischer Versuch," 176.
50 Ibid., 183–203.
51 Abraham Geiger's fundamental lecture on Jewish literary history also mentions Herder, saying that, through his specifically aesthetic perspective, Herder reintroduced the Jews to their pure, unadulterated Hebrew. Abraham Geiger, *Der Israelit des 19. Jahrhunderts* 7 (1846): 83.

immemorial. Certainly, they regretted the fact, easily recognized by any objective observer, that the names had no power of distinction and could not provide a reliable tool for governmental handling of intolerance. Reason prevailed, however, and they drew the necessary conclusions from the irrefutable evidence. They released all given names for both Christians and Jews, except for those names that referred literally to the savior (*Christian, Christoph*, and so forth). A very similar delineation attempt, namely, to return to the usage of addressing Jews officially with the title of "Jew," was decisively rejected by both the ministries and the rulers themselves.[52]

In summary, we can say that the governmental sector, although it responded in an entirely anti-Semitic and reactionary manner on many points, remained liberal at first in the area of language, where the Jews were making particular efforts at assimilation. This was true until, precisely at the turn of the twentieth century, it took a fateful step in the direction of racism in the matter of names. It is impossible to understand how the authorities were forced into this without first taking a closer look at reactions of anti-Semites to issues of language and names.

THE REACTION OF THE ANTI-SEMITES TO THE GERMAN OF THE JEWS

Positive government rulings and the support of the government in language matters were by no means the end of the story. There was often a great discrepancy between the intentions of government offices and the actual behavior of the citizens on a cultural and sociopsychological level. The result, then, depended decisively on how the government responded to such a gap. This will play a decisive role below when we discuss subsequent developments in the issue of names. For now, let us pursue the question of Yiddish and *jüdeln* to the point where one could no longer speak of the German Jews having their own idiom.

Corruption by Jüdeln: The Contamination of the German Language, the Anti-Semitic Imagined Language Behind the Real One

It is undisputed that there was a striking difference between Jews and Christians in the German states at the time of emancipation, and this

---

52 Bering, *Der Name als Stigma*, 74–9, citing several sources.

was true on all levels. The resolutely anti-Jewish Johann Ludolf Holst describes this, as do many others, in an extremely graphic manner. The men, he said, would appear in semi-Eastern garb, nearly all of them with dirty, disgusting beards down to their waists,

> as if they were not already more than characteristic, more than highly conspicuous with the coal-black, curly hair, the arching eyebrows, . . . the sharp crooked Eastern noses, the mouth more open due to those repugnant guttural sounds that are so peculiar to the Hebrews, . . . the Jewish dialect made unignorable by its piercing, bellowing sound.[53]

It is worth noting that even at this early date the loud voice was interpreted as an attempt at suppression. However, it was conceded even for the period before 1818 that, as a result of Lessing's and Herder's efforts, the more civilized Jews had begun "to move closer and closer to the Christians, to pass through the doors of public assembly places, and to make the differences less noticeable in clothing, in conduct and even in regard to that revolting, unbearable language,"[54] a process that was not necessarily viewed with approval.

The date at which pure High German became the general norm among Jews remains uncertain. In his fundamental work on *Die Sprachverhältnisse der heutigen Juden* (1844), Rée stated that even in the progressive Hamburg of his day, a typical Jewish manner of speaking still came through. In contrast, Abraham Geiger, the emphatic adherent of reform, stated the following in 1846:

> The Hebrew language is no longer a part of Jewish lives, and it is no longer the language of the educated. Their intellectual life now flows to them freshly in the language of the fatherland, which has become the medium for thoughts and outlooks on life. . . . Jews no longer need a special, distinctively cast institution for general education; they participate intellectually in everything that stirs the German people; they receive directly what the Germans produce, and they produce right along with them. For their religious matters, . . . for those alone, special journals have begun to appear recently in rapid succession, but all in German, although the tenor of such publications may be extremely traditional. This alone should be proof that Germany's Jews, to the extent it is within their control, have become Jewish Germans in the fullest possible sense.[55]

---

53 Conrad F. von Schmidt-Phiseldek, *Über das Verhältnis der Juden zu den Christen in den deutschen Handelsstädten: In weltbürgerlicher Hinsicht vorgetragen, und allen Staatsmännern des gesammten Vaterlandes zu ernsthaften Prüfung dargelegt* (Leipzig, 1818), 11–12.

54 Ibid., 98–9.

55 Lecture by Rabbi Dr. Geiger before the Silesian Society for Culture of the Fatherland on Feb. 3, 1846, published in Geiger, *Der Israelit des 19. Jahrhunderts* 7 (1846): 84.

Rée's assessment may have been too pessimistic, as was claimed in reviews at the time, and that of Abraham Geiger may have been premature.[56] It is certain, however, that actual developments were proceeding in the direction he described. However, precisely in times of high pressure for homogeneity, precisely when there is a standard of pure language that stands as a symbol for the entire (cultural) nation, it is completely plausible that a despised dialect would produce exactly the kind of reactions Rée forcefully described:

> Even the most casual contact of a stranger with an individual distinguished by the dialect in question brings on ridicule and derision; we are not concerned here with whether or not this is just; . . . one could storm the batteries or be Horatius Cocles II, all that would be insignificant compared to the heroism involved for even a person of clear insight and a loving heart to patiently endure the laughter that is apparently licensed by custom. . . . One mocking expression from the Christian, and the Jew, even the best and the mildest, will be miles away from that heart.[57]

Just such experiences, however, which educators like Rée compiled into comprehensive works on the systematic fight against the Jewish manner of speaking, plus the unlimited will to do their utmost to assimilate, brought German-born Jews at least by the 1870s to precisely that level of linguistic competence that Geiger had claimed for them in the 1850s.

Jacob Toury argued convincingly in an essay that the Jews in particular were strongly identified with High German. All Germans spoke some dialect which, even if it was not valued particularly highly, was at least a permissible means of expressing oneself. The Jews, rather, parted ways

---

56 Critical reviews have said that the "strange publication" takes its subject all too seriously and exaggerates if it believes that all social reforms depend on the Jewish dialect; it will disappear automatically "as soon as a truly educated spirit and genuine patriotic sense is impressed on the hearts of our youth," certainly the easier view to defend linguistically (*Der Israelit des 19. Jahrhunderts* 6 [1885]: 63–4). A more positive assessment came eight issues later in the same journal, 121–4. The reviewer for the *Allgemeine Zeitung des Judentums* comes out against Rée, while expressing admiration for him. For seventy years, he argues, the Jews have made "enormous" progress on the road to assimilation; their entire reality has been "miraculously transformed"; "There may still be a good bit of *mauscheln* among the Jews, but for the most part, their speech is correct and proper" (*Allgemeine Zeitung des Judentums* [Leipzig and Berlin, 1837–1922] 9 [1845]: 142). Regarding very early progress in linguistic assimilation made during Lessing's time, although admittedly lost to some degree after emancipation, see Holst, *Über das Verhältnis der Juden zu den Christen*, 99. Leopold Zunz is certainly far ahead of his time when he reports, in the chapter on "The Present" in his famous book *Die gottesdienstlichen Vorträge der Juden* (Berlin, 1832), that the Jewish-German dialect departed with the Polish teachers (449), and that Jewish German has been "completely" displaced since the "emancipation of the Jews coincided with civilized laws which always favor the German language" (452) – here again the emphasis on the helpful hand of the government in matters of language.

57 Zunz, *Die gottesdienstlichen Vorträge der Juden*, 40–1.

entirely with their completely reviled idiom. Just as they were perhaps particularly pure Germans because they lacked the old roots as Bavarians, Hessians, and Prussians (the Jews did not become citizens of these states until the states had already begun to move in the direction of "empire"), they were in fact often the speakers of the purest German as well. In Toury's words, "A German professor could speak Saxon, Swabian, Viennese, or the German of Berlin or Goethe's Frankfurt. But an educated Jew spoke High German. . . . For [he] did not belong to the autochthonous language group of his place of residence."[58] Toury then modified his statement:

And when he spoke Viennese, for example, a suggestion of his mother and father tongue was often mixed in – as in his High German intonation as well. The initiation of language in the larynx, the vowel shading, the linguistic melody of early childhood can be overcome only by the most musically talented of people, and then only after much practice and disappointment.[59]

Modern linguistics confirms this analysis, with a few corrections, and draws from it decisive conclusions. The limit for irreversible idiosyncrasies is puberty. In other words, unrestricted command of not just one but several languages, with completely pure pronunciation, is possible for those who speak them before puberty. This had radical consequences for the Jewish minority, as well as for the strategies of rejection. The generation born after emancipation, and certainly that born around 1840–50, were unlimited in their linguistic competence. Therefore, whereas representatives of the majority culture during Rée's time were able to react as he had described, later anti-Semites had to look for angles other than linguistic ones – at least as long as they remained realistic.

In the case of Richard Wagner, we find a specific trick for disconnecting from linguistic reality. In his anti-Jewish pamphlet *Das Judenthum in der Musik* (Jews and music) of 1850, barely a decade after Rée, he stated, "The Jew speaks the language of the nation in which he lives from generation to generation, but he always speaks it as a foreigner. . . . To truly write literature in a foreign language has never yet been possible, even for the greatest geniuses." "We" are particularly offended by the strictly sensual proclamations regarding the Jewish language. It was said to be a "foreign and unpleasant," "hissing, shrill, droning, bungled kind of

---

58 Toury, "Die Sprache als Problem," 84. Also of interest is his general thesis that "Although they, i.e., the Jews, assimilated to the local dialect, they did so on a higher level than the local residents," who spoke their local dialect, while the Jews tended to speak the supraregional dialect (87).
59 Toury, "Die Sprache als Problem," 84.

sound," in short, "gibberish."[60] Spurious linguistic argumentation (foreign, hissing, shrill) progressed quite openly to pure insult (bungled, gibberish). More important still was the apodictic tone of the judgment. It was not restricted to Jews who retained a Yiddish element in their speech, and there was no special role for the increasing number who spoke pure German. It applied to *everyone* – despite centuries of putting down roots.

In this way, the position held by Wagner offered a handle when these linguistic attributes were obviously *not* evident (any longer). One could flee into mysticism: "He is not speaking as a German." A quotation from the anti-Semitic literary scholar Otto Hauser will show that this arch of reasoning, of which another anti-Semitic literary scholar, Adolf Bartels,[61] considered himself a pillar, stretched to 1933: "Nothing separates the Jew – any Jew – so sharply from the Aryan German as his complete inability to speak and write German in a German manner."[62]

60 Richard Wagner, "Das Judenthum in der Musik" (1850/1869) in Richard Wagner, *Gesammelte Schriften und Dichtungen*, 10 vols. (Leipzig, 1872), 5:70–1. His remarks are similar regarding Jewish music, the essence of which he relates to that of Jewish language: "[Regarding music in the synagogue], who has not been seized by the most objectionable sensation, a mixture of horror and absurdity, when hearing that gurgling, yodeling, babble which is a confusion to mind and spirit, and which no intentional caricature could contort more repugnantly" (76). The thesis that the intonation of the Jews, in particular, was inescapably un-German was still being defended in the Weimar Republic, e.g., by Wilhelm Stapel, *Über das seelische Problem der Symbiose des deutschen und des jüdischen Volkes* (Hamburg, 1928), 42, and by the race researcher Günther (see Römer, *Sprachwissenschaft und Rasseideologie*, 172). See also the complaint by Stapel, *Über das seelische Problem*, 42, regarding the many gutturals and the aggressive sentence rhythm of Jewish speakers. Early on, Nathan Birnbaum introduced the argument that this alleged dissonance could only be perceived by "ears accustomed to German" (Nathan Birnbaum, "Die Sprachen des jüdischen Volkes," in Nathan Birnbaum, *Ausgewählte Schriften zur jüdischen Frage*, 2 vols. [Czernowitz, 1910], 2:319).

61 As did many others, Adolf Bartels, *Nationale oder universale Literaturwissenschaft: Eine Kampfschrift gegen Hanns Martin Elster und Michard M. Meyer* (Munich, 1925), 37, cited the popular theory of the mimicking nature of the Jews, which allowed *any* visible manifestation, apparently including pure High German speech, to be denounced as mere pretense. "Even we laymen know that Jewish literature in German has a different sound than true German literature . . . and we recognize Jewish German prose as such: e.g., we sense quite clearly where Ludwig Börne slips into Yiddish, as well as certain Judaisms in modern newspaper style" (ibid., 42). "But those without German blood can also not have a full share of the German language" (ibid., 94); "the German language is essentially a foreign tongue for him, and remains so even though he appears to have a command of it" and "Are these really natural sounds in Heine?" (Adolf Bartels, *Heinrich Heine: Auch ein Denkmal* [Dresden, 1906], 95, 231); see also 215, about Heine's language.

62 Adolf Bartels, *Geschichte der deutschen Literatur*, Kleine Ausgabe, nos. 11, 12 (Hamburg, 1933), 16. These were not just occasional outpourings from the nationalist/academic milieu. Ignaz Goldziher, e.g., reports in his journal on August 14, 1894, of having to listen to the following appraisal of the Countess Levetzow in the Tutzinger Castle during his vacation: "None of them [those of the 'Jewish race'] knew German; even Ebers' writings were edited by Guthe in Leipzig; you can tell right away from the style that the author is a Jew" (Ignaz Goldziher, *Tagebuch*, ed. A. Scheiber [Leiden, 1978], 179). Even mysticisms of this sort were only offshoots from much more comprehensive thought structures. As early as 1905, an article on "Stärkung des deutschen

Naturally, a position that was so extremely counter to the clear visual and audible evidence carried with it an inconvenience, or more precisely, the need for a process of reinterpretation. Two such routes were taken. The first shall be explored now, the second later. It was a special application of the assumption investigated by Sander L. Gilman that was repeatedly made about the Jews – that they had their own, albeit concealed, language.[63] When the variation was no longer actually audible, then one had to show the Jewish manner of speaking *behind* the external facade, and then the *jüdeln* suddenly appeared again after all. I list cases of this sort, as well as others that served a similar function. One very well documented case is that of Edith Krohn, an actress whose career was jeopardized in 1910 when it was discovered that she was a Jew, for from this time forward many people began to hear that her speech was indeed not quite clear but had a trace of the Jewish in it.[64] Yiddish expressions were inserted contemptuously into the statements of Jews: Bartels called the reasoning of his opponents *Geseiere*.[65] Anti-Semitic pamphlets in the 1890s were often still written entirely in derisive *jargon*,[66] and those that were written in High German were liberally sprinkled with Yiddish expressions and orthography. A single exclamation such as "*Weh!*" or "*haisst*" (spelled with *ai*) had an exposing function.[67] Dramas and novels included characters speaking in a Jewish manner in order to show the reality of the Jews behind their facade and to prove that they really cannot be assimilated.[68] When even the distortionary

Wesens durch die deutsche Schule" in *Der Hammer: Blätter für deutschen Sinn* (no. 4, 272), the anti-Semitic journal with the widest circulation, began with the following amazing statement (which is a very effective rejection tool): "It is not to be denied. The character of the German man today has taken on many un-German features. It is hard to argue with those who claim that the thinking, emotions, and actions of the majority of Germans are no longer German at all." Such mysterious notions were capable of pulling the rug out from under people's own forthright self-assessment as well as from the objective facts. In 1913, for example, *Der Hammer* made the following pronouncement regarding Eastern Jews and the cultural life of Berlin: "[The Eastern Jew] himself – in his words – has overcome the obstacles of a foreign land and a language that was often foreign to him" (299). Of course, such odd claims were not backed up by concrete linguistic analysis.

63 Sander L. Gilman, *Jüdischer Selbsthass: Antisemitismus und die verborgene Sprache der Juden* (Frankfurt/Main, 1993), pt. 3: *Assimilation and Race Theory*, 95–262.

64 Bering, *Der Name als Stigma*, 207, 247, as well as the Nazi judgment of the "German" of the true verbal powerhouse Alfred Kerr, n. 70.

65 Yiddish for "ramblings."

66 E.g., Ernst Stusslieb, *Der Aufgeblasene Talmudlöwe: Ergötzliche und lehrreiche Gespräche des Herrn Schochet Isidor Eisenstein mit seinem Sohne Moritz* (Würzburg, 1892).

67 See, e.g., *Der Mauscheljude, von einem deutschen Advokaten: Ein Volksbüchlein für deutsche Christen allen Bekenntnisse*, 4th ed. (Paderborn, 1880), 4, 10, 13–14, 21.

68 E.g., Hans Peter Althaus, "Soziolekt und Fremdsprache: Das Jiddische als Stilmittel in der deutschen Literatur," *Zeitschrift für deutsche Philologie*, special issue: *Jiddisch* 100 (1981): 226, regarding

powers of the anti-Semites were no longer able to make out anything Jewish in the apparently pure speech, then the "language problem . . . became a problem of intention and content." *Mauscheln* – that is, speaking like Mausche (Yiddish for Moses) – became a pseudolinguistic category that, in reality, was intended only to mean the pernicious content of the speech.[69]

Of course, knowledge of the Jewish dialect and thus the chance to simply impose Yiddish or Jewish *jargon* were also kept alive by the collections of jokes in circulation,[70] by the special lingo of certain tradesmen – for example, livestock dealers[71] – and by the newly arrived Jews from Poland and Eastern Europe, who often, in fact, did still retain the old way of speaking.[72] The negative tradition alone, however, would have been sufficient to make the anti-Yiddish polemics work flawlessly against people speaking not Yiddish but the finest High German. This was done, for example, in Goebbels's rabble-rousing newspaper *Der Angriff*, which stated in 1928 that one could correspond with the Berlin police headquarters only in Yiddish, because that was the only language understood there.[73] The same publication later called Alfred Kerr "the *beeg* literary authority of Mosse."[74] With the exclamation "new Goiman all around," party leader Marauhn was said to have ingratiated himself

---

Dinter's composition "Die Sünde wider das Blut"; Mark H. Gelber, "Das Judendeutsch in der deutschen Literatur: Einige Beispiele von den frühesten Lexika bis Gustav Freytag und Thomas Mann," in Stéphane Moses and Albrecht Schöne, eds., *Juden in der deutschen Literatur* (Frankfurt/Main, 1986), 165: "Jewish German functioned as an important, recurring element in German literary anti-Semitism," and regarding the de facto anti-Semitic effect of the Yiddish in Gustav Freytag's *Soll und Haben* (3 vols. [Philadelphia, 1855]), see 170, 175.

69 Derived from Toury, "Die Sprache als Problem," 92, certainly the most in-depth article on the issues addressed here.

70 E.g, Chaim Jossel, *Schabbes-Schmus: Schmonzes Berjonzes*, 41st ed. (Berlin, 1912); *190 gepfefferte Jüdische Witze und Anekdoten* (Weissensee bei Berlin, n.d.).

71 See Althaus, "Die jiddische Sprache," *Germania Judaica*, n.s. 14, no. 4 (1965): 1–23, and n.s. 23, no. 1 (1968): 1–2; E. Bischoff explains the necessity of his *Jüdisch-Deutscher Dolmetscher: Ein praktisches Jargon-Wörterbuch*, 3d ed. (Leipzig, 1901), 6, by saying that knowledge of Jewish *jargon* was "indispensable for everyone in close commercial contact with the lower Jewish business classes, e.g., with livestock dealers, produce and second-hand goods dealers, peddlers, etc." See also Toury, "Die Sprache als Problem," 87, regarding this essentially ritualized merchants' language.

72 The Berlin anti-Semitism conflict popularized Treitschke's dictum regarding the "trouser-selling Eastern Jew" who soon weaseled his way to the top with shadowy business deals in order to occupy the nerve centers of the German economy. On this subject, see Trude Maurer, *Ostjuden in Deutschland* (Hamburg, 1986), 29, especially regarding the Jews' "ugly and ridiculous language, their clothing and anything else that seems worthy of derision and indignation."

73 *Angriff* 49 (1928): 5.

74 Ibid., 22 (1929): 2, where this oft-assailed man is especially scorned for actually defending Yiddish (quite rightly) with the argument that it is a "good old piece of linguistic heritage from the Middle Ages," which was said to be correct insofar as "the 'German' of Mr. Kerr is a throwback to certain infantile areas of linguistic imperfection."

with the Reichsbanner and promptly founded the "Goiman State Party,"[75] all of this garnished with the recurring "*Weh!*": for example, "Lenchen Mayer with the soft 'ay' fell into disfavor with Herr Böss. Oi, weh!"[76]

Or what was considered Yiddish was simply put directly into the mouth of despised persons such as Leopold Jessner, the Berlin director who carried out a thorough modernization and chose not to degenerate amid the dust-covered props and interpretive stuffiness of the grandiose Wilhelmine theater. For this, he was badgered in the theater column of *Der Angriff*: "Who says Schiller, Goethe and Shakespeare meant it like dat? Couldn't we say dey meant it some udder vay? – And Reb Ephraim Leopold Jessner Jeiteles determined that the classic authors coulda meant it some udder vay."[77] Everyone understood what was intended in each case: They do not belong to us; they will remain Jews forever because they do not have command of the code that creates the culture and the nation and that is the proof of Germanness. Indeed, they scoff at things German.

This was certainly an effective strategy of exclusion, effective because it did precisely what was impossible in view of the facts. It denied all of the assimilation that the Jews had accomplished and made them what they actually no longer were – unassimilated Jewish Jews. I demonstrate subsequently that anti-Semitism could behave even more radically without this spurious reasoning, which was patently false and could so quickly be revealed as a pretext. In other words, we will see how the Jews could be excluded without any explanation whatsoever but simply by means of aggressive rejection. First, though, let us look at one more area in which the battle was waged with spurious reasoning. The older argument that the Jewish language was contemptible because it was primitive, backward-looking, and existed prior to any linguistic refinement is immediately revealed as completely baseless when we look at exactly the opposite rejection technique, the claim of the "corruptive modernity of Jewish language usage."

---

75 Ibid., 61 (1930): 1; see also "Daitsche Staatsbirger jiddischen Glaubens," ibid., 62 (1930): 9.

76 Ibid., 24 (1929): 13 (refers to the Jewish fencer and the Lord Mayor of Berlin); see also the manner of speech of a Jewish moneylender in ibid., 72 (1930): 9: "*Se nehmen m'r nur mai Zait!*" [You're just wasting my time!] (regarding the actual, more phonetically accurate transcription, see top of page); for the abundant use of the signal "*Weh*," I cite the following from ibid., 1 (1927): 3; 24 (1928): 5; 23 (1928): 5; 39 (1929): 3; 42 (1929): 3; 35 (1929): 6, 12; 52 (1930): 2, among many.

77 Ibid., 36 (1929): 6.

Progressive Corruption: The Jewish Language of the Press

There can be no dispute regarding the functional goal of anti-Semitism. Those, such as nationalist conservatives, who did not want to accept reality had to find reasons for the pervasive phenomena of the period of industrial restructuring, that is, for the phenomena specific to the bureaucratic state and mass culture, and these reasons did not disclose the actual basis of the upheaval. "The Jews are our misfortune." This dictum from one so apparently serious as Heinrich von Treitschke set the tone, and not only in relation to politics and economics. Who was to thank for such "un-German" developments as (1) the press, that public institution without which life is unimaginable; (2) the mass press, that unavoidable consequence of increased participation in opinion-making, ultimately by all classes; and (3) the daily press, with its unique topical requirements, with a style increasingly removed from that middle-class elite language promoted as the continuation of distinguished, refined classical diction? For anti-Semites, the answer was always the same.

That Jews played a prominent role in the German press as publishers, journalists, and indeed as bearers of German culture generally was not a figment of the anti-Semitic imagination.[78] In 1893 H. K. Lenz published the following rhyme on the subject in an 1893 anti-Semitic pamphlet:

> Herr Zwiebeles, Herr Knobeles,
> Herr Schimpfeles, Herr Lobeles,
> Herr Schundeles, Herr Pfandeles,
> Herr Spotteles, Herr Schandeles,
> These are the masters of critique,
> The noble roundtable;
> They praise each new work.
> It smells like the same old group.[79]

---

78 The prominent position of the Jews, particularly in the liberal press, has often been emphasized; see Peter Gay, "Der berlinisch-jüdische Geist: Zweifel an einer Legende," in Peter Gay, *Freud, Juden und andere Deutsche: Herren und Opfer in der modernen Kultur* (Munich, 1989), 190–3, and Barbara Suchy, "Die jüdische Presse im Kaiserreich und in der Weimarer Republik," in Julius H. Schoeps, ed., *Juden als Träger bürgerlicher Kultur in Deutschland* (Stuttgart, 1989), 169, 311–28. Hortzitz, *"Früh-Antisemitismus" in Deutschland*, 90, 225 shows the use of the term "newspaper Jew" even during the early anti-Semitic period. Regarding anti-Semitic language in the area of the press, see Christoph Cobet, *Der Wortschatz des Antisemitismus in der Bismarckzeit*, Münchner Germanistische Beiträge, no. 11 (Munich, 1973), 72–6. Accusations of Yiddishisms in the press are found in essentially every anti-Semitic pamphlet; see, e.g., the chapter "Fort mit der Mauschelpresse," in *Der Mauscheljude* (1880), 27–30; in the anti-Semitic press, see also *Der Hammer*, no. 5 (1906): 510; no. 9 (1910): 58; no. 10 (1911): 265, and many other occurrences.
79 "Herr Zwiebeles" refers to an onion and "Herr Knobeles" refers to garlic (*Knobel* is idiomatic for *Knoblauch* or garlic) – both allude to the supposed garlic breath of Jews; "Herr Schimpfeles" and "Herr Lobeles" refer to *Schimpf* (insult) and *Lob* (praise), respectively, and allude to Jewish

Thus, the critic "Schundeles" also promoted low quality. Although that may well have been the primary substantive intent here, as elsewhere,[80] the Jews were also expressly charged with having internalized the stylistic modernism of the newspapers. Ferdinand Kürnberger, who was the first (in 1860 and 1876) to study the linguistic modernization phenomenon in the press, saw not *only* bad sides to these changes, which he said aired new levels of style and language. Kürnberger forecast that the "written language will be more and more the language of journalism."[81] To be sure, he wrote, the progressive integration of conversational and lower-register elements of popular speech yielded greater strength and emphasis, which the press definitely needed.[82] However, he added, it was still a "disaster." He titled the chapter "Vulgar Newspaper Style." He described the second aberration, the increasing militancy of the language of opinion in the press, as follows: "Having grown old with *tjost* and *buhurt*,[83] we see the famous knight Aaron Mendel *tilting* for the duty-free import of yarn and 'Simon Frankel' even 'breaking his lance' for the duty-free import of rags."[84]

The concept that a modern, democratic public (long delayed in the German lands) should thrash out ideas was generally thought by the conservatives to be merely a Jewish maneuver aimed at destroying the language of the old elite idiom, which had promised unity. For modern researchers, however, at least since the publication by Otto Brunner, Werner Conze, and Reinhart Koselleck of *Geschichtliche Grundbegriffe* (Historical basic terms and concepts), it has been an obvious characteristic of language since the nineteenth century. The scapegoat theory was thus at work here, too. Jewish manipulations were simply all there was to modern newspaper language. Since the Jews were also notable exponents of the modern culture of large cities,[85] and the modern newspaper

"masters of critique"; "Herr Schundeles" and "Herr Schandeles" refer to *Schund* (pulp literature) and *Schande* (disgrace). See H. K. Lenz, *Judenliteratur und Literaturjuden: aus Sebastian Brunner's Werken dargestellt* (Münster/Westphalia, 1893), 33.

80 Similar style and polemical use of names in the article "Eine Schwäche unserer nationalen Presse," *Der Hammer*, no. 3 (1904): 50: "They praise one another right out of the mud. What Cohn writes, Levy and Meyer immediately interpret as 'brilliant.'"

81 Ferdinand Kürnberger, *Feuilletons*, selected and with an introd. by K. Riha (Frankfurt/Main, 1967), 25; see the selections "Sprache und Zeitungen," 1866 and "Die Blumen des Zeitungsstils," 1872.

82 Kürnberger, *Feuilletons*, 10.

83 Middle High German terms used by knights in jousting.

84 Kürnberger, *Feuilletons*, 4–5.

85 An often described fact; see Reinhard Rürup, *Emanzipation und Antisemitismus: Studien zur "Judenfrage" der bürgerlichen Gesellschaft* (Göttingen, 1975), 166, 823, which has so far been acknowledged only by Toury, "Die Sprache als Problem," 89ff., with respect to the linguistic consequences.

industry was genuinely connected to these congested areas, all the pieces once again appeared to fit together. The Jews were the profiteers and orchestrators of modern city life, which was considered a monstrosity born of civilization and the destruction of German culture, and the Jews spoke only in a "language of civilization," in which "concepts bound by blood" did not exist.[86] A deep tradition plus the firmly fixed relationship to basic consciousness-structuring ideas (antithesis of culture and civilization) yielded a situation in which the appeal in 1927 of *Der Hammer: Blätter für den deutschen Sinn*, the best-known anti-Semitic journal, seemed plausible to more than just the most intractable anti-Semites:

When the unsophisticated German-Teutonic man speaks, he speaks German which is true to its blood; when the Jew speaks "German," he speaks "Jewish German." Reducing all of this to a short formula: if we remove the dominating influence of the Jews from the German newspaper and publishing industry, we will immediately heal all of the damage to German newspaper language.[87]

Such absurd assertions gain further internal plausibility when one remembers that, for example, the "readiness," the urgency of topicality in the press, which indeed subjected language usage to new standards, was attributed by this same anti-Semitic journal as early as 1906 to typical Jewish cunning, zeal for profit, and cold-heartedness.[88] These properties, the journal explained, were what made it possible to write about anything and everything on an ad hoc basis, whereas Germans faced with some catastrophic event might first falter or even waste time offering assistance. For people whose ideas were based on such a foundation, it was of course consistent to hope that a "healing of the national life" would result from reform of the press, where "on a daily basis thousands of counterfeiters and poisoners are still allowed to inject their caustic drops into our minds unimpeded." Their concrete appeal, then, as

---

86 Quotations in Ruth Römer, *Sprachwissenschaft und Rassenideologie in Deutschland* (Munich, 1985), 174.

87 *Der Hammer*, no. 26 (1927): 78, as commentary on the eighteenth competition of the Deutscher Sprachverein (German language society): "Damage to German Newspaper Language, Its Causes and Its Cure." *Der Hammer*, no. 2 (1903): 292–3, had previously proclaimed, following a piece extolling "Wagner's love for humanity," that the French phrase was becoming so disgustingly prevalent in newspaper jargon "that the battle for a respectable, honorable German language has gradually become a vital question for our people"; Wilhelm Stapel made a similar statement in his nationalist-conservative journal *Deutsches Volkstum* (1921): 48–9. "They speak our language, use our concepts. . . . But their blood and soul are Jewish, so language and concepts become an artificial means to express their own tradition," followed by attacks on the strong position of the Jews as art dealers and critics, and in the newspaper and publishing industries. It was consistent with this worldview that the *Alldeutsche Blätter* 4 (1894): 50–1, ran an article on "those of foreign language and race in the German Empire."

88 *Der Hammer*, no. 5 (1906): 506.

early as 1906, was that only "German men be allowed to write German newspapers."[89]

Of course, modern linguists saw only a new stylistic form of the language where many on the Right detected a corruption of the German spirit and German language.[90]

Distinguishing Language and Spirit:
The "Realistic" Interpretation, or the Arrival of Racism

It became increasingly difficult to back up the assertions presented in the last section with the argument that the Jews did not speak proper German. The liberal press, led by the *Frankfurter Zeitung*, the *Vossische Zeitung*, and the *Berliner Tageblatt*, were prime examples. The editorials of a Theodor Wolff, for example, were considered then, and would still be considered, substantive and stylistic masterpieces of journalism. To demonstrate one of the culminations of anti-Semitic illogic, how could the anti-Semites applaud the famous article by the Jewish Moritz Goldstein in 1912, which appeared in *Kunstwart* under the headline "Deutschjüdischer Parnass" (German-Jewish Parnassus)? After all the article demonstrated that the Jews dominated the entire German cultural heritage, theater, and literature. How, then, could anti-Semites continue propagating their thesis that the Jews lacked proper German? With such a crass logical contradiction, which even the feeblest mind could expose, the strategy of rejection had to be placed on a different foundation. I encountered indications of such a change in direction in what is probably the most important anti-Semitic journal, *Der Hammer*, published in Leipzig under the editorial pen of the infamous Theodor Fritsch. Once I was on the track, I systematically combed through ten volumes (1902–13).[91]

Naturally, I found a plethora of statements that fit the discourse presented so far. These included the assertion that the Jews exerted pressure

---

89 Ibid., 510. Although a warning may have been issued not to imagine *too* close a dependency between a specific spirit and a specific language, statements were then added which did more to provoke fear than to reduce hatred of the Jews.

90 See Gerhard Kettmann, "Die Existenzformen der deutschen Sprache im 19. Jahrhundert – ihre Entwicklung und ihr Verhältnis zueinander unter den Bedingungen der industriellen Revolution," in Joachim Schildt, ed., *Auswirkungen der industriellen Revolution auf die deutsche Sprachentwicklung im 19. Jahrhundert* (Berlin, 1981), 34–97. All linguists are unanimous that the language of radio and newspapers has much more influence on the style of language today than the classical language ever did.

91 I am grateful to Christian Kassung for help with the reading.

on the language through the press,[92] and that this was leading to a creeping infiltration of German culture,[93] the linguistic consequence of which was that "the masses stirred into a state of confusion by the Semitic whip associate words with different concepts than we do."[94] When this problem was seen in connection with the old thesis of language as a constituent of the nation, the journal stated, "the sparkling French phrase is becoming so disgustingly prevalent in newspaper jargon that the battle for a respectable, honorable German language has gradually become a vital question for our people."[95]

The gradual transition from a criterion involving style and form to a more content-oriented assault becomes evident, for example, regarding Maximilian Harden's defamatory attack on the aristocratic Counts Moltke and Eulenberg: "How he juggles with the concepts of abnormal male friendships, sexual sensations and sexual activity, hetero- and homosexual, perversion and perversity, etc., is a great credit to his Talmud-trained scholasticism."[96] This is the critical penalty for classifying urgently needed concepts previously only roughly outlined (due to Wilhelmine inhibitions) into a sophisticated terminological system. But the general linguistic competence of the attacker was also addressed:

He, whose style is so un-German that one can only describe as Hebraic his Moritz and Rina cackling, has the impudence to instruct and correct at every opportunity one of the most breathtaking masters of the word whom we possess, such a born orator as Emperor Wilhelm II, for his supposed stylistic errors.[97]

This must indeed have been a sacrilege, because the language was regarded much as the noble House of Hohenzollern itself: It "should be something sacred to us; we should not play with it in frivolous ways."[98]

All in all, the language should never fall victim to the pressures of internationalism, for "it arose from the thought and feeling of the people and is inseparable from the life of the people." This statement was made in 1908,[99] but its ideological substance could easily be dated a hundred years earlier. And the "audacity" as a Jew to place himself stylistically

---

92 *Der Hammer*, no. 2 (1903): 80–1. Another citation regarding Jewish press practices actually misrepresents anti-Jewish poetry; see ibid., no. 3 (1904): 428–9.
93 Ibid., no. 9 (1910): 565ff.
94 Ibid., no. 2 (1903): 142.
95 Ibid.: 293–4.
96 Ibid., no. 6 (1907): 714.
97 Ibid.: 712–13.
98 Ibid., no. 7 (1908): 135.
99 Ibid.: 689.

above even that irreproachable Prussian-German paragon of the articulate man! We are reminded of the statement by Ludwig Börne – "more fervently than you" – and the basic thesis that hate was generated because the well-established "foreigners" had achieved even higher levels than the Germans precisely within the "German" parameters. Viewed from this perspective, even the manic language critic Karl Kraus takes on a new aspect; we now see in him the culmination of a certain position of the Jews toward the German language.

The argument of the Jews' poor German could no longer escape the obvious reality. An escape route was needed. A curiously contradictory position was taken on the problem of foreign words; faced with this "linguistic threat," other journals decided uncompromisingly for the German. Of course, *Der Hammer* also contained tirades against thieves' slang and against garbled French and Latin such as *pardon, adieu,* and "word cripples" such as *aujourd'hui.* Similarly, they also appealed for purification of the language.[100]

Der Hammer, however, also contains articles such as "Von den Sprach-Reinigern und ihren Übertreibungen,"[101] along with astounding statements to the effect that the Germans were trying by means of language purification to emphasize their uniqueness, but that language cannot be used as a measure of spirit.[102] This was a new tone that seemed to be above all a departure from the one that had been introduced in the eighteenth century and developed into the commonly held German opinion regarding language in the nineteenth. Was this a harbinger of the Nazis' well-known opposition to the language purification movement because, betting everything on the propagandistic effectiveness of language, they wanted unrestricted use of the agitating power of language for their own purposes?[103] This thesis is not without merit, for one reads outrageous things along these lines in *Der Hammer* as well. This outrageousness, however, enabled the Nazis to escape the corner into which they had painted themselves by insisting that the German Jews were to be rejected as un-German despite the fact that they obviously spoke exceptional German and were therefore pure Germans according to the "classical" cultural and linguistic theory of the German nation.

---

100 Ibid., no. 9 (1910): 565ff., and no. 10 (1911): 275ff.
101 Ibid., no. 4 (1905): 252–7.
102 Ibid., no. 11 (1912): 291–2.
103 See Peter von Polenz, "Sprachpurismus und Nationalsozialismus: Die 'Fremdwort'-Frage gestern und heute," in Benno von Wiese and Rudolf Henss, eds., *Nationalismus in Germanistik und Dichtung: Dokumentation des Germanistentages in München* (Berlin, 1967), 79–112.

As early as October 1903, we read: "There is a classic example for how little language can do to change the character of a people: Jews. Dispersed throughout all lands, the Jews speak the languages of all the cultures of the world, and yet they have preserved all of the characteristic features of their tribe."[104] This was where the strict correlation between language and national spirit, this awkward legacy of the German idealism of Herder and Humboldt, began to dissolve.[105] Admittedly, this thesis was immediately taken to task in an issue from February 1904,[106] where the undeniable polyglot speech of the Jews was (again) rejected as mere *mauscheln* and the following assertion was made:

> Therefore, the Jew in the middle of a purely Czech area, even if he speaks only Czech, remains Jewish from generation to generation. The language is in reality only a costume for him. For Germans, however, and for all Aryans, . . . their language is more than a piece of clothing; it is – in political terms – the defining stamp of their nation, their coat of arms, the priceless legacy of their fathers; and if they lose it, if it dissolves in the language of foreign cultures, then their existing political-national affiliation is also gone.[107]

This lengthy quotation illustrates once more the conflict that drove anti-Semites to other solutions. Apparently, linguistic disintegration in foreign cultures dissolves national affiliation for the Aryans but not for the "inferior" Jews. The response to this obvious contradiction was a more definitive departure from the basic philosophy of Herder and Humboldt. *Der Hammer* intimated that it was standing by the view that "language represents only the clothing of ideas"; its purpose was clarity and comprehension, which was why one should not shy away from foreign words;[108] the function of language was overestimated in the schools, they stated; it was actually only a means of expressing the spirit. Really, the spirit?[109] Here, too, anti-Semitism had "more modern," at any rate more useful, concepts – useful because the new terminological arsenal freed them even more decisively from reality:

---

104 *Der Hammer*, no. 2 (1903): 451.
105 In 1909, *Der Hammer*, no. 8 (1909): 400, states that language cannot be used as an unerring characteristic of racial origin, since the English speak English but are of Celtic origin, and the Bulgarians descend from the Huns but speak a Slavic language. It goes on: "Many Germans show by their physical attributes – in particular, round heads and black hair – that they have little blood of the Teutons in their veins; but they must be recognized as fellow citizens because of their German mother tongue." This had unfortunate consequences for the Jews.
106 The editorial office explains that the article was directed only at exaggerations; see *Der Hammer*, no. 3 (1904): 61n.
107 Ibid., no. 3 (1904): 62.
108 Ibid., no. 4 (1905): 253.
109 Ibid., no. 11 (1912): 144ff.

And what does language mean for the race of a people? Has it not been changed by many people like the shirt on one's back during the bustling travel of the last thousand years? The German knights taught their Slavic serfs the German language, and in the time of German powerlessness, the Catholic clerics turned into Poles the descendants of the western German and Dutch settlers whom Frederick the Great led to the East.

   – Only the blood, the race, remain stable.[110]

Such statements installed a new strategy of exclusion, an unrestricted racism elevated beyond discussion and based on unqualified aggression, detached from Herder, Humboldt, and all kinds of difficult debate over the essence of language, thought, and culture. It could simply return to mythical concepts like race and blood, or to categories like "taste":

A man who harbors an aversion toward the Jews need not look for logical reasons for it; he is adequately justified by his taste and this perception puts him in the best of company, among those of the deepest and most sensitive natures. For men like Herder, Fichte, Goethe, Frederick the Great, Arndt, Schopenhauer, Richard Wagner, Lagarde, and others have shared this taste.[111]

One sees here the usurpation technique. The farther back one goes, the more questionable the right to cite earlier thinkers in such an unrestricted manner – and certainly Herder, for whom race was by no means a relevant category, as he himself emphasized.

   This new position facilitated the stance of the anti-Semites in yet another regard. They could now openly admit the obvious truth, which even they secretly felt, namely, that the Jews – one thinks of Heine, Börne, Kraus, the reproachful Harden, and many others – were entirely equal to the Germans, and in some cases even superior. For example, the following was written in 1912 with regard to the formerly absolute unity of "language and spirit" and without apology:

The spirit seems to us more important than language. Someone can use the German language quite well and at the root be quite un-German. We have, indeed, among us a class of people who sometimes use the German language more proficiently than many a German and nevertheless have as foreign and

---

110 Ibid., no. 7 (1908): 117. In the essay "Rasse und Sprache," language is seen as merely the expression of a certain racially predetermined thinking capacity, whereby the Indo-Germanic "dialects," such as German, French, Russian, and so forth, all function according to the same structure: subject, predicate, object, with the Altaic language listed in contrast – just as in Nietzsche's *Über Lüge und Wahrheit* (*Der Hammer*, no. 5 [1906]: 547); of interest is a comment right in the middle: "Above all, it is true that one cannot become German by force of language, but only by blood and spirit. A firm spiritual bond is the living nerve of nations, and it is such a bond that *Der Hammer* wants to forge" (ibid., no. 2 [1903]: 454).
111 Ibid., no. 9 (1910): 174.

hostile a relationship to the German nature as can be imagined. . . . We do not believe that someone has become an entirely different person in all respects simply because he has put on a different coat. And it is the same with language and spirit.[112]

Need we emphasize that the particularly German Germans, the Jews, fought for the old view, which was exactly the opposite?[113]

Racism in the Matter of Names

The issue of names also took a racist turn. It was not the discussion in anti-Semitic circles, however, that forced this decisive turn. The Prussian government misstepped, but this must be interpreted in the context of the accusations against the government heard more frequently toward the end of the nineteenth century from the anti-Semites, who charged that because the aristocracy was intermarrying with the Jews, the government authorities had been completely infiltrated by the Jews and were therefore their secret accomplices. The Prussian minister of the interior wished to arm himself against these charges when the following situation arose in May 1900.

The view that Jews could be recognized by their names had been dominant since the 1870s. This caused suffering for both German and Jewish bearers of names stigmatized by the anti-Semites. Applications for name changes were made by the *Cohns*, the *Israels*, and the *Moseses* three times as often by Germans with "Jewish" names as by Jews. As is true of religious conversions, name changes by Jews were actually rare (no more than 2,000 in Prussia since names were adopted in 1812, in contrast to 30,000 changes of Polish names in the Ruhr region alone). Only anti-

---

112 Ibid., no. 11 (1912): 291. This also shows that, although the new racial foundation made possible a new means of anchoring humanity in a category of "spirit," those with an ethnic-national orientation immediately found ways to block this escape route. It is logically true that fascist linguists, e.g., Georg Schmidt-Rohr, later equated language, people, and spirit, thereby laying a foundation on which the Jews could clearly have been defined as members of the German people. However, they paid no attention to whether precisely these correct conclusions were drawn, or whether a variety of excuses was sought so as not to draw these conclusions. Cf. the discussion by Gerd Simon, "Materialien über den Widerstand in der deutschen Sprachwissenschaft des Dritten Reichs: Der Fall Georg Schmidt-Rohr," in Gerd Simon, ed., *Sprachwissenschaft und politisches Engagement: Zur Problem- und Sozialgeschichte einiger sprachtheoretischer, sprachdidaktischer und sprachpflegerischer Ansätze in der Germanistik des 19. und 20. Jahrhunderts* (Weinheim, 1979). Cf. also Ruth Römer, "Mit Mutter Sprache gegen die Nazis?" *Linguistische Berichte* 14 (1971): 68–9.

113 One of many examples is the famous Darmstadt professor Julius Goldstein, who fought with his Zionistically inclined namesake Moritz Goldstein over the "Deutsch-jüdischen Parnass" (citing Goethe no less) and said that it was "not in the least the language which makes the poet German or French" (*Im deutschen Reich* 18 [1912]: 442).

Semitic propaganda talked the numbers to a dizzying height. A contamination of German names was underway, they warned – a special case of linguistic mixing. The (parallel) threat they presented was that all Jews seemed to speak German, but in reality spoke something else; and most Jews seemed to have proper German names, but in reality this was only a deceptive facade, behind which the old "real" Jewish-Yiddish-Hebraic name was hiding. This onomastic facade, they continued, was provided to the Jews by their sidekicks in the governments of the district presidents – for money, not by upright means.

The Prussian minister of the interior, Baron von Rheinbaben, took the opportunity of a name-change case that had caused an outcry across Germany (*Schmuhl* to *Steinhardt*) to put an end to such talk. He did it in a way that was at first latently anti-Jewish and later, in its specific wording, openly so. On May 18, 1900 – take note of the date, for this is the first racist regulation in German history – he ordered that so as to guarantee "desirable uniformity" and thereby justice, all name-change applications by Jews from that day forward had to be submitted to the minister of the interior in Berlin for approval. He did not say simply "Jews," however. Instead, he adopted the terminology used in the argumentation of the anti-Semites and said "Jews and persons of Jewish descent."[114] This was an unprecedented break with the already widely undermined Prussian tradition. The inescapable consequence was a systematic tracing of the roots of Christian applicants to see if one could not perhaps turn up a Jew in the ancestry after all, in which case the application was to be sent to the minister of the interior in Berlin. This was a sort of state processing, an apparently harmless prelude to the later, deadly, deportation procedures against people of Jewish ancestry.

SUMMARY

With this an important leap was taken. It inescapably shows that language, a seemingly harmless terrain, is an especially sensitive area in the German case, containing far-reaching, ultimately hideous, implications. We shall summarize by saying that in the area of language *government*, strategies for ostracizing minorities are perhaps not so effective because language is always a predominantly social phenomenon. With the exception of names, it cannot be controlled *from above*. In the case of the Jews,

---

114 See Bering, *Der Name als Stigma*, 146; regarding the entire case, 145ff.; regarding the number of
    name changes, 176, 198, 378.

therefore, the strategies of rejection are to be found primarily within society. The anti-Semites indeed agitated against Yiddish and *jüdeln* (even where it was only imagined), certainly with significant success with regard to the specific, national-bonding function of the German language. The boundary-setting rejection had to be particularly vigorous because "Jewish" Germans and "German" Germans were quite similar to one another in many respects, particularly language. The educated middle class had virtually defined itself by language and had declared it sacred. This special position of the language in the process of self-definition of things "German" and of "German citizens" explains the unique rejection of the Jews. Remaining doubts about the mechanism presented here can be eliminated by identifying the most resistant core group of anti-Semites. They were exactly the same group as in the last century. In the words of Hans August Winkler, "Anti-Semitism, which became respectable in the late nineteenth century thanks largely to Heinrich von Treitschke, found more ardent admirers among the educated middle class after 1918 than in any other class."[115] This statement is not only factually correct, but there also seems to be an important explanation for it.

What about *government* handling of intolerance? In the early nineteenth century, the government tended mainly to offer assistance in eliminating the age-old linguistic differences in writing, terminology, and names. In the end, however, the government itself first stepped onto clearly racist ground, precisely in the area of language control, and specifically the control of names. Thus, while there was considerable tension at the beginning of the century between societal strategies and governmental measures, the century ended with the government authorities falling into line with anti-Semitism.

---

115 Hans August Winkler, "Die deutsche Gesellschaft der Weimarer Republik und der Antisemitismus," in Bernd Martin and Ernst Schulin, eds., *Die Juden als Minderheit in der Geschichte* (Munich, 1981), 283. Specifically, he counts among the hard core white-collar workers, bureaucrats, and particularly teachers; the leadership of anti-Semitic parties included "a remarkably large number of independent professionals, especially doctors and lawyers" (281).

PART THREE

Race, Gender, Body, Biology

11

Ambiguous Roles

The Racial Factor in American Womanhood

LOIS E. HORTON

Writing about the attitude of black women toward the contemporary women's movement in its early phase in the United States, bell hooks observed: "Contemporary black women could not join together to fight for women's rights because we did not see 'womanhood' as an important aspect of our identity. Racist, sexist socialization had conditioned us to devalue our femaleness and to regard race as the only relevant label of identification."[1] The black woman's identity, she argued, had been "socialized out of existence." In ordinary discourse "men" meant white men, "blacks" meant black men, and "women" meant white women.[2] In the controversial and contested world of American sex roles and gender identification, how did the black woman's womanhood become submerged in her racial identity? The answer lies in the peculiar history of African Americans in the United States, in the roles African-American women played, and in the cultural justifications developed to explain the role of blacks in America. The "scientific," cultural, and philosophical justifications of slavery constituted a dehumanization of African Americans in the white mind. As a part of this process, distinctions between different categories of African Americans were obscured or disappeared from view. Slaveholders often ignored the gender conventions Africans brought to America and considered slave women as well as men suited to hard labor.

The conflict between black society's ability to define individual identity and white society's power to impose identities, combined with the tensions between the realities of black life and prevailing gender ideals, created ambiguous roles for black women in the nineteenth century.

---

1 bell hooks, *Ain't I a Woman: Black Women and Feminism* (Boston, 1981), 1.
2 Ibid., 7.

295

These conflicts were complicated by their existence within the framework of the slave system in a paternalistic society. The conception of the "feminization" of the relatively powerless slave had a profound impact on the image (and the self-image) of black men and lasting consequences for black women. The conflicting ideals and demands on black women in particular continue to echo in contemporary relationships between black men and women and in efforts to organize black women and white women.[3]

The relationship between gender and race in the social structure and social thought of America has had lasting consequences for all groups, but the consequences have been especially profound for the organization of movements to extend human and civil rights to African Americans and to women. In the American consciousness, European Americans have been distinguished by ethnicity and gender; African Americans have been delineated by race. The effects of racial and gender constructions are clearly apparent on the antislavery movement of the nineteenth century, and the civil-rights and black feminist movements of the twentieth century, and they have most often been detrimental to the identity and prospects of black women.[4]

At first glance this seems to contradict the implications of the work of major social theorists and most writing about slavery in America that contend that the institution destroyed, or at least was designed to destroy, black manhood. Indeed, there are historical, political, and philosophical reasons for the connection of enslavement with feminization. Generally, social theorists have seen the earliest occurrences of slavery as intertwined with the history of patriarchy and a male-dominated political hierarchy.[5] With the development of private property, according to Frederick Engels, came the imposition of monogamous marriage to ensure its legitimate inheritance. This gradually transformed women into the possessions of men, and as women became another kind of property, it was a short step to the enslavement of the women of conquered groups. Engels was concerned with explaining the origin of private property and

---

3 See Michele Wallace, *Black Macho and the Myth of the Superwoman* (New York, 1979).
4 For an important treatment of the peculiar role and status of black women in American society and among African Americans, see Rosalyn Terborg-Penn, *Afro-American Women: Struggles and Images* (Port Washington, N.Y., 1978).
5 James O. Horton and Lois E. Horton, "Violence, Protest and Identity: Black Manhood in Antebellum America," in James Oliver Horton, *Free People of Color* (Washington, D.C., 1993), 80–97; James O. Horton and Lois E. Horton, "The Affirmation of Manhood: Black Garrisonians in Antebellum Boston," in Donald M. Jacobs, ed., *Courage and Conscience: Black and White Abolitionists in Boston* (Bloomington, Ind., 1993), 127–53.

class systems of oppression, seeing the subjugation of women as the first instance of a class system, and although later evidence has called the sequence of events he outlined into question, the implications of his theory have remained intact.[6]

After an exhaustive study of nearly 2,500 years of development in Near Eastern societies, arguably the cradle of European culture, Gerda Lerner concluded that the commodification of women actually antedated and was the foundation for the development of private property. Lerner also presented detailed historical evidence that women were the first slaves, enslaved by conquerors who killed the vanquished men of their groups. Thus, there is general agreement among feminists that the subjugation of women provided the precedent and the model for hierarchical social systems and the institutionalization of slavery. Eventually conquered men were enslaved as well, and coupled with the rape of conquered women, Lerner argued, slavery created a "class of psychologically enslaved people," dishonored women, and symbolically castrated men.[7] Slavery feminized men in a patriarchal society by robbing them of the essential capability of manhood – control over their women. It also deprived them of power and autonomy, the corollaries of this manhood.[8]

In this historical and philosophical development, with women already under men's "ownership" and control, the primary changes brought by the slave system seem to have been in the status of enslaved men. As the patriarchal family was the model for the system, enslaved men joined the ranks of the dependent powerless populations, and to them were attributed the characteristics shared by women and children. The full consequence of this phenomenon can be seen in the increasingly explicit justifications for slavery when the institution faced growing opposition in the United States in the nineteenth century. Slaveowners in the South marshaled two different but related defenses against abolitionist arguments. First, they alleged that African Americans were a naturally docile and childlike people, intellectually inferior and incapable of independent living. In other words, they lacked the ability to achieve adulthood and needed the slaveowner's paternal care. South Carolina's George Fitzhugh claimed that southern slavery was a more humane system for black workers than the industrial capitalism that was beginning to emerge in the North because

---

6 Frederick Engels, *Origin of the Family, Private Property, and the State*, trans. Eleanor Leacock (New York, 1972).

7 Gerda Lerner, *The Creation of Patriarchy* (New York, 1986), 80.

8 Mark C. Carnes and Clyde Griffen, *Meanings of Manhood: Constructions of Masculinity in Victorian America* (Chicago, 1990).

it protected them from economic and social competition, for which they were unsuited. Comparing all blacks to white women and children, he argued that slavery, like marriage and the family, provided protection for inherently dependent, childlike creatures.[9]

Second, slaveholders argued that slaves were a bestial subhuman species incapable of higher civilization, and that slavery was necessary for their control. This argument was commonly put forth by southern scholars and scientists during the antebellum period who agreed that "by himself [the African never] emerged from barbarism, and even when partly civilized under the control of the white man, he speedily returns to the same state if emancipated."[10] Thomas Jefferson believed that emancipating slaves without deporting blacks was unwise because he believed blacks would be likely to engage in reprisals against the whites who had enslaved them. "We have a wolf by the ears," he contended, "and we can neither hold him; nor safely let him go. Justice is in one scale, and self-preservation in the other."[11]

As a primitive people, naturally undisciplined and not fully in control of their emotions, blacks could not be counted on for rational, civilized actions. According to this reasoning, Jefferson concluded that African Americans posed a potential danger to democratic government, which relied on the civilized self-restraint of its citizens. This was a powerful justification for the preservation of slavery in the new nation, for the unrestrained emotionality of blacks, in contrast to the self-control of civilized men, demanded close supervision. Thus, the characteristics attributed to African Americans by these justifications, similar to the characteristics attributed to nineteenth-century women and children, were the antithesis of adult masculinity. Such characteristics left African Americans and all women, like children, unfit for independence and citizenship.[12]

The identification of slaves with feminine characteristics has been a powerful force with enduring consequences in the history and experience of gender and race in America, but focusing on this phenomenon illuminates only half the story. An examination of the lives of slave women

---

9 Eric L. McKitrick, ed., *Slavery Defended: The Views of the Old South* (Englewood Cliffs, N.J., 1963).

10 E. N. Elliott, ed., *Cotton Is King and Pro-Slavery Arguments* (Augusta, Geo., 1860), xiii, quoted in George M. Fredrickson, *The Black Image in the White Mind: The Debate on Afro-American Character and Destiny, 1817–1914* (New York, 1971), 83.

11 Quoted in John Chester Miller, *The Wolf by the Ears: Thomas Jefferson and Slavery* (New York, 1977), ix.

12 Anthony Rotundo, *American Manhood: Transformations in Masculinity form the Revolution to the Modern Era* (New York, 1993).

and the roles they were expected to play reveals a powerful source of ambiguity in women's lives. Although there was a division of labor on the slave plantations and some task assignment according to sex, it was common for female slaves to perform fieldwork and other heavy labor. The slave literature abounds with accounts of women who did work requiring great strength, generally considered men's work in white society. Feminized by their powerlessness, black women were also masculinized by the demands for labor under which they worked.

In *Ar'n't I a Woman?* Deborah Gray White examined the complex world of female slave labor. Masters did frequently make distinctions between male and female slaves, she found, at least during a woman's childbearing years. Accounts of life in the slave quarters indicate that slaves maintained traditional divisions of labor after their work in the field was finished, leaving women to do housekeeping tasks such as spinning, weaving, and sewing after their day's labor. There was also some division of labor by sex in agricultural work, although it is difficult to determine whether this was at the slaves' or the slaveholders' behest. Heavier tasks tended to be reserved for men, and pregnant women were often given reduced workloads, but when the growing cycle or the market created a high demand for labor, all slaves were expected to do heavy work.[13] The priorities of the slave system were captured in Jacqueline Jones's conclusion that slaveholders made "efforts to wrench as much field labor as possible from female slaves without injuring their capacity to bear children." Such efforts were unscientific and not always effective, especially since slaveholders were concerned that women, even pregnant women, not use their sex as an excuse to shirk demanding labor.[14] Women past childbearing age needed no protection and could be worked to the limits of their strength. Some women of exceptional strength were assigned tasks according to their abilities without regard to their sex. Solomon Northup, enslaved in Louisiana, reported that four female slave lumberjacks were brought to his owner's lumbering operation to meet heavy demand. They were "excellent choppers," Northup recalled, "equal to any man" at piling logs. Northup also noted that some cotton and sugar plantations in the area were worked entirely with female labor.[15]

Evidence is plentiful that slaves resented slaveowners' lack of respect for the gender sensibilities of African and American cultures and that

13 Deborah Gray White, *Ar'n't I a Woman?* (New York, 1985).
14 Jacqueline Jones, *Labor of Love, Labor of Sorrow* (New York, 1985), 15.
15 Solomon Northup, *Twelve Years a Slave* (Buffalo, N.Y., 1853), 308.

slave men were frustrated by their inability to protect their women. In his incendiary *Appeal*, published in 1829, David Walker wrote of the degradation and ignorance of the American slave, describing how slave-holders' tyranny forced fathers to turn against sons, mothers against daughters, and children against parents. His most powerful and heartrending examples illustrated the vulnerability of women and the painful contradictions the slave system created. Showing the depths to which the slave population had sunk, Walker called attention to the cases in which the protectors of women became the agents of their oppressors. In Walker's words, the observer in the South might see

a son take his mother, who bore almost the pains of death to give him birth, and by the command of a tyrant, strip her as naked as she came into the world, and apply the cow-hide to her, until she falls a victim to death in the road! He may see a husband take his dear wife, not unfrequently in a pregnant state, and perhaps far advanced, and beat her for an unmerciful wretch, until his infant falls a lifeless lump at her feet![16]

Yet, there is evidence that slave women took pride in their strength and their ability to do demanding work. Physical strength gave both men and women an advantage; some slaves were said to be too physically imposing to be whipped. Frederick Douglass recounted the story of one female slave on the plantation where he grew up who stood up to the overseer and gained the tacit understanding that she would not be whipped.[17] Although there was some satisfaction in evading work under the forced labor system, there was also the characteristically human tendency to gain a sense of mastery and self-esteem from difficult work well done. The resulting dignity and strength of character pervades Sojourner Truth's famous 1851 speech in favor of women's rights:

Look at me! Look at my arm! I have plowed, and planted, and gathered into barns, and no man could head me – and ar'n't I a woman? I could work as much and eat as much as a man (when I could get it), and bear de lash as well – and ar'n't I a woman? I have borne thirteen chilern and seen em mos' all sold off into slavery, and when I cried out with a mother's grief, none but Jesus heard – and ar'n't I a woman?[18]

Slaves understood the roles of black women, both as workers and as women. Slaveholders exploited sex differences, using slave women to

16 David Walker, *Walker's Appeal, in Four Articles*, 3d ed. (Boston, 1830), in Herbert Aptheker, *One Continual Cry* (New York, 1965), 84–5.
17 Frederick Douglass, *My Bondage and My Freedom*, ed. William L. Andrews (Urbana, Ill., 1987).
18 *Narrative of Sojourner Truth: A Bondwoman of Olden Time*, comp. by Olive Gilbert (1878; New York, 1968), 133–4.

gratify their need for mastery and their desire for more slaves, and they often adjusted labor assignments in consideration of gender. For abolitionists, the image of a mother torn from her children was a powerful organizing tool. Yet when American womanhood was considered, the lives of black women became invisible. In his record of his travels in America published in 1835, the astute observer Alexis de Tocqueville contrasted women's roles in America with those in Europe. American young women, he contended, were outspoken and independent but lost that independence with marriage. Tocqueville was critical of the Europeans' promotion of gender equality, which he thought resulted in "weak men and disorderly women," and approved of the complementarity between the sexes he saw in America. "In no country," he reported, "has such constant care been taken as in America to trace two clearly distinct lines of action for the two sexes . . . two pathways which are always different." Tocqueville was certainly aware of slavery and the role of blacks in America. He believed the question of race and the status of black people to be the issue that would prove to be the greatest problem for the new nation. Nonetheless, when he wrote of women, they were white women. Except under the exigencies of the frontier, even among the poor, according to Tocqueville, American women were never "compelled to perform the rough labor of the fields, or make any of those laborious exertions which demand the exertion of physical strength."[19] Nor was this inability to see race and gender simultaneously confined to male observers. When Harriet Martineau, friend of the slaves and advocate of women's rights, wrote of the American woman, she explained how "her case differ[ed] from that of the slave."[20]

Theories of the feminization of slaves fail to explain the consequences of the slave system for female slaves. Understanding patriarchies and the operation of their economic inequalities in the institution of slavery may illuminate the condition of male slaves but leaves the particular situation of female slaves unexamined. It seems paradoxical, but to better understand the intersection of race, gender, and the consequences for black women in America, it is necessary to consider the development of racism in the American context. Slave labor contradicted America's founding principles of freedom and equality, and northern states provided for its abolition early in their existence. In response to southern resistance to

19 Alexis de Tocqueville in Ronald W. Hogeland, ed., *Women and Womanhood in America* (Lexington, Mass., 1973), 75. Tocqueville's observations fail to recognize how physically demanding the household labor performed by the average white woman was as well.
20 Harriet Martineau in 1837, in Hogeland, *Women and Womanhood in America*, 78.

abolition, the federal government maintained property rights in slaves and supported state laws that denied human rights to slaves and citizenship rights to all African Americans. The foundation of the racism that provided the justification for American slavery in the face of the nation's dilemma was the dehumanization of black people. To remain true to their principles, American slaveholders (and by extension American politicians) had to define African Americans as a different order of beings, an inferior subspecies, to whom the ordinary rules of human conduct and social organization need not apply.[21]

Understanding the process of the dehumanization of Africans and African Americans in American thought is important for comprehending the combined impact of race and gender because part of the process was the creation of propaganda and perceptions that muted the differences between members of the subordinate group, those who were the objects of racism. The image of blacks in the minds of most white Americans came to lack differentiation by slave or free status, class, ethnicity, or gender. Free blacks recognized this phenomenon in the nineteenth century. They engaged in the fight to abolish slavery for many reasons – slavery violated their moral and religious values, they had friends and relatives in slavery, and they were vulnerable to being kidnapped into slavery. But they also knew their condition and prospects for the future were tied to white conceptions of blacks' "natural" suitability for slavery. Although a sizable racially mixed population existed by the nineteenth century, largely as the result of white-male control over black women, Americans considered blacks and mulattos part of the same population with basically the same characteristics. With regard to gender characterizations, the feminization of black men and the masculinization of black women under slavery can be seen, in part, as another aspect of the denial of difference involved in the process of dehumanization.

At the same time that differences among blacks were muted in white conceptions, differences between whites and blacks were exaggerated. In his compelling analysis of the construction of whiteness in America, David Roediger has demonstrated the utility of exaggerating the differences between the races for the white working class. For Irish immigrants in the nineteenth century, and later for others, a declaration of their whiteness was an establishment of their right to full membership in American society. Whiteness, Roediger points out, was the attribute

---

21 For an exposition of the development of American racism and the justifications of slavery, see Winthrop Jordan, *White over Black* (Chapel Hill, N.C., 1968).

powerful enough to overcome the great diversity of the American work-ing class. It was powerful enough because it allowed new white Amer-icans to distance themselves from degraded blacks. White Americans' attempts to define themselves as the opposites of the blacks they paro-died and stereotyped permeated American culture. Their efforts were evident in public festivals, parades, and processions, and on the minstrel stage. Increasing the social distance between racial groups gave whites greater control over the stereotyped black images they created and main-tained. Black festivals and celebrations, which had been attended by whites for at least half a century, were, by the middle of the 1820s, banned in places like New York and Philadelphia, and the occasionally integrated procession gave way to segregated parades where blacks were harassed by white bystanders. In the quintessential American entertain-ment called minstrelsy, white men masquerading as black men and women performed their own versions of black music and parodied black life before white audiences.[22]

Although color created a bond among many disparate groups in the white working class, greater differentiation among white Americans was especially characteristic of this period. The growth of commerce and indus-try, burgeoning cities, and waves of European immigration all contributed to the delineation of classes and an awareness of disparate class interests. The large numbers of Irish immigrants focused American attention on potential antagonisms based on religious differences, and as immigration progressed, ethnicity was more and more implicated in political opposi-tions. The differences between whites that assumed greater definition also included gender differences.

The gender prescriptions that have come to be known as the "cult of true womanhood," or the ideal of separate spheres, developed at the same time as racial justifications for slavery in the early nation. Few out-side the white middle class were capable of realizing these ideals in their everyday lives, yet they became a powerful prescription for the as-pirations of American women. The revolutionary principles had stirred women's hopes for education, achievement, and political power, and a few had made considerable progress in formerly male areas of classical education. By the nineteenth century, however, women's enthusiasm had generally been channeled into pursuing greater accomplishments in the

22 David R. Roediger, *The Wages of Whiteness* (New York, 1991); Shane White, "'It Was a Proud Day': African Americans, Festivals and Parades in the North, 1741–1834," *Journal of American History* 81, no. 1 (June 1994): 13–50; Noel Ignatiev, *How the Irish Became White* (New York, 1995).

acceptably feminine undertakings of "republican motherhood" and moral reform. In the conception of separate spheres, politics and economics were male concerns, and the household and family were female concerns, although the feminine domain came to be stretched to include anything related to home and family that was not specifically a masculine province. Moreover, this separation was based on what were perceived as immutable differences between men and women.[23]

Catharine Beecher, a woman from a famous reform family and sister of Harriet Beecher Stowe, expressed her belief in the "doctrine of masculine and feminine virtues" in her criticism of women involved in the abolitionist movement. In *An Essay on Slavery and Abolitionism with Reference to the Duty of American Females*, she argued that public work, especially public speaking, was appropriate for men but not for women. Women must accept their natural divinely ordained inferiority. "Heaven has appointed to one sex the *superior*, and to the other the *subordinate* station, and this without any reference to the character or conduct of either."[24] In this essay, Beecher was specifically criticizing the outspoken abolitionist Angelina Grimke. It is interesting that female abolitionists were the white middle-class women most likely to violate the strictures of the separate-spheres doctrine. Following the examples of free black women and female fugitive slaves, white female abolitionists risked vehement disapproval and physical attack by addressing political issues in public forums to "promiscuous" audiences of men and women. With the example of black women who played strong public roles, white female abolitionists were encouraged to transcend the limitations of their ordinary feminine roles. These women not only transgressed the lines dividing proper male and female behavior, their rhetoric also diminished the distance between black women and white women.

Abolitionists, both men and women, called on their audiences to identify female slaves as women. Their speeches were filled with denunciations of the separation of families on the auction block, the impropriety of the nakedness of the female slaves at auction, the sexual exploitation of slave women, and the slaveholders' contravention of slave women's right to fulfill their roles as mothers. Abolitionists especially encouraged white women in the audience to identify with black women as mothers

23 Mary Beth Norton, *Liberty's Daughters: The Revolutionary Experience of American Women, 1750–1800* (Boston, 1980); Ronald Hoffman and Peter J. Albert, eds., *Women in the Age of the American Revolution* (Charlottesville, Va., 1989); Linda K. Kerber, "The Paradox of Women's Citizenship in the Early Republic: The Case of *Martin vs. Massachusetts*, 1805," *American Historical Review* 97, no. 2 (Apr. 1992): 351.
24 Catharine Beecher in Miriam Gurko, *The Ladies of Seneca Falls* (New York, 1974), 42.

who suffered for the loss of their children. Although there were typically American instances of prejudice and discrimination against women and against African Americans within the abolition movement, the abolitionists occasionally went so far as to promote the idea of the sisterhood of black and white women. Black abolitionist Sarah Parker Remond was overwhelmed by her reception by English abolitionists after her first antislavery speech in Britain in 1859. She responded to their tribute saying, "I have been received here as a sister by white women for the first time in my life. I have been removed from the degradation which overhangs all persons of my complexion."[25]

Such affirmations of the primary status of black women as women were extremely uncommon outside of their own communities. Still, the roles of black women were defined by both the white society and the black society, often in conflicting ways. At the same time that black women were accepted by their communities as public speakers and as important, often equal, participants in labor and the household economy, they were admonished by some community leaders for not being properly supportive of black men. From the pages of black newspapers, editors, almost all black middle-class men, instructed women on the duties and desired characteristics of men and women. "Man is daring and confident" they were told, whereas "woman is deferent and unassuming." Although "man has judgement" black women were reassured that "woman [has] sensibility."[26] Further, using her more sensitive nature she was expected to shield the male ego from the assaults of slavery and racial discrimination. It was the responsibility of a black man to "act like a man," and black women were to "encourage and support the manhood of our men." A woman should "never intimidate [the black man] with her knowledge or common sense, let him feel stable and dominant." It was seen as a black woman's duty to the race to allow black men to feel "tough and protective" even if it was unrealistic to expect men to act this way. All women faced sanctions for not living out the demands of the American patriarchy, and many working-class white women also worked outside their homes. The responsibility for promoting black manhood, which accompanied their commitment to racial liberation, was an extra burden carried by black women.[27]

---

25 Vron Ware, *Beyond the Pale* (London, 1992), 78. See also Jean Fagan Yellin, *Women and Sisters: Antislavery Feminists in American Culture* (New Haven, Conn., 1989) and Shirley J. Yee, *Black Women Abolitionists: A Study in Activism, 1828–1860* (Knoxville, Tenn., 1992).
26 *Colored American*, Sept. 14, 1839.
27 Ibid., Sept. 8, 1838.

Economic necessity often forced these women to take on traditional male tasks and become partial breadwinners, while continuing their traditional female tasks at home so as not to force black men to do women's work. Protecting their men from gender-threatening demands was an essential part of black women's responsibility not only to the men but to the race. Sarah Watson of Westerly, Rhode Island, mother of five, understood this responsibility and shielded her husband, Thomas, from the humiliation of having to do women's work even though it meant additional work for her. Thomas was a Revolutionary War veteran who worked as a laborer for most of his life, while Sarah was employed as a domestic servant. When he developed rheumatism, his work became sporadic, and the couple took in boarders to make ends meet. Although Thomas was at home much of the time with his illness, Sarah performed all the work to serve the boarders. One of the Watson's neighbors explained that "of course this kept Sarah plenty busy between working outside, keeping the children and the [male boarders], especially with [Thomas] always in the way." There was no expectation that a black man should help with the household duties.[28]

These gender assumptions weighed heavily on black women. The circumstances of their lives often rewarded strength and a certain kind of independence, or at least a woman's ability to care for herself and her children. The values of the white society prescribed restricted roles for women under the support and protection of men. African and African-American men too held patriarchal values with circumscribed male and female roles, but circumstances generally required flexibility in the way those roles were realized. Abolitionist Martin Delany was a strong supporter of women's rights and especially of women's right to a liberal education. "The potency and respectability of a nation or people," he wrote, "depends entirely upon the position of their women; therefore, it is essential to our elevation that the female portion of our children be instructed in all the arts and sciences pertaining to the highest civilization." He was also supportive of black women as representatives of the black community. When the Emigration Convention, in which Delany played a leadership role, met in Cleveland in 1854 to consider the possibilities of African-American emigration to Africa, six female delegates, including his wife, Catherine Delany, were present. Part of the more gen-

28 Revolutionary War Pension Records (Thomas Watson) cited in Horton, *Free People of Color.*
Slave men, bell hooks explains, "regarded tasks like cooking, sewing, nursing, and even minor farm labor as women's work"; see hooks, *Ain't I a Woman*, 44. See also Ann Firor Scott, *The Southern Lady: From Pedestal to Politics, 1830–1930* (Chicago, 1970).

eral acceptance of black women in these expanded political roles was based on their critical economic position, made necessary by job discrimination against black men, and men's support of this position was often predicated on this necessity. Delany, for example, had strong words for black women "who voluntarily leave their home and become chambermaids and stewardesses." He believed those who worked only to obtain meaningless luxuries reflected the "degradation of the black race."[29]

Concern with the denial of properly powerful roles for black men, in slavery and in freedom, dictated that black women support black manhood. While strong women were celebrated, "masculinized" women were seen as a threat to that manhood. Black women who played a role in the household nearer to an equal role with men were seen as evidence for the existence of a black matriarchy, dominating men and contributing to their continued emasculation. Thus, in the Reconstruction period after the Civil War, when voting rights for African Americans and women were debated, black women were told that gaining political rights for black men was the most important aim. Their interests, leaders argued, lay not with the women's movement for suffrage, but in any social or political change that would strengthen the position of black men. Many feared that including controversial demands for women's rights would jeopardize the assurance of black rights. Later, prominent women's rights organizers alienated black women with arguments for giving white women the vote in order to offset the power of new African-American and immigrant voters. Some were unwilling to give up the fight for women's rights, and a few, like Sojourner Truth, feared that recently freed black women would be trading a tyrant outside their household for another within, but many more postponed demands for their own rights in favor of the rights of black men.

Much has been written about African Americans' communal values founded on the primacy of the family. Born out of African roots in traditional cultures, attacked but not erased by the slave system, nurtured by the necessity of a limited freedom in black communities, such values provided an alternative to the competitive, individualistic society developing in America. Elsa Barkley Brown has recently presented convincing evidence that given this context, black-male suffrage was an element of family and community power. She noted that women participated in unofficial but influential ways in political debates in southern states during

---

29 Sharon Harley, "Northern Black Female Workers: Jacksonian Era," in Sharon Harley and Rosalyn Terborg-Penn, eds., *The Afro-American Woman: Struggles and Images* (New York, 1978), 12.

Reconstruction and argued that men and women saw the "ballot as collectively owned," that it was a wife's expression of choice as well as her
husband's.[30] Without reference to underlying paternalistic values, however, it is unclear why men's voting rather than women's, or both, should
have come to be accepted as expressing the collective will. Brown and
other scholars have made it clear that southern black women participated
in creating their own freedom, but Brown also noted that even within
the black community these women's political rights became more circumscribed during the last quarter of the nineteenth century. The pressure on
African-American women to contribute their strength to bolstering the
besieged manhood of the formerly enslaved males may help to answer
the question Brown has posed concerning "how an explicitly gendered
discourse on citizenship and rights *developed* within late-nineteenth-century
black communities."[31]

Long after all women gained the vote, these gender dynamics remained
to impede collective action based on equal rights to exercise power. During
the mid-twentieth century, civil-rights organizations followed the traditional imperative of empowering black men who dominated the leadership. Even the youthful members of the racially integrated Student
Nonviolent Coordinating Committee, which sought to embody the
values of an egalitarian society by giving each person an equal vote
and reaching decisions by consensus, gave women supporting roles in
political organizing. Patricia Hill Collins recognized that the subordina-
tion of black women's roles and experiences in the civil-rights movement had a long history. "Adhering to a male-defined ethos that far too
often equates racial progress with the acquisition of an ill-defined manhood has left Black Thought with a prominent masculinist bias," she
observed.[32] Whereas many women agreed with Collins's contention that
minimizing women's roles limited black progress, black men were often
explicit about their attempts to gain control over black women. Andrew

---

30 See Elsa Barkley Brown, "To Catch the Vision of Freedom: Reconstructing Southern Black
   Women's Political History, 1865–1880," in Ann D. Gordon et al., eds., *African-American Women
   and the Vote, 1837–1965* (Amherst, Mass., 1997), 66–69. Presumably, single women were represented at the polls by male relatives, but those without male relatives lacked even this indirect
   representation. For additional information on the participation of black women in Reconstruction politics, see Thomas Holt, *Black over White: Negro Political Leadership in South Carolina During
   Reconstruction* (Urbana, Ill., 1977), 34–5, and Noralee Frankel, "Freedom's Women: African American Women and Family in Mississippi, 1860–1870," manuscript, 1994.
31 Brown, "To Catch the Vision of Freedom," n. 39.
32 Patricia Hill Collins, *Black Feminist Thought* (New York, 1990), 8. Black feminists tend to attribute
   the gender prescriptions that call for dominance by black men to African Americans' adopting
   European-American gender roles. I think this underestimates the influence of gender ideals
   rooted in African societies, which are at least as patriarchal as the European cultures.

Young analyzed the discomfort Martin Luther King Jr. felt when facing assertive women in the civil-rights movement by describing the power King's mother had over his father and over Martin and his need to free himself from his mother's domination. Young's explanation of the gender dynamics of the movement included the history of slavery and segregation. "This is a generality," he said, "but a system of oppression tends to produce strong women and weak men."[33] Women needed to remain in the background, he implied, because in the past black men had been dominated by white society and by black women.

It was the blurring of gender differences in the context of a patriarchal society that led to the myth of the black matriarchy, a myth that echoed through Andrew Young's analysis of the attitudes of Martin Luther King Jr. Often forced to be independent, frequently assertive in demanding her rights for herself and her family, and sometimes requiring physical strength for survival, the more equal position of black women in their society compared to the position of white women in theirs came to be seen as female domination. Scientific opinion then typically blamed what was erroneously labeled a black matriarchy for many of the problems of oppressed African Americans. Hence, philanthropic and social science solutions to black problems often focused on the supposed need to strengthen black manhood and restore the black male to his rightful place in the family and community, solutions that implicitly required black women to assume supporting roles. The positive model of the strong black woman, which developed historically through the struggles of many women, was tinged with ambivalent connotations. Anita Hill's assertions against Clarence Thomas in his confirmation hearings for the Supreme Court were framed as an attack on black manhood, a violation of her responsibility as a black woman.

The historical experience and social ideals at the nexus of sex and race have also greatly complicated relationships between black women and white women in American society. The conflicts and misunderstandings arising from racial factors made the organization of the modern feminist movement, for example, much more difficult and complex. Although they often shared similar ideals through the nineteenth and twentieth centuries, their experiences of work and their family roles were generally very different. This was especially true for the middle-class women likely to be involved in social reform.[34] When young white women

---

33 Paula Giddings, *When and Where I Enter* (New York, 1984), 313.
34 Nancie Caraway, *Segregated Sisterhood: Racism and the Politics of American Feminism* (Knoxville, Tenn., 1991); Sara M. Evans and Harry C. Boyte, *Free Spaces* (New York, 1986).

in the civil-rights and antiwar movements of the 1960s began to challenge the men of those movements to share decision-making and public
leadership, it presented a moral dilemma for the black women who had
been sensitized to the importance of their supporting and nurturing
black manhood. Young men like Stokely Carmichael in the Student Nonviolent Coordinating Committee reacted angrily and defensively, accus-
ing the women of losing sight of their appropriate roles in uplifting the
race. Since past oppression had attacked black manhood, women who asserted their own rights risked being seen as undermining racial progress.[35]

Emphasis on their responsibilities to the race was likely to discourage
black women's participation in the women's liberation movement of the
late 1960s. Although opinion polls at the time showed black women to
be far more supportive of the aims of the women's liberation movement
than were white women, and some black women did participate from
the beginning, black women were slower to join the feminist movement.[36]
When black feminist organizations were formed in the mid-1970s,
they emphasized their differences from white feminists. They accused
white feminists of ignoring the racial factor in women's lives, the long
history of black women's working, the economic realities of working-
class women's lives, and concerning themselves with issues appealing
only to the leisurely lives of privileged white women.[37] Divisions in the
American women's movement stemmed partly from the disparate experiences of black women and white women, but the historical construction of gender within each racial group was just as important. Just as
liberation for the black man came to mean constructing his masculine
identity, liberation for the black woman came to mean the ability to
define and assert a feminine identity. For white women, the aim of liberation was to break down the barriers between the sexes, to open the
doors to formerly male occupations and endeavors. For black women,
liberation lay, in one sense, in the ability to be less like men, that is, to be
treated with the dignity and respect accorded to women. Black women
were not willing to give up the strength and independence they had
achieved, but they were determined to have the choices formerly open
to middle-class white women. Most important, black women's liberation
could not be divorced from the struggle for the dignity and the rights of
all members of African-American society. This struggle, with its focus on

35 Collins, *Black Feminist Thought.*
36 Jo Freeman, *The Politics of Women's Liberation* (New York, 1975).
37 Barbara Sinclair Deckard, *The Women's Movement*, 3d ed. (New York, 1983).

black manhood, often obscured the control of both black women and white women by the patriarchal structures of society.

The power of what Michel Foucault terms "totalizing discourses" can be seen in the operation of the philosophical underpinnings of the structures of domination that converged in America to support the slave labor system. The "great truths" about the innate nature of African Americans – the feminized black male, the black matriarch, and the natural dependence of women – reverberate through the centuries and continue to restrict social options in contemporary society. At the heart of the certainties on which oppression rested in America was the idea of manhood and the belief that slavery denied this manhood to black men. Foucault argues that knowledge of the experiences of specific individuals and groups in particular places and times can undermine oppressive commonsense beliefs. An examination of the intersection of gender and race in American thought and experience, through the social history of African Americans and women, discloses the ambiguity in women's roles created by the idea of manhood in a patriarchal slaveholding society. Perhaps an understanding of this process can help free women from the power of such long-accepted truths.[38]

38 Mark Philp, "Michel Foucault," in Quentin Skinner, ed., *The Return of Grand Theory in the Social Sciences* (Cambridge, 1985), 76.

12

Citizenship Embodied

Racialized Gender and the Construction of Nationhood in the United States

EILEEN BORIS

When Barbara Cole visited a social-service center in Orange County, California, in 1991, she

walked into this monstrous room full of people, babies and little children all over the place, and I realized nobody was speaking English. I was overwhelmed with this feeling: "Where am I? What's happened here?" Social services had denied an elderly friend public health benefits; the counselor explained "that lots of those people waiting were illegal aliens and they were getting benefits instead of citizens like my friend."[1]

Cole responded by helping to organize the California Coalition for Immigration Reform that sponsored Proposition 187, the "Save Our State" initiative, as a ballot referendum that would prohibit undocumented immigrants from receiving state-financed social services. Under the initiative, such immigrants could not receive nonemergency health care, prenatal and childbirth services, child welfare, foster care, and public elementary, high school, or college education.[2] Social services, rights that characterize what the British philosopher T. H. Marshall called social citizenship,[3] could go only to citizens. The social wage – all those state-provided services that bolster individual earnings – belonged only to some, not all, who inhabited the nation.

---

1 This is a revised version of my article "The Racialized Gendered State: Conceptions of Citizenship in the United States," *Social Politics: International Studies in Gender, State, and Society* 2 (summer 1995): 160–80.
2 Roberto Suro, "California's SOS on Immigration," *Washington Post*, Sept. 29, 1994, A1; see also Hermann Schwartz, "The Constitutional Issue Behind Proposition 187," *Los Angeles Times*, Oct. 9, 1994, M1.
3 Thomas H. Marshall, *Citizenship and Social Class* (Cambridge, 1952).

"How dare we deny education to the children of women who clean our homes and raise our children?" asked *Los Angeles Times* columnist Robert Scheer in the midst of the resulting political battle over Proposition 187, which voters overwhelmingly approved in November 1994. "Imagine a California that sends mothers to prison for trying to keep their children in school!" exclaimed high-tech entrepreneur Ron K. Unz.[4] The left-liberal Scheer and Republican libertarian Unz equally exposed the gendered subtext that existed in the silences of Cole's recollections – a subtext that further reveals the racialized gendered construction of citizenship that Proposition 187 embodied.

Noncitizen women, overwhelmingly nonwhite, increasingly act as "nannies" so that citizen women, overwhelmingly white and of greater wealth, can combine wage earning with motherhood. Cutting services means denying immigrant women and their children health care and education. While Proposition 187 supporters continued to fear the economic consequences of immigration, they sought an easier terrain for battle: the welfare state already under attack for ostensibly fostering dependence instead of the work ethic among women who supposedly have babies to enjoy its subsidies. In fact, undocumented immigrants do not qualify for what at the time were the major welfare programs: Aid to Families with Dependent Children (AFDC) and food stamps. The amnesty program under the 1986 Immigration Reform Act contains a five-year ban on federal assistance; an 1882 restriction against those "likely to become a public charge" remains, increasingly enforced against Latina women in an attempt to keep them from residency. The immigrant mother, who greedily consumes social services with her children, now symbolizes the unwanted alien, having replaced the immigrant worker, who undermines good wages and working conditions. According to this scenario, both mothers and workers undercut the "American" standard of living even as they make their home in the United States, pay taxes, and become parents of citizens, that is, children born in the United States.[5]

Under the social insurance basis of the American welfare state, only wage earners who pay into the system out of their paychecks earn enti-

4 Robert Scheer, "The Dirty Secret Behind Proposition 187," *Los Angeles Times*, Sept. 29, 1994, B7; Ron K. Unz, "Scaling the Heights of Irrationality," *Los Angeles Times*, Oct. 3, 1994, B7. For the victory of 187, see Roberto Suro, "Proposition 187 Could Open Pandora's Box for GOP," *Washington Post*, Nov. 11, 1994, A24.
5 Grace Chang, "Undocumented Latinas: The New 'Employable' Mothers," in Evelyn Nakano Glenn, Grace Chang, and Linda Rennie Forcey, eds., *Mothering: Ideology, Experience, and Agency* (New York, 1994), 263–5.

tlements: old-age insurance, commonly called social security (which goes to the elderly), and unemployment compensation. Those related to these breadwinners by marriage or their children can also draw upon social security. Nonwage housewives and mothers only qualify for the stigmatized AFDC program. Immigrant mothers appear, like all mothers, as not workers and thus undeserving on the basis of both their citizenship status and lack of earnings.[6]

Who is a citizen? How does the construction of citizenship reflect the racialized gendered order? After the Civil War, the Fourteenth Amendment to the Constitution of the United States redefined the meaning of citizenship. It declared that all persons born or naturalized in the United States were American citizens and citizens of the state in which they resided. This prevented states from excluding African Americans from citizenship, but not other people defined as "nonwhite." Chinese and Japanese would be barred from citizenship; special acts would make Native Americans "citizens" by denying their nationhood and ethnicities. Only white immigrants had been able to become citizens following the Naturalization Act of 1790, but the children of immigrants born in the United States would be citizens no matter what the race or legal status of their parents.[7]

Historians of the United States have begun to chart the racialized boundaries of nationhood. That "America was born nearly free and racist" with the revolution against Britain has become a truism among those who recognize the paradox of independent nationhood emerging along with the development of chattel slavery.[8] Less apparent is how this racialized nation – in which only some belonged to the nation-state – was also gendered. Constructions of citizenship developed out of notions of whiteness, blackness, Anglo-Saxonism, womanhood, and manhood. The concept of "racialized gender" more accurately allows us to assess the relation of persons to the nation-state than the concept of race alone.

6 For the separation of mother from worker, see Eileen Boris, *Home to Work: Motherhood and the Politics of Industrial Homework in the United States* (New York, 1994); on social insurance models, see Linda Gordon, *Pitied but Not Entitled: Single Mothers and the History of Welfare* (New York, 1994), 145–81.

7 Donald G. Nieman, *Promises to Keep: African-Americans and the Constitutional Order, 1776 to the Present* (New York, 1991), 50–77; Lawrence H. Fuchs, *The American Kaleidoscope: Race, Ethnicity, and the Civic Culture* (Hanover, N.H., 1990), 7–16, 37–42, 87–94.

8 See George Rawick, *From Sundown to Sunup* (Westport, Conn., 1972). The classic on this remains Edmund Morgan, *American Freedom, American Slavery: The Ordeal of Colonial Virginia* (New York, 1979); see also Theodore Allen, *The Invention of the White Race* (New York, 1994ff.), vol. 1, who considers racism to be a deliberate ruling-class policy as opposed to Morgan's merely socioeconomic explanation.

I use the concept "racialized gender" to signify the interaction of race and gender. Scholars often attempt to disaggregate the workings of one category from the other, but I wish to emphasize how they have existed in conjunction with each other to profoundly transform the ways in which each works alone. As a term of analysis, race particularly suffers from biologism, from assumptions based on nineteenth-century anthropology that physical characteristics and genetic heritage distinguish one race from another. Such racialist thought usually feeds into racism because it encourages the classification of races based on a hierarchy among them. A historical approach, however, suggests that "white" as well as "black" are constructed terms, imagined communities that have not always embraced the same members even within the United States. Rather than "natural," I emphasize how "race" is a product of historical, social, cultural, and political forces.[9] Whereas much debate revolves around race as a category of analysis, feminist scholarship now takes for granted the creation of gender (and more recently sex), so that the very term signifies the made, rather than the found. Gender is a process and not determined biologically.[10] Ethnicity and nationalism are related terms that we must also problematize, whose meanings we cannot take for granted. We need to explore their histories rather than accept them as unchanging essences.[11] The meanings of all these terms shift over time; they have undergone constructions and reconstructions in light of historical events and in conjunction with each other.

By citizenship, I refer to the status of belonging to a nation-state and having rights and obligations in relation to that state. Following Marshall, recent scholarship has divided citizenship into three components: civil, political, and social. Civil refers to rights before the legal system, such as a jury by one's peers. Political embraces the right to suffrage and participation in the political realm. Social includes "the whole range from the right to a modicum of economic welfare and security to the right to share to the full in the social heritage and to live the life of a civilized being according to the standards prevailing in society." Timing of these

---

9 For an excellent statement of such a position, see Phyllis Palmer, "Review Essay: How We Talk About Race Affects What We Do About Race," *Journal of American Studies* 28 (1994): 255–65.

10 See Linda Nicholson, "Interpreting *Gender,*" *Signs: A Journal of Women in Culture and Society* 20 (autumn 1994): 79–105; Judith Butler, *Gender Trouble: Feminism and the Subversion of Identity* (New York, 1990).

11 A fine analysis of these terms is in Floya Anthias and Nira Yuval-Davis in association with Harriet Cain, *Racialized Boundaries: Race, Nation, Gender, Color and Class and the Anti-Racist Struggle* (New York, 1992).

rights has varied by class, gender, and race or ethnicity. Feminists in particular have modified Marshall by pointing out how these rights must
take different forms for women whose responsibility for bearing and
raising children often undermines economic and political power.[12]

This chapter presents an analytical narrative of the construction of citizenship in the United States in order to suggest how racialized gender –
as concept and material relation – shaped the rights and obligations of
citizens and the divisions of citizens from noncitizens. After considering
the birth of the Republic, I shall focus on naturalization and immigration policy. I shall conclude with a discussion of bodily integrity as a key
component of democratic society that has taken differential form according to racialized gender and immigrant status. Welfare rights represent
not only a form of social citizenship but also a necessary facilitator of
bodily integrity. Thus, Proposition 187 threatens the bodily integrity of
those designated as "the other" by their looks and their names, the un-
welcomed and undocumented who work as maids and housekeepers,
sweatshop garment workers and migrant agricultural laborers, whose
very presence California voters deemed a threat to the body politic.

THE BIRTH OF THE REPUBLIC

From the beginnings of American nationhood, racialized gender marked
citizenship, thus defining the rights of inhabitants. Since the late eighteenth century, the oppressed have appropriated the declaration that "All
men are created equal," but the Founding Fathers actually expressed particular meanings through this universal appeal. They excluded from the
term "men" both subordinate racial groups – Africans enslaved for their
labor power and indigenous peoples removed or exterminated for their
land – and their own mothers, wives, and daughters. Freedom rested on
slavery, and both were gendered. Slavery gave white people an identity in
opposition to black people, who became equated with the slave. Freedom – from control by the king – did not extend to married women,
who still suffered under coverture or legal death through subsumption
under the husband. Nor did freedom from colonial status mean freedom
or equal rights for the enslaved or formerly enslaved. The Founding

---

12 G. Andrews, ed., *Citizenship* (London, 1991); Ian Culpitt, *Welfare and Citizenship: Beyond the Crisis
of the Welfare State?* (London, 1992); Lydia Morris, *Dangerous Classes: The Underclass and Social Cit-
izenship* (New York, 1994), quotes Marshall, 44. For modifications, see also Nancy Fraser and
Linda Gordon, "Contract Versus Charity: Why Is There No Social Citizenship in the United
States?," *Socialist Review* 22 (July–Sept., 1992): 45–68; Ruth Lister, "Tracing the Contours of
Women's Citizenship," *Policy and Politics* 21, no. 1 (1993): 3–16.

Fathers were precisely that: brothers who made a racialized sexual contract as part of the social contract to enter into representative government. Citizenship status distinguished between inhabitants of a geographical area and groups within. Hence the enslaved counted as three-fifths of a person for apportioning congressional representatives; white women counted as a whole person. But neither could vote for the representatives that their numbers helped to determine.[13]

Citizenship depended on individual rights. But what if women were not individuals and counted only in relation to other family members, a throwback to the time when all men were dependents in the households of their betters?[14] As dependents, they could not receive the vote. The service of European-American women to nation building as republican mothers earned them moral power but not the political claim to full citizen rights (suffrage) that men gained through military sacrifice.[15] European-American women possessed a citizenship mediated by their womanhood and the meanings given to that concept.

In law, politics, and public policy, European-American women had meaning through their family relationships (as the bearers or caretakers of children) or through their connections to men (as wives or daughters). As early as the 1630s, Virginia law distinguished them from African-American women who – alone among free, enslaved, or servant women – were taxed for working in the fields along with men. Slave law saw black women as separate but not as individuals in the liberal sense. Slaves lacked the ability to control their own bodies.[16]

Notions of whiteness defined womanhood, motherhood, manhood, and even childlife. African-American women could have their womanhood denied because they were not white. They were judged as workers rather than women, categories growing more distinct by the late eighteenth century. Even their motherhood became work, with their chil-

13 My thought here is influenced by Carol Pateman, *The Sexual Contract* (Stanford, Calif., 1988), which I modify from the perspective of racialized gender; and Linda Kerber, "The Paradox of Women's Citizenship in the Early Republic: The Case of *Martin vs. Massachusetts, 1805*," *American Historical Review* 97 (Apr. 1992): 349–78. On the three-fifths clause, see Nieman, *Promises to Keep.*

14 For the shifting meaning of dependency, see Nancy Fraser and Linda Gordon, "'Dependency' Demystified: Inscriptions of Power in a Keyword of the Welfare State," *Social Politics: International Studies in Gender, State, and Society* 1 (spring 1994), 4–31; see also Nancy Fraser and Linda Gordon, "A Genealogy of *Dependency*: Tracing a Keyword of the U.S. Welfare State," *Signs: Journal of Women in Culture and Society* 19 (winter 1994): 309–36.

15 On Republican Motherhood, see Linda Kerber, *Women of the Republic: Intellect and Ideology in Revolutionary America* (Chapel Hill, N.C., 1980).

16 Paula Giddings, *Where and Where I Enter: The Impact of Black Women on Race and Sex in America* (New York, 1984), 33–55.

dren, as resources for the master, liable to be sold at any time for a profit. Other nonwhite women similarly suffered from lacking the designation of "woman."[17]

Racial slavery mitigated the class divisions that were developing among those increasingly identified as white. After Bacon's Rebellion in 1676, in which English indentured servants and former servants joined with Africans and disgruntled lesser gentry to defy the colonial governor, Virginia passed a series of laws to distinguish a white man from an African. White men, for example, would not be flogged as were Africans; the African could not testify against an Englishman. The planter class reasoned that if Africans were not the same kind of people, then individual rights could coexist with slavery. Likewise, they saw native peoples as outside the boundaries of the state; the indigenous Americans became "noble savages" or increasingly just "savages." Whether or not race was a necessary ingredient of slavery, it was an ingredient; the only slaves were from non-European groups. Significantly, enslavement became measured through the condition of the mother, a solution for miscegenation despite laws prohibiting such interracial connection. Africans became an oversexed people; their supposed bestiality and uncleanliness justified different and inferior treatment and the rule of whites. Enslaved, they suffered social death and could not be citizens.[18]

The American Revolution ushered in notions of citizenship in which working-class "freemen," in the North as well as in the South, benefited from their masculinity and their "whiteness." They began to define themselves against enslaved people and their own women. They were members of the new white Republic in which manliness (derived from skill or pride in craft) and whiteness cemented political life. This had political as well as symbolic consequences, allowing for the incorporation of

17 On mother and worker, see Boris, *Home to Work*; Jeanne Boydston, *Home and Work: Housework, Wages, and the Ideology of Labor in the Early Republic* (New York, 1991). Dorothy Roberts notes how black women have their motherhood denied them in "Racism and Patriarchy in the Meaning of Motherhood," *The American University Journal of Gender and the Law* 1 (1993): 1–38. For black womanhood, see Deborah Gray White, *Ar'n't I a Woman? Female Slaves in the Plantation South* (New York, 1985); Hazel Carby, *Reconstructing Womanhood: The Emergence of the Afro-American Woman Novelist* (New York, 1987). On racial-ethnic women, see Evelyn Nakano Glenn, "Racial Ethnic Women's Labor: The Intersection of Race, Gender and Class Oppression," *Review of Radical Political Economics* 17 (fall 1985): 86–108.

18 Ronald Takaki, *A Different Mirror: A History of Multicultural America* (Boston, 1993), 51–76. For "race" as a category in U.S. history, see Barbara Jeanne Fields, "Slavery, Race and Ideology in the United States of America," *New Left Review* 181 (May–June 1990): 95–118; and her earlier "Ideology and Race in American History," in J. Morgan Kousser and James M. McPherson, eds., *Region, Race, and Reconstruction: Essays in Honor of C. Vann Woodward* (New York, 1982), 143–78; Peggy Pascoe, "Race, Gender, and Intercultural Relations: The Case of Interracial Marriage," *Frontiers* 12, no. 1 (1991): 5–18.

northern European ethnics, including the despised Irish, into the body politic while barring Asians, placing Mexicans in an ambiguous status, and locking out Africans and indigenous people. The citizen of the Republic was the "common" man, and he was "white."[19]

IMMIGRATION AND NATURALIZATION POLICY

The Naturalization Act of 1790 limited naturalized citizenship to whites only. Europeans of both sexes could become incorporated into America; Africans could not. European immigrants would be accepted as citizens if they were white and held onto the beliefs of the Republic, although with voting as the main benefit of citizenship, men more often applied to become naturalized citizens. There would be no citizenship for people of color unless states allowed native-born free blacks to be citizens of their states. Indigenous peoples could not be citizens; Mexicans became defined as white for citizenship purposes, although they faced discriminatory laws in California and other conquered territory that placed them in a second-class status. The government would prohibit Chinese and Japanese immigration through the 1882 Chinese Exclusion Act and 1907 Gentleman's Agreement with Japan. Asians already here could not be naturalized; but they too suffered from race-based legal discrimination, including laws that prohibited intermarriage. Although racialist thought doubted the purity of various European ethnic groups and at different times refused to consider Irishmen, Italians, Finns, and Jews "white," European ethnics could claim whiteness by adopting the racism of the dominant society and distinguishing themselves from Africans, Mexicans, and other people of color.[20]

The history of immigrant restriction contains assumptions about appropriate homes, proper families, and gender roles. Citizens born in the United States would control the immigrant others by shaping their womanhood and manhood; among European immigrants especially, the racialized other could be molded into an American by becoming worthy not only through the work ethic but also through nuclear, heterosexual families with male breadwinners and female housewives who cared for their

19 David Roediger, *The Wages of Whiteness: Race and the Making of the American Working Class* (New York, 1991); Alexander Saxton, *The Rise and Fall of the White Republic: Class Politics and Mass Culture in Nineteenth-Century America* (New York, 1991). On the ambiguous status of Mexicans, see Takaki, *A Different Mirror*, 177–84.

20 Fuchs, *The American Kaleidoscope*, 7–16, 37–42, 87–94. For racialist thought, see Thomas E. Gossett, *Race: The History of an Idea in America* (New York, 1963). See also Rodgers M. Smith, "The Meaning of American Citizenship," *This Constitution* 8 (fall 1985): 14–15.

own children and homes in approved ways.[21] The 1910 report of the U.S. Immigration Commission, for example, concluded that men who migrated with families "exhibit a stronger tendency toward advancement." Those who came alone or "unaccompanied by their families" were associated with a drop in the "American Standard of Living." Although solo men often were saving money to send to families in their country of origin, they seemed to deviate from the pattern of the male breadwinner/ protector because they had left their families behind. (Similarly, undocumented immigrants from the Americas, particularly Mexico, came to work in the 1970s and early 1980s; most were young men who sent back their earnings and used few social services.) Immigrant workers appeared as obstacles to the family wage that the American Federation of Labor sought for its skilled, mostly northern, European male membership. Moreover, through child labor, the industrial work done by mothers in the home, and extended households, immigrant families challenged other gendered understandings of social life. They mixed the home sphere with the work world as they extended the boundaries of kin and family to embrace a greater variety of relationships. In both its nativist-culturalist and economic rationales, immigrant restriction embodied conceptions of womanhood and manhood.[22]

From the start Congress sought to facilitate "the coming together of families as a unit and the reuniting of families whose members did not immigrate at the same time." Permanent immigrants gained preference over "sojourners," those mostly male "birds of passage" who came to the United States during good times to earn money to bring back to their country of origin. The first proposed literacy test for prospective immigrants in 1896 – an attempt to stem the tide of those judged by Anglo-Saxons as having "thoughts and . . . beliefs . . . wholly alien to ours" – exempted alien parents of present and future residents. It harbored a gender distinction that derived from a perceived shortage of domestic servants by applying only to males aged sixteen to sixty; a nongendered literacy test would bar more women than men since women more likely lacked the ability to read and write in their native languages. Then, as now, the low wages of service required "alien" women to "free" citizen

---

21 Gwendolyn Mink, "The Lady and the Tramp: Gender, Race, and the Origins of the American Welfare State," in Linda Gordon, ed., *Women, the State, and Welfare* (Madison, Wis., 1990), 92–122.

22 Gwendolyn Mink, *Old Labor and New Immigrants in American Political Development* (Ithaca, N.Y., 1987); U.S. Immigration Commission, "Brief Statement of the Conclusions and Recommendations of the Immigration Commission" (Washington, D.C., 1910), 30–2; David M. Reimers, *Still the Golden Door: The Third World Comes to America*, 2d ed. (New York, 1992), 230–9.

women, especially white middle-class ones, from the burdens of women's work in the home.[23]

Other restrictive legislation also contained exemptions to promote family maintenance. The 1906 literacy bill expanded the exempt categories to include the wife, mother, fiancée, or father over fifty-five of the immigrant. The 1917 bill that actually became law over President Woodrow Wilson's veto allowed the legal immigrant to bring in his father or grandfather over age fifty-five, wife, mother, grandmother, and unmarried or widowed daughter (but not widower son), whether or not these individuals could read. Such acts considered the immigrant to be a man in his prime work years. Later acts of Congress continued to privilege women related to male citizens or legal male immigrants, perhaps out of the belief that women are men's dependents. Beginning in January 1951, a racially ineligible spouse and children of veterans of the U.S. armed forces could enter the United States if the marriage took place six months after enactment of this law in August 1950.[24] Immigration reform in the 1960s continued to privilege the entrance of family members in keeping with conceptions of social stability.[25]

The legal fiction that a married woman merged her identity into her husband's had ominous implications for the citizenship rights of the woman born in the United States. With their marriages unrecognized by the law, enslaved women had no such problem, but then again, they were not citizens; neither were Native-American women until the Dawes Act of 1887 and the Synder Act of 1924.[26] The immigrant woman on the basis of her relation to an American-born man could have more rights than a woman born in the United States. An 1855 act of Congress provided citizenship to a noncitizen woman who married an American citizen. Courts similarly argued that a woman born in the United States who married a noncitizen suspended her citizenship since a woman's citizenship followed her husband's. Women born in the United States could find themselves treated as noncitizens and stateless if the country of their spouse rejected them as citizens. A 1907 law actually codified court rulings by taking citizenship away from women born in the United

23 Edward P. Hutchinson, *Legislative History of American Immigration Policy, 1798–1965* (Philadelphia, 1981), 117–18, 482, 505.
24 Hutchinson, *Legislative History*, 506–7.
25 On changes in the 1960s, see Reimers, *Still the Golden Door*, 61–91.
26 James S. Olson and Raymond Wilson, *Native Americans in the Twentieth Century* (Urbana, Ill., 1984), 85–6; Dolores Janiewiski, "Learning to Live 'Just Like White Folks': Gender, Ethnicity, and the State in the Inland Northwest," in Dorothy O. Helly and Susan M. Reverby, eds., *Gendered Domains: Rethinking Public and Private in Women's History* (Ithaca, N.Y., 1992), 167–80.

States and married to "aliens." The Cable Act of 1922 provided, only after women's suffrage and a vigorous women's movement, that "the right of a person to become a naturalized citizen shall not be denied to a person on account of sex or because she is a married woman." But if the noncitizen husband of a woman born in the United States was ineligible for citizenship – as were Japanese and Chinese – such a woman would lose hers. This happened to second-generation Japanese Americans. And because they were treated as naturalized citizens, they could lose their citizenship after residing abroad for two years.[27]

For immigrant women married to naturalized men, the Cable Act made it more difficult to obtain citizenship. Less educated than their husbands, they had to take the naturalization exam in their own right. More isolated from the larger society than men, some of these immigrant wives and mothers were hesitant to do so. Others had great difficulty taking English and Americanization courses at night, caring for children, and earning wages at the same time. But without citizenship, immigrant women could not qualify for mothers' pensions, the predecessor to AFDC, which some previously had been able to obtain on the basis of a deceased husband's citizenship (when not discriminated against for being an unworthy immigrant in the first place.) As political theorist Wendy Sarvasy has shown, women reformers like Edith Abbott and Sophinisba Breckinridge urged that formal citizenship not be a prerequisite for pensions and that immigrant women have a choice whether to gain citizenship through their husbands or on their own. Breckinridge argued: "Citizenship is highly desirable for the mothers or other caretakers of children, but the conclusions to be drawn are that the tests of fitness to care for children should be sufficient tests of fitness for citizenship." But in the 1920s, with the triumph of immigration restriction, neither the state nor the public desired to enable immigrant mothers to become citizens on the basis of their gendered experiences. The standard for citizenship would remain geared to men's lives and failed to recognize the work that mothers did to educate and nurture the next generation of citizen-workers.[28]

Thus, immigration and naturalization policy not only was gendered; it also had tremendous implications for family formation. Immigration

27 For a cogent summary, see Kerber, "The Paradox of Women's Citizenship," 377–8; but see also Virginia Sapiro, "Women, Citizenship and Nationality: Immigration and Naturalization Policies in the United States," *Politics and Society* 13 (1984): 1–26.
28 Wendy Sarvasy, "Beyond the Difference Versus Equality Policy Debate: Postsuffrage Feminism, Citizenship, and the Quest for a Feminist Welfare State," *Signs: Journal of Women in Culture and Society* 17, no. 2 (winter 1992): 351–5.

Service regulations promoted legitimacy in childbearing by interpreting the quota act of 1924 to claim that "an illegitimate child had no standing as a stepchild of the mother's American citizen husband who was not the father of the child."[29]

During World War II, the state attempted to regulate marriages of military personnel to noncitizen women. It did not prohibit such "overseas marriages" but left "the question . . . to the sound discretion of the commanding officer concerned." The War Department made it more difficult for such families to remain together by not providing funds or services to transport dependents to the United States upon the discharge of the soldier-husband; neither would it transfer dependents when reassigning the husband during the course of the war. It attempted to discourage commanding officers from granting permissions to marry through distribution of "pertinent facts" that underscore the racialist assumptions behind state policy. Directives reminded commanding officers that

(a) Existing laws . . . prohibit the admission into the United States of aliens ineligible to citizenship. This means that persons of Asiatic or East Indian descent, even though married to American citizens, cannot be admitted to the United States. (b) The laws of a number of States do not recognize as valid any marriage contracted between persons of certain different races, regardless of whether the marriage was valid where contracted.

The War Department also reflected a generalized anti-immigrant bias when it noted that marriage to a citizen did not automatically bring American citizenship and that "the alien wife of an American citizen will be denied admission to the United States if the American consular officer determines that she is likely to become a public charge." In May 1944, the Commanding General, Southwest Pacific Area reported that he had given permission to five African-American "enlisted men . . . to marry white native women" due to "pregnancy."[30]

Insofar as racialist assumptions have driven such policy, they also have affected gender relations within ethnic communities. Women could enter the country as picture brides and already married wives, circumstances that might make them more dependent on men within their families upon arrival. More recently, women who have come into the country by

29 Edith Lowenstein, *The Alien and the Immigration Law* (New York, 1957; reprint, Westport, Conn., 1972), 29–30.
30 War Department, Washington, D.C., Ag 291.1 (Sept. 11, 1943), Subject: Overseas Marriages of Military Personnel; To: The Commander-in-Chief, Southwest Pacific Area, attached to Stanley J. Grogan to Jonathan Daniels, May 22, 1944, in Fair Employment Practice Committee, or FEPC, files, 4245-G, box 4, folder A–J 44, Franklin D. Roosevelt Library, Hyde Park, New York.

virtue of marriage to a man with legal status or citizenship cannot leave that marriage for two years. Otherwise they risk deportation even if they leave the marriage to end a violent or abusive relationship.[31]

BODILY INTEGRITY, CITIZENSHIP, AND DEMOCRACY

Democracy requires the free movement of the citizen; citizenship presumes the integrity of the body. The noncitizen immigrant lacks access to certain jobs and to free movement; leaving the country does not necessarily mean reentry will be possible. In the late 1880s, Chinese men who returned to their homeland to visit or to marry discovered that the Exclusion Act applied to them even though they had lived in the United States for years and had obtained a certificate guaranteeing readmission.[32]

The struggle over citizenship for African Americans occurred on an embodied terrain. Segregation denied their citizenship rights. Jim Crow laws created a geography that mapped power and hierarchy through bodies by denying free movement to African-American men and women and, to a lesser extent, white women. The rape-lynching complex developed as southern white men used the protection of their women as an excuse to control black men, but maintained their manhood rights in raping black women. If bodily integrity is a key component of citizenship rights, then African-American men as well as women lacked full rights. Bodies here played more than a symbolic role.[33]

The Civil War amendments to the Constitution of the United States extended citizenship rights to African Americans but only incorporated black men into the body politic. The Thirteenth Amendment abolished slavery; the Fourteenth Amendment provided citizenship. The Fifteenth Amendment gave black men the right to vote, but not immigrant men, and western states had already excluded Chinese from citizenship. But through terrorism and the law, southern states undercut these amendments, threatening the bodily integrity of the newly emancipated women and men by denying the democratic right to vote, equality before the law, and economic choice. Redeemers snatched away civil and political

---

31 On the family basis of Asian immigration, see Takaki, *From A Distant Shore*; on picture brides, Hyung-chan Kim, *A Legal History of Asian Americans, 1790–1990* (Westport, Conn., 1994), 103; Nilda Rimonte, "A Question of Culture: Cultural Approval of Violence Against Women in the Pacific-Asian Community and the Cultural Defense," *Stanford Law Review* 43 (July 1991): 1311–26.

32 For such an analysis, see Leonard Dinerstein, "The Supreme Court and the Rights of Aliens," *This Constitution* 8 (fall 1985): 27–30.

33 See, e.g., Jacqueline Dowd Hall, *Revolt Against Chivalry*, 2d ed. (New York, 1993).

as well as social citizenship through restrictions in courts, vagrancy ordinances, segregated railroads, and debt peonage.[34]

Central to the concept of bodily integrity, for men as well as women, is safety from harm. Without bodily integrity, participation in other aspects of public life becomes problematic. Derived from classical liberalism, with its emphasis on self-mastery or control, bodily integrity focuses on the individual citizen. But control of one's body becomes an oppositional act under circumstances that deny control based on racialized gender. Bodily integrity depends on the individual's connection to the community and can flourish best in conjunction with the bodily integrity of others. In such a context, it merges the personal with the political, the personalistic with the social.[35]

Questions of bodily integrity continue to block full enjoyment of citizenship. This issue goes beyond the question of reproductive rights – a broader concept, when considered from the standpoint of women of color, that embraces the right to have children as well as legalized, safe, and available abortion. Communities of color, particularly poorer African-American and Latino ones, face police harassment and brutality, invasion of their intimacy by social workers, and occupational and environmental disease. Doctors and police more likely punish substance abuse among poor mothers, disproportionately women of color, confining them in jail during pregnancy and removing children from their custody. Life in inner cities, where poor people of color live, is more dangerous, police protection never adequate.[36]

Bodily integrity also embraces the wholeness of the body, requiring a minimum standard of living and access to health care. The question of who had access to public relief and AFDC depends on racialized gendered citizenship. State-federal relations, along with the courts, determined the shape and the implementation of the New Deal through which the modern welfare state developed. Northern states included African Americans in temporary programs to relieve distress. In contrast, southern states usually discriminated – denying social citizenship just as

---

34 Nieman, *Promises to Keep*, 50–77; Edward Ayers, *The Promise of the New South: Life After Reconstruction* (New York, 1992).

35 In developing this concept I have drawn upon Pateman, *The Sexual Contract*.

36 E.g., Rosalind Pollack Petchesky, *Abortion and Woman's Choice: The State, Sexuality and Reproductive Freedom* (New York, 1984); Dorothy Roberts, "Punishing Drug Addicts Who Have Babies: Women of Color, Equity, and the Right of Privacy," *Harvard Law Review* 104 (1990): 1419–50; Cynthia R. Daniels, *At Women's Expense: State Power and the Politics of Fetal Rights* (Cambridge, Mass., 1993), 97–131. These themes take a different twist when we consider poor men of color; for one example of a black male scholar unpacking race, gender, and state policy, see Troy Duster, "Crime, Youth Unemployment, and the Black Urban Underclass," *Crime and Delinquency* 33 (Apr. 1987): 300–16.

blatantly as they undermined political and civil citizenship. New Deal agricultural policy ultimately undermined the southern racial order by pushing African Americans off the land.[37]

Local implementation of federal relief programs often meant racialized gendered differentials and exclusions. If the cotton crop or beet crop needed pickers, African-American or Mexican women would be dropped from the relief rolls. Many never qualified for either work relief or the dole, since it was assumed that women of color would work as domestic servants. When they were included on federal work projects – and they never were in the numbers that their need demanded – they were channeled into household labor while white women could gain supervisory positions and white-collar jobs. Outdoor work was men's work, unless one was a black woman who might be put on a beautification project, that is, on a trash gang doing road work. Works projects would hire only a male head of household, often excluding women no matter what their race.[38] Exclusion from benefits, then, represents a primary way in which citizenship became denied on the basis of racialized gender.

The Social Security Act of 1935 was no different. As political sociologist Jill Quadagno has pointed out, it "created a racial division in the distribution of benefits to women." Southern congressmen required local control of eligibility as a condition for passage. Thus, most recipients of AFDC initially were white widows. Divided into inclusionary, non–means-tested, and exclusionary, means-tested programs, the New Deal state incorporated a pattern of racial segmentation that depended on the relative exclusion of minority- and female-headed households from the main non–means-tested and private forms of social protection. The elderly received old-age insurance; workers obtained unemployment compensation; widows and survivors of workers gained survivors' benefits; the poor got AFDC or old-age assistance (OAA), actually the largest program until the 1950s. OAA was a local program, and thus African Americans received benefits depending on where they resided.[39]

37 Theda Skocpol, "African Americans and American Social Policy," 26–7, paper presented at the Annual Workshop of the Research Network on Gender, State, and Society of the Social Science History Association, Baltimore, Nov. 1993; on the impact of agricultural policy, see Jill Quadagno, *The Transformation of Old Age Security: Class and Politics in the American Welfare State* (Chicago, 1988).

38 For a critique of the New Deal that adds gender but concentrates on race and class, see Michael K. Brown, "Divergent Fates: The Antinomies of Race and Class in the New Deal," unpublished paper, 1993. For racialized gendered policies, see Jones, *Labor of Love*, 172–97; Sarah Deutsch, *No Separate Refuge: Culture, Class, and Gender on an Anglo-Hispanic Frontier in the American Southwest, 1880–1940* (New York, 1987), 162–99.

39 Jill Quadagno, *The Color of Welfare: How Racism Undermined the War on Poverty* (New York, 1994),

Given the gaps in coverage that resulted from political compromise,
African Americans and many Mexican Americans found themselves excluded from social security and unemployment compensation into the
1960s and 1970s as they concentrated in the uncovered agricultural and
service industries. The public thought that welfare or AFDC went to the
undeserving poor rather than merely the uncovered and underpaid. Because the labor market continues disproportionately to exclude African
Americans from jobs covered by private insurance or public unemployment compensation, they increasingly have ended up on welfare. Some
might call this indirect government discrimination because the sorting
mechanism is the labor market, but government established its programs
in reference to a preexisting labor market segmentation by race and gender.
Access to welfare for African Americans took place only after renewed
migration out of the South during World War II. Then African-American
women could slip past the blatant discrimination of local southern officials. Indeed, the federalizing of some social programs, like AFDC, placed
power with northern machine politicians, an institutional change that
eventually increased benefits for black migrants whose votes maintained
machine rule.[40]

Restrictive welfare rules limited the numbers on welfare until government responded to the organizing efforts of welfare mothers in the
mid-1960s. "Man in the house" rules cut off benefits if the mother was
sleeping with a boyfriend; social workers could enter homes in the middle of the night. Some states cut off welfare during harvest time. As a
way to cut the welfare rolls, states made concerted efforts to withdraw
support from mothers with illegitimate children. Louisiana's 1960 law
stated:

In no instance shall assistance be granted to any person who is living with his
or her mother if the mother has had an illegitimate child after a check has been
received from the Welfare Department unless and until proof satisfactory to the
Parish Board of Public Welfare has been presented showing that the mother has
ceased illicit relationship and is maintaining suitable home.

The Gallup Poll soon afterward reported that a majority found it acceptable to withhold federal support or food money from illegitimate black
babies. But facts and social perceptions often fail to match. AFDC be-

119. See also Mimi Abramowitz, *Regulating the Lives of Women: Social Welfare Policy from Colonial
Times to the Present* (Boston, 1988), 215–40, 313–48.
40 Gordon, *Pitied but Not Entitled*, 183–306. For pensions in general, see Ann Shola Orloff, *The
Politics of Pensions: A Comparative Analysis of Britain, Canada, and the United States, 1880–1940*
(Madison, Wis., 1993).

came stigmatized as a black program because of the growing numbers of black recipients, even though more unwed white mothers received such grants. Meanwhile, immigrant women, especially increased numbers who entered the country illegally, could not even apply for such assistance.[41]

AFDC continued the casework tradition of an earlier era, when social workers investigated the use of relief funds by recipients as part of the process of verifying the worthiness of those aided. In this sense, welfare as constructed allowed agents of the state to invade the privacy and control the bodies (clothing, food, housing) of those who qualified. The "means test" pushed recipients to rid themselves of any resources in order to retain their eligibility or risk lesser payments. Only women on welfare experienced a "morals test" to judge whether their home remained suitable for the care of children. This indirect control of women's sexuality further denied the bodily integrity central to citizenship.[42]

CONCLUSION

After the 1994 American electoral campaign, the Republican-controlled House of Representatives and Republican governors engaged in a bidding war to see who could propose more draconian measures to restrict welfare. The previous summer President Bill Clinton had proposed restrictions on teenagers and a two-year time limit on eligibility. Some states already were experimenting with denying welfare mothers additional benefits for children born out of wedlock or docking their checks if older children skipped school. Such proposals prefigured others that would punish the mother for her behavior by removing children or the funds enabling her to fulfill her responsibilities as a mother. Lawmakers assumed that women had babies in order to obtain welfare checks that did not provide an adequate standard of living anywhere in the country. They would use welfare to shape morality and reshape sexual behavior. They would punish those who refused to abide by the work ethic even if the only available jobs sank women deeper into poverty because they failed to pay a wage adequate to support a household.[43]

---

41 Rickie Solinger, *Wake Up Little Susie: Single Pregnancy and Race in the Pre-Roe vs. Wade Era* (New York, 1992); see also Rickie Solinger, "Race and 'Value': Black and White Illegitimate Babies, 1945–1965," in Glenn, Chang, and Forcey, eds., *Mothering: Ideology, Experience, and Agency*, 287–310. For immigrant women, see Chang, "Undocumented Latinas."

42 For a fine analysis of these matters, see Gordon, *Pitied but Not Entitled*, 293–9.

43 For one state battle, see Michael Cooper, "Tough Welfare Restrictions Proposed for Massachusetts," *New York Times*, Feb. 4, 1995, A1, 6; for a critique of such proposals, "Women Academics Concerned About Welfare," political advertisement in *New Republic*, Jan. 23, 1995.

Women used to gain citizenship for their work as mothers. But in the 1990s debates over welfare reform, such labor brought scorn from those who argued that welfare mothers should find jobs. In the public's mind, these mothers were not just any random group of lazy women, but young minority women whose race and gender together lessened their worth. Like "illegal" immigrants, unwed mothers were judged "undeserving," condemned for draining the resources of those who played by the rules and took responsibility for their lives. As the United States sought to rethink its welfare state, racialized gendered concepts continued to define the nation, determining access to citizenship in the process.

13

Body Matters

Race, Gender, and Perceptions of Physical Ability from Goethe to Weininger

PATRICIA VERTINSKY

INTRODUCTION

In *Fables of Desire*, Helga Geyer-Ryan shows how every racist discourse in a patriarchal society necessarily includes a discourse on the sexuality (or, rather, the nonsexuality) of that society's representative woman. To be accurate, she says, the race problem as such exists only as a sexual problem, as was illustrated in Goethe's 1779 version of *Iphigenia in Tauris*, which retained such cultural power in German literary tradition. *Iphigenia* can be read as a subtle discourse on social and racial control through the inscription of the two main images onto the reader's perception: First, the white woman is sexually threatened by the barbarian; and second, the barbarians are really yearning for all that is Greek.[1]

The function and importance of the appeal of these images derive, Geyer-Ryan suggests, from their capacity to mold the subject into a specific patriarchal and ethnic identity. Because Germany in the eighteenth century was not yet a nation-state that could construct an identity in opposition to other ethnic groups, it employed a vague notion of European identity reaching back into the classical heritage of Greece to

I wish to acknowledge the support of the Social Sciences and Humanities Research Council of Canada in the preparation of this chapter, and the helpful suggestions of Allen Guttmann, Arndt Krüger, and Gertrud Pfister.
1 Among the vital changes Goethe introduced into his version of Euripides' *Iphigenia in Tauris* was the transformation of Thoas, the barbarian king, into a noble barbarian king who also took a sexual interest in Iphigenia. "Thoas longs for the socially elevated woman and always will because he cannot attain her, and the cult central to the national identity stays back in Tauris with the effigy of Artemis." In the end, "Thoas is left with empty hands – a circumstance which tacitly assumes the Scythian desire for the Greek" (Helga Geyer-Ryan, *Fables of Desire: Studies in the Ethics of Art and Gender* [Cambridge, 1994], 134).

find the imaginary body of European culture. The appropriation of this heritage, including the ideal Greek male body as a subject position of cultural superiority, helped provide moral justification for embodying German racism, sexism, and imperialism during the nineteenth century and into the twentieth. By the time of the Third Reich, German fascism had translated the preracialist topos of culture-versus-barbarism into pure racism. "Jews and Slavs, both from the East, have become a sub-human race. Both have been endowed with an aura of abnormal sexual appetite."[2] The German woman had become the white desexualized mother-sister ideal, guardian of culture and morals and guarantee and basis of a patriarchal identity. The ideal German man was not only a reflection of the classical Greek warrior-hero-athlete, he had become a "Wagnerian Siegfried," lithe and tall, with steel-hard muscles and firm flesh, blond hair, blue eyes, and a particular clarity of skin.[3]

Nowhere is this better illustrated, perhaps, than in Sander Gilman's discussion of Erik Erikson's parody of Hitler's racial typology as a simple dichotomy between the German (soldier) and the Jew:

The Jew is described as small, black and hairy all over; his back is bent, his feet are flat; his eyes squint, and his lips smack; he has an evil smell, is promiscuous, and loves to deflower, impregnate, and infect blond girls. The Aryan is tall, erect, light, without hair on chest and limbs; his glance, walk and talk are *stramm*, his greeting the out-stretched arm. He is passionately clean in his habits. He would not knowingly touch a Jewish girl except in a brothel. This antithesis is clearly one of ape man and superman.[4]

George Mosse has suggested how, from the start, modern nationalism was concerned with sexual control and restraint as part of the larger effort to cope with the complex social and political changes wrought by industrialization and revolution.[5] Parker and others similarly argue in *Nationalisms and Sexualities* that nationalism and questions of sexuality and gender are interrelated phenomena, having been inappropriately separated by philosophical and critical traditions that tacitly accepted the

2 Ibid., 136.
3 Albert Speer, *Inside the Third Reich* (New York, 1970), 96. Lois Banner notes how patriarchy has consistently been able to readjust itself to threats against its hegemony by reinventing idealizations of the masculine heroic. In *Full Flower: Aging Women, Power and Sexuality* (New York, 1993), 19.
4 Sander Gilman, *Difference and Pathology: Stereotypes of Sexuality, Race and Madness* (Ithaca, N.Y., 1985), 32.
5 George L. Mosse, "Nationalism and Respectability: Normal and Abnormal Sexuality in the Nineteenth Century," *Journal of Contemporary History* 17 (1982): 222; George L. Mosse, *Toward the Final Solution: A History of European Racism* (New York, 1978), 111.

categorization of the latter as private matters having little to do with the public realm of nation building.[6] The emergence of the modern state stimulated new imperatives to control and discipline the body as the idea of nationalism and the emerging concept of national identity became potent devices to define the boundaries between normality and deviancy, masculinity and femininity, health and sickness, beauty and ugliness, and to provide an appropriate vocabulary for the sense of difference. Difference is what threatens order and control, suggests Gilman, hence the idea of the pathological becomes a central marker for difference. He relates, no doubt, to Freud, who claimed that "we are so made that we can derive intense enjoyment only from a contrast and very little from a state of things."[7]

German nationalism, according to Mosse, offered ideals and standards of beauty, along with stereotypes of the ideal classical Greek male body. "The beautiful body as the personification of the beautiful nation was supposed to transcend its own sexuality."[8] With the help of sanitized masculine Greek models in the national stereotype manifesting chastity and restraint as well as harmony, proportion, beauty, athleticism, vigor, and the best qualities of a soldier, a nervous age might be controlled and disciplined.[9] Maintaining the ideal of masculinity as opposed to unrestrained sexuality and effeminacy was seen as essential to the order and health of the nation. "Masculine comportment and a manly figure exemplified the transcendence of the so-called lower passions."[10] Thus, nationalism used racist, sexist, and anti-Semitic stereotypes to redirect passion from the individual body to the body politic of the nation.[11]

Efforts to revive masculinity were typically embedded in a larger critique of European society and the lure of a compulsively antimodernist sentiment that included a particular rejection of the industrial city as a place of sin, loose morals, and a sapper of virility. As the nineteenth century advanced:

6 Andrew Parker et al., eds., *Nationalisms and Sexualities* (New York, 1992), 2.

7 Gilman, *Difference and Pathology*, 15–29; Sigmund Freud, *Civilization and Its Discontents*, trans. and ed. James Strachey (1930; reprint, New York, 1961), quoted in James A. Boon, *Other Tribes, Other Scribes: Symbolic Anthropology in the Comparative Study of Cultures, Histories, Religions, and Texts* (Cambridge, 1982), 3.

8 George L. Mosse, "Nationalism and Respectability," 223; for a discussion of sexual abstinence and Greek athletes, see Wilfried Fiedler, "Sexuelle Enthaltsamkeit griechischer Athleten und ihre medizinische Begründung," *Stadion* 11, no. 2 (1985): 137–75.

9 Mosse, "Nationalism and Respectability," 223.

10 George L. Mosse, *Nationalism and Sexuality: Respectability and Abnormal Sexuality in Modern Europe* (New York, 1985), 13.

11 Isabel V. Hull, "The Bourgeoisie and Its Discontents: Reflections on 'Nationalism and Respectability,'" *Journal of Contemporary History* 17 (1982): 257.

The concepts of degeneration and the survival of the fittest became embroiled with European racism [in such a way that] the characterization of inferior races was similar in almost every respect to that applied to so-called sexual degenerates. The stereotypes of beauty and ugliness were the same, and so were the fears that inspired them. . . . First Blacks and then Jews were endowed with excessive sexuality, a female sensuousness said to transform love into lust. They lacked manliness: Jews were said to have female characteristics, just as homosexuals were generally called effeminate. Both . . . were estranged from the healing power of nature, strangers to Greece.[12]

The compulsive reassertion of traditional masculinity resonated with renewed yearning for the symbols of classical Greece, and the imagery of manly athleticism and military toughness demanded the height of physical vigor among German men. It also provided a compelling foil for the further demonstration of the interrelated physical inadequacies of women and Jews painted by the Viennese Jewish intellectual Otto Weininger in 1903.[13]

Weininger's portrayal of the imaginary impaired Jewish body despised by the anti-Semite has been called a classic case of Jewish self-hatred. In *Sex and Character*, Weininger drew widely upon scientific arguments in Germany and elsewhere in Europe to insist that there was a fundamental homology between the pale, ugly, and lecherous Jew and the weak, passive, and potentially hysterical woman, the woman being a negative force incapable of positive and productive force and totally preoccupied with her sexuality. Adding a racial argument to his thesis of female inferiority, he located the female at the far end of the continuum from the male and placed the Jew beside her as a total contrast to the real male, who exemplified normalcy and self-control yet knew how to fight.[14] He could then link the concept of degeneration to that of sexuality to conclude that the Jew might well be regarded as a degenerate woman. Weininger saw the wellspring of their own degeneration hidden within the insatiable sexuality of both.[15] "To be either a Jew or a woman was a physiological state that could not be cured."[16] Weininger's book, suggests Gilman, was "a mad diatribe against the specters of the woman and the Jew which haunted his own imagination" but his work was in many ways a reflection of popular scientific and medical attitudes toward the

---

12 Mosse, "Nationalism and Respectability," 230.
13 While recognizing that Austria and Germany became separate countries, I refer in this paper to Austrians such as Weininger and Freud as "culturally" German.
14 Otto Weininger, *Sex and Character*, authorized translation from 6th German ed. (London, 1906), 301–20, 106–7.
15 Sander Gilman, *Jewish Self-Hatred: Anti-Semitism and the Hidden Language of the Jews* (Baltimore, 1991), 19.
16 Mosse, *Nationalism and Sexuality*, 145.

impaired body of the woman, the Jew (and people of color), which were the mirror image of the ideal German male stereotype, the beautiful Greek warrior-athlete-hero melded with the historic "Aryan" type.[17] Weininger's "Aryan" male was exemplified by classical models, says Mosse, "not only as part of the 'Aryan' ideal type but also as an unambivalent reference point in a confused and complex world."[18]

Weininger, the arch anti-Semite, has been called the psychobiographer's dream come true because of the way he dealt with his own despair over his homosexuality and his Jewishness, but his work does provide a particularly convenient focus for historical investigations of racism, sexism and the body, and the role of analogy in shaping body images of racial and sexual difference. *Sex and Character* (which perhaps owed its popularity to Weininger's sensational suicide in Beethoven's house) has been viewed as a critique of modern culture and as "a symptomatic text of the fears, concerns, and prejudices of fin-de-siècle Europe," framed as it was in response to contemporary biological and medical texts.[19] Their influence upon Weininger's discourse was significant, but the science articulated within them was, of course, significantly influenced by cultural factors. Within their numerous texts and in response to the political pressure of emerging feminist movements, scientists and medical men repeatedly tried to demonstrate that a female's morphology and physiology constrained her physical potential and limited the possibility of improvement in her intellectual and social status. By locating the Jew on the female end of the gender continuum, Weininger located the problem of the Jew's physical ineptitude and social status in his nervous and unstable body as well. The Jew, Weininger said, is preoccupied, like a woman, with his sexuality; he has no soul, no moral sense, nor does he sing or engage in sports.[20] The hopelessness of the Jew's bodily circumstance ruled out, of course, the possibility of Weininger's own improvement. In despair he decisively canceled his own Jewish embodiment by killing himself.[21]

---

17 Gilman, *Difference and Pathology*, 55.
18 Mosse, *Toward the Final Solution*, 109.
19 Chandak Sengoopta, "Science, Sexuality, and Gender in the Fin de Siècle: Otto Weininger as Baedeker," *History of Science* 30 (1992): 249–79. Nancy Leys-Stepan and Sander L. Gilman concur that however bizarre Weininger's work may appear to be, in his own time he was understood as a scientific investigator whose ideas, although controversial, were nevertheless taken as contributions to scholarship, not as examples of psychosis. "Appropriating the Idioms of Science: The Rejection of Scientific Racism," in Sandra Harding, ed., *The "Racial" Economy of Science: Toward a Democratic Future* (Bloomington, Ind., 1993), 180.
20 Weininger, *Sex and Character*, 170.
21 How a man feels about himself is closely related to how he feels about his body, and homosexuals, for example, have been shown to place an elevated importance on aspects of a man's physical self. See Marc E. Mishkind et al., "The Embodiment of Masculinity," *American Behavioral Scientist* 29 (May–June 1986): 545–62.

Weininger's analogy between the Jew and the woman was effective not because the associated commonplaces or constructed systems of implications were at all true, but because they were readily and freely evoked.[22] The analogy, or interactive metaphor as it has been described by Max Black, selects, emphasizes, suppresses, and organizes features of reality, highlighting aspects of human experience otherwise treated as unimportant and making new features into signs of inferiority.[23] What was significant in the scientific and medical discourse on human difference, suggests Nancy Leys-Stepan, was that interactive metaphors and race-gender analogies implied a similar cause of the resemblances between races and women and of the differences between both groups and white males. Scientists were led to make particular choices in selecting physical differences for study and to suppress or exaggerate information gained from their research. Not surprisingly they then interpreted their information according to their own mental representations of the world, constructing bodies to perpetuate the racial and gendered status quo.[24] "The analogies were used by scientists to justify resistance to efforts at social change on the part of women and 'lower races' on the grounds that inequality was a fact of nature and not a function of the power relations in society." Where the science of human difference was concerned, by the late nineteenth century "the system of implications evoked by the analogy linking the lower races and women was not just a generalized one concerning social inferiority, but the more precise and specialized one developed by years of anthropometric, medical and biological research."[25] Thus the scientific and medical debates about race, sex, and gender that provided such substance to Weininger's desperate arguments about weak women and effeminate Jews not only were deeply structured by the stereotyping discourses of the day but also were in many respects the already ripe development of efforts over more than a century to naturalize physical (and mental) differences between and among the races and the sexes and to prescribe differential roles and activities to sustain them.

Recent studies of the Enlightenment and new insights into modernization have begun to reveal why the scientific and medical community was so preoccupied with delineating precise gender and racial differences

22 Nancy Leys Stepan, "Race and Gender: The Role of Analogy in Science," *ISIS* 77 (1986): 268.
23 For Max Black's interaction theory of metaphor, see Max Black, *Models and Metaphor* (Ithaca, N.Y., 1962), 44. See also Mary Hesse, *Models and Analogies in Science* (Notre Dame, Ind., 1966), 159–60.
24 Gilman, "Difference and Pathology," 27.
25 Leys Stepan, "Analogy in Science," 268, 275.

in the context of earlier scientific, medical, and social developments.[26] By the late eighteenth century the imprint of race and gender upon the human body had already become the object of intense scrutiny as "the Enlightenment project of building society according to nature's laws fanned the desire to see physical differences between the sexes [and races] as a blueprint for their social relations."[27] In particular, repeated and sustained attempts were made to attribute negative characteristics to the bodies of selected groups, and "scientifically" identified anatomical and physiological differences began to form part of the measure of the capabilities of the woman, the black, and the Jew (among others), along with attempts to define their physical aptitudes and limit their physicality as well as their social and economic opportunities. Of interest was the way in which scientists and medical men moved easily between investigations into racial differences and studies of sexual differences, using similar methods and reasoning to draw deterministic conclusions about the nature and capabilities of people's bodies.

It may be useful, therefore, to examine those formative aspects of the extensive post-Enlightenment scientific discourse on gender and racial differences, and the analogies drawn between them. This discourse observed the bodies of women and Jews in Germany, selected specific anatomical and physiological markers of immobility or impaired physical ability, and then used these markers as reasons to uphold "nature's verdict" concerning their inability to perform physical tasks or join the exercise and athletic opportunities of the "white" European male (thus confirming their different or lesser position in the social hierarchy). I will limit my investigation to two specific markers of physical difference, the female pelvis and the Jew's foot, where the language of science and medicine was used in particular and suggestive ways during the late eighteenth and nineteenth centuries to carry and validate an ethos of physical impairment and disability – an ethos that had an enduring effect on popular perceptions of athletic aptitudes, exercise, and sporting opportunities for women and Jews.

In my discussion I will draw upon Bob Connell's argument that neither naturalistic nor social constructionist approaches to the study of the body are fully able to grasp the importance of human embodiment

---

26 See, e.g., Elaine Showalter, *Sexual Anarchy: Gender and Culture at the Fin de Siècle* (New York, 1990); Thomas Laqueur, *Making Sex: Body and Gender from the Greeks to Freud* (Cambridge, 1990); Ludmilla Jordanova, *Sexual Visions: Images of Gender in Science and Medicine Between the Eighteenth and Twentieth Centuries* (Madison, Wis., 1989).

27 Londa Schiebinger, *The Mind Has No Sex? Women in the Origins of Modern Science* (Cambridge, 1989), 223.

to the constitution of social systems.[28] Connell notes that the fact that major inequalities in society are based on socially determined criteria without permanent foundation in the body has not prevented biology from serving as an ideological justification for these divisions.[29] In such cases, biological differences are either fabricated or exaggerated. The subsequent distortion, far from being an expression of natural difference, is based on the suppression of physical similarities and the exaggeration of bodily differences and is used to support racist and sexist classificatory schemes.[30] In his analysis of the construction of the gendered body, Connell terms this argument the process of negation, in which social categories define people as different by negating the similarities that exist between their bodies and highlighting differences that foster the development of stereotypes. However, he continues, the body is also transformed through social practices, since it is an object of people's own labor and can therefore be built up or left to deteriorate. Different opportunities for physical activity and muscle use such as gymnastics and weight training play an important part in developing and transforming bodies, hence gendered and racist images of physical disability or muscular power can themselves become embodied. Finally, in a self-fulfilling prophecy, this embodiment can itself serve to justify and legitimate the original categories defining impairment or weakness. Hence the processes of negation and transcendence have been vital in providing an ideological justification for physical gender and racial differences and in sustaining the myth that not only are men biologically superior to women but "white" European males are physically superior to men of "other" groups whom they have chosen to designate as a race.

---

28 Bob Connell, *Gender and Power* (Cambridge, 1987).
29 In addition, Philip Cohen has shown how there is nothing natural about categorizing people on the basis of particular characteristics. Social factors invariably enter into the construction of selected peoples as "visible" or lacking certain physical or mental qualities (Philip Cohen, "The Perversions of Inheritance," in Philip Cohen and Harwant S. Bains, eds., *Multi-Racist Britain* [London, 1988]). Indeed, if racial or gender groups are not naturally different, why have elaborate institutional arrangements and regulations been needed in order to enforce that difference? See Sarah Kofman, "Rousseau's Phallocentric Ends," in Nancy Fraser and Sandra Lee Bartky, eds., *Revaluing French Feminism* (Bloomington, Ind., 1992), 46–59.
30 To be sure, says Thomas Laqueur, "difference and sameness, more or less recondite, are everywhere; but which ones count and for what ends is determined outside the bounds of empirical investigation. The fact that at one time the dominant discourse construed male and female bodies as hierarchically, vertically, ordered versions of one sex and at another time as horizontally ordered opposites, as incommensurable, must depend on something other than even a great constellation of real or supposed discoveries" (Laqueur, *Making Sex*, 10).

REINVENTING THE BODIES OF WOMEN AND JEWS

> Bodies are constructed in different ways for different social
> groups, these differences often being a function – at least
> in part – of interlocking formations characterized by race,
> gender, class, ethnicity and nationality.[31]

According to Michel Foucault, a dramatic epistemic shift toward the end of the eighteenth century made possible the emergence of the embodied individual as we know him today, a man who was to become the measure of all things and against which "others" were to be measured, or mismeasured.[32] Language, and the body as its object, emerged together within the complex network of social, political, and economic relations that signaled the emergence of the modern European state.[33] A narrative of culture in anatomical disguise began to be woven as the "new" body that was gradually being created (or reinvented) was "constructed from the same materials of the social imagination that went into the making of a new society."[34] This body was increasingly scrutinized as the positivist sciences, having extended their mastery over nature, attempted to master the body with systematic discourses and through visual inspection.[35]

Anatomical illustration flourished as the emergent medical sciences laid increasing stress upon empiricism, and as art lent medicine a repertoire of realist tropes designed to convince viewers of the "truthfulness" of unimpeded sight.[36] As the medical gaze became more dominant, the

---

31 Leslie A. Adelson, *Making Bodies, Making History: Feminism and German Identity* (Lincoln, Neb., 1993), 35.

32 For a discussion of Foucault's views of this changing episteme, see Hubert L. Dreyfus and Paul Rabinow, *Michel Foucault: Beyond Structuralism and Hermeneutics* (Chicago, 1983), 27; Stephen Jay Gould, *The Mismeasure of Man* (New York, 1981).

33 Michel Foucault, *The Order of Things: An Archaeology of the Human Sciences* (New York, 1973), 211.

34 Barbara Duden, *The Woman Beneath the Skin: A Doctor's Patients in Eighteenth-Century Germany* (Cambridge, 1991), 26. As Bryan Turner has explained, during the late eighteenth and early nineteenth centuries the rationalization of Western society found a new object of exploration and control in the human body itself. Bryan S. Turner, *The Body and Society: Explorations in Society Theory* (Oxford, 1984), and *Regulating Bodies: Essays in Medical Sociology* (London, 1992). As Foucault explained in the case of France, a modernizing, industrializing state required control over individual behavior. The individual thus became an important focus for political and scientific concern, a concern motivated by the desire to find specific ways of regulating the space and action of the body on behalf of society's needs (Michel Foucault, *Discipline and Punish: The Birth of the Prison* [New York, 1979]).

35 William Coleman, *Biology in the Nineteenth Century: Problems of Form, Function and Transformation* (Cambridge, 1977), 15; Barbara M. Stafford, *Body Criticism: Imaging the Unseen in Enlightenment Art and Medicine* (Cambridge, Mass., 1991), xviii. Such vision, says Haraway, was not a passive reflection: "All eyes . . . are active perceptual systems, building in translations and specific ways of seeing, that is, ways of life" (Donna Haraway, "Situated Knowledges: The Science Question in Feminism and the Privilege of Partial Perspective," *Feminist Studies* 14 [fall 1988]: 583).

36 David Lomas, "Body Languages: Kahlo and Medical Imagery," in Kathleen Adler and Marcia

laboratory and then the clinic became spaces for investigating and classifying diseases and physical disabilities. In striving for systematic human
improvement, "the health of nations became an integral part of European
geopolitics, and education of the masses in such matters a high priority."[37]
Questions of health and lifestyle were propelled to a much larger role
in social policy through increased medicalization and the assistance of
what German physician Wilhelm Rau called "medical police."[38] Johann
Peter Frank's *A Complete System of Medical Policy*, for example, demanded
unprecedented regulatory functions from German-speaking governments
in 1783 on the basis that, from now on, nobody could "retain natural
freedom in social life without curbs."[39] Furthermore, the doctor's role as
health regulator was not to be a limiting one but was expected to encompass a vast array of methods for managing the people's health and developing the quality of the population and the strength of the nation.[40]

Londa Schiebinger has suggested that late-eighteenth-century politics
might most appropriately be called "body politics par excellence" due to
this accelerating interest of scientists in scrutinizing and regulating the
human body, and the desire of the age to rationalize natural hierarchies,
order, and stability and hence its ability to justify the social status quo.[41]
The felt need to justify social inequality within liberal thinking of the
time demanded that science explain sex and race differences as natural,
hence the representation of natural anatomical and physiological differences between the sexes and races became significant to the extent that

Pointon, eds., *The Body Imaged: The Human Form and Visual Culture Since the Renaissance* (Cam-
    bridge, 1993), 6.
37 Guenter Risse, "Medicine in the Age of Enlightenment," in Andrew Wear, ed., *Medicine in Soci-
    ety: Historical Essays* (Cambridge, 1992), 195. See also the concept of medicalization as advanced
    by Foucault and members of the Annales School in France, in "La Politique de la Santé au
    xviiie Siècle," in Michel Foucault et al., eds., *Les Machines à Guerir* (Paris, 1978), 11–21.
38 Cited in Ludmilla Jordanova, "Medical Police and Public Health: Problems of Practice and Ide-
    ology," *Society of the Social History of Medicine Bulletin* 27 (1980): 15–19. The term medical police
    was used in a variety of ways in the late eighteenth and early nineteenth centuries. It applied to
    the administration of the health and well-being of the population, the control of medical prac-
    tice and practitioners, legal medicine, and the science of hygiene. The real issue, suggests Jor-
    danova, was citizenship. A good citizen was knowledgeable about health and put his knowledge
    into practice through a deep sense of civic responsibility. "Policing good health was, it could be
    argued, an integral part of the broader transition from political arithmetic to political economy"
    (16, 18).
39 Johann Peter Frank, *System einer vollständigen medicinischen Polizey* (Mannheim, 1780); E. Lesky,
    "Johann Peter Frank and Social Medicine," *Annales Cisalpines d'Histoire Sociale* 4 (1973): 137–44.
40 Jacques Donzelot, *The Policing of Families*, trans. Robert Hurley (New York, 1979), 6–7. See also
    Ute Frevert, "The Civilizing Tendency of Hygiene," in John C. Fout, ed., *German Women in the
    Nineteenth Century* (New York, 1984), 320–44.
41 Londa Schiebinger, *Nature's Body: Gender in the Making of Modern Science* (Boston, 1993), 9. See
    also William F. Bynum, "The Great Chain of Being After Forty Years: An Appraisal," *History of
    Science* 13 (1975): 1–28.

these differences were seen as politically important. Optimism among underprivileged groups, such as women and Jews, that the declarations of the French Revolution on the rights of man would engender universal rights and freedoms was thus confronted with scientific communities who believed that the rights-bearing individual was embodied as a man even though this embodiment complicated women's claims for equal rights.[42] Debate also ensued over the exclusion of certain classes of men, some of whom obtained only limited forms of citizenship because of hidden or visible characteristics of inferiority posited by scientists who generated "countless examples of racial misreadings of the human body."[43] Scientific racism and scientific sexism thus shared many key features: "Both regarded women and non-European men as deviations from the European male norm. Both deployed new methods to measure and discuss difference. Both sought natural foundations to justify social inequalities between the sexes and races."[44] While racial science interrogated males and male physiology, sexual science focused largely on European women. And in the developing racial and sexual hierarchy the European male invariably occupied the high ground.

Reinventions of the German male body that were a conscious reinstatement of the classical beauty of the ideal type, symbol of the perfect human body and the combative military potential of man, provided a new and common standard against which the bodies of women and races (including Jews) could be measured. The Greeks knew the human body more from the outside than the inside. They honed it at gymnastics and athletic festivals, and they especially associated geometric measures of the body with beauty. They had determined that a man was truly beautiful when he possessed a body that was at once fit for warlike exercises and agreeable to the sight.[45] For them, health and beauty naturally occurred together. Furthermore, strength and size were matters of paramount importance to male physical beauty, and the classical beauty of Greek sculpture was taken as clearly defining the proper anatomical

---

42 Joan Wallach Scott, "French Feminists and the Rights of Man: Olympe de Gouge's Declaration," *History Workshop Journal* 28 (autumn 1989): 1–21.

43 Johann Gottlieb Fichte, for example, enthusiastically greeted the early beginnings of the French Revolution and admired the egalitarian drives of the French nation, but he excluded the German Jews from his notion of a nation-state. See Alfred D. Low, *Jews in the Eyes of the Germans: From the Enlightenment to Imperial Germany* (Philadelphia, 1979), 144.

44 Schiebinger, *Nature's Body*, 144. See also Max Horkheimer and Theodor W. Adorno, *Dialectic of the Enlightenment* (New York, 1988).

45 Jean E. Chryssafis, "Aristotle on Physical Education," *Journal of Health and Physical Education* 1, no. 1 (1930): 3–8; Jean E. Chryssafis, "Aristotle on Kinesiology," *Journal of Health and Physical Education* 1, no. 7 (1930): 14–56.

proportions required for a good German.[46] Thus the emerging ideal German male was heroic, regularly presented in postures of action, combat, or struggle with muscles tensed and visible, sculpted through gymnastic exercises and healthy from physical training. He stood at the top of an arbitrary and ascending scale of perfection and was the standard against which the woman and the Jew were to be measured and found impaired and unworthy of participating fully in those political, social, cultural, and especially physical activities that constituted his dominant world.[47]

In the case of women, the superior build of the male European body was presented as visible proof that men should be masters of women, and an intensifying focus upon the anatomical and physiological differences between men and women helped demonstrate that European male privilege was natural, certain, and universal.[48] As emerging representations of the gendered body in the late eighteenth and nineteenth centuries focused in detail on a distinctly female anatomy that emphasized the form and function of the broad female pelvis, scientific and medical discourse repeatedly used the language of anatomy and physiology to support and validate the ethos of the disabled female and to label women's particular disadvantages in the domain of exercise and physical activity.

As anatomists, physiologists, and psychologists grew increasingly concerned in the nineteenth century with attempts to classify individuals according to types with sharply differing constitutions and aptitudes, the Jew's unhealthy body, especially his flat feet, became the subject of invidious comparisons with the ideal German male soldier–athlete stereotype. Science and medicine thus became potent weapons of anti-Semitism, again using the language of anatomy and physiology to label and validate the Jew's particular disadvantages in the domain of physical activity with a special focus on his poor athleticism and lack of military skills.

46 See Mosse, *Nationalism and Sexuality*, 13, 138. See also Erwin Panofsky, "The History of the Theory of Human Proportions," in Panofsky, ed., *Meaning in the Visual Arts: Papers in and on Art History* (New York, 1955), 55–107.
47 Peter Brooks, *Body Work: Objects of Desire in Modern Narrative* (Cambridge, Mass., 1993), 17. Notes Leon Poliakov, "The European, called by his high destiny to rule the world, which he knows how to illumine with his intelligence and subdue with his courage is the highest expression of man and at the head of the human race" (*The History of Anti-Semitism*, trans. Miriam Kochan, 4 vols. [New York, 1965–75], 3:181).
48 Schiebinger, *Mind Has No Sex*, 216.

THE FEMALE PELVIS

> For anatomists . . . it was the pelvis (and its procreative
> virtues) that ultimately emerged as the universal measure
> of womanliness.[49]

In the case of the female body, Thomas Laqueur has argued that late-eighteenth-century political events and changing epistemes encouraged a revolutionary reinterpretation of sexual difference that had a significant impact upon scientific and medical attitudes toward female physicality.[50] Although he may have overstated the extent of this change, it does appear that the emergence of comparative functional anatomy and its many biopolitical offspring based upon the concept of the body as a machine caused a gradual abandonment of Galen's hierarchical model as science began to flesh out the categories of "male" and "female" by basing them firmly upon biological differences.[51] Count de Buffon, the great eighteenth-century naturalist, laid the basis for the delineation of these categories in his multivolume opus *Histoire Naturelle* (Natural history, 1749–1804). In comparing the bodies of men and women he had been able to cite few empirical measurements to support his descriptions. This had not deterred him, however, from prescribing that a man's body *should* be angular with strongly etched muscular contours whereas a woman's *should* be rounder and smoother. "Man has strength and majesty," he said. "Graces and beauty are the appendages of the other sex."[52]

In the ensuing decades, medical men increasingly represented the differences between male and female form and function as a series of

---

49 Schiebinger, *Nature's Body*, 156; see also Schiebinger, *Mind Has No Sex*, 197, 209, 212, 214.
50 Laqueur, *Making Sex*, 35, 52. Until this time, European physicians had relied upon a hierarchical approach to conceptualize male and female difference by accommodating Galen's accounts of the body and his belief that men and women were positioned along a spectrum of heat where the female was simply a cooler, less perfect version of the male. Hence, from the instant of conception women were imperfect men – mutilated males, as Aristotle put it, who would always be weaker and less perfect. See Susan C. Lawrence and Kate Bendixen, "His and Hers: Male and Female Anatomy in Anatomy Texts for U.S. Medical Students," *Social Science and Medicine* 35, no. 7 (1992): 926. For the inability of woman ever to achieve physical maturity or perfection, see Mary Dove, *The Perfect Age of Man's Life* (Cambridge, 1986), 21. Galen's system is explained in Galen, *On the Usefulness of the Parts of the Body: De usu partium*, trans. and introd. Margaret T. May, 2 vols. (Ithaca, N.Y., 1968), 2:628–30.
51 Laqueur, *Making Sex*, chap. 5. For a discussion of the analogy of the machine, which allowed the body to be analyzed, classified, and segregated into its constituent parts, see Donna Haraway, "Investment Strategies for an Evolving Portfolio of Primate Families," in Mary Jacobus et al., eds., *Body/Politics, Women and the Discourses of Science* (New York, 1990), 148; and Samuel Osherton and L. Amara Singham, "The Machine Metaphor in Medicine," in Elliot G. Mischler et al., eds., *Social Contexts of Health, Illness and Patient Care* (Cambridge, 1981), 1.
52 Georges-Louis Leclerc, Comte de Buffon, *Histoire Naturelle, Générale et Particulière*, 73 vols. (Paris, 1749–1804), vols. 3–4, supp.

binary oppositions. They drew for support on the new work of European anatomists and physiologists who claimed the unassailable reality of bones and organs as they looked for fundamental sex differences in various parts of the body.[53] Jakob Ackermann, seeking to describe the distinctively female body in 1788, called upon his fellow German anatomists to list all the differences they could find in order to discover "the essential sexual difference from which all others flow."[54]

As anatomical illustrations of distinctly female skeletons began to appear for the first time in German and French medical texts, much discussion ensued about appropriate modes of representation of the female body. Anatomists targeted and debated essential sex differences by closely examining the female skeleton and showing a marked preference for representations with a small skull (less ability for deep thought), short trunk and narrow ribs (since a sedentary lifestyle required less ability to breathe vigorously), and a wide pelvis (to better represent the female's procreative function).[55] Drawings of the female skeleton by female anatomist Marie Thiroux D'Arconville in 1759 provided a particularly distorted baseline for later pelvic studies, for she accentuated an already wide pelvis by narrowing and distorting the rib cage.[56] German anatomist Samuel Thomas von Soemmerring's more accurate artistic rendition of a female skeleton in 1796 was less excessive in its pelvic roominess but quite distinctively female, for he chose as his model a twenty-year-old woman who had proved her femininity by giving birth.[57] Joseph Wenzel, one of Soemmerring's students, approved, noting that he had "always observed that the most beautiful and womanly in all its parts is one in which the pelvis is the largest in relation to the body."[58]

Anatomical drawings thus increasingly labeled, idealized, and in other ways privileged certain parts of the female anatomy over others. To the early anatomists, sex differences such as the wider female pelvis were

---

53 Patricia Vertinsky, "The Social Construction of the Gendered Body: Exercise and the Exercise of Power," *International Journal for the History of Sport* 11, no. 2 (1994): 147–71.

54 Jakob Ackermann, *Über die körperliche Verschiedenheit des Mannes vom Weibe, ausser den Geschlechtstheilen*, trans. Joseph Wenzel (Koblenz, 1788), 2–5.

55 Londa Schiebinger, "Skeletons in the Closet: The First Illustrations of the Female Skeleton in Eighteenth-Century Anatomy," *Representations* 14 (spring 1986): 62.

56 Ludwig Choulant, *History and Bibliography of Anatomic Illustration* (Chicago, 1920), 304–6.

57 Samuel Thomas von Soemmerring, *Tabula Sceleti Feminini, Juncta Descriptione* (Frankfurt/Main, 1797). For Soemmerring, the anatomically normal was the most beautiful, and in his quest to twin art with anatomy, he compared his rendition of the female skeleton to the statues of Venus de Medici and the Venus of Dresden. See Marcia Pointon, "Interior Portraits: Women, Physiology and the Male Artist," *Feminist Review* 22 (Feb. 1986): 9.

58 Joseph Wenzel, preface in Ackermann, *Über die körperliche Verschiedenheit*, 5.

nature's ruling on women's place and women's duties.[59] Physical and intellectual strength belonged to the man whereas the female body was suited to motherhood.[60] Just as the superior build of the male body constituted male authority in society, it was posited that newly discovered aspects of the female skeleton demonstrated that women should remain subordinate within the state and that their destiny was to have children and nourish them in the private sphere of the home. Woman, the passive side of the partnership, would henceforth complete, not compete with, the more active male.

As this sexually complementarian literature was exported to Germany along with the general unrest following the French Revolution, so too was the belief that "women could best serve the state through their bodies by bringing forth a robust, numerous, and handsome population."[61] Few anatomists or medical men tried to correct exaggerated claims of sexual difference.[62] Masculinity was privileged by both complementarians and those seeking measures of equality for women, for both saw female differences as the source of their handicap and the male body, the Greek-styled athletic and muscled hero, as the measure of all things.[63] And for all the rhetoric of complementarity, scientific and medical discourse continued to define women and femininity as "other than" and "less than" men and the masculine. Johann Jacob Sachs nicely summed up the prevailing attitude in 1830:

The male body expresses positive strength . . . sharpening male understanding and independence and equipping men for life in government, in the arts and sciences. The female body expresses womanly softness and feeling . . . the roomy pelvis ordains women for motherhood. The weak soft limbs and delicate skin are witness of woman's narrower sphere of activity, of domesticity and peaceful family life.[64]

59 Soemmerring defined racial differences in much the same way as he viewed sexual difference. Seeking diversity deep in the anatomy, he believed that race and sex permeated the entire human organism. The body, he was sure, literally spoke for itself (Schiebinger, *Mind Has No Sex*, 213).

60 Coleman, *Biology in the Nineteenth Century*, 4; Schiebinger, *Mind Has No Sex*, 191.

61 Jakob Mauvillon, *Mann und Weib nach ihren gegenseitigen Verhältnissen geschildert: Ein Gegenstück zu der Schrift: Über die Weiber* (Leipzig, 1791), 9. See also Duden, *The Woman Beneath the Skin*, 17.

62 Schiebinger, *Mind Has No Sex*, 227; see also George S. Rousseau and Roy Porter, eds., *The Ferment of Knowledge: Studies in the Historiography of Eighteenth-Century Science* (Cambridge, 1980).

63 For egalitarians this meant that women's only route to improvement was to become more masculine since female limitations, demonstrated by science, were not challenged; Theodor Hippel, mayor of Königsberg, for example, championed women's rights but like most others did not consider challenging anatomical evidence, suggesting that more supportive evidence for women remained to be discovered (Schiebinger, *Mind Has No Sex*, 229).

64 Johann Jacob Sachs, *Ärztliches Gemälde des weiblichen Lebens im gesunden und krankhaften Zustande aus physiologischem, intellektuellem und moralischem Standpunkte* (Berlin, 1830).

As new views on sex and gender brought with them a greater appreciation of women's unique sexual characteristics, the subsequent emergence of evolutionary thought during the nineteenth century commonly accepted the ranking of both sexes and the races along a single axis of development. Using the pelvis and the skull as indices of human progress, women's development (like that of lower races) was assumed to have been arrested at an earlier stage of evolution. Craniometrist Gustave Le Bon, for example, on the basis of the measurements of just thirteen skulls concluded that "women represent the most inferior forms of human evolution and . . . are closer to children and savages than to an adult, civilized man. . . . A desire to give them the same education and as a consequence to propose the same goals for them is a dangerous chimera."[65] Woman, it seemed, was childlike because she was unable to reach full human maturity. Her head was big like a child's, her brain was small like a child's.[66] In fact, John Barclay, a Scottish anatomist and physician whose work was very influential in Germany and throughout Europe, claimed it was obvious that the skeletal characteristics of woman and child were essentially equivalent but for woman's most distinguishing feature, her wide accommodating pelvis. This was a feature, he complained, that even Soemmerring had inadequately represented for "it is in the pelvis and the pelvis alone that we perceive the strongly marked and peculiar characteristics of the female skeleton."[67]

When debate arose over whose skeleton was the best representative of a European woman, the size of the pelvis was Barclay's main concern. In *Anatomy of the Bones of the Human Body* (1829) he carefully selected examples of European anatomical drawings of male and female skeletons for the sake of comparison and compared each to an animal that might best highlight their distinctive features. He chose Albinus's skeleton of the perfect male (which had been given the particularly long legs the Greeks admired) and matched it with George Stubb's rendering of the musculature of a horse for its strength, speed, and agility.[68] To high-

---

65 Gustave Le Bon, "Recherches Anatomiques et Mathématiques sur les Lois des Variations du Volume du Cerveau et sur leurs Relations avec l'intelligence," *Revue d'Anthropologie*, 2d ser., 2 (1879): 62; Stephen Jay Gould notes that Le Bon, "chief misogynist of Broca's school[,] used these data to publish what must have been the most vicious attack upon women in modern scientific literature" (Gould, *Mismeasure of Man*, 104).

66 This comparison of women with children was reminiscent of Aristotle, who had held that a woman could never be more than a child. See Aristotle, *The Politics*, trans. H. Rackham (London, 1932), 63.

67 John Barclay, *A Series of Engravings Representing the Bones of the Human Skeleton*, ed. E. Mitchell (Edinburgh, 1819), 29.

68 Hendrik Punt discusses this point in *Bernard Siegfried Albinus, 1697–1770, on Human Nature:*

light the female he selected Thiroux D'Arconvilles's female skeleton and matched it with an ostrich, the animal with the largest known pelvis, a long neck, and a very small head.[69] This was powerful visual imagery. Images of the horse in European nineteenth-century art and literature were replete with meaning. The linking of the passions, the horse, and the bodily trappings of masculinity with the increasing desire for man to control nature frequently positioned the horse (like the woman) in a new and subservient relationship to man's control, underscoring the growing assumption that the bodies of women, like the bodies of horses, needed reining in.[70] The ostrich was a less common image, but its enormous pelvis was patently declared woman's dominant procreative function, and its small skull was an obvious allusion to her limited brain power.[71] Given that the wide female pelvis was to be used repeatedly as a reason why women could not run speedily or well, one wonders how many knew about the ostrich's remarkable running ability.

As the bones of the human body took on additional tones of masculinity and femininity, craniologists were able to further clarify that the large female pelvis (while a handicap to skilled movement) was necessary to accommodate the large male skull in the birth canal.[72] The pelvis is the part that most corresponds to the skull, said Carl Vogt in his *Lectures on Man* in the 1860s. "In the pelvis as in the skull the sexual differences are very evident, but they are most distinct in the former as this part of the skeleton is so immediately concerned with parturition."[73] This was an important dimension to the debate about the female pelvis that incorporated views on race. Petrus Camper, the father of craniometry, had already measured a variety of female pelvises in the 1750s and concluded that women in warm climates gave birth more easily, even though the African women he measured seemed to have cruder, narrow pelvises.[74] During the 1830s Moritz Weber of Bonn tried to sort pelvises

Anatomical and Physiological Ideas in Eighteenth-Century Leiden (Amsterdam, 1983), 13. For a wonderful discussion of George Stubb's drawings of horses, and the growing belief that men and animals held certain characteristics in common, see Stephen Deuchar, *Noble Exercise: The Sporting Ideal in Eighteenth-Century British Art* (New Haven, Conn., 1982).

69 John Barclay, in Edward Mitchell and Robert Knox, eds., *The Anatomy of the Bones of the Human Body* (Edinburgh, 1829), plates 1, 32, 34. See also Schiebinger, *Mind Has No Sex*, 204–5.

70 Whitney Chadwick, "The Fine Art of Gentling: Horses, Women and Rosa Bonheur in Victorian England," in Adler and Pointon, *The Body Imaged*, 89–108.

71 Laqueur, *Making Sex*, 168.

72 See Elizabeth Fee, "Nineteenth-Century Craniology: The Study of the Female Skull," *Bulletin of the History of Medicine* 53 (1979): 426.

73 Carl Vogt, *Lectures on Man, His Place in Creation, and in the History of the Earth*, ed. James Hunt (London, 1864), 119.

74 Camper decided that Africans had narrower pelvises than Europeans because their heavy skulls

into distinct racial types and suggested that African women gave birth easily, not because they had wide pelvises but because the skulls of African babies, housing few brains, were so small.[75] Willem Vrolik put forward the view that the size of the pelvis was a characteristic of the perfecting of the races; European women had larger pelvises than Negro women in order to give birth to larger skulled babies.[76] It was proof of high evolution and the promise of capable maternity. With this idea in mind, at the end of the century the influential sexologist Havelock Ellis ranked the races by size of female pelvis and claimed that the large and padded buttocks of black women were simply a simulation of the wide pelvis of higher races, having a compensatory function something like the face powder he believed black women used to lighten their skins to attract mates.[77]

THE PELVIS AND PHYSICAL ACTIVITY

> While the man's form seems to be instinctively seeking
> action, the woman's falls naturally into a state of
> comparative repose, and seems to find satisfaction in an
> attitude of overthrow.[78]

The prolonged focus on pelvic width and the received notion that the outer pelvis of the female was absolutely, as opposed to relatively wider in women than in men was particularly unfortunate in light of the ramifications drawn by doctors and physical educators for female physicality and movement. Medical interest in comparative anatomy had suggested from the start that body structure might provide pertinent clues to female health and disease. Jakob Ackermann, for example, who had been a pupil of Soemmerring, believed that differences in body build were bound to affect a patient's lifestyle and the course of disease.[79] This was also the

---

pressed them down during childhood. He also measured Greek statues to examine pelvic measurements (Petrus Camper, *Vermischte Schriften* [Lingen, 1801], 342–3).

75 Moritz Weber, *Die Lehre von den Ur- und Racen-Formen der Schädel und Becken des Menschen* (Düsseldorf, 1830), 5.

76 Willem Vrolik, *Considérations sur la Diversité des Bassins de Différentes Races Humaines* (Amsterdam, 1826), 11. For differences in the pelvises of women of various races, see René Vernan, *Le Bassin dans les Sexes et dans les Races* (Paris, 1875); Hermann H. Ploss, *Das Weib in der Natur- und Völkerkunde: Anthropologische Studien*, ed. Maximilian C. A. Bartels, 2 vols., 3d rev. ed. (Leipzig, 1891), 1:115.

77 Havelock Ellis, cited in Sander Gilman, *Sexuality: An Illustrated History* (New York, 1989), 295.

78 Havelock Ellis, *Man and Woman*, 2d ed. (London, 1897), 32.

79 Ackermann, *Über die körperliche Verschiedenheit*, 2.

argument of Roussel, Moreau, and Cabanis, prominent moral anthropologists of the French Revolution who made early suggestions that corporeal differences grounded in nature demanded distinct lifestyles.[80] Pierre Roussel, whose work was translated into German by C. F. Michaelis in 1786, believed that the differences in the male and female skeleton literally shaped the lives of men and women.[81] Hence, the well-being of each sex was easily seen as dependent on establishing a lifestyle that matched its anatomy and physiology. Health precautions such as diet, exercise, and hygienic regimen became more centered upon the female function of reproduction and child-rearing and increasingly distinct from health-related prescriptions for males, who had a much broader range of possible roles.[82] Women, said Pierre Cabanis in his influential *Oeuvres Philosophiques*, were characterized by physiological properties such as passivity, sensitivity, and softness, leading to "a muscular feebleness that inspires in women an instinctive disgust of strenuous exercise." One could add, he noted, in relation to their distinct anatomical form, that "the separation of their hips makes walking more painful for women, thus ensuring their passivity and dependence upon males."[83]

Echoing these views, German physicians sought to protect and bolster the maternal health of their bourgeois patients by offering rules for observing good health, including exercise prescriptions for healthy motherhood.[84] Indeed, middle-class women were the most important constituency for medical health propaganda. Göttingen physician Johann Peter Frank spoke of the need to promote the physical strengthening of the female sex, and physical educator Johann Christoph Friedrich Guts Muths, extolling the hardy virtues of the ancient German race, praised the rugged birth in the open field and urged exercise for girls to become hardy mothers.[85] Women were not, however, expected to participate in strenuous

---

80 Laqueur, *Making Sex*, 196.
81 Pierre Roussel, *Système physique et moral de la femme, ou tableau philosophique de la constitution, de l'état organique, de tempérament des moeurs, et des fonctions propres au sexe* (Paris, 1775), 2; see also Ludmilla Jordanova, "Natural Facts: A Historical Perspective on Science and Sexuality," in Carol P. MacCormack and Marilyn Strathern, eds., *Nature, Culture and Gender* (Cambridge, 1980), 42–69.
82 Pierre J. G. Cabanis, *Oeuvres Philosophiques*, 2 vols. (Paris, 1956), 1:275.
83 Ibid., 1:278.
84 See, e.g., Christoph W. Hufeland, *Makrobiotik oder die Kunst, das menschliche Leben zu verlängern* (Berlin, 1796; reprint, Munich, 1978); Franz Anton May, *Medicinische Fastenpredigten, oder Vorlesungen über Körper- und Seelen-Diätetik zur Verbesserung der Gesundheit und Sitten*, 2 vols. (Mannheim, 1792–4); Ute Frevert, *Krankheit als politisches Problem* (Göttingen, 1984).
85 Johann Peter Frank, *System einer vollständingen medicinischen Polizey* (Mannheim, 1780), special chapter on physical education, "Von der Wiederherstellung der Gymnastik"; Johann C. F. Guts Muths, *Gymnastik für die Jugend* (Schnepfenthal, 1793).

exercise and gymnastics, which were designed to develop manly character expressed through physical strength and dominance. "No formal gymnastics for girls," said Guts Muths, "but daily movement out in the open, happy and active chores at home."[86] Phokian Clias held a similar view. In *Kalisthenie* (Calisthenics, 1829), he advocated moderate exercise for women but rejected ball games because they required running, throwing, and excessive muscle use, which might damage the reproductive system.[87]

As scientific research on women's bodies made it increasingly clear that female exercise had to be carefully constrained to match the body structure and physiological functioning of the female (as represented by the wide pelvis), *Turner* (gymnastic) teachers such as Eiselen and Werner advocated gymnastics courses to improve women's health in the 1830s. But these were orthopedic or corrective gymnastics to remedy women's weak body structure, not the *Turner* exercises developed by *Turnvater* Jahn as a singularly German activity for men exalting physical strength and military fitness and promoting the Greek ideal of harmonious bodily proportions.[88] Moritz Kloss, who represented the mainstream of *Turnen* wrote in *Die weibliche Turnkunst* (The art of female gymnastics, 1855) that calisthenic exercises for women should emphasize the desire to be delicate and graceful and "not sacrifice tender femininity for the sake of Spartan toughness."[89] Activism in sport was clearly a masculine preserve.

Although anatomical studies of the pelvis focused medical attention almost exclusively upon the form and function of the female's reproductive system and the fact that a wide pelvis affected a woman's mobility, physiologists further highlighted the female reproductive economy in terms of the weakening and sickening nature of the menstrual cycle. When Theodor Bischoff in the 1840s observed the process of dogs in heat and postulated that females must ovulate during their menses, "he

86 Nicolaas J. Moolenijzer, *Johann Christoph Friedrich Guts Muths and His Gymnastik für die Jugend* (New York, 1970), 41.
87 Edmund Neuendorff, *Geschichte der neueren deutschen Leibesübung vom Beginn des 18. Jahrhunderts bis zur Gegenwart*, 4 vols. (Dresden, 1930), 3:29–30. See also Allen Guttmann, *Women's Sports: A History* (New York, 1991), 92.
88 George L. Mosse, *The Nationalization of the Masses* (New York, 1975), 130–3; George L. Mosse, *The Crisis of German Ideology* (New York, 1964), 116; John M. Hoberman, *Sport and Political Ideology* (London, 1984), 103; Horst Ueberhorst, ed., *Friedrich Ludwig Jahn: 1778–1978* (Munich, 1978); H. Bernett, "Sport History: Sport and National Socialism: A Focus of Contemporary History," in Herbert Haag, Ommo Grupe, and August Kirsch, eds., *Sport Science in Germany* (Berlin, 1992), 445; Fred Eugene Leonard, *A Guide to the History of Physical Education* (Westport, Conn., 1947), 96.
89 Moritz Kloss, quoted in Neuendorff, *Geschichte*, 3:538; Gertrud Pfister, *Geschlechtsspezifische Sozialisation und Koedukation im Sport* (Berlin, 1983), 61.

was providing a scientific explanation for the principle most medical men had already come to accept."[90] Like a bitch in heat, menstruation signaled a woman's capacity to conceive as well as her recurrent energy loss and inability to behave rationally. The emerging medical model of reproductive difference, while based on totally erroneous knowledge that was not to be corrected until the twentieth century, shackled a woman to her body and propelled the menstrual cycle and the ovaries to the forefront of her being, the driving force of her economy. Menstruation came to be seen as a primary cause of disease, a periodic wounding that required appropriate physical and social adjustment. Concerns about the preservation of the body's vital and finite energy supply led to fears that any activity other than reproduction might overtax the woman. Females, even the most healthy ones, appeared to be irremediably handicapped in their attempts to participate in anything other than "feminine" activities. As "monthly cripples" they required close medical supervision over the nature and extent of physical activity that was required to sustain their precarious health.[91]

The medical profession, notes Pfister, felt authorized to speak on almost all aspects of women's lives, including *Turnen* and sport. Physicians reasoned that the delicate female physiology must be protected from vigorous exercise while encouraging certain kinds of therapeutic movements. The view of women as inherently sick and disabled was emphasized, for example, in a number of Institutes of Orthopedic Gymnastics that flourished in the 1850s as part of a growing market in women's physical culture.[92] Here middle-class girls and women were advised to combat deformities of the spine and diseases of the reproductive system by exercising gently, but they were warned emphatically against overexertion, which might lead to physical collapse. That women were the weaker sex and inferior to men in bodily structure and function was confirmed by experts of the Berlin Medical Association in 1864, who

---

90 Theodor L. von Bischoff, *Das Studium und die Ausübung der Medicin durch Frauen* (Munich, 1872); see also Mary Poovey, *Uneven Developments: The Ideological Work of Gender in Late Nineteenth-Century England* (Chicago, 1988), 7.

91 See George Bernstein and Lottelore Bernstein, "Attitudes Toward Women's Education in Germany, 1870–1914," *International Journal of Women's Studies* 2, no. 5 (1979): 473–88. August Strindberg, for example, explained that "no creature (woman) that spent so much of its life procreating (or at least menstruating) could possibly develop in any other direction" (quoted in Bram Dijkstra, *Idols of Perversity: Fantasies of Feminine Evil in Fin de Siècle Culture* [New York, 1986], 170). For a discussion of vitalist concepts and the menstrual disability theory, see Patricia Vertinsky, *The Eternally Wounded Woman: Women, Doctors and Exercise in the Late Nineteenth Century* (Chicago, 1994).

92 See Gertrud Pfister, "The Medical Discourse on Female Physical Culture in Germany in the 19th and Early 20th Centuries," *Journal of Sport History* 17, no. 2 (1990): 183.

regarded the weaker organization of the female as self-evident.[93] At an 1880 Congress in Berlin, pediatrician Dr. Levy complained about rope jumping for girls, arguing that it caused flat feet. After the age of ten, another pediatrician concluded, "girls should no longer do gymnastic exercises with equipment because they are scarcely decent and are often injurious."[94] Fears of potential injury invariably focused on the pelvic area and the dangers to female reproduction:

> Every exercise that requires sudden and jerking movements is to be avoided on account of the particular position of the female's reproductive organs. One should not overlook the fact that the female body, because of its particular function, is open at the lower end so that vigorous physical exercise might cause a prolapse to occur.[95]

Such medical reservations helped to shape exercise norms for girls and women in everyday situations to the extent that, in 1908, German school-girls were still being cautioned by some of their teachers not to run for more than five minutes, not to sprint, not to throw, and not to jump higher than fifty centimeters.[96] When Fred Eugene Leonard, a pioneer of American physical training, visited Germany in 1896 he criticized particularly the low intensity of free exercises he witnessed in girls' gymnastics classes in Frankfurt.[97] The clear supposition behind attempts to restrict young women to gentle exercise and graceful motion was that vigorous sports were essentially masculine – symbols of virility and dominance, while females were expected to do just enough calisthenics to remain healthy as they developed domestic skills and prepared their bodies for childbirth.

The uses to which a focus upon the oversized pelvis and the ideology of menstrual disability were put in medicalizing and controlling bourgeois women's bodies to thwart educational, professional, and personal development matched in creativity and fervor the diverse attempts of German women from many walks of life to prove that they could study, work, exercise, and play sports without succumbing to an unsteady gait,

---

93 *Deutsche Turnzeitung* 9 (1864): 341. See also Esther Fischer-Homberger, *Krankheit-Frau und andere Arbeiten zur Medizingeschichte der Frau* (Bern, 1979), 49–84.
94 Neuendorff, *Geschichte*, 3:120; Gertrud Pfister and Hans Langenfeld, "Die Leibesübungen für das weibliche Geschlecht: ein Mittel zur Emanzipation der Frau?" in Horst Ueberhorst, ed., *Weltgeschichte der Leibesübungen*, 6 vols. (Berlin, 1972–88), 3:485–521.
95 Kloss, cited in Adolf Bluemcke, *Die Körperschule der deutschen Frau im Wandel der Jahrhunderte* (Dresden, 1928), 141.
96 Neuendorff, *Geschichte*, 3:238, 419.
97 Roland Naul, "Studies of the Turner System by an American: Fred E. Leonard's Visits to Germany, 1896, 1900–1, 1913," in Roland Naul, ed., *Turnen and Sport: The Cross-cultural Exchange* (Münster, 1991), 121–46.

nervous exhaustion, infertility, insanity, or masculine tendencies.[98] Toward the end of the nineteenth century, both working-class and bourgeois women were participating in increasing numbers in gymnastics, games, and sports and demonstrating that vigorous exercise could be beneficial rather than injurious to their general health. Although the Deutsche Turnerschaft (German Gymastics Organization) remained more tradition-bound than most European exercise systems, the pervasive Darwinianism and militarism of the late nineteenth century increasingly pressed doctors to acknowledge that the strong were born of strong mothers and that women must therefore require more vigorous and strength-promoting physical activity and sport. Some women doctors did speak out clearly on behalf of women's rights to unrestricted physical activity, but not until well after the turn of the twentieth century. Dr. Alice Profé from Berlin, for example, was to brush aside the complaints of "prejudiced old men who propagated old wives' tales about nervous prostration and stiffened pelvic musculature," suggesting in 1912 that "there is no such thing as male *Turnen* or female *Turnen* – the same exercises have the same effects on the human organism. Men will always err if they try to explain to women what female attributes are."[99]

Nevertheless, the prolonged medical focus on the female pelvis had left the enduring impression that because of its width the gait and bearing of woman were affected in a way that clearly indicated the passive state nature had designed for her. "Women everywhere reveal somewhat less capacity for motor energy than men and less degree of delight in its display," said Havelock Ellis who was widely cited by German physicians.[100] The largeness of the pelvis and the approximation of the knees influenced the female gait and rendered it vacillating and unsteady.[101]

---

98 E.g., see John C. Fout, ed., *German Women in the Nineteenth Century: A Social History* (New York, 1984).

99 Pfister, "Medical Discourse," 191; Guttmann, *Women's Sports*, 129–34; Profé, cited in Gertrud Pfister, *Frau und Sport* (Frankfurt/Main, 1980), 35–6. Feminist and antifeminist discourse in Germany at this time is discussed in Richard J. Evans, *The Feminist Movement in Germany, 1894–1933* (London, 1976). The struggle for female doctors to enter the profession and treat women is discussed in James C. Albisetti, "The Fight for Female Physicians in Imperial Germany," *Central European History* 15, no. 3 (1982): 99–123.

100 Havelock Ellis, *Man and Woman*, 150.

101 Nineteenth-century discourse on women's locomotive system is captured nicely in Scottish physiologist Alexander Walker's widely circulated *Beauty in Women: Analysed and Classified*, 5th ed. (1836; reprint, Glasgow, 1892), which was favorably reviewed in Germany. Walker underscored the fact that the pelvis was the center of woman's being and that locomotive beauty was associated with action and movement, which did not fit the sedentary lifestyle needed by women. "Happily," he said, "the athletic temperament does not occur in women" 199. See also Adolph Carl Peter Callisen, *Medicinisches Schriftsteller-Lexicon der jetzt lebenden Verfasser: Nachtrag*, 33 vols. (Altona, 1845), 33:205–6.

"The obliquity of the legs, resulting from the breadth of the pelvis compelled women to run by alternate semicircular rotations of the legs, hence to run nature did surely not construct her."[102] For men, running was natural; their bodies were constructed to make running swift and efficient. Women's bodies, however, were constructed for reproduction and nurturing. Their attempts to run displayed "a kind of precipitate waddle with neither grace, nor fitness nor dignity."[103]

Doctors and the scientists who informed women about their movement difficulties tended to look at women rather than listen to them tell about their own needs and experiences and thereby unlock the truth of nature's secrets by decoding what they saw within the female body. Long-standing notions of patriarchal dominance were translated into the language of modern science as theories of sexual difference helped determine what they saw and knew. Images of women's bodies that they projected through their discourse and practice distinguished gender as a central medical metaphor and circumscribed the female preserve in sport and physical activity.

THE JEW'S FOOT

We all recognize the Jewish type . . . it is always possible to recognize him . . . because he always bears some characteristic of his race.[104]

Sander Gilman addresses the issue of the Jew's foot in *The Jew's Body*. In a work described by Daniel Pick as a virtuoso phenomenology of stereotypes, Gilman explores the racial biology of the Jew. In particular he examines the construction of medical and scientific discourse proclaiming the perceived unfitness of a Jew to march as a foot soldier in the nineteenth-century armies of Europe, as well as linking the pathological nature of the gait of the Jew to his inability to undertake physical labor.[105] Gilman reminds us that when we look at nineteenth-century racist characterizations of the Jew's body, "we are not speaking about realities but about their representations and the reflection of those representations in the world of those who stereotype as well." Nevertheless,

---

102 Havelock Ellis, *Man and Woman*, 50, 150.
103 Wendy Mitchinson, *The Nature of Their Bodies: Women and Their Doctors in Victorian Canada* (Toronto, 1991), 14.
104 Richard Andree, *Zur Volkskunde der Juden* (Bielefeld, 1881), 37.
105 Sander L. Gilman, *The Jew's Body* (New York, 1991); Daniel Pick, "Review of *The Jew's Body*," in *Medical History* (July 1993): 352.

the meanings that came to be attributed to the Jew's foot and gait (and their social implications) were more than "a 'footnote' to the development of general representations of the pathophysiology of the Jew."[106] In a number of ways they had an enduring effect on the patterns of sport and physical activity adopted by Jews in Germany and elsewhere in the Diaspora, in Eretz Israel, and later on in Israel itself. In a people with such supposed physical deficiencies, who could expect physical agility and strength, the essence of athletics?[107] In Western society, which continues to be acutely race conscious and is increasingly body conscious and sport infatuated, the ideological determinants of lasting "racial" images about physical impairment and incapacity for particular sporting and exercise activities merit closer investigation than they have received so far.

Just as with women, perceived signs of Jewish impairment tended to emerge at times when Jews made efforts toward greater emancipation, especially beginning in the late eighteenth century. After centuries of persecution, the image of the male Jew, says Gilman, was already one who was physically handicapped, clearly identifiable by his physiognomy and a host of other physical markers, including his flat feet and impaired gait.[108] But from this time, suggests Mosse, with increased controversy about German Jews' emancipation and their assimilability, the so-called characteristic features of the Jews entered the polemical literature and fed an emerging scientific racism that scavenged widely for evidence.[109]

This may have begun with the insubstantial claims of Johann Friedrich Blumenbach, German pioneer of physical anthropology, when he pointed out in 1775 that the Jewish race represented the most notorious and least misleading example of physiognomy, which can be easily recognized everywhere.[110] However, it was a large step, in 1783, for Johann David Michaelis from Göttingen (responding negatively to Christian Wilhelm Dohm's call for Jewish emancipation in *On the Civic Improvement of the Jews*) to argue that the Jews as a race were much too short to meet the criteria (5 feet, 2 inches) of modern European armies.[111]

106 Gilman, *The Jew's Body*, 1, 39.
107 Bernard Postal, Jesse Silver, and Roy Silver, *Encyclopedia of Jews in Sports* (New York, 1965), 3.
108 Sander L. Gilman, *The Case of Sigmund Freud: Medicine and Identity at the Fin de Siècle* (Baltimore, 1993), 115. See also Harvey Mitchell and Samuel S. Kottek, "An Eighteenth-Century Medical View of the Diseases of the Jews in Northeastern France: Medical Anthropology and the Politics of Jewish Emancipation," *Bulletin of the History of Medicine* 67 (1993): 248–81.
109 George L. Mosse, *Germans and Jews* (New York, 1970), 64.
110 Johann F. Blumenbach, *The Anthropological Treatises of Johann Friedrich Blumenbach* (London, 1865), 98–9.
111 On the debate between Dohm and Michaelis, see Michael K. Silber, "The Enlightened

To be sure, eighteenth-century recruiters from many regiments had begun to identify height with strength and fitness by imposing a minimum height on recruits. (For example, the shortest mean height recorded for recruits to the Habsburg armies was 62.6 inches.)[112] The Prussian military had also long preferred tall soldiers to short ones, since they could march in step, cover more ground with longer strides, and load their bayonets more easily. The Prussian obsession with physical size, suggests Tanner, stemmed partly from the recorded notions of Tacitus and Julius Caesar about the tallness and strength of the Germanic tribes in ancient times – their fighting prowess derived, it was believed, from their sexual abstinence in early manhood.[113] Despite the attraction of these historic myths of super-barbarians and the stringent military height restrictions of certain ceremonial guardsmen, in practice conscripted recruits were eagerly sought after and seldom held to stringent height requirements. The notion that Jewish males consistently failed military height requirements clearly contradicted the fact that many Jews could be found in the armies of Europe. Yet the fiction that Jews were worthless as soldiers because of their (inadequate) physical stature and thus could not possibly become physically able, hence true citizens, in the emerging modern state was to be repeated throughout the nineteenth century and into the twentieth.[114] The soldier archetype was, after all, an important way for man to express and preserve traditional male characteristics by literally embodying them.

As the idea of race came to play a critical role in determining how people saw themselves, the issue of who Jews were and how they related to the larger society grew increasingly controversial. And as discussions of anatomical and physiological differences among different races began to slip easily into debates about "historical" racial worth and the ranking of different races and groups, scientists were quickly induced to endow physical differences with explanatory powers well beyond their original

Absolutist State and the Transformation of Jewish Society: Tradition in Crisis? State Schools, Military Conscription and the Emergence of a Neutral Polity in the Reign of Joseph II," 12–14, paper presented at the conference, "Tradition and Crisis Revisited: Jewish Society and Thought on the Threshold of Modernity," Harvard University, Oct. 11–12, 1988. See also Poliakov, *The History of Anti-Semitism*, 3:177.

112 J. Komlos, "Stature and Nutrition in the Habsburg Monarchy: The Standard of Living and Economic Development in the Eighteenth Century," *American Historical Review* 90 (1985): 1149–61; see also Roderick Floud, Annabel Gregory, and Kenneth Wachter, *Height, Health and History: Nutritional Status in the United Kingdom, 1750–1980* (Cambridge, 1990).

113 James M. Tanner, *A History of the Study of Human Growth* (Cambridge, 1981), 98–102.

114 Istvan Deak, "Jewish Soldiers in Austro-Hungarian Society," *Leo Baeck Institute Year Book* 34 (New York, 1990): 3–29.

taxonomic purposes.[115] Through observation and comparison they determined that nature must be the arbiter of morality, and a dark skin and particular physiognomy came to be readily associated as natural signs of inferiority.[116] Moses Mendelssohn was in no way born to be an athlete, commented Johann Kaspar Lavater, who was one of many scientists of the late eighteenth century to air a fascination with human physical difference and a growing admiration for the classical Greek beauty of the male body.[117] Lavater, the physiognomist, was a colleague of Petrus Camper, the Dutch anatomist, who drew conclusions from his measurements of facial angles that left no doubt as to the racial superiority of the European ideal type over others, based upon the beautiful and harmonious proportions of the tall and athletic Greek body. Why, asked Camper rhetorically, is a tall person so much more beautiful than a small one?[118] It would not take many decades for racist ideologues in Germany to identify the male "Aryan" by a physical form and a fair skin that typified the Germanic, Greek-inspired ideal of beauty and strength and showed the Jew, "the enemy from within," to be his exact opposite – ugly, dark, small, and disproportioned, with crooked legs, flat feet, and impaired gait.[119] One of the cornerstones of scientific racism thus became

115 Poliakov, *History of Anti-Semitism*, 3:140.
116 Christoph Meiners, for example, in anticipation of the formulation of the Aryan concept, simply divided humankind into two types – the fair and beautiful and the dark and ugly, the latter representing insensitivity and hardness and evoking disgust. Christoph Meiners, *Grundriss der Geschichte der Menschheit* (Lemgo, 1785), 123–4.
117 Johann Kaspar Lavater, *Physiognomische Fragmente zur Beförderung der Menschenkenntniss und Menschenliebe* (Leipzig, 1775–8); Moses Mendelssohn has been called the prototype of the German Jew in the late eighteenth and nineteenth centuries – the archetypal figure of Jewish liberation in Germany and the archetypal fighter for Jewish civil rights. The important role he played in developing the consciousness of what was a German Jew rendered criticism leveled against his physique and motor ability particularly important. Alexander Altmann, "Moses Mendelssohn as the Archetypal German Jew," in Jehuda Reinharz and Walter Schatzberg, eds., *The Jewish Response to German Culture: From the Enlightenment to the Second World War* (Hanover, N.H., 1985), 17–31.
118 Thomas Cogan, *The Works of the Late Professor Camper: A New Edition* (London, 1821), 9. Size to the Greeks was a matter of paramount importance in physical beauty. "Those who are too small even though well proportioned, can never be called beautiful" (Aristotle, *Nicomachean Ethics*, IV, 7, 11,236, in Chryssafis, "Aristotle on Physical Education," 4).
119 Robert Proctor, "From Anthropologie to Rassenkunde in the German Anthropological Tradition" in George W. Stocking, ed., *Bones, Bodies, Behavior: Essays in Biological Anthropology* (Madison, Wis., 1988), 139. By the late nineteenth century, says Gilman, scientists were claiming that Jewish anthropometric difference was an absolute that could be seen and measured, and it was mirrored as well in the kinds of diseases linked to Jews (Gilman, *Case of Sigmund Freud*, 14–15); Gustav Klemm's variation of Camper's notion of beauty and superiority further fostered notions of racial difference. Klemm divided races into "active" and "passive," where active races were "masculine," thriving in cold climates, whereas passive races, in warm climates, were effeminate (Gustav Klemm, *Allgemeine Cultur-Geschichte der Menschheit*, 10 vols. [Leipzig, 1843–52], 1:196–7).

its elevation of notions of beauty and ugliness to legitimate scientific categories of classification and underscore physical markers of difference such as the Jew's foot.[120]

Those who looked back to Greece for inspiration in the formation of the German ideal male stereotype acknowledged that the Greeks attached considerable importance to the foot in the development of a perfect human being. Before the male child was sent to the Palaestra at five, his mother was expected to modify the shape of his foot by making him walk on the inside of his foot with his toes planted in a straight line with his heel. This careful training was believed to be part of the explanation for the beautiful Greek foot that was evident from Greek statuary and so admired by the Germans. Students of Greek form were able to explain that the more perfect the development of the human form, the more rudimentary the little toe became. Anthropologists conjectured that proof of this could be deduced from studies of the gradual development of the ape. As he became erect, the weight of his body forced his knees out and threw his weight onto the outside of his foot forcing a widening of the toes and a developed little toe. A precarious balance was thus maintained by a projecting heel and a widened toe base. Only as the body evolved and straightened would the toes narrow and the heel diminish, and because the feet were the first to register any alteration in balance, they were the first parts of the body to require training.[121]

The assignment of flat feet to apes, and then by analogy to the lower races of Negroes and Jews, was as much a development of post-Enlightenment racial science as was the assignment of a wide(r) pelvis to the German woman in its sexual-science discursive counterpart. Anthropologist Carl Vogt was one of many who came to support such conjectures in racial science, in this case through his comparisons of the Negro and the German male – two human types who stood, he opined, at the extreme limits of the human group. Quoting the work of ethnologist Karl Hermann Burmeister, Vogt suggested that the Negro's external characteristics afforded "a glimmer of the ape beneath the human envelope – stooped posture, bent knees, bandy legs and ugly feet." Indeed, everything about his foot was ugly: "the flatness, the projecting heel . . . the spreading

---

120 John M. Efron, "Scientific Racism and the Mystique of Sephardic Racial Superiority," *Leo Baeck Institute Yearbook* 38 (1993): 93.
121 Diana Watts, "The Essential Training of the Foot as Base," in Diana Watts, ed., *The Renaissance of the Greek Ideal*, 2d ed. (New York, 1914), 14–18.

toes." Said Vogt, "The Negro is a decided flat-foot . . . and such persons with flat feet are poor walkers and are rejected as recruits."[122]

The notion that Jews were poor walkers and foot soldiers, not only because of their puny size but also because of weak or flat feet, was aired early in the nineteenth century and then with growing conviction after midcentury as Jewish "problems" increasingly became a topic of medical as well as military and political discussion. Weak feet were cited in 1804 by Joseph Rohrer as the reason why so many Jewish soldiers under the Austrian monarchy were hospitalized or released, although as Ainsztein's detailed survey of the Jew as soldier has indicated, questions of Jewish emancipation largely colored the perceived success or failure of German Jews in the army.[123] Although Jews volunteered for, and fought well in, the German Wars of Liberation, they were still subject to criticisms of physical weakness and cowardice at the hands of their Christian comrades-in-arms. Indeed, Caroline von Humboldt's strident charges against the Jews and their inherited lack of courage in the duty of war stood in sharp contrast to the repeated acknowledgment by military sources of Jewish courage and fortitude in the war against France.[124]

After midcentury the ideas of French historian Ernest Renan, who characterized the "Semites" as an incomplete race lacking physical courage and public spiritedness, slid easily into the growing anti-Semitic rhetoric in Germany about the Jew's unmilitary body – a rhetoric to which Jewish scientists such as Heinrich Steinthal contributed.[125] Reviewing Renan's arguments, Steinthal accepted that "Our body is predetermined to have a specific gait because of our nature, that is, because of our anatomical construction. . . . [Only the soldier] who is trained and schooled in his pattern of exercise walks naturally."[126] Contrasted thus against the soldier with his natural walk and even gait who resembled health, normality, and self control was the lame and unhealthy Jew indelibly marked by his racial lineage and further hampered by the pressures of urban civilization.

122 Carl Vogt, *Lectures on Man: His Place in Creation, and in the History of the Earth*, ed. James Hunt (London, 1864), 172, 181.

123 Rueben Ainsztein, *Jewish Resistance in Nazi-Occupied Eastern Europe, with a Historical Survey of the Jew as Fighter and Soldier in the Diaspora* (New York, 1974), 89–102; see also Paul Breines, *Tough Jews: Political Fantasies and the Moral Dilemma of American Jewry* (New York, 1990), pt. 2.

124 Low, *Jews in the Eyes of the Germans*, 138.

125 Although Ernest Renan, *Etudes d'Histoire Religieuse* (Paris, 1862), 85, 87, 89, did not intend to make negative comments about the Jews, his study was extensively used by anti-Semites in Germany. See also Raphael Patai and Jennifer Patai, *The Myth of the Jewish Race* (Detroit, Mich., 1989), 10.

126 Heinrich Steinthal's comments are discussed in Gilman, *Case of Sigmund Freud*, 117.

Accusations of weak feet not only continued to condemn the foot soldier but were, in addition to other difficulties, experienced by Jews in
becoming officers after they had been formally emancipated and granted
the right to serve in the armed forces. Although the Prussian General
Staff made no secret that Jewish soldiers had fought well against Napoléon
in 1815 and had made a significant contribution to Prussia's victory in
1866, the regulation that no Jew was to be promoted to a commissioned
officer was never changed in Prussia until World War I.[127] Young Jews,
forced to live with the stigma of their Jewish descent and repeated questions about their loyalty to the state, often made it their ambition to
strive for those Teutonic ideals of virile virtues deemed important by the
average German – courage, physical strength, and discipline. Soldierly
experiences of march, battlefield, and camp (as well as the importance
placed by academic fraternities upon swordsmanship and dueling) drove
home the need and social value of physical skill and efficiency. Such
qualities, Jewish students believed, might best be achieved by testing
their courage in dueling and through physical training in the *Turner* clubs.
In this respect they referred naively to Friedrich Ludwig Jahn, who had
become one of the forerunners of German racialism through the cultivation of German gymnastics, which retained the Greek notion of beauty
as an ideal type, exalted the physical strength and disciplined hardness
of the Germanic form, and denigrated the lower races as unmanly parasites on the body of the fatherland.[128] For Jahn, "father of gymnastics,"
Jews were never missing from among those he assailed, yet paradoxi-
cally, his name and praise for his ideas would appear often in the ranks
of the Jewish gymnastic movement that developed in the early twentieth
century.[129]

In 1881, German philosopher Eugen Dühring focused on the degenerating Jewish body in *The Jewish Problem as a Question of Racial Characteristics*, which was designed to provide further arguments to deny Jews
access to the officer corps and to reaffirm the unlikelihood of Jews ever
becoming accepted as Germans.[130] Johannes Nordmann also highlighted

---

127 Adolph Asch and Johanna Philippson, "Self-Defence at the Turn of the Century: The Emer-
    gence of the K. C.," *Leo Baeck Institute Year Book* 3 (London, 1958): 133.
128 Mosse, *Nationalization of the Masses*, 75; Poliakov, *The History of Anti-Semitism*, 3:100. The Jew,
    Jahn had said, was a "bodiless, airy phantom without volkdom" (quoted in Hans Kohn, *The
    Mind of Germany: The Education of a Nation* [New York, 1960], 88).
129 Low, *Jews in the Eyes of the Germans*, 164–5; Friedrich Ludwig Jahn, *Kleine Schriften* (Leipzig,
    1906), 26.
130 Eugen Dühring, *Die Judenfrage als Racen-, Sitten-, und Kulturfrage* (Karlsruhe, 1881). See also
    Steven Beller, *Vienna and the Jews, 1887–1938: A Cultural History* (Cambridge, 1989), 191.
    Dühring followed such pronouncements as that of Bruno Bauer who saw the Jew as a "white

the Jews' unfitness for military responsibilities in his pamphlet *Israel in the Army*, stressing the physical disenfranchisement of the Jew and presenting the image of the Jew's foot as a salient marker of Jewish difference.[131] The status associated with the Jew's role as soldier was paralleled by the increasingly intense anti-Semitic critique of the Jew's lack of soldierly qualities so that Mark Twain, after a visit to Austria, could discuss unabashedly "the common (though erroneous) reproach that the Jew is willing to feed upon a country but not fight for it."[132]

The intensification of nationalism in Europe toward the end of the nineteenth century further stimulated discussion about racial differentiation and provided the impulse for renewed attacks upon the integrity of the Jew's body. Many German anthropologists were professors of medicine, and the close links between anatomy and anthropology allowed racial concepts to become an integral part of medical thinking to explain determinants of health and disease, justify medical prescriptions for preserving health and exercise, and in some cases demonstrate that Jewishness was closely associated with physical disability, mental disease, and hypersexuality.[133] Evolutionary theories, while mitigating beliefs about innate racial differences, nevertheless did not eliminate faith in race as a biological entity. Those scientists and physicians, such as Rudolph Virchow, who did not accept the notion of innate racial differences but saw races as pathological variations from the perfect type were not able to stifle the view that alien cultural forces and degenerate racial poisons were causing a disintegration of society, sapping German energy, and undermining national unity.[134] Concern about industrialization and rapid urbanization, coupled with Darwinian notions about the survival of the fittest and an emphasis upon the inheritance of acquired characteristics, heightened a growing anxiety about widespread physical and psychological degeneration. And, as the word degeneration became an integral part

negro" with different blood from the Christian peoples of Europe. The Jew, therefore, could never become a Christian and a German (Low, *Jews in the Eyes of the Germans*, 318).

131 Johannes Nordmann, *Israel im Heere* (Leipzig, 1893).

132 Gilman, *Case of Sigmund Freud*, 117; Mark Twain, *Concerning the Jews* (New York, 1899; reprint, Philadelphia, 1985), 30.

133 Proctor shows that most of Germany's premier anthropologists were physicians by training, since anthropology was generally studied as a subdiscipline of medicine (Proctor, "From Anthropologie to Rassenkunde," 141).

134 Paul Weindling, *Health, Race and German Politics Between National Unification and Nazism* (Cambridge, 1989), 37–59. Virchow was by no means anti-Semitic, although his survey on school children which separated out the Jews showed how a negative attitude toward the Jews was implicit in German nineteenth-century medicine. See John M. Efron, "Defining the Jewish Race: The Self-Perceptions and Responses of Jewish Scientists to Scientific Racism in Europe, 1882–1933," Ph.D. diss., Columbia University, 1991, 29.

of the vocabulary of nationalism "as a means of classifying and circum-
scribing those who would not, or could not, progress," the stigmata of
degeneracy were presented as "yet another chapter in the story of body
divination."[135]

The degenerate was easily recognized because his deformed body
manifested internal decay.[136] Distortions of ear shape, facial asymmetry,
supernumerary digits, and high-domed palates were examples of physical
stigmata accompanied by a long list of mental symptoms – all considered
to be deviations from the norm due to the inheritance of characteristics
acquired from parents in a faulty environment.[137] These "badges of ser-
vitude" illuminated by, for example, the work of Italian criminologist
Cesare Lombroso, included vast numbers of physical identifiers of degeneracy and criminality, among which the flat feet and impaired gait of the
Jew became medically observable signs of a degenerating and contaminat-
ing group within German society.[138] Such outward signs were identified
by medical experts as symbols of nervous exhaustion and sexual deviance
or abnormality to which Jews and women were particularly susceptible.
Both were thought to possess "a basic biological predisposition to specific forms of mental illness."[139] Ambroise Tardieu spoke of the feminine

135 Mosse, "Nationalism and Respectability," 230; Nancy Leys Stepan, "Biological Degeneration:
     Races and Proper Places," in J. Edward Chamberlain and Sander L. Gilman, eds., *Degeneration:
     The Dark Side of Progress* (New York, 1985), 97–120, 290; Richard Walter, "What Became of
     the Degenerate? A Brief History of a Concept," *Journal of the History of Medicine* 11 (Oct.
     1956): 427.
136 Mosse, "Nationalism and Respectability," 230.
137 The result, summed up depressingly by Max Nordau in *Degeneration* (London, 1895), was that
     a severe mental epidemic was in progress due to the vast fatigue of a civilization subject to very
     rapid change. With the idea that the German race was threatened by degeneration, Otto
     Ammon undertook extensive surveys to investigate racial degeneration in detail, concluding
     with a racial anthropology that advocated selective breeding (see Weindling, *Health, Race and
     German Politics*, 100).
138 There were, said Charles Dana, "at least seven distinct ways in which the ear could be wrong,
     each corresponding to a particular sin and two doctors had examined the toes of hundreds of
     normal people, idiots and criminals to infer that intelligence was indicated by the distance
     between the toes" (Charles L. Dana, "On the New Use of Some Older Sciences," *Transactions
     of the New York Academy of Medicine* 11 [1894]: 479, 484). For a discussion of Cesare Lombroso
     and degeneracy, see Robert A. Nye, *Crime, Madness, and Politics in Modern France: The Medical
     Concepts of National Decline* (Princeton, N.J., 1984), 99–119; see also Gould, *Mismeasure of Man*,
     122–42.
139 Sander L. Gilman, "Jews and Mental Illness: Medical Metaphors, Anti-Semitism, and the Jew-
     ish Response," *Journal of the History of the Behavioral Sciences* 20 (1984): 157; see also Edward
     Shorter, "Women and Jews in a Private Nervous Clinic in Late Nineteenth-Century Vienna,"
     Medical History 33 (1989): 150. Shorter seems to believe that women and Jews were more ner-
     vous and depressed. Jews "obscurely but correctly perceived that indeed they were at greater
     risk from some disorders. . . . If nineteenth-century women found themselves melancholic [it
     was because] they were exposed to a hostile disease environment – in the form of pelvic con-
     tractions from rickets . . . and damage from childbirth" (183).

appearance of the diseased body, sapped of its virility in the spermatic economy through excessive sexual activity.[140] Physicians such as Jean-Martin Charcot saw both women and Jews as lacking control over their sexuality because of their weak nervous system; thus female characteristics were easily projected onto the Jews.[141] From their physical appearance it could be conjectured that male Jews, confined in the degenerate city, lacked the self-discipline to curb their perverse sexuality and, drained of manliness, took on "feminine" characteristics of softness, physical frailty, and timidity.[142]

With their poor physicality and lack of manly strength, "Jews walk with their toes pointed forward and need to lift their flat feet more than we do, like the dragging gait of a lower-class individual," explained Hermann Schaaffhausen in 1888.[143] Even more derogatory was the warning given to Jews about their body image by Jewish self-hater Walther Rathenau:

You should . . . be careful not to walk about in a loose and lethargic manner, and thus become the laughingstock of a race brought up in a strictly military fashion. As soon as you have recognized your unathletic build, your narrow shoulders, your clumsy feet, your sloppy roundish shape, you will resolve to dedicate a few generations to the renewal of your outer appearance.[144]

PHYSICAL TRAINING, NATIONALISM, AND THE JEW'S FOOT

The response of Jewish scientists to such stereotypes was first to produce statistics to prove that Jews had served ably as soldiers in German

---

140 Ambroise Tardieu, *Die Vergehen gegen die Sittlichkeit in staatsärztlicher Beziehung* (Weimar, 1860), 140. See also Mosse, *Nationalism and Sexuality*, 142. One of the sites in which the perceived damage of urban culture was understood to be registered was the woman's body, whose fertility and maternalism were feared to be at special risk (Adler and Pointon, *The Body Imaged*, 86).

141 George Beard's influential treatises on neurasthenia, which were promoted by Charcot in Paris as well as by German and Austrian somatic psychiatrists such as Richard von Krafft-Ebing, drew a clear relationship between sexual behavior and nervous exhaustion. In *Sexual Neurasthenia* he explained that "the strong, the phlegmatic, the healthy, the well balanced temperaments – those who live out-doors and work with the muscle more than the mind – are not tormented with sexual desire to the same degree . . . as the hysterical . . . the nervous – those who live in-doors and use the mind much and muscle very little" (George M. Beard, *Sexual Neurasthenia: Its Hygiene, Causes, Symptoms and Treatment, with a Chapter on Diet for the Nerves* [New York, 1884], 102–3). See Richard von Krafft-Ebing, *Psychopathia Sexualis: A Medico-Forensic Study*, trans. Harry E. Wedeck (Stuttgart, 1886; reprint, New York, 1965).

142 See Gilman, *Difference and Pathology*, 158, for a discussion of how Jewry were accused of sexual perversity because of their marriage patterns.

143 Hermann Schaaffhausen, "Die Physiognomik," *Archiv für Anthropologie* 17 (1888): 337.

144 Walther Rathenau, "Hear O'Israel," in Paul R. Mendes-Flohr and Jehuda Reinharz, eds., *The Jews in the Modern World: A Documentary History* (New York, 1980), 232; original source: Walther Hartenau, "Hoeve Israel," trans. J. Hessing, *Zukunft* 18 (Mar. 16, 1897): 454–62.

armies throughout the nineteenth century, and second, in a scientifically apologetic manner, to attempt to explain how and why, from a medical point of view, the Jew's body had become misshapen and unmilitary.[145] According to Dr. Elias Auerbach, who was heavily influenced by *völkisch* (national) ideology, sport was the best solution to address the very real problem of the Jew's degeneracy and impaired gait. For orthopedist Gustav Muskat, writing in 1909, the flat feet of the male Jew came not as a racial gift but rather from the result of a poor lifestyle and insufficient physical activity in crowded urban living arrangements.[146] That environment affected human behavior, and the shape of the body, was also the view of Anglo-Jewish scholar Joseph Jacobs, the first Jewish physical anthropologist who, in trying to combat the popular belief that Jews had an innate aversion to manual labor, explained that had Jews been forced to become blacksmiths "one would not have been surprised to find their biceps larger than those of other folks [but] as they have been forced to live by the exercise of their brains, brain size rather than muscle size is the result."[147] This, he concluded, explained the relative shortness of Jews as well as their narrow chest measurements which must be the result of poverty, city dwelling, and a general lack of exercise.[148]

The medical rationalization of Jewish physical impairment was further stimulated by Max Nordau, physician and convinced Darwinian, who like his contemporaries believed that just as "the physical horizon of the body was identified with the moral horizon of the species, the moral infirmity of the subject was proportional to the debilitating effects of fatigue."[149] Viewing a man's conduct in life to be determined by his physical constitution and reflected in his bodily structure, Nordau saw the Jews as victims of modern life desperately in need of discipline to control lascivious thinking and improve the body. Although he said nothing about Jewishness in *Degeneration,* once he became attached to Zionism,

---

145 For a discussion, see Gilman, *Case of Sigmund Freud,* 119.

146 Elias Auerbach, "Die Militärtauglichkeit der Juden," *Jüdische Rundschau* 50 (Dec. 11, 1908): 491–2; for a discussion of ideology and sport, see John M. Hoberman, *Sport and Political Ideology* (Austin, Tex., 1984).

147 Joseph Jacobs, "Are Jews Jews?" *Popular Science Monthly* 55 (May–Oct. 1899): 507.

148 American anthroplogist Maurice Fishberg interpreted the statistics Sniggers collected on Jews in Russia and Poland between 1875 and 1877, showing small stature and narrow chest measurements, as the result of the fact that young Jews, fearful of armed service, would present themselves for measurement at a much younger age than the required twenty years in hopes of being rejected (Maurice Fishberg, *The Jews: A Study of Race and Environment* [New York, 1911], 29).

149 Anson Rabinbach, "The Body Without Fatigue: A Nineteenth-Century Utopia," in Seymour Drescher, David Sabean, and Allan Sharlin, eds., *Political Symbolism in Modern Europe* (New Brunswick, N.J., 1982), 44.

the thesis of his book was clearly reflected in his slogan that Jews must become men of muscle instead of remaining neurasthenic slaves to their nerves.[150] He thus drew a conceptual link between the virtues of physical training and national revival, where sport assumed the status of a therapeutic strategy.[151] What was needed, he said, was muscle, manliness, dignity, and self-respect: "Jews cannot afford to be seen as physically weak for in such weakness the Gentile world sees proof of Jewish inferiority."[152]

The nationalistic impulse of Zionism clearly reflected German preoccupation with the style and imagery of manly athleticism and military toughness. When Theodor Herzl founded the World Zionist Organization in 1897 his stated aim was to transform Jews into tough soldiers. Max Nordau, an early recruit to the movement, "promptly emerged as a theorist of the tough Jew in a most precise sense."[153] At the Second Zionist Congress in 1898, Nordau and his colleague Max Mandelstamm proposed a physical culture program for Jewish youth designed to nurture hardy, athletic Jewish bodies in which to house the new Jewish national spirit. In his manifesto on Jewish toughness, Nordau proclaimed, "We must once again create a muscular Jewry. . . . [L]et us once again become deep-chested, sturdy, sharp-eyed men."[154]

Just like *Turnvater* Jahn (father of the gymnastics movement) earlier in the century, Nordau cast himself in the role of a nation builder in the German style, who took seriously, if not literally, the metaphor of the body politic and sought the ideals of controlled sexuality, strength, masculinity, and beauty of the warrior-athlete-hero in a new Jewish nation. Zionistic athletic nationalism was thus a profoundly compensatory movement for the impaired Jewish body, designed in many ways to triumph over the perceived mental and physical ills brought on by degeneration and worsened through excessive sexual activity. "It is through the articulation of Nordau's views about the reconstitution of the Jewish body that the first Jewish gymnastic society, the Makkabi-Turnverein, was founded," reports Sander Gilman.[155] Bar Kochba Berlin was formed on October 22,

---

150 See George L. Mosse's introduction to Max Nordau, *Degeneration* (Berlin, 1892; reprint, New York, 1968), xxviii.

151 See, e.g., Nye, *Crime, Madness and Politics*, 321–9.

152 Max Nordau, quoted in *Körperliche Renaissance der Juden: Festschrift zum 10 jährigen Bestehen des "Bar Kochba"* (Berlin, 1909), 12.

153 Breines, *Tough Jews*, 142; see also P. M. Baldwin, "Liberalism, Nationalism and Degeneration: The Case of Max Nordau," *Central European History* 13 (1980): 99–120.

154 Max Nordau, "Muskeljudentum," *Jüdische Turnzeitung* 4 (Aug. 1903): 138, cited in Flohr and Reinharz, *The Jews in the Modern World*, 434.

155 Gilman, *Case of Sigmund Freud*, 124. See also Paul Yogi Mayer, "Equality – Egality: Jews and

1898, with the slogan "Openly facing the world, we confirm our nationality, which we want to retain, but we are also conscious of our duties as
citizens!"[156] Such duties focused very much on a bodily renaissance that
would seek through sport and physical culture to mirror an "Aryan"
form and beauty through strength, discipline, and military prowess. The
promise of regeneration thus depended on revitalizing the frail and
limping Jew in the image of the mythically robust and racially superior
German "Aryan" male, who in turn was styled on the classical Greek
soldier-athlete-hero archetype.[157]

"In the genesis of the twentieth-century Jew," suggests Breines, Weininger's destructive, self-hating *Sex and Character* is the "great countertext
to Nordau's *Muskeljudentum* (The muscular Jew)."[158] Of course, their strategies for dealing with the stereotype of the impaired body of the Jew
differed radically. Whereas Nordau called for a strategy of Jewish national
and racial renewal through physical culture, Weininger saw no possibility for the Jew "saturated with femininity" to achieve the manliness of
the productive and combative "Aryan." The effects of each message were
to have widely different and far-reaching consequences in the Nazis'
organized killing of the Jews and the Israeli army's successes, but at the
turn of the twentieth century both Weininger and Nordau accepted the
pervasive images of the Jew's inferior physical condition, which had
been decisively shaped by Gentile, often anti-Semitic bodily aesthetics.
Both readily internalized the physical and psychological ideals of the
dominant culture, which idealized the strength and masculine beauty of
the German male (and his imagined classical Greek heritage), forgetting
"that far from being self-evident cultural universals, these ideals [were]
predicated on a series of exclusions and erasures" – especially of women
and Jews.[159]

Sport in Germany," *Leo Baeck Institute Year Book* (London, 1980): 221–41; Moshe Sasson and
Barbara Schrodt, "The Maccabi Sport Movement and the Establishment of the First Maccabiah
Games, 1932," *Canadian Journal of the History of Sport* 16 (May 1985): 67–90.

156 Mayer, "Jews and Sport," 229.
157 Between 1898 and 1903 many Jewish gymnastics clubs were set up in Berlin, Freiberg, Vienna,
Basel, and smaller Jewish communities all over Germany. In 1903 a Jüdische Turnerschaft
(Jewish gymnastics organization) was organized "to foster gymnastics as a medium to build up
physical fitness as part of the Jewish National Idea." In 1921, this became the Maccabi World
Union (Arthur Hanak, "The Historical Background of the Creation of the 'Maccabi World
Union,'" in *Physical Education and Sport in the Jewish History and Culture: Proceedings of an International Seminar, Wingate Institute, July 1973* [Netany, Israel, 1973], 150).
158 Breines, *Tough Jew*, 149.
159 Ibid., 167.

CONCLUSION

> It is on the body itself that we look for the mark of
> identity . . . the bodily marking not only serves to
> recognize and identify . . . the body can be made to bear
> messages of all kinds.[160]

The eighteenth century paved the way for a host of somatic distortions and exaggerations as taxonomic schemes and naturalized models of cultures and physical differences slid easily from Enlightenment designs of racial and sexual hierarchy into evolutionary schemes that began with a primitive state. Evolutionists then "embroidered Enlightenment concepts into a texture of fantastic stereotypes," assuming all the while that their scientific impressions could be charted as natural, measurable differences.[161] The creation of racial and gendered stereotypes around the bodies of German Jews and women, however, was anything but natural. Culture, not nature, influenced assumptions about physical differences, such that "the most creative theories [were] often imaginative visions imposed upon facts."[162] From the late Enlightenment throughout the nineteenth century, scientific comparisons and somatic interpretations in Germany were more often based on a complex combination of aesthetic acceptability, sexual anxieties, and political concerns as gender and race worked their way deeply into nature's body.

The perceived flat feet and impaired gait of the Jew, his supposed inability to handle forced marches in the army as the German man could, and the German woman's wide pelvis and reproductive requirements, which limited her mobility and energy for strenuous exercise (of body or mind), were images of impairment meticulously constructed as markers of difference from the physically strong and dominant European German male. There is no better proof of the social and political impulses to render women and Jews inadequate to the physical tasks and competences of the "Aryan" male (and therefore undeserving of the same benefits and opportunities) than the way in which the traditional Greek archetype of masculinity – the soldier-athlete-hero figure – co-opted to assist with the development of a German national consciousness, underwent a series of pragmatic transformations during the nineteenth century.

From the start the Greek image of manliness, which included that erotic and homosexual element that made the young male body the

160 Brooks, *Body Works*, 21–2.
161 Boon, *Other Tribes*, 40–1.
162 Gould, *Mismeasure of Man*, 21–2.

measure of beauty, was seen as antithetical to the increasingly felt German need for self-discipline and respectability. At those moments in history when sexuality is an issue of public concern and private anxiety, discussions about the nature, meaning, function, and effects of human beauty become matters of argument and debate.[163] As aesthetic notions of beauty stood in for ordered sexuality, the Germans incrementally transformed the Greek ideal body, producing a desexualized lightness and corporeal linearity by adding or emphasizing features such as blond hair, blue eyes, and a light skin that corresponded to their aesthetic notions of beauty and ostensibly distinguished themselves from other groups, but that had little to do with a physical, athletic, or soldierly function. The embodied masculine ideal of the German "Aryan" was thus essentially subverted to include distinct though irrelevant physical markers that were deemed to signify moral as well as heroic and physical powers and that easily distinguished the Teutonic male from both his female counterpart and the dark, ugly, and small males of "Other" races, especially the Jews. It was critical that the identity of the German male be recognizable by his body, which represented at the same time his external reality.

Athletics were an important key to the embodiment of the German male. Physical culture played a constructive role in sustaining his identity and fostering the reality of the male national stereotype in developing the healthy (that is, sexually controlled) human being described by Paul Julius Möbius in *Sexuality and Degeneration* (1903) as "mostly lithe and tall[;] his face is never ugly."[164] The German *Turner* movement by the second half of the century had come to include drilling and disciplined body work, which dulled the sex drive and submerged the individualism while developing solidarity, paramilitary skills, and a honed body. "Who does not recognize in the high-shouldered, deep-chested, thin-flanked frame, in the melancholy disposition, in the unity and solidarity of the German youth, the effect of his favorite gymnastic apparatus and the posturing and pyramiding of the *Turnplatz* [gymnastic field]?" commented the eminent American physical educator Dudley Sargent admiringly.[165] Thus, suggests Connell,

the concern with force and skill becomes a statement embedded in the body, embedded through years of participation in social practices like organized sport

---

163 Robyn Cooper, "Victorian Discourses on Women and Beauty: The Alexander Walker Texts," *Gender and History* 5 (spring 1993): 34.

164 Paul Julius Möbius, *Jahrbuch für sexuelle Zwischenstufen* (Leipzig, 1904), 6:499.

165 Dudley A. Sargent, *Physical Education* (Boston, 1906), 16.

[and physical training]. . . . The meanings in the bodily sense of masculinity concern, above all else, the superiority of men to women, and the exaltation of hegemonic masculinity over other groups of men which is essential to the domination of women.[166]

Threats to either the image or the embodiment of the German male were met by both a refashioning of the German "Aryan" body and through real or perceived restrictions on opportunities to participate in the activities of the dominant male culture, including their strength-acquiring and power-building physical training activities. At those moments during the nineteenth century that Jews and women made determined efforts for greater access to the physical training and sporting culture of the German male, their efforts were sometimes resisted. After 1848, Jews were not always welcome in the Deutsche Turnerschaft, were often abused by anti-Semitic student organizations, and were periodically discouraged from participating fully in German sports organizations, whereas women tended to be channeled into corrective exercises insufficient to develop any significant strength and endurance and were warned about the dire medical consequences of strenuous and competitive sports as well as about the danger of taking on "masculine" tendencies.

For Jews and women, facing society's limits on their bodies was a chilling real-life confirmation of Roland Barthes's claim that "the ultimate field of symbolism is the human body."[167] Sport was the art, said Baron de Coubertin, of virilizing bodies and souls.[168] Virility was manliness, manliness meant normality, and those who were not, could not, or should not demonstrate their manliness were deemed impaired or diseased. Jews tried, says Mosse, "to embrace the ideal of manliness and bodily strength as part of their embourgoisement, but this imperative did not silence the suspicion of cowardice and bodily weakness that followed the emancipated Jew as a potential outsider."[169] In aspiring for greater mobility and seeking to participate in the physical and sporting world of the "normal" male, and hence in pressing against the sexual norms defined for her, the white woman is punished for having abandoned her

---

166 Connell, *Gender and Power*, 85. See also the discussion about sport, gender, and the civilizing process in Jennifer Hargreaves, "Sport, Power, and the Body in Sport and Leisure: Has There Been a Civilizing Process?" in Eric Dunning and Chris Rojek, eds., *Sport and Leisure in the Civilizing Process* (London, 1992), 161–82.
167 Roland Barthes, *S/Z* (Paris, 1970), 220.
168 Pierre de Coubertin, *Essais de Psychologie Sportive* (Lausanne, 1913), 79. See also Eugen Weber, "Pierre de Coubertin and the Introduction of Organized Sport in France," *Journal of Contemporary History* 5 (1970): 3–26.
169 George L. Mosse, "Jewish Emancipation: Between Bildung and Respectability," in Reinharz and Schatzberg, *The Jewish Response to German Culture*, 13.

subjection to the white patriarchal law, which can only be defined by the subjection of woman. Her threat to his cultural identity (or what is subjectively felt as such) must, in order to be effective, be mediated by a reinvocation of repressed female sexuality.[170] Weininger asked for no less, and National Socialism came to insist upon it.

One cannot assume that individuals remained passive to the imprint of culture. Nor should one assume that the exercise of agency on the part of oppressed groups is always evidence of resistance.[171] Nevertheless few can escape the affective resonance of a determining text. Cultural representations are often accepted even when their ideological messages are cognitively understood by the recipients.[172] Oppression leaves its traces, not just in people's minds but in their muscles and skeletons as well, and in their feet and their widening pelvises.[173] Culture, in this sense, is inscribed both on and in the body, and people often knowingly cooperate in their own oppression by the ideologies of others, even if some resist the dominant culture at the level of their bodies by refusing to occupy the socially encoded spaces of the "feminine body" and the "Jew's body." One may, therefore, fruitfully explore the history of the body as a narrative of culture in anatomical disguise, "a parable of culture, of how the body is forged into a shape useable by civilization despite, not because of itself."[174]

170 Geyer-Ryan, *Fables of Desire*, 133.
171 Mariana Valverde, "As if Subjects Existed: Analysing Social Discourses," *Canadian Review of Sociology and Anthropology* 28, no. 2 (1991): 182. Many German Jews, for example, viewed the student fraternities and the *Turner* clubs as positive reference groups, which they tried to join by conforming to the prevailing mores. However, assimilation through sport, notes Eisen, was doomed to failure, because it would be repudiated by increasingly intense nationalism and anti-Semitism (George Eisen, "The Maccabiah Games: A History of the Jewish Olympics," Ph.D. diss., University of Maryland, 1979, 19).
172 D. J. Scholle, "Critical Studies: From the Theory of Ideology to Power/Knowledge," *Critical Studies in Mass Communications* 5 (1988): 33; see also Theodor Adorno, "Cultural Industry Reconsidered," *New German Critique* 6 (1974): 13–19.
173 Brian Fay, *Critical Social Science* (Ithaca, N.Y., 1987).
174 Thomas W. Laqueur, "Amor Veneris, vel Dulcedo Appeletur," in Michael Fehrer, ed., with Ramona Naddoff and Nadia Tazi, *Fragments for a History of the Human Body*, 3 vols. (New York, 1989), 2:94.

14

A Horse Breeder's Perspective
Scientific Racism in Germany, 1870–1933

ARND KRÜGER

In the discussion of the recent resurgence of nationalism, racism, and xenophobia in Germany, Hubert Markl called the insistence of German law on defining *German* along racial rather than cultural lines "a horse breeder's perspective." He also claimed that biologically founded xenophobia is a "half truth that leads to full error."[1] In modern American sperm banks any male semen can be ordered for artificial insemination, not only according to the skin color and ethnic origin of the donor, but also according to his IQ.[2] For a surcharge, the semen of a Nobel Prize winner in the natural sciences is available.[3] Although this may also be called a horse breeder's perspective, it is obvious that in the former case it is a decision of a national parliament, whereas in the latter case it is a decision of the individual. As can be seen in the debate over AIDS, blood is still a very special liquid that threatens not only the individual but also ethnic groups and entire nations.[4]

Nationalism is most vividly expressed in warfare and, falling short of that, in the ritualized form of sport.[5] Flag-waving fans have become a trademark of national encounters and are televised around the world. In the context of this chapter, I do not discuss why television sports editors

---

1 Hubert Markl, "Das missbrauchte Wirgefühl," *Die Zeit*, 49 (1994): 7, 40; for a fuller discussion, see Nora Raethzel, "Germany: One Race, One Nation," *Race and Class* 32, no. 3 (1990): 32–48.
2 For the racial implications in an international context, see Gajendra K. Verman and Christopher Bagley, eds., *Race and Education Across Cultures* (London, 1975); James M. Lawler, *IQ, Heritability, and Racism* (New York, 1978).
3 Charles Oswald Carter, "Eugenic Implications of New Techniques," in Charles Oswald Carter, ed., *Developments in Human Reproduction and Their Eugenic, Ethical Implications* (London, 1983), 205–12.
4 J. Philippe Rushton and A. F. Bogaert, "Population Differences in Susceptibility to AIDS: An Evolutionary Analysis," *Social Science and Medicine* 28 (1989): 1211–20.
5 Arnd Krüger, "The Ritual in Modern Sport: A Sociobiological Approach," in John M. Carter and Arnd Krüger, eds., *Ritual and Record* (Westport, Conn., 1990), 135–52.

seem to think that nationalism can be used to sell an athletic contest, transforming it into a highly emotional and important event. The problem is that spectators around the world understand this form of nonverbal communication and accept it as an expression of the public discourse on individual, national, and often racial talent and superiority.[6] A sporting contest on a high international level is still taken as an indicator of national strength and vitality – even if for the individual it is only a sign of personal success.[7] The highly praised selection process for scientific talent in the former German Democratic Republic (GDR)[8] was based on *anthropometry*,[9] a science that had originally been used to measure racial differences. But this is far from being the only field in which the foundations of *scientific racism* continue to be part of today's discourse.[10]

In this chapter, I look at horse breeding, blood, and sports in order to analyze how social biology[11] – that is, scientific thinking in racial terms and the involvement of government in essentially private matters – was different in Germany from that in other countries. I assume that this background in the history of popular culture[12] and science will be helpful to show some of the peculiarities of the German *Sonderweg* (special path) in the field of scientific racism. The history of science only makes sense in a political context and should not be regarded separately. Where scientific knowledge becomes general knowledge and influences behavior, it becomes a part of hegemonial thought.[13] The development of the breeder's perspective as a part of civil society is therefore more at the

---

6 Arnd Krüger, "Cui bono? Die Rolle des Sports in den Massenmedien," in Arnd Krüger and Swantje Scharenberg, eds., *Wie die Medien den Sport aufbereiten* (Berlin, 1993), 24–63; see Neil Blain, Raymond Boyle, and Hugh O'Donnell, *Sport and National Identity in the European Media* (London, 1993).

7 Arnd Krüger, "On the Origin of the Notion That Sport Serves as a Means of National Representation," *History of European Ideas* 16 (1993): 863–70.

8 Doug Gilbert, *The Miracle Machine* (New York, 1980).

9 Kurt Tittel and Heinz Wutscherk, *Sportanthropometrie* (Leipzig, 1973).

10 Cf. Halford H. Fairchild, "Scientific Racism: The Cloak of Objectivity," *Journal of Social Issues* 47 (1991): 101–15.

11 Heinz-Georg Marten, *Sozialbiologismus: Biologische Grundpositionen der politischen Ideengeschichte* (Frankfurt/Main, 1983); Robert W. Bell and Nimrod J. Bell, eds., *Sociobiology and the Social Sciences* (Lubbock, Tex., 1989).

12 Tony Bennett, Colin Mercer, and Janet Woolacott, eds., *Popular Culture and Social Relations* (Milton Keynes, 1986); John Fiske, *Understanding Popular Culture* (London, 1989); Chandra Mukerji and Michael Schudson, eds., *Rethinking Popular Culture* (Berkeley, Calif., 1991); John Storey, *An Introductory Guide to Cultural Theory and Popular Culture* (Hemel Hempstead, 1993).

13 Thomas Bates, "Gramsci and the Theory of Hegemony," *Journal of the History of Ideas* 36, no. 2 (1975): 351–65; Marc Landy, "Cultural Politics and Common Sense," *Critical Studies* 3, no. 1 (1991): 105–34; T. J. Jackson Lears, "The Concept of Cultural Hegemony: Problems and Possibilities," *American Historical Review* 90, no. 3 (1985): 567–93; for debate, see *Journal of American History* 75, no. 1 (1988): 115–57.

center of this chapter than are interior differentiations between the various branches of scientific racism.[14]

Scientific racism, particularly its main German form of racial hygiene (*Rassenhygiene*), has been analyzed quite thoroughly in recent years in studies that have taken the direct political implications into account.[15] However, considering the internationality of the scientific community, there are relatively few comparative studies.[16] Even fewer studies have analyzed scientific racism in the context of the contemporary cultural discourse.[17] Although the rising influence of the medical profession, with its power to interpret natural events, should not be underestimated,[18] it seems facile to view Nazi euthanasia as an aberration involving some three hundred medical doctors[19] or to point out that the medical profession profited from German anti-Semitism and thus supported Nazis more than most other professions.[20] The basic assumptions of scientific racism were so deeply rooted in the discourse of elites as well as in that of the general public that their ruthless application in the Nazi period was not seriously questioned. The achievement of such consensus on this issue was possible only because the intellectual ground had been sufficiently prepared in the years before the Nazis came to power.

14 For the best study, see Paul Weindling, *Health, Race and German Politics Between National Unification and Nazism, 1870–1945* (Cambridge, 1989).

15 Some of the better studies include Martin Beutelspacher et al., eds., *Volk und Gesundheit: Heilen und Vernichten im Nationalsozialismus* (Frankfurt/Main, 1988); Jürgen Kroll, "Zur Entstehung und Institutionalisierung einer naturwissenschaftlichen und sozialpolitischen Bewegung: Die Entwicklung der Eugenik/Rassenhygiene bis zum Jahre 1933," Ph.D. diss., University of Tübingen, 1983; Georg Lilienthal, "Rassenhygiene im Dritten Reich: Krise und Wende," *Medizinhistorisches Journal* 14 (1979): 114–33; Robert Proctor, *Racial Hygiene: Medicine Under the Nazis* (Cambridge, Mass., 1988); Christian Pross and Götz Aly, *Der Wert des Menschen: Medizin in Deutschland, 1918–1945* (Berlin, 1989); Hans-Walter Schmuhl, *Rassenhygiene, Nationalsozialismus, Euthanasie* (Göttingen, 1987); Peter Weingart, Jürgen Kroll, and Kurt Bayertz, *Rasse, Blut und Gene* (Frankfurt/Main, 1988); S. F. Weiss, "The Race Hygiene Movement in Germany," *Osiris* 3 (1987): 193–236; Johannes Zischka, *Die NS-Rassenideologie: Machttaktisches Instrument oder handlungsbestimmendes Ideal?* (Frankfurt/Main, 1986).

16 Bernd Heuer, "Eugenik/Rassenhygiene in USA und Deutschland," M.D. diss., University of Mainz, 1989; Loren R. Graham, "Science and Values: The Eugenics Movement in Germany and Russia," *American Historical Review* 82 (1977): 1133–64; William Schneider, "Toward the Improvement of the Human Race: The History of Scientific Racism in France," *Journal of Modern History* 54 (1982): 268–91; David Kohn, ed., *The Darwinian Heritage* (Princeton, N.J., 1985), pt. 3, "The Comparative Reception of Darwin," 641–754.

17 Kohn, *The Darwinian Heritage*, pt. 2, "Darwin in Victorian Context," 435–640.

18 See Alfons Labisch and Reinhard Spree, eds., *Medizinische Deutungsmacht im sozialen Wandel* (Bonn, 1989); Claudia Huerkamp, *Der Aufstieg der Ärzte im 19. Jahrhundert* (Göttingen, 1985).

19 Andrew Convay Ivy, "Nazi War Crimes of a Medical Nature," in Stanley Joel Reiser et al., eds., *Ethics in Medicine: Historical Perspectives and Contemporary Concerns* (Cambridge, Mass., 1977), 267–72.

20 According to Michael H. Kater, *Doctors Under Hitler* (Chapel Hill, N.C., 1989) the average income of medical doctors rose between 1933 and 1937 by about 40 percent, and seven times as many M.D.'s belonged to the NSDAP than the national average of all the population.

SCIENTIFIC RACISM

Descriptions of race in human beings are at least as old as Greek antiquity,[21] but the knowledge and acceptance of different races do not constitute racism. Yet, Aristotle said that

whereas the peoples living in the cold climate of northern Europe were conspicuous for their spirit and bravery, their lack of intelligence [made them unfit
for] political organization and dominion. Asiatics were intelligent and inventive,
but they lacked spirit. The Greeks were geographically intermediate, and therefore naturally fitted to rule the earth.[22]

Is this already racism? "Race is a matter of careful scientific study; racism
is an unproved assumption of the biological and perpetual superiority of
one human group over another."[23] In relatively modern form, scientific
racism was invented to prove this "unproved assumption" by means of
exact empirical data and (pseudo) scientific theory. The work of scientists in this field "is 'scientific' inasmuch as they use the paraphernalia
of science . . . to demonstrate differences; but it is 'racist' inasmuch as it
purports to show inherent differences in advance of good evidence, and
often makes policy proposals as a result of this research."[24] It may be contrasted with older forms of racism based on general observations (often
skin color and national origin)[25] and religious difference.

The origin of scientific racism probably lies in Henri de Boulainvilliers's posthumously published claim of 1732 that the noblemen of
France were the descendants of the long-headed Franks of the time of
Charlemagne, whereas the round-headed Celtic Gauls made up the
lower estates of the French society.[26] These racial differentiations were
used to maintain the privileges of the nobility and later gave rise to the
science called craniology, the science of measuring and evaluating skulls.
Craniology was used by Samuel Morton in 1839 to claim that Indians,
blacks, and women were intellectually inferior because their heads were

---

21 See Robert Miles, *Racism* (London, 1989), 14ff.
22 Quoted by Otto Klineberg, *Race Differences* (New York, 1935), 2.
23 Ruth Benedict, *Race and Racism* (London, 1983), vii.
24 Christopher Bagley, "On the Intellectual Equality of Races," in Gajendra K. Verma and Christopher
    Bagley, eds., *Race and Education Across Cultures* (London, 1975), 31.
25 The Spanish and Portuguese had a very elaborate system of names and descriptions to differen-
    tiate between at least twenty-one possible mixtures of Iberian, Indian, and black parentage, taking
    into account the last five generations; cf. Magnus Moerner, *Race Mixture in the History of Latin
    America* (Boston, 1967).
26 Henri de Boulainvilliers, *Essais sur la noblesse de France* (Amsterdam, 1732), quoted in Patrik von
    zur Mühlen, *Rassenideologien: Geschichte und Hintergruende* (Stuttgart, 1977), 33.

smaller than those of the Anglo-Saxon male.[27] Eventually, such notions became so popular that Bertolt Brecht even wrote a sarcastic play about them.[28] The new science of statistics was applied on a wide scale by Adolphe Quetelet, who developed an index of human physical development in his *Recherches sur la loi de la croissance de l'homme* (1831),[29] which is still used as a maturity index in the selection of sporting talent.[30]

Seymor Drescher has shown that the end of the European slave trade coincided with the evolution of European scientific racism. He posits that the abolition gave rise to new questions and anxieties that paved the way for new forms of racism.[31] But this argument, of course, cannot be applied to eighteenth-century racism.[32] Karl von Linné (1707–78) had already included mankind in his system of mammals a century earlier and thus originated the theory that reduced the biblical uniqueness of human beings to an empirical paradigm.[33] In 1853–5 Arthur de Gobineau published his *Essay on the Inequality of the Human Races*, which was the first work of history to explain world history not in terms of "great men," geopolitical factors, or military inventions but in terms of "racial vitality."[34] In 1859 Charles Darwin[35] filled in the gaps and thereby fostered speculation that the same modes of breeding that had been known for a long time in the animal world could now be applied to mankind.[36] His theory applied the models of the sciences that had become the dominant creed of the Industrial Revolution and thus paved the way for the new racial theories.

In the following decades these ideas were combined to produce what Richard Hofstadter later called "social Darwinism" – the idea that the survival of the fittest, which Darwin had described for the animal world,

---

27 Samuel George Morton, *Crania americana* (Philadelphia, 1839); cf. Stephen Jay Gould, *Der falsch vermessene Mensch* (Frankfurt/Main, 1988), 48ff.

28 Bertolt Brecht, "Die Rundköpfe und die Spitzköpfe: Ein Greuelmärchen," in Bertolt Brecht, *Gesammelte Werke* (London, 1938; reprint, Frankfurt/Main, 1967), 908–1040.

29 Richard H. Shryock, "The History of Quantification in Medical Science," *Isis* 52 (1961): 215–37.

30 Tittel et al., *Sportanthropometrie*.

31 Seymor Drescher, "The Ending of the Slave Trade and the Evolution of European Scientific Racism," *Social Science History* 14, no. 3 (fall 1990): 415–50.

32 Harold E. Pagliaro, ed., *Racism in the Eighteenth Century* (London, 1973).

33 Fritz Lenz, "Die soziologische Bedeutung der Selektion," in Gerhard Heberer and Franz Schwanitz, eds., *Hundert Jahre Evolutionsforschung: Das wissenschaftliche Vermächtnis Charles Darwins* (Stuttgart, 1960), 368–96.

34 Arthur Graf Gobineau, *Versuch über die Ungleichheit der Menschenrassen*, 5th ed., 4 vols. (Stuttgart, 1939–40).

35 David Kohn, ed., *The Darwinian Heritage* (Princeton, N.J., 1985).

36 See Karl Eduard Rothschuh, *Physiologie: Der Wandel ihrer Konzepte, Probleme und Methoden vom 16. bis 19. Jahrhundert* (Freiburg/Breisgau, 1968).

also operated in the human species among different races and people.[37]

During the second half of the nineteenth century, the quantifiable experiment became the dominant research design. Medicine, biology, anthropology, and psychology all used empirical "hard" data and borrowed heavily from the modern science of statistics for progress in their field. Rudolf Virchow, the leading pathologist of his time, confirmed this when he said, "We have the unity of method. We are looking for the laws of human development, being, and activity with the same means."[38] Darwin's cousin Francis Galton (1822–1911) used the family histories of famous generals, poets, mathematicians, scientists, musicians, theologians, wrestlers, and others to introduce statistics into the study of human development. In his *Inquiries into the Human Faculties and Its Development* (1883), Galton came to the conclusion that superior as much as inferior intelligence (he scored on a table from 1 to 7) was rare in any given population.[39] His collaborator, Karl Pearson, became professor of biometrics at Cambridge University, and the two were among the founders of the Eugenic Education Society in 1907.[40] For them, and for practically the entire scientific community at that time, quantification was the only scientific method capable of explaining the world.

Although the basic theories of scientific racism at the turn of the century were similar the world over, there was one marked difference: Racism in France was softened by the pre-Darwinian theories of Jean-Baptiste Lamarck (1744–1829), who insisted on the inheritance of acquired characteristics, whereas for the true racist changes could take place only through breeding and not training. The typical example for Lamarck was the giraffe, which was supposed to have developed such a long neck since for generations it had had to eat leaves from the upper branches of trees or starve. In contrast, Germany was influenced by the theories of Gregor Mendel (1822–84), whose research on the inheritance of characteristics in the growth pattern of peas had remained limited to the world of botany for thirty-five years and only then spread out to

---

37 Richard Hofstadter, *Social Darwinism in American Thought, 1860–1915* (Philadelphia, 1944).
38 Quoted by Heinrich Schipperges, *Utopien der Medizin: Geschichte und Kritik der ärztlichen Ideologie des neunzehnten Jahrhunderts* (Salzburg, 1968), 86.
39 Edwin Garrigues Boring, "The Beginning and Growth of Measurement in Psychology," in Harry Woolf, ed., *Quantification: A History of the Meaning of Measurement in the Natural and Social Sciences* (Indianapolis, Ind., 1961), 108–27. Galton also established statistics on the performance of horses and optimistically concluded that by breeding and training they would get faster from generation to generation (cf. Francis Galton, "The American Trotting Horse," *Nature* [May 10, 1883]: 28).
40 Michael Billig, *Die rassistische Internationale: Zur Renaissance der Rassenlehre in der modernen Psychologie* (Frankfurt/Main, 1981).

become the dominant theory of human development.[41] His theory is the basis of the current chromosome theory of inheritance.

In 1900 Friedrich Krupp helped define the state of the art in Germany when he held a competition for the best essay on the question, "What can we learn from the principles of the theory of the descent of man in relation to domestic political development and state legislation?" For a handsome price of 30,000 marks (or the contemporary equivalent of approximately $7,500) and after much publicity, sixty essays were submitted. Some essays revived the dormant theories of Mendel. None of the essays showed a trace of Lamarckianism. It was clear to German researchers that you could cut off the tail of certain dogs for hundreds of years or circumcise Jewish males for three millennia, but that these traits would not be inherited; rather, they were believed to be acquired.[42]

Ernst Haeckel (1834–1919), the major biologist and philosopher of racial hygiene, was the head judge of the competition. His role is somewhat surprising since he believed – like Darwin – in the inheritance of acquired characteristics. Haeckel's theory of radical monism combined Darwin's theory of evolution with a strong anticlerical position, claiming that the church stood in the way of the development of science.[43] For Haeckel, "selection" was the most important point of all racial theories.[44] This was incorporated into August Weismann's (1834–1914) germ plasma theory. Weismann was the first to differentiate in men (just like Mendel had done for plants) between genotype and phenotype, the germ plasma and the individual,[45] stressing that it was impossible to improve our progeny's condition in the long run through physical or mental training – but only through selection.[46]

The First International Hygiene Exhibition in Dresden in 1911, which led to the establishment of the German Hygiene Museum, provided an avenue for bringing German notions of racial hygiene (a term created by Ploetz in 1895) to the attention of the majority of the population. It was here that connections were drawn and established between hygiene and

41 J. Gregor Mendel, *Versuche an Pflanzenhybriden: Zwei Abhandlungen* (Leipzig, 1865).
42 Burchard von Oethingen, *Die Zucht der edlen Pferde in Theorie und Praxis* (Berlin, 1908), 187.
43 Ernst Haeckel, *Die Welträtzel: Gemeinverständliche Studien über monistische Philosophie* (Bonn, 1899) had a circulation of over 400,000 in German alone and was translated into twenty languages (cf. Hans-Günter Zmarzlik, "Der Sozialdarwinismus in Deutschland als geschichtliches Problem," *Vierteljahreshefte für Zeitgeschichte* 11 [1963]: 246–73).
44 Wilhelm Bölsche, *Ernst Haeckel: Ein Lebensbild* (Berlin, 1905).
45 Frederik Churchill, "August Weissmann and a Break from Tradition," *Journal of the History of Biology* 1 (1968): 91–112.
46 Hermann Werner Siemens, *Die biologischen Grundlagen der Rassenhygiene und der Bevölkerungspolitik* (Munich, 1917).

physical culture, hygiene and the decline in birth rates, and hygiene and everyday life.[47] It should be noted, however, that contemporary science took a positivistic approach and did not claim the superiority of any of the races, only their inherent differences.[48]

In 1918 Hermann Werner Siemens pointed out that Germans generally believed Lamarck's theories to be mere "superstition" and that anybody who still believed them was ignorant of modern science.[49] After the French Revolution, the French believed in the inheritance of culture, that anybody who absorbed French culture would eventually become French and would thus become *better*.[50] This theory became the basis of Lamarckianism. Britain's leading Lamarckian was Herbert Spencer (1820–1903), who was not only a biological theorist involved in research on the organic mutability of the species but also a philosopher of science engaged in explaining "cosmical" progress. In *Synthetic Philosophy*, Spencer tried to summarize all of the knowledge of the time in the fields of biology, psychology, and sociology and to explain its development in terms of progress, thus supporting political notions of laissez-faire and optimism.[51]

World War I can be seen as a turning point in the development of scientific racism in Germany. The death of many of the best young men was interpreted as a negative selection and a danger for Germany,[52] particularly since those who survived were by definition – or claimed to have been – unfit for war. Before the war, there had already been a lengthy discussion in Germany and in western Europe in general on population decline and its unfavorable consequences as the socially less desirable groups tended to have more children than the upper classes.[53] The measures taken against this included support for both positive[54] and

47 Max von Gruber and Ernst Rüdin, eds., *Fortpflanzung, Vererbung, Rassenhygiene: Illustrierter Führer durch die Gruppe Rassenhygiene der Internationalen Hygiene Ausstellung 1911 in Dresden* (Munich, 1911).

48 E.g., Wilhelm Schallmayer, *Vererbung und Auslese in ihrer soziologischen und politischen Bedeutung* (Jena, 1910), 318ff., praises the racial characteristics of the Chinese and explains "racial hatred" in economic terms, refuting suggestions that this might be racially inherent.

49 Hermann Werner Siemens, "Was ist Rassenhygiene?" *Deutschlands Erneuerung* 2 (1918): 280.

50 George Ward Stocking, "Lamarckianism in American Social Science, 1890–1915," *Journal of the History of Ideas* 23 (1962): 239–56.

51 James R. Moore, *The Post-Darwinian Controversies* (Cambridge, 1979).

52 The same argument had already been voiced elsewhere since the American Civil War; cf. David S. Jordan and Harvey E. Jordan, *War's Aftermath* (Boston, 1914).

53 Jean Borntraeger, *Der Geburtenrückgang in Deutschland: Seine Bewertung und Bekämpfung* (Würzburg, 1913); Walter Claassen, "Die Abnehmende Kriegstüchtigkeit in Deutschland in Stadt und Land von 1902–1907," *Archiv für Rassen- und Gesellschaftsbiologie* 6, no. 1 (1909): 73–7; John Edwin Knodel, *The Decline of Fertility in Germany, 1871–1939* (Princeton, N.J., 1974).

54 E.g., the *Deutscher Bund zur Volkserhaltung* was fighting against birth control and abortion of per-

negative eugenics.[55] This dying-out of a people (*Völkertod*) could be counteracted only through measures of "artificial" selection. This could be achieved either by eliminating the *bad* germ plasma from reproduction by means of sterilizing the feebleminded, epileptics, and the nearly 10 percent of the population considered to be unsuitable for procreation,[56] or by encouraging the *best* to procreate more.[57] Much research and discussion went into the question of the diseases that were indeed inheritable and those that were not.[58] In many cases, the laws of various American states[59] and other European countries[60] were cited to show the general acceptability of such measures.

It is also in this context that racism became more virulent. This was expressed either in the form of anti-Semitism – since a smaller percentage of Jews had fought in the war than their percentage in the overall population – in the discussion surrounding the so-called Rhineland bastards,[61] or by stressing the racial differences between the Nordic and the "eastern" (*ostisch*) peoples, assuming the racial superiority of the former. Because France had sent, in addition to white Frenchmen, troops from its African colonies to occupy the Rhineland, in most of Germany – with the notable exception of the Rhineland itself – there was a discussion about the possible damage done to the German gene pool on account of children of mixed parentage. In cases of rape the widespread recommendation was abortion or compulsory sterilization of the offspring.[62]

During the war, there had also been much propaganda against the "eastern peoples" (*Ost-Völker*) and even against the "yellow peril."[63] In all, almost twenty national organizations worked in eugenics in some manner by the end of the war.[64] This trend was reinforced by the fact that from the summer semester 1920 onward, instruction in racial hygiene at

sons having potentially healthy offspring; cf. Jean Borntraeger, *Der Geburtenrückgang in Deutschland: Seine Bewertung und Bekämpfung* (Düsseldorf, 1913).

55 Max von Gruber, *Ursachen und Bekämpfung des Geburtenrückgangs im Deutschen Reich* (Munich, 1914).

56 See Fritz Lenz, *Menschliche Auslese und Rassenhygiene* (Munich, 1921), 125ff.; Otto Krankeleit, *Die Unfruchtbarmachung aus rassenhygienischen und sozialen Gründen* (Munich, 1929).

57 Geza von Hoffmann, *Krieg und Rassenhygiene: Die bevölkerungspolitischen Aufgaben nach dem Kriege* (Munich, 1916).

58 Krankeleit, *Unfruchtbarmachung*, 52–61.

59 Geza von Hoffmann, *Die Rassenhygiene in den Vereinigten Staaten von Nordamerika* (Munich, 1913).

60 Krankeleit, *Unfruchtbarmachung*, 83–95.

61 Reiner Pommerin, *Sterilisierung der Rheinlandbastarde* (Cologne, 1979).

62 Sally Marks, "Black Watch on the Rhine: A Study in Propaganda, Prejudice and Prurience," *European Studies Review* 13 (1983): 297–334.

63 Max von Gruber, "Rassenhygiene, die wichtigste Aufgabe völkischer Innenpolitik," *Deutschlands Erneuerung* 2, no. 1 (1918): 17.

64 Jürgen Kroll, "Zur Entstehung und Institutionalisierung," 254ff.

German medical schools, including lectures for students of all faculties as part of the general program of studies, trebled when compared to the prewar era. It had again doubled by 1933.[65]

Darwin had discussed race in purely neutral terms:

> namely the amount of difference between them, and whether such differences relate to few or many points of structure, and whether they are of physiological importance; but more specifically whether they are constant. Constancy of character is what is chiefly valued and sought for by naturalists. Whenever it can be shown, or rendered probable, that the forms in question have remained distinct for a long period, this becomes an argument of much weight in favour of treating them as species. Even a slight degree of sterility between any two forms when first crossed, or in their offspring, is generally considered as a decisive test of their specific distinctness.[66]

Much of the debate about scientific racism is concerned with the issue of whether humans originated in one, or more than one, species. Questioning the Christian notion of creation and the assumption of the inequality of the "races" is far easier if one can prove that the races do in fact belong to distinct subspecies. Although from the turn of the century onward anthropology had shown that the polygenetic theory was not feasible,[67] German science was animated by the idea of likewise refuting the monogenetic theory. However, unlike their colleagues in the social sciences,[68] those in the international natural-sciences community agree that humans as biological beings are far more determined by biological functions, and thus genetic functions, than is often thought.[69]

The racial hygienists in Germany can be divided into two groups: those who claimed that racial hygiene knew neither racial hatred nor class hatred,[70] and those who believed the question was not just of being different but of being superior or inferior.[71] It should be noted, how-

---

65 Maria Günther, "Die Institutionalisierung der Rassenhygiene an den deutschen Hochschulen vor 1933," Ph.D. diss., University of Mainz, 1982, 61.
66 Charles Darwin, "On the Races of Man," *The Works of Charles Darwin*, 29 vols. (London, 1986–9), 21:172.
67 Heinz-Georg Marten, *Sozialbiologismus*, 183ff.
68 Robert M. Young, "Darwinism Is Social," in David Kohn, ed., *The Darwinian Heritage* (Princeton, N.J., 1985), 609–38.
69 Krüger, "The Ritual in Modern Sport"; Eugene G. D'Aquili et al., *The Spectrum of Ritual: A Biogenetic Structural Analysis* (New York, 1979); Charles D. Laughlin and Eugene G. D'Aquili, *Biogenetic Structuralism* (New York, 1974); Edward Osborne Wilson, *Sociobiology: The New Synthesis* (Cambridge, Mass., 1975).
70 E.g., Hermann Werner Siemens, *Vererbungslehre, Rassenhygiene und Bevölkerungspolitik* (Munich, 1930), 131.
71 E.g., Gobineau, *Versuch über die Ungleichheit*; Ludwig Woltmann, "Die anthropologische Geschichts- und Gesellschaftstheorie," *Politisch-Anthropologische Revue* 2 (1903–4): 11–15, 115–34, 284–8, 379–83, 451–6, 547–53; Hans Friedrich Karl Günther, *Der nordische Gedanke unter den Deutschen* (Munich, 1925).

ever, that the whole differentiation of *races* within Germany is mostly an invented tradition that, according to Hobsbawm, means

a set of practices, normally governed by overtly or tacitly accepted rules and of a ritual or symbolic nature, which seek to inculcate certain values and norms of behavior by repetition, which automatically implies continuity with the past. In fact, where possible, they normally attempt to establish continuity with a suitable historical past.[72]

Since Roman times, Germany itself had been a "melting pot" of Roman, Germanic, and Slavic peoples with an influx of Huns and others. Accordingly, ethnic stability was achieved only where such an influx could not take place, that is, in remote mountain areas. The differentiation between various Germanic "races," which were described according to their facial and bodily characteristics, was doubtful at best. Whereas Darwin preferred to call the races "subspecies" and mentioned various theories that differentiated between two and as many as sixty-one different races,[73] German anthropology became very specific about the "action-oriented" "Nordic" (*nordisch*), or Germanic races, and the rather passive eastern races. Some of this was the consequence of the constitutional analysis of Hans Günther[74] and later of Ernst Kretschmer,[75] which assumed that certain character traits accompanied certain body types. Anthropologists measured these body types by anthropometry. The old craniology was still used, but measurements of limb length and width, body ratios, hair color, and pigmentation were added. "Races" were then defined as groups of people that had the same physical characteristics and thus the same "character."

After 1870 anti-Semitism became racially defined; yet it confounded all attempts to find any racial differences between Jews and Germans.[76] A great deal of research in this field and attempts to differentiate between the two subraces of Jews, the eastern Ashkenazic and the western Sephardic Jew, a distinction accepted even by Jews themselves,[77] could

72 Eric Hobsbawm and Terence Osborn Ranger, eds., *The Invention of Tradition* (Cambridge, 1983), 1.

73 Darwin, *On the Races*, 180–1.

74 Hans Günther, *Grundlagen der biologischen Konstitutionslehre* (Munich, 1922); Hans Günther, *Adel und Rasse* (Munich, 1927).

75 Ernst Kretschmer, *Körperbau und Character* [1929], 26th ed., enlarged by Wolfgang Kretschmer (Berlin, 1977).

76 See Wilhelm Marr, *Der Sieg des Judenthums über das Germanenthum: Vom nicht konfessionellen Standpunkt aus betrachtet*, 8th ed. (Bern, 1879).

77 Felix von Luschan, "Die anthropologische Stellung der Juden," *Allgemeine Zeitung des Judentums* 56 (1892): 816–18, 628–30; Ignacy M. Judt, *Die Juden als Rasse: Eine Analyse aus dem Gebiete der Anthroplogie* (Berlin, 1903); Ignaz Zollschau, *Das Rassenproblem unter besonderer Berücksichtigung der theoretischen Grundlagen der jüdischen Rassenfrage* (Leipzig, 1910).

not distinguish Jews from Germans by anthropological means[78] – in spite of the search for different shapes of heads, feet,[79] or noses.[80] In the largest anthropological enterprise of the time, Virchow and his colleagues measured 6.7 million schoolchildren, including 75,000 German-Jewish children. They found that neither a typical German nor a typical Jew emerged. Virchow was forced to conclude that there was no German race, and also no Jewish one.[81]

German racism was different from American racism in that differences were not as easily drawn as between black and white, upper class and lower class. In Germany, racial superiority had to be defined in a far more sophisticated manner than in the United States. "Western" Jews in Germany were often among the best-educated part of German society and had worked their way into the *Bildungsbürgertum* (educated middle class).[82] The recent Jewish immigrants from the East, by contrast, had a difficult time earning a living and were considered a source of cheap labor. A racial theory that wanted to fold both groups into one "race" had to be far more complex. It therefore stressed such socially undesirable traits as meanness and slyness as typically Jewish, regardless of where the people actually came from, the East or the West. As part of the invented tradition, racial purity was praised, whereas Jews from eastern Europe were claimed to have a racial mixture that was "Near Eastern, oriental, east Baltic, eastern, deepest Asian, Nordic, Hamitic, and Negroid" (*"vorderasiatisch-orientalisch-ostbaltisch-ostisch-innerasiatisch-nordisch-hamitisch-negerisch"*).[83]

The question, of course, is one of why the invention of the tradition of a Jewish race was so readily accepted and why it took root as a notion that was completely at odds with factual research. In fact, to some extent positivistic scientific research into racial difference showed the opposite of what was ideologically desirable for racists and the Nazis. It might have been expected that the textbook of *Rassengünther* ("Hans Günther," a nickname given because of his racism) would have gone through many

---

78 For the best overview, see Maurice Fishberg, *Die Rassenmerkmale der Juden* (Munich, 1913).

79 See Sander Gilman, "The Jewish Foot: A Foot-Note to the Jewish Body," Gilman, *The Jew's Body* (London, 1991), 38–59.

80 Georg Lilienthal, "Die jüdischen 'Rassenmerkmale': Zur Geschichte der Anthropologie der Juden," *Medizinhistorisches Journal* 28, nos. 2–3 (1993): 173–98.

81 Rudolf Virchow, "Gesamtbericht über die von der deutschen anthropologischen Gesellschaft veranlassten Erhebungen über die Farbe der Haut, der Haare und der Augen der Schulkinder in Deutschland," *Archiv für Anthropologie* 16 (1886), 275–466.

82 Irma L. Cohen, *The Intelligence of Jews as Compared with Non-Jews* (Columbus, Ohio, 1927).

83 Hans Friedrich Karl Günther, *Rassenkunde des jüdischen Volkes* (Munich, 1930), 191; cf. Günther, *Die Rassenkunde des deutschen Volkes* (Munich, 1930).

new printings in the Nazi period and that much new research would have attempted to refute authors such as Maurice Fishberg, who had shown the similarity between Jews and Germans – but the opposite was the case. Actual anthropological measurements of Jews were no longer used, and the Nuremberg racial laws resorted to defining a Jew by religion rather than by anthropology. To a greater or lesser extent, this new development was initiated by racists such as Siegfried Passarge[84] and Ludwig Schemann, who showed that racial differences alone could not explain different attitudes. They therefore drew on history to show that orthodox Jews supposedly had remained "archaic and primitive like early men in their thinking and feeling."[85]

It might therefore be argued that the German scientific preoccupation with race did not differ much from general international developments. In the mid-1920s, for example, Sir Julian Huxley began to stress the formative impact of education and claimed that the action of man was not 80 percent genetically predetermined but only 50 percent.[86] Yet, there were considerable differences between Germany and the Western democracies in the social discourse about race and racism.

THE BREEDERS

Darwin had gathered much of the information for his work from discussions with lay breeders of bees, cows, sheep, and horses.[87] As a nation that had only recently made the transition from an agrarian to an industrial country, Germany still cultivated a breeding discourse in all spheres of agriculture.[88] The discourse regarding horses continued to play a large role within aristocratic social circles as well as the newly affluent upper-middle classes.[89] Although most animals on all farms were bred for excellence, in society at large selective breeding and certain pedigrees were

---

84 Siegfried Passarge, *Das Judenthum als landschaftskundlich-ethnologisches Problem* (Munich, 1929).
85 Ludwig Schemann, *Die Rassenfragen im Schrifttum der Neuzeit* (Munich, 1931), 375–9.
86 See Elazar Barkan, *The Retreat of Scientific Racism: Changing Concepts of Race in Britain and the United States Between the World Wars* (Cambridge, 1992).
87 James A. Second, "Darwin and the Breeders: A Social History," in David Kohn, ed., *The Darwinian Heritage*, 519–42; according to the index of the *Works*, Darwin mentions horses 125 times.
88 E.g., Hugo Werner, *Die Rinderzucht*, 2d ed. (Berlin, 1902); Ernst August Brödermann and Gottfried Freyer, *Der Werdegang des deutschen weissen Edelschweines, seine Züchtung, Beurteilung und Verbreitung* (Berlin, 1930); Richard Reinhardt and Josef G. Vaeth, *Das Katzenbuch: Rassen, Züchtung, Haltung sowie Krankheiten der Katze* (Hanover, 1931); Bruno Dürigen, *Die Geflügelzucht* (Berlin, 1927).
89 Observing the physique of his models, Sascha Schneider exclaimed, "How much better than this human material is a horse of race" (Felix Zimmermann, "Sascha Schneiders Kunstschaffen," *Die Schönheit* 17 [1921]: 490).

discussed about horses more widely than about any other animal. There were special journals for horse breeders, thorough-breeding registers were kept, the racial advantages of horses were reported in the daily press more frequently – for example, on the sports pages – than was the case for cows or other domesticated animals. Because of this widespread interest, I limit myself in this chapter to the discourse on horses. The history of the public discourse on breeding, and with it the obsession with what constituted the best horse, had enjoyed a hundred-year history before the Nazis prohibited the crossbreeding of different races of German horses.[90] The same discussion about the best physical military training, "scientific exercises," *Turnen* (gymnastics), or sport, finds its equivalent in the world of horses.[91] The first horse races took place in Germany only in 1825, and between 1837 and 1853 horse racing became a major social phenomenon.[92] For its first fifty years, the discourse on horse breeding centered on the various functions of horses – and in terms of race, only on Arabian and German stock.[93] In horse breeders' terms, one was obviously speaking about "blood."

The war of 1870–1 was a turning point. Because nearly one-third of German horses died during the war or in its immediate aftermath,[94] the discussion about the decline of the German horse and its military implications preceded by a generation the discussion about the decline of the German human population. In both cases, the point of comparison was France.[95] The various German states took action by trying to use the occasion to raise the quality of breeds of horses for military purposes. In a concerted action, horses for the various military purposes (cavalry, artillery, and so forth) were bred. To ensure a high degree of uniformity of the breed at the optimal level of military performance, the states tried to monopolize stallions for use in general breeding. This was done in

90 Paragraph 19 of the *1. Verordnung zur Förderung der Tierzucht* (May 26, 1936), e.g., the horses of Oldenbourg were supposed to become particularly useful for drawing artillery; see Josef Jaspers, *Züchterische und wirtschaftliche Bedeutung der Hengsthaltung* (Bonn, 1940), 39.
91 Otto Dijon von Monteton, *Wie entspricht die deutsche Pferdezucht am besten dem Staatsinteresse?* (Berlin, 1880), 7ff.
92 In Berlin the first races were held in 1829. In 1837 there was racing in twenty different towns, and by 1849 the number had expanded to forty-two towns, with a total of 116 races featuring 482 horses. By 1853 the figures had grown to 245 races in 37 towns, with 1,020 horses for 22,177 gold francs prize money and 60 valuable cups. At the same time there were 1,474 races in England with 1,686 horses for £188,314. See Georg Friedrich Bandow, *Pferdezucht und Pferderennen: Ein Wort zur Aufmunterung* (Berlin, 1854), 22.
93 See General Csekonics, *Praktische Grundsätze die Pferdezucht betreffend* (Pesth, 1817), 45ff.
94 Karl Ableitner, *Positive Vorschläge zur Hebung der Pferdezucht mit Privat-, Staats- und Landgestüten* (Vienna, 1871), 49; according to the tables of Heinrich Dade, *Zum Schutz der deutschen Pferdezucht* (Berlin, 1900), 20ff., the figure must have been smaller.
95 Friedrich Oetken, *Zur französischen Pferdezucht* (Berlin, 1902).

accordance with the breeding practice for race horses, where the performance of the stallion was taken more into consideration than that of the mare, and where the hiring-out of stallions from one stable to the next was an established practice. In some of the states, there had been crown, or later state-owned, stables for over two centuries; in others, they were founded for the purpose of controlling the breeding in a distinct region after the Franco-Prussian War.[96] The attempt on the part of the governments to monopolize the better breeds for military purposes failed, however, but not because it was impractical. In the end, about 50 percent of the new breed of military horses had state-owned and -operated stallions as fathers and were thus standardized, even if the mares belonged to private breeders. The other horses continued to be the usual crossbreedings that the private breeders produced among themselves.[97]

Because of heavy government involvement, inbreeding shaped the German horse to produce a multitude of what would later be called "races," such as the Trakehner, Friesisch, or the Hanoverian.[98] Whereas these German horse races were still in the process of being invented immediately after the war of 1870–1,[99] in 1890 the first all-German exhibition of the German horse took place, which firmly established the newly invented races.[100] The formation of a Landespferdezuchtverein (State Horse-Breeding Association) in the various German states played a major role.[101] Horse races were being defined at the same time as attempts were being made to define human races biologically. The 1900 World Exposition in Paris was accompanied by the Second Olympic Games as an exhibition of "manpower"[102] not unlike the exhibition of horses in 1890.[103] This was not a purely German matter. The main

---

96 Gustav Fröhlich and Gustav Schwarznecker, *Lehrbuch der Pferdezucht*, 6th ed. (Berlin, 1926), 130ff.

97 For the development of the breeders' organizations, see Christian von Stenglin, ed., *Deutsche Pferdezucht: Geschichte-Zuchtziele* (Warendorf, 1983).

98 About the value of inbreeding, see Axel de Chapeaurouge, *Einiges über Inzucht und ihre Leistung auf verschiedenen Zuchtgebieten* (Hamburg, 1909).

99 Whereas Hermann Settegast, *Die Thierzucht* (Breslau, 1872), vii, claimed racial consistency (*der Racen unverwüstliche Constanz*), Hermann von Nathusius, in his *Vorträge über Viehzucht und Rassenkenntnis* (Berlin, 1872), xvii, objected, since "the definition of *Linné* according to which the species are the original form as created by God, is no longer feasible. The process of the formation of races is never ending and continuously in progress."

100 *Deutschlands Pferde im Jahre 1890: Bericht über die 1. allgemeine deutsche Pferdeausstellung, 12–22. Juni 1890* (Berlin, 1891).

101 At its fiftieth anniversary in 1927 the one for Hesse had the most members, with 1,000; see von Westerweller, *Die Pferdezucht im Grossherzogtum Hessen* (Darmstadt, 1927).

102 Coubertin was against the inclusion of women in the Games, and in 1900 they only participated in tennis and golf. See Uriel Simri, *Women at the Olympic Games* (Netanya, Israel, 1979).

103 In Paris the races of East Prussia, Holstein, Mecklenburg, Oldenburg, East Friesland, Schleswig,

American publication devoted to eugenics, the *Journal of Heredity*, started out under the title *American Breeders' Magazine* and was only renamed with a slight shift in emphasis in 1913. Likewise, the American Breeders' Association was renamed the American Genetic Association at about the same time.[104]

Although knowledge of animal races – in this case of horse breeds – and scientific racism are not equivalents, it should not be overlooked that, for the first time and for military reasons, German state governments took concerted action in breeding that in other countries was left completely to individual initiative. From this it is also possible to see that the inventions of the traditions of horse races and human races took place in parallel. The laws of heredity of horses were publicly discussed and thoroughly recorded in terms of character, color, and acquired traits[105] – but also, as with human beings, in terms of inheritable diseases.[106]

Horse breeders also anticipated the discourse on racial characteristics: The longer the line of horses with the same character, the more certain the inheritance of particular traits. In the discourse about human races this argument would be repeated: A pure race is better than a mixed one.[107] Scientists also discussed the inheritance of acquired traits, such as speed, in horses. In 1908 it seemed clear to the horse breeders and many educated laymen that acquired traits could be passed along to some degree.[108] In short, the discourse on races of horses made it easier to discuss races of human beings. In fact, the horse breeder's perspective was shared not only by people who actually bred horses but by the general public in Germany as well.

TURNEN AND SPORT

Since the time of Friedrich Ludwig Jahn at the beginning of the nineteenth century, fitness of males has been closely associated with the strength of an entire nation. By the beginning of the twentieth century,

and the Rhineland were present, see Landwirthschaftlicher Centralverein, ed., *Catalogue: Collection des Chevaux exposée par le "Landwirthschaftlicher Centralverein,"* 7 vols. (Paris, 1910).

104 Heuer, *Eugenik/Rassenhygiene*, 76.

105 In Prussia the commission in charge was founded in 1875; see Oskar Knispel, *Die Verbreitung der Pferdeschläge in Deutschland* (Berlin, 1915), 4.

106 Edmund Suckow, *Erbfehler in der Pferdezucht: Studien aus der Praxis* (Berlin, 1924).

107 *Johann Christoph Justinus – hinterlassene Schriften über die wahren Grundsätze der Pferdezucht* (Vienna, 1884), 16–17.

108 Von Oethingen, *Die Zucht*, 190ff., also explains that a long line of forefathers with the same traits guarantees the perpetuation of a certain trait.

the *Turner* and sport movements in Germany had more than a million members and were by far the largest fitness movements in the world.[109] Here I examine in this connection, the origins of the notion that sports can be used for international propaganda about national and racial superiority. Throughout most of the nineteenth century, the notion of superiority was not self-evident. Countries compared themselves in wars, technology and modernization, military potential beyond the actual battlefield, imperial reach in peacetime, or in world expositions. Since the first exposition in London in 1851, seventeen others with an international ranking followed until 1904.[110] The expositions in Paris (1900) and St. Louis (1904) incorporated the Olympic Games as a demonstration of the world's best human physical performance, much as they assembled many outstanding accomplishments in other fields, including, of course, horses.[111]

A conference in Berlin in 1912 established the actual conditions under which these expositions were to take place, their classification as "world" or "regional" expositions, their tax-exempt status, and so forth. Such expositions were being codified at the same time as international sporting events.[112] It is therefore not surprising to find Theodor Lewald in both fields as a representative of the German interior minister at the Chicago, Paris, and St. Louis expositions, and later in a similar role at international sporting events.[113]

The St. Louis Exposition and associated Olympic Games also contained, "Anthropological Days" in which the way of life and the performances of ethnic groups from around the world were presented. In an era of growing nationalism, the "Anthropological Days" served to show the superiority of the white person and the desire to compare, much as with animals, the various species of human being.[114] Although sport had originally been an individual matter, the discourse about it had and still has nationalistic and racial connotations.

To ensure the importance of sports, it has been essential that there are

---

109 Arnd Krüger, *Sport und Politik: Von Turnvater Jahn zum Staatsamateur* (Hanover, 1975).

110 *Meyers Lexikon* (Leipzig, 1924), 1:1193.

111 Richard D. Mandell, *Paris 1900: The Great World's Fair* (Toronto, 1967).

112 In charge of the conference was Dr. Theodor Lewald, who later became IOC member for Germany and the president of the Organizing Committee of the 1936 Olympic Games; see Bundesarchiv, Abteilung Potsdam, Nachlass Lewald, vol. 136, Conférence Diplomatique relative aux Expositions Internationales, Oct. 10–25, 1912.

113 Rolf Pfeiffer and Arnd Krüger, "Theodor Lewald: Eine Karriere im Dienste des Vaterlands oder die vergebliche Suche nach der jüdischen Identität eines 'Halbjudens,'" *Menora: 6. Jahrbuch für deutsch-jüdische Geschichte* (Munich, 1995).

114 Matti Goksoyr, "An Image of the Third World in the White Man's Arena: The Anthropological

international competitions with which the citizens of a country can identify. This means not only that the competition must be at a somewhat representative level, but also that it must be widely reported in the news media. The rise of a sports press took place at different times in the various countries. The 1906 Olympic Games in Athens appear to have had a considerable importance in Germany, ten years after the establishment of the modern Olympics. By the time of the Athens games many international sporting federations had been founded, and newspaper coverage was significant. The Greek crown prince served as one of the judges, which gave the events high visibility.[115] The professionalization of sports journalism helped broaden the contemporary discourse on the masculine vigor or decadence of a nation and a race, although articles on these subjects appeared in a different section of the newspaper.[116] In most countries the early sports newspapers also covered horse racing.

Although sports is considered an individual matter, the sporting press raised many questions about nationalism. For the *Times* of London the argument was an easy one:

> There is also the consideration that the national reputation is more deeply involved than perhaps we care to recognize in the demonstration of our ability to hold our own against other nations in the Olympic contests. . . . Whether we took the results very seriously ourselves or not it was widely advertised in other countries as evidence of England's "decadence."[117]

The same opinion was voiced in the United States. The president of the U.S. Olympic Committee, Colonel Thompson, explained, "Instead of the individual athlete being first consideration, the nation now directs the actions of the athletes, and this . . . will result in better competition, world-wide interest, and add to the importance of the Olympic games."[118]

Germany was the first country to provide direct state financial support for its Olympic athletes to ensure that nobody would think about German "decadence." The country that had placed only sixth at the Stockholm Olympic Games in 1912 was to become number one. In line with the notion of German superiority, the emperor himself encouraged the

---

Days in St. Louis, 1904, and Their Aftermath," in Roland Renson et al., eds., *The Olympic Games Through the Ages: Greek Antiquity and Its Impact on Modern Sport* (Athens, 1991), 229–40.

115 Athanasios Tarassouleas, *Jeux Olympiques à Athènes: 1896–1906* (Athens, 1988), 115ff.

116 See Arnd Krüger, "100 Jahre Olympische Idee: Wettkampf der Rassen oder Fest der Sportler?" *Damals* 26, no. 6 (1994): 66–70.

117 *Times* (London), editorial, Aug. 18, 1913, 7:4.

118 *New York Times*, July 4, 1914, 8:5.

imperial and Prussian governments to allocate money (in the Prussian case, 100,000 reichsmarks) for the selection and preparation of athletes. This was more than any other participating country had ever done for its Olympic team. As a simple matter of sponsorship, other governments had certainly given money for the construction of stadiums, the preparations, or the actual staging of the games. But Germany not only wanted to be a good host, it planned to win the games in order to demonstrate national strength in this highly symbolic contest. Considering the international amateur code of the time, direct financial support of athletes and their coaches by governments was of questionable legality.

In preparation for the 1916 Olympic Games, scheduled to take place in Berlin, a new stadium was built. It was financed privately by the same Berlin Union Club that had financed the 1890 horse exhibition. According to the contemporary slogan, the new sports stadium would be a "super stadium for super Germans."[119] The emperor himself officiated at the dedication, stressing in his speech the national importance of sports. This point was also underscored by the German press:[120]

The Olympic Games are a war, a real war. You can be sure that many participants are willing to offer, without hesitation, several years of their life for a victory of the fatherland. . . . The Olympic idea of the modern era has given us a symbol of world war that does not show its military character very openly, but – for those who can read sports statistics – it gives ample insight into world ranking.[121]

The Olympic Games were considered particularly useful for this purpose, since each athlete could maintain his national identity and show his national feelings. The laurels were won for the fatherland, and the games represented a competition of country against country.[122] After some discussion, the German parliament voted by a clear majority to finance the training of German athletes.[123]

The value of the German emperor's taking a public position on Olympic matters and the parliament's discussing the funding of elite sports should not be underestimated. They were part and parcel of the discourse on the individual, the nation, and the race. We should differentiate,

---

119 *Daily Mail* quoted in the *New York Times*, June 9, 1913, 3:3.
120 *New York Times*, June 8, 1913, sec. 3, 2:8.
121 Martin Berner, "Der olympische Gedanke in der Welt," *Fussball und Leichtathletik* 14 (1913), 495–6.
122 Erich Mertin (Deutsche Reichspartei), *Stenographische Berichte zu den Verhandlungen des deutschen Reichstags* (Berlin, 1914), 292:7342.
123 Feb. 17, 1914, in Mertin, *Stenographische Berichte zu den Verhandlungen des deutschen Reichstags*, 293:7386.

however, between the discourse on sports and the discourse on gymnastics. In athletic competition, it was easy to compare and measure differences in performance. Since German Jews were on the whole less inclined to participate in amateur sports at a competitive level and since their percentage among top athletes was below their percentage in the population, anti-Semitism in competitive sport was the exception rather than the rule before 1933.[124] Accordingly, the discourse on race in the United States, with its talented African-American athletes, was much more developed and led to racial segregation and separate Negro leagues in baseball, the national pastime.

This was no different in the gymnastics movement, which in 1904 had split over the question of anti-Semitism and an "Aryan" paragraph that forbade Jewish membership in the southern German and Austrian Deutscher Turnerbund (German Gymnastic Federation). The much larger Deutsche Turnerschaft (German Gymnastic Union) accepted Jewish membership. Since gymnastics symbolized military readiness, that is, a more general fitness of the population and not top performance, a physical differentiation was not as easily drawn. This also led to the formation of a Jüdische Turnerschaft (Jewish Gymnastics Organization) stressing *Muskeljudentum* (muscular Jewishness) as opposed to "muscular Christianity."[125]

The discourse on sports is of particular importance because it is here that genetic endowment and the influence of training have been most thoroughly studied. It also helps us differentiate between scientific racism, the scientific study of anthropometric measurements, and genetic endowment. In the discourse on athletic performance from the late 1920s, it became clear to many that if one is not sufficiently gifted, no amount of training or favorable environmental factors will make one into a champion. Because of the diversity of sports, it was also thought important to guide an individual into choosing a sport for which he was genetically best endowed.[126] By 1933, a racism defined by physical traits had not caught on in Germany, a country with six million dues-paying members of sports organizations, as much as in North America. Soccer, the German national sport and the spectator sport that drew the largest crowds, showed that physical appearance and racial characteristics were not

---

124 Arnd Krüger, "'Wenn die Olympiade vorbei, schlagen wir die Juden zu Brei': Die Olympischen Spiele 1936 und die Juden," *Menora: 5. Jahrbuch für deutsch-jüdische Geschichte* (Munich, 1994), 83–98.

125 Hartmut Becker, *Antisemitismus in der Deutschen Turnerschaft* (Sankt Augustin, 1980).

126 See Carl Krümmel, "Eignungslehre," in Carl Krümmel, ed., *Athletik: Ein Handbuch der lebenswichtigen Leibesübungen* (Munich, 1930), 84–123. The first book linking sport and race directly was not published until the Nazi era; see Lothar Tirala, *Sport und Rasse* (Munich, 1936).

important to win. Yet this is also a sport in which the struggle for survival of the fittest individual was emphasized in other ways. In Germany, however, the national government intervened in order to stress national rather than individual strength, bending an international code of ethics to do so.

BLOOD

"Blood" is crucial from the horse breeder's perspective, since racial traits are supposed to be carried by the blood – hence the "full-blooded" horse. Landsteiner had discovered the ABO blood types in 1901[127] (incidentally the same as in horses),[128] realizing that in the case of blood transfusion, donor and recipient had to have the same blood type. In 1910 it was established that blood types were hereditary, following the laws of Mendel. This was important in forensic medicine as well as in everyday discourse, since legal paternity cases could usually be decided far more clearly with the aid of blood typing.[129] Blood typing became a major asset in World War I, eventually leading to an identification tag on which the blood type of each soldier was printed to speed up the search for donors. Toward the end of the war, Hanna and Ludwik Hirszfeld discovered racial dissimilarities in blood typing in a camp on the Macedonian front in their analysis of blood from sixteen different nationalities.[130] They left out blood type O and expressed their results as a "race index" – (OA + OAB):(OB + OAB). If a region had more blood type A than B, the higher the index figure above 1; if there was more B than A, the lower the figure below 1. Mapping the blood types in Europe, they found a sharp drop at the eastern German border, from an A-dominated Germany with a race index of more than 5 in some areas, to a B-dominated Poland, with a race index of as low as one-fifth (0.2). According to their interpretation, there were two original races of humankind, a group A originating in the West (later associated with blond hair and blue eyes) and a group B, originating in the East.[131]

127 Pauline M. H. Mazumdar, "The Purpose of Immunity: Landsteiner's Interpretation of the Human Isoantibodies," *Journal of the History of Biology* 8 (1975): 115–33.
128 Oluf Thomsen, "Die Serologie der Blutgruppen," in Paul Steffan, ed., *Handbuch der Blutgruppenkunde* (Munich, 1932), 100–2.
129 Emil Dungern and Leo Hirschfeld, "Über Nachweis und Vererbung biochemischer Strukturen," *Zeitschrift für Immunforschung* 4 (1910): 531–46; 6 (1910): 284–92.
130 Hanna Hirszfeld and Ludwik Hirszfeld, "Serological Differences between the Blood of Different Races: Result of Researches on the Macedonian Front," *Lancet* 197 (1919), 675–9.
131 W. H. Schneider, "Chance and Social Setting in the Application of the Discovery of Blood Groups," *Bulletin of the History of Medicine* 57 (1983): 545–62.

This led to an enormous amount of research devoted to mapping Europe according to blood type. In 1932 Paul Steffan published an international bibliography on blood typing that has been of great clinical importance. Yet, of the 2,979 titles in the bibliography, 710 used the medical research for racial, not medical, purposes and presented research that discussed racial differences measured by blood types.[132] Since the wrong blood type could be lethal in a transfusion, there did not seem to be any doubt about the validity of blood type theories – and the racial theories that went with them. Researchers soon discovered that Jewish blood was not racially different and that it differed relatively little from the blood types of non-Jews. This gave rise to the theory of Jews being "parasites" who preyed on their host countries. The existence of blood types supported the notion of two different origins of human beings, since erythroblastosis due to the incompatibility of parental blood led to infant mortality – a form of sterility defined by Darwin as necessary for the existence of two races.[133] This, however, was a result not of ABO blood typing but of the racially neutral Rhesus factor and, therefore, did not support the hypothesis of blood superiority.

Blood type research did much to spread the notion of scientific racism among the general population. A survey of the contemporary literature makes clear that Germans (as well as Poles and Japanese) were far more concerned with this line of scientific research than were most other national groups. Although it helped to give scientific racism greater credibility, it was not taken as a basis for practicable action. Günther warned of its being just one trait out of many,[134] the Nuremberg Laws did not use it, and it was not used even in the attempts to germanize Poland because it was considered too crude. Blood grouping stressed the horse breeder's perspective, but it also helped show that race is seldom "pure."

CONCLUSION

Scientific racism in Germany had similar roots and covered many of the same topics as the rest of the international scientific community. It was already losing much of its influence before the Nazis came to power, and eventually there remained only one group of scientists struggling for Nazi approval and research funds. Their racial criteria were not applied

---

132 Paul Steffan, "Die Bedeutung der Blutgruppen für die menschliche Rassenkunde," in Steffan, *Handbuch*, 382–452.
133 Darwin, "On the Races of Man."
134 Günther, *Rassenkunde des deutschen Volkes*, 182ff.

when persecuting Jews, but their techniques of sterilization and "euthanasia," that is, murder of people deemed unfit, found their way into the Nazi agenda.

Many of the differences between German research and other research on this subject are to be explained by the different reception of Darwinism. In Germany it meant the survival of the fittest race, whereas in the Anglo-American world it meant the survival of the fittest individual.[135] The different role of the state in matters of race and breeding – and the general social acceptability of state intervention in Germany – has also become clear in the foregoing discussion.[136]

We should also not overlook the fact that medical experimentation on human "guinea pigs" was until midcentury the rule rather than the exception. Experiments were frequently conducted on people first and on animals only later – since people were cheaper to come by.[137] This chapter has shown that many of the elements the Nazis could rely on in their general support after 1933 had already existed in many fields of science and popular culture. Horses were important because the discourse about their breeding patterns preceded that about humans by a generation and strongly influenced the general knowledge on the value of blood. Horses can be considered the test case. The organization of the breeding of horses for military purposes by allowing reproduction only among those considered most suitable preceded the Nazi plan to eliminate those humans considered unsuitable. Of course, there are differences between the different actions, but the breeding of horses demonstrated the effectiveness of such measures and fostered the acceptance of government intervention in a matter that in other countries was left in private hands.

Blood typing helped provide a pseudoscientific basis for the differentiation between the various "races" of humankind. Since there was a widespread discourse on blood types because of paternity cases and the problems of blood transfusion, there seemed to be a scientific basis for assuming differences between races. Between the West and the East, there

135 Richard Hofstadter, "Darwinism and Western Thought," in Henry L. Plaine, ed., *Darwin, Marx and Wagner* (Columbus, Ohio, 1962), 53–5; I have shown the same in the case of comparative nudism; cf. Arnd Krüger, "Zwischen Sex und Zuchtwahl: Nudismus und Naturismus in Deutschland und Amerika," in Norbert Finzsch and Hermann Wellenreuther, eds., *Liberalitas: Festschrift für Erich Angermann* (Stuttgart, 1992), 343–65.
136 See Helmut Böhme, *Prologema zu einer Sozial- und Wirtschaftsgeschichte Deutschlands im 19. und 20. Jahrhundert* (Frankfurt/Main, 1968); Michael Hughes, *Nationalism and Society: Germany, 1800–1945* (London, 1988), 130–63.
137 Reinhard Steinmann, "Die Debatte über medizinische Versuche am Menschen in der Weimarer Zeit," M.D. diss., University of Tübingen, 1975.

seemed to be a racial, that is, biological, barrier and not just a cultural one. The brutality of the German Wehrmacht in the East, as much as the killing of many more Eastern than Western Jews, had its origins in these seemingly scientifically proven differences. Racial superiority toward the people of the East was for many Germans more than a slogan; blood typing seemed to prove that one really had a better biological origin. The presumed racial superiority seemed to supply the legitimization for those Germans who on a purely cultural basis would never have considered themselves superior. Racial differences thus became part of German hegemonial thought toward the East even before 1933.

Whereas elite sports are mainly on a national level in the United States — for example, the World Series is almost always played between two American teams — in Europe, elite sports have been closely associated with demonstrating not only the relative strength and vitality but also the putative decadence of a particular nation. Countries compared themselves with other nations in the symbolic sphere of international sports. National identities are formed and maintained through sports.[138] Although sports were considered a private matter in many countries, in Germany it was readily accepted that the state should intervene to demonstrate national superiority in such highly symbolic contests as the Olympic Games. Germans applauded the fact that German sports organizations and the German government flouted international rules in order to show national strength and effectiveness. Much scientific effort went into the preparation of athletes to demonstrate German superiority.[139] After World War II, this kind of government intervention became normalized; yet Germany was the first to introduce an active government role in international sports competition.

The 1936 Olympic Games in Berlin, the so-called Nazi Olympics, ended with Germany triumphant. Germany's success in the medal count translated into even more popular support for the Nazis, since the games seemed to prove the correctness of Nazi theories regarding the differences among the human races.[140] The selection of talent at an early age on the basis of scientific tests and anthropometry was the German way of interpreting the survival of the fittest race. The Germans attempted to

138 E.g., Grant Jarvie and Graham Walker, eds., *Scottisch Sport in the Making of the Nation: Ninety-Minute Patriots?* (Leicester, 1994).
139 John Hoberman, *Mortal Engines: The Science of Performance and the Dehumanization of Sport* (New York, 1992).
140 Arnd Krüger, *Die Olympischen Spiele 1936 und die Weltmeinung* (Berlin, 1972); Reinhard Rürup, ed., *1936: Die Olympischen Spiele und der Nationalsozialismus* (Berlin, 1996).

find genetically endowed individuals and train them to create super-champions.[141] In the United States and in Great Britain, the selection of the fittest individual was accomplished through individual competition. In these countries, where scouting and training were considered more important than racial or genetic endowment, sports promoters tried to identify junior champions in order to develop them into world-class athletes. In Germany, genetic determination in the arena of elite sport was part of popular hegemonial thought, written up in the sports media and discussed in neighborhood bars. With the rise of the sports pages in German newspapers, genetic theories, on which much scientific racism was based, became widespread. The average person in the street, not just the scientist in the laboratory, eagerly participated in this discourse on race and genetics.

Horse breeding, blood typing, and elite sports were thus examples of the popularity of notions about racial differences based on blood. Belief in these notions, moreover, continues in many quarters. This "horse breeder's perspective" was one of the bases for the popular support of the Nazis in fields where Nazi policies would otherwise have been rejected on moral grounds.

---

141 Krümmel, "Eignungslehre." Carl Krümmel, a dedicated Nazi, was elected president of the German Physical Education Teachers' Association in 1925. On Krümmel, see Horst Ueberhorst, *Carl Krümmel und die nationalsozialistische Leibeserziehung* (Berlin, 1976).

15

The Thin Line Between Eugenics and Preventive Medicine

PETER WEINGART

THE ISSUE

The history of science in the late nineteenth and twentieth centuries has a special place for "racism" – its origins, its causes, and its perseverance. Political history does as well. Racism and its consequences are one of the very few issues where both histories meet in an obvious and explicit fashion. Since the beginning of the nineteenth century, "race," whatever other origins and uses it had, has been a scientific term.[1] The history of the applied science of eugenics, or race hygiene, as it was called in Germany and the Scandinavian countries, has been connected to racism, and owing to its history, so has its heir, human genetics. Racism, particularly anti–Semitism, although it has many roots, has become equated with "scientific racism," that is, with race biology and race hygiene. The closest link is undoubtedly the use of elements of biology and anthropology in Nazi ideology, so much so that the scientists involved labeled National Socialism "applied biology." But there is also a different tradition implied with eugenics – that of preventive social medicine. It too, primarily because of the Nazi experience, has been linked to social discrimination or "social racism." The specter of this legacy continues to haunt contemporary human genetics and has cast a shadow over recent technological advances in the mapping of the human genome.

This chapter asks whether the sciences are responsible for racism in society, and if experiences in the fairly recent past can guide present-day judgments about the potential racism of scientific research. The answer is twofold: It is at best much too simple and at worst misleading to apply the categories of the past, that is, German race hygiene, to judge the

---

1 Nancy Stepan, *The Idea of Race in Science: Great Britain, 1800–1960* (London, 1982).

present and future of human genetics; but a reflection on past experience can provide guidance as to how we should evaluate present developments. Rather than assuming a unilinear causation between scientific theories and racism in society and politics, the analysis shows that predominant categories in science and their interpretative potential co-evolve with the social values embedded in the political culture.

RACE AND HYGIENE: THE TWO TRADITIONS IN EUGENICS

The history of eugenics has been told many times and need not be repeated, with the exception of pertinent episodes.[2] The early history of eugenics is instructive with respect to the two traditions that later merged into one movement: the anthropological and the medical. Alfred Ploetz initiated interest in eugenics in Germany in 1895 with a book that alluded to both "the fitness of our race" and the "protection of the weak."[3] The concepts of "race" and *Volk* were not clearly distinguished; the use of "race" ranged from morphological type ("Nordic race") to species ("physical and intellectual racial fitness"). Ploetz's and then Wilhelm Schallmayer's concepts of "race hygiene," as they termed eugenics, emerged in the context of a discourse on "race," which, again, was made up of two components. Anthropology in Germany and on the Continent was generally physical anthropology and had become primarily the anthropometric study of racial "types." By the turn of the century, anthropology had entered into a symbiotic relationship with conservative nationalist circles under the banner of Gobineau's Aryan racism. Popularized by various nationalist associations and Ludwig Woltmann's *Politisch-Anthropologische Revue*, this part of the discourse shaped its distinctly nationalist-racist expressions.

With Gobineau, Lapouge, and many other less well-known authors who engaged in the nationalist and anti-Semitic discourse that glorified the Aryan race, humanists had gained influence in an area that was otherwise dominated by physicians and natural scientists. Furthermore, keen interest in Aryan science was not limited to Germany but pervaded to a greater or lesser extent most of the European nations and the United States. The question of its popular impact has not been answered author-

---

2 Daniel J. Kevles, *In the Name of Eugenics* (New York, 1985); Peter Weingart et al., *Rasse, Blut und Gene, Geschichte der Rassenhygiene und Eugenik in Deutschland* (Frankfurt/Main, 1988); Paul Weindling, *Health, Race and German Politics Between National Unification and Nazism, 1870–1945* (Cambridge, 1989).

3 Alfred Ploetz, *Die Tüchtigkeit unserer Rasse und der Schutz der Schwachen* (Berlin, 1895).

itatively, but it can be assumed to have been marginal in the United States and in the Catholic countries and somewhat greater in Germany and the Scandinavian countries.

In spite of its pervasiveness, this "racist" component of the discourse on race, when it joined with the newer, more modern eugenic discourse, did not render eugenics inherently "racist." Schallmayer, although a social Darwinist by today's standards, not only ridiculed the "Nordic" movement but also rejected in clear terms its goal of purifying the race or giving priority to the "Nordic elements" as a legitimate objective of eugenics.[4]

A clear indication of the parallel and ultimately conflicting constellation of the anthropological and the medical components of eugenics is the development of the respective scientific and professional organizations and their programs. In 1925 a competitor to the German League for Race Hygiene (Deutscher Bund für Volksaufartung und Erbkunde) was founded, an organization whose membership base was composed of civil servants of the registry offices. Several of its officers worked in responsible positions in the Prussian welfare bureaucracy. The eugenicists themselves spoke of the division of the movement into a conservative "Munich" faction oriented toward race hygiene and a more moderate "Berlin" faction. When the two societies merged in 1931, the original goal to "improve the race" had been reformulated into the more mundane "eugenic formation of family and *Volk*."

The concurrent development can be witnessed in the foundation of the Kaiser Wilhelm Institute for Anthropology, Human Genetics, and Eugenics (Kaiser-Wilhelm-Institut für Anthropologie, menschliche Erblehre und Eugenik) in 1927, which was accompanied by declarations from scientists and policymakers alike that it would maintain its distance from the nationalist and racist leanings associated with the race hygiene movement before and during the war.

Whereas this political configuration suggests a rough equation between the anthropological race-hygiene orientation and the political right, on the one hand, and the medical eugenic orientation and the political left, on the other, the situation is more complicated. To understand the subsequent fate of eugenics under National Socialism, one has to consider both the scientific and political developments and the convictions of its practitioners.

---

4 Wilhelm Schallmayer, *Vererbung und Auslese: Grundriss der Gesellschaftsbiologie und der Lehre vom Rassedienst*, 3d ed. (Jena, 1918), 375ff.

From its beginnings, physicians were the most numerous supporters of race hygiene. Fischer, Grottian, Rüdin, Ploetz, and Schallmayer, to name the most influential, were all trained physicians. When the League for Race Hygiene was admitted to the Society of German Naturalists and Physicians (Gesellschaft deutscher Naturforscher und Ärzte, or GDNÄ) in 1913, it was categorized in the medical section.

The majority of German eugenicists was nationalistic, perhaps even *völkisch*, racist, and, later on, National Socialist. The profile of their political convictions probably did not differ from that of the rest of the medical profession, nor was there any difference between geneticists and eugenicists. The common denominator was the elitism shared by the "Mandarins" at the German universities.[5] Even those who aligned themselves with the political Left, such as Schallmayer and Grottian, remained "biologistic" in their outlook, and their value orientations differed in no relevant point from those of the race hygienists leaning to the Right. In other words, the spectrum of political options available to contenders in the eugenic discourse in the 1920s was fairly narrow and did not include the fundamental opposition that emerged only after World War II. This is also true, albeit to a lesser extent and for a shorter time period, for Anglo-Saxon eugenicists.[6]

To this configuration of anthropology and medicine another important component has to be added that emerged with the new science of genetics and the technological and political perspectives it provided practitioners. Mendelian inheritance theory only slowly gained ground after its rediscovery in 1900. Eugen Fischer published his *Rehobother Bastards* in 1913 and, with it, became the leading young anthropologist in the country, having demonstrated the fruitfulness of the new theory in its application to the study of racial miscegenation. The theory of heredity constituted a revolution in the sterile anthropometric research program, but it also gave focus to the hitherto diffuse fears of degeneration and the effects of racial mixing. All kinds of physical traits as well as psychological dispositions were believed to be heritable – from common diseases to criminal behavior, alcoholism, and even the drive to go out to sea. For a while, the search for unambiguous criteria of racial differentiation and delineation seemed to be a promising research program when moved to the level of genetics and blood groups.

The obsession with racial impurity had its parallel in the fear of de-

---

5 Jonathan Harwood, *Styles of Scientific Thought: The German Genetics Community, 1900–1933* (Chicago, 1993).
6 Diane Paul, "Eugenics and the Left," *Journal for the History of Ideas* 45 (1984): 567–90.

generation, and both were amplified by the perspective of the theory of heredity. Until genetics was put on a more secure foundation through the work of the experimental Morgan School in the United States and subsequent reception of this school's findings in Germany, the more speculative approach of German race hygienists to heredity left ample room for political value judgments to enter into policy recommendations.

In short, the link between the debates about racial mixture in anthropology and degeneration in social hygiene and medicine was provided by the new genetics, or theory of heredity, as it was still called. This scientific modernization proved highly attractive to demographers and social medicine professionals. The social and political environment determined which elements of the scientific discourse spread beyond the narrow confines of academia into the realm of politics.

The liberal and welfare-minded middle years of the Weimar era did not foster selectionist arguments as promoted by race anthropologists and race hygienists. This changed suddenly with the world economic crisis. In Germany, the drop of the Gross National Product (GNP) by 25 percent over four years and the rise of unemployment from 1.8 million, in 1929, to 5.6 million, in 1932, prepared the ground for a high receptivity for cost-saving schemes in the public health sector. Comparative cost-benefit analyses of different strategies, notably sterilization, became common. Their targets were patients with physical or mental disabilities believed to be hereditary. Soon alcoholics, criminals, and whoever fell into the category of "socially unfit" were included. Likewise, in an atmosphere of rapidly disappearing tolerance, the anthropological discussion about racial mixture dovetailed with the growth of anti-Semitism and played on its political leverage. Social and racial discrimination, although distinguishable in terms of their disciplinary origins and their targets, had the same methodological basis and profited from the same political climate.

The interest of the state medical administration in race hygiene as a preventive strategy coincided with a paradigm shift in public medical care. Arthur Gütt, its main proponent, called for a shift from what he deemed to be an exaggerated individual and social hygiene-oriented system of medical care to one that would be based on heredity (genetics), race hygiene, and population policy (*Bevölkerungspolitik*).[7] This fundamental

---

7 Alfons Labisch and Florian Tennstedt, *Der Weg zum "Gesetz über die Vereinheitlichung des Gesund-heitswesens" vom 3. Juli 1934: Entwicklungslinien und -momente des staatlichen und kommunalen Gesund-heitswesens in Deutschland*, Schriftenreihe der Akademie für öffentliches Gesundheitswesen in Düsseldorf, no. 13 (Düsseldorf, 1986).

reorientation of the system of medical care implied its reorganization from a diversified communal to a unified state administration. When the National Socialists assumed power in 1933, Gütt became the most influential medical administrator and the architect of a new law unifying the public medical care system in which heredity and race care (*Erb- und Rassenpflege*) were integral parts. The law, put into effect in 1934, provided the framework for the infamous Nuremberg laws passed in 1935, which contained the core provisions of Nazi race policy.

Until recently, historians who were probably unaware of the history of anthropology and eugenics and who all too readily believed accounts of the supposed ad hoc character of the Nuremberg laws did not realize that they were merely the implementation of more than twenty years of discussion in the two fields.[8] Far from inventing them, the Nazis (or, rather, Hitler himself) had only translated race-hygienic and race-based anthropological postulates into the party program. The "Law for the Protection of German Blood and German Honor" reflected concerns about racial purity and prohibited marriage and sexual intercourse (*Blutsgemein-schaften*) between Germans and members of foreign races. The "Law for the Protection of Hereditary Health of the German People," in turn, was supposed to put marriage under a eugenically motivated state control through the issuing of marriage permits. This law was intended to complement the sterilization law of 1934. An indication of the inherent connection between "protection of blood" and "protection of heredity" may be seen in Gütt's report of September 1935, in which he stated that the state originally planned to regulate in one law the prohibition of marriages with members of ethnically unwanted groups and with eugenically unwanted groups.[9]

Whereas the implementation of the eugenic control of marriages ultimately failed, the "protection of German blood" was one of the several steps taken toward the Holocaust. When the war ended in 1945 and the full extent of the horror committed in the name of race biology and race hygiene became publicly known, the political tide turned against biologistic thinking in general and against the concept of race as a legitimate term for policymaking in particular. More fundamental than that, at least in the West, was the revulsion against authoritarianism and its glorification of the state above the individual, as seen at the core of the different brands of fascism. Eugenics and race biology had provided Na-

---

8 Weingart et al., *Rasse, Blut und Gene*, 498ff.
9 Gisela Bock, *Zwangssterilisation im Nationalsozialismus* (Opladen, 1986), 101; Weingart et al., *Rasse, Blut und Gene*, 502–3.

tional Socialism with its specific characteristics among the fascist ideologies. As a result, they both lost their legitimacy at the same time. In conjunction with the overwhelming moral indictment, the crucial factor was the restoration of the rights of the individual and not, as is often claimed by the scientific community, the prevalence of "good science" over "bad science" or the end of the "abuse" of science by corrupt political regimes.[10] The best indicators of this are the UNESCO (United Nations Educational, Scientific, and Cultural Organization) statement on race and scientists' postwar attitudes toward sterilization and other eugenic measures.

To appreciate the significance of the value changes that pervaded the international political culture in the aftermath of the war, one has to consider the inherent link between eugenics and the authoritarian state. Fritz Lenz, one of the leading German geneticists and race hygienists, had explicitly and correctly claimed an "essential relationship" (*Wesensverwandtschaft*) between race hygiene and the "fascist idea of the state": "Whereas the liberal, and in essence, also the social democratic ideas of the state are based on an individualistic 'weltanschauung,' fascism does not recognize the value of the individual. Its ultimate goal is eternal life, which is perpetuated through the chain of generations, and that means the race," he wrote in 1931. He took pride in the fact that Hitler had taken many of his ideas from his own writings.[11] Indeed, the selectionist rationale of race hygiene would have required a fundamental restructuring of a whole host of social institutions to avoid their counterselective effects and orient them to the goal of hereditary health. Many of these changes were discussed in the scholarly literature in Germany and elsewhere throughout the first decades of the century, and some were ultimately put into practice under the National Socialists. Examples include the redistribution of land to large families, the nativist reform of income and inheritance tax laws, and, of course, the medical control of marriages. All these measures of a eugenic social technology had a centralist, authoritarian state as their prerequisite. Lenz was correct in his diagnosis, and it is no accident that the race hygienists welcomed and supported the Nazis.

UNESCO resolved in 1949 to abolish racial discrimination with a statement on the state of research on race. In retrospect this enterprise illustrates the continuity of the scientific discourse and the inability of

---

10 Peter Weingart, "Science Abused? Challenging," *Science in Context* 2 (1993): 555–67.
11 Fritz Lenz, *Menschliche Auslese und Rassenhygiene (Eugenik)*, 3d ed. (Munich, 1931), 451.

the German race hygienists in particular to face up to their political involvement and to comprehend the value changes that had occurred in
the political arena. A first version of the declaration formulated by social
scientists that suggested the replacement of the concept of "race" by that
of "ethnic groups" met with resistance from geneticists and anthropologists. A second attempt to find a consensus provoked a heated debate
among the geneticists now leading the effort and revealed the community's internal conflicts, notably the resistance of some members to abandoning the race concept. They clung to the fear of racial mixture and
objected to the human-rights formulation that all men were created
equal. In the end the document was published containing the modern
definition featured by the population geneticists, according to which
"races" can only be sensibly defined as populations that differ in the frequency of one or several genes.[12] But this was not yet the consensus
among the genetics and anthropology communities. Given the lack of
clear scientific evidence, only the change in the political context had
suddenly rendered the supposed dangers of racial mixture unimportant.[13]
After having been delegitimized by changes in political context, the
problem of racial mixture that for so long had plagued the anthropologists was also simply dissolved by population genetics.

PROFESSIONAL TRANSITION AND SCIENTIFIC ADVANCEMENT

The reluctance of the anthropologists and geneticists to give up their
morphological race concept had its parallel in the eugenicists' reluctance
to relinquish their reliance on state surveillance of the reproductive process. The moral indictment of racism had its deeper roots in the reinstatement of the sovereign individual. The recovery of human rights in the
political arena implied a denunciation of the kind of authoritarian state
control implicit in eugenic social technology. But the profession was slow
to move and to adapt to the new times.

The shift that took place over a decade and a half can be described as
the transition from a state-interventionist eugenics oriented toward the
gene pool to a human genetics based on individual choice and focused
on disease. (The term "human genetics" had been coined by the German
geneticist Günther Just in 1940.) After the war, American geneticists
took the lead when Herman J. Muller, himself a professed eugenicist

---

12 Leslie C. Dunn and Theodosius Dobzhansky, *Heredity, Race and Society* (New York, 1958), 118.
13 William B. Provine, "Genetics and the Biology of Race Crossing," *Science* 182 (1973): 790–6.

and experimental geneticist, tried to remove the taint of eugenics from human genetics. His strategy was to situate human genetics closer to medicine by offering its services for medical diagnosis, therapy, and prophylaxis of rare genetic defects. Muller continued to believe that eugenics would remain an important task, but he was realistic enough to see that "the heat and the misunderstandings of present political controversy, and the prejudices rampant in all existing societies, make very bad soil for the development of sound eugenic policies at the present time."[14] Thus, whereas Muller wanted to have human genetics put under the legitimating shield of a consensual concept of disease, he had by no means abandoned the hope for a human eugenics. And he held on to this perspective with the same benevolent posture with which the prewar eugenicists had considered the political infeasibility of their plans for mandatory sterilization and marriage permits. Muller, it should be noted, was a progressive among human geneticists. But his attitude describes fairly well the ambivalence expressed in the late 1940s and through the 1950s of the generation of human geneticists trained before the war.

The crucial issue for human geneticists at the time, and one that determined the position on the political spectrum, was anxiety about the quality of the gene pool. In essence, this was the translation of the old eugenic creed into modern scientific categories. It also decided on the central issue of the practice of human genetics, that is, whether genetic counseling should be directive or nondirective. Although the democratic value system favored individual self-determination, the gene-pool orientation of the genetics "experts" called for directive counseling in order to influence individual reproductive behavior for the benefit of the gene pool as a whole. Obviously, the "direction" given to patients depended on the state of the art in genetics and the value convictions of the experts. It can be shown that the gradual shift toward "medicalization" of human genetics was driven primarily by advances in genetics, supported by the political environment. For a while, the convictions of the human-genetics community lagged behind.

The ambivalence expressed during this time of transition is exemplified by Lee R. Dice, the director of the first heredity clinic in the United States (founded in 1940 at the University of Michigan). Dice saw the difference between the old eugenics and the new practice in the "voluntary cooperation of the citizen," and he expressed the slowly growing trust of

---

14 Herman J. Muller, "Progress and Prospects in Human Genetics," *American Journal for Human Genetics* 1 (1949): 1–18.

the geneticists in the rationality of individuals' choices. But like Muller he continued to be oriented toward the quality of the gene pool. Human geneticists, in his view, were not only interested in the "decrease of harmful genes, but also in the increase of desirable ones."[15]

Muller himself was instrumental in fueling the fear for the quality of the gene pool with his diagnosis of a rising load of mutations resulting from the effects of modern medicine and the increasing radiation in the environment.[16] Although this argument revived older eugenic topoi, there was also one important difference: The dysgenic effects he diagnosed were devoid of all categories of class and race. But Muller's view was apocalyptic and seemed to call for drastic intervention nonetheless. Ultimately, the perceived threat was defused by two other geneticists, Dobzhansky and Wallace, who showed that, contrary to Muller's conviction, the individual variability in a population, that is, the high degree of heterozygocity in individuals, proved to be an adaptive advantage, notwithstanding the deleterious nature of some ephemeral genes in a homozygot state.[17] But this debate remained unresolved for several years.

Locked in between his eugenic convictions and a changed environment of political values, Muller looked for a "technological fix" that would be acceptable in a democratic context and suggested "germinal choice" by "artificial insemination" as the solution.[18] The old idea had become technically feasible: Male sperm could be frozen for an indefinite time. The reactions to this explicitly eugenic vision are a good indicator of the eugenic potential that still existed in the human genetics community around 1960. Rather than drawing harsh criticism, he drew supportive comments from such leading scientists as Francis Crick, James F. Crow, J. B. S. Haldane, Ernst Mayr, and Frederick Osborne. One of the few critics of his "benevolent utopia" was the geneticist Leslie C. Dunn, who pointed to the "historicity" of the value judgments implied in any breeding concept.[19]

---

15 Lee R. Dice, "Heredity Clinics: Their Value for Public Service and for Research," *American Journal for Human Genetics* 4 (1952): 6.

16 Herman J. Muller, "Our Load of Mutations," *American Journal for Human Genetics* 2 (1950): 111–76.

17 Theodosius Dobzhansky and Bruce Wallace, "The Problem of Adaptive Differences in Human Populations," *American Journal for Human Genetics* 6 (1954): 199–203.

18 Herman J. Muller, "Germinal Choice: A New Dimension in Genetic Therapy," *Proceedings of the 2nd International Congress of Human Genetics (Rome, Sept. 6–12, 1961)*, 3 vols. (Rome, 1963), 3:1968–73.

19 Leslie C. Dunn, "Cross Currents in the History of Human Genetics," *American Journal for Human Genetics* 14 (1962): 1–13.

The subsequent fundamental change in the discipline of human genetics was initiated by the decoding of the chromosomal basis of three frequent abnormalities, the Down, Klinefelter, and Turner syndromes.[20] In retrospect, this was interpreted as the birth of clinical genetics and the fusion of human and medical genetics. The significance of this medicalization of human genetics was made explicit by Victor McKusick a decade and a half later, when he stated that "medicine has given focus, direction and purpose to human genetics."[21] Indeed, the more human genetics concentrated on severe disorders and diseases, the greater was its focus; thus, it could here find its purpose under the protection of the established legitimacy of the medical profession. But the same techniques that provided the potential for therapy also posed the dangers of preventive medicine with their specific ethical dilemmas and opened the prospects for new eugenic visions. It is evident that this development, which took shape in the mid-1960s, characterizes the situation in human genetics down to the present.

The rapid expansion of diagnostic capabilities that allowed the diagnosis of hitherto unknown, rare, and less serious disorders has continued to test the troubled line of demarcation between medicalized human genetics and eugenics. Prenatal diagnosis by amniocentesis, which was introduced in 1966, did not only pose the ethical problems connected with abortion implied in the method; it also triggered the debate among human geneticists over the classic eugenic problem of modern medicine's neutralizing selective mechanisms and thus contributing to the gradual degeneration of the gene pool, that is, whenever parents risk births of phenotypically healthy carriers of their genetic defects.

The human geneticists experienced another ambiguity of the new biomedical technology with routinized screening programs, applied first to "inborn errors of metabolism," phenylketonuria, then to Tay-Sachs and sickle-cell anemia.[22] Whereas the implementation of the last two screening

---

20 Down syndrome, or trisomy 21, earlier called mongolism: chromosome 21 appears three times and leads to mental retardation and lower life expectancy. Klinefelter (XXY) syndrome: like Down Syndrome an autosomal trisomy in men, expressed by lack of male hormones and sterility, not necessarily obvious phenotypically. Turner syndrome: X0-Karyotype, phenotypically a very complex syndrome, most obvious is small body height, and the majority of X0-women are sterile.

21 Victor A. McKusick, "The Growth and Development of Human Genetics as a Clinical Discipline," *American Journal for Human Genetics* 27 (1975): 261–73.

22 Inborn errors of metabolism (Phenylketonuria) is a hereditary (autosomal recessive) disease of metabolism that leads to debility if untreated; Tay-Sachs is a recessive disease leading to debility and to death in early childhood; sickle-cell anemia (thalassemia) is a grave disturbance of beta-

programs seemed to fit into the medical paradigm, it revealed the context dependence and value-ladenness of this technique as well as the political naiveté of the scientists involved. Tay-Sachs screening proved to be a success because it was administered to a well-educated, higher-income group in the population: Jews, to whom the defect poses a fatal threat. Sickle-cell anemia, in contrast, failed in the quagmire of race politics: The genetic defect appears primarily among blacks and groups in the population whose origin is in countries with a high incidence of malaria and who are socioeconomically underprivileged on average. The difference between the genetic defect that has no negative effect and the disease that can be fatal was not always clear. Since prenatal diagnosis was not yet available, carriers could only refrain from having children to avoid the risk, a suggestion that at a time of increasing racial disturbances exposed human genetics to the suspicion of racism. The groups concerned had not been involved in the preparation of the program. All of these issues contributed to its failure and demonstrated how thin the line between preventive medicine and eugenic policies was, at least in the eyes of the groups concerned.

With the emergence of every new technology, especially in the realm of medicine, the number of options calling for decisions is increased. Human genetics, bolstered by the new DNA-recombination techniques and their prospect of genetic manipulation, cannot eradicate memories of its eugenic precursor. Therefore, eugenic options are inherently connected with techniques such as prenatal diagnosis, genetic screening, in-vitro fertilization, and, ultimately, genetic engineering. Threats, allegations, and the suspicion that human genetics would return to eugenic practices have beset the field ever since its inception. In some cases these were justified or at least reasonable, for example, when Hans Nachtsheim in Germany proposed to uphold the 1934 sterilization law,[23] or in the case of the XYY debate in the United States. There is no "built-in" barrier that could prevent these techniques from starting down the "slippery slope." Such a barrier has to be erected from outside, that is, by the political system. Such was precisely the case in 1983 when, through the "Report of the President's Commission for the Study of Ethical Problems in Medicine and Biomedical and Behavioral Research," eugenic

---

globin synthesis appearing in tropical and subtropical populations that – if it appears homozygotic – leads to destruction of red blood cells with serious secondary effects.

23 The debate triggered by Nachtsheim lingered on between 1952 and the early 1960s as a backdrop to the restitution legislation; cf. Hans Nachtsheim, *Für und Wider die Sterilisierung aus eugenischer Indikation* (Stuttgart 1952); Hans Nachtsheim, "Eugenik im Lichte moderner Genetik," Forschung, Praxis, Fortbildung 17 (1966): 3–8.

value references, that is, orientation to the quality of the gene pool, was delegitimized. Screening and genetic counseling were declared "medical procedures" that could be chosen by the individual as an aid in personal medical and reproductive decisions.[24]

To leave reproductive and medical decisions in the hands of the individual, even if this implied social costs and deterioration of the gene pool as the ethical and political baseline, was also supported by science itself. As early as 1917, population geneticists had maintained that the expected effects of sterilization in eliminating disease had been mistaken. Model computations of a phenotypically curable recessive genetic disease, such as PKU, showed that under certain conditions it would take a hundred generations for the initial incidence to quadruple. Those are time ranges far beyond any political perspective, and certainly beyond the range of any legitimate claim to eugenic control.

THE HUMAN GENOME PROJECT: A RENAISSANCE OF EUGENICS?

Any assumption that the conjunction of medicalization and political support would resolve the issue of the "specter of eugenics" implicit in modern human genetics research and practice has been premature. In 1988 the Commission of the European Community, responding to a challenge from the United States and Japan, proposed a fifteen-year research program on the analysis of the human genome as an effort in predictive medicine. The official U.S. Human Genome Project was launched by the U.S. Department of Energy and the National Institutes of Health in 1990. In the same year the international Human Genome Organization (HUGO) was created. National research foundations and research councils have set up their own programs. This multibillion-dollar research program was initiated in anticipation of large returns for the biotechnology industry and was more than welcomed by the research community as an umbrella for long-term funding. The primary justification of the program is, however, as its title suggests, to identify genes that are connected with diseases, to isolate them, and to analyze their structure.

The proposal of the EC Commission revealed that the structure of the problem has not changed in principle, only in detail, and that ambiguities that were previously avoided reappear. It is evident to all actors in the "human genome" game that the project will result in an "enormous

---

24 *President's Commission for the Study of Ethical Problems in Medicine and Biomedical and Behavioral Research, Screening and Counseling for Genetic Conditions* (Washington, D.C., 1983).

expansion of information" about the human genetic makeup, which, in turn, will provide cheaper and more efficient screening methods for all kinds of genetic dispositions, many of which will not be covered by current concepts of disease. It is easy to predict that this kind of information will continue to fuel the dynamics of social definitions of disease and will open an entirely new arena of interpretation about "normality" – highly dependent on the actors and interests involved.

The initial focus of the project, it is suggested, will be on well-defined diseases with a clear genetic base. These monogenetic defects are comparatively rare. Altogether their incidence is approximately 2.5 percent of West European births. The claim of relevance goes beyond this, however, into the realm of multigenetic defects and more common diseases that have a strong environmental component. The rationale here is more ambiguous: Since it is improbable that environmental risk factors can be controlled, let alone eliminated, it appears desirable to know as much as possible about factors of genetic predisposition in order to identify endangered individuals and to avoid transfer of their dispositions to subsequent generations.[25]

The Human Genome Project has triggered a public debate that still continues and is unlikely to end very soon. The criticisms launched against the project invariably appeal to the past experiences with eugenics translated into more modern forms of social discrimination.[26] There is no doubt that the new knowledge will provide precisely the means that the old eugenics lacked for their practical application. The ability to diagnose genetic diseases before they are expressed or even just carriers of recessive defects is crucial to any effective eugenic program. The diagnosis of disorders for which there is no foreseeable therapy calls for eugenic elimination of the genetic material in question. The availability of this knowledge and technology is therefore seen in reference to the old eugenic program, and the fit seems compelling. In particular, eugenic discrimination is foreseen in job recruitment and health insurance. Jobs could be denied to individuals with risk dispositions to specific work conditions. Insurance companies could determine rates or even admission on the basis of genetic screening. And beyond these predicted dangers lies the specter of an oppressive government that will put the new technologies to eugenic uses, repeating the history of race hygiene. Recent

25 *Kommission der Europäischen Gemeinschaften, Vorschlag für eine Entscheidung des Rates über ein spezifisches Forschungsprogramm im Gesundheitsbereich: Prädiktive Medizin: Analyse des Menschlichen Genoms* (Brussels, 1988), 3.
26 Neil A. Holtzman and Mark A. Rothstein, "Invited Editorial: Eugenics and Genetic Discrimination," *American Journal for Human Genetics* 50 (1992): 457–9.

eugenic programs in China and Singapore are cited as cases that are supposed to demonstrate the immediacy of the threat.

Fears and anxieties about new knowledge and technologies are commonplace. Like scouts in unknown territory, speculation about possible dangers runs in all directions in order to find the safest path. This is a necessary and helpful activity to cushion inevitable risks. But the human genome project is different from other types of knowledge in one important respect: Its relation to its eugenic ancestor points to the mistakes made in a different historical experience. Memory allows learning. Past experiences with eugenic policies provide a fairly detailed map of roads to avoid. The challenge of the new technology is to give the map a proper reading.

In spite of the enormously increased knowledge in human genetics and its almost certain expansion in the near future, it is not likely to result in eugenic uses in the style of the 1920s and 1930s for two reasons: First, the knowledge proper has become more complex and does not lend itself to the same primitive social categorizations for which it was used during the first half of the century. Scientific knowledge does not necessarily give legitimacy to the discrimination of races, ethnic groups, and social deviants. And even where overzealous scientists cross that border, as in the debates over IQ and XYY, another check is in place, namely, the political context and the associated value system that reject the unwarranted "biologization" of social categories. Many past experiences show that the political sensitivity about eugenic uses of new genetic technologies is high. In Germany, where the historical experience with eugenics is most vivid, public awareness and press coverage reveal an unusual level of information given the esoteric nature of the subject.[27] In other words, the fit that existed between eugenics and the political value system in the 1930s no longer exists.

This does not mean that the issue is closed. As research on the human genome continues, new options will appear, new types of decisions will have to be made, and new ethical dilemmas will be posed. It is probably also unavoidable that laymen and policymakers alike tend to turn to biological explanations when social problems seem inscrutable. The borderline between the "natural" and the "social" itself, as defined by the respective scientific disciplines, is in constant flux. Given the scientific profession's quest for new knowledge, its application, and the social control that it confers, a certain amount of whistle-blowing is a good check on

---

27 *Büro für Technikfolgenabschätzung beim Deutschen Bundestag, TA-Projekt "Genomanalyse": Chancen und Risiken genetischer Diagnostik: Endbericht* (Bonn, 1993), 183ff.

technocratic expansionism. It reflects the conflict between different values and interests. But from the vantage point of a social evolutionist, one can look beyond this stage. Two paradoxes emerge in the assessment of the human genome project. First, critics frequently point out that the genetic approach is reductionist with respect to social and environmental conditions, that individual predictive strategies foreclose social and ecological problem solutions. This is, indeed, one implication, but another may be less comfortable to admit. The implicit appeal by the critics to far-reaching social and ecological solutions is an appeal to political authority that would be in the position to exert such power as to implement the respective rearrangements. This leads right back to strategies suggested by the earlier eugenics movement: On the basis of a selectionist "social biology," it envisaged the reform of a host of social institutions in order to achieve a healthy gene pool.

Second, the slow turning away of the genetics community from an authoritarian eugenics to an individualist human genetics with its abdication to the gene pool as a legitimate concern and its reliance on individual decisions may, and probably will, have effects on the population because of shared value orientations concerning health and physical fitness. Thus, the paradoxical outcome of the "democratization" of human genetics, of the political condemnation of authoritarian eugenics and its anti-individualist values, may well be that the consumer orientation toward reproductive technologies and genetic therapies could lead to the realization of the very eugenic ideals that the eugenicists of the early twentieth century had in mind. Only this time it would be consonant with our value system, an outcome of individual choices within the population.

Index

413

In a world of increasingly heterogeneous societies, matters of identity politics and the links between collective identities and national, racial, or ethnic intolerance have assumed dramatic significance — and have stimulated an enormous body of research and literature. This research seldom transcends the limitations of a national perspective, however, and thus reproduces the limitations of its own topic; comparative studies are rare, if not altogether absent. *Identity and Intolerance* is an effort to shift the focus toward comparison in order to show how German and American societies have historically confronted and currently confront matters of national, racial, and ethnic inclusion and exclusion. The comparative perspective sheds light on the specific links between the cultural construction of nationhood and otherness, the political modes of integration and exclusion, and the social conditions of tolerance and intolerance. The contributors to this book also attempt to integrate the largely separate approaches offered by the history of ideas and ideologies, social history, and discourse theory.